TORS · ART & ANTIQUE FAIRS · ARTS DE LA TABLE · ART

EUR SERVICES · COOKERY SCHOOLS · COSMETIC SURG

ES · FLORISTS · GARDEN DESIGNERS · GOLF CLUBS · H

SIC FESTIVALS · NANNIES · PARTY ORGANISERS & CATE

TY CONSULTANTS · RACING, TRAINERS AND BLOODSTO

SULTANTS · SPAS & CLINICS · SPECIALIST SHOPS · SPORT

WINE MERCHANTS · WINES, CHAMPAGNES & SPIRITS ·

RTER · ANTIQUE DEALERS · ARCHITECTS & DECORATO

ON HOUSES · CASINOS · CASTLES & VILLAS · CHAUFFE

MESTIC EMPLOYMENT AGENCIES · FASHION & ACCESSO

ITY · HOTELS · JEWELLERY & WATCHES · MUSEUMS · M

TURE DEALERS · POLO CLUBS · PRIVATE BANKS · PROP

NTS · RESTAURANTS & BARS · SCHOOLS · SECURITY CO

SPORTS CLUBS & GYMS · TRAVEL CONSULTANTS · WINE

ERS, DESIGNERS & BUILDERS · YACHT CLUBS · AIR CH

TIQUE FAIRS · ARTS DE LA TABLE · ARTS DE VIVRE · AU

ES · COOKERY SCHOOLS · COSMETIC SURGEONS · DOM

TS · GARDEN DESIGNERS · GOLF CLUBS · HAIR & BEAU

VALS · NANNIES · PARTY ORGANISERS

LTANTS · RACING, TRAINERS AND B

· SPAS & CLINICS · SPECIALIST SHO

HANTS · WINES, CHAMPAGNES & SPIRITS · YACHT BRO

IQUE DEALERS · ARCHITECTS & DECORATORS · ART &

ES · CASINOS · CASTLES & VILLAS · CHAUFFEUR SERVIC

PLOYMENT AGENCIES · FASHION & ACCESSORIES · FLO

S · JEWELLERY & WATCHES · MUSEUMS · MUSIC FESTI

RS · POLO CLUBS · PRIVATE BANKS · PROPERTY CONS

TS & BARS · SCHOOLS · SECURITY CONSULTANTS · SPA

CLUBS & GYMS · TRAVEL CONSULTANTS · WINE MERCH

RS & BUILDERS · YACHT CLUBS · AIR CHARTER · ANTIQ

EUROPE'S ELITE 1000

THE ULTIMATE LIST

THE MILLENNIUM ISSUE

Inspired by Gabrielle Rose O'Mahony Kelly. A truly stylish woman.

First Published in October 1998 and **revised in October 1999** by
Cadogan Publications Limited
50 Hans Crescent, London SW1X ONA, UK
Telephone: +44-20-78 23 74 45

British Library Cataloguing in Publication Data
A catalogue record for this book is available from The British Library
ISBN **0 9534276 1 7**

Publisher: Kevin Kelly

Acknowledgements and Picture credits: See page 336

Designed by Gowers Elmes Publishing Limited
Colour origination by Graphic Facilities
Printed and bound in Italy by Mondadori Printing S.p.A - Verona

FRONTISPIECE: *Interior designed by François–Joseph Graf–Ariodante*
TITLE PAGE: *The garden at Villa Reale, near Lucca, Italy*

EUROPE'S ELITE 1000

THE ULTIMATE LIST

THE MILLENNIUM ISSUE

EDITED BY
SANDRA LANE

CP

CADOGAN PUBLICATIONS

FOREWORD

Having been, for centuries, the cradle of Western culture and civilised living, Europe remains the source of and the standard-bearer for most of the world's finest luxury products and services. This unique guide - the second of an annual series - lists the most prestigious companies and individuals in Europe, who are maintaining and building upon that tradition of excellence.

Europe's Elite 1000 has been researched, written and edited by a team of distinguished contributors, whose specialised, local knowledge has enabled us to give you the definitive, inside story on every name listed.

For this second edition our editorial team reviewed every name which was included in last year's Listing of the Elite 1000; some did not make the grade this time and have been replaced by companies which have either raised their standards during the past year or have been newly discovered by our contributors. In addition, the 100 Best-Kept Secrets and 100 Rising Stars Listings are entirely new, as are all the editorial features.

Recognising the limitations of the many guide books, on a variety of subjects, which already exist, *Europe's Elite 1000* has been created to fulfil two purposes.

First, it has been designed as a stylish source-book, which will provide an invaluable reference-point when travelling to or within Europe, guiding you in the direction of the best, and only the best, providers of an enormously broad range of luxury goods and services – all brought together in a single volume.

Second, having been created in this visually arresting format and containing eight editorial features in addition to the Listings, it will make an elegant and long-lasting prestigious addition to your library or coffee table.

Whatever your particular interests, as long as you are a lover of the finer things in life, you will not only be inspired by this book but also, we hope, will make many exciting new discoveries throughout its pages.

KEVIN KELLY
CHAIRMAN AND EDITOR-IN-CHIEF

EUROPE'S ELITE 1000

THE LISTINGS

Europe's Elite 1000 comprises three Listings sections – The Elite 1000, 100 Rising Stars and 100 Best-Kept Secrets – each of which includes names chosen by our editorial team from all sectors of luxury goods and services. Every company or individual proposed for inclusion has been checked and cross-checked by our network of contributors, advisers and contacts, to ensure that its inclusion is merited. The names have been selected on the basis of the current excellence of their products and services, rather than, simply, a high profile or impressive past reputation. Equally, all names have been judged against a pan-European standard of excellence, rather than being selected on a country-by-country basis. All of the entries are reviewed and updated annually.

EUROPE'S ELITE 1000

While it includes the acknowledged 'greats', the List of *Europe's Elite 1000* also contains many less predictable names. Some readers may, however, be surprised to find certain famous names missing from the list. If they did not qualify, it is because they appear to have succumbed either to the temptation of resting on their laurels, rather than constantly reviewing and upgrading their standards, or to the temptation of becoming too commercial and populist.

100 BEST-KEPT SECRETS

While the Elite 1000 listing contains a significant number of names that are well known only to those who are truly 'at home' in Europe or those with a specialised knowledge of a particular sector, this list of secrets is more of a 'Little Black Book'. Names on this sometimes quirky list constitute real insiders' tips, such as a favourite hideaway hotel, a marvellous beautician or a jeweller who works only to private commission. Some of the names are already well-established but, we believe, deserved to be more widely known.

100 RISING STARS

While some of the Rising Stars may be well-established and may already have achieved considerable success, we believe that they have even greater potential and will make it to the very top of their particular field. Others – relative newcomers – may not have yet fulfilled their potential or proved that they have real staying power but their commitment to excellence is unquestioned. Many of these names will make it into the Elite 1000 List – perhaps as soon as next year.

HOW TO USE THIS BOOK

Each of the above lists is published in alphabetical order, across all product categories. The names are cross-referenced in three indexes, to enable you to use this book in a variety of ways. For example, if you are travelling to a particular country, you would use the Country Index to discover the best of everything in that country. On the other hand, if you are seeking the best in a certain field – say jewellers or antique dealers – you would use the Product Category Index, which will list all European names under the relevant category heading. In addition, there is a straight Alphabetical Index of all names which have been included in the Listings sections of the book.

CONTENTS

BEYOND THE STYLE,
THE EMOTION

PIAGET

GENEVE 1874

PIAGET ALTIPLANO

18K WHITE GOLD, ULTRA-
THIN, PIAGET'S OWN
MECHANICAL MOVEMENT

CHATEAU MARGAUX

By Nicola Mitchell

*Under the direction of Corinne Mentzelopoulos, this
legendary château has overcome its problems of the 1970s to reclaim
its place among the finest of all first-growth Bordeaux.*

Sitting at a large, highly polished desk in her penthouse office overlooking Paris' supremely chic avenue Montaigne, Corinne Mentzelopoulos stretches out an elegant arm and extracts a red leather folder from the impressive pile in front of her. Pulling out a clutch of invoices, she says, with fitting solemnity, "This one is for screws; that one is for safety gloves for the cellar master; these are little things to disinfect the barrels; that is for the château roof; this is for a tractor repair; and that for the metal that is fixed around the barrels; this, pipes for the workshops; plumbing in the museum; drainage in the garden; flowers for dinner; sandpaper..." She could go on.

The daily arrival of these *billets-doux* at the headquarters of Château Margaux is a major clue to how the label, a struggling *grand cru classé* in the late Seventies, has today become arguably the finest of the five first growth Bordeaux wines, nudging ahead of Lafite-Rothschild, Mouton Rothschild, Latour and Haut-Brion.

"Our work is all about details, a million little details," says this 46-year-old dynamo, who owns 25% of Margaux, with an important interest in the 75% stake held by the holding company Exor Group, which is controlled by the Agnelli family. However, if Mentzelopoulos has shown the relentless discipline necessary to turn an historic first growth around, it is thanks to her late father, the Greek-born multi-millionaire financier André Mentzelopoulos, that she has the opportunity to prove her mettle in the rarified world of *grands vins*.

Mentzelopoulos *père* was a major shareholder in France's oldest grocery chain, Félix Potin and also had substantial shares in Vins Nicolas. In 1977 he read in the *Financial Times* that the Ginestet family, who had owned Château Margaux since 1934, had put the estate on the market.

Deeply attached to Margaux, the Ginestets had gone to considerable lengths to restructure the vineyards, regaining the boundaries of 1855, the year that Napoleon III classified Bordeaux wines. These parcels of land, or *terroirs*, which were originally assembled by the Lestonnac family in the 16th- and 17th centuries, are still considered to be among the best in the Médoc. However, a series of bad harvests, the world's relative indifference to Bordeaux wines at the time and the pressure of heavy succession duties forced the family to sell up.

Surprisingly, Félix Potin, alias André Mentzelopoulos, was the only French company

prepared to meet the Ginestets' conditions, which included the guarantee of continuing employment for the staff. After a brief tour of the estate and lunch at the château, the financier shook hands on a sale price equivalent to $13 million at today's values; 23 years on, the 650-acre estate is worth at least 20 times that figure.

Although responsible for setting in motion the vast scheme of restoration work at Château Margaux, which began in 1977 and continued through the Eighties, André Mentzelopoulos sadly saw few of his projects come to fruition, as he died from a stroke at the age of 65 in 1980. One key contribution he made to the estate's success, however, was the appointment of Professor Emile Peynaud as the main consultant to Château Margaux.

Until his retirement in 1989 this eminent academic and great communicator – previously director of Bordeaux's prestigious Institut Oenologique – offered invaluable advice for improving the wines. Peynaud's first and most important recommendation was to introduce a stricter selection for the *grand vin*.

To make this possible, the estate's second wine, the Pavillon Blanc du Château Margaux was redefined and the Pavillon Rouge du Château Margaux – discontinued around 1932 due to the fallout from the Wall Street Crash and Prohibition – was reintroduced. Thus, Château Margaux would be better placed once again to produce wines of the calibre that made even Friedrich Engels sigh. (His idea of bliss was an 1848 Château Margaux.) Indeed, within a year of reimplementing this system, Margaux's 1978 vintage was hailed as the best Bordeaux wine of the year.

Corinne Mentzelopoulos was just 27 when she took over the Château with her French mother, Laura, after her father's death. Within a few years, when her mother remarried and moved to New York, she found herself in complete control. Although young and inexperienced, she was better equipped than many to run a great, classic vineyard; she had tremendous drive, as well as a sense of refinement, an economics degree from the highly respected School of Political Science in Paris and a passion for ancient history and culture. She had originally specialised in the Humanities but, she explains, "as all my conversation with my father revolved around the Dow Jones, I finally gave up and switched to business".

Her first major undertaking was the realisation of one of her father's main projects – the building of a

Above: Corinne Mentzelopoulos, who took over the running of Château Margaux following the death of her father, André, in 1980. Right: The little-known northern façade of the château, designed by Louis Combes in 1810.

"*Château racehorse*

Margaux is like a thoroughbred that few past owners have known how to handle."

second *chai*, or cellar, to provide the best possible conditions for barrel ageing in the second year, before bottling. The original *chai*, with its oak roof supported by 18 white stone columns, had impressed her deeply when she first visited the estate. "I found the mix of classical architecture, the smell of the oak barrels mingled with the wine, the darkness and tranquillity quite spectacular," she recalls. Naturally, she wanted the second one to match its splendour. Designed by Mazières, a local architect, it was the first underground cellar in Bordeaux and a masterly blend of classical architecture and modern, practical details; Mentzelopoulos is particularly pleased with the hidden elevator system that takes the barrels down from the first-year cellar, thereby keeping wine disturbance to a minimum.

In 1983, Mentzelopoulos matched her father's skill in choosing an exceptional oenologist. Paul Pontallier not only had an extensive technical understanding of wine-making, honed through his studies at the Ecole Oenologique, he also had a more worldly approach to developing the first growth potential than was usually the case in Bordeaux; most importantly, he was the same age as Mentzelopoulos, which made communication easier.

Carrying on the work that André Mentzelopoulos had begun, Pontallier got to grips with the soil, which had been rather neglected before the financier's arrival. A section of Cap de Haut, one of Margaux's most precious *terroirs*, was cleared for the first time in 70 years. A brave move, it was just the start of an ambitious replanting programme, which is continuing to this day. "After you replant it takes three years before we can call the wine a Margaux," Mentzelopoulos explains. "It then takes six to 14 years before you start producing a really complex wine – the older the better. So if you make a mistake you have lost at least 15 years."

Pontallier's second task was to adjust the balance

Left: The Empire-style salon was, like the rest of the château, restored by the great decorator, Henri Samuel, during the 1980s. Above: The entrance hall.

13

Main picture: The enfilade of reception rooms, looking from the dining room towards the salon. Given the dining room's capacity for only 18 guests, invitations to dine at Château Margaux are rare and much coveted.

of grape varieties, with "a little less Merlot and a little more Petit Verdot". This added pinch of Verdot, which he describes as "rustic, tender and quite spicy", restored the *grand vin* to its centuries-old balance: 75% Cabernet Sauvignon, 20% Merlot, 5% Petit Verdot and Cabernet Franc. Not that today's *grand vin* is entirely the same as in the past. "Margaux carries the indelible trace of its genes," explains Pontallier, "but there are certain elements which have evolved – in the same way that, although we have not changed genetically, we have done so culturally." Taking the point that Margaux is considered the most 'feminine' of the first growth wines, he continues, "It is not the same 'feminine' character of 50 years ago, when women were more fragile; it is a wine with more power, depth and strength, yet still full of charm – as women are today."

Replanting to help the soil to "re-express its quality", fine-tuning the grape varieties and reducing the yields still further were just the start of improvements. Margaux's 60-strong staff also introduced new drainage systems in the vineyards using 18th-century-style clay pipes, stricter pruning, better control of the temperature in the vats, the use of new barrels for maturing the wines and bottling in a maximum of two weeks to ensure a consistent quality.

The weather, though, was one thing they couldn't fine tune. "We are peasants at the end of the day," says Mentzelopoulos in her characteristically forthright manner. "We may not look like peasants," she adds, elegantly spreading her hands to indicate her immaculate grey trouser suit, "but you have to remember that the only real progress we have made is learning to cope better with what nature gives us. We

could have frosts or hail, an invasion of bugs or disease. Until the last grape is in the vats we don't know how the harvest is going to turn out." However, she adds, Margaux wines can never be bad. "Since, genetically, the soil is the equivalent of Einstein or Van Gogh it has to be good."

All the same, Margaux, like the Médoc in general, experienced relatively good harvests through the Eighties and Nineties. Pontallier agrees that this is a Golden Age for Bordeaux wines but he sees Margaux as being particularly blessed. "Thanks to André Mentzelopoulos' foresight, it was in a perfect position to benefit from Bordeaux's return to favour around 1983 and the revival of the world economy." Those buying Margaux's *grand vin* of 1978 as an investment would have seen this liquid gold outperform the FTSE 100 index by more than

100% in the following ten years. That vintage has been followed by a run of superb wines, notably the 1982, 1983, 1985, 1986, 1990, 1995 and 1996; the last is Pontallier's personal favourite, "for its purity, tranparency and crystalline finesse".

It is more than just the wines that make Margaux special, however. The estate is a completely self-sufficient entity. Besides the key people who collaborate directly with Pontallier, including the assistant director Philippe Bascaules, *Chef de Culture* Jean-Pierre Blanchard and *Maître de Chai* Eric Marin, there are dozens of craftsmen and technicians on the estate. "We have a cooper, a plumber, a roof repairer, an electrician; this is important, as we are 15 miles from Bordeaux and need help immediately if something needs to be fixed," says Mentzelopoulos.

Yet, despite all the activity, an uncanny tranquillity

reigns over Margaux. This is partly the result of the impeccable restoration work that the Mentzelopoulos family has carried out over the past 20 years. Bernard Fonquernie, head architect for France's historic monuments, with responsibility for approving architectural changes on the estate (it was declared a classified monument in 1946) is among the many people impressed by Corinne Mentzelopoulos' "intelligence, sensibility and perseverance" during the long process of reviving the *domaine*. "Chateau Margaux is like a thoroughbred race horse that few past owners have known how to handle," he says.

The estate was built for the Marquis de la Colonilla in 1810 by the Bordeaux architect, Louis Combes. Thanks to a profusion of drawings found in the château's archives, it was possible to restore the buildings, courtyards and garden in perfect harmony

Left: The harvest. Like the rest of the Médoc, Margaux experienced relatively good harvests throughout the Eighties and Nineties. Above: The château's 'vinothèque', built in 1810, serves as the Margaux archive; it contains almost 100,000 bottles, dating back to 1848, which are taken out for special tastings or dinners. Right above: A pair of limestone sphinxes guards the château's principal, southern entrance. Right below: Viewed from the main entrance, a long allée of plane trees leads to the château.

with Combes' original vision. A devotee of neo-classicism in its purest form, the architect was particularly influenced by the Greek tradition; this is particularly evident in the fine neo-Doric features around the doorways in the Cour des Artisans. The sublime honey-yellow of the courtyard walls and the Napoleonic cobblestones in the Cour des Chai add to the extraordinary harmony of the estate.

The legendary château itself, depicted on Margaux's labels, lies at the end of a tree-lined drive, set apart from the main working area. Although Palladian in style, the singular finesse of the structure, with its impressive staircase leading to the facade's graceful columns, along with the sweeping rear stairwell, makes it clearly the work of a Frenchman.

The great decorator, Henri Samuel, restored the mansion's three reception rooms, each furnished with unusually elegant pieces of Empire furniture, upholstered in subtle pastel shades. The main bedroom is decorated in a *chinoiserie* style, popular during that period. There are leather-bound books belonging to Alexandre Aguado, the Marquis de las Marismas, who purchased the estate from Colonilla's children in 1836, and Mentzelopoulos has added a music cabinet presented by Napoleon to Murat after his victory at the Pyramids.

Although the dining room holds only 18 people, this has its advantages, Mentzelopoulos explains. "It allows us to say, 'Sorry, we would love to have you, but it is impossible.' We don't want to be rude; we simply want to keep Margaux special and help people understand that it is special. We are not 'the inn at Margaux'; the château is a symbol of the prestige of the wine and it is there thanks to the fame of Margaux's vines – not the other way around."

The privileged VIPs who do receive an invitation to one of her rare receptions in the château will find the park a dream, with its lush, sprawling lawns and views over the meadows beyond the moat where Margaux's cows – the suppliers of crucial manure for the vines – graze. And all around are the vineyards, so impeccably pruned that they could be part of the gardens. "Following the Bordeaux tradition of edging the vines with roses, I thought of planting some, as I felt the estate was too green in summer," says Mentzelopoulos. "Bernard Fonquernie put a stop to that. '*Roses,* Madame,' he said, 'surely not'."

Thus Louis Combes' motto, "unity, simplicity and aptness" was not dishonoured. Mentzelopoulos did find a compromise, though. She planted a species of

American beech tree which has a partly rust-coloured trunk. "These contrast beautifully with the green of the lawns and, in the autumn, they reflect the tones of the vines," she explains.

Tempting as this pastoral idyll might appear, Mentzelopoulos stays at the château only for short periods, preferring to live and work in Paris, where she was born and raised. When she can get away, she takes off with her stockbroker husband, Hubert Leven and their three children Nathalie, Alexandra and Alexis, for holidays in the French Alps, where she skis avidly, and Greece.

It is not long, though, before she is back at her avenue Montaigne office, "at the service of a fabulous heritage". "When I leave it," she continues, "I would like to think that I have left the estate in perfect shape. I certainly couldn't say I had improved it. When Thomas Jefferson was Ambassador for the United States in 1787 he wrote: 'There cannot be a better wine produced in Bordeaux.' So who are we compared to that heritage? I simply feel that it is my responsibility to make sure the soil and its surroundings — meaning the architecture — stand up to the name of Margaux."

And, to that end, she is still putting Margaux through its paces. An even more severe selection process has been introduced, often with well over half of the wine being declassified as Pavillon Rouge. More serious still, she has hired her second-generation oenologist, the brilliant young Vincent Millet. "He is there to question our methods, so that we don't lapse into a routine," she says briskly.

Although she calls it "a great privilege" to be in charge of Château Margaux, Mentzelopoulos has one regret — that the Agnelli family is not more involved in the estate, "simply because they have such taste". One wonders, though, what more the family could do; the château again merits its past title — the 'Versailles of the Médoc' — and the 1995 *grand vin* was awarded 100 points by *Wine Spectator* magazine, a reminder of 1855 when Château Margaux was the only first growth to receive 20 out of 20 at a blind tasting.

How long the Golden Age will last Paul Pontallier can't say but, like Mentzelopoulos, he is determined that Château Margaux will be prepared for the day when nature deals another harsh blow, perhaps similar to the disastrous 19th-century phylloxera invasion. "Some new disease is bound to come along one day. It is inevitable. But Château Margaux has such a strong foundation now, it will survive very well." E

Left: Château Margaux under snow. For all of the improvements which have been introduced during the last two decades, Corinne Mentzelopoulos admits, "the only real progress that we have made is learning to cope better with what nature gives us".

THERE ARE PEOPLE WH•

A FEW ASPIRE TO. Th

DESIGN CARS TO C

MASERATI 3200 GT. THE POWER OI

V8 boosted by mixed flow turbines, traction control also in the spo

OVE TRUE EMOTIONS. A TYPE OF EMOTION THAT ONLY

E ARE ALSO CAR MANUFACTURERS WHICH PLAN AND

E THESE PEOPLE WHAT THEY ARE LOOKING FOR.

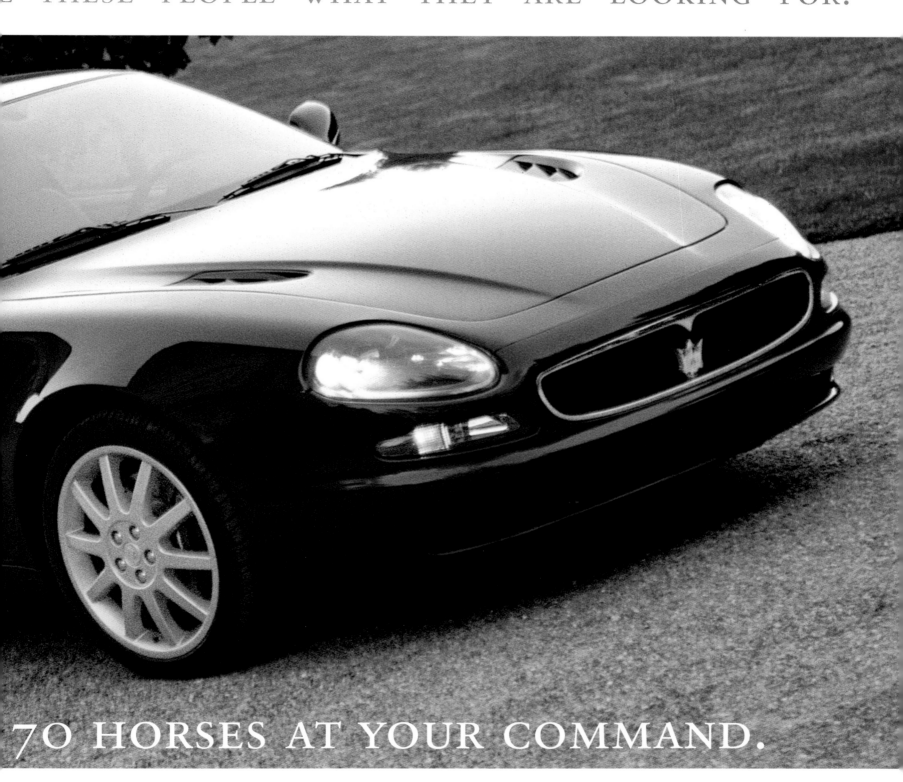

70 HORSES AT YOUR COMMAND.

sion, drive-by-wire, Connolly leather upholstery, true four seater.

LUXURY AT SEA

By Sandra Lane

The last decade of the 20th century has seen an unprecedented boom in the construction of very large private yachts and their design has evolved into an elegant, modern classicism.

Jon Bannenberg is sitting on a teak-and-canvas sofa in his design office, a mass of large-scale photographs spread on the low table in front of him. "This is beautiful," he says with quiet conviction, picking out a black-and-white print of the saloon of the 1904 royal yacht, *Victoria and Albert III*. "Do you see how relaxed it is – all that loose furniture? I would love to do a yacht like that. It's a shame that so many modern yacht designs stick to the notion of built-in furniture – rather like the cabinets in a fitted kitchen," he muses.

As he has done throughout the 30-odd years since he effectively invented the profession of yacht designer as we now know it, Bannenberg is constantly asking himself questions about the stylistic possibilities of yachts, searching for different ways of doing things, pushing the boundaries. And, in doing so, he looks backwards as well as forwards, in search of references.

While it is unquestionably contemporary, the interior of *Talitha G*, John Paul Getty's 235-foot yacht that Bannenberg recreated within a 1929 hull, is filled with 'yacht-like' elements which are clearly informed by the past: leaded-glass skylights, for example, and working gas-flame fireplaces.

During the 1980s and early 90s, once yacht design had broken out of its straight-jacketed adherence to the old nautical cliché of teak-with-everything, a whole new generation of yachts appeared. But, ironically, with them came a new cliché: interiors that had more in common with a Park Avenue apartment (or, indeed, a Miami disco) than a place to relax on the sea.

However, the 1990s generation of large yachts clearly reflects a more casual opulence.

"We [yacht designers] are all guilty of having created environments which are wrong for a swimsuits-and-T-shirts way of life," acknowledges Terence Disdale. "But our clients' tastes are definitely evolving. Fashion has had a big influence on the way people define luxury – in the sense that it has become more understated – and, as they travel, they are sampling the less glitzy style of some of the new, luxury hotels. Consequently, we are now able to steer them towards a softer style."

For one of his current projects, a 140-metre yacht for a Middle Eastern client – the owner's third yacht – Disdale is using natural wood for the floors and lots of rattan.

"It's almost a beach house look," he says. "The owner has been through glitz and now has the

Previous page: The 118-foot 'Globana', designed by Ron Holland and built by Abeking & Rasmussen. Right: The 50-metre, 40-knot 'Thunder' was launched in 1998. Designer Jon Bannenberg has taken a softer approach to the signature 'flying wedge' shape that he introduced for his fast yachts in the 1980s.

Fashion has a big luxury... yach lines, are steering

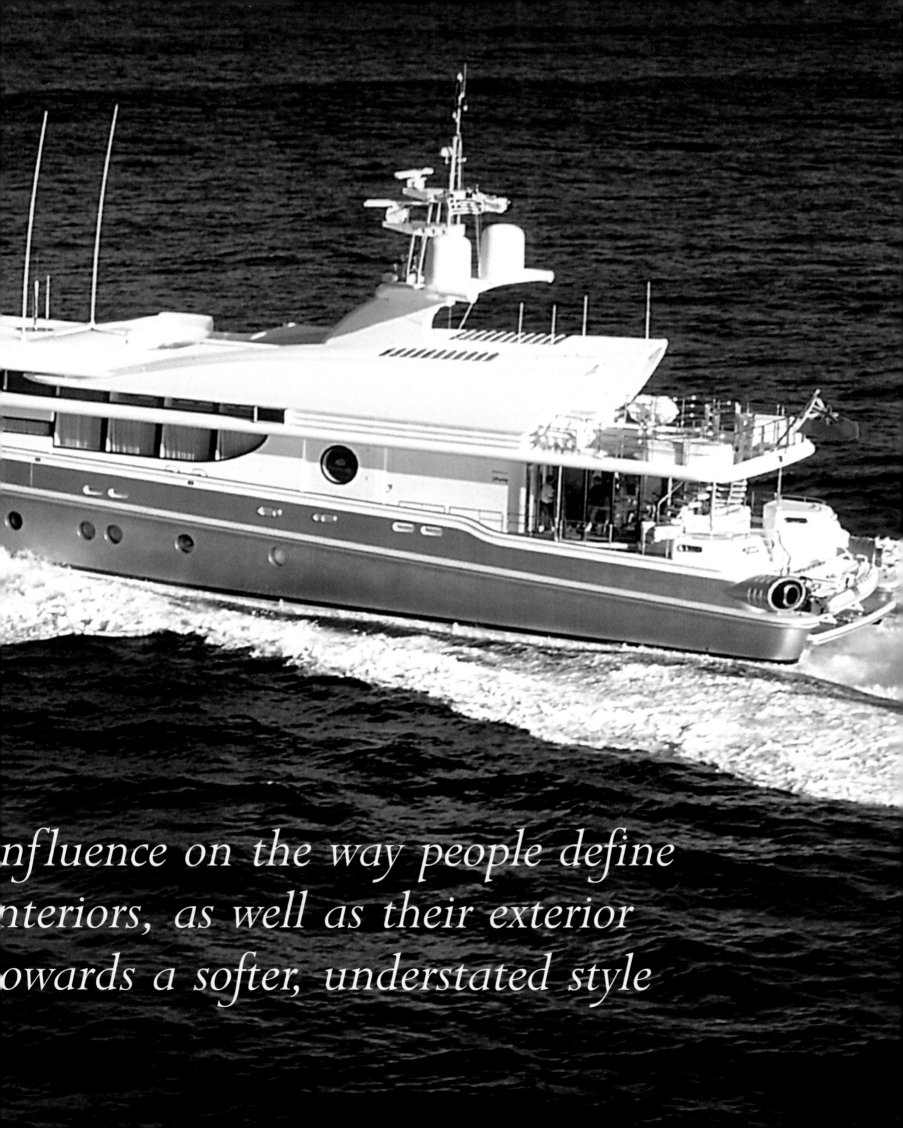

nfluence on the way people define nteriors, as well as their exterior owards a softer, understated style

confidence to go for a more relaxed ambience. He's very excited about it."

In a similar vein, Jon Bannenberg based his design for *Coral Island*, a 72-metre yacht built by Lürssen, around the owner's exceptional collection of tribal art. The result is a world away from what the designer terms "the typical handwriting of a modern yacht interior".

"With sophisticated owners, we see a theme running through their houses, their yachts and even their planes," observes Nick Edmiston, director of the eponymous brokerage firm. "There is a common thread – though it can be very subtle." One such owner is Sir Anthony Bamford who, with his wife, Carole, commissioned Colefax & Fowler to redecorate the 62-metre *Virginian*, which they bought from John Kluge. The same taste is evident in their superb houses, among them Daylesford in the English countryside and Herons Bay in Barbados.

It is not only interiors that have evolved; the exterior lines of yachts have developed into a 'new classic' idiom; clean-lined and classically proportioned, they have come a long way from the exotic extremes of the 1980s yet, at the same time, are not merely a reprise of earlier designs. Even Jon Bannenberg, whose radically aggressive 'flying wedge' designs shook the yachting world ten or twelve years ago, has refined the styling of the speed machines at which he excels. *Thunder*, a 50-metre, 40-knot gas turbine-powered flyer launched in 1998, owes a clear debt to his earlier designs but their brutalism has been tempered by a softer hand.

As well as the simple matter of aesthetics ("We refer to a yacht as 'she' and I really believe that, like a woman, she should look soft and pretty," remarks Terence Disdale), there is probably a financial motivation for this evolution.

"Extreme yachts taught us expensive lessons,"

Above: Perini Navi's 53-metre 'Independence' clearly demonstrates the current preoccupation of designers and owners alike with greater areas of shaded outdoor space and more privacy on deck.
Right: Jon Bannenberg rebuilt the 235-foot 'Talitha G' inside a classical 1920s hull, translating many traditional, yacht-like motifs into a stylish and unmistakably modern idiom.

acknowledges Nick Edmiston, citing the 72-metre Martin Francis-designed *Eco*. "She cost $60 million to build in the late Eighties and sold, after sticking on the market for years, for less than half that amount." And this in a market where good second-hand yachts regularly fetch more than they cost to build.

However, the big change over the last decade is as much about the sheer size of large yachts as it is about style. "Size does matter," says Jonathan Beckett, of the leading brokerage firm, Nigel Burgess. "Ten years ago, a 50-metre motor yacht was regarded as very big; anything larger was exceptional. Now there are more than 35 yachts over 65 metres. At the other end of the scale, a 30- to 35-metre yacht, once considered quite large, is no longer even part of the same market."

The real reason for the increase in size is not to have more people on board, Terence Disdale maintains, "It is because, nowadays, technology means that it really is possible for people to use a yacht like a second home. Spending more time on board requires more kit – and more toys."

Also, he points out, there are a lot of owners who hate going in and out of port. "The Antibes marina is like a caravan park," he laughs, "and Monte Carlo is like a goldfish bowl – all those

sightseers. They would rather be at anchor offshore." According to this logic, a wide-beamed 70-metre yacht is a lot more comfortable at anchor than a 50-metre one.

A similar explosion in size has occurred with sailing yachts. Ron Holland currently has two 61-metre yachts being built, one at Abeking & Rasmussen for a British client and one in the USA for an American, while Perini Navi's largest project to date, *Taouey*, tips the 59-metre mark. Even at a 'mere' 53 metres, Perini's *Independence* is huge, owing to its 12-metre beam and three-deck interior layout.

Technology, above all, has been responsible for this new generation of sailing yachts. The watershed came in 1984-85 when, coincidentally, Perini Navi

Right: Jon Bannenberg's solution for the swimming pool on board 'Thunder' is ingenious. While the yacht is under way this well houses its tenders; once at anchor it is filled with sea-water. Its position on the foredeck affords the owner and his guests total privacy. Far right: a table-setting on board the award-winning 52-metre 'Solemates', designed by Andrew Winch and launched in December 1998 by Feadship.

launched its 40-metre *Felicita* and Royal Huisman launched the Ron Holland-designed *Whirlwind XII*. Both were revolutionary. By incorporating the captive winch system (a Perini invention which fully automates sail handling) the need for huge crews was eliminated; it would simply have been impossible to accommodate the vast numbers required to sail a conventional yacht of this size. At the same time, Ron Holland, whose pedigree is in racing yacht design, hit on the simple logic of combining high performance hulls with the large-volume interiors and larger superstructures traditionally associated with motor yachts. Suddenly a yacht owner could think Bentley Azure, rather than Ferrari or, its polar opposite, Daimler saloon.

As size increased, so interiors became more lush. However, the interior design of sailing yachts has changed less dramatically than that of motor yachts. "Sailing yacht interiors are generally more unified; there is more joinery and less decoration than on a motor yacht," explains Andrew Winch, who designs both genres.

"Rather than a dramatic change in style," adds Ron Holland, "the biggest change has been in the degree of luxury inside. The people who come to us

are generally more connected to the traditions of sailing and this is reflected in their taste." A case in point is Perini's 52-metre *Liberty*. If you were deposited, blindfolded, into its main saloon you would be hard-pressed to determine whether it was a sailing or motor yacht. It is flooded with daylight and, while not opulent in the grand and gilded sense of the word, it whispers 'class' and exquisite comfort.

Quite apart from the issues of aesthetics and performance, many of the changes that we are now seeing in the design of large yachts relate to the way in which people want to live on board. "Thanks to the huge amount of information available to them nowadays, the owners themselves are far more aware of this," says Jim Gilbert, Editor-in-Chief of *Showboats International* magazine, "and it is manifested in a greater variety of design solutions."

The shift in the distribution of wealth to a younger generation has resulted in yachts which are better suited to a sporty lifestyle: cut-away transoms, with bathing platforms at water level are now commonplace. The desire to live a more 'outdoors' life on board has given us more extensive open-air

The glitzy interiors of the 1980s have given way to a far more relaxed approach, favouring a neutral colour palette and an atmosphere of casual opulence.
Above: Andrew Winch's concept drawing for the owner's suite of the 49-metre 'Avalon', currently under construction at Oceanco in Holland.
Opposite: The study on board 'Thunder'. Below: The dining room of 'Independence'.

Above: Terence Disdale has emphasised natural materials and the use of texture rather than colour to achieve this cool and clean-lined interior on the 50-metre 'Tigre d'Or'.

Below: Stairwells provide designers with an opportunity to flood yacht interiors with natural light. On 'Solemates' (below) Andrew Winch has used hand-carved limestone panelling for the walls and limestone treads for the stairs, while Jon Bannenberg has used the reflective qualities of stainless steel to great effect on 'Thunder' (below left). A Matisse painting provides the focal point.

dining areas while, at the same time, the widespread awareness of melanoma has led to a demand for greater shaded areas on deck. Even indoors, owners want to feel more in touch with the sea environment – hence the advent of much larger areas of glass.

"It's a mystery that, for so many years, we simply accepted the idea that yachts had to have small port-holes," reflects Jon Bannenberg. "There was no real reason for it – only convention."

The desire for greater privacy has led to a total re-think of deck arrangements. Ten years ago it was almost unthinkable to house the tenders on the main aft deck. This – in full view of dockside spectators – was the main outdoor living area; the tenders were hoisted to the upper deck. Today the exact reverse is the norm. Sailing yachts, too, reflect this change. Perini's *Liberty* features a large, shaded seating area on the foredeck, rather than the traditional cockpit

layout (made possible by the new winch system which leaves the decks free of ropes and tackle). Jon Bannenberg's solution for *Thunder* is even more ingenious; a well on the foredeck, which houses the tender, converts into a swimming pool when the tender is in the water.

"With a yacht, form very much follows function," asserts Andrew Winch. "The location of the features then determines the yacht's exterior lines." Thus, when the owner of the 52-metre *Solemates*, launched in 1998, explained to Winch that he didn't want to "miss out on the fun" when working on board, the designer moved the owner's office from its conventional position, down low next to the master suite, to the top deck, next to the main outdoor living and dining area. In the process he gave it floor-to-ceiling windows so that the owner could also enjoy the view.

"My starting point is always to talk to a client about the life he wants to live on board," says Winch. "The design process means having to work on very intimate level – I literally know which side of the bed a client sleeps on and what his bathing habits are. But it is all part of finding the right solution."

A change, too, in where people want to use their yachts, exploring more remote places rather than sticking to the conventional 'show-off' destinations, has given rise to an entirely different genre – what Jim Gilbert terms "expeditionary yachts".

Kerry Packer's *Arctic P* is one example; utilitarian on the outside, it is stuffed with comforts inside. These yachts are entirely self-sufficient, able to stay at sea for months at a time, thanks to their huge storage capacity for provisions and fuel.

While such changes in the concept of large yachts are slow to filter into the general design vocabulary (due, not least, to the fact that from concept to delivery is a three-year process) both owners and designers clearly have more confidence to explore new solutions.

"The process is becoming increasingly client-driven." says Ron Holland. "They are more sophisticated – more willing to push the level further."

They are also discovering that the design process is tremendously enjoyable in itself. Sir Donald Gosling, who currently owns the 75-metre *Leander*, is working on a new project with Terence Disdale. Whether he eventually gets the boat built is

Perini Navi's 53-metre 'Independence', sailing off the Italian coast. The development of automatic winches, which mean that such yachts no longer require an army of crew to operate them, has led to an explosion in the building of very large sailing yachts during the 1990s.

almost beside the point and those who know Gosling well say that he is right in his element. What is clear is that the era of building large private yachts is here for some time to come. As the supply of money continues to grow and it becomes increasingly difficult – or inappropriate – to build very large houses, yachts provide a logical outlet. The very newness of many of these fortunes – and the lack of preconceptions that often come with the territory – is what excites Jon Bannenberg when he considers the future of his profession.

"To build anything is the *greatest* luxury," he says, "and, as every yacht is individual, hand built and very expensive, it seems like a cop-out not to think what you can do – where you can go – with it. Our job is to release and to realise a client's fantasy. I wouldn't be doing my job if I didn't try to adapt, expand and explode that fantasy." 𝗘

Quality through Independence

Our primary concern
is not the next shareholders' meeting.
It's the next generation.

The character of a bank is determined most strongly by the principles developed from its own history. Our experience has taught us that independence is crucial to the quality of private asset management.

We believe it enables us to best identify with your personal goals, while avoiding conflicts of interest. Our main focus is on preserving the value of your personal assets for the next generation. Short-term profits, in our opinion, are no substitute for long-term success.

It may also interest you to know that, since its establishment in 1789, our bank has experienced four revolutions, half a dozen wars and five currency reforms. Today, it is one of Europe's leading private banking houses. And one of the very few still in the hands of its founding family – financially independent and unprejudiced in its advice.

Sal. Oppenheim jr. & Cie.

Privatbankiers seit 1789

COLOGNE · FRANKFURT · MUNICH · HAMBURG · DUBLIN · LONDON · LUXEMBOURG · NEW YORK · VIENNA · ZURICH

Sal. Oppenheim jr. & Cie. · Unter Sachsenhausen 4 · D–50667 Cologne · Tel. +49 (0)221 14501

Until now, why would you have wanted to leave your hotel?

To tempt our guests away from the luxury within, we now offer luxury without: two Rolls-Royce and two Bentley motor cars bearing the unmistakable crest of the Savoy Group.

Because, despite the undoubted allure of the attractions outside all our hotels, our guests have often found the comfort and calm of their accommodation difficult to leave.

You could, of course, be met on arrival at the airport by one of these four luxurious motor cars, and once at the hotel, you may be more eager to go out shopping, sightseeing or to the theatre.

By providing you with a Rolls-Royce or

THE SAVOY GROUP
England's most distinguished and individual hotels

Bentley, we give you the same splendour you're used to at home when you're away. And no matter how much pleasure you find in their familiar luxury, we know, from long and happy experience, you will soon return to the luxury of your hotel.

More cosseted than previously, perhaps, but delighted as always by our welcome.

For reservations contact (020) 7872 8080, in the USA 800-63-SAVOY, www.savoy-group.co.uk or your travel agent.

THE BERKELEY   CLARIDGE'S   THE CONNAUGHT   THE SAVOY   THE LYGON ARMS   Members of *The Leading Hotels of the World*

THE TREASURES OF EUROPE'S MUSEUMS

Research by Ruth Hillenbrand

*An exploration of Europe's smaller museums yields much
interest for art-lovers. We asked 15 in-house experts to select a
seminal work from their collections and explain its significance.*

EDOUARD MANET

Boy Blowing Bubbles, 1867

Museu Calouste Gulbenkian, Lisbon, Portugal

Calouste Sarkis Gulbenkian (1869-1955), the oil magnate, assembled one of the 20th century's finest art collections. The museum was opened to the public in 1969 and holds a remarkably wide-ranging selection, of which the highlights include celebrated 19th-century French painting and impressive Islamic art.

Boy Blowing Bubbles by Edouard Manet (1832-83) is one of the museum's most important 19th-century French works. It depicts in very light shades the painter's stepson, who is seen blowing bubbles, in sharp contrast to the dark background. Manet's use of opposites immediately attracts the viewer's attention and creates an impressive effect of improvisation. It is also typical of a painter influenced by the lines and contrasts of Japanese prints, and its psychological theme – the innocence of youth – is characteristic of Manet's interest in real, human topics. His desire to paint ordinary subjects shows the effect of Velásquez and Goya on his work.

This painting places Manet firmly among the most important pre-Impressionist artists. His technique of describing the natural immediacy of the eye's perception was to prove seminal in the evolution of French painting. Although he never exhibited with the Impressionist painters, Manet's impact on their work was profound.

João Castel-Branco Pereira, Director

REAL FABBRICA DI CAPODIMONTE

Salottino di Porcellana, 1757-79

Museo di Capodimonte, Naples, Italy

The Museo di Capodimonte is a magnificent palace set high above the city of Naples and housing three main collections: the precious art of the house of Farnese, received as inheritance from King Charles Bourbon; Neapolitan art dating from 1200 to 1800; and a collection of furniture and decorative art from Bourbon residences. Among the museum's Renaissance works are pieces by Michelangelo, Titian, Raphael and Caravaggio.

Within the royal apartments section, we find the *Salottino di Porcellana* (Porcelain Sitting Room), a masterpiece made by royally-appointed craftsmen from the 18th-century workshop, Reale Fabbrica di Capodimonte. It was made between 1757 and 1759 for the private quarters of Queen Amalia of Saxony in the Royal Palace in Portici and transferred back to Capodimonte in 1866. This room, with walls entirely covered by porcelain tiles, was planned, executed and decorated by a group of artisans, including Giuseppe Gricci, Giovan Battista Natali, Sigmund Fischer and Luigi Restile. The decorations represent scenes of daily life in China, depicting musical instruments and scrolls with Chinese poems, some of which eulogise King Charles. The decorations are an interpretation of the Chinese style, which influenced many artisans at that time, including those of Real Fabbrica di Capodimonte.

Luisa Ambrosio, Curator, Royal Apartments

CLAUS SLUTER AND CLAUS DE WERVE, JEHAN DE LA HUERTA AND ANTOINE LE MOITURIER

The Tombs of the Dukes of Burgundy, 14th and 15th century

Musée des Beaux-Arts, Dijon, France

This museum is regarded as one of the finest in France outside Paris with a fabulous collection of paintings and art treasures, notably from the 15th century when Dijon was a leading art centre and the capital for the Dukes of Burgundy. Two of their tombs – both magnificent works of medieval craftsmanship – are included in the collection.

In 1381 the Duke, Philippe le Hardi, charged his head craftsman, Jean de Marville, with making his tomb. On the death of the artist in 1389, the sculptor Claus Sluter, originally from Haarlem in the Netherlands, took over the commission. The tomb was not finished by the time of the Duke's death in 1404, nor when Sluter died two years later.

This memorial, completed by Sluter's nephew and pupil, Claus de Werve, is highly original; it breaks with the previous dependence on architectural rules and abandons conventional form. On the four sides of the tomb one can see a depiction of the funeral procession carrying the Duke's remains as it makes its way from Halle, near Brussels (the place of his death), to Dijon, where he had to be buried. The mourners are pictured walking under alabaster arches with diagonal rib vaulting and an ornamental canopy. The weeping figures are created with a realism which captures their attitude – and all are given individualised expressions.

The second tomb, that of John the Fearless and Margaret of Bavaria, was commissioned by their son, Philip the Good, after his father was assassinated in 1419. It illustrates, notably in the sculpture of its raised platform, a style more flamboyant than that of its predecessor, from which it takes its inspiration directly. The Aragonese sculptor, Jehan de la Huerta, started the tomb in 1443 and it was completed by Antoine le Moiturier in 1470.

These two major works reflect the importance of the patronage bestowed by the Dukes of Burgundy, who gathered together work by Dutch and other foreign artists, making Dijon one of the principal centres for Christian art.

Emmanuel Starcky, Director

Above: Edouard Manet, 'Boy Blowing Bubbles', 1867.
Above left: Claus Sluter & Claus de Werve, Jehan de
la Huerta & Antoine le Moiturier,
The Tombs of the Dukes of Burgundy,
14th and 15th century.
Left: Real Fabbrica di Capodimonte,
Salottino di Porcellana, 1757-59.

Above: Maestro de Caberstany, 'The Apparition of Jesus Christ to His Disciples in the Sea', 1275-99.
Above left: Angelica Kauffmann, 'Henrietta Laura Pulteney', 1777.
Left: Francis Bacon, 'Last Unfinished Portrait', 1992.

MAESTRO DE CABESTANY

The Apparition of Jesus Christ to His Disciples in the Sea, 1275-99
Museu Frederic Marès, Barcelona, Spain

Frederic Marès I Deulovol (1893-1991) was a sculptor and prodigious collector who came to Barcelona and never left.

In the 1940s, the city created a museum to house his extensive collection of religious sculpture. It now holds the main national collection of Hispanic sculpture from the Roman period to the 20th century.

A key work is Maestro de Cabestany's *The Apparition of Jesus Christ to His Disciples in the Sea* from the last quarter of the 12th century, which forms part of Catalonia's important medieval heritage. During the Roman period, numerous monasteries were constructed, including the Monastery of Sant Pere de Rodes in Girona, from which the sculpture originates; it was originally positioned on a monumental façade.

On the reverse of the sculpture is a relief which makes it clear that the work was sculpted from one piece of marble. More interestingly, however, the marble itself is almost certainly antique and had been used before this sculpture was created, possibly for another medieval work.

The façade of Sant Pere de Rodes was practically dismantled at the end of the 18th century. The best quality pieces from the façade can be found in the Frederic Marès Museum, together with a relief of an ancient key from the vault which is dedicated to 'the Lamb of God'.

Pilar Vélez, Director

ANGELICA KAUFFMANN

Henrietta Laura Pulteney, 1777
Holburne Museum, Bath, UK

The core of the museum's fine and decorative art collection was formed by Sir William Holburne (1793-1874), a native of Bath. His connoisseurship was typically 19th-century: Renaissance ceramics, 17th-century French bronzes and Flemish Masters paintings and English Regency china. In 1955 Ernest Cook, another Bath resident, bequeathed masterpieces by Raeburn, Turner and Gainsborough to the collection.

Henrietta Laura Pulteney by Angelica Kauffmann (1766-1808) is the only surviving image of the daughter of Sir William Johnstone Pulteney, famous developer of 18th-century Bath. Heir to the Pulteney family fortune, Henrietta Laura, whose business acumen was considerable, later played an active part in the management of the Bathwick estate.

Pictured here aged 11, she became a colourful personality in later life – "censurably neglectful of dress" and lacking the "embellishments" in conversation expected among ladies of rank, according to a contemporary writer. She was described in her youth as an "indefatigable dancer" and it is this carefree spirit which the fashionable Swiss artist, Angelica Kauffmann, captured with her typical delicacy of touch in this portrait of 1777.

The celebrated architect Robert Adam may have created the link between Sir William Johnstone Pulteney and Angelica Kauffmann, who was renowned for her portraits of children. It was he whom Pulteney engaged to design Pulteney Bridge, the first and key step in the development of the Bathwick Estate, while the painter had also been associated with Adam in a number of decorative schemes.

Barley Roscoe, Director

FRANCIS BACON

Last Unfinished Self-Portrait, 1992
Hugh Lane Municipal Gallery of Modern Art, Dublin, Ireland

The Hugh Lane Municipal Gallery of Modern Art was created by the Earl of Charlemont, who built the place as his townhouse in 1762, and the collector and art dealer Sir Hugh Lane, who decided at the beginning of the 20th century that the city should have a museum for modern art.

The collection today includes many late 19th- and early 20th-century works from France and Ireland.

In 1998 the gallery received one of its most significant donations ever: Francis Bacon's studio. Bacon was born in Baggot Street, Dublin, in 1909. As part of the gift to the Municipal Gallery, Bacon's heir, John Edwards, gave the artist's *Last Unfinished Self-Portrait*.

This painting is unique in the artist's œuvre. No other work in its elementary stages of composition exists; it was discovered on the easel in his studio in London after he died in 1992.

The beginnings of a self-portrait, the painting portrays Bacon's distinctive left profile, which he favoured. Placed within a cage-like structure – a recurrent feature of Bacon's paintings – the beautiful, interlaced curved lines reveal a strong central composition. The face and torso are clearly defined. The detailed modelling of the head is splendid, with the assured slash of paint across the cheek violently disrupting any suggested atmosphere of contemplation.

Bacon was in his eighties when he began the work and internationally acclaimed as one of the greatest artists of the 20th century. However, there is no perceived sense of satisfaction as he contemplates his own appearance; as in all his great works, this self-portrait is a ruthless exploration of the image.

Barbara Dawson, Director

JOAN MIRÓ
The Morning Star, 1940
Fundació Joan Miró, Barcelona, Spain

Since it opened in 1975, the Fundació Joan Miró has pursued a dual aim: the study and exhibition of the artist's work and support for other contemporary art. The gallery, designed by Miró's friend, Josep Lluís Sert, holds over 10,000 pieces by the artist, which include paintings, sculptures, textiles, ceramics, original prints and drawings.

One of the most notable works by Miró (1893-1983) is *The Morning Star*, part of a series of 23 gouaches known as the Constellations (1940-41). These paintings, whose visual complexity makes it difficult to focus on them, contain the essential elements of the language of signs that is so characteristic of Miró's art.

Started in 1940 in the Normandy village of Varengeville-sur-Mer, where Miró sought refuge after the outbreak of World War II, *The Morning Star* reflects a longing for harmony and universal solidarity, in contrast to the dramatic events unfolding in the terrible discord around him. In Varengeville he found temporary peace and the splendours of a starry sky, immersing himself in the music of Bach and Mozart.

Taking as his reference the reflections seen in water, he improvised a figure that determined the placing of additional figures until the entire surface was filled. These incorporeal figures, which still retain characteristics of the tormented beings Miró saw on the eve of the Spanish Civil War, are here idealised as free, transparent creatures who grow and are transformed naturally in symbiotic harmony with the diversity of the sky.
Jordi Joan Clavero,
Head of the Education Department

CONSTANTIN BRANCUSI
The Beginning of the World, 1924
Rijksmuseum Kröller-Müller Museum, Otterlo, Netherlands

Rijksmuseum Kröller-Müller, based in the national park, De Hoge Velvive, is well-known for its fine collection of Impressionist paintings and over 200 Van Gogh paintings.

Its sculptures are equally exceptional, with pieces by Rodin, Brancusi, Henry Moore and Barbara Hepworth.

The Beginning of the World (1924) is one of Constantin Brancusi's most abstract sculptures. With his superior feeling for form, colour and texture, combined with his highly-developed technical ability, Brancusi (1876-1957) introduced abstraction and modernism to sculpture.

He is credited with setting the standard for successive generations of artists throughout the 20th century, including Modigliani, Hepworth, Nicholson and Moore, all of whom drew inspiration from Brancusi's work.

The Beginning of the World marks the end of a series of works on the theme of a reclining head. Brancusi, who was born in Romania but worked in Paris, embarked on the series in 1906 with a study of a sleeping child's head. This was followed by the head of Prometheus (1911), the head of a new-born infant (1915) and a sculpture for the blind (1920). In the course of the series, the anatomical elements by which the sculptures can be recognised as heads were eliminated one by one. What is left is a smooth, elongated egg shape.

The title of the work prompts associations with the birth of the spiritual and the material, of art and of life. By that token, it is strongly representative of one of Brancusi's favourite themes: the manifestation of source, of inception, as a metaphor for the creative act of the artist.
Evert J van Straaten, Director

GIROLAMO VIRCHI
Cittern, 1570
Musée de la Musique, Paris, France

The Musée de la Musique, which opened in 1997, houses a rich permanent collection of instruments from the Renaissance to the modern era.

Its primary mission is to make the manifold aspects of music-making as accessible to the public as possible. And within the fascinating Renaissance collection is a beautiful cittern by Girolamo Virchi (c.1523-74), illustrative of the techniques for musical craftsmanship at the time.

Small instruments with a high-pitched sound and six double metal strings plucked with a plectrum, citterns were widely used in Italy in the 16th and 17th centuries. Judging by the four citterns we know that he made, Girolamo Virchi showed extraordinary mastery and a taste which was influenced by the Brescia craftsmen of around 1570.

The elegant outline of the soundbox, the fluted shell shape carved in the maplewood back, the numerous designs — such as a woman's face with a delicate smile and a couple hugging amid intricate foliage at the back of the pegbox — all demonstrate a rare virtuosity in woodcarving which adds to the overall, pleasurable experience of the instrument and its music.

The label glued inside the soundbox and dated 1700 suggests that this instrument would certainly have been in Antonio Stradivari's workshop. For a long time he was thought to have made the instrument, even though the cittern was out of fashion at the time.
Anne Houssay, Conservationist, Stringed Instruments

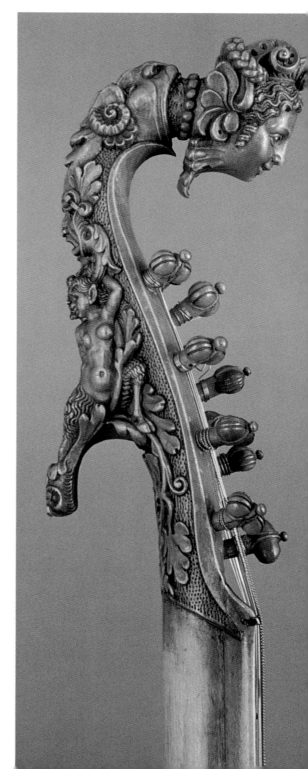

Right: Joan Miró, 'The Morning Star', 1940.
Below right: Constantin Brancusi,
'The Beginning of the World', 1924.
Below: Girolamo Virchi, Cittern, 1570.

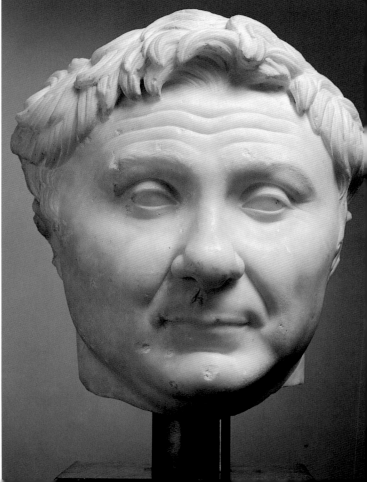

*Above: Claude Monet, Impression,
Soleil Levant, 1873.
Left: The Portrait of Gnaeus
Pompeius, 2nd century AD.
Far left: Piero della Francesca,
San Nicola da Tolentino, 1454-70.*

PIERO DELLA FRANCESCA

San Nicola da Tolentino, 1454-70

Museo Poldi Pezzoli, Milan, Italy

The house of Milanese nobleman and collector, Gian Giacomo Poldi Pezzoli (1822-79), became a museum in 1881. During his lifetime, Pezzoli's fabulous collection was the talk of Milan. Among its precious treasures are sculptures, *objets d'art*, a superb fabric collection and important Renaissance masterpieces by Piero della Francesca, Botticelli, Mantegna and Bellini.

Della Francesca's *San Nicola da Tolentino* represents a canonised friar wearing a black tunic. His right hand is in a benedictory position; his left holds the rule-book of the Agostinian Order.

The bright light in the blue sky of the background recalls the legend that a star appeared when San Nicola was born; behind the saint is a marble slab decorated with palm leaves. Della Francesca's interpretation of San Nicola departs from traditional depictions of him with the star on his chest and a lily in his hand.

The painting belongs to an original four-panel polyptych which della Francesca (c1420-92) was commissioned to make for the Church of the Agostinian Monks in Borgo San Sepolcro in 1454 and finally completed in 1470. The polyptych is believed to have been divided up in 1555.

Thought originally to have been centred around a lost painting of the Madonna and Child with saints on each side, the depiction of San Nicola is all that survives of the set in Italy. The three remaining paintings are housed in New York, London and Lisbon.

Annalisa Zanni, Director

CLAUDE MONET

Impression, Soleil Levant, 1873

Musée Marmottan, Paris, France

As well as housing medieval tapestries and manuscripts and Empire paintings and furniture, the Musée Marmottan has one of the world's finest collections of Impressionist paintings.

One of the museum's greatest treasures is Monet's *Impression, Soleil Levant*, which he presented at the first exhibition for the *Société anonyme des artistes peintres, sculpteurs et graveurs* in 1874. A view of the old harbour at Le Havre, it shows the influence of the Turner paintings he had seen in London three years earlier. The exhibition, which included work by Degas, Cézanne, Pisarro, Renoir and Sisley, was a showcase for pieces which would otherwise have gone unnoticed.

The 1874 exhibition was a great success, despite discouragement from the press, which was keen to avoid any perceived support of a movement deemed morally subversive.

Impression, Soleil Levant was taken as part of an armed robbery of the Musée Marmottan in 1985. This is ironic when we consider that the painting had fetched only 210 francs when it was sold to a doctor in 1878. It has now reclaimed its original pride of place in the museum.

From his first paintings at the edge of the Seine in Argenteuil to the *Water Lilies* series at the end of his life, Monet felt passionately about the changes of light and colour in the sky, the shimmers on the water and anything without a definite shape. His creative method was meticulous, often involving observation of the effect of light on a particular scene over many months, and he was always particularly determined to capture the dialogue between water and light. As Zola noted in 1896, "For Monet, water is alive, deep and very real." *Impression, Soleil Levant* is a perfect expression of this fascination and is seen by many as a defining symbol of the Impressionist movement. *Arnaud d'Hauterives, Director*

THE PORTRAIT OF GNAEUS POMPEIUS

2nd century AD

NY Carlsberg Glyptotek, Copenhagen, Denmark

The heart of NY Carlsberg Glyptotek is the private collection of the brewer Carl Jacobsen (1842-1914), who founded the museum. It houses extensive collections of sculpture and portraits from ancient Egypt, Greece and Rome; its Etruscan Department is considered to be among the most important outside Italy.

There are also significant groups of 19th-century French and Danish sculptures and painting. Of particular note are works by Rodin and Gauguin.

The Portrait of Gnaeus Pompeius is one of the principal works in the Roman collection. Gnaeus Pompeius (106-48BC), the Roman general, was popularly known as Pompey and took the appellation Magnus. The head was found in the Tomb of the Licinii in Rome in 1885 and depicts Pompey at the age of 50.

This is the best-preserved portrait of the general and is probably a marble copy of the bronze portrait which stood in the Senate Building on Rome's Field of Mars. Made at the beginning of the 2nd century AD, the portrait radiates the authority, determination and amiability characteristic of the popular military leader.

In 48 BC Pompey lost the Battle of Pharsalos in northern Greece to Julius Caesar and fled to Egypt, where he was murdered on the beach the moment he arrived. His corpse was decapitated and the head sent to Caesar, who had it cremated; the ashes were laid to rest by the general's widow. Pompey's motto – To sail is necessary: to live is not – perfectly sums up his active life and dramatic death.

Søren Dietz, Director

MAX BECKMANN
Self-Portrait with Quappi, 1940-41
Stedelijk Museum, Amsterdam, Netherlands

Stedelijk Museum is Amsterdam's finest modern art museum, with works by Mondrian, Rieteveld and other members of the 1920s De Stijl movement, as well as work by young, up-and-coming artists.

In *Self-Portrait with Quappi*, we see the German painter, Max Beckmann, with his wife, Quappi. The artist presents himself as a man of the world, without embellishment. He paints with hard, expressive colours and black contours.

Beckmann (1894-1950) was a man who felt a deep affinity with modern urban life which, in the Germany of the first part of the 20th century, was marked by war and the rise of Nazism. Many of Beckmann's scenes are set in cafés, music halls and theatres and, in them, he mercilessly lays bare the pretence and superficiality of fashionable life by also showing its other faces, especially loneliness.

Self-Portrait with Quappi, painted at the beginning of World War II, also bears witness to the difficult and uncertain circumstances in which he found himself. In 1937 Beckmann fled the Nazis and, having failed to obtain an entry visa for America, ended up in Amsterdam, where he led an isolated existence for the next ten years. After the war he finally got to America, where he spent the last three years of his life.

Beckmann's importance lies primarily in his capacity to unite the visible with the instinctive, without false sentiment or inflated mysticism. The Nazis declared that this raw, objective approach to art – adopted by many other Expressionists – was *entartet* or 'censored'. *Self-Portrait with Quappi* offers a probing reflection of the artist's personal situation, while also forcing us to define our place in the world.

Maarten Bertheux, Assistant Director

Left: Max Beckmann, 'Self-Portrait with Quappi', 1940-41.
Top Right: Marcello Bacciarelli, 'Portrait of King Stanislaw Augustus', 1771.
Far Right: Albrecht Dürer, 'The Feast of the Rosary', 1506.

MARCELLO BACCIARELLI
Portrait of King Stanislaw Augustus, 1771
Zamek Królewski, Warsaw, Poland

Zamek Królewski, Warsaw's Royal Castle, was the royal residence and the seat of the Seym (Parliament) of the Commonwealth of the Two Nations (Poland and Lithuania). Its richly decorated interiors show the history and traditions of the Polish State. Demolished on Hitler's orders during World War II, it was rebuilt in the Baroque style between 1971 and 1984.

One of the treasures which escaped the demolition is the *Portrait of King Stanislaw Augustus* by Marcello Bacciarelli (1731-1818). The painting shows the monarch, Stanislaw II Poniatowski, in full coronation dress and has a Latin inscription dedicated to the memory of kings.

Bacciarelli worked throughout Eastern Europe but settled in Poland, where he became the king's principal painter, and was ennobled in 1786. He supervised the decoration of the king's residence and looked after the royal collections; in his time he was also responsible for painting portraits of the entire aristocratic community in Poland, kings and queens from previous centuries and scenes from Polish history.

He is thus seen as the Polish monarchy's chief interpreter of artistic policy in the second half of the 18th century.

Bacciarelli's portraits show his preference for clean outlines, a single tonality and simple backgrounds. The *Portrait of King Stanislaw Augustus* confirms Bacchiarelli's place as the founder of an 18th-century Polish national iconography, based on authentic historical records and his own keen eye.

Andrzej Rottermund, Director

ALBRECHT DÜRER

The Feast of the Rosary, 1506

Šternberský Palác, Prague, Czech Republic

Šternberský Palác, home to several impressive galleries, includes icons and religious art from the 3rd to the 14th century, as well as works by Dürer, Holbein, Van Dyck, Canaletto and modern masters.

Albrecht Dürer's *The Feast of the Rosary* marks a turning-point, not only in his own work but in the whole of North European Renaissance painting. The subject of the painting is linked with the growth and spread of the cult of the Rosary, influenced mainly by the Dominican Order, in the second half of the 15th century. We see, therefore, besides the Virgin and Child, Saint Dominic and several angels distributing crowns of roses to a congregation of believers symbolising one of the fraternities of the Rosary founded at the time by the Dominicans. The Pope and Emperor, representing spiritual and temporal power, and also the figures kneeling around the throne, have been depicted with the precision of portraits although the models are difficult to identify.

As well as its importance in the works of Dürer (1471-1528), this is the earliest North European painting in which Renaissance ideas prevail, despite vestiges from the past. These include a strongly marked analytical tendency, a delight in detail, a somewhat loose rhythm and an accumulation of figures within the picture.

The painting was in the Church of San Bartolomeo in Venice until 1606 when it was bought by Emperor Rudolph II of Austria. The Czech State acquired the work in 1934.

Gere Fajt, Director **E**

Wentworth

Mats Wilander has called it "the perfect setting for the game of tennis", while Severiano Ballesteros puts Wentworth at "the very top of my list of favourite places, alongside Augusta". The real joy of Wentworth – for them, as for its members – is not simply the club's world-class sporting facilities; it has a uniquely seductive magic.

With its three suberb 18-hole courses, the club has, of course, become synonymous with golf – yet it was always about much more than that. Created seventy five years ago by the visionary Walter Tarrant, in classical American country club style, its present incarnation is due to the latter-day vision of Chairman, Elliott Bernerd, and Chief Executive, Willy Bauer. Taking ownership in 1988, they were determined to create one of the world's finest sporting and leisure clubs.

That vision was made manifest in January 1999 with the opening of Wentworth's spectacular new tennis and health centre. Built on the site of the original tennis pavilion and overlooking the 11 outdoor courts, it incorporates an indoor pool, a gymnasium and dance studio, saunas and steam rooms, as well as offering a vast range of spa treatments. Its sleek modernity – a blend of wood, limestone and polished marble – is a perfect complement to the discreet and relaxed elegance of the famous, castellated clubhouse – itself sensitively and subtly restored in 1993.

As the 21st century dawns, Wentworth provides, more than ever, a perfect escape from the pressures of an increasingly hectic world.

Wentworth Club
Wentworth Drive, Virginia Water, Surrey GU25 4LS, UK
Tel: +44-1344-84 22 01   Fax: +44-1344-84 28 04

A MATTER OF CLASS

By Sandra Lane

*The mystique and mores of the British upper classes
have long fascinated outsiders. We look at their style and,
in this egalitarian age, their future.*

The subject of the British class system – in particular, the mystique and mores of the upper classes and the question of their survival – is one which has long fascinated observers and, if we are to believe some of the more excitable sections of the media, it is about to be consigned to history.

The upper classes' sporting strongholds are under siege: fox-hunting is under threat of a ban and the grouse moors echo with the mobile phones and estuary accents of Johnny-come-lately City traders – clad, to a man, in brand-new tweeds. Practically anyone (even divorcees, shock! horror!) can get into the Royal Enclosure at Ascot these days, rendering

Eton College has always been the cradle of élite education in Britain; today it attracts a mix of aristocracy and serious new money. Previous page: Schoolboys in their distinctive white-tie-and-tails uniform. Above: Festivities at Eton's 'Fourth of June' open day for parents include boat races on the Thames.

the borrowing of a friend's name badge to gain entry – for which Joan Collins was famously thrown out a few years ago – not only undignified but quite unnecessary. (The last bastion of smartness at that race meeting nowadays is White's tent.) And, the final nail in the coffin, Britain's present Prime Minister (ironically the first for over 30 years to have received a private education – a traditional marker of upper-classness if ever there was) is in the throes of abolishing the House of Lords.

But just what is a member of the upper classes? (One never talks of the 'upper class'; middle class and working class, yes, but 'upper' is always plural). This, of course, is a question that has, for many generations, exercised the minds of ambitious American mothers with daughters of marriageable age – in their country, after all, 'Earl' is merely a christian name. An aristocrat, obviously, is one but a Life Peer, quite likely, is not – particularly these days when so many are superannuated MPs or the Prime Minister's cronies – although he or she can be counted among the Establishment, which is not at all the same thing.

In truth, the subject is fascinating, most of all, to

those who do not – for reasons either of style and profession or of nationality – belong to these classes. Ask most members of the British upper classes what defines them and they have genuine difficulty answering (quite apart from being too well-mannered to discuss such matters).

"Although the title under which I sit in the House of Lords is only three generations old, my Scottish ancestor, John Sinclair, was created a baronet in 1786," says Viscount Thurso. "I went to Eton and Oxford but, as a hotelier, I work in service. Am I an aristocrat? I don't know."

Lord Sieff, on the other hand – a Life Peer with a background in trade (Marks & Spencer) – has all of the credentials of a blue-blood; like Thurso, he is clever, discreet, immensely cultured and has impeccable manners. He is also a major philanthropist and a Trustee of the National Gallery.

So how to decide who really is who? Lady Apsley, whose husband is heir to the Earl of Bathurst, puts it succinctly. "Quite simply, class is always in the eye of the beholder."

"It has a lot to do with manners and style and is absolutely not a question of money," she adds. "In the US, where the system is entirely money-based, you can go up and come back down very quickly; here, if you go up, you tend to stay up. You are not sidelined if you run out of money." This, quite possibly, helps to explain one notable characteristic of the British upper classes: a sense of sureness, a quiet confidence. There is neither pretence nor pretentiousness – that is the preserve of the wannabes.

Those who aspire certainly are far more class-conscious than those who already belong. The Duke of Devonshire tells a revealing story about Evelyn Waugh. "He desperately wanted to be Lord Sefton [a very grand and stylish member of White's club at the time] but would turn up at White's in the wrong kind of checked suit. Mind you," he adds with a twinkle, "it would have mattered far more to Waugh than to the other members if it had been pointed out."

It is their confidence which gives the very grand their famous nonchalance about dress. The aristo who looks like a gardener in his old tweed jacket is an enduring – and perfectly accurate – image; he doesn't need clothes to demonstrate his worth. His antennae are, however, finely tuned to quality. "A gent, no matter how poor, will wear a good suit," points out Lord Mancroft. "Not necessarily a new one but a good one, made by a proper tailor."

The same goes for the women. Traditionally reticent about putting on any sort of 'show', a true English aristocrat is oblivious to trends, preferring to follow her own codes. By this measure, the late Princess of Wales, the daughter of an Earl and a world-class clothes-horse, was far less typical of her class than is the non-titled Camilla Parker-Bowles. However, in

Left: The late Princess of Wales broke with the British upper class tradition of discreet, classical elegance in favour of high-octane designer glamour. Top: The Duke of Devonshire. Above: A tailor at Huntsman, one of Savile Row's élite establishments. A true gent will always wear a good suit, made by a proper tailor, rather than a designer label.

Above: Oxford University, a key stage in the education of a member of the élite. Right: In wigs and ermine, the Lords file into the House for the State Opening of Parliament.

this age of cash and flash, Diana's style was, quite simply, easier for the public – both British and international – to understand. These days it is a millionaire footballer or hairdresser – the very apex of the working class – who will be in head-to-toe Versace or Prada. "Designer labels demonstrate their form of class-consciousness," explains historian Andrew Roberts.

It's not just a matter of dress, either. Sir Paul McCartney, despite his title (only a knighthood, admittedly), his wealth, his press-shy lifestyle and his ownership of thousands of prime Sussex and Scottish acres, will never be as 'aristocratic' as Mr Mick Jagger or Mr Bryan Ferry, both of whom slid smoothly into the embrace of the upper classes many years ago.

Accents probably remain the easiest shorthand by which to separate the classes and are largely a product of the public (i.e. private) school system. "Accent gives everything away," agrees MP Alan Clark, "and there is still a strange vigilance. You notice it in the House of Lords when a new peer is sworn in; there is a ripple across the benches, as the real ones categorise the newcomer by the peccability of his speech."

As anyone who has aspired (successfully or otherwise) to join the British upper classes will have discovered to their chagrin, it is, quite simply, impossible to acquire what they may perceive to be the 'right' accent. Quite apart from the vowel sounds, there are those very grand quirks, such as the dropped 'g' in shootin' and fishin' and the dropped 'th', as in got 'em; some may be eerily similar to working-class speech but, make no mistake, there is never, ever a glottal stop. Foreigners can't do it and the point is that neither they nor the Mick Jaggers of this world have to try. The late Lady Tryon, for instance, who became a confidante of Prince Charles and married a peer, never felt a need to play down her Australian accent — or, indeed, her breezily outspoken Antipodean manner. Her outspokenness was, on the contrary, both natural and endearing to her English friends. Without fear or favour, the upper classes have always called a spade a spade.

But, these examples of successful assimilation aside, are the British upper classes as impenetrable as some would have us believe?

"The class system is massively misunderstood," asserts Andrew Roberts. "Its critics imply that, because of the class system, poor people can't get to the top. That is so obviously untrue; the class system is very porous."

Just ask Derek Laud. Born in south London of Jamaican parents and brought up alone by his mother after his father left home, he spent the best part of the last two decades at the heart of the Tory government, becoming the first and only black member of the Right-wing Monday Club, and is now a successful venture capitalist in the City of London. Last spring he became Master of the New Forest Foxhounds — the top slot in a sport which is regarded, quite wrongly, as the bastion of upper-class privilege and snobbishness.

Hunting is, in fact, far more socially inclusive than many other sports; it was always a farmers' sport, becoming 'upper class' only in some areas after 1850. Among its adherents today, the wealthy and titled are still vastly outnumbered by farmers and country people of every stripe.

What hunting - like shooting and fishing - does demonstrate, though, is the extent to which the British upper classes have maintained their traditional closeness to the countryside; those aristocratic families whose fortunes have waned are far more likely to have given up the town house rather than the country seat, whereas the opposite applies in, say, Germany or Italy. This also partly explains the passion of the upper classes (men and women) for gardening; country houses mean rolling acres in which to create their visions of Arcadia. Yet, like hunting, gardening knows no social boundaries; at the Chelsea Flower Show and countless smaller events around the country, aristocrats swap notes with allotment holders.

Despite the experience of the present Lord Carrington's ancestor, the ruling class has never excluded new wealth. When his family was ennobled in the 18th century the entire House of Lords walked out in protest at the elevation of this common banker. That was a mere blip, however, and the family has since held a central position both politically and socially; Carrington himself, the 6th Baron, has been, variously, British Foreign

Secretary, Nato Secretary-General and Chairman of Christie's. Even the bluest blood had murky beginnings and much of the 'old' money in Britain is post-Industrial Revolution and Empire; the Lords Vestey, Cowdray and Rothschild, for instance, all owe their position to 19th- and 20th-century fortunes.

What's more, unlike, say, the high French aristocracy, the British bring in new blood by marrying outside their class. Lady Haden-Guest, one of the most elegant peeresses at last year's State Opening of Parliament, is none other than American actress Jamie Lee Curtis and, while they may have been excellent financial marriages, the previous Duke of Marlborough's union with Consuelo Vanderbilt and the Earl of Strathmore's marriage to a member of Hong Kong's Keswick family are outside the strict boundaries of their social class.

Although an egalitarian-minded American, German or Frenchman would probably be horrified by the notion, the truth is that every country has a class system — it's just that they go by a different name. And, in those countries, some circles are

The British passion for gardening crosses all class barriers. Above: Princess Margaret at the Chelsea Flower Show, greeted by her son, the furniture designer David (Viscount) Linley.

far less accepting of outsiders than are the British upper classes.

In Germany, apart from the few big land-owning families (Hanover, Hesse, Schaumburg-Lippe and Wurttemburg, for instance) titles are irrelevant. However, the ruling class is, arguably, an even more solid fraternity; as a result of Germany's convention of cross-networking between banking and industry, members of each sector hold positions on each others' boards.

Money may be the driving force of America's meritocracy but, even there, regardless of how much cash you have, you can't break into certain élites; the Kennedys were always outsiders until JFK became

The Queen presents Prince Charles with a prize, following a polo match at Smith's Lawn.

President and Hollywood's or Washington DC's (largely self-appointed) A-Lists – not to mention New York's 'old money' Knickerbocker Club – are far more exclusive, in the true sense of the word, than are White's or Pratt's.

There is, of course, an element of snobbery here – a trait of which the British upper classes are often accused. When Alan Clark, in a light-hearted attempt to explain why Michael Heseltine (then Deputy Prime Minister) was not acceptable to the governing class, said that Heseltine "bought all his own furniture and can't shoot straight", the remark was seized upon by the media with great glee, as proof of Clark's snobbery.

"We are all snobs of some kind," laughs the Duke of Devonshire. "There are wine snobs, I'm a literary snob – it's human nature to want to belong to a group which excludes others."

As Andrew Roberts points out, the lower middle class is far more defensive of its non-working class status than the upper classes are of their position. Ask most peers who are the grandest people in the

House of Lords and they will most likely agree: the doormen.

It comes back to that sense of sureness and confidence; the British upper classes simply don't feel the need to throw their weight around. And here they have an advantage over their European counterparts. While their existence is more formalised, due to the continuing presence of the monarchy, the aristocracy does not depend on the House of Lords for its validity and while, as Andrew Roberts points out, "the political class has, for years, had more power than the upper classes", this has come about by evolution rather than revolution.

The result? "A gent treats nobody any differently," says Lady Apsley. "He is gracious without ever being condescending or patronising." Hence that old chestnut about Dukes and dustmen getting along famously; both are entirely sure of their position.

In contrast, perhaps because it has less upon which to anchor its sense of validity – not to mention six sets of titles, conferred by different regimes over the course of a century – the French aristocracy is notoriously snobbish.

"Like all countries in Europe where titles are purely social, it is totally governed by protocol," says Alan Clark. "They perpetuate it amongst themselves, like a sect; their only life is manoeuvring within the remit of the Almanach." Thus it was that former President Valéry Giscard d'Estaing was famously blackballed from the Paris Jockey Club, not because he wasn't a real aristocrat but because his title was somehow not quite right.

"While the British upper classes may not welcome an outsider into the centre of their world with open arms, they are, unlike the Germans, very open-minded and tolerant – probably as a result of several generations of education and travel and their heritage of Empire," observes one German aristocrat who is a long-time London resident. "There is a great willingness here to allow parallel societies to coexist."

This probably makes Britain the ideal society in which the traditional upper classes can happily survive. And just as well, because things are certainly not what they used to be. Noblesse oblige has been replaced by a reverence for nouveau-riche glamour. And the nouveaux are drawn from a more varied background than ever – sports stars, porn kings, pop stars and a floating population of Euro-rich, as well as industrial entrepreneurs and financiers – and they have created an 'aristocracy' all of their own.

These days the Duke of Norfolk can step out of his car unnoticed; it's the new celebrity class that gets all the attention. And revels in it.

For anyone grand, a generation ago, it was unforgivable to have one's name in the newspapers, except to announce births, marriages and deaths. Now the Age of Gossip is upon us and, although

Top: Fox hunting, mistakenly regarded by many non-participants as a toffs' sport, unites country people of all social levels. Left and Above: Pheasant shooting at Wiscombe Park in Devon.

Above: Viscountess Linley and Princess Alexandra arrive in the traditional royal procession at Ascot.

some traditionally grand families keep their counsel (who has heard of the Earl of Yarborough, for instance, who inherited £180 million in cash and has 11 Stubbses hanging in his house) the likes of Henry Dent-Brocklehurst (whose inheritance was a cool £50 million and a 15th-century pile, even though his great-grandfather had given up the title) happily court the press.

The 'new aristos' are flash and they are brash. You won't see them lunching at Wilton's or the Savoy Grill; they're probably not out of bed yet and, anyway, they have their own hangouts – Daphne's, Titanic and the Met Bar. They may be buying country mansions but their idea of field sports is the

Cartier Polo Day or Ascot. They may, indeed, get their suits made – though by Richard James, Ozwald Boateng or Timothy Everest, rather than Huntsman.

That said, new money generally tries to look like old money as quickly as possible; give them time – just a little time – and they will be buying country estates, restoring grand houses and acquiring collections of fine art and fine wines.

The really telling moment is when the new aristos become parents. They rush to put their children's names down for the smart schools (good both for the accent and for future networking).

Lord Hanson (made a life peer by Margaret Thatcher) who began his life as, simply, James,

the son of a Yorkshire trucker, sent his own son, Robert, to Eton; Madonna has chosen that bastion of tradition, Cheltenham Ladies' College, for her daughter, Lourdes, and even the doorman at Annabel's sent his son to Harrow.

Of course, not every teenaged son or daughter of a property magnate or pop star integrates fully at Eton

or Harrow, Roedean or Benenden but that probably has more to do with their manners (or lack of them) and fact that they flaunt their money than with their parents' accents. "If you have good manners," insists Lady Apsley, "you can be accepted into any class."

It's simply a question of attitude – or what royal couturier, Sir Hardy Amies (by his own admission, "a suburban boy made good") calls "appropriateness at all times".

"There are," Sir Hardy is fond of saying, "ladies and gentlemen and then there are the others." He, as much as anyone knows that having class, as distinct from belonging to a particular class, will always be the most important social marker. **E**

The British aristocracy has, over the years, regularly brought in 'new blood' by marrying outside its own class. Above: The wedding of HRH Prince Edward and the former Miss Sophie Rhys-Jones.

Your Eternal Cut diamond
will perfectly set off the green of their eyes.

The new 81-facet Eternal Cut diamond, shown here as part of the
Stellar Collection, can be found only at Asprey & Garrard.
Available with matching ring and bracelet, it creates a circle of pure,
brilliant, perpetually-moving light. The effect is magical.

Asprey & Garrard 167 New Bond Street W1 Tel: 0171 493 6767 www.asprey-garrard.com

ASPREY & GARRARD

LONDON

EUROPE'S ELITE 1000

*The 1000 names on the following list are the Editors' choice of the finest
shops, services and luxury goods that Europe has to offer.
We give you an insider's report on each and every one of them.*

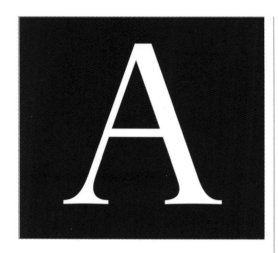

A. UGOLINI & FIGLI

This illustrious menswear shop in the heart of Florence was founded in 1896 by managing director Niccolo Ugolini's grandfather, Arturo. This select little operation – which also has a woman's branch along the road – sells clothing in a range of seasonal fabrics and has welcomed gentlemen from the highest echelons of Italian society, including Prince Umberto of Savoia, Riccardo Muti and Walter Chiari.

A. Ugolini & Figli
via Calzaiuoli 65, 50122 Florence, Italy
Tel: +39-055-21 44 39 Fax: +39-055-21 23 91

ABEKING & RASMUSSEN

Founded in 1907 by Henry Rasmussen (grandfather of the yard's current President, Hermann Schaedla) and Georg Abeking, this shipyard developed its technical expertise through the construction of naval and commercial vessels before turning to custom-built yachts. These skills have enabled it to produce masterpieces as diverse as Gianni Agnelli's classically inspired wooden-hulled sailing yacht, the Bruce King/Andrew Winch-designed *Hetarios*, and, currently under construction, a 58m Don Starkey-designed steel and aluminium motor yacht.

Abeking & Rasmussen
P.O. Box 1160, D-27805 Lemwerder, Germany
Tel: +49-421-673 3532 Fax: +49-421-673 3115

ACIUGHETA

The touristy-looking exterior of this trattoria belies the fact that this is a taste of the real Venice; drop in for *cichetti* (bite-sized local specialities, such as *Sarde in saor* – marinated sardines) and a glass of excellent wine – a dozen different reds and whites are opened each day for tasting. Next door, owner Gianni Bonaccorsi has opened Bar Europa, where he sells a remarkable selection of fine wines, oils and coffees.

Aciugheta
Campo San Filippo e Giacomo 4357, 4509 Venice, Italy
Tel: +39-041-522 4292 Fax: +39-041-520 8222

ADLER

With boutiques as far afield as Hong Kong and Tokyo, Geneva-based Adler's reputation has spread around the world. Jacques Adler founded the company in Istanbul in 1886 and his descendants, brothers Carlo and Franklin Adler oversee the business to this day. Adler prides itself on the rare quality of its stones, the fine design of its original and made-to-measure creations in the "purest tradition", and its personal service. Increasingly, Adler is noted for its striking advertising campaigns which emphasise a love of multi-cultural influences and contrasting artistic traditions. Innovative combinations of coloured stones and baguette diamonds on a grand scale are Adler's signature, while their growing collection of young, affordable jewels features such pieces as the 'Leyla' ring, designed by Franklin's wife.

Adler
23 rue du Rhône, CH-1204 Geneva, Switzerland
Tel: +41-22-819 8025 Fax: +41-22-819 8020
E-mail: info@adler.ch
Also in Gstaad (+41-33-744 6680)
and London (+44-20-74 09 22 37)

ADLON, HOTEL

Within two year's of its 1997 reopening the Adlon had welcomed Clinton, Kissinger and Kohl, the Dalai Lama and Pierce Brosnan. Its two Presidential Suites, overlooking the Brandenburg Gate, have astonishing security, including bulletproof windows, private entrances and rooms for bodyguards. In 1999 a Terrace restaurant (also facing the Brandenburg Gate) and an exclusive outside catering service were inaugurated, and in the Autumn, a gourmet restaurant opened under the direction of chef, Karlheinz Hauser.

Hotel Adlon
Unter den Linden 77, D-10117 Berlin, Germany
Tel: +49-30-22 610 Fax: +49-30-22 61 11 60

ADMIRABLE CRICHTON, THE

This party organiser specialises in transforming any social event – be it a shop launch in New York, a film premiere in London or a wedding in Venice – into a fantasy world and the results are unforgettable. Supported by a wonderfully creative kitchen and a troupe of engaging staff, its imagination and attention to detail impress hosts and guests alike.

The Admirable Crichton
6 Camberwell Trading Estate, Denmark Road
London SE5 9LB, UK
Tel: +44-20-77 33 81 13 Fax: +44-20-77 33 72 89

ADRIAN SASSOON

Although primarily a glass and porcelain dealer, Sassoon recently arranged a world-record sale of a 17th-century Savonnerie carpet made for Louis XIV. In his capacity as an art advisor he has also outfitted a 288-foot super-yacht with works of art. He was the first exhibitor to sign up for the New York 20th Century Arts Fair, held at the end of 1999.

Adrian Sassoon
14 Rutland Gate, London SW7 1BB, UK
Tel: +44-20-75 81 98 88 Fax: +44-20-78 23 84 73

AGATA E ROMEO

With its high, vaulted ceiling, ancient walls and comfortable seating, this is an oasis of serenity in one of Rome's busiest quarters (a charming detail: antique mirrors as table centre-pieces). And it's one where you can enjoy authentic, yet refined versions of the classical Roman dishes more usually found in simple trattorie – Fresh artichokes with peas and broad beans; Steamed skate with grapes, walnuts and pignoli and a *Millefeuille* of sheep's milk cheese.

Agata e Romeo
via Carlo Alberto 45, 00185 Rome, Italy
Tel: +39-06-446 6115 Fax: +39-06-446 5842

AgenC, THE

Top-flight domestic staff are Jann McKeague-Green's speciality and staff placed by her company, The AgenC, are found in the highest echelons of service. Although it no longer provides yacht crews,

MCKEAGUE-GREEN
INTERNATIONAL PLACEMENTS

the company has both expanded and relocated during 1999. Its security division handles a broad range of related tasks, from computer fraud and specialist forensic services to high security vehicles and VIP protection.

The AgenC McKeague-Green
2nd floor, 55A Knightsbridge
London SW1X 7RA, UK
Tel: +44-20-72 45 65 55   Fax: +44-20-72 45 62 22
Email: agenc@cocoon.co.uk

AGRY

Engravers to the aristocracy since 1825, Agry designs family crests to order, using time-honoured methods. Catherine Hacquebart, an ancestor of the founder, is passionate about heraldry, attributing the resurgence of interest in it to society's feeling that it has become distanced from its roots. Having created the insignia, Agry will apply it to seals and stationery, porcelain, signet rings, cufflinks, buttons for blazers and hunting clothes. The tiny shop is, itself, a step into the past with rich, Charles X-style maplewood panelling.

Maison Agry
14 rue de Castiglione, 75001 Paris, France
Tel: +33-1-42 60 65 10   Fax: +33-1-42 60 48 92

AIDAN O'BRIEN

The supernova of Irish racing, trainer Aidan O'Brien is married to Anne-Marie — herself the Champion Irish Jumps trainer for 1992/3 — and together the pair have three children. O'Brien broke the Irish prize money record in his first season and has also been enormously successful in England. Adept at both jumpers and flat racers, his relative youth has never stood in his way.

Aidan O'Brien
Ballydoyle, Cashel, Co. Tipperary, Ireland
Tel: +353-62-62 615   Fax: +353-62-61 260

AIMO E NADIA

To understand Aimo Moroni's passion for food and the warmth of his hospitality, it helps to know of his past; he arrived in Milan as a 12-year old in 1946 — penniless, hungry and alone. His wife Nadia's cooking (Fettucine with prawns, sole and wild fennel; deep-fried artichokes and prawns with potatoes) will reduce a grown man to tears. Regulars — including Milan's top movers and shakers — are, thoughtfully, always given the same table.

Aimo e Nadia
via Montecuccioli 6, 20146 Milan, Italy
Tel: +39-02-41 68 86   Fax: +39-02-48 30 20 05

AIR HARRODS

Established in 1997, Air Harrods owns and operates two luxuriously appointed helicopters, the most technically advanced in their respective classes — a Sikorsky S76A++ and a Twin Squirrel. It also arranges top-of-the range charters for both helicopters and fixed-wing aircraft. By acting as a broker rather than owning its own fleet, Air Harrods is able to offer clients the maximum possible flexibility; anything from a 767 to a Citation can be sourced, anywhere in the world, for both long and short-term use. In addition, the company undertakes aircraft management; the owner of a Gulfstream IV is among the clients currently enjoying its benefits.

Air Harrods
First Avenue, Stansted Airport, Essex CM24 1QQ, UK
Tel: +44-1279-66 08 00   Fax: +44-1279-66 08 80

AKELARE

So stunning are the views of sea and sky from this glass-fronted restaurant that Pedro Subijana designed his ultra-modern kitchens to share the same outlook. He encourages guests to visit both the kitchens and the gardens, where he grows most of his own herbs and vegetables. Subijana's seafood-based menu, a creative adaptation of classical Basque cuisine, includes such masterpieces as a Ragoût of asparagus, octopus and baby vegetables with foie gras.

Akelare
Paseo del Padre Orcolaga 56, E-20008 San Sebastian, Spain
Tel: +34-943-21 20 52   Fax: +34-943-21 92 68

AL PINO

Superb salami and home-made foccacia are harbingers of the treats which follow: a masterful Vegetable *millefeuille* with tuna sauce and Veal kidneys with artichokes. Mario Musoni is also a wizard with risotto — his sublime squid-ink version is one of five, which change each season. His English wife, Patricia, oversees the restaurant; set on the first floor of this white villa, its modern decor is offset by fine carpets inside and views of the surrounding fields outside.

Al Pino
via Pianazza 11, 27040 Montescano, Pavia, Italy
Tel & Fax: +39-0385-60479

AL RODODENDRO

This jewel of a restaurant — decorated in soothing tones of blue — is a fairy-tale setting for owner-chef Maria Barale's sublime cooking. So passionate is she about the quality of her ingredients that she insists on doing all of the buying herself; her finds include superb Piedmontese lamb (roasted whole), wild boar and little-known local cheeses. They are serious about wine here, too, and sommelier Carlo presides over an exceptional cellar.

Al Rododendro
via San Giacomo 73, 12012 Boves, Cuneo, Italy
Tel: +39-0171-38 03 72   Fax: +39-0171-38 78 22

AL SORRISO

In 1981 Luisa Valazza started teaching herself to cook and, within months, Michelin awarded her a star. Now she has three and the Valazzas' little inn — imbued with a charmingly old-fashioned gentility — has become a member of Relais & Châteaux. If *fassone* is on the menu, you must order it; a rare type of Piedmontese veal, it can be cut with the side of a fork. Equally, if Angelo Valazza recommends a bottle of anything by Anselmi, trust him; you are in for a treat.

Al Sorriso
via Roma 18, 28018 Soriso, Italy
Tel: +39-0322-98 32 28   Fax: +39-0322-98 33 28

ALAIN BLONDEL, GALERIE

In just 20 years, Blondel has displayed work by more than 30 new figurative artists. Apart from discovering artists, he has wide experience in cataloguing works of art. His software package, 'Encyclia', is essential for cataloguing and gallery management. Blondel has won numerous awards, notably in 1998, when he became a *Chevalier des Arts et des Lettres*.

Galerie Alain Blondel
4 rue Aubray le Boucher, 75004 Paris, France
Tel: +33-1-42 78 66 67   Fax: +33-1-42 78 47 90

ALAIN CHAPEL

The great Alain Chapel was certainly a hard act to follow but the confidence which Chapel's widow, Suzanne, placed in Philippe Jousse has been amply rewarded; Jousse has brought his own subtle nuance to the master's classic dishes, while adding such perfectly balanced creations as Warm foie gras with a lightly peppered compote of fennel. The service at this serene, flower-filled country retreat, led by maître d' Hervé Deronzier, is silky smooth and sommelier Christoph is particularly inspiring.

Alain Chapel
01390 Mionnay, France
Tel: +33-4-78 91 82 02   Fax: +33-4-78 91 82 37

ALAIN DEMACHY

Having trained at l'Ecole Spéciale d'Architecture et d'Urbanisme, Demachy worked as a journalist for the Match magazine group before becoming a decorator. Prestigious projects soon flooded in, from corporate work for Hôtel Le Bristol, Banque Rothschild and Nina Ricci in Paris to designs for such private clients as Serge Dassault and Prince Albert and Princess Paola of Belgium. Specialising in the restoration of old buildings, Demachy indulges his passion for antiques through his gallery, Camoin Quai Voltaire.

Alain Demachy
11 quai Voltaire, 75007 Paris, France
Tel: +33-1-42 61 82 06   Fax: +33-1-42 61 24 09

ALAIN DUCASSE

'Simplicity' is the mantra of this über-chef but the plain titles of his dishes, identified only by their principal ingredient — simple ingredients but the best quality on the planet — belie the extraordinary *tours de force* behind their presentation. Laurent Gras oversees the kitchens when the master is away, shuttling between Nice (his home) and Monaco (his *Restaurant Louis XV*). Simple does not, however, describe the setting — an extravagant turn-of-the-century *hôtel particulier* — or the 40,000 bottle cellar.

Alain Ducasse
59 avenue Raymond Poincaré, 75116 Paris, France
Tel: +33-1-47 27 12 27   Fax: +33-1-47 27 31 22

ALBERGO GIARDINO

Set in lush, scented gardens, this is a magical hideaway. The pink ochre of the Mediterranean-style building is echoed on the hotel's bicycles and motor launch — and even flamboyant Director Hans Leu's Harley Davidson is painted to match. Leu greets and bids farewell to every guest in person — part of the memorable service which hs established 80 per cent of his guests repeat visitors. A nice touch is the hotel's Enoteca, where guests are able to sample wine before ordering for dinner.

Albergo Giardino
via Segnale, CH-6612 Ascona, Switzerland
Tel: +41-91-791 0101   Fax: +41-91-792 1094

ALEXANDRA BELLINGER

German-born Alexandra Bellinger's passion for jewels has been nutured by her extensive travels. She has absorbed the richness of different cultures and landscapes while studying jewellery and gemmology in Paris, Bangkok and Los Angeles, as well as Madrid, where she established a successful business before moving to London two years ago.

Alexandra Bellinger owes her elite status not to oversize and costly gems but to a combination of her immense charm and discretion (she works, by appointment only, from a chic second-floor studio in Chelsea) and a highly creative eye, based on a perfect understanding of the lifestyles of contemporary women and the individual jewellery which will really work for them.

Her varied sources of inspiration vary from nature, *objets trouvés*, and fine art curiosities to the pure impact of great simplicity. These are transformed into baroque rings, gold hoops with interchangeable pendants, beaded earrings with clever clasps, weighty bauble necklaces and striking brooches or pendants. One of her signature pieces is the 'Bomellang' necklace; available in a wide range of permutations, it consists of long, multiple strings of freshwater pearls or coral beads tipped with gold wire-work spheres. Alexandra is exacting in the quality and colours of the precious and semi-precious stones which she uses, often varying them with the seasons, emphasising pastel to bright shades in the summer and more settled hues in winter.

Alexandra Bellinger
117 Walton Street, London SW3 2HP, UK
Tel: +44-20-72 25 20 04   Fax: +44-20-75 84 55 50
Email: ab@abellinger.u-net.com   Website: www.abellinger.u-net.com

ALBERTA FERRETTI

Alberta Ferretti remains true to her whimsical, dressmaking roots for both her own label and Philosophy collections this season. For the former, girlish dresses and high-waisted coats were the order of the day, while for the latter, will 'o the whisp models paraded in felt skirts, devoré dresses and unlined loden coats, accessorised with fur slippers and woodman's boots.

Alberta Ferretti

via Donizetti 48, 20122 Milan, Italy

Tel: +39-02-76 05 91   Fax: +39-02-78 41 90

ALBERTO DI CASTRO, ANTICHITA

This gallery, established in the late 19th century, is still run by the di Castro family. Its speciality remains exquisite 17th- and 18th-century paintings, furniture and objets d'art. It keeps company with other prestigious antique dealers through its annual participation in the Basel art fair, TEFAF.

Antichità Alberto Di Castro

Piazza di Spagna 5, 00187 Rome, Italy

Tel: +39-06-679 2269   Fax: +39-06-678 7410

ALBERTO PINTO

Studies at the Ecole du Louvre and time spent taking photographs for decorating magazines set this self-taught decorator on the path to his present exalted position. He loves to think big; apart from four

private jets, none of the 20-odd projects to which Pinto is currently applying his lush style is under 300 square metres. His work is found from the Middle East (where he works for royalty) to South America and clients include the Chiracs (for whom he did the private apartments at the Elysée Palace), David & Julia Koch, the David-Weills and Flavio Briatore.

Alberto Pinto

61 quai d'Orsay, 75007 Paris, France

Tel: +-33-1-45 51 03 33   Fax: +33-1-45 55 51 41

ALDO COPPOLA

Hairdressing supremo Aldo Coppola and his talented team are responsible for innumerable catwalk coiffures and the hair in countless advertisements and films. Private clients count on Matteo or Aldo himself for perfect cutting. In conjunction with his daughter Monica, Coppola produces a glossy annual art book – the most recent photographed by Javier Vallhonrat and much praised by Vogue.

Aldo Coppola

Corso Garibaldi 110, 20121 Milan, Italy

Tel: +39-02-657 2685   Fax: +39-02-29 00 66 27

ALFONSO XIII, HOTEL

Redolent of Seville's Moorish past, the lush courtyard garden of the Alfonso XIII, with its tiled arcades and gushing fountains, is a magical retreat from the heat and bustle of the city. During the past year, its new General Manager, Héctor Salanova, has overseen the redecoration of all the bedrooms – in a variety of styles: from Moorish to classically Spanish – and has introduced a 24-hour butler service.

Hotel Alfonso XIII

San Fernando 2, E-41004 Seville, Spain

Tel: +34-95-422 2850   Fax: +34-95-421 6033

ALFRED DUNHILL

Dunhill's insistence on an old-fashioned code of quality for all its traditional products and menswear, has not prevented it from some forward thinking. The AD2000 collection is its most avant-garde range to date and consists of writing implements and gentlemen's accessories which take their inspiration from acclaimed icons of British 20th-century architecture, automobiles and household items.

Alfred Dunhill

48 Jermyn Street, London SW1Y 6LX, UK

Tel: +44-20-78 38 81 18   Fax: +44-20-72 90 86 55

ALICE CADOLLE

Founded in 1889, this is the last remaining *sur mesure* lingerie house in Paris, making beautiful hand-stitched bras and nightdresses for likes of the Baroness de Rothschild. Poupie Cadolle's great-grandmother, Alice Cadolle, invented the first bra and also specialised in custom-made corsets. In the late Eighties Poupie relaunched several models, inspiring Thierry Mugler, Christian Lacroix and Mr Pearl to experiment with corsets ever since.

Alice Cadolle

14 rue Cambon, 75001 Paris, France

Tel: +33-1-42 60 94 94   Fax: +33-1-49 27 92 30

ALOIS DALLMAYR

One of Europe's great delicatessens, this family business has been a Munich institution since the early 18th century; it is a destination for visitors and local gourmets alike, who come to savour such delights as caviar, oysters, smoked salmon and foie gras. The store also offers a splendid range of wines and spirits and a selection of teas and coffees that is both classic and exotic.

Alois Dallmayr

Dienerstrasse 14-15, D-80331 Munich, Germany

Tel: +49-89-21 350   Fax: +49-89-213 5167

ALTAIR

This outstandingly good travel bookshop also stocks a comprehensive selection of books on subjects ranging from world music to photography. Not content with books alone, Altaïr publishes an award-winning magazine of the same name and has recently brought out a travel literature series, Altaïr Viajes, in collaboration with Peninsula Publications.

Altaïr

Gran Via de les Corts 616

E-08007 Barcelona, Spain

Tel: +34-93-454 2966   Fax: +34-93-451 2559

AMBASCIATA

Opulent and extravagant are the words which spring to mind here – from the wonderful flowers, the lace and crystal on the tables and Francesco Tamani's flamboyant service to the rich flavours and generous portions of his brother Romano's cooking, based on the Mantua region's traditional ingredients and dishes. A glass wall separates restaurant and kitchen, so you can watch Romano and his team at work. The marinated rabbit is divine but, for real excess (of calories), try the all-pasta menu.

Ambasciata

via Martiri di Belfiore 33, 46026 Quistello, Italy

Tel: +39-0376-61 90 03   Fax: +39-0376-61 82 55

AMBASSADEURS, LES

So cosmopolitan are the high-rolling members who frequent this elegant gaming club (like all UK casinos, membership must be obtained in order to gain entry) that the menu comprises Arabic, Indian, Thai, and classical European dishes, each cooked by a native-born chef from the country in question. The grand, panelled Library and Salle Privée are a legacy of its origins as a Rothschild mansion and its courtyard garden is a pretty retreat in the summer.

Les Ambassadeurs
London W1, UK
At the time of writing, UK law prohibits the publication of contact details for British casinos. The law is currently under review.

~

AMBROISIE, L'

Conceived by François-Joseph Graf, the decor of this sophisticated and supremely elegant restaurant (honey-coloured walls hung with Aubusson tapestries and good pictures, wonderful lighting, parquet floors) is a perfect foil for Bernard Pacaud's sublime cooking. An appetiser of baby octopus in a bordelaise sauce sets the scene for a sequence of classically-inspired and perfectly judged dishes. Pierre le Moullac oversees a cellar-full of great vintages and Danièle Pacaud is a most gracious hostess.

L'Ambroisie
9 Place des Vosges, 75004 Paris, France
Tel: +33-1-42 78 51 45

~

AMELS

Drawing on the technical expertise and financial strength of the Damen ship-building group, of which it has been a part since the mid-1980s, Amels specialises in the construction of ocean-going steel and aluminium motor yachts. With a dry dock capable of building vessels of up to 120 metres under cover, Amels has recently launched the 71-metre *Boadicea* and a 52-metre motor yacht, the latter in September 1999.

Amels Holland BV
P.O. Box 1, 8754 HA Makkum, The Netherlands
Tel: +31-515-23 25 25   Fax: +31-515-23 27 19

~

AMHUINNSUIDHE

Jonathan Bulmer's romantic baronial castle on the Isle of Harris is set in a breathtaking wilderness of hills, lochs and white shell sand beaches – designated under European legislation for its wildlife. Here, resident chef, Rosemary Schrager, who trained under Pierre Koffman and Jean-Christophe Novelli, runs five-day cookery courses in May, June and October. The hands-on courses centre on the island's incredible range of fresh produce – lobster, scallops and langoustines – as well as classic wines and Scottish

cheeses. Amhuinnsuidhe also offers some of Scotland's best sea trout and salmon fishing for parties of up to 15 guests in July, August and September – when excellent red deer stalking is also available.

Amhuinnsuidhe Castle
Amhuinnsuidhe, North Harris
Western Isles HS3 3AS, UK
Tel: +44-1876-50 03 29   Fax: +44-1876-50 04 28

~

AMPLEFORTH COLLEGE

Piers-Paul Read, Rupert Everett and the late Cardinal Hume all attended this ultra-conservative bastion of Catholicism. Ampleforth life centres on a Benedictine monastic community and the teachings of St Benedict continue to determine the ethos of this school, which has a powerful sporting and academic record. Its coffers have lately been boosted by the monks' best-selling recordings of plainsong.

Ampleforth College
North Yorkshire YO6 4ER, UK
Tel: +44-1439-76 60 00   Fax: +44-1439-78 83 30

~

AMSTEL INTERCONTINENTAL

The soaring white pillars of the lobby set the scene in this grand palace, which has received a top-to-bottom overhaul in the last couple of years. Rooms on the western side overlook the Amstel, as does the glass-walled indoor pool, whose water is at the same level as the river outside. In the restaurant, La Rive, Robert Kranenborg produces the only cooking in Amsterdam to be deemed worthy of two Michelin stars.

Amstel Intercontinental
Prof Tupplein 1, 1018 GX Amsterdam, The Netherlands
Tel: +31-20-622 6060   Fax: +31-20-622 5808

~

ANANOV

Having survived Russia's economic crisis, Ananov is celebrating a decade in the jewellery business with a new flagship in St. Petersburg's main thoroughfare. Ananov is the first jeweller and artist to be honoured with the State Premium of Russia in Art and Literature, amongst other awards from France and Italy. His series, 'Easter Eggs – Cathedrals of Russia', rivals Fabergé in expertise.

Ananov
31 Nevsky Prospect, St. Petersburg 191011, Russia
Tel: +7-812-110 5592   Fax: +7-812-235 3276

~

ANASSA

After a highly successful first year in business, the Michaelides family's gorgeous, £33 million resort has rightfully claimed its place as the jewel of the eastern Mediterranean. Built on a beach – so deserted it feels private – in the Northwest coast of Cyprus, its cool, creamy and hugely spacious rooms all have views of the sea, even while lying in bed. Fifteen suites have their own, private pools and a thalassotherapy spa was opened in spring 1999.

Anassa
Latsi, CY-8840 Polis, Cyprus
Tel: +357-6-88 80 00 Fax: +357-6-32 29 00

~

ANDERSON & SHEPPARD

"We don't really change with the fashions, as the firm maintains the same silhouette, fabrics and colours that have always distinguished us" maintains a spokesman for top people's tailor Anderson & Sheppard. Clearly this approach works because it continues to be the *sine qua non* of the Savile Row elite, enjoying but never exploiting the patronage of princes.

Anderson & Sheppard
30 Savile Row, London W1X 1AG, UK
Tel: +44-20-77 34 14 20   Fax: +44-20-77 34 17 21

ANDRE DE CACQUERAY

Although this decorator's background as an art historian and antique dealer leads him instinctively towards classical – and particularly French – furniture and fabrics, he is at home in any period. "Far more important than any specific period," he asserts, "are the appropriateness of items to their setting and the appropriateness of the setting to the personalities who live in it." Based this philosophy, de Cacqueray's involvement in a project may extend to the exterior and gardens, in order to place a house in its best cotext. De Cacqueray's recent projects range from a large, classically styled London house for collectors of contemporary art to a Polish country house, designed in traditional, hunting lodge style. For the latter clients

he is working on a new house in Spain, which he describes as "a blend of reclaimed wood with summery linens and pastel colours".

A noted perfectionist – despite his deceptively easy-going style – de Cacqueray takes on only two or three projects at any one time, all of them referred by word of mouth.

His clients speak of the fun that they have, being inspired constantly to evolve and refine their ideas. Even de Cacqueray's richest schemes are underpinned by his belief in the value of simplicity.

"Simplicity can be either stylish or banal," he says. "Where it succeeds is in the detail."

André de Cacqueray
227 Ebury Street, London SW1W 8UT, UK
Tel: +44-20-77 30 50 00   Fax: +44-20-77 30 00 05

ANDRE FABRE

Chantilly-based André Fabre is the first man to have trained five winners of the Prix de l'Arc de Triomphe in the race's 78-year history. France's most celebrated trainer has had numerous successes on both sides of the Channel and so dominates French racing that he wins, on average, one in every three national group races.

André Fabre
14 avenue de Bourbon, 60500 Chantilly, France
Tel: +33-3-44 57 04 98   Fax: +33-3-44 58 14 15

ANGLO-GERMAN CLUB

Designed very much on the English 'gentleman's club' prototype, the elite Anglo-German Club is a paragon of old-world values. Situated in Hamburg's most exclusive quarter, it is distinguished by the distinctly male bias and immovable dress-code of its members. Fine pictures and leather sofas fill the club's beautiful old rooms.

Anglo-German Club
Harvesterhudeweg 44, D-20149 Hamburg, Germany
Tel: +49-40-45 01 55 12

ANDREW WINCH DESIGNS

After 20 years in the business, Andrew Winch prides himself that neither the interiors or exteriors of the yachts designed by his practice conform to a single, recognisable style.

"If I have a signature, it is an almost obsessive attention to detail, rather than a particular look," he says. "My starting point is always the question of how the owners want to live on board."

The result has been award-winning projects as diverse as the 52m motor yacht, *Solemates* launched in 1998 and the futuristic, 42m ketch, *Surama*. Combining creativity with technical expertise, Winch – unusually – excels equally in both the

sailing and motor yacht genres. His current projects include two sailing yachts being built at Royal Huisman, a modern 50m motor yacht at Oceanco and a classical cherrywood interior for a 62m Feadship.

Andrew Winch Designs Ltd
The Old Fire Station, 123 Mortlake High Street
London SW14 8SN, UK
Tel: +44-20-83 92 84 00   Fax: +44-20-83 92 84 01
Email: Info@andrew-winch-designs.co.uk

ANITA SMAGA

This elegant boutique is a sartorial feast for Geneva's most discerning women, who have implicit trust in Smaga's ability to edit the best pieces from each season's collections of the designers that she stocks. Her impeccable selection now includes clothes by Giorgio Armani, Ungaro, Prada and Dolce & Gabbana, in addition to collections from her old favourites, Yves Saint-Laurent, Christian Lacroix and Calvin Klein.

Anita Smaga
51 rue du Rhône, CH-1204 Geneva, Switzerland
Tel: +41-22-310 2655   Fax: +41-22-311 5680

ANGELICA FRESCOBALDI

"I find it difficult to categorise my style because it is constantly evolving," says this talented decorator, "Classical with a contemporary twist sums it up best." Indeed, her inspiration comes from myriad sources: books, films, antiques and travelling. Frescobaldi's interiors all share a clean-lined, uncontrived elegance and a sense of intimacy – as if the owners have lived there for ever. Colour is another vital component; Frescobaldi may use several shades together with employing sharp contrasts to add colour and dimensions to her rooms.

Many of the distinctive details in Frescobaldi's schemes – lamps, picture frames, small items of furniture – are the product of her own *atelier*; working with a group of highly skilled craftsmen and employing many almost-forgotten artisanal techniques, she produces both one-off commissions and a range of items for sale.

Having spent the past 11 years working on houses and apartments, Frescobaldi recently designed several offices, enjoying "the challenge of fitting functional needs into a warm, almost residential environment." She now commutes between her Milan workshops and her design studio, which she relocated to London in September 1999.

Angelica Frescobaldi
29 Kensington Gate, London W8, UK
via del Carmine 7, 20121 Milan, Italy
Tel & Fax: +39-02-87 79 47   Email: a.frescobaldi@iol.it

ANNE SÉMONIN

Anne Sémonin has worked her beauty magic on everyone from Princess Grace of Monaco to Princess Marie-Chantal of Greece. Her holistic skincare line is completely natural and tailor-made to clients' needs and the ministerings at her Paris *atelier de beauté* are legendary – travellers swear by her jet-lag treatment!

Anne Sémonin
2 rue des Petits Champs
75002 Paris, France
Tel: +33-1-42 60 94 66 Fax: +33-1-47 05 39 30

ANNELIE, PIZZI E RICAMI

This boutique, which opened in 1992, is a wondrous source of monogrammed embroidery and exquisite lace, sought out by its Austrian-born owner, Annelie. In the last year, the range has been extended to include beautiful, made-to-measure tablecloths in cotton and linen, christening robes and dresses for little girls up to the age of two.

Annelie, Pizzi e Ricami
Calle Lunga San Barnaba
2748 Dorsoduro, Venice, Italy
Tel & Fax: +39-041-520 3277

ANNABEL'S

Many people describe Annabel's owner, Mark Birley, as "the quintessential Englishman"; Birley, on the other hand, often describes himself as a "most unlikely nightclub owner". Annabel's – the cornerstone of Birley's group of four London clubs and still, after 37 years, one of the world's top night places – was conceived in 1962, when Birley's friend, John Aspinall, took over the last remaining private house in Berkeley Square for his gaming club and Birley "thought it might be fun" to have a bar in the basement.

The secret of Annabel's longevity is that it is a meeting place, rather than a nightclub in the conventional, noisy, disco sense of the word (the dance floor is tucked away at the back, surrounded by a glass screen). Founder

members – mainly Birley's friends – who still pay the original 5 guineas annual subscription, meet and mingle with a unique blend of film stars and foreign potentates, Dukes and bankers, supermodels and quietly chic ladies in little black dresses. Here they can eat – and eat well – late into the night or simply drop in for a glass of champagne or a cigar.

The surroundings – stylish, comfortable and unpretentious – are deeply reassuring, the sense of belonging enhanced by the presence of staff members who have worked there for decades.

Annabel's
Berkeley Square, London W1X 8NR, UK
Tel: +44-20-76 29 10 96 Fax: +44-20-74 91 18 60

ANNICK GOUTAL

Annick Goutal worked as a model for David Bailey before discovering her true vocation – perfumery – in her late twenties. Remarkably, less than two months after commencing training with Robertet in Grasse, Goutal had developed a 'nose' and created Folavril, the first of numerous sensual offerings, which she dispenses from her own, charming boutiques in Paris, as well as selling internationally.

Annick Goutal
14 rue de Castiglione, 75001 Paris, France
Tel: +33-1-42 60 52 82   Fax: +33-1-40 71 20 70

ANOUSKA HEMPEL COUTURE

The exotic ambience of Anouska Hempel's jewel-box *atelier* reflects the designer's dramatic personality, which finds such elegant expression in the creation of her clothes. A strong believer in what she terms "the

architecture" of her clothes, Hempel conterbalances the deceptively simple designs and rigorous tailoring of her suits and ballgowns with opulent fabrics, meticulous attention to detail and the use of many techniques largely lost to modern manufacturing.

In her current collection, Hempel uses dramatic blacks, reds and whites for bolero-jacketed suits, tiny bustiers under cardigans and dramatic ostrich-feather evening skirts. Underlining her success, the *couturière* is shortly to expand her shop, having recently bought the adjacent property.

Anouska Hempel Couture
2 Pond Place, London SW3 6QJ, UK
Tel: +44-20-75 89 41 91   Fax: +44-20-75 84 18 00

ANTHONY D'OFFAY GALLERY

This gallery continues to dazzle with its range of international contemporary art. In 1999, there were exhibitions of pieces by Warhol and Beuys and, ever keen to take on different projects, D'Offay continues to accept work by new artists. His list of represented artists is long and prestigious – ranging from Roy Lichtenstein to Gilbert & George.

Anthony d'Offay Gallery
9, 23 and 24 Dering Street, London W1R 9AA, UK
Tel: +44-20-74 99 41 00   Fax: +44-20-74 93 44 43

ANTICHI MAESTRI PITTORI

Giancarlo Gallino founded this gallery in 1978. His preference for staging exhibitions of hand-picked Renaissance art has been particularly marked in recent years, with viewings of Donatello's early work and newly-discovered pieces by Beato Angelico; in the year 2000, the early model for Canova's Three Graces will be on display.

Antichi Maestri Pittori
via Andrea Doria 19/a, 10123 Turin, Italy
Tel: +39-011-812 7587   Fax: +39-011-812 7612

ANTICO SETIFICIO FIORENTINO

Owned and run by the Pucci family, this company has produced hand-woven silk on the same premises for over 300 years. Today's production includes damask, brocades and lampass, all woven on hand looms to original Renaissance patterns. 'Ermisino' – a very light taffeta typical of the 15th century – is produced on the company's 19th-century mechanical looms and used today for curtains.

Much of the work undertaken is bespoke, although an impressive range of designs is available in the beautiful, old showroom; exclusivity is guaranteed, for none of these fabrics is available elsewhere. While clients as far afield as Australia have ordered fabrics for their homes, the firm's work is found in many castles and palaces and, in 1999, the Kremlin's restored Grand Palais was added to its prestigious client list.

Antico Setificio Fiorentino
via L. Bartolini 4, 50124 Florence, Italy
Tel: +39-055-21 38 61   Fax: +39-055-21 81 74

ANTICA OSTIERA DEL PONTE

A grand fireplace is the focal point of one room of this romantic, 300-year old inn outside Milan, while a second room opens onto a broad verandah and lovely garden. Ezio and Maurizio Santin's constantly evolving menu includes a sublime brandade of cod, perfumed with new season's olive, an unforgettable tartare of prawns and sea bass and an extraordinary dish of goose, boned and stuffed with foie gras. The superb service is led with considerable passion by Ezio's wife, Renata.

Antica Osteria del Ponte
Piazza G. Negri 9
20081 Cassinetta del Lugagnano, Italy
Tel: +39-02-942 0034   Fax: +39-02-942 0610

ANTIQUORUM

The world's leading auctioneer of collectors' time-pieces – everything from watches to marine chronometers – Antiquorum was set up in 1974. Among the firm's innovations was the idea of selling wristwatches at auction – considered radical when

Antiquorum dreamed it up in 1980 – and the notion of 'thematic' auctions devoted to one particular subject. Its ten auctions a year, held in Geneva, Hong Kong and New York and dedicated to watches, clocks and jewellery, regularly achieve record prices.

Antiquorum
2 rue du Mont-Blanc, CH-1201 Geneva, Switzerland
Tel: +41-22-909 2850   Fax: +41-22-909 2860
Email: geneva@antiquorum.com

ANTONIETTA MAZZOTTI EMALDI

Decorated with flowers, Renaissance motifs and mythological animals, Antonietta Mazzotti Emaldi's ceramics pay homage to the history of Faenza (where faïence was first developed). With her husband, Tomasso Emaldi, an expert in ancient majolica, Antonietta constantly searches out old documents, in order to produce historically accurate shapes and patterns. Delicately hued, they are all hand-painted, either as private commissions or in limited editions and she has worked for several of the world's most important museums.

Antonietta Mazzotti Emaldi
Villa Emaldi, via Firenze 240, 48018 Faenza, Italy
Tel: +39-0546-43199   Fax: +39-0546-43156

ANTONIO RAVA

Soon after graduating as an architect, Antonio Rava won a Fulbright scholarship to research new art conservation techniques in the US. After restoring the Palazzo Barberini for the Italian Ministry of Culture, he established his own business in 1984 with three partners. While Studio Rava specialises in the restoration of modern art (and advises on hanging and transportation techniques) it also has an in-depth knowledge of older works of art, especially stucco, frescoes and works in stone.

Studio Rava
via Castilione 6 bis int. 4, 10132 Turin, Italy
Tel: +39-011-819 3739   Fax: +39-011-819 1542

APICIUS

Described by one critic as a "playboy of the stoves", the charismatic Jean-Pierre Vigato achieves a remarkable balancing act between absolute clarity and great subtlety in his cooking. His pressed rabbit, accompanied by shavings of beetroot, is superb, as is his *Turbot rôti aux épices* and there is a particularly rich wine list to accompany them. The restaurant, decorated in contemporary style, enlivened by abstract paintings, is overseen with immense charm by Madame Vigato.

Apicius
122 avenue de Villiers, 75017 Paris, France
Tel: +33-1-43 80 19 66   Fax: +33-1-44 40 09 57

APOLLONI, GALLERIA ANTICHITA

Founded by Vladimiro Apolloni in 1926 and now run by his son, Fabrizio, this gallery is a very important centre for Italian paintings and sculpture from the 16th to the 19th century. Its impeccable record includes the sale of works to the Palazzo Braschi and the Galleria Nazionale d'Arte Antica in Rome.

Galleria Antichità Apolloni
via del Babuino 132/134, 00187 Rome, Italy
Tel: +39-06-36 00 22 16   Fax: +39-06-36 00 22 17

ARABELLA LENNOX-BOYD

Since establishing her practice in 1971, garden designer Arabella Lennox-Boyd has won four gold medals at Chelsea; her world-wide projects range from small townhouse plots to vast rural landscapes. A trustee of Kew Gardens and Castle Howard Arboretum Trust, the Italian-born Lady Lennox-Boyd is also the author of two books. Recent projects include the spectacular modernist roof garden of No.1 Poultry in the City of London.

Arabella Lennox-Boyd
45 Moreton Street, London SW1V 2NY, UK
Tel: +44-20-79 31 99 95   Fax: +44-20-78 21 65 85

ARCHIDUC, L'

A legend among jazz lovers while owned by Stan Brenders in the 1950s and 60s, this intimate bar was given a new lease of life when Jean-Louis and Nathalie Hennart bought it from Brenders' widow in the mid-1980s. The Hennarts have done little to change its unique atmosphere and celebrities – major, minor and wannabe – sit in the old velvet armchairs beneath the soaring pillars in a setting unchanged since 1937, sipping the best espresso in town. Hennart's 'Round About Five' series of Saturday and Sunday concerts continues the jazz tradition.

L'Archiduc
8 rue Antoine-Dansaert, B-1000 Brussels, Belgium
Tel: +32-2-512 0652

ARNYS

As has been the case for over 70 years, most of the seven tailors in Michel and Jean Grimbert's *atelier* are Italian. Their suits are distinguished by 'natural' shoulders, a high-cut jacket and slanted button-holes. The brothers love to give linings an individalistic burst of colour or add a quirky detail for the wearer's secret appreciation. Arnys' shirts are hand made and the ready-to-wear line comes out of the same workshop as its bespoke clothing, making for remarkable quality. Its twice-yearly collections of ties are specially numbered, with only 40 models made for each design.

Arnys
14 rue de Sèvres, 75007 Paris, France
Tel: +33-1-45 48 76 99

ARPEGE, L'

Alain Passard fully deserves his recent elevation to membership of Relais & Châteaux. Inspired to cook by his Breton grandmother, he spends his entire life in the kitchen, testing, tasting and evolving his ideas. While constantly experimenting (using tomatoes as a dessert, for instance) he eschews exoticism for its own sake. The restraint of his cooking is echoed in the decor: walls of sleek pear-wood with Lalique panels. The wine list mixes classic vintages with lots of surprises.

L'Arpège
84 rue de Varenne, 75007 Paris, France
Tel: +33-1-45 51 47 33   Fax: +33-1-44 18 98 39

ARS ROSA

One of the most elegant shops in Milan, Ars Rosa will tempt you with delicious lingerie. Clients can choose from a vast array of underwear styles and colours or chose to have something made-to-measure in hand-sewn silk, linen and cotton. Other ideas include beautiful nightwear, bridal pieces and slips as well as splendid household items.

Ars Rosa
8 via Montenapoleone, 20121 Milan, Italy
Tel: +39-02-76 02 38 22   Fax: +39-02-76 02 22 86

ART BASEL

The world's most prestigious contemporary art fair, this is the annual meeting place for leading artists, dealers, collectors and curators. Modern masterworks are shown, along with contemporary art – especially cutting-edge work by emerging artists. The event's selection procedure is rigorous and its coverage ranges from large-scale sculptures and installations to painting, photography and video art. Established 30 years ago, the fair has played a pivotal role in the emergence of Basel as a vibrant art capital.

Art Basel
Schweizer Mustermesse
CH-4021 Basel, Switzerland
Tel: +41-61-686 2020   Fax: +41-61-686 2686
Annually for five days in June

ART COLOGNE

This annual art fair specialises in classic 20th-century pieces and, increasingly, sculpture and works by new artists. 1999 marked its 33rd anniversary. Attracting more than 250 exhibitors from over 20 countries, Art Cologne is considered a Mecca for art-lovers and a significant date on the international art calendar.

Art Cologne
Cologne Exhibition Centre, Rhineside Halls
D-50532 Cologne, Germany
Tel: +49-221-821 2907   Fax: +49-221-821 3446
Every November

ARTIOLI

The process of creating a pair of these hand-made shoes involves 200 separate operations, the skills of 30 craftsmen and up to 40 days of hand-work. Famously described as "refreshing" shoes, they have a special absorbent lining – after traditional slow-tanning, the precision-cut leather is treated with vegetable compounds to enable the feet to breathe. Run together by three generations – Severino, Vito and Andrea Artioli, the firm also produce very high quality leather goods and belts.

Artioli
via Oslavia 3, 21049 Tradate, Italy
Tel: +39-0331-84 13 22   Fax: +39-0331-84 45 64

ARTS, HOTEL

Beyond Frank Gehry's celebrated fish sculpture, the view from the second-floor terrace and pool of this ultra-modern 33-floor hotel (one of Ritz-Carlton's first European footholds) is of endless sea and sky. In May 1999 the top ten floors were opened as luxurious apartments; all duplexes, they range from one to three bedrooms. The staff here are notably young, warm-hearted and supremely professional.

Hotel Arts
Carrer de la Marina 19-21, E-08005 Barcelona, Spain
Tel: +34-93-221 1000   Fax: +34-93-221 1070

ARTUR RAMON

Founded in 1941, this art and antiques dealership is now run by Artur Ramón Sr., his son, Artur Jr., and daughter Monica. It specialises in drawings and paintings by Old Masters from the Renaissance to the Enlightenment; the decorative arts, ceramics

and glassware from the 17th to the 19th centuries, and works by late 19th- and early 20th-century Spanish and Catalan artists.

Artur Ramón Anticuario
Palla 23-25, E-08002 Barcelona, Spain
Tel: +34-93-302 5970   Fax: +34-93-318 2833
Email: aramon@retemail.es

ARZAK

The facade of this restaurant – founded in 1897 – is unprepossessing and the interior – softened by good, old pictures on the walls – a little severe, but the cooking of Juan-Mari Arzak and his daughter Elena is sublime. Based on the Basque classics, it is full of surprises – imaginative but never gratuitous; the foie gras mayonnaise which accompanies the langoustines and rice vermicelli, for instance, is a brilliant success, as is the pigeon with leeks and sage.

Arzak
Alto de Miracruz 21, E-20015 San Sebastian, Spain
Tel: +34-943-28 55 93 Fax: +34-943-27 27 53

ASPINALLS

Richly re-decorated, the expanded Aspinalls is well worth a visit – if you can cadge an invitation from a member! The gaming club now comprises a series of baroque rooms in two adjoining Mayfair town-houses. Here, fortunes are made and lost by the likes of magnate Kerry Packer. The personality of animal-lover and owner John Aspinall pervades the establishment.

Aspinalls Club
Curzon Street, London W1Y 7AE, UK
At the time of writing., UK law prohibits publication of contact details for British casinos. The law is currently under review.

ASPREY & GARRARD

Asprey & Garrard have more to celebrate than ever this year. Fresh from last year's successful merger, the company has unveiled the Eternal Cut diamond, which has an extraordinary 81 facets and was designed exclusively for the company by world authority and master-cutter Gabi Tolkowsky. The number of facets added to the unique petal design around the cutlet increase the quality of light to a soft, diffused brilliance. The stone is spendidly offset in 'Stellar' and 'Electra', two major pieces, as well as the smaller jewels of the diffusion line. In keeping with the spirit of the age, Asprey & Garrard has also produced the Celebration Silver collection which features the special millennium hallmark on sterling silver pieces, including party poppers, champagne flutes, stoppers, ice-buckets and vintage champagne gift-cases. The famous Bond Street show-rooms now offer customers the service of a new Watch and Clock Room where they will find limited editions, commemorative sets and many unique jewelled pieces from Switzerland's top houses. In addition, Asprey & Garrard creates some of the most covetable gifts on earth – suitcases lined in the softest suede and other items made up in their house leather, Peppercorn, and a range of luxury games such as bridle-hide backgammon sets and mahogany skittles in the shape of silver-topped champagne bottles.

Stellar

Asprey & Garrard
165 New Bond Street, London W1Y 0AR, UK
Tel: +44-20-74 93 67 67
Fax: +44-20-74 91 03 84
Website: www.asprey-garrard.com

ATHLETIQUE CLUB BOULOGNE BILLANCOURT

For the last 20 years this beautiful riding club in the Bois de Boulogne has been the destination of choice among genteel Parisian women and their *soignée* daughters. With three jumping arenas and some 40 horses, the club is the only place in Paris to specialise in eventing at all levels. Exclusivity is guaranteed by a membership of just 200.

Athletique Club Boulogne Billancourt
Parc Rothschild, 35 quai Alfonse le Gallo
92100 Boulogne, France
Tel: +33-1-48 25 59 80   Fax: +33-1-48 25 75 77

AUBERGE DU PERE BISE

Breakfast on the balcony of your room at this 19th-century coaching inn is a magical moment; the absolute peace and the heart-stopping beauty of Lake Annecy are utterly seductive. Sophie Bise, the fourth generation of her family to run the kitchens, turns out such delights as *Tarte fine de langoustines aux légumes gratinée au pistou*. New maître d'hôtel, David, is joined by gifted sommelier, Jean-Marie and Sophie's mother, Charlyne, oversees all with serene charm.

L'Auberge du Père Bise
Route du Port, 74290 Talloires, France
Tel: +33-4-50 60 72 01   Fax: +33-4-50 60 73 05

ATELIER LUMONT

Jean-Jacques Coron, ceramics restorer par excellence, took over this workshop in 1979. He is among the most sought-after craftsmen in his field, with clients across Europe and America. Specialising in porcelain, earthenware and terracotta ceramics, he has also worked on statues at the Palace of Versailles.

Atelier Lumont
12 rue Cacheux, 92400 Courbevoie, France
Tel: +33-1-47 89 56 90

AUBERGE DU RAISIN

Adored for his genial character as much as his brilliant cooking, Adolfo Blokbergen – universally known as 'Bloki' – is justly celebrated for his pared-down and subtly balanced French-inspired classics. His Charlotte de coquilles Saint-Jacques au caviar is the stuff of dreams. During the winter cosy fireplaces set the scene in this lovely old inn – a member of Relais & Châteaux – and, in summer, tables are laid out on the terrace overlooking Lake Geneva.

Auberge du Raisin
1 Place de l'Hôtel de Ville
CH-1096 Cully, Switzerland
Tel: +41-21-799 2131   Fax: +41-21-799 2501

AUBERGE ET CLOS DES CIMES

You wind through miles of pine forests to reach Régis and Michèle Marcon's inn and, once there, the view stretches forever. Utterly unpretentious, the charm of the place lies in its delicious simplicity and the warmth of its owners. Régis Marcon greets his guests before cooking their dinner – not to show off, you sense, but because he greatly values the human touch. He is a genius with mushrooms and his Puy lentil ragoût is unforgettable. The Auvergne and Ardèche cheeses, too, are a revelation.

Auberge et Clos des Cimes
Place de l'Eglise, 43290 St-Bonnet-le-Froid, France
Tel: +33-4-71 59 93 72   Fax: +33-4-71 59 93 40

AUBERGE DE L'ILL

You can set your watch by the swans here, which arrive at the foot of the garden, morning and evening, to be fed by Jean-Pierre Haeberlin. The bucolic charm of this scene pervades every aspect of his family's delightful inn, with its pale wood-panelled bedrooms and pretty river-bank terraces. Marc Haeberlin's menu, a masterful updating of the Alsace tradition, includes a heavenly Mousseline of frog's legs and a sublime *Assiette d'oie "non grasse" sous toutes ses façons*.

Auberge de l'Ill
rue Collonges, 68970 Illhaeusern, France
Tel: +33-3-89 71 89 00   Fax: +33-3-89 71 82 83

AUBERGE DE L'ERIDAN – MARC VEYRAT

Marc Veyrat's controversial utterances, gleefully pounced upon by the French media, belie his true genius as a chef. Inventive in the purest sense of the word, he uses the little-known herbs which he gathers on his walks in the alps as the centrepiece of such dishes as a (pasta-free) Raviolis de légumes aux saveurs de sous-bois et prairie. The terraces of his luxurious Relais & Châteaux inn, lead down to a private beach on the edge of Lake Annecy.

Auberge de l'Eridan - Marc Veyrat
13 vieil Grande Assietteyrier-du-Lac, France
Tel: +33-4-50 60 24 00   Fax: +33-4-50 60 23 63

AUBUSSON

The town of Aubusson has been synonymous with hand-woven carpets and tapestries since the 16th century. More recently, artists such as Léger, Dalí and Picasso breathed new life into the craft and, like them, Robert Four – a fifth-generation master weaver – is passionate about tapestry. As well as producing carpets (often made-to-order) his company repairs any Aubusson piece. Four's gallery on Paris' Left Bank has served as a 'shop window' for his *atelier* for 32 years.

Aubusson
Galerie Robert Four, 8 rue des Saints Pères
75007 Paris, France
Tel: +33-1-40 20 44 96   Fax: +33-1-40 20 44 97
Email: rfour@club-internet.fr

AUDEMARS PIGUET

This 125 year-old firm is justifiably proud of its technical expertise, which has enabled it to incorporate the largest Tourbillon calibre movement of its type into its recently-launched Tourbillon Canapé watch. The Jules Audemar Minute repeater

Tourbillon Chronographe Rattrapante is as complicated as its name indicates and the 'Promesse' collection for ladies was introduced in 1999.

Audemars Piguet
6 avenue August Forel, CH-1110 Morgs, Switzerland
Tel: +41-21-802 4955   Fax: +41-21-845 1400

AVELINE, GALERIE

Having originally trained to be a lawyer, Jean-Marie Rossi opened his first gallery in 1956. Clients can rely on his unfailing eye for antique pieces – his personal taste ranges from Russian Imperial art to works by the Victorian Aesthetes – although he also has considerable expertise in contemporary art. In September 1999 Rossi moved to grand new premises across the road from his original showroom.

Galerie Aveline
94 rue du Faubourg Saint-Honoré, Place Beauvau
75008 Paris, France
Tel: +33-1-42 66 60 29   Fax: +33-1-42 66 45 91

ASHFORD CASTLE

Under the brilliant leadership of Rory Murphy, this charming castle dating from the 12th century on Lough Corrib, has all the grace and antiquity of the old world with none of the inconvenience. The grounds of which were used as the setting for the movie classic *The Quiet Man* and a guest list from Princess Grace, the Reagans to John Travolta, this hotel offers spectacular wide open spaces both indoors and out. The grounds comprise 300 acres of peace and tranquility and the mildness of the climate encourages rare plants to flourish the whole year round, including a Japanese garden and sporting facilities (hunting, shooting, fishing, riding and a 9 hole golf course are on-site).

Ashford Castle
Cong, County Mayo, Ireland
Tel +353-92-46 003   Fax +353-92-46 260

AXEL VERVOORDT

The flamboyant Axel Vervoordt has moved part of his antiques business from its base in a historic castle to a new five-acre site. This will provide greater space for restoring and displaying the thousands of *objets d'art* which come his way. These range from Ancient Egyptian stone vessels and Renaissance bronzes to 18th-century furniture and contemporary paintings.

Axel Vervoordt
Kasteel van's Gravenwezel, St. Jobsteenweg, 2970's
Gravenwezel, Antwerp, Belgium
Tel: +32-3-658 1470   Fax: +32-3-658 3781

AZIMUT

In 1969 Paolo Vitelli founded Azimut to import yachts into Italy; five years later he began building his own fibreglass boats. Massive investment in the development of new materials and cutting-edge design has made it a world leader in its field – one of the first yacht-builders to offer a five-year guarantee. Designer Stefano Righini's distinctive elliptical windows and curved lines have made Azimut's recent introductions, the *AZ85* (late 1997) and the *AZ39* (late 1998) instantly recognisable.

Azimut SpA
viale dei Mareschi 14, 10051 Avigliana, Turin, Italy
Tel: +39-011-936 7272   Fax: +39-011-936 727

BACCARAT

Established in 1764, Baccarat commands almost 50 percent of the French crystal market. Its crystal jewellery collection – a runaway success since its introduction in 1997 – has seen the addition of a 'bridge' collection, combining crystal with 18-carat gold. Also new are the 'Mille Nuits' collection of hand-cut, halogen-lit chandeliers and the 'Simplissimes' collection of glasses, decanters and *objets*. Including both reproductions and new designs, their pure and uncomplicated form highlights the flawless purity of the crystal.

Baccarat
30 bis rue de Paradis, 75010 Paris, France
Tel: +33-1-47 70 64 30   Fax: +33-1-42 46 97 08

BAD DRIBURG

Centred around its original, 200 year-old buildings and natural springs, this spa has expanded to offer golf tennis and a rehablilitation centre, in addition to invigorating and relaxing spa treatments. The owner, Graf Oeynhausen-Sierstorpff, and his management team also arrange concerts and special-occasion balls for their guests.

Gräfliches Gesundheits-und Fitness Bad-Bad Driburg
Im Kurpark, D-33014 Bad Driburg, Germany
Tel: +49-52-53 95 25 25   Fax: +49-52-53 95 25 75

BADIA A COLTIBUONO

This thousand-year-old abbey was founded by Benedictine monks and made famous by the dynamic Stucchi Prinetti family. A producer of world-famous food and wine, it is now the venue for select summer courses in Italian gastronomy given by the current châtelaine, the acclaimed cookery writer Lorenza de'Medici.

Badia a Coltibuono
Gaiole in Chianti, 53013 Siena, Italy
Tel: +39-0577-74 94 98   Fax: +39-0577-74 92 35

BADRUTT'S PALACE

Johannes Badrutt invented the ski Season when he brought winter tourists to St. Moritz in 1864; 32 years later his son, Caspar, opened what has become the spiritual home of the shiny set. Still family-owned, it joined the Rosewood group in spring 1999. Its most charming rooms are those decorated in traditional alpine style and its King's Club is one of the few nightclubs in Europe to have remained fashionable for over 35 years.

Badrutt's Palace Hotel
CH-7500 Saint-Moritz, Switzerland
Tel: +41-81-837 1000   Fax: +41-81-837 2999

BALBO

A shining beacon in the gastronomic desert which Turin has inexplicably become, Balbo continues to produce wonderfully classy food. Star dishes include such traditional Turin specialities as 'plini' – mini-agnolotti infused with truffles – and a Ragout of chicken giblets. The room is refined and elegant; tables are set with Riedel glasses and fine silverware and corollas of flowers complement the sinuous vine-leaf motif embroidered on the linen curtains.

Balbo
via A. Doria 11, 10123 Turin, Italy
Tel: +39-011-839 5775   Fax: +39-011-815 1042

BALLINACOR

The waiting list for guns on the few commercial days at Lord Jack Ardee's excellent pheasant shoot is long indeed – and with good reason. Not only is it unsurpassed for the number and level of the birds, it is also extremely well-organised. Set in lovely countryside south of Dublin, the shoot is enjoyed by the King of Sweden, who leads one syndicate here on a regular basis; the other is made up of passionate Irish huntsmen and women.

Ballinacor House
Greenane, Rathdrum, Co. Wicklow, Ireland
Tel: +353-404-46 186   Fax: +353-404-46 123

BALLYBUNION

Founded in 1893, the beautiful dune-lined, coastal sweep of the Ballybunion Golf Club is the Mecca of Irish links golf. Many leading professional golfers stop off here to hone their games before the British Open. Five-times Open Champion Tom Watson will lead the Club as Captain in the millennium year.

Ballybunion Golf Club
Ballybunion, Co. Kerry, Ireland
Tel: +353-68-27 146   Fax: +353-68-27 387

BALLYMALOE COOKERY SCHOOL

The school's beautiful gardens contain an airy new café and, nearby, is its soon-to-be-organic 130-acre farm which, for much of the year, keeps it self-sufficient. Pupils have the benefit of a new wood-burning oven and courses include a millennium day class for aspirant new year self-caterers.

Ballymaloe Cookery School
Shanagarry, Co. Cork, Ireland
Tel: +353-21-64 67 85   Fax: +353-21-64 69 09

BALMAIN

Balmain's newly appointed ready-to-wear supremo, Gilles Dufour (formerly of Chanel) enjoyed rave reviews for his first collection – tiny tweed jackets, Argyll-sleeved knits and ruched dresses all found favour. Meanwhile, inspired by the beauties of Proust's day and the paintings of Watteau, Oscar de la Renta's '*Jolie Madame*' creations for Balmain are very much in the grand tradition of haute couture.

Pierre Balmain
44 rue Francois 1er, 75008 Paris, France
Tel: +33-1-47 20 35 34   Fax: +33-1-47 23 40 11

BALOYE SOLNTSE PUSTINYA

Decorated with vivid the carpets and textiles of Central Asia, this opulent restaurant – named after the famous Russian adventure film, *White Desert Sun* – offers the greatest culinary delights of that region. Delicately spiced, it is based on such staples as rice, beans, aubergines and cheesy breads, as well as wonderful meat dishes. Coming from a culture where hospitality is an art form, its owners and staff treat their guests like royalty.

Baloye Solntse Pustinya
Nezlinnaya Street 29/14, 9213833 Moscow, Russia
Tel: +7-095-200 6836

THE BALVENIE

Many call this the finest malt whisky available, yet only recently has The Balvenie earned the respect that has been its due since its creation in 1892. During maturation, its 'new-make spirit' is subjected to different environments — from port wood to vintage cask — for differing periods of time. The delightful aroma of its single barrel bottlings presages an intense palate, which combines great backbone with a lovely rounded flavour. The Balvenie Double Wood won a 1997 International Wine & Spirit Competition Gold Medal.

The Balvenie

William Grant & Sons, 84 Lower Mortlake Road
Richmond, Surrey TW9 2HS, UK
Tel: +44-20-83 32 11 88   Fax: +44-20-83 32 16 95

BANKHAUS B. METZLER SEEL. SOHN & CO.

Founded in 1674, Germany's oldest family-owned bank has 325 years of experience in providing customised financial services for clients. It offers all the services of a modern, international investment bank, including asset management and related counselling services, for institutional clients as well as high net worth individuals. These clients are

provided with a broad range of asset management arrangements geared to meet their individual needs and preferences. Metzler's management style emphasises long-term preservation and growth of capital in order to protect clients from unpleasant surprises. It places a strong emphasis on long-term relationships with its clients and its centuries-old tradition of total independence allows their needs to remain its central concern, thus enhancing its already excellent reputation.

B. Metzler seel. Sohn & Co
Grosse Gallustrasse 18
D-60311 Frankfurt-am-Main, Germany
Tel: +49-69-21 04 46 12   Fax: +49-69-21 04 47 77

BANNERMAN

Having recently completed a project for Lord Lloyd-Webber, Isabel and Julian Bannerman are increasingly emphasising architectural elements in their garden designs. Inspired by what Julian describes as "the genius of each place", they are working at Houghton for the Marquess of Cholmondeley, on the restoration of the gardens at Asthall (former home of the Mitfords) and for the Prince of Wales — creating a huge fern pyramid as well as a sculpture crafted by Isabel.

Isabel and Julian Bannerman
Hanham Court, Hanham Abbots, Bristol BS15 5NT, UK
Tel & Fax: +44-117-961 1202

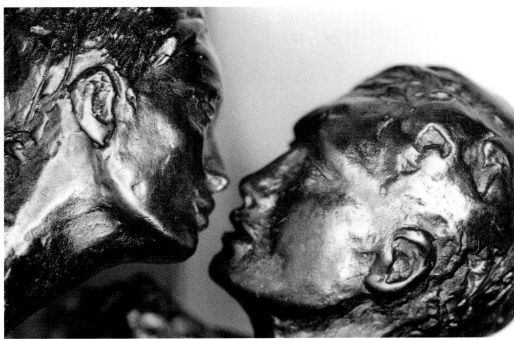

BASRA, DEV

Dev Basra is something of a media darling, having appeared on many a magazine's 'A List' of cosmetic surgeons; he has also been recommended by the recently-published *Beauty Bible* and his portrait has featured in a millennium photographic exhibition. Author of *The Ageing Skin* (with a foreword by Christiaan Barnard), he is the pioneer of 'Botox', having now used the wrinkle-prevention technique for 12 years. A number of patients have expressed appreciation for his talent at reinterpreting face-lifts previously performed by what they describe as "less talented surgeons". Post-op he gives – not sells – patients one of his arsenal of aromatic oils to help healing and takes great pains to educate patients about their skin. To this end he administers vitamin therapy in order that patients are in peak condition before and after surgery. Educated in India and the UK, Basra's off-duty passion is art; an accomplished sculptor, he was commissioned to do the first portrait bust of John Major when the latter became Prime Minister in 1993 and was commissioned to do a sculpture for UNICEF and a portrait head of Sir Cliff Richard for EMI Records.

Dev Basra
111 Harley Street, London W1N 1DG, UK
Tel: +44-20-74 86 80 55   Fax: +44-20-74 86 24 17

BARBIZON, RESTAURANT

This beautiful villa, on the edge of the Soignes forest, has been a Mecca for epicures since it was built by the great chef, Jacques Deluc, 40 years ago. Today his son, Alain – who studied with Troisgros and Chapel – and his delightful wife, Myriam, preside over this serene 'Relais Gourmand'. Respecting his father's classical legacy, Alain Deluc brings his own imaginative twist to such sublime dishes as *Carré de veau de lait braisé, persillade aux quatre épices et primeurs à l'estragon*.

Restaurant Barbizon
95 Welriekendedreef, Jezus-Eik
B-3090 Overijse, Belgium
Tel: +32-2-657 0462   Fax: +32-2-657 4066

BAREISS

For those seeking peace and solitude, the fields and forests surrounding the Bareiss family's hotel are a perfect antidote to urban stress. For those in search of entertainment there are concerts in the evenings, wine tastings in the 20,000-bottle cellar, a magical play-house for children and special golf days. The restaurant here is consistently ranked among Germany's 10 best and, in 1999, the already vast spa and pool area was further extended.

Hotel Bareiss im Schwarzwald
D-72261 Baiersbronn-Mitteltal
Germany
Tel: +49-7442-470   Fax: +49-7442-47320

BARON'S COURT

This wonderful 5000-acre estate, owned – along with the fairy-tale Belle Isle Estate – by the Duke and Duchess of Abercorn, offers Northern Ireland's best stalking and pheasant shooting. On the edge of the Sperrin mountains, Baron's Court is also a perfect place for salmon fishing with its mile-long stretch of the River Mourne. Game, tended to by the illustrious Sam Pollock (a Laurent-Perrier award-winner for game management) includes a wild herd of pure-bred Japanese sika deer, as well as excellent pheasant.

Baron's Court
Newtownstewart, Co. Tyrone
Northern Ireland BT78 4EZ, UK
Tel: +44-28-81 66 16 83   Fax: +44-28-81 66 20 59

BAUR AU LAC

It is not only its superb lakeside location in the heart of Zürich which makes this hotel exceptional. Owned by the Kracht family since the 1840s and brilliantly

BATH & RACQUETS CLUB

Quite simply the smartest – and most discreet – men's gym in London, The Bath & Racquets' 250 carefully-vetted members (among them Ralph Lauren, Prince Michael of Kent, Tim Jefferies and George Michael) come here to work off the excesses of wining and dining at Mark Birley's other three clubs: Harry's Bar, Mark's Club and Annabel's.

Birley's renowned good taste is evident throughout. Sleek oak panelling, onyx and marble are offset by good pictures and, in the dressing-room, deep sofas and Turkish carpets. And there is not a sweat-stained tracksuit or vividly lycra-clad body to be seen; members are issued with crisp white shirts and shorts (prepared for them in the club's own state-of-the-art laundry) on each visit – a code which Birley rigorously enforces.

However, the real point of the Bath & Racquets is not mere style; it takes the business of fitness very seriously indeed; members jealously monitor each other's performances and the squash and fitness contests are hotly competed for. Birley has applied his legendary connoisseurship to the choice of exercise machines – which are regularly updated – and a hand-picked staff, which includes eight instructors, a barber, a barman, a physiotherapist and a masseur, whom members describe as the best on the planet.

The Bath & Racquets Club
49 Brook's Mews, London W1Y 1LE, UK
Tel: +44-20-74 99 90 44   Fax: +44-20-76 29 51 66

managed by Michel Rey, it was completely refurbished in 1998. Its top-floor gym has an inspiring view of Lake Zürich – one shared by the hotel's best rooms. (The Deluxe Suites, with numbers ending in -21 are particularly lovely). The Rive Gauche restaurant and bar, with its East-West cooking, is a favourite watering hole for bankers and ladies-who-lunch alike.

Hotel Baur au Lac
Talstrasse 1, CH-8022 Zürich, Switzerland
Tel: +41-1-220 5020   Fax: +41-1-220 5044

BEAU-RIVAGE PALACE

After seven years of painstaking restoration (representing a 70 million Swiss Franc investment by its majority shareholder, the Sandoz family foundation), this *grande dame* – Switzerland's only true palace hotel – has reclaimed her place among Europe's greats. The splendid recreation of its original Belle Epoque style – with exquisite frescoes, plaster-work and stained glass – has won the 1999 'Historic Hotel of the Year' award.

Each of the hotel's 175 rooms is decorated differently. Suite 409, for instance, is furnished with original Le Corbusier and Mies van der Rohe pieces, while the Somerset Maugham Suite (much in demand for its private roof terrace) is decorated in Napoleon III style and the Imperial Suite (created especially for Emperor Hirohito) is Louis XV.

A vital part of the Beau-Rivage's magic remains, however – its wonderful sense of history. The setting, too, is magical; 10 acres of wide lawns and immaculately tended gardens overlook the lake and the Alps beyond. Noel Coward and Somerset Maugham were so entranced that the hotel featured in their writing and Coco Chanel's affection for the place was such that she buried her beloved poodle in the hotel's pet cemetery. Many people, it seems, cannot bear to leave; the Beau-Rivage has a growing number of permanent residents and over 30 percent of the staff have been there for more than a decade.

Beau-Rivage Palace
CH-1006 Lausanne-Ouchy, Switzerland
Tel: +41-21-613 3333   Fax: +41-21-613 3334
Email: info@beau-rivage-palace.ch

BAROVIER & TOSO

This glass producer, which is constantly researching new materials and techniques, can trace its roots back to 1295, when Jacobellus Barovier set up the business. His descendents have always been innovative; Angelo Barovier is credited with inventing Venetian crystal in the 15th century. The Toso family joined in 1936. With a range that includes glasses and ornaments, as well as custom-designed lighting, the company has been showered with awards, including two entrepreneurial 'knighthoods' for different managing directors.

Barovier & Toso
Fondamenta Vetrai 28, 30141 Murano, Venice, Italy
Tel: +39-041-73 90 49   Fax: +39-041-527 4385

BAYERISCHER HOF

The X-factor at this dignified hotel is surely its stunning roof terrace and swimming pool, from which you feel that you can almost touch the spire of Munich's famed Frauenkirche. The Bayerischer Hof opened in 1841 and, at the end of the 19th century, was bought by the Volkhardt family. Far from being an absentee landlord, Innegrit Volkhardt is an inspired and very hands-on General Manager, whose close involvement in all aspects of the hotel no doubt explains its intimate warmth, despite its large size.

Bayerischer Hof
Promenadeplatz 2-6, D-80333 Munich, Germany
Tel: +49-89-21 200   Fax: +49-89-212 0633

BENETTI

The takeover of this shipyard (founded in 1873 by Lorenzo Benetti) by Paolo Vitelli's Azimut Group in 1985 secured its status as one of the world's finest custom-builders of steel and aluminium yachts of 40-70 metres. In addition, Azimut provided expertise in GRP construction; the first of its 35m GRP semi-custom 'Benetti Classics' series was launched in late 1998. Recent custom-builds include the 50m Disdale-designed *Queen Anne* and the 64m *Ambrosia*.

Benetti
via Michele Coppino 104, 55049 Viareggio, Italy
Tel: +39-0584-38 21   Fax: +39-0584-39 62 32

THE BERKELEY

The Berkeley's quiet elegance is what attracts such low-key celebrities as Liam Neeson and Robin Williams. Its residential ambience has been enhanced by designers such as John Stefanidis and Tessa Kennedy, who have created a different scheme for every room. The stunning Pavilion Suite, with its conservatory and vast terrace, overlooks St. Paul's Church, while the new Park Suite has its own private entrance and glorious views of Hyde Park. Pampering is given high priority, whether in the form

of the Spa (the only Christian Dior spa in Europe) and roof-top pool or the provision of personal shopping services at the smartest boutiques of nearby Knightsbridge. Pierre Koffman recently moved his celebrated restaurant, La Tante Claire, to The Berkeley, complementing Vong, which opened here in 1995.

The Berkeley
Wilton Place, London SW1X 7RL, UK
Tel: +44-20-72 35 60 00   Fax: +44-20-72 35 43 30
Email: info@the-berkeley.co.uk

BERLUTI

This bespoke shoe-maker, founded in 1895, opened a branch in London in the summer of 1998. The hand-workmanship and exquisitely subtle colourings more than justify the cost of these heirloom-like acquisitions. (Indeed, some Berluti clients still wear shoes handed down to them by their fathers and grandfathers.) Now part of the LVMH group, Berluti is still very much the personal fiefdom of Olga, the formidable granddaughter of the founder, who, with remarkable accuracy, can deduce a client's character – and practically tell his fortune – from the shape of his foot.

Berluti

26 rue Marbeuf, 75008 Paris, France

Tel: +33-1-43 59 51 10   Fax: +33-1-42 89 57 92

BERNARDAUD

Although based in Limoges, this porcelain manufacturer is famous for its Paris *salon de thé*, where tea and cakes can be bought, along with the china on which they are served. Established in 1863 and still family-run, Bernardaud crafts fine votives, as well as tableware. Based on early 19th-century designs, the votives are sculpted from fine bisque, non-enamelled porcelain, in a range of styles from 'Grenadiers' to 'Japanese Gardens'.

Bernardaud

11 rue Royale, 75008 Paris, France

Tel: +33-1-47 42 82 66   Fax: +33-1-49 24 06 35

BERNHEIMER

Regarded as Germany's leading dealer in Old Master paintings, ranging from the 16th to the 19th century, Konrad Bernheimer recently moved his gallery to a neo-classical mansion in Munich. Paintings can now be viewed against opulent backgrounds, along with the gallery's other speciality, Chinese porcelain. The family art business was established in 1864 and after taking over in 1977, the ebullient Konrad Bernheimer spent the next decade moulding it to suit his distinctive vision.

Konrad O. Bernheimer Fine Old Masters

Briennerstrasse 7, D-80333 Munich, Germany

Tel: +49-89-22 66 72   Fax: +49-89-22 60 37

BERRY BROS & RUDD

The last decade has seen huge modernisation at this most distiguished of wine merchants. Computer terminals now adorn the 300 year-old premises – with the screens neatly framed in wood, of course – and it has, according to oenophiles, the best website in the business. Its first shop outside the UK opened in Dublin, Ireland, in spring 1999.

Berry Bros & Rudd Ltd.

3 St James's Street, London SW1A 1EG, UK

Tel: +44-20-73 96 96 00   Fax: +44-20-73 96 96 41

BESINS, DR. THIERRY

Dr. Besins has a confident approach to facial rejuvenation, and reduces the process to a series of steps: repositioning, rather than getting rid of, flesh; filling in facial flaws through lipostructure; and never altering a woman's hairline too radically. ("Having lots of hair is an important part of being a woman," he says.) A natural look is always achieved, whether he has performed complicated surgery or simply removed pouches under the eyes.

Dr Thierry Besins

124 rue de la Faisanderie, 75116 Paris, France

Tel: +33-1-40 72 86 00   Fax: +33-1-40 72 75 23

BERNARD & BENJAMIN STEINITZ

Any lover of French *boiserie* and parquet flooring who spies the magnificent Louis XIV panelling, which fills one room of this breathtaking antiques gallery, and the splendid examples of parquet underfoot – one with a trellis pattern, another with wood-work as intricate as an oriental carpet – will be instantly hooked.

After 40 years in the business, Bernard Steinitz and his son, Benjamin, have an excellent eye for the rarest and most beautiful objects of the 17th and 18th centuries, such as commodes by Riesener, Marie Antoinette's favourite cabinet maker, superb neoclassical consoles, Chinese porcelain vases and a portico with masterful *rocaille* sculpture. Madame Steinitz insists, however, that the gallery does not specialise in specific periods because, she stresses, "A house shouldn't be decorated like a museum. The Rothschilds mix Haute Epoque pieces with Louis XIV or Louis XV furniture but also with a down-at-heel Napoleon III sofa, simply because it is comfortable."

Searching for a 20th-century masterpiece to illustrate her point, Madame Steinitz heads for her office, which is dominated by a superb 1950s desk, possibly designed by Hermès or Arbus. Still, you suspect that, like another of her clients, Hubert de Givenchy, she has a soft spot for French decorative arts from *le siècle des lumières*.

Bernard & Benjamin Steinitz

9 rue du Cirque, 75008 Paris, France

Tel: +33-1-42 89 40 50   Fax: +33-1-42 89 40 60

BERSAGLIERE

Antipasti such as Marinated eel with a herb salad and Baked scallops with *caponata* set the standard for the treats to follow. Outstanding main courses include Roasted kid goat with thyme and Pigeon with *fruits des bois*. The room which, in summer, opens out onto the riverbank, is grand and beautifully set up and the wine list intelligent and sensibly priced. Notwithstanding occasional hiccups in service recently, this remains one of Italy's best restaurants.

Bersagliere
via Statale Goitese 260, 46044 Goito, Mantova, Italy
Tel: +39-0376-68 83 99   Fax: +39-0376-68 83 63

BERTHAUDIN

If the staff at this first class wine merchant seem unusually passionate about their trade, it is probably due to the fact that the Berthaudin family is Switzerland's leading wine-maker. Its products feature on the wine lists of both Swissair and Badrutt's Palace hotel. In addition to their eponymous Swiss wineries, Claude Berthaudin owns the Clos de Roussillon domaine in Southern France; its Tartegnin 1997 was very well-reviewed in the 1999 Hachette Wine Guide.

Marcel Berthaudin SA
11 rue Ferrier, CH-1202 Geneva, Switzerland
Tel: +41-22-732 0626   Fax: +41-22-732 8460

BIENNALE INTERNAZIONALE DELL'ANTIQUARIATO

The luxurious rooms of the late Florentine-baroque Palazzo Corsini, still home to the Corsini family, are an inspiring setting for this international antique fair. Now in its 39th year, it is the oldest of its kind in Italy and one of the most important in the world. Italy's finest picture and furniture dealers exhibit a diverse range of pieces here from all periods and styles.

Biennale Internazionale dell'Antiquariato
Piazza Strozzi 1, 50123 Florence, Italy
Tel: +39-055-28 26 35   Fax: +39-055-21 48 31
In September of every unevenly numbered year

BEZZOLA, DR. ALAIN

Appointed President of the Swiss Federation of Dermatological Surgeons in 1998, surgical wizard Alain Bezzola will hold the prestigious seat for three years. In addition to undertaking more traditional procedures, he is well-versed in such staple treatments as Botox, collagen and laser treatments and is pioneering the use of soft-form implants for deep wrinkles.

Dr. Alain Bezzola
53 Rue Ernest-Bloch, CH-1207 Geneva, Switzerland
Tel: +41-22-736 1242   Fax: +41-22-736 2785

THE BEST IN ITALY

With a portfolio of over 80 of the most spectacular houses in Italy for holiday rentals or outright purchase, Count Girolamo Brandolini d'Adda and his American-born wife, the Countess Simonetta, are driven, above all, by their desire to find a perfect fit between client and property. To this end, they prefer to meet prospective clients, gaining a clear understanding of their tastes and lifestyles, before attempting to match them to a property.

For those intending to buy properties, the Brandolinis attend meticulously to every aspect of the process, finding the best local architects, craftsmen, decorators and art experts to complete the job. They also manage the properties when their owners are not in residence, ensuring maximum financial returns for their clients. Rental clients are offered a range of special cultural events, often being given access to places not usually open to the public; art tours are led by world-class experts, hand-picked by the Brandolinis.

This highly personalised service, combined with charm, efficiency and an encyclopaedic knowledge of their (very rarified) end of the business, has brought the Brandolinis a glittering client list, including several Hollywood stars. In 1999, several new properties – mainly in Tuscany and Umbria – were added to the company's existing portfolio.

The Best in Italy
via Ugo Foscolo 72, 50124 Florence, Italy
Tel: +39-055-22 30 64   Fax: +39-055-229 8912   Email: thebestinitaly@thebestinitaly.com

BIENNALE INTERNATIONALE DES ANTIQUAIRES

Featuring 120 leading international dealers, this fair offers works from all of the major periods and locations in art history. A significant cultural event attracting art lovers, museum curators and international dealers, it embraces African and pre-Colombian art, Oriental treasures, rare books, European furniture, ceramics, paintings, jewellery and sculpture.

Biennale Internationale des Antiquaires
Carrousel du Louvre, 99 rue de Rivoli
75001 Paris, France
Tel: +33-1-47 20 31 87   Fax: +33-1-47 23 51 83
In September of every evenly numbered year

BIRGER CHRISTENSEN

If, like Danish or Swedish royalty you require a little something run up in sable, squirrel or seal, then Birger Christensen is for you. This furrier extrordinaire was established in Copenhagen in 1869 and, in addition to selling bespoke or ready-to-wear models, it will alter as well as store furs for its clients. The famous flagship store also stocks a range of designer brands – the most recent addition being J.P Tods.

Birger Christensen A/S
Østergade 38, DK-1100 Copenhagen K
Denmark
Tel: +45-33-11 55 55   Fax: +45-33-93 21 35

BLANCPAIN

Blancpain's watchmakers have cherished the brand's heritage and culture since 1735 though, despite their disdain for quartz movements, never at the expense of progress. Its 'Ladybird' model, featuring the world's smallest mechanical movement, was launched in 1956 and countless record-breakers have since characterised the company including the launch of the sophisticated – yet understated – 1735 wristwatch which, historically, featured all six masterpieces of the watchmaker's art housed in a single case.

Blancpain
CH-1094 Paudex, Switzerland
Tel: +41-21-796 3636   Fax: +41-21-796 3637

BLAKES

The song-bird which greets you as you enter this discreet and ineluctably glamorous hotel is a harbinger of the cosseting, escapist world that lies behind its dark green façade. So seductive is Blakes that countless celebrities have made it their London 'home'. Blakes – which effectively invented the boutique hotel genre 15 years ago, when it was opened by the multi-talented Anouska Hempel – perfectly reflects its owner's love of fantasy. Its rooms evoke Russian Imperial palaces, the Silk Route and the romance of the old Colonies. The courtyard garden is a magical hideaway for summer breakfasts and lunches, while the restaurant and adjoining Chinese Room are a sophisticated setting for Blakes' eclectic cuisine.

Blakes
33 Roland Gardens, London SW7 3PF, UK
Tel: +44-20-73 70 67 01   Fax: +44-20-73 73 04 42

BLANDINGS

Established 13 years ago, Blandings stands out as much for the quality of the properties that it offers for short-term or holiday rental as for its founder, Layla Paterson's attention to detail. Nothing goes onto Blandings' books without a personal vetting by Paterson and she makes regular return visits to ensure that standards are being maintained. Having focused initially on UK country houses, Blandings' portfolio now includes the Iberian Peninsula, France and several privately-owned London townhouses.

Blandings (UK & Europe) Ltd
Musgrave Farm, Horningsea Road, Cambridge CB5 8SZ, UK
Tel: +44-1223-29 34 44   Fax: +44-1223-29 28 88

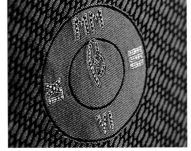

BOBADILLA, LA

Under the auspices of its new General Manager, Klaudios Hech, this lovely retreat has refurbished 15 of its 60 rooms, first stage of an ongoing programme. Set in a virgin landscape of hills, valleys and holm-oak forests, the hotel's Moorish-style buildings are clustered around flower-decked courtyards. Two of its three Imperial Suites are particularly stunning; you can soak in their private jacuzzis with uninterrupted views over La Babadilla's 350-acre estate.

La Bobadilla
Apartado 144, E-18300 Loja, Granada, Spain
Tel: +34-958-32 18 61   Fax: +34-958-32 18 10

BRIONI

Nazareno Fonticoli, who co-founded this tailoring company in 1945, numbered Peter Sellers, Robert Wagner and Henry Fonda among his clients – a showbusiness tradition that continues today with Brioni's designs for James Bond. With Umberto Angeloni – Fonticoli's grandson-in-law – at the helm, the business is growing apace; a new Milan flagship and Brioni's first store in China have opened in the past year. Brioni has also stolen a march on its competitors by obtaining sole rights within the menswear field to use Escorial, the sensational ultra-soft, high-performance wool produced by a rare breed of sheep in New Zealand, which is being hailed as "the new cashmere".

In Brioni's current collection, a salmon-toned double-headed plaid suiting, as well as the 'Edward' tuxedo shirt have been inspired by its recent acquisition of pieces from the Duke of Windsor's wardrobe. Unconstructed, double-face sports jackets, a natty line of hunting clothes and the limited-edition 'Millennium' range of formal wear also star, in the finest fabrics and a rich palette of colours. Each piece is cut, sewn and pressed by hand. Brioni is justifiably proud of the latter technique, by which the component parts are gently coaxed together and shaped by heat and steam, moulding them to the wearer's body and preserving the shape for posterity.

Brioni Roman Style Spa
via Barberini 50
00187 Rome, Italy
Tel: +39-06-462 0161   Fax: +39-06-487 3301

BLOHM & VOSS

Blohm & Voss has been restructuring its yacht-building division under the expert direction of Jürgen Engelskirchen and, at the time of writing, was negotiating the construction of three projects of between 70 and 150 metres. Established in 1877 and now part of the Thyssen group, its reputation is based on its employment of the most technically-sophisticated solutions, coupled with unmatched quality and professionalism. Its credits include *Lady Moura*, still the largest private motor yacht afloat.

Blohm & Voss
P.O. Box 10-07-20, D-20005 Hamburg, Germany
Tel: +49-40-31 19 13 01   Fax: +49-40-31 19 33 38

BON LLOC

Run by Bocuse d'Or winner Mathias Dahlgren, this smart Stockholm restaurant, opened in 1997, is permanently booked up. Its cuisine is eclectic and international: Swedish dishes predominate at lunch-time while, in the evening, Spanish ideas are prominent – with *pata negra* from Salamanca and a delectable prawn *gazpacho* with avocado sorbet and chilli oil as *tapa* and starter respectively. These are complemented by hearty main dishes and some irresistible desserts, while the interesting cellar provides many discoveries, as well as good classics.

Bon Lloc
33 Bergsgaten, Kungsholmen, 11228 Stockholm, Sweden
Tel: +46-8-650 5082   Fax: +46-8-650 5083

BONPOINT

Bonpoint's collections reflect owner Marie-France Cohen's instinctive understanding of the fine line between style and a too-strong fashion element in children's clothing. Tempering modernity with a dash of bon chic bon genre classicism, these beautifully-made clothes – for babies and boys and girls up to the age of 15 – are treasured by sophisticated mothers for their superb fabrics, clever detailing and original sense of colour.

Bonpoint
67 rue de l'Universite, 75007 Paris, France
Tel: +33-1-45 55 63 70   Fax: +33-1-45 56 02 61

BOGNER

The It-wear of the slopes, Bogner ski clothes are sported by gilded Europeans in resorts everywhere. Along with the company's other sportswear ranges, Bogner designs are distinguished by their sophisticated lines and glamorous styling, which makes them instantly identifiable and much in demand. Today Willy Bogner's company is represented in 35 countries and produces over 3000 new styles a year.

Willy Bogner
Sankt-Veit-Strase 4, D-81673 Munich, Germany
Tel: +49-89-43 60 63 14   Fax: +49-89-43 60 64 37

BOWEN, DR. JOHN

"When a patient asks me to perform any procedure," says this respected cosmetic surgeon, "I always ask myself whether I would go ahead if she was my daughter." This remark perfectly sums up John Bowen's rational approach to his profession. Eschewing many of the more fashionable and exotic high-tech procedures (which he regards as insufficiently tried and tested), Bowen excels at creating faces which look noticeably younger, yet entirely natural. His deeply reassuring bedside manner is an added bonus.

Dr. John Bowen
Flat 1, 30 Harley Street, London W1N 1AB, UK
Tel: +44-20-76 36 09 55

BLUMEN COMPANY

Lush, lavish flower arrangements, ranging in style from the baroque to the contemporary, are the signature of Julius Linke's company. Linke, who was originally a costume designer for television and theatre, refuses to accept artificially-grown flowers, and uses garden roses from Italy and elegant tulips from the Côte d'Azur instead. Munich's branches of Bulgari, Rena Lange and Gucci are among his regular clients and he also creates masterfully elaborate floral confections for weddings, parties and banquets.

Blumen Company
Rumfordstrasse 43, D-80469 Munich, Germany
Tel: +49-89-29 16 10 55   Fax: +49-89-29 16 10 59

LE BRISTOL, HOTEL

Notwithstanding the magnificent Gobelin tapestries and Baccarat chandeliers which hang in the lobby or the monumental staircase, which soars to the first floor, the atmosphere here is one of restrained elegance.

Elegant – almost impossibly luxurious – it may be but what is it about Le Bristol that causes 80% of its guests to return? Could it be the glass-walled sixth-floor pool? Reminiscent of an ocean liner, it has a wonderfully evocative view of the Paris rooftops. Or the 46 superb suites, notably the two Terrace Suites, with their vast roof gardens, and the palatial bathrooms, the biggest in Paris – a sybaritic fantasy in pink or white marble? Perhaps it is waking, in the heart of Paris, to the sound of birdsong floating up from the magnolias in the ravishing courtyard garden. Or is it one of the best wine cellars in France and Michel Del Burgo's Mediterranean-accented cooking? In his hands such a deceptively simple dish as chicken roasted with truffles under its skin becomes truly sublime and, like the entire menu, it can be ordered through Room Service.

Above all, though, Le Bristol's discreet and utterly unpretentious staff remember even the tiniest quirks and foibles from your past visits, giving you a deeply reassuring sense of being at home.

Hôtel Le Bristol
112 rue du Faubourg St-Honoré
75008 Paris, France
Tel: +33-1-53 43 43 00   Fax: +33-1-53 43 43 01

BOLLINGER

The flavour of Bollinger's Special Cuvée is challenging and uncompromising – you grow to like it, it does not change to suit you. Further up the scale, the 1999 Grande Année is a triumph; singular and forceful, with its ravishing Pinot Noir characteristics, it is as good an expression of this vintage as you are likely to get.

Bollinger
B.P.4, 51160 Ay, France
Tel: +33-3-26 53 33 66   Fax: +33-3-26 54 85 59

BORGES

Thanks to its survival as a family firm, Borges continues to produce wines that preserve Madeira's once-great quality. Concentrated and intense, pungent and piercing, they are a stirring reminder of the great diversity to be found in wine if only we are prepared to look. Let them age 10 years and they provide an exceptional drinking experience.

H.M. Borges
Rua 31 Janeiro 83, Apartado 92
9000 Funchal, Madeira, Portugal
Tel: +351-91-22 32 47   Fax: +351-91-22 22 81

BOURGUIGNON FLORISTS

Brothers David and Peter Bourguignon run this elite florists, which has been in their family for 70 years. In addition to their stunning range of cut flowers, the brothers' passion for orchids is refelcted in the dozens of varieties on display. Bourgignon's two Madrid branches are complemented by a garden centre and landscaping service.

Bourguignon Florists
Almagro 3, E-28010 Madrid, Spain
Tel: +34-91-319 2692   Fax: +34-91-319 2998

BRACHOT, GALERIE

The Brachots' gallery, which was founded in 1915, currently deals with works by Belgian sculptor Panamarenko. Mr. and Mrs. Brachot are excited by their involvement in what they call the "evolution" of such artistic talent. Isy Brachot, who is a world expert on Magritte, Delvaux, Opalka and Broodthaers, is also Vice-President of the Belgian Chamber of Experts on Works of Art. The Gallery regularly participates in the Basel Art Fair and Art Brussels.

Galerie Christine & Isy Brachot
8 rue Villa Hermosa, B-1000 Brussels, Belgium
Tel: +32-2-511 0525   Fax: +32-2-514 3335

BREGUET

Under new management for the last few years, this 225-year old company is committed to making a significant, ongoing contribution to the art and science of mechanical watchmaking. Founder, Abraham-Louis Breguet – known as 'the father of modern watchmaking', thanks to his invention of the tourbillon regulator – would doubtless be proud of the company's latest models, including the Héritage, a barrel-shaped men's chronograph, and a Classique model with date, based on a double-barrel self-winding movement.

Montres Breguet S.A.
46A avenue Général Guisan, CH-1009 Pully, Switzerland
Tel: +41-21-728 2001   Fax: +41-21-728 2484

BRENNER'S PARK

Recent guests at this legendary, 125 year-old hotel and health resort range from Daniel Barenboim and Bryan Adams to Giorgio Armani and Nelson Mandela. Its Penthouse Suite, with a private elevator, has ravishing views over the hotel's park and the Honeymoon Suite, a top floor duplex, overlooks the elegant town. In 1999 Director Richard Schmitz upgraded the already-excellent spa to include a new fitness centre and sauna and a private 'Spa Suite' within the complex. New chef Christian Melcher's *cuisine légère* menu is a big hit, too.

Brenner's Park Hotel & Spa
Schillerstrasse 6, D-76530 Baden-Baden, Germany
Tel: +49-7221-90 08 30   Fax: +49-7221-38 772

BREGENZ FESTIVAL

This open-air festival on the shores of Lake Constance continues to dazzle audiences every year, from late July to mid-August, with its floating stage and diverse programme. In 1999, visitors were treated to Verdi's *Un Ballo in Maschera* and Martinu's *The Greek Passion* while, for orchestral *cognoscenti*, there was music by Beethoven, Elgar and Prokofiev, performed by the Vienna Symphony Orchestra.

Bregenzer Festspiel
Postfach 311
A-6901 Bregenz, Austria
Tel: +43-55-74 40 72 30   Fax: +43-55-744 5770

BREIDENBACHER HOF

A focal point of Düsseldorf since 1812, this distinguished hotel is undertakjng a total restoration; such is the magnitude of the work that it closed down completely in June 1999. The signs are that, upon re-opening in Spring 2000 it will set new standards of distinction, under the guidance of highly respected General manager, Welf Ebeling.

Breidenbacher Hof
Heinrich-Heine-Allee 35
D-40213 Düsseldorf, Germany
Tel: +49-21-11 30 30   Fax: +49-21-11 30 38 30

BROWN THOMAS

Ireland's leading department store, Brown Thomas was established in 1884 and is *the* destination for shoppers requiring anything from the cream of current women's and men's designer collections to cutting-edge telecommunications products. Owned by Canadian retail magnate Galen Weston (whose elegant wife, Hilary, is Irish) the store has always attracted celebrities – Princess Grace, Rita Hayworth and Prince Ali Khan were all customers in their day. Today's *cognoscenti* can choose from top names such as Prada, Chanel, Armani and Joseph, as well as up-and-coming Irish designers. The homeware department, spanning two floors, offers everything from cooking gadgets to designer furniture and linens, while Brown's Bar is a favourite rendezvous for stylish shopaholics.

BT2, Brown Thomas' fashion-forward, designer sportswear store, located a few doors along from the flagship store, recently celebrated its first anniversary and, having won the 1998-99 UK and Ireland 'Department Store of the Year' award for its Cork store, Brown Thomas is capitalising on its success with the introduction of a range of own-name products, including chocolates, oils and spices. In addition, the company's Limerick store completed the first phase of its refurbishment, opening new cosmetic and fragrance halls in the spring of 1999.

Brown Thomas
Grafton Street, Dublin 2, Ireland
Tel: +353-1-605 6666
Fax: +353-1-679 5260
BT2, Grafton Street,
Dublin 2, Ireland
Tel: +353-1-605 6707
Fax: +353-1-605 6755

BREITLING

Breitling's rugged chronograph wristwatches are worn by men of action, including many private, commercial and military pilots. The company made history in March 1999 when its *Breitling Orbiter 3* balloon, piloted by Brian Jones and Bertrand Piccard, made the first non-stop circumnavigation of the globe.
Breitling SA
P.O. Box 1132, CH-2540 Crenchen, Switzerland
Tel: +41-32-654 5454 Fax: +41-32-654 5400

BRUNO LAFOURCADE

A self-taught architect/builder-cum-decorator, Bruno Lafourcade is steeped in the sensibility of the southern French countryside – as it was 200 years ago. It is his unerring instinct for context that enables him so successfully to breathe new life into the buildings on which he works, creating – out of virtual ruins – the embodiment of the late 20th–century Provençal dream. Lafourcade's wife, Dominique, is equally talented, transforming the outdoors into ravishing gardens, whose strong 'bones' provide a foil for gentle harmonies of green and silver.
Bruno Lafourcade
10 boulevard Victor Hugo
13210 St-Rémy-de-Provence, France
Tel: +33-4-90 92 10 14 Fax: +33-4-90 92 49 72

BUEREHIESEL, RESTAURANT

Anton Westermann's genius lies in his ability to modernise regional dishes and make them his own; his menu always features one or two 'granny' dishes – slowly-simmered, convivial recipes. On the wine list classic vintages are complemented by excellent, and rarely seen, Alsace wines. A favourite of Helmut Kohl whenever he visited the European Parliament, just across the park.
Restaurant Buerehiesel
4 Parc de l'Orangerie, 67000 Strasbourg, France
Tel: +33-3-88 45 56 65 Fax: +33-3-88 61 32 00

BY TERRY

Formerly a celebrity make-up artist with Carita and creator of the emblematic *Touche Eclat* while Creative Director of YSL cosmetics, Terry de Gunzburg is enjoying even greater success with her latest venture. Her boutique offers both a 'Ready to Wear' and a 'Haute Couture' line; the latter is made to order following a personal consultation and comes in sleek pewter compacts with your name engraved on the lid.
By Terry
21 Passage Véro-Dodat, 75001 Paris, France
Tel: +33-1-44 76 00 76 Fax: +33-1-44-76 00 79

BUÇACO

Probably the hardest of all great wines to come by, this extraordinary wine is made at the Palace Hotel, near Coimbra in Portugal, and is available only to guests there. The huge range of vintages, both red and white, dates back over 50 years. A 'young' red, such as the 1963, will deliver a chewy mouthful of flavour, far removed from the modern style of fruit-dominated wines.
Buçaco
Hotel Palace Buçaco, 3050 Mealhada, Portugal
Tel: +351-31-93 01 01 Fax: +351-31-93 05 09

BVLGARI

Descended from a family of Greek silversmiths, Sotirio Bulgari founded the Bvlgari family business when he opened his first shop in Rome in 1884. His sons Constantino and Giorgio took over the burgeoning jewellery business and, in the first decades of the 20th century, Bvlgari evolved its distinctive signature – a style inspired by Greek and Roman classicism, the Italian Renaissance and the 19th century Roman school of goldsmiths. The house now combines these elements alongside cutting-edge contemporary motifs and manufacture; in combination they inspire remarkable and inimitable jewellery which is recognised the world over. Overseen by brothers Paolo and Nicola Bulgari and their dynamic nephew Francesco Trapani, it has become the third largest jewellery company in the world, expanding from its base to incorporate a range of luxury goods which include silk and leather accessories, eyewear and fragrance. In tune with fashion, some of Bvlgari's jewellery designs for the millennium are small and perfectly formed. They include the gem-set 'Astrea' ring collection, the delicate 'Goccia' ring and earring variations, and the 'Corona' and 'Bvlgari-Bvlgari' diamond solitaire and diamond pavé pendants. In a departure from its signature style, using yellow gold and coloured stones, Bvlgari has introduced the platinum and diamond 'Nuvole' range into its high jewellery collection. Another new development is the 'Home Designs' range of porcelain which features motifs inspired by David Pizzigoni's water-colours, as well as crystal, barware and silver flatware manufactured in conjunction with Rosenthal.
Bvlgari Spa
via dei Condotti, 10, 00186 Rome, Italy
(flagship store) Tel: +39-06-679 3876
Lungo Tevere Marzio 11, 00186 Rome, Italy
Tel: +39-06-68 81 01 Fax: +39-06-68 81 04 00
Internet: www.bulgari.it

BUCARO

The Pastega sisters, Isabel and Marta, have been florists to Madrid's élite for 25 years. (They designed the flowers for Princess Elena de Borbón's 1995 wedding, for instance.) Influenced by the English look, they generally work with flowers from a single part of the colour spectrum, mixing them with abundant greenery. They also stock a wide variety of containers and accessories.
Bucaro
Capitán Haya 26, E-28020 Madrid, Spain
Tel: +34-91-556 4221 Fax: +34-91-556 4540

BUHLERHOHE SCHLOSSHOTEL AND IMPERIAL RESTAURANT

Politicians, business czars and fashion stars flock to this elegant 19th-century castle where, from the vast terrace of its Japanese Suite they have breathtaking views of the Rhine valley. The marvellous spa treatments are a perfect antidote to the irresistible excesses of the Imperial Restaurant, where Klaus Erfort has taken over as chef - in the process retaining its 18/20 rating by Gault Millaut. A new Cigar Lounge and Champagne Lounge were added in 1999.
Bühlerhöhe Schlosshotel
Scwarzwaldhochstrasse 1, D-77815 Bühl/Baden-Baden, Germany
Tel: +49-7226-550 Fax: +49-7226-55777

CHANEL

C&C

This shop is discreetly tucked away and you ring the door-bell to gain entry. But what wonders await! Run by Emanuele Castellini, cousin of the celebrated architect, Piero Castellini, C&C is a marvellous source of textiles, linens, furniture and *objets*. Changing every season, its warmly toned and luxuriously textured household items range from elegant bed-linens, rich duvets, bed covers and cashmere plaids to precious table settings and sophisticated unisex pyjamas.

C&C
via della Spiga 50, 20121 Milan, Italy
Tel: +39-02-78 02 57 Fax: +39-02-78 05 01

CALA DI VOLPE, HOTEL

A secluded oasis just outside Porto Cervo, this is a favourite haunt of the glossy set. Its magic lies in its understated, seemingly artless style. Designed in the Sardinian vernacular by architect Jacques Couelle, it is built around a private marina, its turrets, terraces and archways, footbridges of rough-hewn wood and the sunburnt colours of its walls giving it the look of a fishing village that might have been here for centuries. Built in 1963, it was extended in 1971 and completely renovated in 1996.

The lovely rooms, all with their own terraces, are filled with sunshine and fanned by the breeze; decorative details are minimal: exposed beams, rough, whitewashed stone walls and simple, Sardinian-styled furnishings. (Its *pièce de résistance*, the three-bedroomed Presidential Suite, is hidden away in the tower with its own private pool overlooking the sea.) The simplicity is deceptive, however, for every detail has been perfectly thought out.

There is a huge sea-water swimming pool and a private, sandy beach – five minutes away by shuttle boat. Cala di Volpe has a good formal restaurant but its laid-back elegance is best reflected in its famous poolside buffet; barbecued fish is complemented by superb pasta – dressed with local specialities *bottarga* or *granchio* (crab) – and it offers some of the best people-watching on these celebrity-studded shores.

Cala Di Volpe
07020 Porto Cervo, Sardinia, Italy
Tel: +39-0789-97 61 11 Fax: +39-0789-97 66 17

CAMERON-SHAW

Ranging from the whimsical to the daring, Russell Longmuir's highly imaginative dried flower arrangements are increasingly sought after by an international *côterie* of decorators and private clients. Longmuir now incorporates glass, fibre-optics, water and stainless steel into his sculptures, and has diversified into land-design and earth-sculpture. His designs have travelled as far afield as Moscow and Japan, while Gordon Ramsay has commissioned pieces for his two new London restaurants.

Cameron-Shaw
279 New Kings Road
London SW6 4RD, UK
Tel: +44-20-73 71 81 75 Fax: +44-20-73 71 81 78

CAMPER & NICHOLSONS

Established over two hundred years ago, in 1782, London-based Camper & Nicholsons now has offices from France to North America. Its charter services cover a remarkably broad range, from a 24m motor yacht based in New Zealand to a 40m sailing yacht in the Mediterranean. The firm's other services include a brokerage division, which encompasses New Construction and a Yacht Management, and a Technical Services division, which takes care of maintenance and operations.

Camper & Nicholsons
25 Bruton Street
London W1X 7DB, UK
Tel: +44-20-74 91 29 50 Fax: +44-20-76 29 20 68

CAMPAGNA

In the autumn of 1999 Gianni Campagna moved his headquarters to an 18th-century *palazzo* in the heart of Milan, a fittingly grand setting for his celebrated tailoring business. Signalling the company's plans for international expansion, the custom-made suits are joined by a new ready-to-wear line, as well as sportswear, accessories and bespoke shirts and ties, all hand made.

Campagna's destiny was decided early; as a child in Sicily he spent his days at the local tailor's and his evenings at the cinema, where his sense of style was conditioned by the Hollywood stars of the era. Since then he has become renowned among his elite, international clientele for his exceptional 'eye' – his ability

to recognise immediately upon meeting a person the clothes that will suit him (or her) best. The Hollywood connection remains strong and Campagna is much in demand by stars such as Jack Nicholson, Pierce Brosnan and Charlton Heston – as well as high flyers Henry Kravis and Ronald Perelman and women, including Sharon Stone, who appreciate fine, menswear-inspired tailoring.

Now working with his sons, Angelo and Andrea, Campagna still cuts every one of his bespoke suits in person. Made in the finest fabrics – cashmere, vicuña and Super 150 and Super 180 wools – and always lined in pure silk, each suit (the only ones still to be entirely made by hand) is sewn by a single tailor.

Gianni Campagna
via Palestro 24 (corner of Corso Venezia), 20122 Milan, Italy
Tel: +39-02-76 02 23 60   Fax: +39-02-76 00 41 03

CAMPIGLIO, DR. GIANLUCA

This respected plastic surgeon is a busy man. With a string of awards and scholarships to his name, he is a highly able cosmetic surgeon, both in private aesthetic operations and restorative work after accidents, at his main base, the Niguarda Hospital in Milan; he is also a prolific teacher and researcher and has even found time recently to set up a private scientific foundation.

Dr. Gianluca Campiglio
Casa di Cura Privata del Policlinico, via Dezza 48
20144 Milan, Italy
Tel: +39-02-48 59 34 00   Fax: +39-02-48 59 35 19

CAMPILLO SAN JUAN

The breathtaking scenery which surrounds this private sporting estate 200 kilometres south of Madrid, attracts many top sportsmen to shoot stag, moufflon, wild boar and partridge. Visitors to Campillo San Juan can also enjoy horse-riding and tennis. The charming house has ten guest rooms and the superb cooking, as may be expected, is based on game.

Campillo San Juan
Paseo de Moret 7
E-28008 Madrid, Spain
Tel: +34-91-549 1862   Fax: +34-91-543 9332

LE CAPRICE

Le Caprice may have been Catherine Zeta-Jones' and Michael Douglas' choice of London rendez-vous to go public about their romance but the delight of the place is its unself-consciousness about its celebrity hang-out status. Despite now owning two more (equally successful and star-studded) restaurants – The Ivy and J. Sheeky's – Jeremy King and Chris Corbin spend time at Le Caprice every lunch and dinner without fail, greeting their guests like old friends. The cooking (simple, modern) and service remain faultless.

Le Caprice
Arlington House, Arlington Street, London SW1A 1RT, UK
Tel: +44-20-76 29 22 39

CARITA

Since the Carita sisters founded their salon in 1947, it has become a Paris institution; Terry de Gunzburg trained here and a host of others have gone on to be beauty stars in their own right. Famous faces continue to flock here to be ministered to by super-manicurists Marie-Françoise, Karen or Ruth and massage-maestro Ronald Crooks, although Carita will gladly send a beautician to your hotel upon request.

Carita
11 rue du Faubourg Saint Honoré, 75008 Paris, France
Tel: +33-1-44 94 11 11   Fax: +33-1-44 34 11 25

CARLO ORSI, GALLERIA

This fabulous gallery, founded by Alessandro Orsi in 1950, has been managed by his son, Carlo, for over 20 years. Its speciality is Old Master paintings and sculpture from the Renaissance to the 18th century and works have been sold to the Sforza Castle Museum in Milan, *inter alia*.

Galleria Carlo Orsi
via Bagutta 14, 20121 Milan, Italy
Tel: +39-02-76 00 22 14   Fax: +39-02-76 00 40 19

THE CARNEGIE CLUB

Set on a 7,500 acre estate, Skibo Castle, former Scottish home of Andrew Carnegie, is the cornerstone of entrepreneur Peter de Savary's expanding network of members-only hideaways. The two big draws here are golf (the championship links course was Golf World's "Best new course in the British Isles" in 1996) and networking. Considering that you may find yourself at the communal dining table next to Daniel Patrick Moynihan, Charles Schwab, Jack Nicholson or Greg Norman, the attraction is obvious.

The Carnegie Club
Skibo Castle, Dornoch, Sutherland IV25 3RQ
Scotland, UK
Tel: +44-1862-89 46 00   Fax: +44-1862-89 46 01

CARTIER

After a much-praised 17-year run, Alain Dominique Perrin has been succeeded as President of Cartier by Richard Lepeau and the world's largest jewellery company looks set for further expansion. Still the *sine qua non* of the Riviera set, Cartier's contemporary watches and baubles capitalise on its rich, creative history; the runaway success of the latest variations on the Tank watch has ensured Cartier's pole position among jewellers for the 21st century.

Cartier
13 rue de la Paix, 75002 Paris, France
Tel: +33-1-49 26 17 00   Fax: +33-1-42 18 53 05

CASINO DE DIVONNE

Opened in 1954 this *Belle Époque*-styled casino has, under the direction of Jean-Claude Aaron, become one of the top-ranked casinos in France. With its strong interest in the renewal of traditional games, it attracts a mixed clientele of French, smart Swiss and international Geneva-area residents, who flock over the border just a few kilometres away, in search of the high life.

Casino de Divonne
avenue des Thermes
01220 Divonne-les-Bains, France
Tel: +33-4-50 40 34 34   Fax: +33-4-50 40 34 24

CARACENI

Through the work of its founder, Domenico Caraceni, this illustrious company has played a key role in creating the Italian school of bespoke tailoring. Domenico Caraceni opened his first shop in Rome in 1913 and, following a hiatus during the First World War, eventually made his way to Milan in 1928, later opening a branch in Paris.

To be "dressed by Caraceni" has been considered a status symbol for over 70 years. Onassis and Niarchos, Tyrone Power, Cary Grant and Gary Cooper all wore Caraceni's hand-made suits, as did both of Italy's last two kings and the future Edward VIII in the 1920s – although the latter had to do so in secret, for fear of arousing the jealousy of Savile Row! Prince Rainier of Monaco, Gianni Agnelli and Sophia Loren – who loves menswear-inspired tailoring – remain faithful clients today.

The Caraceni *atelier* is staffed by team of almost 50 highly-skilled tailors, many of whom were trained by Domenico himself. Indeed, so distinctive are the cut, stitching and drape of the suits that, even after the master died, clients called the head tailor "Mr. Caraceni". The superb craftsmanship and the classical elegance of the house's style are a fine tribute to the founder's legacy.

Domenico Caraceni
Piazza San Babila 4/A, 20121 Milan, Italy
Tel: +39-02-76 00 28 24   Fax: +39-02-76 00 13 10

CASINO DE MONTE-CARLO

Despite the introduction of slot machines, this is still one of the world's grandest gaming houses, in whose ornate Salles Privées large fortunes are won and lost. A Belle Epoque palace designed by Charles Garnier, it was originally the haunt of the crowned heads of Europe and has subsequently become synonymous with the Principality.

Casino de Monte-Carlo
MC-98000, Monaco
Tel: +377-92-16 21 21   Fax: +377-92-16 38 57

CASSEGRAIN

Quintessentially French and *ancien régime*, this jewel of a stationery shop has been the place to go for exquisite gold-leaf edged note-books, copper-plate calling cards and monogrammed paper since 1919. Cassegrain will engrave your château or country house onto your notepaper and, if none of its myriad type-faces and inks quite suits, you can commission your own.

Cassegrain
422 rue Saint-Honoré
75008 Paris, France
Tel: +33-1-42 60 20 08   Fax: +33-1-42 61 40 99

CARRE DES FEUILLANTS

"My one regret," says Alain Dutournier, "is that each day lasts for only 24 hours." The son of innkeepers in the Landes region of south western France, this chef is a man of many passions – rugby, bull-fighting, travelling but, most of all, food and wine. His cellar impressed even Robert Parker and the honesty and unpretentiousness of his cooking – with duck, game, foie gras and truffles in the starring roles – belie its technical brilliance. One is left in awe, for instance, by his soft-boiled egg, encased in a feather-light beignet of asparagus and truffles. Dutournier's restaurant, on the site of a medieval convent, is as straighforwardly elegant as his cooking, the service silken smooth yet without a trace of obsequiousness.

Carré des Feuillants
14 rue Castiglione, 75001 Paris, France
Tel: +33-1-42 86 82 82   Fax: +33-1-42 86 07 71

CASTEL

The most *soigné* club in Paris, Castel nevertheless maintains an almost family atmosphere. The elders among the members – who've known Jean Castel since he ran a nightclub in a grocery shop in the early 1960s – spend their evenings musing in the cosily unpretentious ground floor bar. Parisian grandees dine upstairs in the formal restaurant while, in the basement disco, the young jet set dance into the small hours.

Castel
15 rue Princesse, 75006 Paris, France
Tel: +33-1-40 51 52 80   Fax: +33-1-40 51 72 74

CASTEL THALASSO

"A haven of peace between sky and sea" is how this discreet and perfectly-run retreat describes itself – fitting for an institution devoted to health and well-being, located on a spectacular part of the Brittany coast. Castel Thalasso attributes the success of its weight loss and anti-stress treatments, for men and women, to the clear sea air, combined with its remarkable seaweed and mud treatments. Most clients stay in the adjoining Relais & Château, Castel Clara.

Castel Thalasso
Goulphar, Belle-Ile-en-Mer, 56360 Bangor, France
Tel: +33-2-97 31 84 21   Fax: +33-2-97 31 51 69

CAZATUR

Since 1976, this company has organised bird shooting and big game hunting at some of Spain's finest sporting estates. Guests of the company are entertained at the Roman Water Dam Finca, 20 minutes from Toledo and are accompanied by first-

class, multi-lingual guides. The estate is close to an extraordinary variety of top quality game, including ibex, boar, mouflon, red, fallow and roe deer and offers trips for chamois. Eduardo de Araoz, Vice-President of the International Professional Hunters Association, who bought the company in 1987, also organises hunting trips around the globe.

Cazatur
Jose Abascal 55, 28003 Madrid, Spain
Tel: +34-91-422 3775   Fax: +34-91-442 8643
Email: eduardoaraoz@cazatur.com

CELIA KRITHARIOTI

With her clothes worn by the cream of Greek society, Celia Kritharioti is, at the tender age of 29, the most talked-about fashion designer in Greece.

Since this venerable Haute Couture house, established in 1906, was bought by her father 17 years ago, Kritharioti has breathed fresh life into it, creating sexy, refined and utterly feminine day and evening wear. This, along with her show-stopping wedding dresses, is all hand made in one of her three ateliers. A fourth workshop creates her famous embroideries, using pearls, sequins, Swarovski crystals and semi-precious stones, worked with silver and gold thread.

Celia Kritharioti
Dedalou 8, 11258 Plaka, Athens, Greece
Tel: +30-1-322 1318   Fax: +30-1-323 0689

CELINE

Meg Ryan is a devotee of the newly re-vamped Céline label under Michael Kors who has brought a touch of American slickness to this venerable French house. Both the clothes and the beautifully finished accessories are now highly covetable. His winter collection ranged from extravagant chinchilla, cashmere and pheasant feather coats, to practical lumberjack checks.

Céline
38 Avenue Montaigne, 75008 Paris, France
Tel: +33-1-49 52 12 12   Fax: +33-1-49 52 12 00

CERAMICA SANTA ANA

The quality of the craftsmanship at this ceramic works has attracted a celebrity clientele and a stream of private commissions since it opened in 1870. Its beautiful, hand-painted tiles include *monteria*, a Seville speciality and *brenacimiento*, available in all colours but best known as the blue-and-white tiles traditionally used for country houses. Fountains draw on classical and Moorish influences and plant pots carry traditional depictions of natural scenes.

Cerámica Santa Ana
Calle San Jorge 31, 41010 Seville, Spain
Tel & Fax: +34-95-433 3990

CERCLE DE L'UNION INTERALLIE

This most private of private clubs toasts the cream of French society. Founded in 1917, it provides its carefully vetted members with complete discretion, first-class cuisine and perfect service. The club also hosts lavish balls – and for those who wish to keep fit, the gymnastic facilities are excellent.

Cercle de l'Union Interallié
33 rue du Faubourg Saint-Honoré
75008 Paris, France
Tel: +33-1-42 65 96 00   Fax: +33-1-42 65 70 34

CERRUTI 1881

Patriarch of the eponymous company which was started by his grandfather, Nino Cerruti has been in the fashion business for over 30 years. He oversees both the Arte collection and the less expensive Cerruti 1881 range. The former has been designed by Peter Speliopoulos for the past four seasons and currently features 'futuristic patchworks' – a modern mix of pieces with decorative square-shaped embellishments.

Cerruti 1881
3 Place de la Madeleine
75008 Paris, France
Tel: +33-1-53 30 18 81   Fax: +33-1-53 30 19 43

CAZENOVE & LOYD

This company stands out as much for its encyclopaedic knowledge of sub-Saharan Africa as it does for the meticulous attention that it applies to every detail of its safaris. The tailor-made trips in which it specialises are based on meticulous research (the company uses only people and places which are personally known to its directors) and detailed consultation with clients, to ensure that their precise wishes are fulfilled.

Accommodation, for instance, may range from close-to-nature simplicity to the ultimate in luxury (tents with four-poster beds, fine silver and Persian rugs) and itineraries may include elephant riding in the Okavango Delta or camel safaris in North Kenya, canoeing in Zimbabwe or walking in Southern Tanzania.

Whether a private mobile tented safari, a camp and lodge safari or a special-interest trip, Cazenove & Loyd's itineraries place a strong emphasis on getting to know the real Africa; by taking you off the beaten track – independently or in very small groups – with guides whose love of the country is inspirational.

The company shares a philosophy with its sister company, Cazenove & Loyd Expediciones. In late 1999, it introduced a new programme of trips to Argentina, Chile, Bolivia, Peru, Ecuador and the Galapagos. Like the African programme, everything is tailor-made to give the very best each country has to offer. Private journeys with English speaking guides can open up a South America that is only accessed by a privileged few.

Cazenove & Loyd Safaris
3 Alice Court, 116 Putney Bridge Road, London SW15 2NQ, UK
Tel: +44-20-88 75 96 66   Fax: +44-20-88 75 94 44   Website: www.caz-loyd.com
Geneva representative office: Tel: +41-21-311 0021

CESARE ATTOLINI

Giuseppe Attolini considers the jacket which hangs in his office to be the prototype of the modern Neapolitan style. Made by his grandfather, Vincenzo, in the 1930s, it has the signature narrow, high-notched lapels, light construction and sloping shoulder line which characterise the look. The present-day company, founded by Giuseppe's father, Cesare, in 1989, produces three collections, the finest of which, bearing the Cesare Attolini label is hand-made in the firm's workshops outside Naples.

Cesare Attolini
Corso Garibaldi 329, 80028 Grumo Nevano
Naples, Italy
Tel: +39-081-395 2211   Fax: +39-081-395 2250

CHALET BRAMES

After a hard day on the pistes there can be few things more blissful than sinking into this sumptuous chalet's outdoor jacuzzi. However, if Chalet Brames' private ski guide has pushed you too hard, there is a physiotherapist on hand to soothe aching muscles. Pampering and luxury are absolute here, from the excellent service to the palatial bedrooms and superb cooking. Secluded, private and very secure, the chalet is just a stone's throw from the centre of Méribel village.

Chalet Brames
Méribel, France
Contact: Villas and Apartments Abroad, 420 Madison Avenue, New York, NY 10017, USA
Tel: +1-212-759 1025   Fax: +1-212-755 8316

CHALET DU MONT D'ARBOIS

Owned by Nadine de Rothschild, this delightfully intimate Relais & Châteaux lodge is a delight in both winter and summer. Set on the mountainside overlooking Megève, it is decorated in exquisite taste, its bedrooms bursting with character. The service is faultless, yet the notably warm welcome gives it the feel of a private home rather than a hotel. An excellent wine cellar (especially Rothschild labels) complements the classic yet original cooking.

Chalet du Mont d'Arbois
447 chemin de la Rocaille, 74120 Megève, France
Tel: +33-4-50 21 25 03   Fax: +33-4-50 21 24 79

CHALUPA & MARSCHALL

Chalupa & Marschall's real estate services range from brokerage to consultancy and appraisal. Catering to a clientele that includes private individuals, embassies and blue-chip companies, its multi-lingual team deals in exclusive residential properties for rental and sale in and around Vienna, ranging from exceptional country properties to villas and luxury apartments. Its affiliation to Sotheby's International Realty ensures a strong connection to the international real estate network.

Chalupa & Marschall
Schottenbastei 6, A-1010 Vienna, Austria
Tel: +43-1-533 9545   Fax: +43-1-533 9538

CHAMPNEYS

Restored and expanded in 1998, Britain's finest health resort enjoys a bucolic setting amidst 170 acres of parkland barely an hour from London. In addition to its list of over 100 treatments – including numerous complementary therapies – it offers a vast range of mind-body-and-soul enhancing activities. Chef Adam Palmer's imaginative cooking is better than you could ever imagine 'healthy food' to be. Champneys opens a Brussels outpost in early 2000.

Champneys
Wigginton, Tring, Hertfordshire HP23 6HY, UK
Tel: +44-1442-29 11 11   Fax: +44-1442-29 11 12

CHANEL HAUTE JOAILLERIE

Chanel's 'Prestige' *Haute Joaillerie* range is distinguished by its bold designs and technical complexity; the Winter 2000 collection is based on a theme of 'Passage', expressed through changing colours. In Spring 1999 a new collection was launched comprising deliciously tiny earrings (charmingly named *les puces d'oreilles*) and sleek gold rings – all of which feature Chanel's classic iconography. A range of 'Jour et Nuit' steel watches with patent leather straps has also been introduced.

Chanel Haute Joaillerie
18 Place Vendôme, 75001 Paris, France
Tel: +33-1-55 35 50 31   Fax: +33-1-55 35 50 51

CHANEL

Chanel's headquarters at 31 rue Cambon - the address chosen by Mademoiselle Chanel herself in 1910 - epitomise the spirit of the brand. Elegant, refined and utterly feminine it is, nevertheless imbued with youthfulness, originality and humour. Thanks to the clarity of its vision Chanel has expanded, perhaps more successfully than any other brand, beyond clothing to embrace accessories, perfumes, cosmetics, watches and, most recently, luggage. When seen all together, as they are here, every product forms part of a coherent whole. This address is the centre of Chanel's world; on the floors above the boutique are the Design Studio, the Haute Couture workshops and the apartment of Mademoiselle Chanel, still decorated just as she left it.

Arguably the most influential name in 20th-century fashion, the house of Chanel has always been defined by the values of freedom, daring and modernity. Under the legendary Gabrielle 'Coco' Chanel, its seminal creations included the tweed cardigan-suit, jersey dressing and costume jewellery; today, its Creative Director, Karl Lagerfeld, has inspired a new generation of clients, not only reinterpreting the brand's distinctive iconography in a totally modern way but also introducing radically new ideas, such as the 2005 handbag, to reflect – and sometimes even anticipate – the changing *zeitgeist*.

Karl Lagerfeld has often said that "not too much respect and a little bit of humour are indispensible for the survival of a legend" and this philosophy may well be the key to Chanel's unique success story.

Chanel
31 rue Cambon, 75001 Paris, France
Tel: +33-1-42 86 28 00
Fax: +33-1-47 03 43 61

CHARVET

Christian Louboutin loves Charvet so much that he has even used its tie fabrics in his women's shoe collection. Founded in 1838, this shirtmaker to Paris' elite stocks an intoxicatingly varied selection of shirts and ties on its ground floor. In the serene calm of its upstairs room clients are fitted for hand-made shirts, choosing from over 6,000 fabrics. Produced at Charvet's own factory outside Paris, each garment takes 30 days to complete.

Charvet
28 Place Vendôme, 75001 Paris, France
Tel: +33-1-42 60 30 70   Fax: +33-1-42 96 27 07

CHATEAU DE PUYRICARD

This serene 17th-century château, beautifully restored and decorated with French antique furniture, is available for limited private rental. Located four miles from Aix-en-Provence, it is set in 12 acres of grounds,

with formal gardens, antique fountains and sweeping lawns. It has a 12th-century tower, a 16th-century chapel and a spectacular swimming pool, set against the ruins of the palace of Archbishop Jérome de Grimaldi, who held court here from 1655 to 1685.

Château de Puyricard
Aix-en-Provence, France
Contact: Western & Oriental, 11 Westbourne Grove
London W2 4UA, UK
Tel: +44-20-73 13 66 00   Fax: +44-20-73 13 66 01

CHATEAU DE BAGNOLS

"A desperate indulgence but an unmissable opportunity" is how Lady Hamlyn describes her four-year restoration of this magnificent 13th-century castle; for her pains she has been made a Chevalier de l'Ordre des Arts et des Lettres. Each of the 20 bedrooms has its own character, with magical, Renaissance murals, sumptuous furniture and rich antique silks and velvets. The gardens are equally dreamy, with their cherry trees and allées of lavender. A swimming pool will be completed in 2000

Château de Bagnols
69620 Bagnols-en-Beaujolais, France
Tel: +33-4-74 71 40 00   Fax: +33-4-74 71 40 49

CHATEAU SAINT-MARTIN

This exquisite Relais & Châteaux hotel, which nestles amid olive groves near the Matisse Chapel, was described by Konrad Adenauer as "the ante-chamber to paradise" and, with its sweeping views over the hills and Mediterranean coastline, it's easy to see why. Originally the residence of the Knights Templar, it now offers perfect, peaceful guestrooms and suitably excellent cuisine. Its seclusion and tranquillity continue to make it a magnet for publicity-shy celebrities.

Château Saint-Martin
Avenue des Templiers, 06140 Vence, France
Tel: +33-4-93 58 02 02   Fax: +33-4-93 24 08 91

CHATEAU DE TOURREAU

Located in the heart of Provence, this spectacular, eight-bedroomed 18th-century château is set on 20 acres of grounds, with ornamental lakes, gardens and even an exquiste chapel. The cool and airy 'Japanese'

salon opens onto a ravishing view of the formal gardens and fountain, while the 'Chinese' salon provides a cosy retreat for cooler evenings. Fully staffed, it has its own squash and tennis courts, as well as a superb pool and pool-house with a summer dining room.

Château de Tourreau

near Avignon, Contact: Agence Avignon Provence, 85 rue Joseph Vernet, B.P.67, 84005 Avignon Cedex 1, France

Tel: +33-4-90 85 90 95   Fax: +33-4-90 85 84 16

CHAUMET

Founded in 1780, Chaumet has been a favourite of discerning connoisseurs and European crowned heads since the days when its founder, Marie-Etienne Nitot, was court jeweller to Napolean I. Ever in the forefront of fashion, their latest designs – worn amongst others by Catherine Deneuve – include the 'Fidelité', and 'Liens de Chaumet' lines and the 'Khesis' watch.

Chaumet

12 Place Vendome, 75001 Paris, France

Tel: +33-1-44 77 24 00   Fax: +33-1-42 60 41 44

CHELTENHAM LADIES' COLLEGE

One of Cheltenham's first principals, Dorothea Beale, believed that the education of girls was as important as that of boys and, under her guidance, the school's reputation for academic excellence was established. Madonna's choice for her daughter Lourdes' education, this distinguished boarding school has a new art and technology block and competition-sized indoor swimming pool, while polo has recently become an option. Girls are known locally as 'Greenflies', after their loden coats!

Cheltenham Ladies' College

Cheltenham, Gloucestershire GL50 3EP, UK

Tel: +44-1242-52 06 91   Fax: +44-1242-22 78 82

CHESTER JONES

This distinguished architect-cum-decorator may not be a household name but that is because his clients are the sort of people whose houses never, ever appear in the press. Furthermore, despite turning away "a job every month", Jones insists on keeping his practice small. While he describes his great love as the 20th century, Jones regularly works on older houses. Current projects include a spectacular, 18th-century William Chambers house in Berkshire (the most expensive house sold in the UK last year), a house on Nantucket and the London home of Bill Gates' partner, Paul Allen.

Chester Jones

240 Battersea Park Road, London SW11 4NG, UK

Tel: +44-20-74 98 27 17   Fax: +44-20-74 98 73 12

CHEVAL BLANC, CHATEAU

Serve 1947 Cheval Blanc at your millennium celebration and nobody, but nobody, will accuse you of

lack of taste, for this legendary wine is widely regarded as one of the best ever made, anywhere. Containing an unusually high proportion of Cabernet Franc it is, in youth, quite delicious and almost irresistible. Forbearance, however, will be rewarded for, in maturity, the wine is rich and seductive. Taken over in 1999 by Belgian financier, Albert Frére and Bernard Arnault's LVMH Group, the quality should remain as high as ever.

Château Cheval Blanc

33330 Saint-Emilion, France

Tel: +33-5-57 55 55 55   Fax: +33-5-57 55 55 50

CHEZ NICO AT 90 PARK LANE

In the 30-odd years since he began cooking in London, Nico Ladenis has been showered with accolades, culminating in three Michelin stars. Never afraid to express his stringent views about anything from the 'celebrity-chef' syndrome to the behaviour of diners, Ladenis is, however, best judged by his masterful, classically-based cooking. His elegant restaurant plays host to a diverse blend of celebrities, power-brokers and gourmets and offers a splendid baronial-style private room for up to 20 guests.

Chez Nico at 90 Park Lane

90 Park Lane, London W1A 3AA, UK

Tel: +44-20-74 09 12 90   Fax: +44-20-73 55 48 77

CHLOÉ

Camilla Parker-Bowles' presence in the front row and that of her daughter, Laura, backstage, gain Stella McCartney's fourth collection for Chloé something of an establishment seal of approval. The winter styles are raunchy rather than royal, however, with a sexy take on such British upper crust classics as tweedy gamekeeper jackets, jumbo cord trouser suits and Sherlock Holmes capes.

Chloé

54-56 rue du Faubourg St Honore, 75008 Paris, France

Tel: +33-1-44 94 33 33   Fax: +33-1-47 42 60 50

CHOPARD

A creative force in jewellery since 1860, Chopard's present-day image is closely identified with the runaway success of its 'Happy Diamonds' watch, introduced in 1976. Owned by the Scheufele family for three decades, the company employs 720 craftsmen, who undertake hundreds of private commissions each year in addition to Chopard's regular collections. In 1996, the company returned to its roots in the Swiss Jura, creating its own fully-fledged watch manufacturing operation.

Chopard Genève

8 rue du Veyrot, CH-1217 Geneva-Meyrin, Switzerland

Tel: +41-22-719 3131   Fax: +41-22-719 3135

CHEWTON GLEN

Martin & Brigitte Skan's refined taste and legendary attention to detail permeate every inch of their superb Relais & Châteaux property. Cary Grant and Orson Welles led the Hollywood A-List here in the hotel's early days and a new generation of stars has been equally seduced. Who are they? The super-discreet Skans will not breathe a word, for this is a very private bolt-hole. Suffice to say that over 70 percent of its first-time guests come by word-of-mouth recommendation.

This, along with service (under the inspired direction of Managing Director, Peter Crome) which is almost telepathic in its anticipation of guests' wishes, yet is never intrusive, creates an atmosphere which is more family home than elegant hotel.

Set in a tranquil landscape of gardens and woodlands, a 20-minute walk from the coast, Chewton Glen is a

marvellous place to relax and unwind. In addition to both indoor and outdoor tennis courts and its own Par 3 9-hole golf course, it has an excellent spa, centred around a magnificent, classically-styled indoor pool.

With their hotel winning top billing in the *Condé Nast Traveller* readers' awards and a Michelin star for Pierre Chevillard's cooking, there seems little that the Skans can do to improve upon something so close to perfection. However, reflecting their deeply-held belief that a happy staff means happier guests, they have invested a considerable sum in behind-the-scenes improvements during the past year.

Chewton Glen - The Hotel, Health & Country Club
Christchurch Road, New Milton, Hampshire BH25 6QS, UK
Tel: +44-1425-27 53 41   Fax: +44-1425-27 23 10
Email: reservations@chewtonglen.com   http://www.chewtonglen.com

CHRISTIAN BONNET

Christian Bonnet hand-crafts exquisite, made-to-measure eyeglass frames in real tortoiseshell, a skill passed down to him by his father. His clients have included François Mitterand and Jacques Chirac, while his father worked for the likes of Jacqueline Kennedy and Yves Saint Laurent. Recognised for its artistry, Bonnet's work recently formed the centrepiece of a tortoiseshell exhibition in the south of France.

Christian Bonnet
60 rue Lepeletier de Saint-Fargeau, 89100 Sens, France
Tel: +33-3-86 95 22 70   Fax: +33-3-86 65 40 88

CHRISTIAN DIOR

Soft tailoring and a passion for knitwear characterize winter 1999 at Christian Dior. Designer John Galliano showed a preference for rich mustards and soft reds for graceful bias-cut dresses and Edwardian-style sailor suits. The other big news at the house is the launch of Dior's fine jewellery line this year, with its own boutique on Paris' Avenue Montaigne.

Christian Dior
30 avenue Montaigne, 75008 Paris, France
Tel: +33-1-40 73 54 44   Fax: +33-1-47 20 00 60

CHRISTIAN LACROIX

With the support of Bernard Arnault's conglomerate, LVMH, Christian Lacroix burst onto the fashion scene in 1987. His cosmopolitan confections have drawn inspiration from his home town of Arles, employing a melting-pot of fabrics, patterns, colours and embroidery, while his wedding dresses have found favour with the grandest brides. While no one contests his genius, returns from Arnault's investment have, alas, been slower than expected and rumours abound that the axe may soon fall.

Christian Lacroix
73 rue du Faubourg Saint-Honoré, 75008 Paris, France
Tel: +33-1-42 68 79 00 Fax: +33-1-49 24 99 41

CHRISTIAN LIAIGRE

Single-handedly responsible for the current craze for wenge wood, this exponent of cool 'post-minimalism' is among the world's most sought-after

interior designers. After studying painting at the Ecole des Beaux Arts in Paris, Liaigre looked after family interests before establishing his own business in 1987. While it is no surprise that Liaigre's pared-down style should appeal to Calvin Klein, it has also seduced such erstwhile lovers of extravagance as Valentino and Karl Lagerfeld. Recent projects include a new furniture line and a book about his work.

Christian Liaigre
42 rue du Bac, 75007 Paris, France
Tel: +33-1-53 63 33 66 Fax: +33-1-53 63 33 63

CHRISTIAN LOUBOUTIN

A disciple of the late, great cobbler Roger Vivier, Christian Louboutin's creations are worn by aristocrats and film stars. With shops in Paris and London, he now has designs on Madison Avenue where, as usual, he will oversee the boutique's style. His shoe range features some 120 exotic, inventive and utterly covetable models.

Christian Louboutin
19 rue Jean-Jacques Rousseau, 75001 Paris, France
Tel: +33-1-42 36 05 31 Fax: +33-1-42 36 08 56

CHRISTIAN STEIN

Owner Christian Stein has been exhibiting *avant garde* artists since the 1960s, becoming celebrated for showing the best that the contemporary art scene has to offer. He owns two spaces in Milan- showing artists' exhibits in Corso Monforte, which is open to the public, while via Amedei is reserved for private clients by appointment only.

Christian Stein
Corso Monforte 23
20122 Milan, Italy
Tel: +39-02-66 98 24 44   Fax: +39-02-76 00 71 14

CHRISTIE'S

Continuing to give arch-rival Sotheby's a run for its money and still holder of the record for the highest price for a work of art at auction ($82.5 million for van Gogh's Portrait of Dr Gachet), Christie's sales range from pictures and furniture to wine, motor cars, teddy bears and celebrity memorabilia. Its first sale of cigars, held in London in 1999, raised more than double the estimate; a box of 50 Diplomat Trinidads signed by Fidel Castro, for instance, went for £13,200.

Christie's
8 King Street, St James's, London W1Y 6QT, UK
Tel: +44-20-78 39 90 60   Fax: +44-20-78 39 70 26

CHRISTOFLE

The 19th-century elite's silversmith of choice, Christofle expanded rapidly after pioneering the use of electro-plating in 1842. In addition to its wide range of flatware, hollow-ware and objets, Christofle's craftsman produce a limited-edition range of haute orfevrerie – including reproductions from the Christofle Museum – in workshops that the firm has occupied continuously since 1830. Today Christofle also produces crystal and a Christian Lacroix-designed range of porcelain.

Christofle
9 rue Royale, 75008 Paris, France
Tel: +33-1-49 33 43 00   Fax: +33-1-49 33 43 84

CHRISTOPHE ROBIN

His fame as hair colourist to the most super of supermodels may explain why Robin is so much in demand among glamorous Parisians. Appointments must be booked well in advance but are worth the wait; within his gem of a salon, you receive painstaking attention, large doses of charm and a colour which not only blends perfectly with your skin tone but lasts twice as long as normal.

Christophe Robin
7 rue du Mont Thabor, 75001 Paris, France
Tel: +33-1-42 60 99 15   Fax: +33-1-42 60 99 14

CICERI

Now owned by Brioni, this firm became the ceremonial and evening shirt supplier to the Italian royal family soon after its inception 100 years ago. Using the same, complex and highly skilled methods today to produce its classical white-tie-and- waistcoat sets, it is the secret behind the on-stage elegance of Herbert von Karajan, Riccardo Muti and Claudio Abbado. Having somewhat incongruously initiated the 1960s craze for matching beach shirts and shorts, Ciceri also now makes wonderful silk dressing gowns.

Tel: +39-06-462 0161 (for stockists only)

CHRISTOPHER FOLEY

This ultra-discreet dealer is an authority on English 17th- and 18th-century portraits and sporting pictures, about which he writes for the MacMillan Dictionary of Art. He has sold works by Reynolds and Constable and was recently responsible for the rediscovery of an important missing Turner painting. Foley's clients, who come to him by personal recommendation, include many celebrated international collectors, as well as other dealers.

Christopher Foley
8 Drayton Gardens, London SW10 9SA, UK
Tel & Fax: +44-20-73 73 31 30
By appointment only

CHRISTOPHER GIBBS

This highly successful and ultra-discreet antique dealer has been in the business for over four decades. A key to his success is his refusal to disclose the identities of his clients (many of whom are celebrities, from diverse fields). Gibbs' speciality is beautifully-crafted furniture from the 17th and 18th centuries.

Christopher Gibbs Ltd.
3 Dove Walk, Pimlico Road, London SW1W 8PH, UK
Tel: +44-20-74 39 45 57   Fax: +44-20-77 30 84 20

CHRISTOPHER HODSOLL

Renowned for his taste and connoisseurship, antique-dealer-cum-decorator Christopher Hodsoll fills his shop with a rich mixture of 18th- and 19th- century English furniture. The fine tables, chairs, mirrors and bookcases – both gothic and neo- classical in style – are offset by over-scaled Roman marble busts and Oriental porcelains. Hodsoll's design company, Soane, formed in partnership with Lulu Lytle, produces furniture, lamps and accessories, all which draw on a classical inspiration.

Christopher Hodsoll
89-91 Pimlico Road, London SW1W 8PH, UK
Tel: +44-20-77 30 33 70   Fax: +44-20-77 30 15 16

CIPRIANI, HOTEL & PALAZZO VENDRAMIN

There is hardly a celebrity worth the name who hasn't enjoyed the sanctuary of this great hotel. A four-minute boat ride from the hubbub of St. Mark's Square, it is set in a ravishing, three-acre garden with the only tennis court and swimming pool (salt water, Olympic-sized) in Venice. Its Meridiana Suite has a private garden and pool, while the 15th-century Palazzo Vendramin and adjoining Palazzetto Nani Barbaro are perfect for those whose privacy is non-negotiable. Above all, though, the Cipriani is soothing and inviting rather than grand and overbearing and, for this, credit goes to Natale Rusconi, arguably the greatest hotel director on earth.

The Cipriani's autumn cookery courses, run by Julia Child, have become as renowned as the hotel itself. Excursions – to markets, winemakers and private *palazzi* for dinner – are an integral part of the courses.

Hotel Cipriani
Giudecca 10, 30133 Venice, Italy
Tel +39-041-520 7744   Fax +39-041-520 3930

CIRENCESTER PARK POLO CLUB

The Earl of Bathurst's beautiful Gloucestershire estate is home to England's oldest polo club, founded in 1894. Its season includes many important games and endowed trophies, notably the Warwickshire Cup, presented by the inhabitants of nearby Leamington Spa at the club's inception. Although it maintains a low-key atmosphere, the club also hosts glamorous sponsored days and is regularly used by Prince Charles. The current chairman is Major Christopher Hanbury.

Cirencester Park Polo Club
Cirencester Park, Gloucestershire GL7 2BU, UK
Tel: +44-1285-65 32 25 Fax: +44-1285-65 50 03

CIRCOLO DEL GOLF DI ROMA

Founded in 1903 by the British Ambassador to Rome, this discreet and exclusive club, located just a few kilometres from the city centre, is Italy's oldest. The 18-hole course was built in 1918 and the club retained a very British feel for its first 20 years. Quietly influential Romans come here to enjoy the seclusion and beautiful surroundings, which include a unique view of the Aqueduct of Appio Claudio from the 4th hole.

Circolo del Golf di Roma
via Appia 716/a, 00178 Rome, Italy
Tel: +39-06-78 61 29 Fax: +39-06-78 34 62 19

CLAIRE BATAILLE & PAUL IBENS

Sought-after both in their native Belgium and internationally, these architects-cum-designers have been in successful partnership since 1968. Making maximum use of space and natural light, their style favours the traditions of Bauhaus and Le Corbusier. Bataille and Ibens work extensively on private homes and projects in 1999 included two houses on the Côte d'Azur, as well as Galerie Hufkens in Brussels, and top-grade boutiques in Brussels and Antwerp.

Claire Bataille & Paul Ibens Design N.V.
Vekestraat 13 Bus 14, B-2000 Antwerp, Belgium
Tel: +32-3-231 8620 Fax: +32-3-213 8639

CLAIREFONTAINE, RESTAURANT

In the historic heart of Luxembourg, this prestigious restaurant is a feast for the eye as well as the tastebuds. Diners, many of whom are financiers and political leaders, enjoy chef Tony Tintinger's original and stylish dishes – many based on fish – while luxuriating in the opulent Louis XIV-style surroundings. The establishment is run by a close-knit team; Margot Tintinger welcomes guests and oversees the smoothly efficient service

Restaurant Clairefontaine
9 place de Clairefontaine, L-1341 Luxembourg
Tel: +352-46 22 11 Fax: +352-47 08 21

CLAUDIA GIAN FERRARI ARTE CONTEMPORANEA

This fascinating gallery for international and contemporary Italian art continues its exciting range of exhibitions. Highlights of the 1998-9 season were 'Conversation Pieces', an exhibition of paintings by English artist Martin Maloney (showing for the first time in Italy), and photography displays by Italian Loris Cecchini and American Tim Hailand.

Claudia Gian Ferrari Arte Contemporanea
via Brera 30, 20121 Milan, Italy
Tel: +39-02-86 46 16 90 Fax: +39-02-80 10 19

CLARIS, HOTEL

Decorated in striking colours, the contemporary styling of the Claris' interior contrasts with its neo-classical, 19th-century façade. The X-factor here, though, is the hotel's extraordinary private collection of Egyptian and Roman artefacts; you can sip drinks beneath a stunning 4th-century mosaic or meet in the shadow of a 4000 year-old Pharaonic frieze. A small pool and gym on the roof offer great views of the city.

Hotel Claris
Pau Claris 150, E-08009 Barcelona, Spain
Tel: +34-93-487 6262 Fax: +34-93-215 7970

CLEVERLEY, G.J.

Of the 130 bespoke shoe-makers in central London at the turn of century, few companies remain; G. J. Cleverley is one. Born into a shoe-making family in 1898, George Cleverley opened his first business in Mayfair in 1958. He became famous for creating the refined 'Cleverley' shape which, along with other classics, is still part of the range today. Clients have included Rudolph Valentino, Winston Churchill and Jackie Stewart.

G.J. Cleverley
12 The Royal Arcade, Old Bond Street
London W1X 3HB, UK
Tel: +44-20-74 93 04 43 Fax: +44-20-74 93 49 91

CLINIQUE LA PRAIRIE

Famous for its anti-ageing fresh-cell therapy, pioneered by Dr Niehans, this most elite of spas sticks resolutely to the aim with which it was established in 1931: to envelop you in mental and physical well-being. However, it has consistently expanded both its facilities (to include a state-of-the-art Medical Centre) and the range of treatments it offers (from cosseting massages to full-scale cosmetic surgery). Its original building, The Residence, has recently been refurbished and the Imperial and Bellevue Suites offer ravishing views of the lake.

Clinique La Prairie
CH-1815 Clarens-Montreux, Switzerland
Tel: +41-21-989 3311 Fax: +41-21-989 3333

CLIVEDEN

Designed by Sir Charles Barry (whose father was the architect of London's Houses of Parliament) and built in 1666, Cliveden was once the home of the Astors, who entertained Churchill, Lawrence of Arabia, Kipling and Charlie Chaplin here. Now a grand hotel, this spectacular stately mansion has stylish, 18th-century rooms and a menu dedicated to the best contemporary cuisine. Cliveden's gardens, with lovely views over the River Thames, are a treat.

Cliveden
Taplow, Berkshire SL6 0JF, UK
Tel: +44-1628-66 85 61 Fax: +44-1628-66 18 37

CLONGOWES WOOD COLLEGE

Established in 1814 and immortalised by James Joyce in *A Portrait of the Artist as a Young Man*, this traditional, all-boys' boarding school is set among splendid woodlands. Traditional it may be, though the days of harsh discipline and bleak comfort are long gone. A splendid new residential block with an expansive refectory opened in 1999. Students are encouraged to do social work but sport is also a priority; the school even has its own nine-hole golf course.

Clongowes Wood College
Naas, Co. Kildare, Ireland
Tel: +353-45-86 82 02 Fax: +353-45-86 10 42

CLOS ST-DENIS

This exquisite Relais & Châteaux restaurant, opened in 1984, nestles in the midst of the Limburger countryside. Connoisseurs flock here from all over Europe to sample the cooking of Christian Denis and his son-in-law Wim. In 1999 Monsieur Denis shared some of his secrets in the exquisitely-produced book, *Les meilleures recettes du Clos St. Denis*, featuring such sublime house specialities as *Charlotte de pointes d'asperges, homard et caviar* and *Crème bavaroise à l'ananas confit*.

Clos St-Denis
Grimmertingenstraat 24, B-3724 Kortessem, Belgium
Tel: +32-12-23 60 96 Fax: +32-12-26 32 07

CLARIDGE'S

How can you preserve the unique beauty of this hotel's Victorian and Art Deco fixtures (many of them under preservation orders) while introducing 21st-century technology and services? Claridge's answer, during its £40 million refurbishment, included picking the tiny mosaic tiles off the bathroom walls, sending them away for restoration and replacing them one by one after the new plumbing and wiring were completed.

This attention to detail perfectly encapsulates Savoy Group Managing Director Ramón Pajares' determination to create "a seamless conjunction of the past, the present and the future" – a policy which

has seen the conversion of the hotel's sixth floor into a magnificent suite of private dining rooms, the beautifully designed Olympus Health and Fitness Suite and what are now regarded by many as London's finest accommodation: the Brook and Davies Penthouses. Some things, though, remained unchanged – like the presence here of Court Florist, Edward Goodyear.

Claridge's has always been the hotel of choice for Heads of State, European royalty, and American industrialists but its Restaurant is also the prime breakfast venue for London power-brokers and the Mayfair style mafia. The latter now return in the evenings to Claridge's new Bar – where fine wines and champagnes are served by the glass or bottle and a superb selection of cigars is available – making it one of London's hottest venues.

Claridge's
Brook Street, London W1A 2JQ, UK
Tel: +44-20-76 29 88 60   Fax: +44-20-74 99 22 10   Email: info@claridges.co.uk

CLUB 10

A compelling reason for staying at the Hotel Principe di Savoia is the privilege, shared with Milan's fashion and business elite, of access to this luxurious roof-top gym and health club. Its facilities include everything from Turkish baths, sauna and massage rooms (regulars rave about Manuel's invigorating deep-tissue massages) to a beauty treatment area, an open-air solarium and a pool with breathtaking views of Milan.

Club 10
Hotel Principe di Savoia, 20124 Milan, Italy
Tel: +39-02-62 301   Fax: +39-02-659 5838

CLUB DE CAMPO VILLA DE MADRID

The sports club of choice for Spain's gilded society, this centre offers everything from golf to polo; it was founded in 1930 and is a huge oasis just outside Madrid. Royal endorsement came first from Alfonso XIII and Juan Carlos I has since praised the club's "traditional and progressive spirit" and excellent facilities.

Club de Campo Villa De Madrid
Carretera de Castilla, Km 2
E-28040 Madrid, Spain
Tel: +34-91-550 2010   Fax: +34-91-550 2031

CLUB 55

Beneath Patrice de Colmont's great charm and apparently nonchalant informality lies a fixed determination to remain true to his vision of perfection in simplicity. The result? His beach restaurant is one of those rare places which, after more than two decades at the epicentre of fashionable life, has never become a fashion victim. Here, the *beau monde* lunches on impeccably

prepared staples such as grilled sardines or *daurade* and perfectly-sauced pastas – washed down with the best rosé and concluded with a fine cigar.

Club 55
Plage de Pampelonne, boulevard Patch
83350 Ramatuelle, France
Tel: +33-4-94 79 80 14

COLEFAX & FOWLER

Joint Heads of the decorating division of this legendary firm, Wendy Nicholls and Vivien Greenock have an international array of celebrity clients keen to benefit from their expertise and refined aesthetic sense. Although discretion is their watchword, names that have emerged include American designer Tommy Hilfiger, Sir Anthony Bamford and the Goulandris family. The firm's 'English' look ranges from the traditionally countrified to pared-down sophistication and is based always on solid architectural foundations. Current projects range from France to the Caribbean.

Colefax & Fowler
39 Brook Street, London W1Y 2JE, UK
Tel: +44-20-74 93 22 31   Fax: +44-20-73 55 40 37

COLLEEN B. ROSENBLAT

After she left university in the early Eighties Rosenblat's fascination for jewels led her on a lengthy tour of the gem-stone mines of Australia and Indonesia. Later, having trained as a goldsmith,

she used the fruits of her peripatetic lifestyle to inspire a range of "archic" jewellery. With undertones of the monumentalism which distinguishes the rings and necklaces of ancient civilisations, her new designs feature 22-carat gold in a variety of finishes, inset with sapphires, emeralds, rubies and tanzanites. After working largely for private clients in Germany and America for a decade or so, Rosenblat opened a showroom in the heart of Hamburg in October 1998, designed by America's "Prince of Minimalism", Michael Gabellini.

Colleen B. Rosenblat
Mittelweg 49A, D-20149 Hamburg, Germany
Tel: +49-40-448 0860   Fax: +49-40-448 0864
http/www.Rosenblat.de

COLLEGE DU LEMAN

Teaching in both English and French, the Collège du Léman has, for forty years, been one of Europe's leading boarding and day schools. It provides a stimulating and broad-ranging education, enriched by the wealth of experiences offered by an international community. of 1150 students representing 100 nationalities currently enjoy its beautiful 20-acre campus.

Collège du Léman
74 Rue de Sauverny
CH-1290 Versoix-Geneva, Switzerland
Tel: +41-22-775 5555   Fax: +41-22-775 5559

COLLETT-ZARZYCKI

In a rare blend of disciplines, this architectural practice, which has worked on projects across Europe, America and the Far East, also undertakes interior design and decoration. Typical clients are high-profile and of a high net worth – Conrad Black and Lord Palumbo have both benefited from the firm's expertise. Recognised for its attention to detail and use of high-quality materials, Collett-

Zarzycki's work is based on the classical idiom which, it says, gives it the freedom to be more adventurous.

Collett-Zarzycki
Fernhead Studios, 2B Fernhead Road
London W9 3ET, UK
Tel: +44-20-89 69 69 67   Fax: +44-20-89 60 64 80

COLNAGHI

Practically every major museum in the world has a painting or drawing which has passed through Colnaghi's hands. Enjoying royal patronage in the 19th century, the gallery was a regular haunt of artists such as Constable and Bonington. Early this century it was a catalyst in the formation of the great American collections. Its current director, the dynamic Jean-Luc Baroni, is a notable expert in Old Master drawings.

Colnaghi
15 Old Bond Street
London W1X 4JL, UK
Tel: +44-20-74 91 74 08   Fax: +44-20-74 91 88 51

COMME CHEZ SOI

Run by the Wynants family since 1926, this legendary Brussels restaurant is renowned equally for its unique interior, designed in the style of Art Nouveau pioneer Victor Horta, and Pierre Wynants' superb cooking. Wynants trained at the Savoy in Brussels, and then worked in Paris at Le Grand Véfour and La Tour d'Argent, before returning to Brussels. His style is a perfect balance between French classicism and pan-European modernism, with a distinctly Belgian accent.

Comme Chez Soi
23 Place Rouppe, B-1000 Brussels, Belgium
Tel: +32-2-512 2921   Fax: +32-2-511 8052

COMTE GEORGES DE VOGÜE, DOMAINE

After a lull in the mid-1980s this domaine is right back on song and its fabled Musigny Vieilles Vignes is once again a wine of Burgundian legend. Years such as 1945, 1947 and 1966 are still spoken of in hushed tones and, in future, so will 1989 and 1990; the former is more voluptuous and forthcoming while the latter is sterner, more forceful and destined for years of life yet. The 1991 was made in tiny quantities due to hail damage in the vineyards. It is reported that, immediately after the hailstorm, a team of 60 people armed with eyebrow tweezers went through the vineyards removing damaged grapes. Now that's attention to detail.

Domaine Comte Georges de Vogüe
rue Sainte Barbe
21220 Chambolle-Musigny, France
Tel: +33-3-80 62 86 25   Fax: +33-3-80 62 82 38

COMTES LAFON, DOMAINE DES

For nearly 20 years Dominique Lafon has modestly, and with infinite patience, worked to produce the best possible wines from his vineyards. As they mature in the barrel in his famously cold cellar they are subject to as little manipulation as possible. The results are wondrous: white wines full of intense flavours and equipped with a superb ability to age.

Domaine Des Comtes Lafon
Clos de la Barre, 21190 Meursault, France
Tel: +33-3-80 21 22 17   Fax: +33-3-80 21 61 64

THE CONNAUGHT

The liveried 'greeter' - his peaked cap embroidered with The Connaught's name – who (upon request) meets you at Heathrow is a fitting introduction to the exceptional civility of this most English of hotels.

More club than mere hotel, The Connaught is 'home' to American aristocrats of every stripe, from Vanderbilts and Astors to Jack Nicholson and Ralph Lauren, as well as grandly stylish Italians. So low-key is it that members of the Royal Family regard it as an extension of their homes; The Queen Mother has even dined in Executive Chef Michel Bourdin's kitchens. More usually, though, they join the blue-bloods and blue-chip businessmen in the mahogany-panelled Restaurant or more intimate Grill, to dine on unapologetically traditional and perfectly executed French and English dishes.

Like the oak-panelled American Bar (an unintentionally ironic name for this great London 'secret') and the rest of the hotel, these rooms are not so much 'decorated' as the product of years of care, with antiques and pictures acquired over many decades and wood-work buffed to mirror-like brilliance by two full-time French polishers.

Regulars have good reason to praise the service. Butlers are in attendance on every floor; if you come to England to shoot, The Connaught will store your guns from one season to the next; and Head Concierge, Alan Bromley, can open practically every door in London.

The Connaught
Carlos Place, Mayfair, London W1Y 6AL, UK
Tel: +44-20-74 99 70 70   Fax: +44-20-74 95 32 62
Email: info@the-connaught.co.uk

CONRAD INTERNATIONAL HOTEL

Since it opened in 1993 the Conrad has become the destination for the diplomats and Heads of State who gather in this Euro-capital. Completely rebuilt behind a 19th-century façade, it is decorated in classically elegant style and is notable for the large size of all of its rooms. Talented chef, Pascal Sliman, has taken over at the gourmet restaurant, La Maison de Maître and Champneys will open a three-floor spa in the hotel in early 2000.

Conrad International Hotel
Avenue Louise 71
B-1050 Brussels, Belgium
Tel: +32-2-542 4242   Fax: +32-2-542 4200

CONTROL RISKS

With a stated mission to enable its clients "to succeed in complex or hostile environments" this security firm has, since its inception in 1975, established a gold-plated reputation, working in over 130 countries for thousands of clients – 91 of which figure in the Fortune Top 100 companies. Active in political and security risk analysis, confidential investigations, security consultancy and crisis response, it is particularly renowned for the quality of its travelling bodyguards.

Control Risks Group
83 Victoria Street, London SW1H OHW, UK
Tel: +44-20-72 22 15 52   Fax: +44-20-72 22 22 96

CONNOLLY

Under the watchful eye of Creative Director Isabel Ettedgui, this family-owned leather specialist, Connolly, has metamorphosed into a luxury 'destination' store selling utterly desirable objets, accessories and clothes. So successful has the

transformation been that Isabel's husband – fashion retailing guru, Joseph – has taken a majority stake in the company. Snap up the Connolly's latest driving glasses and its Sebastian Conran-designed Ladies' Toolkit before they sell out!

Connolly
32 Grosvenor Crescent Mews, London SW1X 7EX, UK
Tel: +44-20-72 35 38 83   Fax: +44-20-72 35 38 38

CORNETTE DE SAINT CYR, DR. BERNARD

Despite the graphic and somewhat alarming pictures in this cosmetic surgeon's salon, Bernard Cornette de Saint Cyr practises his art with the sole aim of making clients look as naturally attractive as possible. While he performs body and breast surgery with great skill, Cornette de Saint Cyr is most celebrated for his facial work. He specialises in deep-tissue facelifts, which involves filling out cheekbones with fat and muscle from the jowls; this results in a far more natural look than a facelift, where the skin is simply pulled back. Similarly natural-looking results are achieved around the eyes, through a combination of eyelid lift and under-skin laser treatment to smooth out bags.

Dr. Bernard Cornette de Saint Cyr
15 rue Spontini, 75116 Paris, France
Tel: +33-1-47 04 25 02   Fax: +33-1-47 04 60 66

COS D'ESTOURNEL, CHATEAU

The dramatic oriental towers of Cos d'Estournel's chai are no mere fripperies, for this is one of the most serious estates in all of the Médoc. Its big, powerful wine is balanced by an elegance and suppleness which ensure that the plaudits continue to roll in, especially for such vintages as 1985 and 1986. The domaine was sold by the Prats family last year for some £60 million, although Jean-Guillaume Prats' appointment as General Manager ensures continuity.

Château Cos d'Estournel
33180 St-Estèphe, France
Tel: +33-5-56 73 15 50   Fax: +33-5-56 59 72 59

CORVIGLIA

Retho Mathis - son of the quasi-legendary Hartly - probably has a better take on the social ups and downs of St Moritz's habitués than anyone, thanks to his ownership of this clutch of four restaurants,

perched on the mountains at 2500 metres above sea-level. La Marmite's unique atmosphere makes it a magnet for the town's social elite, who come for Retho's Engadine cooking and a gossip-filled break from skiing.

Corviglia
7500 St. Moritz, Switzerland
Tel: +41-81-833 6355   Fax: +41-81-833 8581

COSA TRAVEL

George Müller, who trained as an engineer, had travelled all over the world before turning his passion into a business, setting up this travel agency in 1979. Specialising in tailor-made trips to the world's most luxurious and exotic locations, his

expertise has won him a high profile international clientele. Cosa Travel's impressive offices were designed by Italian architect Ettore Sottsass. Müller, who is also Consul-General of Japan in Zürich, has a stake in Zürich's Travel Book Shop, run by Gisela Treichler.

Cosa Travel Ltd
Utoquai 55, P.O.Box 5077
CH-8022 Zürich, Switzerland
Tel: +41-1-269 4040   Fax: +41-1-269 4044

COWDRAY PARK POLO CLUB

This club stands on the sprawling estate of Viscount Cowdray, whose late father was largely responsible for the post-war revival of polo in England. Although the atmosphere here is pure country-house polo (i.e. no fancy clubhouse) the Gold Cup — the most significant match of the English season — attracts a glamorous following. 1999's stars included Gillian Johnston and long-time champion Adolfo Cambiasso, "arguably the best in the world", according to Cowdray.

Cowdray Park Polo Club
Cowdray Estate Office, Midhurst
West Sussex GU29 OAQ, UK
Tel: +44-1730-81 32 57   Fax: +44-1730-81 73 14

COUTTS & CO

More than 300 years old and one of Britain's oldest private banks, Coutts' modern emphasis on what it describes as a "holistic" service has won it clients as far afield as Miami and Singapore, ranging from young entrepreneurs to those with established fortunes. Confident enough to accept that its approach may not suit everyone, Coutts tailors an individual strategy around each client, in order to grow their assets.

Coutts & Co.
40 The Strand, London WC2R OQS, UK
Tel: +44-20-77 53 10 00   Fax: +44-20-77 53 10 11

COYS

1999 was Coys' 80th year in the vanguard of classic car dealing. In addition to leading in the sales and auction market, Coys has expanded into auto-memorabilia, including accessories, models and art. Under the dynamic directorship of Jeffrey Pattinson, the company also organises and sponsors historic car competitions throughout Europe.

Coys of Kensington
2-4 Queens Gate Mews
London SW7 5QG, UK
Tel: +44-20-75 84 74 44   Fax: +44-20-75 84 27 33

CREDIT SUISSE HOTTINGUER

Neither Hottinguer's time-tested expertise in private wealth management nor its highly personal style of service have suffered since the bank's 1998 merger with Credit Suisse. Committed to fulfilling the highest standards required by its discerning clients, Credit Suisse Hottinguer is, on the contrary, continuing to supervise the wealth of individuals from an enforced position of strength – that provided by a premier international financial group.

Credit Suisse Hottinguer

38 rue de Provence, 75009 Paris, France

Tel: +33-1-49 70 58 00   Fax: +33-1-49 70 58 80

CRIQUETTE HEAD

On behalf of owners such as Sheikh Al-Maktoum and the Wertheimer family, Criquette Head has won classics in both France and England since taking over her father's yard about 12 years ago. A member of France's top racing dynasty (her father is now retired from training but still an active owner and breeder and her brother is jockey-turned-trainer Freddy), her easygoing style belies a thorough professionalism.

Criquette Head

32 Avenue du Général Leclerc, 60500 Chantilly, France

Tel: +33-3-44 57 01 07   Fax: +33-3-44 58 53 33

CRISTALLERIES SAINT LOUIS

One of the oldest producers of fine crystal in France, this firm's history dates back to 1586, when it was established under the name of Munzthal. The name change came when the firm was appointed verrerie royale to Louis XV. Its most recognisable designs have echoes of that period, with rich, precious-metal filigree, deep cutting and, often, intense colours; however, the influence of its present owner, Hermès, can be seen in its new, distinctly contemporary ranges.

Cristalleries Saint Louis

13 rue Royale, 75008 Paris, France

Tel: +33-1-40 17 01 74   Fax: +33-1-42 44 13 88

CRN ANCONA

Specialising in steel and aluminium motor yachts, this shipyard has, over 35 years, built up an impressive reputation, for both its new construction and its refitting work. By retaining direct or indirect control of all subcontracting companies, CRN maintains a high level of quality control. Recent projects include the 50-metre Paolo Scano/François Zuretti-designed *Pestifer*, launched in late 1998 and the 61-metre *Numptia*, also by Scano and Zuretti, due for launching at the end of 1999.

CRH Ancona

via E. Mattei 26, 60125 Ancona, Italy

Tel: +39-071-20 17 54   Fax: +39-071-20 00 08

CROCKFORDS

The beautiful interiors of this casino, with their magnificent plaster-work and panelling are a fine setting for the world's oldest private gaming club, established (at another address) in 1828. Once the headquarters of Wedgwood ceramics, Crockfords' current premises, designed by Robert Adam in the 18th century, contain some fine Wedgwood pieces bequeathed to them by the previous owners.

Crockfords

London, UK

At the time of writing, British law prohibits the publication of contact details for British casinos. The law is currently under review.

CUCINARIA

Describing itself as "a temple to the kitchen", Cucinaria is a wonderful source of elegant kitchenware and fine condiments. Set up by Rolf Jehring, the company's motto is to provide superb cooking and storage equipment for inspiring surroundings. Clients can buy everything from cake moulds to special knives for preparing sushi and sashimi. There are also regular cookery courses, which are much in demand.

Cucinaria

Ludwigstrasse 12

D-20357 Hamburg, Germany

Tel: +49-40-43 29 07 07   Fax: +49-40-43 29 07 09

CVM

That Baron Maximilian Riedesel zu Eisenbach's company is only seven years old does nothing to diminish its excellent reputation as an importer and retailer of fine wines and champagne. It has a remarkable list of rarely-seen grand-cru champagnes from family-run vineyards, in addition to its other speciality, white and red Bordeaux (including, notably, Vieux Château Ferron-Pomerol). Another strong suit is its distinguished selection of Italian white, rosé and red wines.

CVM

Rimloserstrasse 67, D-36341 Lauterbach, Germany

Tel: +49-6641-18 520   Fax: +49-6641-18 550

CUTLER & GROSS

Cutler & Gross has been instrumental in the transformation of spectacles from a medical necessity into a glamorous accessory. Founded in 1969 by two opticians, Tony Gross and Graham Cutler, who were frustrated by the lack of elegant glasses on the market, the company now has a range of over 450 frames in a vast range of colours and materials. Hugely influential, its chic yet original take on the most traditional of styles has made it a cult brand among the fashion elite worldwide.

Cutler & Gross

16 Knightsbridge Green

London SW1X 7QL, UK

Tel: +44-20-75 81 22 50   Fax: +44-20-75 84 57 02

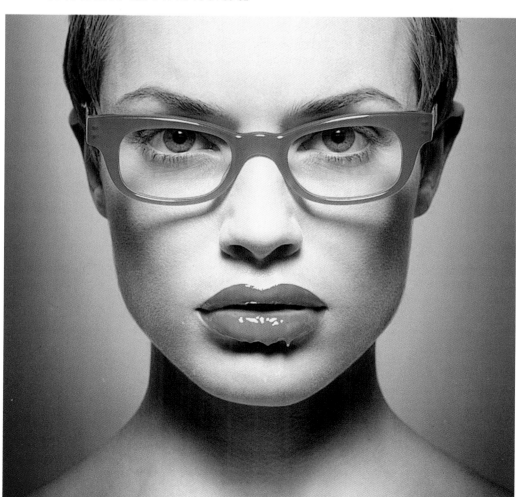

DA GIACOMO

The street outside may be a little shabby but the crowd inside is anything but. At lunchtime the restaurant is filled with smart bankers and fashion industry folk while, in the evening, a glossy social set takes over. The atmosphere is peaceful, the decor (by Renzo Mongiardino) beautifully thought-out but, with tables quite close together, it's buzzing and informal. Cooking is simple but delicious – tagliolini with herbs, linguine with scampi and zucchini flowers, good fish and meat.

Da Giacomo
via Pasquale Sottocorno 6, 20129 Milan, Italy
Tel: +39-02-76 02 33 13   Fax: +39-02-76 02 43 05

DA GUIDO

The late Guido Alciati would burst with pride at the way his wife, Lidia, and sons, Piero, Ugo and Andrea, have continued his heritage. It is not the setting which is remarkable but the cooking – regional dishes of unequalled brilliance. Lidia brings the benefit of 35 years of home cooking to her craft, while her sons maintain their father's passion for the finest and rarest local products. (The roast kid goat – capretto – comes from a farmer who knows all of his animals by name.) The wine list continues to improve, with the big names complemented by exceptional local growths.

Da Guido
Piazza Umberto I 27, Costigliole d'Asti, 14055 Asti, Italy
Tel & Fax: +39-0141-96 60 12

DAL PESCATORE

This place makes you forget there is a real world outside. Its riverbank setting is magical and, beyond the pretty new courtyard garden, you find a peaceful haven - with widely spaced tables and staff who treat you like a king. Nadia Santin's classical cooking is brilliantly executed; the Pumpkin tortelli are a perfect balance of sweetness and salt, the local river Pike with Tuscan oil, anchovies and capers judged with absolute precision. There is a new 'secret' room with an open fire, perfect for smoking your post-prandial cigar.

Dal Pescatore
Loc. Runate 17
46013 Canneto sull'Oglio, Mantova, Italy
Tel: +39-0376-72 30 01   Fax: +39-0376-70 304

DALI THEATRE-MUSEUM

This museum, inaugurated in 1974, was built on the site of the old theatre of Figueras in northern Spain. Conceived and designed by Dalí himself, it offers a unique glimpse into his fascinating world and houses such outstanding pieces as Soft Self-Portrait with Fried Bacon (1941). Seen as a Dali-esque 'playground' as much as a gallery, it also contains works by other artists, hand-picked by Dalí, including El Greco, Fortuny and Missonier.

Dalí Theatre-Museum
Plaça Gala-Salvador Dalí 5
E-7600 Figueras, Spain
Tel: +34-972-51 18 00   Fax: +34-972-50 16 66

DALLOYAU

Founded in 1802, this exquisite pâtissier, confectioner and traiteur in the heart of the Quartier de la Madeleine also has its own café, offering dishes which range from omelettes with langoustines and artichokes to the famous Dalloyau profiteroles. Other specialities are marrons glacés, miniature macarons and a huge variety of chocolate truffles - and the shop packs them in beautifully-crafted gift boxes.

Dalloyau
99-101 rue du Faubourg St-Honoré, 75008 Paris, France
Tel: +33-1-42 99 90 00   Fax: +33-1-45 63 82 92

DAN PEARSON

Garden designer Dan Pearson is also a noted broadcaster and the author of *The Essential Garden Book* in collaboration with Sir Terence Conran. He visited Chelsea Flower Show from the age of six, trained at Wisley and subsequently visited a wide variety of plant communities overseas. With the help of unusual materials (notably grasses) and bold plantings he has played a significant role in redefining contemporary garden design. Large, naturalistic drifts of perennials are Dan Pearson's current passion.

Dan Pearson
80c Battersea Rise, London SW11 1EH, UK
Tel & Fax: +44-20-79 24 25 18

DANIEL GALVIN

Born into a hairdressing family, Daniel Galvin trained with some of London's most innovative 1960s hairdressers and was one of the first people to specialise in colour. He joined Leonard and, after becoming a partner, left to start his own specialist colour salon in 1978. A favourite of the stars – Michael Caine, Nicole Kidman and Catherine Zeta-Jones among them – he has capitalised on his success with a best-selling Designer Hair Care range.

Daniel Galvin
42-44 George Street, London W1H 5RE, UK
Tel: +44-20-74 86 86 01   Fax: +44-20-74 87 26 16

DANIEL KATZ

Daniel Katz's passion for bronzes from the Renaissance to the 18th century was triggered by the purchase of a French 19th-century bronze animal. Having dealt privately for many years, he opened his gallery in 1996, staging bi-annual exhibitions. Katz has the knack of turning up rare and beautiful objects and, in 1981, discovered Giambologna's marble Bathsheba – carved in the mid-1560s and lost, in a Swedish country house, since 1632.

Daniel Katz Ltd
59 Jermyn Street, London SW1Y 6LX, UK
Tel: +44-20-74 93 06 88   Fax: +44-20-74 99 74 93

DANIEL MALINGUE, GALERIE

For private collectors and museums around the world, Daniel Malingue's gallery is a byword for taste. The leading artists of the 19th and 20th centuries from Renoir and Monet to Chagall and Picasso are all represented by Malingue, who has been in the business for over three decades.

Galerie Daniel Malingue
26 avenue Matignon
75008 Paris, France
Tel: +33-1-42 66 60 33   Fax: +33-1-42 66 03 80

DAVID COLLINS

Having established his own practice in 1985, architect/designer David Collins has become best-known for creating such high profile London restaurants as Marco Pierre White's Mirabelle and Pierre Koffman's La Tante Claire, as well as hairdresser John Barrett's New York salon. However, at the same time he has completed numerous residential projects on both sides of the Atlantic. Collins' philosophy is to use simple, natural materials of quality and endurance to create

beautiful spaces and to seek out artists and craftsmen, from whom he commissions bespoke furniture, fixtures and lighting, in order to give each project its own, clear identity. The result is a clean-lined, contemporary glamour with a confident sense of colour.

David Collins Architecture & Design
6-7 Chelsea Wharf, Lots Road, London SW10 OQJ, UK
Tel: +44-20-73 49 59 00   Fax: +44-20-73 52 72 84

DANIEL ROTH

Daniel Roth's delight connoisseurs of fine watches with his 'Masters' collection, which combines distinctive contemporary styling with high-end complications. Lately, the Manufacture has show-cased the 'Papillon' which features an ingenious jumping hour with a novel minute display involving two retractable hands mounted on a centrally located disc. Roth is broadening his horizons, too. This year he introduced the new 'Vantage' range of innovative timepieces aimed at a wider public.

Daniel Roth
4 rue de la Gare, CH-1347 Le Sentier, Switzerland
Tel: +41-21-845 1555   Fax: +41-21-845 1566

DANIEL SWAROVSKI

Scion of the famous crystal manufacturing family, Daniel Swarowski has, since 1989, more than proved his pedigree by creating a fantastical range of handbags, jewellery and other accessories. Created out of costume gems and crystals, his delicate chainmail jewels faceted rings and intricate coach, tote and woven evening bags are utterly arresting. For winter 1999 Swarovski makes opulent use of inlaid fur, hand-painted, embroidered velvets, metallic lace and cashmere.

Daniel Swarovski
39 rue Marbeuf, 75008 Paris, France
Tel: +33-1-42 56 29 84   Fax: +33-1-45 61 17 67

DAVIDE HALEVIM

Dealing in carpets from the 16th- to the 19th century and Renaissance tapestries, Davide Halevim opened his first gallery in Milan in 1977. Since then, in the belief that "only when free of the pressures of urban life can one truly appreciate such beautiful things", he has expanded to Monte Carlo, St Moritz, Capri, Porto Cervo and Cortina d'Ampezzo. He exhibits at several prestigious international art

fairs, including the Biennale des Antiquaires in Paris, where he is the only Italian in this sector to have been invited twice running.

Davide Halevim
via Borgospesso 5
20100 Milan, Italy
Tel: +39-02-76 00 22 92   Fax: +39-02-78 43 28

DAVIES, DR. DAI

Popular and hugely respected both in and out of the operating theatre, surgeon Dai Davies is one half of Harley Street's highly regarded Plastic Surgery Partners. The partnership has the UK's only private teaching practice in cosmetic and reconstructive surgery. Davies' surgical skills are complemented by a unique combination of specialists, nurses, clinical psychologists and medical aestheticians.

Dr. Dai Davies
Plastic Surgery Partners, 55 Harley Street
London W1N 1DD, UK
Tel: +44-20-76 31 39 27   Fax: +44-20-76 36 65 73

DAVID MLINARIC

David Mlinaric's famously cerebral approach to interior design has won him clients such as Lord Rothschild and Mick Jagger, Conrad Black and Christopher and Pia Getty. Combining rigour with brilliant taste, he creates a unique (and haute luxe) blend of ease and formality, always with close reference to the architectural framework. As well as private projects in the US, Britain and France, his 1999 credits included work on the Royal Opera House, the Victoria & Albert Museum, and the National Portrait Gallery. Tino Zervudachi (at 36, a future decorating superstar) opened the firm's Paris office in 1991.

Mlinaric
Henry & Zervudachi Ltd, 38 Bourne Street
London SW1W 8JA, UK
Tel: +44-20-77 30 90 72   Fax: +44-20-78 23 47 56

DE CRILLON, HOTEL

Commissioned by Louis XV in 1758 and nowadays owned by the Taittinger family, this grand establishment has just been re-styled by Sonia Rykiel. The present King of Morocco rode his toy cars along the corridors as a child and, more recently, Madonna, Pavarotti and Meryl Streep have been to stay. The best rooms – 553/5 and 547/9 – have balconies facing the Place de la Concorde. In the two-Michelin-starred restaurant, 'Les Ambassadeurs', Dominique Bouchet wows le tout Paris with his Sea urchins in caviar aspic.

Hotel de Crillon
10 Place de la Concorde, 75008 Paris, France
Tel: +33-1-44 71 15 00   Fax: +33-1-44 71 15 02

DAVIDOFF OF LONDON

Davidoff is justly celebrated for the fine quality of its tobacco products and smoking accessories — everything from cigars, pipes and cigarettes to humidors and other smokers' accessories — all of which are stocked in its wood-panelled London store. The ebullient and highly respected Edward Sahakian rules the roost here, celebrating 20 years on the site in the year 2000. Known to epicureans the world over (and a favourite of the late King Hussein of Jordan) Sahakian rejoices that "interest in cigars has never been stronger for both men and women".

The company's history dates back to 1911 when, exiled from its native Kiev, Zino Davidoff's family opened a specialist tobacco shop in Geneva that quickly became a centre for fellow exiles, including Lenin. After travelling around South America, Zino returned to Switzerland and opened his own store — the first to have a special cellar for cigars — in 1929. Then, in 1946, he created the famous 'Châteaux' range and, in 1970, in alliance with his great friend Dr Ernest Schneider, began a decisive period of expansion. In the late 1980s production was moved from Cuba to the Dominican Republic, to ensure quality. Davidoff's latest offerings are the *Short T* and the *Special R*.

Davidoff of London
35 St James's Street, London SW1A 1HD, UK
Tel: +44-20-79 30 30 79   Fax: +44-20-79 30 58 87

DOLCE & GABBANA

Domenico Dolce and Stefano Gabbana's success story began with the opening of their first studio in 1982. Their flamboyant and highly creative designs have since enjoyed enormous success and are characterised by a sexy femininity and attention to detail — notably the use of cutting-edge fabrics. By 1990 Dolce & Gabbana had

DOLCE & GABBANA

debuted a menswear collection followed, over the years, by a whole range of accessories, fragrances and the young line, D&G. They now have shops in many of the world's most prestigious locations; one of the most recent to open is on London's Old Bond Street. For the millennium, the pair have added a party theme to their signature 'Sicilian' tailoring, which employs an exciting mélange of colours, fabrics and styles.

Dolce & Gabbana
(Milan flagship stores)
via della Spiga 2, 20122 Milan, Italy
Tel: +39-02-76 00 11 55
via della Spiga 26, 20122 Milan, Italy
Tel: +39-02-79 99 50

DELAMAIN

Delamain is seldom first on anybody's list of the great cognac houses. But don't be fooled, for this small family-owned house is amongst the very best. The style is mellow and elegant with good fruit characteristics and lovely balance. Keep an eye out for Delamain's rare vintage cognacs. Highly regarded by connoisseurs, they are great expressions of the distiller's art.

Delamain
B.P.13, 16100 Garnac, France
Tel: +33-5-45 81 08 24   Fax: +33-5-45 81 70 87

DELPHI LODGE

Set in a spectacular, unspoilt valley, this is one of western Ireland's hidden treasures, offering top quality fly fishing for salmon and sea trout over an unusually long season. British Royals and Swiss and German tycoons are among those who enjoy Peter and Jane Mantle's exceptionally warm hospitality, though rank is irrelevant here; dinner is served around a single, large table. The 12-bedroom house is also let for private houseparties and there are several self-contained cottages on the estate.

Delphi Lodge
Leenane, Co Galway, Ireland
Tel: +353-95 42211   Fax: +353-95 42296

DERMOT WELD

Champion trainer on the flat for the ninth time, tennis fanatic Dermot Weld's ambition for the 21st century is to be the all time highest-winning trainer in Ireland; currently No.2, he hasn't far to go! His son, Mark, affirms that the family is also looking for "some nice races to be won with top horses" in South Africa and South America. Weld has recently been engaged as trainer by US-based computer magnate Satish Sanan.

Dermot Weld
Rosewell House, The Curragh, Co. Kildare, Ireland
Tel: +353-45-44 12 73   Fax: +353-45-44 11 19

DESCO, IL

The appearance of chef-proprietor Elio Rizzo alongside his delightful wife to take your order adds to the charm of this lovely restaurant. Set in an exquisite, late-medieval palazzetto in a hidden corner of Verona, it is deeply cosy, with beamed ceilings and old paintings. Rizzo's cooking is a masterful reinterpretation of traditional Veronese cucina; star dishes include Artichoke and pigeon soup and a sublime Braised guanciale (cured pork cheek) with Amarone and polenta.

Il Desco
via Dietro San Sebastiano 7, 37121 Verona, Italy
Tel: +39-045-59 53 58   Fax: +39-045-59 02 36

DE LAMERIE

Named after the famed silversmith of the rococo age, Paul de Lamerie, the company which bears his name today still uses some of his original moulds and dies. The company has developed beyond silverware to include a complementary range of lavishly-decorated china and crystalware. For bespoke pieces, De Lamerie specialises in traditional forms of English cresting as well as calligraphy. Master craftsman Stefan Nowaki oversees a specialist team of hand decorators.

De Lamerie
9A Windsor End, Beaconsfield
Buckinghamshire HP9 2JJ, UK
Tel: +44-1494-68 04 88   Fax: +44-1494-68 09 00

DIAMS

With its highly-trained team of bodyguards, DIAMS protects the stars who come annually to the Cannes Film Festival; in 1999 this meant sending 250 staff to the Festival to keep watch over 90 celebrities. The company also serves the wealthy élite of the Côte d'Azur and Monaco. An undisputed leader in its field, DIAMS recently opened two new offices in London and Paris.

DIAMS
37 rue d'Antibes, 06400 Cannes, France
Tel: +33-4-93 38 48 00   Fax: +33-4-92 98 44 72

DEBAUVE & GALLAIS

Messieurs Debauve and Gallais were chemists to Louis XVI and their chocolates were considered a healthy confection, as they had no added sugar – still

the case today. Indeed, the 40 varieties of chocolates now offered are still produced in the traditional way in copper vats. Although the shop has a delivery service, the building is worth visiting as it is a fine example of the work of Percier and Fontaine, the architects of Malmaison and the Carrousel du Louvre.

Debauve & Gallais
30 rue des Saints Pères, 75007 Paris, France
Tel: +33-1-45 48 54 67   Fax: +33-1-45 48 21 78

DIDIER AARON & CIE

A third generation family business, Didier Aaron is patronised by international art lovers, of which some two-thirds are American. Specialising in 18th-century furniture and works of art, Aaron acquired several pieces of note in 1999, among which were a Louis XIV desk by Jean-François Leleu and a gilded vacuum pump (a scientific instrument) from 1730. Aaron's next crop of masterpieces will be exhibited at the Biennale des Antiquaires in 2000.

Didier Aaron & Cie
118 rue du Faubourg Saint-Honoré
75008 Paris, France
Tel: +33-1-47 42 47 34   Fax: +33-1-42 66 24 17

DELBRUCK & CO.

This historic bank, founded in 1712, gave financial advice to Frederick the Great. While maintaining its august traditions, it has also moved with the times, focusing resources on small- to medium-sized family-run companies, as well as private clients and institutional investors (Delbrück Asset Management GmbH specialises in advice for this group). Recent results have shown a consistently-improving performance, even with the switch to the euro and new information technology systems in 1999.

Delbrück & Co
Rankestrasse 13, D-10789 Berlin, Germany
Tel: +49-30-88 46 10   Fax: +49-30-88 46 12 22

DOMAINE DE SOUVILLY

Comte Jean de Béarn inherited this beautiful seven-hectare estate in Normandy from his great-great-grandfather and its forest of beech, fir and oak trees provides excellent deer and boar-hunting. For eight days every year from November to January parties of up to 16 guns are entertained in considerable style. As may be expected of a member of the Roederer champagne dynasty, the count is a marvellous host, providing copious food and wine and marvellously comfortable accommodation.

Domaine de Souvilly
Bérnécourt, 27160 Breteuil-sur-Iton, France
Tel: +32-2-32 29 70 54   Fax: +32-2-32 35 25 39

DE GRISOGONO

Having wowed the world with last year's introduction of his spectacular collection of black diamond-encrusted jewellery, the flamboyant Fawaz Gruosi is in expansionist mood. Having opened a London boutique at the end of 1998, supplementing his Paris showroom and Moscow representative office, he is hoping to launch in New York during the year 2000.

de Grisogono
108 rue de Rhône, CH-1204 Geneva, Switzerland
Tel: +41-22-317 1080   Fax: +41-22-317 1088

DISCOUNT BANK AND TRUST COMPANY

Since it was established in 1952, this private bank, which has its headquarters in Geneva, has expanded into over 60 countries and now has branches in many of the world's most attractive tax regimes, from Lugano to Buenos Aires and Bahrain to Grand Cayman. The bank, which is wholly owned by the Recanati family (whose other interests include holding companies in America and the Middle East), describes its policy as a "blend of prudence and trust".

The bank's special area of expertise is asset management. The array of investment funds that it holds is extensive and is tailor-made to suit clients' individual needs. This enables the bank, on its client's behalf, to achieve an optimal asset allocation and a superior return on investment.

Unsurprisingly, with this degree of dedication, the bank has won a string of awards and has a long list of loyal and influential clients. The services offered are comprehensive and the bank has a first-class reputation for the standard of its legal advice, not least because the Discount Bank and Trust Company has put together its own, highly skilled team of specialists, whose expertise covers all issues relating to company, tax or inheritance law.

Discount Bank and Trust Company
Quai de l'Ile 3, CH-1204 Geneva, Switzerland
Tel: +41-22-705 3111   Fax: +41-22-310 1703

DOMAINE DU ROYAL CLUB EVIAN

Notable for its greener-than-green fairways and breathtaking views of Lake Geneva, this golf course figures on the Women's PGA Tour. It is the centrepiece of a beautiful resort, which also offers sailing, tennis and archery, a celebrated spa, a grand casino and two first-class hotels: the recently renovated Royal and the Hermitage. The Evian Music Festival is hosted here every year by Mstislav Rostropovich.

Domaine du Royal Club Evian
Rive sud du lac de Genève, BP 8
74502 Evian-les-Bains, France
Tel: +33-4-50 26 85 00   Fax: +33-4-50 75 61 00

DOMAINE DES HAUTS DE LOIRE

This is a classic Relais & Château retreat — luxurious, though never ostentatious, and imbued with the utterly genuine charm of its owners, Pierre-Alain and Marie-Noëlle Bonnigal. The cooking — centred on beautifully judged and perfectly balanced classics — is what one would expect of a Relais Gourmand. Built as a hunting lodge in 1860 and hidden away in beautiful parkland, it was rated No 1 in Europe for its setting in Condé Nast Traveler's 1999 readers' poll.

Domaine des Hauts de Loire
Route de Herbault, 41150 Onzain, France
Tel: +33-02-54 20 72 57   Fax: +33-02-54 20 77 32

DM PROPERTIES

With 22 years' experience dealing in top-of-the-range properties in the Marbella area, Argentine-born Director Diana Morales has built up a first-class reputation for her integrity and expertise, becoming affiliated to Sotheby's International Realty in 1987. Her multi-lingual team employs its encyclopaedic knowledge of the area to assist clients

to find not only the right property but also the best architects, builders, decorators and landscapers and, on request, to supervise construction.

DM Properties
Los Portales 2, Avenida Ricardo Soriano 72-B
E-29600 Marbella, Spain
Tel: +34-952-76 51 38   Fax: +34-952-77 18 71

DOM PERIGNON

Such is the fame of Dom Pérignon that many people don't realise that it is actually the prestige cuvée of Moët et Chandon. Renowned for the 'mouth-feel' with which winemaker Richard Geoffroy works assiduously to imbue it, DP (as it is known to aficionados) is soft, elegant and seamless. Some of the older vintages are legendary, especially the fabulous 1961, magnums of which were disgorged for the Prince of Wales' wedding in 1981. The 1982 is also splendid, a bewitching blend of chardonnay and pinot noir that demands your undivided attention. Never pass up a bottle of DP Rosé, lest it is the last you will ever come across.

Dom Pérignon, Moët & Chandon
20 avenue de Champagne BP140
F-51333 Epernay Cedex, France
Tel: +33-3-26 51 20 00   Fax: +33-3-26 54 84 23

DOM RUINART

In the first years of the 18th century his uncle, the priest and scholar Dom Thierry Ruinart, watched his fellow Benedictine, Dom Pérignon, at the Abbey of Hautvillers, conjure up a form of gaseous wine which was without precedent. Ruinart confided this knowledge to his nephew, Nicolas, who founded the first champagne house in 1729.

The house's unique cellars – the only ones in Champagne to be listed as an historic monument – are approached by a formidable staircase, which descends more than 30 metres into the earth. A network of galleries opens onto the Gallo-Roman *crayères*, or chalk pits, where the wine undergoes its second fermentation.

Ruinart uses only the first pressing. Characterised by an unusually high proportion of chardonnay (100% in its Blanc de Blancs), they are appreciated by the cognoscenti for their depth, fullness and superb bouquet. Of particular note are the Blancs de Blancs Vintages from 1988 and 1990 or the rich and complex Rosé 1986; unusually, the latter also has a remarkably high chardonnay content. L'Exclusive, created by Ruinart for the millennium, is a unique blending of six *grands crus* and great vintages presented in an elegant magnum designed in 18th-century style and encased in a filigree of silver-plate.

Champagne Ruinart
4 rue de Crayères, 5110 Reims, France
Tel: +33-3-26 77 51 51   Fax: +33-3-26 82 88 43

DON ALFONSO 1890

If Livia and Alfonso Iaccarino's parents had had their way, the couple would never have become restaurateurs – and the world's gourmets would be the poorer for it. Their restaurant has been showered with accolades, three Michelin stars and Relais & Châteaux membership among them. This is

a magnificent place – supremely elegant yet filled with laughter and warmth. The Iaccarinos are passionate about the history of cuisine and products (they grow their own herbs, fruit and vegetables) and the results, on the plate, are stunning. The wine list, too, is exceptional and the cellar itself a marvel, housed in a three-level natural cave directly beneath the restaurant.

Don Alfonso 1890
80064 S. Agata sui Due Golfi, Naples, Italy
Tel: +39-081-878 0026   Fax: +39-081-533 0226
Email: donalfonso@syrene.it

DONALD STARKEY

Having trained as an architect, Donald Starkey worked in partnership with fellow yacht designer, Terence Disdale, before establishing his own practice in 1989. Recent projects include the 64m Lady Marina (his second yacht for the same owner), launched at De Vries in summer 1999, the 50m Feadship Blue Moon, due to be launched in early 2000, and a large private house in Florida. Starkey describes his approach to design as one of "common sense...with a touch of theatre".

Donald Starkey Designs
The Studio, 2 Richmond Road
Isleworth, Middlesex TW7 7BL, UK
Tel: +44-20-85 69 99 21   Fax: +44-20-85 69 98 62

DORMEUIL

Originally a fabric trading business, Dormeuil is now run by the sixth generation of its founding family. Its first off-the-peg suits appeared in 1960 and, today, as well as fabrics by the metre, it offers both the 'Paris-London' ready-to-wear range and the newer 'Boutique' collection, designed by hip British tailor Timothy Everest.

Dormeuil
14 avenue du 1er Mai, B.P.76
91123 Palaiseau Cedex, France
Tel: +33-1-69-32 82 00   Fax: +33-1-69-32 82 95

DROMOLAND CASTLE

Dromoland oozes history and romance, tracing its roots directly to the 10th-century kings of Ireland. The bedrooms all have soul-restoring views of the lake, the 360 acres of walled parkland or the formal gardens. You come here, above all, to unwind – whether that means golf on the hotel's own 18-hole course, challenging, instructor-led off-road driving, trout fishing on the loch and private stream or simply curling up in front of a roaring fire.

Dromoland Castle
Newmarket-on-Fergus
Co. Clare, Ireland
Tel: +353-61-36 81 44   Fax: +353-61-36 33 55

THE DORCHESTER

Overlooking Hyde Park, this unashamedly opulent hotel has been a London landmark since 1931. It continues to attract the world's stars — nowadays Cate Blanchett and Julia Roberts, rather than Marlene Dietrich and Gloria Swanson, though it remains Elizabeth Taylor's "London home-from-home". Its Spa is equally favoured — though so discreet that you are unlikely actually to see George Bush (jet-lag treatments), Demi Moore (manicures) or Goldie Hawn (the full-works). The hotel's lavish restoration, in 1990, returned it to more than its former glory. The Promenade, with its peach marble columns and lifesize blackamoors, and the Oliver Messel Suite, which was created by the celebrated theatre designer in 1953, are particularly stunning. It is a tribute to its management that every inch of the place still looks as fresh as the day the wraps came off.

The Dorchester
Park Lane, London W1A 2HJ, UK
Tel: +44-20-76 29 88 88   Fax: +44-20-74 09 01 14
Website: www.dorchesterhotel.com

DROTTNINGHOLM OPERA FESTIVAL

Every summer this perfectly-preserved 18th-century theatre, in the magical setting of the Swedish Royal Family's palace, stages a season of operas and ballets from — appropriately — the 18th century. Every detail is perfect, from costumes and authentic instruments right down to period-style fireworks. Last season saw productions of Mozart's *Il Re Pastore* and Gluck's *Don Juan*.

Drottningholms Slottsteater
Box 27050, S-10251 Stockholm, Sweden
Tel: +46-8-660 8225   Fax: +46-8-665 1473
Website: www.drottningholmsteatern.dtm.se

DRUIDS GLEN

No expense has been spared to restore Woodstock House, the focal point of Druids Glen Golf Club, to its original splendour. It successfully combines historical elegance with all the modern facilities that one would expect of one of Ireland's finest clubs. Designed by Tom Craddock and Pat Ruddy the 400-acre inland course staged the Murphy's Irish Open for the past four years, until 1999.

Druids Glen Golf Club
Newtownmountkennedy, Co Wicklow, Ireland
Tel: +353-1-287 3600   Fax: +353-1-287 3699

DUBERNET

Based in the Aquitaine, the Dubernet family has been producing foie gras and curing fine meats since before the French Revolution but the present-day company was founded in 1863. The firm's Paris shop is a Mecca for gourmets in search of savoury preserves — all perfectly packaged in white porcelain dishes and jars. Its 240 specialities range from *pâté de foie à l'Armagnac* to cassoulet and a range of truffle delicacies.

Dubernet
2 rue Augereau, 75007 Paris, France
Tel & Fax: +33-1-45 55 50 71

DUBOIS NAVAL ARCHITECTS

Ed Dubois' expertise as a naval architect is based on his extensive yacht racing experience. Having cut his teeth on smaller, Admiral's Cup-winning yachts after establishing his practice in 1977, he now specialises in one-off commissions for large sail and motor yachts, undertaking both exterior styling and internal space-planning. His collaboration with

award-winning New Zealand builder, Sensation Yachts, has been enormously successful and recent projects include the 50m motor yacht, Turquoise, scheduled for launching at the end of 1999.

Dubois Naval Architects Ltd
Beck Farm, Sowley, Lymington
Hampshire SO41 5SR, UK
Tel: +44-1590-62 66 96   Fax: +44-1590-62 64 58

DUCRU BEAUCAILLOU, CHATEAU

A previous owner, M. Ducru, appended 'Beaucaillou' (meaning beautiful pebbles) to his name and thus was born one of the best-loved of all clarets. Vigorous and full bodied, with the classic scent of cedar, it inspires contented reflection rather than rapturous adulation. The 1970, still a lovely garnet colour, has developed superbly over the years, as should the 1986 — a splendid tribute to the efforts of the Borie family.

Château Ducru-Beaucaillou
33250 Saint-Julien-Beychevelle, France
Tel: +33-5-56 59 05 20   Fax: +33-5-56 59 27 37

E. GUTZWILLER & CIE

This influential private bank, established in 1886, has played a central role in the foundation of some of Switzerland's most important financial institutions. The bank, one of only 15 members of the Swiss Association of Private Bankers, is known for its efficient and personalised service and rigorous selection of investment vehicles. Gutzwiller staff are extremely loyal to the firm, which translates into the expertise which comes from long experience.

E. Gutzwiller & Cie Private Bankers
Kaufhausgasse 7
CH-4051 Basel, Switzerland
Tel: +41-61-205 2100   Fax: +41-61-205 2101

ECOLE ACTIVE BILINGUE

Founded in 1954, this school educates over 2000 pupils from cosmopolitan backgrounds. Based in five establishments around Paris' Arc de Triomphe, it describes itself as a 'crossroad of cultures' and espouses bilingualism as a founding precept of its educational plan. General knowledge, environmental studies and new technologies all form part of the curriculum and children have the use of 100 computer terminals.

Ecole Active Bilingue
117 boulevard Malesherbes
75008 Paris, France
Tel: +33-1-45 63 62 22   Fax:+33-1-45 63 30 73

L'ECOLE ALSACIENNE

This excellent private school is so-called because of its roots in a famous Strasbourg college, founded in the 16th century. Its vision is to provide an all-round, liberal education and this may explain its appeal to parents with socialist leanings – many French cabinet ministers send their children here. Language-teaching is a particular speciality, with English taught from primary school onwards.

L'Ecole Alsacienne
109 rue Notre-Dame des Champs, 75006 Paris, France
Tel: +33-1-44 32 04 70   Fax: +33-1-53 29 02 84

EDMISTON & COMPANY

Respected as much for his expertise, gained over many years as the Managing Director of one of the world's leading yacht brokerage firms, as for his straight-talking approach to business, Nicholas Edmiston has established his three-year old firm as a major player in the yacht business.

Specialising in both sailing and motor yachts of over 28 metres, he provides a fully-integrated service, from chartering and management to yacht sales, new construction and refits. Edmiston's philosophy of limiting his team to a small group of hand-picked experts ensures an exceptionally high degree of professionalism, flexibility and personal service. They go to great lengths to determine every detail of a client's tastes and priorities before proceeding with a project. In the case of chartering, for instance, this means a perfect match of client to yacht and destination.

This approach has not only won the firm more new clients – the sale of the 50-metre gas-turbine Feadship *Sussurro*, for instance – but a high degree of repeat business, such as the sale of the 50-metre *Louisianna* for the third time. New projects include a new, 60-metre, Donald Starkey-designed motor yacht, about to begin construction in Holland and a spectacular, $30 million refit of the classic 1930s steam yacht, *Nahlin*, famously associated with Edward VIII and Mrs Simpson.

Edmiston & Company
51 Charles Street, London WIX 7PA, UK
Tel: +44-20-74 95 51 51   Fax: +44-20-74 95 51 50   Email: edmiston@btinternet.co.uk
Monaco office: 9 avenue d'Ostende, MC 98000, Monaco
Tel: +377-93 30 54 44   Fax: +377-93 30 55 33   Email: edmiston@infonie.fr

EDOUARD CONSTANT

Established in 1964, this successful private bank has been owned by the Sandoz Family Foundation since 1994. Banque Edouard Constant offers an inheritance advisory service, skilled risk management and tailor-made investment strategies. Above all, clients can expect excellent, personalised treatment. BEC has played a pioneering role in the Swiss electronic stock market and in 1997 began a collaboration with Tempus Private Bank in Zürich to deal with the German-speaking market.

Banque Edouard Constant SA
11 Cours de Rive , CH-1211 Geneva 3, Switzerland
Tel: +41-22-787 3111   Fax: +41-22-735 3370

EFG PRIVATE BANK

The motto of this private bank – "total wealth management" – perfectly expresses its priorities, namely to provide a wide range of specialised services, tailored to meet the individual requirements of its clients. It places great emphasis on service, based on the tenets of security, confidentiality and accessibility. Owned by Latsis family interests, it has more than 1.7 billion Swiss Francs in capital and the responsibility for 20 billion Swiss Francs of client assets.

EFG Private Bank
24 quai du Seuget, CH-1211 Geneva 2, Switzerland
Tel: +41-22-319 1313   Fax: +41-22-319 1401

EDEN, HOTEL

Located a stone's throw from both via Condotti and the Villa Borghese, the Eden has, since 1889, stood at the hub of Rome's political, cultural and social life. During the 1960s it was where the jet set lived out *la dolce vita* and Federico Fellini treated it as a second home. Today, following total renovation in the mid-1990s, it plays host to a new generation of stars, such as Cruise and Kidman, Anthony Hopkins and Liam Neeson.

Why do they come? For its muted elegance, certainly, but above all for the ineluctable glamour of its rooftop terrace and restaurant, with its magical views over the Eternal City. Renowned for his 'modern Mediterranean' cuisine, Enrico Derflingher – formerly personal chef to the Prince and Princess of Wales – has made La Terrazza one of Rome's finest restaurants.

Hotel Eden
via Ludovisi 49, 00187 Rome, Italy
Tel: +39-06-47 81 21 Fax:+39-06-482 1584

EL SALER

When you consider that it takes every shot imaginable to make your handicap on this often breezy course, Bernhard Langer's achievement – 62 in the 1984 Spanish Open – is all the more astonishing. Javier Arana's par-72 design was inspired by the best British courses; spanning 6355 yards, it has subtle bunkering and a marvellous blend of links and wooded holes. Connoisseurs praise it as one of the most challenging in Europe.

Campo de Golf El Saler
Parador Nacional Luis Vives
El Saler, E-46012 Valencia, Spain
Tel: +34-96-161 1186 Fax: +34-96-162 7016

ELEGANT RESORTS

Based on a selection of the finest hotels and villas in the world's most sought after and exotic locations, this 11-year old company specially tailors luxury holidays for those who prefer greater independence and levels of service. Clients praise the company's professionalism and its honesty in describing the destinations being offered. Building on its success, Elegant Resorts has now added a skiing division providing top-of-the-range destinations in Europe and North America.

Elegant Resorts
The Old Palace, Chester CH1 1RB, UK
Tel: +44-1244-35 04 08 Fax: +44-1244-89 75 50

ELENA BENARROCH

An internationally recognised and award-winning figure in the fur trade, Elena Benarroch opened her first Madrid shop in 1979. Her innovative and informal shaping of pelts, in particular mink, has introduced fur to a whole new generation. In addition, she stocks a selection of cutting-edge accessories by the likes of Christian Louboutin, Etro, Bottega Veneta and Malo. Benarroch is working on the launch of a signature fragrance named after her daughter, Yael.

Elena Benarroc
José Ortega y Gasset 14, E-28006 Madrid, Spain
Tel: +34-91-435 5144 Fax: +34-91-431 4960

ELIE BLEU

Using the skills employed by the great 18th-century cabinet-makers, Elie Bleu creates some of the world's most covetable cigar humidors; not only are they exquisitely beautiful, they work extremely well. The company's range includes a variety of other boxes for storing jewellery and keepsakes, as well as desk sets and even tea caddies. All are made in precious woods, such as Indonesian amboyna, Macassar ebony and Brazilian rosewood.

Elie Bleu
8 rue Boissy d'Anglas, 75008 Paris, France
Tel: +33-1-47 42 12 21 Fax: +33-1-47 42 03 98

EMILE GARCIN

Saint-Rémy born and bred, Emile Garcin brings his encyclopaedic knowledge of Provence to the task of matching clients to the perfect property. His success is based on two principal tenets. First, that the setting of a house is vitally important (you can always redesign the building, he points out). Secondly, his understanding of the locals gives him considerable wisdom – he has an unerring instinct for whether the buyers, mostly urbanised outsiders, will get along with their Provençal neighbours.

SARL Emile Garcin Provence
8 Boulevard Mirabeau, Saint-Rémy-de-Provence, France
Tel: +33-4-90 92 01 58 Fax: +33-4-90 92 39 57

ELIZABETH GAGE

"Whenever I find a coin, I wonder how many hands it has passed through and what stories it could tell," says the goldsmith Elizabeth Gage, whose distinctive

pieces have had a significant influence on jewellery design for over two decades. She transforms *objets trouvés* - intaglios, shells, fossils, carvings — into intriguing pieces, ranging from gem-set pins to bombé rings. A recent bracelet, for instance, featured five green tourmalines, each engraved with different species of trees.

Elizabeth Gage
20 Albermarle Street, London W1X 4LB, UK
Tel: +44-20-74 99 28 79   Fax: +44-20-74 95 45 50

ELOUNDA BEACH

The service in the Royal Suites of this complex - virtually a self-contained resort village set in 40 acres on Crete's Mirabello Bay — is spectacular; helicopter transfers from Athens, private gyms with saunas, private indoor and outdoor pools, a chauffered limousine, even private fashion shows in the suiteand one's own pianist are all part of the service.

Many of the other suites (three levels of accommodation are divided between a main building and bungalows dotted about the grounds) have private pools and some have direct access to the sea. Watersports are the focus here and children are exceptionally well-received. The resort's fifth restaurant – this one Polynesian, set on the water's edge – opened recently.

Elounda Beach Hotel
72053 Elounda, Crete, Greece
Tel: +30-841-41 412   Fax: +30-841-41 373

EMMANUEL MOATTI

This leading art dealer displays magnificent Old Masters, some 40 percent of which are sold to museums. Over the years, Moatti's legendary eye has led him to some important discoveries of forgotten works. Recently, the gallery has also exhibited works by contemporary artists. The summer of 1999 saw a show of paintings based on 'antique' themes, such as the art of Russian palaces, by American artists Clare Potter and James M. Steinmeyer.

Emmanuel Moatti
20 rue de l'Elysée, 75008 Paris, France
Tel: +33-1-44 51 67 67   Fax: +33-1-44 51 67 68

ENDTENFANG

The stately, baroque Fürstenhof Celle - a Relais & Châteaux hotel near Hannover owned by the Grafen Hardenberg family — is the setting for this superb restaurant. Generally acknowledged to be one of Germany's best culinary talents, Chef Hans Sobotka bases his repertoire on classical French dishes. The setting is supremely elegant, with panelled walls, lovely moulded ceilings and sumptuous tapestries, yet you are made to feel like a private guest rather than simply a client.

Endtenfang
Fürstenhof Celle, Hannoverschestrasse 55-56
D-29221 Celle, Niedersachsen, Germany
Tel: +49-5141-20 10   Fax: +49-5141-20 11 20

ENGEL & VOLKERS

The market leader for top-of-the-range property in Germany, this agency, established 20 years ago, also has a strong presence in Mallorca and has recently set up a successful collaboration with Sotheby's International Realty. Director, Christian Völkers, applies his talent for publishing to the lifestyle quarterly, Grund Genug, which coincidentally provides a fine showcase for the company's properties.

Engel & Völkers
Stadthausbrücke 5, D-20355 Hamburg, Germany
Tel: +49-40-36 13 10   Fax: +49-40-36 13 11 23

ENOTECA LA FORTEZZA

Lovers of Brunello di Montalcino will think they have died and gone to heaven if they ever get to visit Enoteca la Fortezza. The listings go on and on, including a good smattering of wines from legendary producer Biondi Santi. A fine old vintage will cost a lot but drinking it will be a unique experience. Stock up also on local specialities, such as grappa, olive oil and cheeses.

Enoteca La Fortezza
Piazzale Fortezza, 53024 Montalcino, Siena, Italy
Tel & Fax: +39-0577-84 92 11

ENOTECA RONCHI

One could almost do a tour of the world's major wine producing regions simply by visiting this marvellous emporium. But its real strength lies in the huge selection of Italian wines assembled by fifth-generation owner, Maria Luisa Ronchi — who

was Europe's first qualified female sommelier. Barbarescos and Barolos, Chiantis and Brunellos are all here — in myriad vintages and plentiful supply. The Ronchi wine library contains vintages which date back to 1790.

Enoteca Ronchi
via San Vincenzo 12, 20123 Milan, Italy
Tel: +39-02-89 40 26 27   Fax: +39-02-58 10 35 59

ENOTECA TRIMANI

Despite being refurbished in the early 1990s, the historic interior of the Trimani family's wine shop is richly redolent of the past; a beautiful price chart from 1919, lettered in gold leaf, still hangs behind the Carrara marble counter. In addition to its 4,500 listings, which include wines from throughout the world, fine cognacs and champagne, there is a marvellous selection of teas and coffees, exotic fruit, pasticcini and olive oil.

Enoteca Trimani
via Goito 20, 00185 Rome, Italy
Tel: +39-06-446 9661   Fax: +39-06-446 8351

ENOTECA PINCHIORRI

Set in a 16th-century palazzo, this is not so much a restaurant as an unforgettable gastronomic landmark. Giorgio Pinchiorri is a remarkable host; his place oozes class and refinement, his wine cellar is awesome (including over 30 wines available by the glass) and his waiting staff almost balletic in their elegance. Above all, though, in Annie Feolde he has a chef of rare brilliance. A succulent Red mullet stuffed with foie gras and presented on a bed of raw porcini and toasted pine kernels? That's just an amuse-bouche! Pigeon in a toasted bread parcel is breathtakingly good and, for pudding, a sublime fruit soup comes with handkerchiefs of crisp pasta and perfect vanilla ice-cream.

Enoteca Pinchiorri
via Ghibellina 87, 50122 Florence, Italy
Tel: +39-055-24 27 57   Fax: +39-055-24 49 83

ERMENEGILDO ZEGNA

Ermenegildo Zegna specialises in dressing the world's smartest clothes-horses – John Travolta, Bruce Willis and Kenneth Branagh have all donned the label. The London flagship store doubled its size in 1999, and the company's new limited-edition 'Zegna Millennium Collection' of superfine wool suits and separates, and a new incarnation of the 'Zegna Sport Collection' are planned for 2000.

Ermenegildo Zegna
Via Forcella 5, 20144 Milan, Italy
Tel: +39-02-58 10 37 87   Fax: +39-02-58 10 39 01

ERSEL

This private bank, founded by the Giubergia family more than 60 years ago set up the first unit trust company in Italy in 1984. Its highly respected unit trust arm is regarded within Italy as the only serious competitor to the American multinationals which dominate that market; in February 1999, it won the award from Il Sole 24 Ore (Italy's leading financial paper) for Best Three-Year Performance by a management company.

Ersel
via Roma 255, 10123 Turin, Italy
Tel: +39-011-552 0362   Fax: +39-011-552 0222

ESKENAZI

Having formerly dealt also in Japanese work, London's premier Oriental art dealer now specialises in early Chinese art alone. This family firm, founded in Italy in 1925, shot to international prominence with Giuseppe Eskenazi's arrival in London in 1960. The gallery's Georgian façade contrasts with the sleek Jon Bannenberg-designed space within, where 51 highly specialised exhibitions have been held to date. Additional exhibitions are held each March in New York.

Eskenazi Ltd.
10 Clifford Street, London W1X 1RB, UK
Tel: +44-20-74 93 54 64   Fax: +44-20-74 99 31 36

ESPACE HENRI CHENOT

Henri Chenot's renowned spa is based at the Hotel Palace & Schloss Maur in the beautiful northern Italian town of Merano. This is the hotel where Kafka stayed in 1920 and came home rejuvenated; Chenot's health regime now achieves something very similar. His Energy Detoxicating Diet, which

earned him an honorary doctorate of science, is popular with sportspeople and has attracted 50,000 patients. Assisted by his wife, Dominique, and a team of doctors, he offers many other revitalising options, from spa-water pools to aromatherapy and mud-wraps.

Espace Henri Chenot
via Cavour 2-4, 39012 Merano, Italy
Tel: +39-0473-27 10 00   Fax: +39-0473-27 1100

L'ESPERANCE

The past year may have been tough for Marc Meneau, with the loss of his third Michelin star, but that does nothing to detract from the charm of his restaurant or his undisputed talent as a chef. Entirely self-taught, Meneau continues to evolve his robustly sensual style of cooking; while most of his dishes reflect his Burgundian roots, he is also a wizard with seafood, as demonstrated by his sublime *Red mullet comme à Cancale*, with beetroot and queen scallops.

L'Espérance
89450 St-Père-sous-Vézelay, France
Tel: +33-3-86 33 39 10   Fax: +33-3-86 33 26 15

ETON

Despite some well-publicised scandals, Eton remains a byword for breeding and academic excellence. Founded in 1440, the school's affirmed aim has always been the "training of young men to the service of the church and state". It continues to offer an unparalleled springboard for public life and was the obvious choice for Princes William and Harry. Random drug testing has recently been introduced.

Eton College
Windsor, Berkshire SL4 6DB, UK
Tel: +44-1753-67 12 49   Fax: +44-1753-67 12 48

ETRO

The exoticism which characterised Etro's first paisley decorating fabrics, introduced in 1981 and subsequently developed in over 2000 variations, continues to be reflected in every product that it has since created. Shawls and luggage were followed by decorative accessories, perfume and clothing. The latter, introduced in 1988, brings a luxuriantly bohemian elegance to a look which is essentially hippe-deluxe.

Etro S.p.A.
via Spartago 3, 20135 Milan, Italy
Tel: +39-02-76 00 50 49   Fax: +39-02-76 02 27 31

ETUDE TAJAN

Jacques Tajan has a lifetime of experience as an auctioneer, earning him the respect of colleagues, buyers and contemporaries. In association with this son, François, his Paris auction house, which has additional offices in Lausanne and Monaco, undertakes around 150 sales a year and maintains a worldwide business network with 400,000 catalogues sent out annually. The company's 12 separate departments deal with 21 categories as diverse as old master paintings, modern art and objects, jewellery, archaeological pieces, wines, memorabilia. Recent highlights included the sale of paintings by Canaletto, Renoir and Chagall, medieval English religious sculptures, an early map of Constantinople and the documents surrounding the Dreyfus *cause célèbre*.

Etude Tajan
37 rue des Mathurins, 75008 Paris, France
Tel: +33-1-53 30 30 30   Fax: +33-1-53 30 30 31

FALKENSTEIN

A home-from-home for Hamburg's elite, this golf course, which was inaugurated in 1906 and survived two world wars with no significant impact, has been hailed a masterpiece of golfing architecture. Long-time golfers will endorse Bernhard Langer's view, that playing this Harry Colt classic is an unforgettable experience. The 18 holes are perfectly integrated into the beautiful heathland surroundings, providing challenging obstacles and exciting contrasts between short and long playing areas.

Falkenstein

In De Bargen 59, D-22387 Hamburg, Germany
Tel: +49-40-81 21 77   Fax: +49-40-81 73 15

FALLANI

"The study of antiquity," says Carlo-Maria Fallani, "is a great adventure of the spirit." For many generations, members of his family have shared this sentiment, distinguishing themselves in several areas

connected with art — as sculptors architects, prelates, curators and antiquarians. Established as antique dealers for 200 years, specialising in Greco-Roman art and numismatics, Fallani's forbears served a cross-section of society united in their passion for ancient art — enquiring students and illustrious archaeologists once rubbed shoulders with the King of Italy and Sweden. In keeping with this spirit, Fallani now caters to the world's most discerning museums and private collectors.

Fallani

via del Babuino 58A

00187 Rome, Italy

Tel: +39-06-320 7982   Fax: +39-06-320 7645

FALSLED KRO

This serenely beautiful hotel in the midst of lovely Danish countryside was created by talented chef Jean-Louis Lieffroy and his partner, Sven Grønlykke. Following his untimely death at the end of 1998, Grønlykke will be much missed. Lieffroy, meanwhile, continues to delight guests with his classical French dishes, to which he lends a subtle Scandinavian twist. Room 1 has a sea view from its terraces, while the duplex suites, with their open fireplaces, are cosy havens in winter. Yevgeni Primakov and Catherine Deneuve are among those who have recently enjoyed this secluded retreat.

Falsled Kro

Assensvej 513, Falsled, DK-5642 Millinge, Denmark
Tel: +45-62-68 11 11   Fax: +45-62-68 11 62

FARAONE

Since being bought by Tiffany, Faraone may have a dynamic new management but the company has maintained the Florentine heritage of opulent jewellery which first brought it to international prominence. The house's discreet, signature line of watches and silverware — both traditional and modernist — provide a fine counterpoint to its superb crystal, coral, pearl and gem-set high-jewellery stalwarts. A whimsical 'ladybird' collection contrasts with grand, Renaissance-inspired pieces.

Faraone

via Montenapoleone 7/A, 20121 Milan, Italy
Tel: +39-02-76 01 36 56   Fax: +39-02-78 41 70

FARMACIA DI SANTA MARIA NOVELLA

With 700 years of Florentine culture behind it, this former monastic sanatorium is one of the world's most ancient pharmacies. Time-worn implements of the pharmaceutical trade, together with pure floral essences and exquisitely-scented soaps, creams and unguents — many made to the original recipes —

are arrayed beneath glorious frescoes to create a unique amosphere. Run by four generations of the same family since 1866, the Farmacia now sells its delicious products through boutiques in Rome, Milan, London and Paris.

Officina Farmaceutica di Santa Maria Novella

via della Scala 16, 50123 Florence, Italy

Tel: +39-055-230 2649   Fax: +39-055-28 86 58

FARNESE

For almost 50 years Mario Di Donato has been creating beautiful reproductions of ceramics, frescoes and mosaics, inspired by models dating from antiquity to the 18th-century. The finished pieces are produced from a variety of materials, including enamelled terracotta and rare marble. Di Donato now heads a dynasty of craftsmen and, such is the demand for their talents, there are now Farnese galleries in Rome, Milan and Los Angeles, with additional shops planned for London and New York.

Farnese

47 rue du Berri, 75008 Paris, France

Tel: +33-1-45 63 22 05   Fax: +33-1-45 63 68 87

FARR VINTNERS

Wine brokers rather than simply merchants, Stephen Browett and Lindsay Hamilton have, since 1978, built up a business which turns over some £40 million worth of wine a year — more than Christie's and Sotheby's combined. Despite its unprepossessing appearance, their catalogue reads like a lexicon of the finest and rarest wines on the planet — among them 20 from the Crimean Massandra collection. This winery was established specifically to supply the Tsar of Russia; now the wines are available, at fabulous prices, for all to sample.

Farr Vintners

19 Sussex Street, London SW1V 4RR, UK

Tel: +44-20-78 21 20 00   Fax: +44-20-78 21 20 20

FEAU

Associated with the auctioneer, Christie's, this real estate consultancy works throughout France. However, it is within Paris that its detailed knowledge of the high-end property market comes into its own. Given that demand for prime property in the French capital far exceeds supply, insider advice is essential. Right Bank property is handled through the firm's eighth arrondissement head office, while Philippe Chevalier, director of the St-Germain office knows every inch of the Left Bank.

Féau

132 boulevard Haussman

75008 Paris, France

Tel: +33-1-40 08 10 00   Fax: +33-1-40 08 11 22

FEADSHIP

Renowned for the exceptional quality of the yachts it produces, Feadship comprises the De Vries and Van Lent shipyards, along with De Vogt

International Ship Design and Engineering. Feadship's signature style has always been classical, displacement yachts. However, in a departure from tradition, De Vries launched the 50-metre *Susurio* at the end of 1998; by De Vogt and Don Shead with a Terence Disdale interior, she is capable of 46 knots. The same yard is building the gas turbine-powered *Detroit Eagle*, a 46-metre craft inspired by American sport-fishing boats, due for launching in late 2000. Meanwhile, Van Lent will launch a 50-metre De Vogt-Donald Starkey motor yacht in January 2000.

Feadship Holland
Aerdenhoutsduinweg 1, P.O.Box 70
2110 AB Aerdenhout
The Netherlands
Tel: +31-23-524 7000   Fax: +31-23-524 8639

FEINKOST KAFER

Michael Käfer is the third generation of his family to run this business; founded by his grandparents in 1930 as a tiny delicatessen, it has become a catering institution in Munich. In addition to its famous bistro restaurant Käfer-Schänke, with its 12 private dining rooms, it has a splendid delicatessen and gift shop. Käfer's prestige catering division has a distinguished clientele ranging from the Munich eilte to visiting dignitaries.

Feinkost Käfer GmbH
Prinzregentstrasse 73, D-81675 Munich, Germany
Tel: +49-89-41 681   Fax: +49-89-416 8207

~

FELDAFING

Facing onto the banks of Lake Starnberg, this 18-hole golf course sits amid idyllic surroundings. The lake and the Bavarian Alps form a wonderful backdrop for those members of the Munich elite fortunate enough to have membership. The course, which was upgraded four years ago, has every possible facility, including an impressive driving range, putting green and pitching area as well as a superb clubhouse and children's play area.

Feldafing Golf Club
Tutzingerstrasse 15, Feldafing, D-82340 Munich, Germany
Tel: +49-8157-93 340   Fax: +49-8157-93 34 99

~

FELIX MARCILHAC

Gallery owner Félix Marcilhac is known for his sharp eye and impeccable taste but, above all, for his love and unparalleled knowledge of Art Nouveau and Art Deco. For many years, he was practically the sole champion in France of these periods. In his formative years, Marcilhac knew such leading lights as Joseph Czaky and Henri Navarre personally; his definitive work on glassmaker René Lalique was published to critical and popular acclaim.

Félix Marcilhac
8 rue Bonaparte, 75007 Paris, France
Tel: +33-1-43 26 47 36   Fax: +33-1-43 54 96 87

~

FERRAGAMO

Ferragamo's factories have turned out an unparalleled range of cutting-edge accessories and luxurious sportswear for the last 60 years. These are busy times for the company, with recent shop openings in Mexico and Bogota, a new eyewear license and a planned millennium flagship in the pipeline. In addition, Massimo Ferragamo was awarded a friendship prize for Italian-American relations in Washington this autumn.

Salvatore Ferragamo Italia S.p.A.
via dei Tornabuoni 2, 50123 Florence, Italy
Tel: +39-055-33 601   Fax: +39-055-336 0215

FERNANDO BUSTAMANTE

Fernando Díaz de Bustamante owns what is generally regarded as the finest partridge shoot in Spain. Many sportsmen believe great Spanish partridge shooting to be on a par with grouse; however, a big bag day in Scotland would be a small day here, where bags between 800 and 3,000 birds are the norm. Some exclusive private shooting days can be let and big game programmes (including ibex and stags) are also organised.

Guests are received with great warmth by Fernando and his charming and aristocratic family, who have owned these unspoilt lands since the 14th century, having been honoured over the centuries with various noble titles by Spain's Kings and Queens. They are housed in a magnificent medieval castle, which was restored by a member of the Witney clan, and the food and wine provided by Fernando are of the highest levels. The castle, surrounded by wonderful medieval cities of great artistic and historic interest, may also be let to private parties for a few weeks between February and September.

Fernando Díaz de Bustamante y de Ulloa
E-10184 Torremocha
Cáceres, Spain
Tel: +34-927-19 01 30   Fax: +34-927-19 01 29

FERME SAINT-SIMEON, LA

In the 19th century, this lovely oasis in Normandy was a meeting-place for such artists as Monet and Sisley. Here, the Boelen family has skimped on nothing to transform its 17th-century manor house into the ravishingly pretty and ineluctably romantic Relais & Châteaux hotel which they have run for the past ten years. A few steps from the sea, surrounded by gardens that overflow with flowers, it preserves all the peace and charm that captivated the Impressionist painters.

La Ferme Saint-Siméon
rue Adolphe-Marais, 14600 Honfleur, France
Tel: +33-2-31 81 78 00   Fax: +33-2-31 89 48 48

FERMES DE MARIE, LES

Once a tiny farming hamlet, Jean-Louis and Jocelyne Sibuet's supremely cosseting mountain retreat is more than merely luxurious. It oozes character and style, with roaring log fires in winter, wild flowers in summer, scented candles, piles of books, frescoes in the dining room and antique wood panelling everywhere. The service is extraordinarily considerate and the privacy almost absolute. Small wonder, then, that recent guests included Ringo and Barbara Starr, Jacques Chirac and Barbra Streisand – although those with a yen for extra privacy chose one of the Sibuets' luxurious chalets nearby, all with full hotel service.

Les Fermes de Marie
Chemin de Riante Colline, 74120 Megève, France
Tel: +33-4-50 93 03 10   Fax: +33-4-50 93 09 84

FERRETTI

Founded in 1968 by brothers Alessandro and Norberto Ferretti, this company has become a world leader in the production of motor yachts of 39 to 82 feet and, through its 'Custom Line' division, from 92 to 164 feet. Ferretti's success in offshore racing has not only raised the company's profile (Norberto Ferretti was World Offshore champion in 1994) but provides a test-bed for research and development, with many ideas being successfully adapted for the production boat ranges.

Ferretti
via Ansaldo 5, 47100 Forli, Italy
Tel: +39-0543-47 44 11   Fax: +39-0543-78 24 10

FESTIVAL INTERNATIONAL D'ART LYRIQUE

With its historic architecture and beautiful light, Aix-en-Provence is the perfect venue for a summer festival. Established in 1948, the event has traditionally been an important forum for understanding Mozart and Rossini and, even after its recent relaunch under Stephane Lissner, there is still a strong educational aspect to the festival. 1999 saw masterclasses on Mozart's The Magic Flute, as well as the return of the acclaimed Claudio Abbado/Peter Brook production of Don Giovanni.

Festival International d'Art Lyrique et l'Académie Européene de Musique, Palais de l'Ancien Archevêché
13100 Aix-en-Provence, France
Tel: +33-4-42 17 34 34   Fax: +33-4-42 63 13 74

FINE ART TRAVEL

The tours organised by this exclusive company aim for individuality and eclecticism, giving its clients access to rarely seen private collections, as well as celebrated sites. The most frequent destination is Italy which, according to company founder Lord Charles FitzRoy, formerly of Christie's, provides endless cultural inspiration. Attracting a sophisticated clientele, many of whom return year after year, Fine Art Travel also offers tours to a number of carefully-considered cultural centres in Spain and France.

Fine Art Travel
15 Savile Row, London W1X 1AE, UK
Tel: +44-20-74 37 85 53   Fax: +44-20-74 37 17 33

FINOLLO, E.

Although its staff was allowed to dispense with formal wear some years ago, this celebrated Genoese shirtmaker has, otherwise, scarcely changed since its establishment in 1899. This means that the welcome is still that uniquely local brand of slightly aloof courtesy but, most importantly, that the standards of craftsmanship are as high as ever. Under the direction of head designer, Daniela Finollo, everything is still made by hand, from the finest cotton fabrics. The firm celebrates its heritage in a book published to mark its centenary.

E. Finollo
via Roma 38R, 16121 Genoa, Italy
Tel: +39-010-56 20 73   Fax: +39-010-54 32 37

FISCHERZUNFT

There are few happier sensations than sitting on the terrace of Andrea Jaeger's restaurant on a warm afternoon, bathed in the afterglow of his stunning cooking. Set in a splendid 17th-century house, it is suffused with light reflected off the Rhine, which rushes by almost within reach. Jaeger, who worked for several years in Hong Kong, is one of those rare European chefs to have succeeded brilliantly at combining Eastern influences with Western gastronomic traditions.

Rheinhotel Fischerzunft
8 Rheinquai, CH-8202 Schaffhausen, Switzerland
Tel: +41-52-625 3281   Fax: +41-52-624 3285

FENDI

The runaway success of its "Baguette" and "Croissant" bags has propelled Fendi back into the limelight making its distinctive 'F' logo a must-have for a new generation of trend-setters. Originally celebrated for the unparalleled quality

of its fur coats, the house started life as a small leather and fur workshop in Rome in 1925. Today the five inimitable Fendi sisters have strengthened its clothing and accessories lines to considerable effect under the aegis of Karl Lagerfeld since the mid-1960s.

Fendi
via Cornelia 498
00166 Rome, Italy
Tel: +39-06-61 41 01   Fax: +39-06-624 6838

FIORERIA BAGNI

This renowned Tuscan florist has been run by the same family for more than five decades. The nearby Pescia flower market is the source of much of the shop's raw material. From there, it is the artistry and experience of the Bagnis that create the stunning mixed bouquets and lavishly intricate arrangements so loved by local families and elite summer residents for their villas and for special occasions.

Fioreria Bagni
via del Giglio 16, 50053 Empoli, Italy
Tel & Fax: +39-0571-73 770

FLEURIOT

Fleuriste de Classe, this company has been garlanding Swiss high society since it was founded by Charles Fleuriot in 1920. Now owned by the Millo family, the celebrated florist offers a highly personalised service and its range of orchids, houseplants and bonsai is second to none. Not only will Fleuriot create ravishing bouquets, it also designs flower arrangements for concerts, parties, hotels and banks. A plant-hire service is also offered.

Fleuriot
26 rue de la Corraterie, CH-1204 Geneva, Switzerland
Tel: +41-22-310 3655   Fax: +41-22-310 2072

FLEXJET EUROPE

With around 100 aircraft at its disposal world-wide, this European corporation, a member of the Bombardier Aerospace group, was established in early 1999. Through its fractional ownership programme it can guarantee availability of a plane from any of 5000 airports in Europe or North America within six or four hours respectively. While able to draw on its American experience, its European management team has an intimate understanding of the different needs, culture and service philosophy of clients on this side of the Atlantic. Furthermore, taking into account Europe's different tax environment, the company has pioneered a lease structure specifically designed for this market. The aircraft, all built and maintained by Bombardier-owned or authorised companies, range from the eight-passenger Learjet 31A to the ultra long-range Global Express.

Bombardier Flexjet Europe
Centaur House, Ancells Business Park, Fleet, Hampshire GU13 8UJ, UK
Tel: +44-1252-76 10 12   Fax: +44-1252-76 11 02

FMR

Celebrated publisher Franco Maria Ricci produces the eponymous cult magazine, as well as a library full of luxuriously produced art tomes, which provide erudite coverage of all manner of aesthetic subjects. Both publications are sold exclusively from his elegant bookshops in several European capitals.

Franco Maria Ricci Editore
via Montecuccoli 32, 20147 Milan, Italy
Tel: +39-02-48 30 12 46   Fax: +39-02-48 30 14 73

FOUR SEASONS MILAN

This superb hotel was formerly a monastery and vestiges of its past remain – particularly in the impressive frescoes and cloistered courtyard. Opened in 1993, the hotel recently had another revamp when interior designer Pamela Babey-Mouton, who worked on the hotel originally, organised the complete refurbishment of the already-stylish lobby and bar areas. Showered with awards since its opening, The Four Seasons has an illustrious following – it is the hotel of choice for visiting celebrities, from Robert de Niro to Baroness Thatcher.

Four Seasons Hotel Milan
via Gesù 8, 20121 Milan, Italy
Tel: +39-02-77 088   Fax: +39-02-77 08 50 07

FLEURS DU CHATELAIN, LES

The talented and charming proprietrice of this floral boutique, France (who is known only by her first name), has prepared the flower arrangements for the best private parties in Brussels – and for Calvin Klein, Porsche and the EU – since she set up seven years ago. Her shop is a medley of beautiful scents, colours and exotic ideas and every creation is unique.

Les Fleurs du Chatelain
39 Place du Chatelain, B-1050 Brussels, Belgium
Tel & Fax: +32-2-537 1369

FPD SAVILLS

This UK-based real estate company, founded by Alfred Savill in 1855, deals in important London properties as well as country houses. The scope of the firm is wide: its agency, management and consultancy services span the residential, commercial and agricultural sectors. Its 1998 union with Hong Kong-based First Pacific Davies was the company's first stage of its strategy to become a global player.

FPD Savills
25 Finsbury Circus
London EC2M 7EE, UK
Tel: +44-20-74 99 86 44   Fax: +44-20-74 95 37 73

FLIPOT

Having had the courage to close their restaurant for a complete rebuilding, Gisella and Walter Eynard have made it more beautiful than ever – though it still retains its warm and welcoming soul. The central room, facing the romantic little courtyard garden, is warmed by wall hangings, rustic wood and a quarry-tiled floor. In the kitchen, Walter adds a dash of imagination to his traditional approach, as evidenced by the delicate Sturgeon terrine in a tomato coulis and the Frog-leg soup with herbs. The cheeses, from tiny local farms, are superb.

Flipot
Corso Gramsci 17, 10066 Torre Pellice, Italy
Tel & Fax: +39-0121-91 236

FONDATION BEYELER

This art foundation holds the treasures privately amassed by art dealers Hildy and Ernst Beyeler over 50 years and covers every seminal 20th-century artist from Kandinsky to Klee and Mondrian to Matisse. The gallery has several special exhibitions every year. 'Face to Face to Cyberspace' was an extravagant display which ran from May to September 1999.

Fondation Beyeler
Baselstrasse 101, CH-4125 Riehen, Switzerland
Tel: +41-61-645 9700   Fax: +41-61-645 9739

FRANÇOIS LEAGE

Antique dealer, François Léage is renowned for his rigorous selectivity. Not surprisingly his collection of 18th-century French furniture and *objets d'art*, displayed in an impressively spacious showroom, is among the best in the city and attracts major art institutions worldwide, including the Getty Museum.

François Léage
178 rue du Faubourg St Honoré
75008 Paris, France
Tel: +33-1-45 63 43 46   Fax: +33-1-42 56 46 30

FRANCK MULLER

For almost a decade, the personable Franck Muller has been creating distinctively designed watches for discerning collectors, who clamour for such limited-edition pieces as his 'Master City' watch. Here, period furniture, antique clocks and ancient workbenches are counter-balanced by state-of-the-art equipment and technical wizardry. His latest 'Blackwatch', in an edition of 50, has been produced exclusively in collaboration with London jeweller, Theo Fennell.

Franck Muller
22 route de Malagny, CH-1284 Genthod, Switzerland
Tel: +41-22-959 8888   Fax: +41-22-959 8882

FRANCO BOMPIERI

This is Milan's celebrity barber par excellence. Bompieri has been cutting the hair of Italy's most powerful men for almost 60 years and his reputation remains undimmed. In his time, such luminaries as Luchino Visconti, Marcello Mastroianni and even Giacomo Puccini have passed through his doors. With such impeccable credentials, Bompieri is, naturally, in huge demand and appointments must be booked long in advance.

Franco Bompieri at Antica Barberia Colla
via Morone 3, 20100 Milan, Italy
Tel: +39-02-87 43 12

FRANKONIA JAGD

From its genesis as a small family enterprise 90 years ago, Frankonia Jagd has grown to become Germany's leading supplier of high-quality clothing for traditional outdoor sports. In addition to hunting and shooting clothes, its 14 shops across the country sell a fine range of shotguns. The company has recently added fashionable country-inspired clothes, including such international labels as Barbour, to its range.

Frankonia Jagd
Randersackererstrasse 3-5, D-97064 Würzburg, Germany
Tel: +49-931-80 00 70   Fax: +49-931-80 07 10

FRIEDRICH

Founded in 1947 by Karl Friedrich, this important jeweller is now run by his sons, Stephan and Christoph. The company is renowned for its unusual designs and fine craftsmanship; many of its pieces have found their way into national museums and private collections. Winner of 30 important accolades, including three Diamonds International Awards, Friedrich has held exhibitions in Tokyo, Istanbul, St. Moritz and Berlin.

Friedrich
Goethestrasse 9, D-60313 Frankfurt, Germany
Tel: +49-69-28 41 41   Fax: +49-69-28 41 22

FULMINE

Close to Milan yet a world apart, this is an enclave where the region's traditional cooking is treated with extraordinary respect by the gifted Clemi Bolzoni. With modest charm her husband, Gianni, brings one delicacy after another to your table: Goose liver *alla cremasca*, in white wine with cabbage and lardons, Galantine of eel, sturgeon and salmon, Pigs trotters with tomato salsa and polenta. On summer evenings you eat al fresco in the small garden but during the winter this restaurant – and its cooking – are truly at their best.

Fulmine
via Carioni 12, 26017 Trescore Cremasco, Italy
Tel & Fax: +39-0373-27 31 03

FRETTE

Founded in France, by Edmond Frette, in 1860 this company moved to Italy five years later. It quickly became celebrated for its exquisite bed-linen – and particularly its signature jacquard weaves – woven from the finest linens and cottons. Tapping into the passion for all things 'lifestyle' Frette introduced a ready-to-wear collection in 1999. Simple, sober and luxurious, it features easy separates, jacquard-edged pareos, whisper-soft suede slippers and cashmere underwear.

Frette
via Dante 15, 20049 Concorezzo, Italy
Tel: +39-039-60 461   Fax: +39-039-604 6440

GRIMA

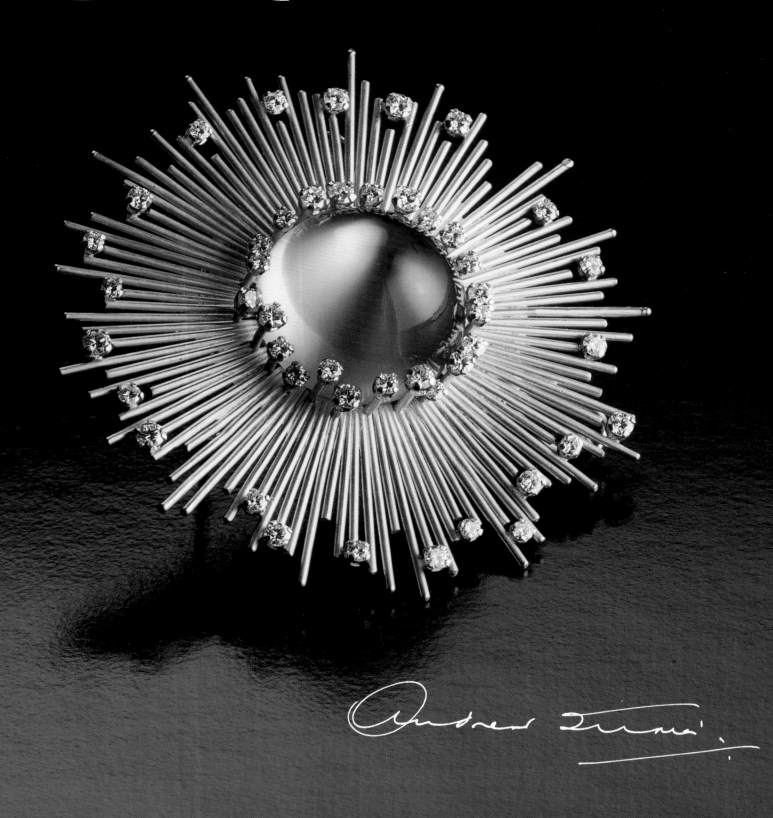

GABHAN O'KEEFFE

Decorator Gabhan O'Keeffe is as flamboyant as the schemes he creates; a sense of fun and a love of extravagance are prerequisites for a happy collaboration. So is patience, since O'Keeffe is booked up years ahead. His projects range from New York apartments (Nan Kempner et al) to a Bavarian palace (Gloria von Thurn und Taxis). His latest – completed in autumn 1999 – is the total re-building of a vast Knightsbridge house, where he has created an environment in which its owners will live, he says, "very much the way an Italian Renaissance family would have lived".

Gabhan O'Keeffe
3 Kinnerton Place South, London SW1X 8EH, UK
Tel: +44-20-72 59 56 58   Fax: +44-20-72 59 56 14

GAGGIO

Emma Gaggio's showroom is a feast of luxurious textiles. The family business spans four generations and Gaggio has skilfully preserved the ancient techniques – first introduced from the East by Marco Polo – that are the company signature. Painted silks and unforgettable hand-blocked velvets are her forte, with private commissions – from cushions to yacht interiors – are readily undertaken. Gaggio has a string of successes to her name, including Adnan Kashoggi's Paris residence.

Gaggio
Piscan San Samuele, San Marco 3415, 30124 Venice, Italy
Tel: +39-041-522 8574   Fax: +39-041-522 8958

GAJA

Since taking over his family business in 1970, Angelo Gaja has flown in the face of convention while in the pursuit of excellence. 'Foreign' grape varieties such as cabernet sauvignon and chardonnay have been planted and he has wrested magnificent flavours from them. His Barbarescos are also superlative, especially the 1990 Sorí Tildin which ranks with the greatest wines in the world.

Angelo Gaja
via Torino 36B, 12050 Barbaresco, Italy
Tel: +39-0173-63 52 55   Fax: +39-0173-63 52 56

GALERIE THOMAS

For the last 35 years this internationally-recognised gallery has been a leading exponent of German Expressionism and classic 20th-century art. It has been responsible for major shows of work by the group of artists known as 'Der Blaue Reiter' – including Kandinsky and Jawlensky – as well as individual exhibitions in 1999 devoted to Max Ernst, German Expressionist painter Lionel Feininger, German calligrapher and meditative painter Julius Bissier and Greek sculptor Ioannis Avramides.

Galerie Thomas
Maximilianstrasse 25, D-80539 Munich, Germany
Tel: +49-89-22 27 41   Fax: +49-89-29 14 04

GALIGNANI

This book shop has been a Paris institution since the early 19th century, when Stendhal wrote that one of his greatest pleasures was to read the English newspapers there. The Galignani heritage is a rich one: texts by Byron, Walter Scott, Thackeray and other great Victorian literary figures were all

published here at a time when this was the city's key English-language book shop. Now selling over 50,000 titles, Galignani deals in French as well as English books in all areas, from history to gardening and tourism to children's stories and is an especially good source of large-format illustrated books on the decorative arts and design.

Galignani
224 rue de Rivoli, 75001 Paris, France
Tel: +33-1-42 60 76 07   Fax: +33-1-42 86 09 31

GALLERIA BORGHESE

"A universal theatre, a collection of wonders" – the poet Scipione Francucci's description of the Borgheses' art collection in 1613 still holds true. The early 15th-century villa which houses it was built for Cardinal Borghese, who began the family tradition of acquiring works of art. The collection contains celebrated sculpture by Bernini and paintings by Raphael, Caravaggio, Rubens and Titian. Paolina, wife of Camillo Borghese and Napoleon's sister, is immortalised here as Canova's *Venus Victorious*.

Galleria Borghese
Piazza Scipione Borghese 5, 00197 Rome, Italy
Tel: +39-06-854 8577   Fax: +39-06-884 4756

GAMBERO ROSSO

The subtle luxury of this restaurant is a perfect foil for Fulvio Pierangeli's brilliant and imaginative cooking. *Lasagnette alla marinara* (tiny packages of clams, mussels and crayfish delicately flavoured with fennel), Leek tortellini with freshwater shrimps and foie gras or Tuna soup with figs are followed by a lightly seared *Daurade* (caught to order) or Suckling pig, flavoured with myrtle and served boned, followed by its head. The wine list is monumental, fully meriting its 1998 'Best Cellar of the Year' award from the Italian Sommeliers' Association.

Gambero Rosso
Piazza della Vittoria 13, 52027 San Vincenzo, Italy
Tel: +39-0565-70 10 21   Fax: +39-0565-70 45 42

GASTHOF POST LECH

Kristl Moosbrugger, owner of this delicious alpine retreat, says, "It's my life's work. I can't think of anything I would rather do." It shows. She and her son, Florian, are wonderful hosts (they won Relais & Châteaux's Welcome Trophy in 1994) and their hotel is a perfect blend of cosiness and chic, with its mix of hand-painted panelling, alpine antiques and hunting trophies. In winter, European royals – taught to ski by the Post's Manfred Felsner – make it a home from home. Some people who come – like Sandra Strasser – never leave; Head Receptionist for five years, she married Florian Moosbrugger last spring.

Gasthof Post Lech
A-6764 Lech am Arlberg, Austria
Tel: +43-5583-22 060   Fax: +43-5583-22 06 23

GASTINE RENETTE

This historic gunsmith traces its roots back to 1812, when it began to build up a world-class reputation for duelling pistols. Its enduring dedication to quality is reflected in the beautifully-crafted hunting rifles on offer, as well as its range of elegant and functional shooting accessories. Monsieur Guené, the shop's owner since 1989, is the scion of a family which has been dedicating its energy to patrician sporting pursuits and the art of fine gun-making since the French Revolution.

Gastine Renette
39 avenue Franklin D. Roosevelt, 75008 Paris, France
Tel: +33-1-43 59 77 74   Fax: +33-1-42 56 21 11

GAVROCHE, LE

Established in 1967 by Albert Roux, Le Gavroche's kitchens passed into the hands of his son, Michel Jr, in 1991. Young Roux continues the tradition of luxurious, classical cuisine that makes a visit to this restaurant such a treat and Silvano Giraldin continues to demonstrate just what it is to be a king among maître d's. Mingle with the likes of Lord Attenborough over a *Poulette de Bresse en vessie*, washed down with a triumphal bottle from the cellar.

Le Gavroche
43 Upper Brook Street
London W1Y 1PF, UK
Tel: +44-20-74 08 08 81   Fax: +44-20-74 09 09 39

GELOT

Hat-makers to the French élite since 1835, Gelot came to international prominence when King Edward VII became a client in 1920. Since then its classically elegant style has attracted numerous high-profile clients – both men and women – including Anthony Quinn, Donald Sutherland, the late President Mitterand and several *Comédie Française* actresses. Using time-honoured techniques, its bespoke and ready-to-wear hats are made of the finest materials, including English and Italian felts in 100 different shades.

Gelot
15 rue du Faubourg St-Honoré, 75008, Paris, France
Tel: +33-1-44 71 31 61

GENEVA LIMOUSINE

This exclusive chauffeur service believes that its clients deserve 'irreproachable' service. Set up in 1995, the company is directed by Philippe Menoud who, having spent more than 15 years in the business, insists that cars from Mercedes-Benz offer the highest quality. Chauffeurs are hand-picked for skill, experience and discretion. The company also offers self-drive cars – principally Mercedes but a selection ranging from prestigious sports cars to small town cars is also available.

Geneva Limousine
3 rue du Levant, CH-1201 Geneva, Switzerland
Tel: +41-22-908 3880   Fax: +41-22-908 3890

GEORG JENSEN

Born in 1866 and trained as both a sculptor and a goldsmith, Georg Jensen opened his first silversmith in Copenhagen at the beginning of the century and, by the time of his death in 1935, had become an internationally acclaimed jeweller and sculptor of *objets*. Jensen broke decisively with the traditions of the day to create silverware inspired by organic forms – a style which became hugely influential – and this tradition is continued by the Jensen workshops today.

Georg Jensen
4 Amagertorv, DK-1160 Copenhagen K, Denmark
Tel: +45-38 14 48 48   Fax: +45-38 14 99 70

GERALD GENTA

A pioneer of the new wave of *Haute Horlogerie*, Gérald Genta established his watchmaking firm in 1969. Five years of development went into creating his revolutionary, 1994 'Grande Sonnerie' in con-

junction with Pierre-Michel Golay, which has been up-dated in 1999 with an inverted mechanical movement. Genta has also created the 'Backtimer' in a limited edition of 456 pieces, which boasts a countdown function to the millennium, and his latest creation, the 'Retro' collection marries technical innovation with casual styling.

Gérald Genta
18-29 rue Plantamour, CH-1201 Geneva, Switzerland
Tel: +41-22-716 0916   Fax: +41-22-716 0917

GEORGES BLANC

Despite turning his village into a veritable Blanc empire (restaurant, inn, shops), George Blanc's heart and soul remain in the kitchen. A great traditionalist – he credits his grandmother, Elisa, with teaching him to cook – Blanc nevertheless has had a seminal influence on the evolution of French cooking. His *Pot-au-feu* with three types of poultry and his *Cuisses de grenouille sauce poulette finement épicées au curry* are unmatchable. The cellar is one of the best in France.

Georges Blanc
Place du Marché. 01540 Vonnas, France
Tel: +33-4-74 50 90 90   Fax: +33-4-74 50 08 80

GERARD BOYER "LES CRAYERES"

Sumptuous is the word – both for Gérard Boyer's refined and classically-based cooking and for the grand turn-of-the-century residence which houses this stately Relais & Châteaux retreat. Elyane Boyer, herself the epitome of French chic, has overseen the decoration of its 19 bedrooms, which overlook the hotel's seven-hectare English-style gardens. Appropriately, given Les Crayères' location, its cellars contain no less than 150 champagnes, from the *grandes marques* to rare bottles from little-known family *domaines*.

Gérard Boyer "Les Crayères"
64 boulevard Henry Vasnier, 5110 Reims, France
Tel: +33-3-26 82 80 80   Fax: +33-3-26 82 65 52

W. & H. GIDDEN

This venerable company, which made the saddle on which the Duke of Wellington rode into battle against Napoleon in 1815, is experiencing a new lease of life under its new owners. Richard Davison, British International Dressage No.1, and entrepreneur Ian Blatchly, an accomplished amateur rider, are re-focusing the company on its core, equestrian products, working from a passionate belief that "luxury goods have no value unless they perform properly".

W. & H. Gidden
15d Clifford Street, London W1X 1RF, UK
Tel: +44-20-77 34 27 88   Fax: +44-20-74 94 23 88

GIAN ENZO SPERONE

This gallery has been a forum for contemporary American art trends – though not simply for American artists but also for Europeans (and, specifically, Italians) influenced by movements in American art since it opened in Turin in 1964. Initially, Sperone focused on works by Rosenquist, Rauschenberg and Lichtenstein but, since his move to Rome in 1971, Sperone's gallery has played host to exciting works by Schnabel, Sachs, Paladino and Boetti.

Gian Enzo Sperone Galleria
via di Pallacorda 15, 00186 Rome, Italy
Tel: +39-06-689 3525   Fax: +39-06-689 3527

GIANNI VERSACE

Catherine Zeta-Jones, Juliette Lewis and Christina Ricci are the latest starlet-converts to the allure of the Versace label, which shows no sign of abandoning its momentum under Gianni's sister Donatella – although she has nixed the Istante range. Rock star razammataz is still the order of the day: the lady's latest look consists of diaphanous dresses – muslin and chiffon – trimmed with mother of pearl, coral or turquoise, all to raunchy effect.

Gianni Versace Spa
via della Spiga 25, 20121 Milan, Italy
Tel: +39-02-76 09 31   Fax: +39-02-76 00 26 35

GIDLEIGH PARK

Set in 45 acres of ravishingly pretty grounds in the North Teign river valley, this quintessentially English country house hotel is, in fact, the creation of an

GINA

Something of a best-kept secret since its foundation in 1954, Gina Shoes opened its first-ever London boutique in 1991 – to the universal acclaim of the fashion élite. Since then Gina has created catwalk collections for designers such as Amanda Wakeley, Hussein Chayalan, Balenciaga and Marni.
Talented brothers, Attila, Aydin and Altan Kurdash, who share the design and manufacturing responsibilities, are the scions of a family whose shoe-making tradition dates back to 1893. Named after Hollywood icon, Gina Lollobrigida, this is the only élite British shoe company that still manufactures in the UK. Each pair of shoes is the result of a dedicated process reliant on outstanding materials, precise cutting and fine sewing.
Gina's signature style is delicate and decorative; the label is known particularly for its jewel-encrusted strappy sandals and shoes. In addition to its main collection, Gina offers a couture service; recently it created an astonishing pair of mules, made from alligator with a buckle in white gold, set with 36 princess-cut diamonds. While acknowledging that they made Sophie Rhys-Jones' shoes for her wedding to Prince Edward, the brothers remain tight-lipped about other clients — although Nicole Kidman is known to be among them. Gina fans can now source their favourites at two boutiques — Gina's second opened in Old Bond Street in Spring 1999 — and in the USA at Saks 5th Avenue and Neiman Marcus.

Gina Boutique
189 Sloane Street
London SW1X 9QR, UK
Tel: +44-20-72 35 29 32   Fax: +44-20-78 38 97 20
Gina Couture Boutique
9 Old Bond Street
London W1X 3TA, UK
Tel: +44-20-74 09 70 90   Fax: +44-20-74 09 18 68

American couple, Paul and Kay Henderson. Passionate about wine, Paul Henderson has built up a quasi-legendary cellar, which perfectly complements Michael Caine's superb cooking. Caine, who joined Gidleigh Park a couple of years ago after training with Raymond Blanc, Bernard Loiseau and Joël Robuchon, earned the hotel Relais Gourmand status and himself a second Michelin star in 1999.

Gidleigh Park
Changford, Devon TQ13 8HH, UK
Tel: +44-1647-43 23 67   Fax: +44-1647-43 25 74

GIEVES & HAWKES

Harrow School's official outfitters, Gieves & Hawkes is looking firmly forward to the 21st century, while cherishing its bespoke tailoring foundation – established more than 200 years ago. New Design Director James Whishaw, fresh from Calvin Klein, has created an updated Millennium Formal Wear collection while, at the same time, 'Gieves', a younger, more accessible line, has débuted. Chinese-themed ties with matching silver and enamel cuff-links accessorise the look.

Gieves and Hawkes
1 Savile Row, London W1X 2JR, UK
Tel & Fax: +44-20-74 34 20 01

GIRARD-PERREGAUX

From its flagship model, the newly-released 'Opera One' – a Tourbillon with Three Gold Bridges and a grand strike with four hammers – to the 'S.F. Foudroyante', which combines a split-second chronograph and jumping seconds with a coaxial pushpiece, Girard-Perregaux continues to break new ground in the development of the watchmaker's art. Under the direction of Luigi Macaluso, this 208-year-old manufactory values painstaking research and development over ostentation, making its limited-edition watches highly sought-after by collectors.

Since 1994, Macaluso – appropriately enough, a former rally car driver – has forged a partnership with Ferrari, which began with a collection of watches characterised by strong, masculine lines. Inspired by the most sophisticated car manufacturing techniques, the Manufactory has created a new line of Ferrari chronographs realised with advanced technology materials like titanium, kevlar, carbon fiber and caoutchouc, produced in a limited series of 1,000 pieces.

The company's rich and innovative history, which began with its founding in Geneva in 1791 by Constant Girard, is celebrated by a permanent display of old, original watches. Created in the spring of 1999, the collection is housed at the Museum Villa Marguerite, a beautiful Belle Epoque-style villa close to the company's headquarters at La Chaux-de-Fonds.

To celebrate the end of the millennium, 999 individually numbered Girard-Perregaux 'Vintage 1999' automatic column-wheel chronographs have also been produced.

Girard Perregaux
1 Place Girardet, CH-2301 La Chaux-de-Fonds, Switzerland
Tel: +41-32-911 3333   Fax: +41-32-913 0480
Email: com@girard-perregaux.ch   www.girard-perregaux.ch

GIOVANNI PRATESI

President of the Italian Antique Dealers' Association, Giovanni Pratesi founded this gallery in 1976. Specialising in Florentine art from the Baroque era, it has been the source of some important sculptures and paintings of the period, which are now found in major museums. Pratesi's photographic archive has formed the basis of an academic art book, *Repertorio della scultura fiorentina del '600 e '700*. He lives in a former Medici villa near Florence, where he produces his own wine and olive oil.

Giovanni Pratesi
via Maggio 14R, 50125 Florence, Italy
Tel: +39-055-239 6568   Fax: +39-055-21 10 96

GISELE CROES

Gisèle Croës is a leading authority on early Chinese art. Her gallery, established 20 years ago, is a showcase for the fascinating pieces that she finds on her frequent visits to China, where she lived for two years. A regular exhibitor at the Biennale Internationale des Antiquaires and the International Asian Art Fair, she was a strong presence at the latter event in 1999, where she displayed outstanding bronze bowls and funerary objects from as early as 1600 BC.

Gisèle Croës Gallery
Boulevard de Waterloo 54
B-1000 Brussels, Belgium
Tel: +32-2-511 8216   Fax: +32-2-514 0419

GILLES SAINT GILLES

Inspired by the artisans with whom he works rather than by any formal architectural training, Gilles Saint Gilles creates dramatic interiors which emphasise light, space and height. Against a backdrop of natural materials such as wood,

terracotta and stone, and fabrics chosen for texture rather than pattern, he mixes myriad styles and periods – North African, Oriental and Moorish, touches of baroque and of tribal art – to create rich and warmly contemporary spaces.

Gilles Saint Gilles
53 avenue Montaigne, 75008 Paris, France
Tel: +33-1-42 25 59 95   Fax: +33-1-43 59 77 56

GIULIANO BUGIALLI

A leading author on the subject of Italian cuisine, Giuliano Bugialli set up Cooking in Florence, his unique cooking school, in 1973. The first to offer classes in English, its original aim – to provide a well-rounded base for studying Italian cooking while having an in-depth look at local culture – has held firm. Lessons, in small classes, take place in the wine and olive oil country outside Florence, to a format which Bugialli varies each year.

Giuliano Bugialli
Cooking in Florence, c/o 60 Sutton Place South
New York, NY 10022, USA
Tel: +1-212-813 9552   Fax: +1-212-486 5518

GIRASOL

"Only those truly in love with their work can provide the best results," asserts Joachim Koerper. By this measure, cooking must be an *amour fou* for this self-taught businessman-turned-chef, recognised by Relais & Châteaux as one of its most talented

GLIN CASTLE

This fairy-tale castle in the south-west of Ireland has been home to the FitzGerald family for 800 years. Set in the middle of a 500-acre estate on the banks of the river Shannon, the castle is now in the capable hands of the 29th Knight of Glin, Desmond FitzGerald, and his wife, Olda, who offer some of the best hospitality of a private country-house anywhere in the world.

Guests are received for overnight stays or, for those who want total privacy, occasional lets of the entire castle (with all staff) can be arranged. It has become increasingly popular with groups of golfers flying into nearby Shannon airport and London bankers who use the castle to celebrate major deals.

As may be expected of the home of the Chairman of the Irish Georgian Society, the castle, built in the late 18th century, is full of stunning interior features, such as a neo-classical entrance hall, a rare example of a 'flying' staircase and a drawing room with an Adam ceiling and Bossi chimneypiece. Equally impressive is the unique collection of Irish 18th-century mahogany furniture.

In the summer, guests can enjoy croquet in the midst of formal pleasure grounds and in view of castellated Gothic folly lodges. All bedrooms have beautiful views over the river Shannon or the gardens. The excellent cooking is based on fine local produce.

Glin Castle
Co. Limerick, Ireland, Tel: +353-68-34 173 Fax: +353-68-34 364
Email: knight@iol.ie Website: www.glincastle.com

members. The refined taste of his wife, Victoria, permeates every detail of their beautiful restaurant, which they established in 1990 in an old hacienda. Here the glow of fine silver, beautiful antiques and polished marble is complemented by mellow colours and rich textures, providing a dream-like setting for Koerper's deceptively simple, sun-infused creations.
Girasol
Moraira-Calpe, E-03724 Moraira, Alicante, Spain
Tel: +34-96-574 4373 Fax: +34-96-649 0545

GLOBAL ASSET MANAGEMENT

Gilbert de Botton, founder of Global Asset Management, pioneered the multi-manager approach to asset management; based on the belief that no single organisation can attract the best fund managers in every sector, the group employs both in-house and external experts. With 10 offices world-wide, it manages over $13.5 billion and offers secure Internet reporting to clients wishing to have 24-hour access to portfolio information.
Global Asset Management Ltd.
12 St. James's Place
London SW1A 1NX, UK
Tel: +44-20-74 93 99 90 Fax: +44-20-74 93 07 15

GIORGIO ARMANI

Having become a charter member of the La Scala Foundation for the princely sum of $2 million, Giorgio Armani continues to be one of fashion's enduring forces, both on the catwalk and in costume design. His winter collection featured brilliant turquoise and jade accents on shrug-coats and kimono jackets for day, as well as show-stopping strapless evening gowns.
Giorgio Armani Spa
via Borgonuovo 11, 20121 Milan, Italy
Tel: +39-02-72 31 81 Fax: +39-02-72 31 84 50

GIVENCHY

In addition to producing a well-received Givenchy collection for the 21st century, Alexander McQueen is also finding time to support Le Petit Prince charity, an organization that grants wishes for terminally ill children. His futuristic designs have more than a touch of the space age about them this season - linear tailoring in leather and glazed fabrics and a catsuit decorated with rhinestone circuitry were notable.

Givenchy
3 avenue George V, 75008 Paris, France
Tel: +33-1-44 31 50 00   Fax: +33-1-47 20 44 96

GIORGIO VIGANO

The *doyen* of Milan's real estate brokers, Giorgio Viganò, today works with his daughter, Benedetta. The sole Italian affiliate of Sotheby's International Realty and leaders of the Italian Network Luxury

Real Estate group covering nine qualified real estates, their firm has unparalleled knowledge of the Milan property market thanks, not least to Viganò's exceptional network of business and social contacts. The Viganòs' expertise extends well beyond that city, however, and their portfolio includes properties from Santa Margherita and Lake Como in the north to Capri and Porto Cervo in the south.

Giorgio Viganò s.r.l.
via Maggiolini 2, 20122 Milan, Italy
Tel: +39-02-76 00 39 14   Fax: +39-02-78 36 18

GLYNDEBOURNE FESTIVAL

Founded in 1943 by Audrey and John Christie, this annual opera festival, characterised by black-tie picnic dinners on the lawns, has become an inviolable part of the English summer season. Featuring world-class performances, the festival – now directed by the experienced and innovative Nicholas Snowman

–has launched the careers of numerous stars. The 1999 and 2000 seasons, the last to be planned by former director Anthony Whitworth-Jones, featured such classics as Mozart's *La Clemenza di Tito* and Massenet's *Manon Lescaut*.

Glyndebourne Festival
Glyndebourne, near Lewes, East Sussex BN8 5UU, UK
Tel: +44-1273-81 38 13   Fax: +44-1273-81 46 86

GLENEAGLES

To most, Gleneagles is synonymous with golf – but there's much more besides. Its three championship courses are wrapped around a grand hotel, which has all the trappings of a five-star resort… and then some. Its shooting school is run by ex-Formula One World Champion, Jackie Stewart, it has a world-class equestrian centre, falconry, two private salmon-fishing beats on the Tay and a loch for trout, a great spa and even its own railway station and its own 18 year-old single malt whisky.

Gleneagles
Auchterarder, Perthshire, Scotland PH3 1NF, UK
Tel: +44-1764-66 22 31   Fax: +44-1764-66 21 34

GMURZYNSKA, GALERIE

One of Europe's most respected private galleries, founded in 1965, has a sister gallery in Zug, Switzerland and a joint venture in New York. It represents leading 20th-century artists, with Picasso, Miró, Kandinsky and Yves Klein among its portfolio. There is a variety of regular exhibitions but the gallery's specialities are classical modern art and the Russian avant-

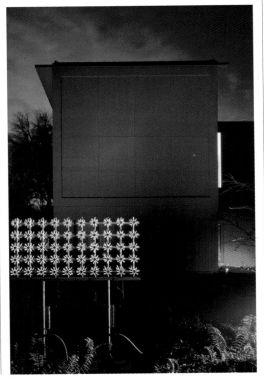

garde, as well as Bauhaus, Constructivism and de Stijl.

Galerie Gmurzynska
Goethestrasse 65a, D-50968 Cologne, Germany
Tel: +49-221-37 64 40   Fax: +49-221-37 87 30
Email: gmurzynska@aol.com

GOFF'S BLOODSTOCK SALES

Ireland's leading bloodstock auction house, Goff's was established in 1866. Michael Osborne, an expert in thoroughbred breeding and racing, and in the management of international bloodstock affairs, took over as Chairman, after Michael Dargan stepped down in 1999. Horses sold by Goff's have enjoyed some notable successes throughout the year, including the victory of *Saffron Waldon* in the Entenmann's Irish 2000 Guineas and it sold another prize-winner, *Hula Angel*, to the BBA Ireland.

Goff's Bloodstock Sales Ltd.
Kill, Co. Kildare, Ireland
Tel: +353-45-88 66 00   Fax: +353-45-87 71 19

GOLF CLUB BIELLA

Set in the midst of woods, this golf course, also known as *Le Betulle* ('The Birches'), was designed in 1958 by John Morrison. At the time, the designer acknowledged that its setting could hardly have been better; nature had already created much of the layout, which weaves through a rocky valley, carved out by glaciers. Its long holes are perfect for golfers who enjoy a technical challenge. Many of the area's leading industrialists are members.

Golf Club Biella
Località Valcarozza, 13050 Magnano, Biella, Italy
Tel: +39-015-67 91 51   Fax: +39-015-67 92 76

GOLF CLUB MILANO

Established in 1928, this is the oldest golf club in the Milan area – a fact reflected in its membership, which includes business leaders, lawyers and members of some of the city's oldest families. The clubhouse is elegant, the service and the cooking top-notch. The golf is fine, too; its 18-hole course has a classical mix of challenging and flattering holes and there is a nine-hole course alongside. Reflecting its traditional values, the club holds to the idea that a natural golfing style cannot be learned.

Golf Club Milano
viale Mulini S. Giorgio 7, 20052 Parco di Monza, Milan, Italy
Tel: +39-039-30 30 81   Fax: +39-039-30 44 27

GOLF DE CANNES-MOUGINS

The easier stretches of this traditionally styled, undulating course – designed by Peter Alliss and Dave Thomas – may lull players into a false sense of security, for there are some wickedly tricky holes as well. Just outside the pretty village of Mougins, the club was the home of the Cannes Open for many years and is one of the chic-est meeting-places in this ultra-chic area. It's where Hollywood royalty rubs shoulders with Euro tycoons and tennis stars taking time out.

Golf de Cannes-Mougins
175 route d'Antibes, 06250 Mougins, France
Tel: +33-4-93 75 79 13   Fax: +33-4-93 75 27 60

GOLF DE CHANTILLY

Stylish Parisians rub shoulders with Chantilly's racing élite at this club, which is overlooked by the magnificent Château de Chantilly. Devised in the early years of this century and revised in the 1920s by Tom Simpson, the course can be played in two configurations. It is a long course on heavy soil, so it requires some stamina – as well as technical prowess on several tricky holes. The clubhouse is as elegant as one would expect in this part of the world.

Golf de Chantilly
Allée de la Menagerie, 60500 Chantilly, France
Tel: +33-3-44 57 04 43   Fax: +33-3-44 57 26 54

ROBERT GOOSSENS

"Designers are the eunuchs of creativity; they lack a crucial element – technique," says septuagenarian goldsmith Robert Goossens. He should know, having helped some of this century's most accomplished couturiers realise their jewel visions. Today his son Patrick is behind the stunning urban armour offered by Thierry Mugler, John Galliano (for Christian Dior) and other fashion luminaries. Meanwhile, Goossens Senior works on his collection of gold and rock crystal pieces, influenced by ancient Egyptian, Etruscan and Byzantine jewels.

Robert Goossens
42 avenue George V, 75008 Paris, France
Tel: +33-1-47 23 99 26

GORDON RAMSAY

It's not that Gordon Ramsay loves cooking so much as that he is obsessed by the desire "to be the best chef in Britain". That, apparently, accounts for his notoriously fiery character. It also accounts to his robust approach to his craft and for the light and intensely flavoured dishes (classically French – with a twist – and beautifully structured) which make tables at his eponymous restaurant among the most sought-after in London.

Gordon Ramsay
68 Royal Hospital Road
London SW3 4HP, UK
Tel: +44-20-73 52 44 41   Fax: +44-20-73 52 33 34

GOLF FACTOR, THE

Set up by passionate golfer Sam Rogers in 1996, this shop (in an out-of-the-way corner of south London) is heaven for those seeking an extra edge to their game – and is where top internationals such as Mark O'Meara and Ian Woosnam come for their custom-fitted clubs. Using a *state-of-the-art* virtual reality simulator, John Palmer – formerly manager of the pro fitting division of Ben Hogan – will analyse your swing and recommend the best equipment for the job.

The Golf Factor
Unit 7, Delta Park, Smugglers Way, Wandsworth
London SW18 1EG, UK
Tel: +44-20-88 75 11 18   Fax: +44-20-88 71 93 14

GRIMA

Andrew Grima's dramatic, futuristic pieces favour bold configurations of gold, often offset by less conventional stones like malachite, quartz, opals and crystallised agate, as well as baroque and coloured pearls. They appeal to a cosmopolitan elite which has included Edith Sitwell, Jackie Onassis and Liz Taylor. Princess Margaret commissioned a brooch based on a piece of lichen and Madame Pompidou received one from The Queen in the form of a sunburst, which starred in Grima's 1991 retrospective at London's Goldsmiths Hall.

A leading light of contemporary jewellery design for 50 years, Andrew Grima held a Royal Warrant from H.M. The Queen from 1966 until 1986, when he moved to his present Gstaad location. He was the first jeweller to win the Queen's Award for Export in 1966 and the only jeweller to win the Duke of Edinburgh Prize for elegant design in the same year. He has won more De Beers Diamond International Awards than any other jeweller and designed a unique 'Prestige' collection of watches for Omega which set new standards in the genre. Sometimes styled the 'Faberge of the 20th century', Grima is self-taught; following military service during the war, he set up in business as a jeweller. A descendent of Bracchi, the sculptor of the central group of Rome's Trevi fountain, he clearly has creativity in his blood. Today, assisted by his wife Jojo, and daughter, Francesca, in the family business, he is looking forward to his next retrospective, which will be in Honolulu in 2001.

Andrew Grima
Vieux Gstaad, CH-3780 Gstaad, Switzerland
Tel: +41-33-744 9050   Fax: +41-33-744 9052

GONZALEZ BYASS

In a world where it seems axiomatic that large companies cannot produce top quality goods, Gonzalez Byass is a refreshing exception. The descendants of the founder, Manuel Maria Gonzàlez Angel (1812-

1887), produce sherries that are considered benchmarks of their type. The most famous is its Fino, Tio Pepe while, at the very top of the range come Matusalem and Apostoles — proof of just how good sherry can be. As for the brandy, Lepanto, forget that it is not French — just revel in its superb flavour.

González Byass
S.A., calle Manuel María Gonzalez, E-11403 Jerez
Cadiz, Spain
Tel: +34-956-35 70 04   Fax: +34-956-35 70 44

GORDON-WATSON, CHARLES

One of the world's leading yearling buyers, bloodstock agent Charlie Gordon-Watson's success is well documented; he has bought six Classic winners, including *Desert Prince*, World Champion

three-year old in 1998, 21 Group One winners and 10 Royal Ascot winners. The Maktoums, the Lloyd-Webbers and the Sultan of Malaysia have all benefited from his expertise. His sister Mary, an Olympic eventing gold medallist, is now an established member of the Jockey Club.

Charles Gordon-Watson
Fairholt House, 2 Pont Street, London SW1X 9EL, UK
Tel: +44-20-78 38 97 47   Fax: +44-20-78 38 97 67
Mobile: +44-385-36 79 27
Website: www.gordon-watson.com

GRAFF

"There is a tremendous amount of power associated with big diamonds," Laurence Graff says and he should know. Blessed with an unerring instinct for the most sublime stones, he works them into classical settings and extraordinary watches. Entirely the architect of his own success, he is acknowledged to have a significant influence on the world market for important stones. Graff is grooming his son, François, to carry the family name into the next generation and has recently begun trade-marking the stones which he sells to the trade.

Graff
6-7 New Bond Street, London W1Y 9PE, UK
Tel: +44-20-75 84 85 71   Fax: +44-20-75 81 34 15

GORDONSTOUN SCHOOL

Gordonstoun's headmaster, Mark Pyper, prides himself on his school's committed staff, who, he believes, give pupils "pastoral care of the highest quality", promoting the "holistic development of every boy and girl". Despite having been the ancestral home of Gordon-Cumming (of card-cheating fame), the school has an outstanding record of community service.

Gordonstoun School
Elgin, Moray 1V30 2RF, UK
Tel: +44-1343-83 78 07   Fax: +44-1343-83 78 08

GOULANDRIS MUSEUM OF CYCLADIC ART, THE

The Nicholas P. Goulandris Foundation was set up to promote Aegean studies — especially the story of ancient Greek art — and the accompanying museum is a showcase for exactly these aims, with more than 1,000 objects, dating from 3,000BC to 400AD. Particularly fascinating are the Cycladic exhibits, of which many are figurines with simple, bold outlines, carved out of island marble — unique examples of prehistoric art, which trace every stage in the development of early Cycladic civilisation.

The Goulandris Museum of Cycladic Art
4 Neophytou Douka St, Kolonaki, GR-10674 Athens, Greece
Tel: +30-1-722 8321   Fax: +30-1-723 9382

GRAND HOTEL EUROPE

This legendary St. Petersburg hotel was a favourite of Tchaikovsky, Anna Pavlova and Gorky and, restored to its former art deco glory, it once again attracts the rich and famous. With a ballroom (especially designed to let in the summer light of the White Nights) and caviar bar, the hotel is the centre of the city's social life and is a short walk from some of St. Petersburg's finest sites, including the Hermitage.

Grand Hotel Europe
Nevskiy Prospekt, Mikhailovskaya Ulitsa 1
191011 St. Petersburg, Russia
Tel: +7-812-329 6000   Fax: +7-812-329 6001

GRAND HOTEL STOCKHOLM

Régis Cadier, personal chef to King Oscar II, founded the Grand in 1874 and, today — standing on the quayside facing the Royal Palace — it epitomises old-fashioned elegance in both style and service. With no less than 21 Royal Suites, the interior — accented by original chandeliers, gold ornamentation and valuable works of art — has been declared a National Heritage Building and in 1996 two penthouse suites were added as part of a major refurbishment.

Grand Hôtel Stockholm
Blasieholmshamen 8, 10327 Stockholm, Sweden
Tel: +46-8-679 3500   Fax: +46-8-611 8686

GRAF – ARIODANTE

"Only by constructing the appropriate architectural proportions will a room work," says Parisian decorator François-Joseph Graf, "and, for that, you need a great knowledge of art history and respect for the past." Beside his expertise in these areas, Graf is a great colourist and, with great skill he mixes furniture and *objets d'art* from many periods, along with fabrics made to order from his archive of Renaissance-to-1930s samples. Clients include Pierre Bergé in Paris and the Kravises in New York and Graf creates rooms sets for several leading dealers at the Biennale des Antiquaires.

François-Joseph Graf – Ariodante
17 rue de Lille, 75007 Paris, France
Tel: +33-1-42 61 39 39   Fax: +33-1-42 61 40 45

GUALTIERO MARCHESI

Branded an iconoclast, Gualtiero Marchesi has the highest media profile of any chef in Italy. Yet his cooking seems remarkably simple – classical, even; his tasting menu is a sequence of contrasting and perfectly judged flavours and textures. So why the "radical" tag? "What I do is to ally the techniques of *haute cuisine* with the Italian tradition; 30 years ago, when I started, that was avant-garde," he explains. Marchesi moved from Milan to his

current location, in the Franciacorta wine-growing region, six years ago. The setting is idyllic – the glass-walled room looks out through woods to Lake Iseo – and the decor *haute* rustic-chic. A tip: ask if there are any 'not-on-the-menu' specials; they will be a treat.

Restaurant Gualtiero Marchesi
via Vittorio Emanuele 11
25030 Erbusco, Italy
Tel: +39-030-776 0562   Fax: +39-030-776 0379

~

GUARDS POLO CLUB

Originally named the Household Brigade Polo Club when it was founded in 1955 with the Duke of Edinburgh as President, the club assumed its current name in 1969. With 160 playing members – many of whom are world-class – the club is the largest in Europe. At its headquarters at the famous Smiths Lawn grounds (apparently named after a 17th-century game-keeper) celebrities and aristocrats mingle with plutocrats and military types.

The Guards Polo Club
Smith's Lawn, Windsor Great Park, Egham
Surrey TW20 OHP, UK
Tel: +44-1784-43 42 12   Fax: +44-1784-47 13 36

GRITTI PALACE, HOTEL

This breathtaking 16th-century Venetian palace, set on the Grand Canal, is one of the world's most celebrated hotels. Imposing yet intimate, its antique-laden rooms have a pronounced sense of history. It was home to the Gritti family, descendants of Andrea Gritti, one of the most famous Doges of Venice and, over the centuries, other noble families as well as writers and artists lived there (John Ruskin wrote *The Stones of Venice* here). The hotel visitors' book is a *Who's Who* of the century's most eminent people, from Elizabeth Taylor to Valentino, Princess Grace of Monaco to General Charles de Gaulle. Today there are few places in the world more sublime than the Gritti's terrace at sunset, gazing across the canal to the beautiful church of Santa Maria della Salute.

Hotel Gritti Palace
Campo S. Maria del Giglio 2467, 30124 Venice, Italy
Tel: +39-041-79 46 11   Fax: +39-041-520 0942

GUINEVERE ANTIQUES

The four theatrical windows and 10 rambling interior showrooms of Guinevere Antiques inspire collectors, compulsive shoppers and interior decorators alike. Aided by her two sons Marc and Kevin, founder Geneviève Weaver has an unerring instinct for the zeitgeist, and her powerful taste and prescience continue to be the driving force behind the company. Celebrity customers abound – Ralph Lauren, Paloma Picasso and Lauren Bacall are among those who appreciate the Guinevere look. A wider circle has been able to admire the house style since the publication in autumn 1999 of *Antiques for Today's Interiors* by Geneviève Weaver and Helen Chislett with photographs by Andreas von Einsiedel. A glossy bible with 200 new colour

photographs, it aims to dispel the image of antiques as rarefied artefacts synonymous only with grand old houses. The authors show them in modern interiors, quoting designers with creative imagination. Glorious acquisitions will always be at the heart of the business, however, and recent canny finds include unique 18th-century olive oil jars from the Gresigne factory, Tang dynasty terracotta 'stick-men' and 200-year-old giant clam shells worthy of Botticelli's Venus. These, along with the current trend for pieces from classical antiquity, perfectly sum up the Guinevere style.

Guinevere Antiques
574-580 Kings Road, London SW6 2DY, UK
Tel: +44-20-77 36 29 17   Fax: +44-20-77 36 82 67
Website: www.guinevere.co.uk

GROSVENOR HOUSE ART & ANTIQUES FAIR, THE

Established in 1934, this is one of the most important events in the international art and antiques calendar. It is characterised by enormous diversity, with exhibits dating from 3000 BC to the present day, at prices from £200 to over £1 million. It is estimated that over £50 million changes hands during its eight day run. A truly eclectic mix, ranging from antiquities to contemporary paintings, Oriental ceramics to English furniture and from garden statuary to carpets and textiles, it provides inspiration to collectors, designers and decorators alike. In David Mlinaric's words, "for anyone interested in the decorative arts, it's not to be missed". Every work of art is stringently vetted to ensure both quality and authenticity.

The Grosvenor House Art & Antiques Fair
Grosvenor House, Park Lane
London W1A 3AA, UK
Tel: +44-20-73 99 81 00   Fax: +44-20-74 95 87 47
Website: www.grosvenor-antiquesfair.co.uk
Annually: 14-20 June 2000   Private preview: 13 June

GRAVETYE MANOR

Peter Herbert's timeless and super-discreet hotel was one of the first – and remains one of the classic – country house hotels. A Elizabethan manor surrounded by forests and fields, it continues to be run like a private home, resisting all the clichés of modern hotel-keeping. As befits the former home of one of the 20th century's greatest garden designers, William Robinson, the grounds are

wonderful. Chef Tommy Raffan, whose vegetable garden is a marvel, was personal chef to the late King Hussein of Jordan for three years.

Gravetye Manor
near East Grinstead, Sussex RH19 4LJ, UK
Tel: +44-1342-81 05 67   Fax: +44-1342-81 00 80

~

GUERLAIN

Based in an exquisite townhouse on the Champs-Elysées since 1914, Guerlain continues to delight with its wonderful beauty treatments and sophisticated products. The launch of the appropriately-named *Champs-Elysées* fragrance in 1996 followed a century of glamorous perfumes. Visiting Guerlain's flagship store and Beauty Institute is a sumptuous visual experience, with the original Franck and Bérard decor and the Giacometti appliqués largely unchanged after more than six decades.

Guerlain
68 avenue des Champs-Elysées
75008 Paris, France
Tel: +33-1-45 62 52 57   Fax: +33-1-40 74 09 91

GUCCI

Helen Hunt looked stunning at the 1999 Oscars in Gucci, confirming Hollywood's love affair with designer Tom Ford. A noted perfectionist, Ford oversees every aspect of the company's image from the clothes collections and accessories to the minutiae of the shops' fittings. The future of his vision now seems assured, with confirmation that Bernard Arnault's hostile takeover bid was beaten by a counter-bid from Francois Pinault in Spring 1999.

Gucci
via Montenapoleone 5, 20121 Milan, Italy
Tel: +39-02-79 54 67   Fax: +39-02-79 58 96

GUILLERMO DE OSMA

This jewel-box of a gallery is notable for its fine, vibrant exhibitions of modern art. These take in every 20th-century school from Surrealism and Constructivism to Pop and abstract art. Recent shows include the collaboration between Surrealist painter Oscar Dominguez and Spanish art critic Eduardo Westerdahl, paintings by Uruguayan José Gurvich and Spanish Pop artist Dis Berlin.

Guillermo de Osma
Claudio Coello 4, E-28001 Madrid, Spain
Tel: +34-91-435 5936   Fax: +34-91-431 3175

GUY ARMENGOL

This French-based bloodstock agent's liking for what he describes as "unconventional choices" has resulted in 30 years of success. His considerable personal charm, undisputed *savoir-faire* and numerous international connections explain the many impressive deals he has made, as well as his long list of important clients. Demand for his expertise has recently taken him to Saudi Arabia, where his horse *Danae de Brulé* has won five King's Cups.

Guy Armengol
8 rue Sédillot, 75007 Paris, France
Tel: +33-1-44 18 72 32   Fax: +33-1-44 18 72 34

A symbol beyond time

JAS HENNESSY & Cº Rue de la Richonne 16100 COGNAC - Tel. (33) 5.45.35.72.72 - Fax (33) 5.45.35.79.

HACIENDA EL BULLI

A chef's greatest critics are his peers and, by that measure, Ferran Adria is a genius; the Pourcel brothers — chef-owners of the three-star Le Jardin de Sens — are among his most avid fans. Adria's menu *dégustation* of 26 tiny courses is, quite simply, astounding. Tucked away in a ravishingly pretty cove at the end of a winding, barely-paved road, this little paradise now offers three-day cookery courses to those who wish to take inspiration home to their own kitchens.

Hacienda El Bulli
Cala Montjol, E-17480 Roses, Gerona, Spain
Tel: +34-972-15 04 57 Fax: +34-972-15 07 17

HALE CLINIC, THE

Leading up to her marriage to Prince Edward, Sophie Rhys-Jones joined the long list of celebrity clients to have visited this clinic for complementary medicine. Founded by Teresa Hale and officially opened by Prince Charles in 1988, the clinic's philosophy is to combine conventional and complementary methods with a constant search for innovation. This may be the reason for its reported success in treating such ailments as asthma and migraine.

The Hale Clinic
7 Park Crescent, London W1N 3HE, UK
Tel: +44-20-76 31 01 56 Fax: +44-20-73 23 16 93

HAMBURGER POLO CLUB

Prince Charles is a great admirer of this fine polo club — founded in 1898 by Heinrich Hasperg, who introduced the sport to Germany. The setting for two major tournaments — the German Championship in May and the Derby Cup in August — the club plays an important role in Hamburg's social and sporting scene (it also offers tennis and hockey). The clubhouse was designed by the architect Heinrich Amsinck, a disciple of Bauhaus.

Hamburger Polo Club
Jenischstrasse 26, D-22609 Hamburg, Germany
Tel: +49-40-82 06 81 Fax: +49-40-82 06 89

HANRO

The brand name Hanro first appeared on the market in 1913, although the company's story began in 1884. Hanro immediately became synonymous with beautifully-made, stylish day and nightwear for women and men. Eschewing flounces and overt sexiness in favour of a clean and discreet elegance, Hanro uses the very finest silk and Egyptian cottons; the great appeal of its garments is their wonderful softness against the skin. Combining high technology with hand-crafted detail, Hanro's latest line is 'TouchFeeling', a range of seamless underwear and smooth-fitting tops made of silky, high-tech microfibre.

Hanro of Switzerland
AG Benzburgweg 18, CH-4410 Liestal, Switzerland
Tel: +41-61-926 5555 Fax: +41-61-926 5533
Email: URSULA_KYBURZ@compuserv.com

HARBOUR CLUB

This health and sports club in a leafy setting close to the centre of Milan offers all the facilities its top-brass members could wish for: 16 tennis courts, two huge swimming pools, two gyms, a squash court, two football pitches and a golf course. There are also scuba-diving courses, a team of first-rate personal trainers, an excellent spa area and a 'concierge' service, which provides everything from priority theatre bookings to car washing.

Harbour Club
via Cascina Bellaria 19, 20153 Milan, Italy
Tel: +39-02-45 28 61

HARDENBERG CONCEPT

With the influx of new business to Berlin in 1989, the demand for exclusive social and business events has soared. Countess von Hardenberg, with her intimate knowledge of Berlin society, has proved the perfect person to fill this niche. She has overseen some of the most important social events to take place in the German capital in the last 10 years, including a special dinner for Prince Charles and the reception for the opening of the Berlin Stock Exchange.

Hardenberg Concept
Burgunderstrasse 5, D-14129 Berlin, Germany
Tel: +49-30-803 8846 Fax: +49-30-803 6163

HAREL

Since 1922, Harel has been supplying the elegant women of Paris with the classiest — and probably best made — shoes in town. Distinguished by their classical femininity, they are available both ready-made and *sur mesure*. Devotees rave about the vast range of colours, from neutrals to brights and pretty pastels, and luxurious materials — from precious leathers to flannel and sequins — as well as the fine service in Harel's three Parisian boutiques.

Harel
8 avenue Montaigne, 75008 Paris, France
Tel: +33-1-47 23 83 03 Fax: +33-1-47 23 90 02

HARROW

Each of Harrow's 11 historical boarding houses has its own particular character and customs. Pupils are educated to the highest standards, passing through five 'blocks' or year groups and the school is particularly rich in endowed prizes and internal scholarships. Drama has been boosted by the new Ryan Theatre and, on the sporting front, rugby is stronger than ever under England coach Roger Uttley.

Harrow School
Harrow-on-the-Hill, Middlesex HA0 3HW, UK
Tel: +44-20-84 22 21 96 Fax: +44-20-84 23 31 12

HARVEY NICHOLS

Regarded as the 'Bergdorf Goodman of London', thanks to its stylish displays and 'only the best labels' policy, Harvey Nichols continues to lead in the glamour stakes. With Hong Kong-based entrepreneur Dickson Poon having increased his stake in the business, its winning blend of cutting-edge designers, glorious household accessories and fine food is set to spread further, with four more British branches slated to open in the near future.

Harvey Nichols
109-125 Knightsbridge, London SW1X 7RJ, UK
Tel: +44-20-72 35 50 00 Fax: +44-20-72 59 60 84

HARRODS

It is hard to imagine that the mighty Harrods began as a humble grocer's shop back at its inception in 1849. "Everything for everyone, everywhere", is its motto and, in keeping with this, £200 million has been spent on a redevelopment programme over the last 10 years. With its state-of-the-art sports floor, superb new menswear department and the cream of women's fashion and jewellery, Harrods is really a world within itself. In addition it offers shop-till-you-drop consumers everything from dry cleaning, interior design to private banking – not to mention gifts galore, sublime food halls and a total of 20 restaurants – from tapas to sushi – in which to refresh themselves!

Harrods Ltd.

Knightsbridge, London SW1X 7XL, UK

Tel: +44-20-77 30 12 34   Fax: +44-20-75 81 04 70

Website: www.harrods.com

HARRY'S BAR

From the Fortuny-covered walls of Mark Birley's supremely refined private dining club, the characters in his unparalleled collection of Peter Arno cartoons survey a glossy and urbane crowd. It is pure, transatlantic A-List: Flicks and Rothschilds, a Kennedy or an Astor, a media mogul, a smattering of plutocrats and faces from the highest echelons of show-business. The club's consummately professional manager, Mario, is the master of *placement* for, with such a group there can be no such thing as a 'bad' table.

Everything in the deceptively simple room is polished to glowing perfection – from the honey-coloured wooden floor to the fine, blue-rimmed glasses and the tiny silver tops placed on the espresso cups to retain heat – and is bathed in soft light from the windows which line one side of the room and an exquisite, old Venetian chandelier. Birley's legendary perfectionism is reflected in every detail, from the specially produced linen to the tables themselves – at low height to encourage a relaxed intimacy.

The brilliantly inventive Alberico Penati's Italian cooking is, likewise, deceptively simple. But the carpaccio, the pasta and the truffles are the finest to be found anywhere and artist sommelier, Valentino – adored for his courtly manners – unfailingly suggests exactly the right wine to complement them.

Harry's Bar

26 South Audley Street, London W1Y 5DJ, UK

Tel: +44-20-74 08 08 44

HATFIELDS

Since 1834, this company has been restoring items of antique furniture (especially French pieces), metalwork and sculpture and now has a network of international clients. Its skills extend from exquisite marquetry and historic clocks to fine bronzes and elaborate *objets d'art*. Contemporary furniture (from 1920 to the present day) can also be restored and pieces can be specially copied. Managing Director Henry Thornhill was an art broker for 10 years before joining the firm in 1998.

Hatfields

42 & 42a St. Michael Street, London W2 1QP, UK

Tel: +44-20-77 23 82 65   Fax: +44-20-77 06 45 62

HATTON CASTLE

The Duff family home for three centuries, Hatton Castle is set within a 1,000 acre agricultural and sporting estate in one of the loveliest parts of

Scotland. The owners, David James Duff – the 12th Laird – and his wife, Jayne, welcome guests to enjoy "the traditional hospitality of country house parties". A renowned pheasant shoot with duck flighting and pigeon shooting are the main winter attractions; the summer offers golf, tennis and stalking and all year round it is a wonderfully peaceful retreat.

Hatton Castle
Turriff, Aberdeenshire AB53 8ED, Scotland, UK
Tel: +44-1888-56 36 24   Fax: +44-1888-56 39 43

HAUT-BRION CHATEAU

Any Irishman worth his salt will try to convince you that the name Haut-Brion derives from O'Brien. Don't believe him but do give this château the serious attention it deserves. Its wines exude an earthy softness and integration of flavours that make them immediately attractive. The oldest of the great Bordeaux châteaux, Haut-Brion was, paradoxically, the first to introduce stainless steel tanks for fermentation, in 1961.

Château Haut-Brion
133 avenue Jean Jaurès, 33602 Pessac, France
Tel: +33-5-56 00 29 30   Fax: +33-5-56 98 75 13

HAWELKA

The most classical of all Viennese cafés, Hawelka has, for over 60 years, had a special place in the hearts of local urbanites, foreign residents and ascendant intellectuals (this was Elias Canetti's 'local' for a time). Its founders, Leopold and Josefina Hawelka, are still on hand to welcome regulars for excellent coffee and fine cakes; among Frau Hawelka's specialities are *Buchteln* (Bohemian dumplings filled with plum jam), available until the early hours of the morning.

Café Hawelka
Dorotheergasse 6, A-1010 Vienna, Austria
Tel: +43-1-512 8230

HAYWARD

At the epicentre of Swinging London in the 1960s (Terence Stamp, David Bailey and the Earl of Lichfield, with whom he once ran a night-club, were – and remain – clients and close friends), tailor Doug Hayward is now a fully paid-up member of the Establishment. He considers his tailoring to be beyond ephemeral trends and, instead, concentrates on the "classic, top quality cloths", expert cutting and subtle colour sense which have always been his trademark.

Hayward
95 Mount Street, London W1Y 5HG, UK
Tel & Fax: +44-20-74 99 55 74

HEESEN

Established in 1978, this Dutch shipyard – which markets its custom-built motor yachts under the name *Diaship* – shot to prominence in 1988 with the launch of the 38-metre *Octopussy*, a 53-knot flyer. 1999 was a busy year for the yard, with the launches of the 46-metre *No Escape in March*, the 38-metre *Red Sapphire* – a sportfishing motor yacht – in June and a 35-metre displacement motor yacht in September. The 37-metre *Alumerica* follows in March 2000.

Heesen Shipyards BV
Rijnstraat 2, 5347 KL Oss, The Netherlands
Tel: +31-412-63 25 10   Fax: +31-412-63 73 85

HEIMSCHULE KLOSTER WALD

Founded in 1946 by the Sisters of the Heiligen Lioba convent in Freiburg, this excellent girls' school seeks to educate the 'whole person'. Religious instruction remains fundamental, with a keen observation of the important dates in the Catholic calendar. Academically, the school has a strong reputation for mathematics and modern languages. Students can also learn woodcarving, dress-making and pottery and, for the sports-

minded, there are basketball, athletics and football, as well as riding, gymnastics and judo.

Heimschule Kloster Wald
D-88639 Wald, Germany
Tel: +49-7578-18 80   Fax: +49-7578-18 81 17

HELLY NAHMAD GALLERY

Helly Nahmad, a graduate of the Courtauld Institute, is the third generation of his family to enter the art world, opening his eponymous gallery in 1998. His gallery impresses with 19th- and 20th-century classics from Monet's *Le Palais Contarini*, Venise to Kandinsky's *The Last Judgement*. Following its successful Picasso exhibition in 1998, the gallery is mounting a major exhibit of Surrealist art.

Helly Nahmad Gallery
2 Cork Street, London W1X 1PB, UK
Tel: +44-20-74 94 32 00   Fax: +44-20-74 94 33 55

HEMMERLE

A family business since 1893, Hemmerle originally found fame reproducing ancient jewellery and supplying medals to the Bavarian Court. Today its exquisite pieces are inspired by flowers, animals and Modernism and the firm is famed for its exceedingly warm welcome. The coolly contemporary look of Hemmerle's present shop, which combines natural materials and neutral colours, was created by artistic director Stefan Hemmerle, in collaboration with Dutch designer Tom Postma.

Hemmerle
14 Maximilanstrasse,
D-80539 Munich, Germany
Tel: +49-89-242 2600   Fax: +49-89-24 22 60 40

HEMPEL, THE

Step into the front hall of Anouska Hempel's ineffably cool temple to East-West minimalism after a stressful day's travelling and your system instantly shifts down a couple of gears. Carved out of five adjoining Georgian houses overlooking a private garden square, its creamy Zen-inspired spaces could not be more different from owner/designer Anouska Hempel's first triumph, the winningly decadent Blakes.

Pure and uncluttered it may be but coldly minimalist it is not; its clean lines are offset by the subtle textures of natural materials – stone, polished plaster, clear-toned woods, linens and cottons – and the hotel's signature white phalaeonopsis orchids adorn windowsills and tables. Anouska Hempel's legendary perfectionism and beady eye for detail are evident in myriad little touches. Oxygen canisters, Berocca vitamins, energy drinks and scented candles provide succour to weary travellers and, no doubt aware of the soothing value of music, CD players are installed in every room – a detail too often overlooked in luxury hotels.

The hotel's restaurant, I-Thai, is an equally stylish setting for its highly individualistic cooking. Based on Anouska Hempel's own ideas, the dishes are visually striking and packed with flavour, combining influences from Italy, Thailand and Japan. Even Valentino – hitherto renowned as a lover of opulence – has been seduced; this was where he chose to celebrate his birthday in the spring of 1999.

The Hempel
31-35 Craven Hill Gardens, London W2 3EA, UK
Tel: +44-20-72 98 90 00   Fax: +44-20-74 02 46 66

HENRY CECIL

Super-trainer Henry Cecil continues to re-write the record books; by the middle of 1999 he had lifted his tally of English Classic winners to 22. First, *Wince* clinched the 1,000 Guineas, then *Ramruma* and *Oath* managed a superb Derby/Oaks double – all of them ridden by champion jockey Kieran Fallon. This was Cecil's second double win in 14 years, a feat that no-one else has achieved, and underlines his status as one of the greatest British trainers in history.

Henry Cecil
Warren Place, Newmarket, Suffolk CB8 8QQ, UK
Tel: +44-1638-66 21 92   Fax: +44-1638-66 90 05

HEREND

The names of Herend's best-known dinner service patterns – Esterházy, Rothschild and Apponyi – are a precise reflection of its early, aristocratic clientele. The porcelain manufactory, established in 1826, shot to prominence from 1839 onwards with the introduction by Mór Fischer of a strongly artistic sensibility and even state ownership during Hungary's communist era (Herend is now 75% owned by its workers) did nothing to dim its reputation. Its signature animal sculptures (150 designs in all) are prized collectors' items.

Herend
H-8440 Herend, Hungary
Tel: +36-88-26 11 44   Fax: +36-88-26 15 18

HERMES

The evergreen luxury goods company, Hermès, purveys stylish definitives to the BCBG crowd and aspirants the world over. Under the visionary direction of Jean-Louis Dumas-Hermès, who employed the Belgian designer, Martin Margiela, two years ago, the company has become more fashion-forward than in the past. Despite his reputation as a radical, Margiela has understood the Hermès ethos perfectly. His current classics include creamy, cowled cashmeres, soft pyjama pants and enveloping stoles.

Hermès
24 rue du Faubourg St Honoré, 75008 Paris, France
Tel: +33-1-40 17 47 17   Fax: +33-1-40 17 47 18

HERMITAGE, HOTEL

This stunning Belle Epoque hotel is as much an historic landmark as one of Monaco's finest hotels. Its sumptuous interiors, which include a magnificent glass dome built by Gustave Eiffel, are surprisingly tranquil. The best rooms – particularly sought-after during the Grand Prix and the mid-summer Fireworks Competition – are those which offer a grandstand view of the port. Another big plus is the Hermitage's direct access to Monaco's spa, Les Thermes Marin.

Hôtel Hermitage
Square Beaumarchais, MC 98000, Monaco
Tel: +377-92-16 40 00   Fax: +377-92-16 38 52

HERNO

Herno has been making superb raincoats – both under its own label and for several of the world's leading fashion designers – since 1948, when the company was founded by Giuseppe Marenzi. Combining state-of-the-art technology with traditional hand-finishing, Herno has, since then, added overcoats to its range (of particular note is its double-face wool or cashmere) and, more recently, full men's and women's clothing collections. Herno's signature style is a sporty classicism – sober, simple and linear.

Herno
via Castello 5, 28040 Lesa, Italy
Tel: +39-0322-77 091   Fax: +39-0322-77 974

HERZOG ANTON ULRICH-MUSEUM

In the 18th century Duke Anton Ulrich was a noted art-lover and prodigious collector. The exhibits in this museum (Germany's oldest, it was founded in 1754) range from Old Master to the decorative arts and provide a fascinating insight into the his tastes. Old Masters – particularly Flemish paintings – are especially strong, with key works by Cranach, Vermeer, Rembrandt, Rubens and Van Dyck. The gallery also displays impressive majolica, enamel work and Oriental art.

Herzog Anton Ulrich-Museum
Museumstrasse 1, D-38100 Braunschweig, Germany
Tel: +49-531-484 2400   Fax: +49-531-484 2408

HENNESSY

This giant of the cognac business was founded in 1765, after Irishman Richard Hennessy joined the Irish Brigade of King Louis XV's army. Now part of the LVMH luxury group, the firm is imbued with tradition; cousins Gilles and Maurice Hennessy are the eighth generation to be involved in the day-to-day management of the company and cellar-master, Yann Fillioux, is the seventh generation of his family to hold the position. However, Hennessy has always been an innovator; it created the cognac grading system in the 1860s, introduced X.O in 1870 and pioneered the use of decanter-style bottles in 1948.

The house's latest release, 'timeless' continues this tradition. Launched in September 1999, it is the result of intense collaboration between Gilles Hennessy, Yann Fillioux and Baccarat crystal's talented designer, Thomas Bastide. Blended from 11 'eaux-de-vie' – the most outstanding one from each decade of the 20th century (with two from the 1950s) – 'timeless' strikes an amazing balance between the fresh, fruity and floral character of the youngest (1990) and the leather, oak, pepper and spice flavours of the oldest (1900). The bottle itself, an ellipse of purest crystal – inspired by the idea of a stone, worn smooth by the centuries – held in an angular casing of brushed metal, is a stunning sculptural *objet d'art* in its own right.

That so much should go into producing a limited edition of just 2,000 bottles of cognac is testament indeed to Hennessy's unflagging commitment to excellence.

Hennessy
1 rue de Richonne, 16100 Cognac, France
Tel: +33-5-45 35 72 72 Fax: +33-5-45 35 79 79

HIGHCLERE THOROUGHBRED RACING

Founded in 1992 by The Hon. Harry Herbert, son of The Queen's racing manager, Lord Porchester, Highclere is Europe's leading racehorse syndication company. It specialises in putting together syndicates with a maximum of 30 owners in any one venture and acts as personal racing manager to each owner. The company currently has 30 horses in training with the likes of Sir Michael Stoute and Roger Charlton and its successes include European Champions *Lake Coniston* (bought for 22,000 Guineas and sold for £2.5 million), *Tamarisk* and *Delilah*.

Highclere Thoroughbred Racing
The Field House, Highclere Park, Newbury
Berkshire RG20 9RN, UK
Tel: +44-1635-25 53 98 Fax: +44-1635-25 50 66

HILDITCH & KEY

"Hilditch & Key shirts are the finest in the world", states owner Michael Booth unequivocally; Karl Lagerfeld, Ralph Lauren, Paloma Picasso and Diana Rigg are among those who evidently agree. Shirts are made to the finest specifications in their Scottish workrooms, and stocked alongside a selection of ties, sleepwear and cashmeres. Not for Booth a plethora of outlets; the company restricts itself to three in London and one in Paris (since 1925), yet turnover has grown by half in the last five years. Hilditch & Key celebrated its centenary in 1999.

Hilditch & Key Ltd.
73 Jermyn Street, London SW1Y 6NP, UK
Tel: +44-20-79 30 23 29 Fax: +44-20-73 21 02 16

HOLGER STEWEN

This antique dealer-turned-interior designer, who now divides his business between Hamburg and Mallorca, has been honing his aesthetic sense for more than 25 years. His eye is influenced by French, Italian and Scandinavian styles and he has a passion for English furniture, opulent materials and the finest Far Eastern art. Recent commissions which bear Stewen's distinctive mark include the interior of Princess Loretta zu Sayn-Wittgenstein's hotel, La Rotana, in Mallorca.

Holger Stewen
Hohe Bleichen 2
D-20354 Hamburg, Germany
Tel: +49-40-34 84 70 Fax: +49-40-348 4727

C. HOARE & CO.

This prestigious bank, established more than 300 years ago, is the only remaining private deposit bank in England. Fiercely proud of its independence, the bank's partners – all direct descendants of the founder – converted themselves in 1929 into a private unlimited liability company, in which they were the sole shareholders. Emphasising its old-fashioned values of integrity, trust and close personal involvement (the partners are in attendance every day), the bank today offers advice on investment, pensions and taxation, in addition to its core deposit-taking business.

C. Hoare & Co.
37 Fleet Street, London EC4P 4DQ, UK
Tel: +44-20-73 53 45 22 Fax: +44-20-73 53 45 21

HEYWOOD HILL

Possibly the world's most patrician book shop, Heywood Hill is owned by the Duke of Devonshire and patronised by the literary elite; Nancy Mitford worked here for three years. It has remained unchanged for over 60 years (still wrapping books in brown paper parcels rather than plastic bags) and its famously knowledgeable staff regard regular customers as "friends".

Heywood Hill
10 Curzon Street, London W1Y 7FJ, UK
Tel: +44-20-76 29 06 47   Fax: +44-20-74 08 02 86

HOLWICK & WEMMERGILL

Record-breaking bags distinguish the twin grouse moors of Holwick and Wemmergill, which hot-shot Sir Tom Cowie leases from Lord Strathmore. Thanks to Cowie's astute management of the 30,000 acres, they remain pre-eminent, even in the face of recent adverse conditions. This, along with the fact that, on the 70-odd shooting days each autumn, an army of 80 people is mobilised (a ratio of 10 to each gun) explains the high cost of joining the lines here.

Holwick & Wemmergill
H&W Sporting Estates, Broadwood Hall, Lanchester
Co. Durham, DH7 0TD, UK
Tel: +44-1207-52 96 63   Fax: +44-1207-52 95 39

HOME FLOWERS

Günter Haluszczak and Thomas Niederste-Werbeck regard their decorating-cum-florist shop as a playground for their ideas, changing its whole look – from wall colour to furnishings – twice a year. House favourites include tightly packed bunches of a single flower, such as white narcissi or multi-coloured roses, and the partners enjoy using such unfashionable flowers as gerberas and carnations, making them 'hot' again. For its special events work Home again uses masses of single varieties, highlighted by their dramatic custom lighting.

Home Flowers
An der Alster 72, D-20099 Hamburg, Germany
Tel: +49-40-24 34 84   Fax: +49-40-280 3845

HORCHER

The reliably good meat – particularly game – and the elegant company are reasons enough to dine at Horcher. But, most of all, you come for its bizarre history. Originally established in Berlin, Horcher became a favourite of the Nazi bigwigs during the war – until things got a little tricky there. With Franco's help the owner fled to Madrid, lock, stock, napkins, china and all and re-opened this facsimile - perfect to the last knife and fork – overlooking the Parque del Buen Retiro.

Horcher
Alfonso XII 6, E-28014 Madrid, Spain
Tel: +34-91-522 0731

HOLLAND & HOLLAND

Founded by Harris Holland as a gunmaking business in 1835, this quintessentially British company's heritage of superb craftsmanship has formed the basis of its transformation into a global luxury goods brand. While retaining its country roots, Holland & Holland has – under the guidance of Véronique Leblanc, General Manager since 1998 – developed a younger, more urban and more fashion-oriented signature.

In an inspired move, designer José Lévy has been appointed to apply his talent to the clothing and accessories collections. His first collection, for Autumn/Winter 1999-2000, included witty references to wood and feathers, for instance, allied to luxurious fabrics. For serious sportsmen, meanwhile, Holland & Holland maintains its renowned service for bespoke shooting suits, as well as made-to-measure sporting guns.

The firm's global expansion will see its existing European shops (two in London and two in Paris) being joined by branches in Germany, Sweden and Italy during 2000 while, in the US, three further shops opened in late 1999.

Holland & Holland is also expanding its already successful travel division. Itineraries range from the sporting – fly fishing in Patagonia and game-management hunts in Zimbabwe – to the sybaritic, such as luxurious African safaris which incorporate flights in a private, vintage plane over the Victoria Falls or trips to Scotland aboard the glorious, Edwardian Royal Scotsman train. All offer a unique blend of style, adventure and exclusivity.

Holland & Holland
31-33 Bruton Street, London W1X 8JS, UK
Tel: +44-20-74 99 44 11   Fax: +44-20-74 99 45 44
Also in: Sloane Street, London SW1 Tel: +44-20-72 35 34 75,
Paris Tel: +33-1-45 02 22 00 and the USA Tel: +1-800-746 2318

HOSTAL DE LA GAVINA

Josep Ensensa opened this 'baby grand' hotel in 1932 – and immediately attracted a galaxy of Hollywood stars. These days Robert de Niro, Eric Cantona, Luciano Benetton and Gianfranco Ferré enjoy its opulence and courtly service. Rich panelling, Gobelin tapestries and fine antiques set the tone. Set on a small peninsula in a smart residential area, it has a superb sea-water swimming pool, shady gardens, tennis courts and its own motor boat for excursions along the coast.

Hostal de la Gavina
Plaza de la Rosaleda, E-17248 S'Agaro Gerona, Spain
Tel: +34-972-32 11 00   Fax: +34-972-32 15 73

HOTEL COSTES

With the help of decorator Jacques Garcia, Jean-Louis Costes transformed an abandoned 19th-century hotel into a seductive and extravagantly stylish Italianate palace – in the process creating a new social Mecca for the Parisian *beau-monde*. The ravishing first floor suites have terraces overlooking the courtyard garden where, in the summer, a table for lunch requires military-style advance planning – or a very good contacts book. The Costes' gym – with its glamorous pool – is among the best in Paris.

Hôtel Costes
239 rue Saint-Honoré, 75001 Paris, France
Tel: +33-1-42 44 50 50   Fax: +33-1-42 44 50 01

HOTEL DE PARIS

Monaco's elegance may not be quite what it was but the Hôtel de Paris remains proudly and defiantly grand – a refuge where silk dresses and big jewels are entirely in keeping. The rooms are all that you would expect of such a place (whether you prefer a view of the sea or of the action in the Place du Casino is entirely a matter of taste) and the welcome is, fittingly, that uniquely Monégasque brand of slightly aloof courtesy.

Hôtel de Paris
Place du Casino, MC-98000 Monaco
Tel: +377-92-16 30 00   Fax: +377-92-16 38 50

HUBLOT

The simple concept that gave the world the Hublot watch in 1980 – named after the porthole design of its bezel – has established Hublot as a cult style statement among cosmopolitan *sportifs*.

The original design has been reworked in myriad permutations, including a rounder, fuller interpretation of its famous case. While it remains the definitively stylish trademark of the company, Hublot's signature black rubber strap – which took three years to develop and can withstand up to 50 kilograms of traction – has been joined by the 'Colonial' bracelet, an alternative in steel, gold or a combination of the two. Using a variety of materials, from yellow, white and pink gold, to steel, diamonds and coloured gem-stones, Hublot's

HOTEL STADT HAMBURG

It is difficult to think of a better escape from everyday life than a stay at this idyllic hotel, on the North Sea island of Sylt; you wake to the sound of gulls and look out over miles of unspoilt white sand. Established in 1869, it is run with great warmth and charm by the founder's great grandson, Harald Hentzschel and his wife, Moni. Its already lovely rooms were redecorated in early 1999 and a spa added at the end of that year.

Hotel Stadt Hamburg
Strandstrasse 2, D-25980 Westerland/Sylt, Germany
Tel: +49-4651-85 80   Fax: +49-4651-85 82 20

range now consists of 'Classics', 'Chronographs', 'Professional', and 'Greenwich Mean Time' collections, as well as a selection of ladies' jewellery watches.

Each year Hublot introduces its latest designs at the Basel Jewellery Fair and, for 1999, a number of exiting new models were presented, including the 'Power Reserve' automatic model and the divers' 'Super Professional'. Particularly well-received were the stunning new face of the Self-winding Chronograph and the animal figures (available in limited editions only) which adorn Hublot's 'Champlevé Enamel' dials.

Hublot
MDM Genève, 44 route de Divonne
CH-1260 Nyon 2, Switzerland
Tel: +41-22-362 1970   Fax: +41-22-362 1617
Website: www.hublot.ch

HOTEL D'ANGLETERRE

Decorated in classical French style, this palatial hotel – established over 150 years ago – underwent a major facelift during 1999. Its 18 suites – each decorated differently – have romantic views over the Kongens Nytorv (King's Square) and the canals. In 1997 the hotel bought its own, classical 42-metre motor yacht, *D'Angleterre II*, which is available for private charter in the Mediterranean and the Caribbean; the service on board is all that you would expect, as both chef and crew are D'Angleterre-trained.

Hôtel D'Angleterre
Kongens Nytorv 34, P.O. Box 424
1021 Copenhagen K, Denmark
Tel: +45-33-12 00 95   Fax: +45-33-12 11 18

HOTEL DU RHONE

The first luxury hotel built in Europe after World War II, the Hôtel du Rhône immediately attracted an élite clientele. Since the Rafael Group bought it

in 1989, the hotel has been beautifully refurbished, its cosy elegance – coupled with excellent service – winning Five-Star Diamond Awards in 1997, 1998 and 1999.

The rooms are decorated in elegant Art Deco-inspired style, complemented by huge and superbly appointed bathrooms and the seventh-floor Mont Blanc Suite – with a private terrace – has 360° views of the city, the lake and the mountains.

Both of the hotel's restaurants have delightful, shady terraces for the summer; Le Neptune is celebrated for its seafood, while the Café Rafael offers some of the best people-watching in town.

Hôtel du Rhône
Quai Turrettini 1, CH-1201 Geneva, Switzerland
Tel: +41-22-909 0000   Fax: +41-22-909 0010

HOTEL DU CAP - EDEN ROC

It helps to book early and it helps to be Somebody (or a regular) if you want to stay at this legendary hotel. The list of celebrities who have not stayed is probably shorter than the list of those who have. It also helps to bring a suitcase full of cash, since plastic is still not regarded as real money here. Owned by the Oetker family, it has been run like a personal fiefdom by Jean-Claude Irondelle for 45 years. The original 1880s building, set regally back from the sea, has the grandest rooms but those in the Eden-Roc 'annexe' are perched right above the sea, a mere step from the swimming pool (possibly the most glamorous on earth) and its star-studded terrace restaurant.

Hôtel du Cap - Eden Roc
Boulevard Kennedy, 06601 Cap D'Antibes, France
Tel: +33-4-93 61 39 01   Fax: +33-4-93 67 76 04

HUMEWOOD CASTLE

One of the finest Victorian country houses in Ireland, the immaculately restored Humewood Castle rests in 480 acres below the scenic Wicklow Mountains. One of the finest sporting estates in the country, it boasts excellent driven pheasant (on its adjoining property, Shillelagh) and superb duck shooting, as well as fishing. There are four lakes, a polo field, a three-day event course and the opportunity to hunt with the prestigious Kildare Foxhounds.

Humewood Castle
Kiltegan, County Wicklow, Ireland
Tel: +353-508-73 215   Fax: +353-508-73 382

THE HURLINGHAM CLUB

The palatial Hurlingham Club was designed by Lutyens and today its 40 acres of grounds boast a grass and synthetic tennis courts, cricket ground, croquet and bowls lawns, an outdoor swimming pool and another pool in the new fitness centre. Members enjoy a number of special events each year which include a tennis tournament and the *Concours d'Elegance* of classic cars.

The Hurlingham Club
Ranelagh Gardens, London SW6 3PR, UK
Tel: +44-20-77 36 84 11   Fax: +44-20-77 31 12 89

HUNTSMAN

Huntsman has recently celebrated 150 years in business as London's pre-eminent tailor, having suited generations of urbane gentlemen. A single-button Huntsman suit, with its restrained waist and tapered trousers, is one of the most quintessentially English of status symbols. Despite costing upwards of £2,500, their elegance and meticulous workmanship more than justify the expense.

H. Huntsman & Sons Ltd.
11 Savile Row, London W1X 2PS, UK
Tel: +44-20-77 34 74 41   Fax: +44-20-72 87 29 37

HOUGHTON CLUB

This club is to trout fishermen what St. Andrews is to golf; the history of the River Test – one of the birthplaces of fly fishing – and its fabled trout is very much a history of the Houghton Club. Mick Lunn, the third generation keeper, grew up on the riverbank and, as a lad, tended to General Eisenhower, who planned D-Day while fishing here. Remarkably, unlike most of the world's top fisheries, this magical spot is in the heart of England rather than some remote wilderness.

Houghton Club
The Grosvenor Hotel, Stockbridge
Hampshire SO20 6EU, UK
Tel: +44-1264-81 06 06   Fax: +44-1264-810 7478

I.B.P

Such is the reputation of this security company, established barely a decade ago, that it has become the leader in the fashion and show-business fields, covering all the Paris couture shows, as well as film premières and major concerts. Director Philippe Golmard also handles personal protection for visiting VIPs and celebrities, whether in Paris or elsewhere in France. James Brown and Lauren Hill are among his star-studded clientele.

International Bafalo Protection
135-137 rue Emile Beaufils, 93100 Montreuil, France
Tel: +33-1-48 70 49 10   Fax: +33-1-48 57 58 44

IM SCHIFFCHEN

A native of the Loire, veteran chef Jean-Claude Bourgueil had already worked at some of Düsseldorf's leading restaurants when he started from scratch at Im Schiffchen (which translates as 'The Little Boat') in 1977 and turned it into one of Germany's most famous addresses. Ten years later, it received its third Michelin star. The sheer excellence of the menu, which includes such delights as *Homard poché à la vapeur de camomille*, attracts local power-brokers and international gourmets alike.

Im Schiffchen
Kaiserswerther Markt 9, D-40489 Düsseldorf, Germany
Tel: +49-211-40 10 50   Fax: +49-211-40 36 67

INES DE LA FRESSANGE

Model-turned-designer Ines de la Fressange offers what she describes as "clothing solutions". From jeans to evening wear, these are chic and indispensable basics of impeccable quality, which reflect the designer's own youthful and free-spirited attitude – as does her collection of china, glass and decorative items. Reflecting the designer's evolving eye, the sugar-plum pastels of her flagship boutique (where the staff are among the most charming in Paris) will be replaced by a sleeker, more neutral look in early 2000. De La Fressange's signature scent was launched in September 1999.

Ines de la Fressange
14 avenue Montaigne, 75008 Paris, France
Tel: +33-1-47 23 08 94   Fax: +33-1-47 23 05 54

INPERSAU

This exclusive chauffeur service is renowned for its attention to detail; Jean-Baptiste and Antoine Aubrun, its owners, positively welcome demanding clients – for whom they even go so far as to customise cars with special hi-fi systems so that their clients (who range from rock stars to royalty) can listen to their favourite music. The company is extremely selective about its drivers, who are mostly bilingual and all trained in security.

Inpersau
51 rue de St. Lazare
75009 Paris, France
Tel: +33-1-53 19 00 66   Fax: +33-1-53 19 00 88

INFANZIA, L'

Visitors to Milan – and beyond – in need of first-class babysitting, whether for a few hours or a year, can do no better than to follow the lead of Milan's smartest families, who recruit their nannies from this excellent school. In addition to training nannies, l'Infanzia operates an excellent pre-school, where children – supervised by child-development and healthcare experts – spend their days learning everything from painting and dance to photography and computing.

L'Infanzia
via Lario 16, 20159 Milan, Italy
Tel & Fax: +39-02-69 00 22 01

IMPERIAL HOTEL, VIENNA

Originally built as a palace for the Duke of Württemburg, The Imperial is grand as they come – a million miles away in both style and spirit from today's hip but sterile designer hotels. However, for all of its grandeur, the service – including butlers for all guests – is remarkably warm and personal. The Imperial is heaven for opera fans; its concierges seem always to conjure up impossible-to-find tickets and you may meet Pavarotti, Carreras or Seiji Ozawa in the lift, for this is where they all stay.

Imperial Hotel
Kärntner Ring 16
A-1015 Vienna, Austria
Tel: +43-1-50 12 34 25   Fax: +43-1-50 12 33 45

INTERCITY IMMOBILIEN

This property consultancy, established in the 1950s and run today by the founder's sons, Herbert and Markus Wüst, offers clients a full range of services, including brokerage, leasing and management. Its 'Exceptional Properties' division (which is affiliated to Sotheby's) handles just that – properties such as the unique Marcel Breuer-designed villa on Lake Zürich, which it sold last year. Specialising in the German-speaking part of Switzerland, Intercity has affiliates throughout the country.

Intercity Immobilien
Zollikerstrasse 141
CH-8008 Zürich, Switzerland
Tel: +41-1-388 5858   Fax: +41-1-422 1535

INTEGRATED MEDICAL CENTRE

Dr. Mosaraf Ali's skills as a homeopath, dietician, irridologist and masseur have made him a favourite of international royalty. Dr. Ali, who trained in medicine in Moscow, has advised the Sultans of Brunei and the Saudi royal family and acted as a medical mentor to Prince Charles. His Integrated Medical Centre – the only one of its kind in Europe – which was established in 1998 and is now staffed by a team of 25, brings together complementary therapies and conventional medicine.

Dr. Mosaraf Ali
Integrated Medical Centre, 46 New Cavendish Street
London W1M 7RG, UK
Tel: +44-20-72 24 51 11   Fax: +44-20-72 24 31 14

IPCA

This prestigious cooking school teaches students how to make classical Italian dishes, from the simplicity of perfect pasta and fish to the complexity of *pasticceria* and regional specialities. International cuisine is also covered. Its classes (128 were organised last cater for everyone from beginners to professionals and seminars are held on the appreciation of raw ingredients, wine, cooking techniques and table etiquette. IPCA also publishes the respected monthly magazine, *La Cucina Italiana*.

IPCA (Istituto per la Promozione della
Cultura Alimentare)
Piazza Aspromonte 15, 20131 Milan, Italy
Tel: +39-02-266 4907   Fax: +39-02-266 5555

IWC

IWC's distinctive and distinguished watches have been coveted by collectors since the pioneering American, Florentine Ariosto Jones, inaugurated the marque in Switzerland in 1868 – in the process introducing new machines and production processes. The latest watch from the creators of the world's first titanium chronograph is the GST Chrono Automatic, an incredibly resilient mechanical chronograph, which is water resistant to 120 metres and features a patented bracelet system.

IWC, The International Watch Company

15 Baumgartenstrasse, CH-8201 Schaffhausen, Switzerland

Tel: +41-52-635 6533   Fax: +41-52-635 6505

INVERLOCHY CASTLE

Elton John, Jessica Lange, Robert Redford and Mel Gibson have all been seduced by this grand and romantic Relais & Châteaux hideaway. Set on a loch in the shadow of Ben Nevis, it was a private residence for over 100 years (Queen Victoria slept in what is now the Honeymoon

Suite) before becoming a hotel in 1969. The ambience created by its genial Director, Michael Leonard is as warm and vibrant as its Michael Priest decor. Chef Simon Haigh fully merits his Michelin star. Just don't ask for Evian; the water comes from Inverlochy's own springs – better than anything from a bottle.

Inverlochy Castle

Torlundy, Fort William, Inverness-Shire

Scotland PH33 6BN, UK

Tel: +44-1397-70 21 77   Fax: +44-1397-70 29 53

22 JERMYN STREET

Under the leadership of Henry Togna, who opened this tiny gem in 1990, this hotel offers countless thoughtful touches including a wad of highly personalised newsletters detailing, for instance, Togna's favourite restaurants, an invitation to join Togna himself at Annabel's and, for children, 'birdie bags' for feeding the ducks in St. James's Park (a legacy of when Mel Gibson stayed *en famille*). Gault & Millau rate it their favourite small hotel in London but Togna doesn't rest on his laurels. A top-to-toe refurbishment will be completed by summer 2000.

22 Jermyn Street

St. James's, London SW1Y 6HL, UK

Tel: +44-20-77 34 23 53 Fax: +44-20-77 34 07 50

JACK BARCLAY

This company has built up a matchless reputation since Jack Barclay began selling Bentleys in 1926, at the tender age of 23. Within three years the Society press had dubbed him "the finest luxury motorcar salesman in the trade". Today, in addition to being the world's largest retailer of Rolls-Royce and Bentley motorcars, Jack Barclay's service division handles over 300 cars each month and an exclusive chauffeur hire division has been added to its portfolio of services.

Since the untimely death of Jack Barclay's youngest son, Victor, in 1993, the company has been through some radical changes and now, as part of the Dutton-Forshaw Group, it is back in private hands for the first time since 1968, under the direction of a young and dynamic management team. However, reflecting its

founder's deeply-held belief in the value of expertise, its salesmen are among the most experienced in the business. The company's coach-building and restoration division is renowned for its superb craftsmanship and, in 1999, a classic Rolls-Royce Phantom III Sedanca de Ville by H.J. Mulliner, which had been restored by Jack Barclay, won both its own class and overall honours in the annual Rolls-Royce Enthusiasts' Club rally.

Jack Barclay Ltd.

18 Berkeley Square, London W1X 6AE, UK

Tel: +44-20-76 29 74 44   Fax: +44-20-76 29 82 58

Website: bbi.co.uk/jackbarclay/

JACQUES GARCIA

The rich textures and vibrant colours which characterise Jacques Garcia's interior schemes are testament to his confidence and imagination. Much of his inspiration comes from the 17th and 18th centuries – especially the Empire school – although he happily mixes styles and periods, marrying classicism with extravagance. For all that, Garcia's interiors are never stiff – looking, instead, as if several generations have passed through. His 1999 projects included two grand town houses in Paris, and restaurants in Beirut, Paris and New York.

Jacques Garcia
212 rue de Rivoli, 75001 Paris, France
Tel: +33-1-42 97 48 70   Fax: +33-1-42 97 48 10

JACQUES GRANGE

Having been decorator of choice for the Saint Laurent set (and a denizen of that social circle) for two decades, Jacques Garcia stepped away from the limelight for a time. However, with Aerin Lauder's commission to do her New York apartment, we will doubtless hear a lot more of him again. Not that Garcia has been idle; as well as undertaking several lower-profile private commissions, he has produced a range of furniture in the meantime.

Jacques Grange
118 rue du Faubourg St. Honoré, 75008 Paris, France
Tel: +33-1-47 42 47 34   Fax: +33-1-42 66 24 17

JACQUES KUGEL ANTIQUAIRES

This fabulous gallery, spread over three floors, houses a collection of precious gold- and silverware dating from the Renaissance to the early 20th century. Its versatility means that the treasures do not end there; paintings, delicate marquetry furniture, and *objets d'art* fashioned from ivory, amber and rock crystal are also on display. After Jacques Kugel's death in 1985, his sons, Nicholas and Alexis, took over and have been successfully running the operation ever since.

Jacques Kugel Antiquaires
279 rue St. Honoré, 75008 Paris, France
Tel: +33-1-42 60 86 23   Fax: +33-1-42 61 06 72

JAIME PARLADE

Decorator, antique dealer and taste arbiter Jaime Parladé – renowned for his use of colour and textiles – honed his eye through travels as a young man around Morocco, the Dominican Republic and throughout Spain. This love of the exotic is expressed in his work, where the Mediterranean-rustic idiom is enlivened with contemporary references and the use of noble materials. Parladé's shop, La Tartana, on the Ronda road behind Marbella, is a wonderful cache of antiques and *objets* – both antique and contemporary – all in the owner's style.

Jaime Parladé
Urb. La Heredia, c/-Miguel Rubiales 10
E-29670 San Pedro Alcantara, Malaga, Spain
Tel: +34-95-278 9057   Fax: +34-95 278 0015

JAEGER-LECOULTRE

One of the elite brand of watchmaking firms to create its own movements and the majority of its parts in-house, Jaeger-Le Coultre was established by Antoine LeCoultre in 1833.

His 'Millionometer' of 1844 was the first instrument capable of measuring components to the nearest micron and the firm continued this innovative tradition with its 'Atmos' clock, which lives on air. Jaeger-Le Coultre is most celebrated,

however, for its 'Reverso' wristwatches; first introduced in 1931, the line now incorporates jewelled, sports and watchmaking specialities.

Jaeger-LeCoultre
8 rue de la Golisse, CH-1347 Le Sentier, Switzerland
Tel: +41-21-845 0202   Fax: +41-21-845 0550

JAMES PURDEY & SONS

Founded by James Purdey over 150 years ago, this celebrated gunsmith is now owned by the Vendôme Group. By Royal Appointment, the firm builds incomparable guns and rifles - each requiring some 700 man-hours to make - and sevices them with equal skill. The Long Room at its headquarters houses Purdey family portraits, as well as a fascinating collection of shooting memorabilia, and the adjacent accessories department offers sportsmen's clothes and accessories.

James Purdey & Sons Ltd.
Audley House, 57-58 South Audley Street
London W1Y 6ED, UK
Tel: +44-20-74 99 18 01   Fax: +44-20-73 55 32 97

JANE CHURCHILL

Having learned the basics of her trade under Michael Raymond at Colefax & Fowler, Jane Churchill inaugurated her interior design business at the age of just 21. Her tasteful interpretation of the classic country-house look has won her such clients as Estée Lauder, Bill Wyman and Earl and Countess de La Warr. During the past year she has worked her magic on projects as diverse as a Kentucky stud, an apartment in Kensington Palace and the London home of Jane Asher and Gerald Scarfe.

Jane Churchill Interiors Ltd.
81 Pimlico Road, London SW1W 8PH, UK
Tel: +44-20-77 30 85 64   Fax: +44-20-78 23 64 21

JAN KRUGIER, DITESHEIM GALERIE

Jan Krugier has galleries in Geneva and New York, both specialising in international contemporary art. The two venues recently hosted in turn the exhibition, 'Paul Klee: Traces of Memory', which reflects Krugier's lifelong interest in the painter's œuvre. 'Les Femmes de Picasso', another recent show, also demonstrates the quality of works on display.

Galerie Jan Krugier
Diteisheim & Cie, 29-31 Grande-Rue
CH-1204 Geneva, Switzerland
Tel: +41-22-310 5719   Fax: +41-22-310 5712

JANET REGER

Superstars (including Jerry Hall, Kate Moss, Madonna and Joan Collins) and housewives alike have become addicted to Janet Reger's lingerie since she first unleashed her deliciously feminine confections on to a grateful British womanhood over 30 years ago. The range has always reflected prevailing fashion trends and the current preoccupation with underwear as outerwear has encouraged Janet and her daughter Aliza – to expand their collection and they have also introduced bed linen and household textiles.

Janet Reger
2 Beauchamp Place, London SW3 1NG, UK
Tel: +44-20-75 84 93 60   Fax: +44-20-75 81 74 60

JARDIN DES SENS, LE

When Jacques and Laurent Pourcel were 14 their mother fell ill and they took over the family's cooking; later, as apprentices, "we blew a lot of our wages eating", admits Jacques. It was clearly worth it, for in 1999 they won a third Michelin star for their richly flavoured Mediterranean cooking. From the outside their restaurant looks rather like a bunker but inside the tables (for which there is a waiting list of several weeks) overlook a beautiful garden which wraps around it on three sides. The twin brothers' partner, sommelier and maître d', Olivier Château, creates a remarkably relaxed atmosphere for such exalted cooking.

Le Jardin des Sens
11 avenue Saint-Lazare, 34000 Montpellier, France
Tel: +33-4-67 79 63 38   Fax: +33-4-67 72 13 05

JEAN-LUC FIGUERAS

French-Catalan chef and restaurateur Jean-Luc Figueras set up this elegant restaurant in the former studio of Cristobal Balenciaga in 1994. His approach is creative; his signature, Mediterranean-style dishes include Sea bass with cod tripe and *butifarra negra* and Chocolate cake with spiced bread ice-cream and chocolate jelly. The main carta changes with the seasons and there is also a superb

tasting menu and a wine list that brings together the best Catalan and Spanish vintages.

Jean-Luc Figueras
Santa Teresa 10, E-08012 Barcelona, Spain
Tel: +34-93-415 2877   Fax: +34-93-218 9262

JAVIER BARBA

A third generation architect, Javier Barba draws his inspiration from nature; his houses disappear into the surrounding landscape, which determines not only their aesthetics but also their orientation to the sun, the views and natural shelter. A Barba house on Minorca looks more like an ancient temple than the

summer retreat of its sophisticated urbanite owner and Barba has also created an idyllic holiday compound on Corfu for the famously demanding Lord Rothschild. Current projects include the Punta San Basilio Hotel in Baja California.

Javier Barba
Plaza Eguilaz, No. 10, Entresuelo 3a
E-08017 Barcelona, Spain
Tel: +34-3-204 4206   Fax: +34-3-204 2697

JEAN BARDET

The Bardets' grand 19th-century villa sits in romantic grounds, complete with stream and a splendid greenhouse and Jean Bardet's celebrated *Aumonière de légumes du potager* and his delicately-flavoured Artichoke heart with peas are the products of his own marvellous vegetable garden.
Sophie Bardet's gentle charm is a perfect foil for her husband's renowned sense of humour and their wine cellar, naturally enough, contains a superb collection of Loire vintages.

Jean Bardet
Château Belmont, 57 rue Groison
37100 Tours, France
Tel: +33-2-47 41 41 11   Fax: +33-2-47 51 68 72

JEAN-PIERRE MARTEL

An intellectual, *bon viveur* and collector of classic cars, this distinguished decorator trained in Paris at the Ecole des Beaux-Arts, moving to Marbella in the 1970s, where he initially worked with Jaime Parladé. His projects in Spain – both hotels and important houses – reflect his sensitivity to traditional Andalucian style (much of his furniture is specially made by local artisans) while private houses he has done in London express an urban sophistication. The recent revival in The Marbella Club's fortunes is attributed, in good measure, to Martel's brilliant re-design.

Jean-Pierre Martel
Martel Castillo S.L., Hotel Marbella Club
Boulevard Principe Alfonso s/n
E-29600 Marbella, Malaga, Spain
Tel: +34-952-82 89 08   Fax: +34-952-82 50 53

JIL SANDER

From her flagship store in what was once Madame Vionnet's couture house on the Avenue Montaigne - as well as over 60 other stores world-wide - Jil Sander spreads her minimalist vision. Her pared-down 1999 winter collection features modernist, techno fabrics like felt, fleece and rayon in fashion-forward shapes.

Jil Sander
32 Osterfeldstrasse, D-22529 Hamburg, Germany
Tel: +49-40-55 30 20   Fax: +49-40-553 3034

JESURUM

Michelangelo Jesurum was almost single-handedly responsible for reviving the art of Venetian lace-making at the end of the 19th century; his company, founded some 130 years ago, created the city's first lace-making 'school'. Europe's royal courts favoured his 'table-clothes' and Jesurum won a gold medal at the 1878 Universal Exhibition in Paris in recognition of his achievements. Having capitalised on these skills, his name became synonymous with exquisite, hand-made lace on household linens for bed, bath and dining. Today, combining these traditional skills with modern technology, Jesurum's collections – many of them custom-made – feature the embroidery and colour typical of the Venetian heritage alongside more contemporary designs.

Jesurum
Venezia Mercerie de Capitello 4856
30124 Venice, Italy
Tel: +39-041-520 6177 Fax: +39-041-520 6085

J.P. TOD'S

Until Diego della Valle applied his talent for creating objects of desire the company founded by his grandfather in 1917 made private-label shoes for American stores. Now, from classic neutrals to Ferrari red leather (given free if you buy an F50), midnight blue velvet and vivid shades of crocodile (made to order), della Valle's shoes have redefined casual chic. Tod's has diversified into handbags (1997) and leather clothing is next, although its bobble-soled 'driving shoes' remain the status staple for the Princess Carolines and Harrison Fords of this world.

J.P. Tod's
corso Venezia 30
20121 Milan, Italy
Tel: +39-02-77 22 51   Fax: +39-02-76 02 29 28

JIMMY CHOO

Shoe designer Jimmy Choo has come of age, his days of working, virtually unknown, in a tiny *atelier* now far behind him. With the aid of his glamorous business partner, Tamara Yeardye, he expanded across the Atlantic in 1999, opening shops in New York and Beverley Hills. Back in London, socialites compete with the fashionocracy for appointments with his couture service, consoling themselves meanwhile with his velveteen Mary-Jane slippers, towering grosgrain stilettos and delicate leather slingbacks.

Jimmy Choo
20 Motcomb Street, London SW1X 9EL, UK
Tel: +44-20-72 35 60 08   Fax: +44-20-72 35 78 68

JO HANSFORD

Jo Hansford opened her Academy of Colour Excellence opposite her Mayfair salon at the beginning of 1999 to propagate her skills to other hairdressers. Dubbed "best tinter on the planet" by American Vogue, her celebrity client list is one that other hairdressers would die for – although her work is so skilful that it is undetectable to observers. Her 1999 triumphs included Cate Blanchett's hair for the BAFTA ceremony.

Jo Hansford
19 Mount Street, London W1Y 5RA, UK
Tel: +44-20-74 95 77 74   Fax: +44-20-74 95 77 47

JO MALONE

Celebrated for having introduced the concept of 'layering' two or more single-note scents, second-generation beautician Jo Malone has expanded across the Atlantic, rising immediately to the top of chic New Yorkers' wish lists – a far cry from the early days, when she mixed potions in her kitchen sink. Her deliciously scented skin creams, bath products, perfumes and candles can also be ordered by mail. Malone opened a swish new flagship store in London's Sloane Street in mid-1999.

Jo Malone
150 Sloane Street, London SW1X 9BX, UK
Tel: +44-20-77 20 02 02 (Enquiries only)

JOAN PRATS, GALERIA

This Barcelona art dealership (with a sister gallery in New York) takes its name from the son of a famous hat maker, who was also a friend and avid admirer of Miró. Prats' collection of Miró pieces is housed elsewhere but the works here, all contemporary, are impressive. Space is given to Catalan artists such as Albert Ràfols Casamada and Joan Hernández Pijoan, but there is also a strong international flavour, with works by Robert Motherwell, Sue Williams and Hannah Collins.

Galeria Joan Prats
S.A. Rambla de Catalunya 54, E-08007 Barcelona, Spain
Tel: +34-93-216 0290   Fax: +34-93-487 1614

LE JOCKEY CLUB

When Valéry Giscard d'Estaing presented himself for election to this club his experience was a lesson in the legendary pickiness of his peers; he was blackballed, not because he isn't a real aristocrat but because he refused to drop the 'd' in his name. This is where the aristocracy comes to escape the hoi polloi – to lunch, to dine or for the simple pleasure of still hearing a white-jacketed waiter announce, "*Monsieur le Comte est servi*".

Le Jockey Club
2 rue Rabelais, 75008 Paris, France
Tel: +33-1-43 59 85 63

JOCKEY

A director of the Ritz during the 1930s, Clodoaldo Cortes had a ready-made clientele of Madrid high society and international socialites when he opened this restaurant just after the war. Now run by Cortes' son, Luis Eduardo, its clientele and its cosily elegant décor have hardly changed. The cooking is classical, too – a mix of French and Spanish – including its justifiably celebrated Sea Bass *en papillotte* and *Tripe Madrileña*. Jockey has seven private dining rooms and one of the finest cellars in Spain.

Restaurant Jockey
Calle Amador de Rios 6, E-28010 Madrid, Spain
Tel: +34-91-319 10 03   Fax: +34-91-319 24 35

JOHN ESKENAZI

John Eskenazi travelled throughout Asia and worked as a stage designer and theatre director before he joined his family's Milan art gallery in 1977. He followed his cousin Giuseppe's lead, moving to London and establishing his own gallery in 1994, specialising in Chinese, Japanese and Indian works. He has sold many pieces to leading museums, including the Art Institute of Chicago, London's V&A and the Museo Nazionale d'Arte Orientale in Rome, and written a number of scholarly articles.

John Eskenazi Ltd.
15 Old Bond Street, London W1X 4JL, UK
Tel: +44-20-74 09 30 01   Fax: +44-20-76 29 21 46

JOHN FRIEDA

John Frieda's hairdressing empire continues to grow; with three London salons and one in New York, he has just opened in Paris, next door to renowned colourist, Chrisophe Robin. He is also a wizard with his product ranges, the latest of which, 'Sheer Blonde', looks set to be another huge success. Diana Ross, Ivana Trump and Raquel Welch simply call on the services of the master in person.

John Frieda
4 Aldford Street, London W1Y 5PU, UK
Tel: +44-20-72 45 00 33   Fax: +44-20-72 35 13 45

JOHN GALLIANO

Thanks to John Galliano, Cate Blanchett was one of the few truly glamorous actresses at the 1999 Oscars. At collection time, the designer luxuriated in feathers, raffia embroidery and Maori motifs, his designs paraded before a construction site backdrop. Fitted knits were notable, along with blanket-coats for daytime, while Galliano's finale of slender, signature, bias-cut evening dresses in a ruby palette stole the show.

John Galliano
Tel: +33-1-55 25 11 11 (for stockists only)

JOHN GOSDEN

Since being lured back from a successful career in America by Sheikh Mohamed, John Gosden has continued to train winners – including two Classics, the St. Leger and, with *Benny The Dip*, the 1997

Derby. 1998 brought a total of 77 wins and, in 1999 Gosden had two winners at Royal Ascot and success at Longchamp, where *Valentine's Waltz* won the 1999 French 1,000 Guineas. Gosden's stables, established at the beginning of the century, were formerly owned by Lord Derby.

John Gosden
Stanley House Stables, Bury Road
Newmarket, Suffolk CB8 7BT, UK
Tel: +44-1638-66 99 44   Fax: +44-1638-66 99 22

JOHN HOBBS

This highly-regarded dealer specialises in 18th- and early 19th-century works of art, from furniture and paintings to statuary and *objets d'art*. John Hobbs brings a lifetime's experience and an exceptionally discerning eye to the difficult job of tracking down the finest works of art from around the world.

John Hobbs
3107A Pimlico Road, London SW1W 8PH, UK
Tel: +44-20-77 30 83 69 Fax: +44-20-77 30 04 37

JOHN LOBB

Not to be confused with the — also very fine — ready-to-wear collection of the same name (now owned by Hermès) this bespoke shoemaker is quite possibly the finest in the world — though, if you want to join their illustrious client list, be prepared to wait six months for your first pair. Founded by former Cornish farmer, John Lobb, in 1849, the firm has made shoes for such luminaries as Guglielmo Marconi, Haile Selassie and Frank Sinatra. John Hunter Lobb, its fourth-generation chairman, who personally oversees every fitting, was joined in the early 1990s by his son, William.

John Lobb
9 St. James's Street, London SW1A 1EF, UK
Tel: +44-20-79 30 36 64 Fax: +44-20-79 30 28 11

JOHN OXX

Former Chairman of the Irish National Stud and the Irish Trainers' Association, trainer John Oxx (son of the great Irish trainer of the same name) has won major races on both sides of the Atlantic on behalf of Sheikh Mohammed and the Aga Khan — notably with *Ridgewood Pearl* (Cartier Horse of the Year in 1995). Remarkably modest, though renowned for his wit, Oxx trained as a vet before setting up his yard in 1979. In 1999 the Oxx-trained *Enzelli* won the Ascot Gold Cup.

John Oxx
Creeve Currabeg, Curragh, Co. Kildare, Ireland
Tel: +353-45-52 13 10 Fax: +353-45-52 22 36

JOHN PAWSON

The godfather of minimalism, John Pawson's search for purity of form, simple materials and clean spaces has had a huge influence on architecture and interior design at the close of the 20th century. In addition to such publicly acclaimed buildings as the Cathay Pacific Lounges in Hong Kong (1998), Pawson has created more than 25 private houses. Work in progress includes a furniture collection for B&B Italia, the de Botton house in Provence, a Long Island house and the London's Young Vic theatre.

John Pawson
Unit B, 70-78 York Way, London N1 9AG, UK
Enquiries to: Fax: +44-20-78 37 49 49

JOHN STEFANIDIS

The style of this hugely respected decorator (Egyptian-born and Oxford-educated) is characterised by grand simplicity, a refined awareness of detail and a sensitivity to texture, rather than by any particular style or period. Indeed, when he established his firm in 1967, Stefanidis' style was boldly modernistic; today, favouring a soft colour palette, his style is a casually elegant interpretation of the English country look, enlivened by a Mediterranean sensibility which reflects his origins

John Stefanidis
7 Friese Green House, Chelsea Manor Street
London SW3 3TW, UK
Tel: +44-20-73 51 75 11 Fax: +44-20-73 52 94 60

JOHN TAYLOR

Owned these days by Monaco property barons, the Pastor family, this real estate agent deals in blue-chip properties on behalf of celebrities, heads of state and the seriously wealthy. With offices in London and Barcelona, as well as the length of the Côte d'Azur, it has come a long way since it was established in 1864 by Englishman John Taylor, who knew the grand Riviera estates and their owners from his work as a gardener there.

John Taylor S.A.
55 La Croisette, 06400 Cannes, France
Tel: +33-4-93 38 00 66 Fax: +33-4-93 39 13 65

JOHN WARREN

Based at Lord Hartington's Side Hill Stud in Newmarket, which he manages, this highly regarded bloodstock agent has recently been appointed Bloodstock Director to the Royal Studs. Also a director of the extremely successful Highclere Thoroughbred Racing syndicate, which is run by his brother-in-law Harry Herbert (son of the Queen's racing manager, the Earl of Carnarvon), Warren has purchased over 80 'black type', or superior performers, including the champion horses *Tamarisk* and *Lake Coniston*.

John Warren
Side Hill Stud, Ashley Rd, Newmarket, Suffolk CB8 8AF, UK
Tel: +44-1638-66 24 01 Fax: +44-1683-66 64 65

JOHNNY VAN HAEFTEN

Johnny Van Haeften deals exclusively in 17th-century Dutch and Flemish Old Masters paintings, from still lives to those with religious and historical themes. He set up this gallery — now one of the most successful in Europe — with his wife in 1977, after ten years at Christie's. Van Haeften exhibits annually at Maastricht and the Grosvenor House Art and Antiques Fairs; December 1999 marks his latest biennial winter exhibition, accompanied by an extensive catalogue.

Johnny Van Haeften
13 Duke Street, St. James's, London SW1Y 6DB, UK
Tel: +44-20-79 30 30 62 Fax: +44-20-78 39 63 03

JON BANNENBERG

This man invented the profession of yacht designer as we now know it. His ideas, now entirely the norm, were radical when he began almost three decades ago — that a designer could carry a project from concept to turnkey delivery (previously a shipyard built the

yacht and a decorator made it look pretty); that yachts need not all look the same and that a large yacht could also be very fast. While some Bannenberg yachts are instantly recognisable (the 'flying wedge' shape) others, such as the Lürssen-built *Coral Island*, are modern classics. Current projects include a 53-metre *Oceanfast* (delivery: July 2000), and a 50-metre *Benetti*, to be launched in April 2001.

Jon Bannenberg
6 Burnsall Street, London SW3 3ST, UK
Tel: +44-20-73 52 48 51 Fax: +44-20-73 52 84 44

JOSEPH

With a recently-acquired majority stake in Connolly, reputed profits of £10 million in 1998 and a rumoured stock exchange flotation, retailing guru Joseph is on a roll. Celebrated for numerous fashion milestones – among them his Joseph Tricot label and his early recognition of Galliano, Gaultier and Yohji Yamamoto – his latest stroke of genius is recognising a woman's yen for trousers. Joseph's pants-only destination stores are set to be another *succès fou*.

Joseph
77-79 Fulham Road, London SW3 6RE, UK
Tel: +44-20-78 23 95 00 Fax: +44-20-78 23 75 34

~

JOHRI'S TALVO

Roland and Brigitte Jöhri's restaurant is a cosy, charming and hugely enjoyable antidote to the full-on glamour of St. Moritz. For privacy and people-watching, the best tables are in a tiny gallery overlooking the main room and – in summer – on the terrace. Roland Jöhri stays close to his (almost local) roots with game, air-dried meats and *pizzokels* (little pasta shapes) but, this being St. Moritz and he being a master of classical French techniques, there is plenty of lobster, caviar and foie gras too.

Jöhri's Talvo
via Gunels 15, CH-7512 St Moritz/Champfer, Switzerland
Tel: +41-81-833 4455 Fax: +41-81-833 0569

~

JULIUS BAER

Founded in 1890, the Julius Baer Group is listed on both the Zürich and Frankfurt Stock Exchanges, although the family and staff control the registered shares and family members are actively involved in its management. Its principal vehicle, Bank Julius Baer, is now one of Switzerland's leading international private banks and manages over £40 billion of assets, of which two-thirds come from private investors. The bank emphasises a consultative approach, in order to arrive at tailor-made solutions for its clients.

Bank Julius Baer & Co. Ltd.
Bahnhofstrasse 36, CH-8001 Zürich, Switzerland
Tel: +41-1-228 5111 Fax: +41-1-211 2560

~

JUSTERINI & BROOKS

Now 250 years old, Justerini and Brooks has held Royal Warrants to eight monarchs. Like all traditional wine merchants the core of its list is claret but top wines from all around the world increasingly compete for attention. Its broking department will go to great lengths to source any wine which is not in stock.

Justerini & Brooks
61 St. James's Street, London SW1A 1LZ, UK
Tel: +44-20-74 93 87 21 Fax: +44-20-74 99 46 53

KARSTEN GREVE, GALERIE

Karsten Greve began dealing in 1969 and now owns four prestigious art galleries: two in Cologne, and one each in Paris and Milan. The Wallrafplatz gallery in Cologne remains his principal centre and hosts exciting shows of avant-garde works every year. French-American sculptor and painter Louise Bourgeois had two exhibitions at the Wallrafplatz in 1999, in the illustrious company of Graubner, Ikemura and Kounellis.

Galerie Karsten Greve
Wallrafplatz 3
D-50667 Cologne, Germany
Tel: +49-221-257 8737 Fax: +49-221-258 0479

THE KILDARE HOTEL & COUNTRY CLUB

One might have thought that creating a world-class hotel, golf and country club would be enough for the Kildare Club's owner, industrialist Dr. Michael Smurfit, who bought this 330-acre estate in 1988. He transformed its centrepiece – an elegant French-style mansion built in the 1830s – into a magnificent hotel, adorning its drawing room with the world's finest private collection of Jack B. Yeats paintings and adding a superb swimming pool and fitness area. To supplement the renowned Arnold Palmer-designed championship golf course (venue of the Smurfit European Open and the Ryder Cup 2005 matches), he added first class sporting facilities, including tennis, archery, clay pigeon shooting, riding and trout fishing on the River Liffey, which winds through the estate. Chief Executive Ray Carroll then assembled a brilliant staff, whose warmth and fantastic eagerness to please give this idyllic retreat the feeling of a wonderfully cosseting private home.

But for a perfectionist such as Dr. Smurfit, this was merely a beginning. Having realised his dream of securing the Ryder Cup – the first time it will be played on Irish soil – Smurfit has set about making the K Club even more spectacular, beginning with the addition of new wing for the hotel, designed to blend seamlessly with the existing building.

The Kildare Hotel & Country Club at Straffan
Co. Kildare, Ireland
Tel: +353-1-601 7200 Fax: +353-1-601 7299
Email: hotel@kclub.ie   Email: golf@kclub.ie
Website: www.kclub.ie

KEMPINSKI HOTEL TASCHENBERGPALAIS

This 18th-century former palace, built by King August the Strong, was rebuilt and opened as a hotel in 1995. Combining baroque style with contemporary elegance, it has the ultimate Dresden location, sandwiched between the Semper Opera House and the castle and cathedral. The decor of its 25 excellent suites, like that of all the rooms, has been drawn from all over Europe: French mirrors and tapestries, Italian marble, English fabrics and carpets.

Kempinski Hotel Taschenbergpalais
Taschenberg 3, D-01067 Dresden, Germany
Tel: +49-351-49 120   Fax: +49-351-491 2812

KENNEMER GOLF & COUNTRY CLUB

Built among the huge dunes that line Holland's North Sea coast, this classical, Harry Holt-designed course is widely regarded as the finest links course outside the British Isles. A brisk sea breeze is an integral part of the game here though, on very windy days, the charming thatched clubhouse is a wel-coming refuge. Established in 1928, Kennemer has hosted many tournaments, including the Dutch Open for the last 16 years.

Kennemer Golf & Country Club
P.O. Box 85, 2040 AB Zandvoort, The Netherlands
Tel: +31-23-571 2836   Fax: +31-23-571 9520

KENNETH TURNER

Turner's revolutionary approach to floral decoration has redefined the art during the last 20 years. Granted a Royal Warrant by Prince Charles in 1996, Turner's list of celebrity clients is endless and recent projects include the opening gala for the Sackler Wing of New York's Metropolitan Museum. While he works on major private commissions from his south London studio, Turner's Mayfair shop provides ravishing bouquets and his signature line of garden and household accessories. The Kenneth Turner Flower School opened in 1998 and a branch in Tokyo followed in 1999.

Kenneth Turner
125 Mount Street, London W1Y 5HA, UK
Tel: +44-20-73 55 38 80   Fax: +44-20-74 95 16 07

KILGOUR FRENCH STANBURY

Kilgour French Stanbury is building on its reputation as a rare bird – a Savile Row tailor with freshly acquired street credibility. Clothiers Holland and Sherry, who own the company, have come up with a revolutionary new Teflon-coated fabric which Kilgour's new designer Carlo Brandelli, has used to create a stylish, water-resistant suit – a star turn of his 'Mayfair 2000' collection.

Kilgour French Stanbury
8 Savile Row, London W1X 1AF, UK
Tel: +44-20-77 34 69 05   Fax: +44-20-72 87 81 47

KNIGHT FRANK INTERNATIONAL

Established in 1896, this property consultancy has acted in the sale of such historic places as Stonehenge, Chartwell (to Sir Winston Churchill) and the All England Tennis Club, Wimbledon. Knight Frank now has over 100 offices in 25 diffferent countries worldwide specialising in top-of-the-range residential property, yet there has been no compromise in its standards; wherever it operates the firm employs staff who combine first-class local knowledge with a real understanding of the global picture.

Knight Frank International
20 Hanover Square
London W1R OAH, UK
Tel: +44-20-76 29 81 71   Fax: +44-20-74 93 41 14

KITON

Ciro Paone's family had been wool merchants for over 200 years but Paone's bright idea, when he established his company, Ciro Paone Spa in 1953, was to adapt these fabrics for the ready-to-wear market. However, although the sleek Kiton factory resembles a modern industrial enterprise, his suits, sportswear jackets and trouser are manufactured using distinctly old-fashioned methods. A team of 220 tailors scissor-cuts and hand-sews and -presses every garment.

Paone, a renowned perfectionist, insists that it should be so, even though these production methods limit the firm's production to fewer than 20,000 suits per year. Only by hand sewing can tailors adjust the tension of the seams where the body moves the most, giving the clothing a unique fit and drape.

Fabrics are of the highest quality; the firm works with the top mills in England and Italy to produce fine linens and tweeds, super 150s merino worsteds and cashmeres - all to its own designs. Its 13.7 micron wool - as fine as cashmere - is garnered from a flock of specially-reared Merino sheep.

Kiton (the name derives from chitone, the ancient Greek tunic) is one of the few firms still producing seven-fold ties and, in recent years, the firm has introduced an outdoor clothing line, hand-made shirts and, since winter 1997, a capsule collection of women's clothing, which reflects the same classical elegance as its menswear.

Kiton
Ciro Paone Spa, viale delle Industrie, 80022 Arzano, Naples, Italy
Tel: +39-081-573 3175   Fax: +39-081-573 5968

KNIZE

Apart from the introduction of some hand-picked ready-to-wear collections, little seems to have changed at this wonderfully traditional shop since it opened in 1858 – attracting royalty and stars, from the Shah of Iran to Marlene Dietrich in the intervening years. The manners of the staff are as courtly as they were in the days of the Austrian Empire and the clientele is as 'establishment' as ever – appreciating the superb quality of Knize's made-to-measure clothing and its timelessly elegant style.

Knize & Co.

Graben 13, A-1010 Vienna, Austria

Tel: +43-1-512 2119   Fax: +43-1-512 2199

KPM

After more than two centuries this celebrated porcelain manufactory shape and paint every piece that it produces – whether traditional or contemporary in style – by hand. So captivated was Frederick the Great of Prussia by this 'white gold' that he gave the company its name and symbol – the royal blue sceptre – in 1763. Delicately moulded and adorned with cherubs, KPM's signature 'Rocaille' service, regarded as one of the most important created in the Rococo period, is available today in 10 designs, including its original floral pattern.

KPM - Königliche Porzellan Manufaktur

Wegelystrasse 1, D-10623 Berlin, Germany

Tel: +49-30-39 00 92 15   Fax: +49-30-391 9034

KRAEMER & CIE

From its base in an elegant townhouse, this family-run business (now into its fifth generation) recently opened a major extension to provide more space for the museum-quality furniture and *objets d'art* that are its forte. Only the choicest 17th- and 18th-century pieces are on display and the Kraemers provide a depth of knowledge that is almost unmatched in Paris, making their gallery a magnet for connoisseurs, curators and celebrities alike.

Kraemer & Cie

43 rue Monceau, 75008 Paris, France

Tel: +33-1-45 63 24 46   Fax: +33-1-45 63 54 36

KRONENHALLE

"If it isn't broken, don't fix it" could be Kronenhalle's motto. Its founder, Hulda Zumsteg, was a legend, Igor Stravinsky was a client, Placido Domingo a more recent one and James Joyce practically lived at this restaurant for eight years. Its simple and unchanging format – unpretentious classical cooking served up in club-like surroundings with great dollops of warm hospitality – remains as popular today with artists and film directors as it is with the grandees of Zürich.

Kronenhalle

Rämistrasse 4, CH-8001 Zürich, Switzerland

Tel: +41-1-251 0256   Fax: +41-1-251 6681

Délicieuse sérénité.

KRUG

Its elegant swan-neck bottle marks Krug out as a champagne of rare style. There is nothing flashy about it; the flavour is complex, rich and marvellously satisfying. The vintages are majestic, seemingly ageless expressions of a perfectionist ideal that is rare in the world today. In the past year ownership of Krug has passed from Rémy-Cointreau to LVMH but the family still remains firmly at the helm.

Krug

5 rue Coquebert, 51100 Reims, France

Tel: +33-3-26 84 44 20   Fax: +33-3-26 84 44 49

KUNSTSTUBEN

Since opening this jewel of a restaurant on the shore of Lake Zürich in 1982, Hamburg-born Horst Petermann has become recognised as a giant among Europe's chefs. His extravagantly flavoured cooking – classically-based and lightened with a hint of the Mediterranean – has won him countless accolades and a clientele whose combined fortunes could buy and sell any bank in Zürich. Yet, reflecting Iris Petermann's unique brand of relaxed sophistication, the intimate room (and, in summer, the lovely garden) is filled with warmth and laughter, rather than the *sotto voce* pretentiousness that is, too often, associated with such exalted establishments.

Kunststuben

Seestrasse 160, CH-8700 Küsnacht, Switzerland

Tel: +41-1-910 0715   Fax: +41-1-910 0495

LA PERLA

In 1999 this luxury lingerie house opened its 22nd shop, this one in London's Knightsbridge. Its chairman, Alberto Masotti, has turned the business founded by his mother, Ada Masotti, in the 1950s into a world leader, in the process redefining glamorous underwear as an integral part of fashion. More recently – aided by his wife, Olga, the chief designer – he has overseen its expansion into swimwear, pret-à-porter and couture, all of which echo the house's signature body-conscious styling.

La Perla

via Montenapoleone 1, 20121 Milan, Italy

Tel: +39-02-76 00 04 60   Fax: +39-02-76 00 24 73

LADUREE

This renowned pâtisserie may have a new address but it still serves its old favourites, from *croissants fourrés*, to scrumptious ice creams, *tarte tartin* and teatime macaroons. Open every day from 8am until 1.30 the following morning, the snug Napoleon III-styled salons also serve light, *terroir*-inspired cuisine at lunch and dinner. Regulars are delighted that they can now purchase Ladurée's own-label range of coffees, teas, jams and dessert wines to take home.

Ladurée

75 avenue des Champs-Elysées, 75008 Paris, France

Tel: +33-1-42 60 21 79

LAFITE-ROTHSCHILD, CHATEAU

More delicate than some of its Pauillac neighbours, Château Lafite is characterised by a delicious perfume and supple flavour, rather than robust power. But this wine's structure renders it capable of ageing and improving for decades. Splendid, circular-shaped cellars were opened in 1987 and thousands of bottles of older vintages are re-corked every 25 years. Grab the 1945 if you get the chance.

Château Lafite-Rothschild

33250 Pauillac, France

Tel: +33-5-56 73 18 18   Fax: +33-5-56 59 26 83

LAGERFELD GALLERY

Taste-maker Karl Lagerfeld's eponymous gallery, designed by Andrée Putman, showcases all his varied interests. Though best known as a fashion designer, Lagerfeld is also an art collector, a quadrilingual bibliophile and a serious photographer. This store-cum-exhibition space, which opened in 1998, displays books and works by various artists (including photographs by Lagerfeld himself) and, downstairs, the designer's own-label clothing line for men and women reflects Lagerfeld's genius for sharp cutting.

Lagerfeld Gallery
40 rue de Seine, 70075 Paris, France
Tel: +33-1-55 42 75 50   Fax: +33-1-40 46 05 95

LAGUIOLE

A Laguiole knife is a perfect marriage of form, function and superb craftsmanship. Jean-Pierre Mijoule is the guardian of a tradition which has been handed down from the Auvergne shepherds who first made these knives, each one of which involves at least 109 stages in its production. The blades are perfectly balanced and the beautifully sculpted handles are made of horn or wood, including rose and olive. Mijoule's son, Benoît, recently opened his own shop in the village, selling hand-crafted horn items.

La Maison du Laguiole
2 Place de la Patte d'Oie, 12210 Laguiole, France
Tel: +33-5-65 48 44 22   Fax: +33-5-65 44 35 59

LAGAVULIN

The name, meaning 'the hollow where the mill is', sounds innocuous enough; however, the contents of the bottle are anything but. Unquestionably a big boy among malt whiskies, Lagavulin 16 year-old is a great mouth-filling drink from the Island of Islay. The rich peatiness in every drop and distinctively sturdy aroma adds to its already evident depth. The result is a whisky of great complexity, full bodied and satisfying.

Lagavulin
United Distillers, Kingsley House
1A Wimpole Street, London WIM 9AG, UK
Tel: +44-20-79 27 53 00   Fax: +44-20-79 27 46 00

THE LADY APSLEY SCHOOL FOR BUTLERS & BUTLER AGENCY

"Having come into contact with so many poorly-trained butlers, I became convinced that there was a need for a first-class training facility," explains Lady Apsley. Her instincts have been proved right and, two years after opening, the school's graduates — some 30 per year — are in tremendous demand.

After a rigorous entrance procedure, students are trained not only in the traditional requirement of anticipating and meeting their employers' needs with discretion and exactitude but also in such modern requirements as computer literacy and administrative skills. The course is led by Robert Watson, the former Head Butler at the Lanesborough Hotel in London, who prepares the students for not only private butlering, but also corporate and hospitality.

The school also provides an agency service for households seeking full-time staff, as well as temporary butlers for both short-term engagements and one-off events.

The Lady Apsley School for Butlers & Butler Agency
Bathurst Estate Office, Cirencester Park, Cirencester
Gloucestershire GL7 2BT, UK
Tel: +44-1285-88 52 83   Fax: +44-1285-65 62 91

LAHUMIERE, GALERIE

Anne Lahumière has worked with French artists all her life, becoming President of the Comité des Galeries d'Art in 1993. Her gallery, which she describes as a "temple for abstract art", was set up in 1963 and specialises in contemporary works. Lahumière continues to look for new talent and has recently represented Bezie, Dubreuil and Gasquet.

Galerie Lahumière
17 rue du Parc Royal, 75003 Paris, France
Tel: +33-1-42 77 27 74   Fax: +33-1-42 77 27 78

LALIQUE

Lalique continues to produce eminently collectible crystalware informed by a strong artistic sensibility which — like period Lalique, has every chance of increasing in value. More recently, the company has successfully expanded into accessories — a return to René Lalique's origins. The 'Interface' collection introduces a line of stylish handbags and travel bags, while the recent 'Lily of the Valley' jewellery line is delicate, fresh and fashionable. Lalique's recent private commissions include several wall panels for Danielle Steele and Tom Perkins' new motor yacht.

Lalique
11 rue Royale, 75008 Paris, France
Tel: +33-1-53 05 12 12   Fax: +33-1-42 65 59 06

LAMELOISE

Set in a 15th-century house on the village square, this charming restaurant is a shrine to classical Burgundy cuisine. Jacques Lameloise's cooking is a subtle evolution from that of his father, whom he followed into the kitchens. His *Pigeonneau rôti à l'émiettée de truffes* and *Rognons au cassis* may be simple but they are simply perfect. Nicole Lameloise is a gracious hostess and her staff has been here almost for ever. The wine list is nothing less than a homage to the greatness of Burgundy.

Lameloise
36 place d'Armes, 71150 Chagny, France
Tel: +33-3-85 87 08 85   Fax: +33-3-85 87 03 57

LANDHAUS SCHERRER

The late Armin Scherrer would be proud to see how his widow, Emmi (Gault Millau's Gastronomic Personality of the Year in 1997) has maintained the standards he set. In an inspired move, she made Heinz Wehmann her chef and business partner and for 18 years they have maintained its status as a gastronomic landmark, reinventing classical North German cooking and winning two Michelin stars in the process. The restaurant's formal style is entirely in keeping with the city's Hanseatic gravitas.

Landhaus Scherrer
Elbchaussee 130
D-22763 Hamburg, Germany
Tel: +49-40-880 1325   Fax: +49-40-880 6260

LALAOUNIS

This renowned Greek jewellery is now in its fifth generation as a family business, with Ilias Lalaounis' four daughters, Katerini, Demetra, Maria and Joanna, at the helm of what has become a major international company.

Every one of Lalaounis' distinctive 22 and 18 carat gold pieces – often studded with diamonds, pearls or cabochon stones – has a soul and story in its symbolism. Many of the house's 45 collections are based on and inspired by the ancient Minoan, Mycenacan, Byzantine and Hellenistic civilisations; the sculptural nature of Lalaounis' jewellery is further emphasised in a series of *avant garde* models based on science and technology and other themes are drawn from nature. In addition the house is gaining increasing recognition for its fine gift items, notably picture frames, bowls and desk accessories in hand-beaten silver, and delicately wrought *objets* in silver gilt and rock crystal, which represent the wild flowers of Greece.

Ilias Lalaounis has been credited with a renaissance of Greece's artistic jewellery tradition,

reviving the ancient goldsmith's techniques of *repoussé*, granulation, gold hammering and hand-weaving – the majority of which are undertaken in the firm's Athens workshops. Some 3000 examples of the company's work are on view to the public at the Lalaounis Museum at the foot of the Acropolis.

Ilias Lalaounis
6 Panepistimiou Avenue
10671 Athens, Greece
Tel: +30-1-361 1371   Fax: +30-1-364 4978

LANCASTER, HOTEL

Unless you stay in this wonderfully intimate hotel, you cannot book a table in its restaurant – or its more recently opened Café Bar, which opens onto the lovely courtyard garden. Why? Its owner, Grace Leo Andrieu, sees The Lancaster as "a club for our guests". When she restored the hotel in 1996, Andrieu personally oversaw every detail of the works, combining the antiques collected by original owner, Emile Wolf, with carefully chosen work by contemporary artisans. The result is a haven for those who prefer quality over ostentation, immaculate taste over fashion.

Hôtel Lancaster
7 rue de Berri, Champs Elysées, 75008 Paris, France
Tel: +33-1-40 76 40 76   Fax: +33-1-40 76 40 00

~

LATOUR, CHATEAU

Not for this giant of the Médoc the easy charms of soft fruit and mild tannins; Latour produces the quintessence of claret – stern and demanding, foursquare and powerful. It needs cellaring for years. When it is finally ready it will give ample justification for the host of superlatives that it has attracted over the years. The fabled 1961 is just about ready to drink now.

Château Latour
33250 Pauillac, France
Tel: +33-5-56 73 19 80   Fax: +33-5-56 33 19 81

LAUDA EXECUTIVE DIVISION

His regular chartering of private aircraft during his Formula One days has, no doubt, been an asset to motor racing legend Niki Lauda, for he understands perfectly the demands and concerns of clients with a similar lifestyle – most particularly flexibility, reliability, safety and discretion. Having established his eponymous airline in 1979, Lauda set up this executive division in 1994, with a fleet comprising a 7-passenger Learjet 60 and an 18-passenger Challenger 601. Services are both wide-ranging and personalised; clients can book short-haul journeys at short notice and can obtain information and make reservations 24 hours a day. Lauda's assertion that "only when you have a feel for the smallest details can you achieve really perfect results" sums up the basis of the company's success.

Lauda Executive Division
P.O.Box 56, 1st Floor, World Trade Centre
A-1300 Vienna Airport, Austria
Tel: +43-1-70 00 77 10   Fax: +43-1-700 057 710
Email: Executive@laudaair.com
Website: www.laudaair.com/e/executive

THE LANESBOROUGH

Built in 1828 and named after a country house that once stood on the site, The Lanesborough, Rosewood Hotels & Resorts' first European property, can justifiably claim its place as one of London's finest hotels. For its fortunate guests, the hotel – a perfectly-restored, stucco-fronted building – is more of a grand private club, with none of the impersonality of many luxury hotels. The service, under the inspired direction of Geoffrey Gelardi, is notably gracious; staff members all know their guests by name and every one of the hotel's 49 rooms and 46 suites have a complimentary butler service, 24 hours a day.

The Lanesborough's elegant public rooms include a fabulously ornate Conservatory restaurant, where the cooking is a perfect match for its casually refined ambience, a peaceful drawing room

and The Library Bar, which has become one of London's most discreetly fashionable watering-holes. As well as its exceptional range of cigars and vintage cognacs it serves one of the best dry martinis in town.

In addition there are five private dining rooms and - essential these days, of course, a state-of-the-art fitness studio. Every room is decorated individually, in a sumptuous rendition of classical English style but The Lanesborough's *pièce de résistance* is the Royal Suite, commanding superb views over the grounds of Buckingham Palace and with its own chauffeured Bentley on call.

The Lanesborough
Hyde Park Corner, London SW1X 7TA, UK
Tel: +44-20-72 59 55 99   Fax: +44-20-72 59 56 06

A. LANGE & SOHNE

Walter Lange, great grandson of the founder of this distinguished watchmaker, has revived the company's fortunes since German reunification in 1990. Such is the cult status of its watches – distinguished by retro-styled faces with an oversized double date – that there is even a Lange Owners' Club. Lange's 'Arkade' model is one of the world's few ladies' watches to house a fine mechanical movement and its new calibre watch, the L951 'Der Chronograph' – the first new chronograph to be designed for 20 years – was a hit at the 1999 Basel Fair.

A. Lange & Söhne
Altenberger Strasse 15
D-01768 Glashütte, Germany
Tel: +49-35053-48 541   Fax: +49-35053-48 544

LE COUP / GERHARD MEIR

This star hairdresser's elegance, wit and refreshingly unpretentious approach mean that, as well as becoming the confidant of Princess Gloria von Thurn und Taxis and Claudia Schiffer, he is invited to make regular television appearances. Meir opened his first salon, in Munich, in 1985 after learning his craft in London, Paris, Milan and New York. He has since added salons in Berlin and Hamburg and brought out a line of beauty products in 1992.

Le Coup / Gerhard Meir
Theatinerstrasse 23, D-80333 Munich, Germany
Tel: +49-89-22 23 27   Fax: +49-89-22 71 15

LE CACHEMIRIEN

It may seem unusual to combine an Italian sense of fashion with the Kashmiri weaving tradition but it's a formula that designer Rosenda Arcioni Meer, has turned into magic. Meer's deep involvement in preserving and developing this ancient tradition started with a wedding present she received when she married

Kashmir born Jan Meer 11 years ago. Produced by Kahmir's most skilled artisans, her pashminas are outstanding for their softness and lightness, exquisite embroideries and wonderful colours.

Le Cachemirien
12 rue de l'Echaudé, 75006 Paris, France
Tel: +33-1-43 29 93 82   Fax: +33-1-43 29 93 60

LEFEVRE GALLERY

This distinguished gallery was formed when Alex Reid – a friend of Vincent van Gogh – joined forces with Ernest Lefevre in 1926. Today, run by Martin Summers and Desmond Corcoran, it maintains the reputation for exhibiting fine Impressionist works which attracted such collectors as Walter Annenberg and Stavros Niarchos. A first floor gallery is dedicated to post-war British and contemporary works, underlining the gallery's eye for the new; in the past it hosted the first London showings of such artists as Dégas (1928), Modigliani (1929), Lucien Freud (1946) and Balthus (1952).

The Lefevre Gallery
30 Bruton Street, London W1X 8JD, UK
Tel: +44-20-74 93 21 07   Fax: +44-20-74 99 90 88

DOMAINE LEFLAIVE

An already high reputation has soared in the 1990s as this estate switched over to biodynamic cultivation under the direction of its châtelaine, Anne-Claude Leflaive. The results are impressive, especially the minuscule quantity (about 280 bottles per annum) of Montrachet. The wines age beautifully but, if you cannot resist them in youth, try decanting them to allow the ravishing array of flavours to open up.

Domaine Leflaive
Place des Marronniers
21190 Puligny-Montrachet, France
Tel: +33-3-80 21 30 13   Fax: +33-3-80 21 39 57

LEMAIRE

Established in 1896, this is the most august cigar merchant in Paris and a magnet for celebrity clients — especially Havana-starved Americans. Cigar aficionado Guy Pihan bought Lemaire in the mid-1990s and brought it right up to date, recently installing a state-of-the-art walk-in humidor on the ground floor, which is linked to both the cave below (built during the 1950s, its stock would do even Fidel Castro proud) and the shop windows.

Lemaire
59 avenue Victor Hugo, 75116 Paris, France
Tel: +33-1-45 00 75 63   Fax: +33-1-45 01 70 65

LENOTRE

Lenôtre's classical French cuisine stars at many of the smartest parties in Paris and its *traiteur-pâtisserie* shops are found in its chicest quartiers. The company now runs three highly-regarded restaurants in the city —

Le Pré Catelan, Le Pavillon Elysée and the newly-opened Le Panoramique, overlooking the Stade de France. Lenôtre is currently running more than 30 gourmet boutiques worldwide — all a far cry from the small pâtisserie which Gaston Lenôtre opened near Deauville in 1947.

Lenôtre
44 rue d'Auteuil, 75016 Paris, France
Tel: +33-1-45 24 52 52   Fax: +33-1-42 30 79 45

LEOVILLE-LAS-CASES, CHATEAU

This wine is restrained, even austere, in youth and can take decades to reach full maturity. Then, having shed its tannic harshness, it will shine like the true jewel that it is. You can expect power and complexity in the flavour and tremendous length on the palate. Enjoy it with simple food, letting the wine take centre stage.

Château Léoville-Las Cases
33250 St-Julien-Beycheville, France
Tel: +33-5-56 72 25 26   Fax: +33-5-56 59 18 33

LAVEZZARI, DR. EMILIO

This multi-skilled cosmetic surgeon originally qualified in medicine at the University of Pavia. A trained dermatologist, Dr. Lavezzari also counts hair transplants as a major part of his work. Within his elegant Milan and Lugano clinics, he can perform complex hair transplants in two to three hours, at no pain to the patient. Any post-operative qualms are quickly soothed by his experienced, gentle 'bedside manner'; his charm and urbanity are considerable. Clients interested in undergoing any treatment can send photographs of themselves by Email - or even link via an audio-visual conference. This state-of-the-art system places Dr. Lavezzari at the forefront of advanced communication between specialist and patient.

He also uses high-definition images to study the key points of the face in the initial stages of skin enhancement, lip augmentation and a host of other treatments. A painstaking identification of the desired corrections is then made, followed by the under-skin insertion of collagen implants or other relevant treatment. Patients can even have this treatment in the morning and wear their 'new' look that same evening. The fact that so many of his patients are repeat clients is powerful testimony to Dr. Lavezzari's ability.

Dr. Emilio Lavezzari
via Montenapoleone 16, 20121 Milan, Italy
Tel: +39-02-79 69 36   Fax: +39-02-76 01 24 93
Email: info@lavezzari.it

LEROY, DOMAINE

This famous estate is synonymous with the chic and truly formidable Madame Lalou Bize-Leroy, who runs it with a legendary eye for detail. Yields in the vineyard are kept criminally low and, in the cellar, both reds and whites are aged in new oak. The result is wines of enormous concentration and power, built for the long haul, as rare as gold dust and priced accordingly.

Domaine Leroy
rue du Pont Boillot, 21190 Auxey-Duresses, France
Tel: +33-3-80 21 21 10   Fax: +33-3-80 21 63 81

LILIANE SICARD

Since it opened in 1988, Liliane Sicard's boutique has been a treasure-trove of contemporary jewellery. Among those she represents are Poiray, Misani, Delaneau and a host of other leading designers whose work ranges from light-hearted fantasy to serious pieces. In addition, clients' jewellery can be adapted or transformed.

Liliane Sicard
10 quai Général-Guisan, CH-1204 Geneva, Switzerland
Tel: +31-22-311 0055   Fax: +31-22-312 0135

LINLEY FURNITURE

Whether a spectacular one-off bookshelf made to private commission or a simple table from his 'off-the-peg' range, David Linley's furniture is timeless and elegant; inspired by classical architecture, it sits perfectly in both period and contemporary settings. While Linley continues to make special commissions, he further expanded his range of less expensive furniture in 1999, with the

introduction of the 'Metropolitan' collection, offering half-moon tables, scroll benches, pedestals and chairs, as well as chic accessories and a signature home fragrance.

Linley Furniture
60 Pimlico Road, London SW1W 8LP, UK
Tel: +44-20-77 30 73 00   Fax: +44-20-77 30 88 69

LINSLERHOF

Hunting is the leitmotif at this delightful inn, owned by the von Boch family for 800 years. It has a falconry school and state-of-the-art shooting range along with a first-class equestrian centre. 17 new rooms were added in 1999. Guests may take home the estate's own eggs, honey, schnapps and steak from its herd of Angus cattle. Brigitte von Boch, whose skills as both a hostess and a decorator would give Martha Stewart a run for her money, assembled her tips in a glossy book, published in 1999.

Linslerhof
D-66802 Überherrn, Germany
Tel: +49-6836-8070   Fax: +49-6836-80 717

LODEN FREY

Established in 1842 by Johann Georg Frey, this elegant clothing store, overlooking the city's landmark Frauenkirche, is at the hub of the Munich fashion scene. Designers represented on its five floors range from such classics as Burberry's and Bogner to Valentino, Versace and Dolce & Gabbana. Its menswear department features the likes of Brioni, Cerruti and Ermenegildo Zegna and it also stocks a wide range of children's wear.

However, the origin of the company's success is the timeless Lodenmantel, the classic Bavarian coat which takes its name from Loden (woven wool which is specially washed and 'fulled' to make it waterproof). Available in grey, green or brown, and in lighter and heavier versions, it has a universal appeal and a unique reputation because of its comfort and durability. Having received royal patronage as long ago as 1850, when King Maximilian of Bavaria wore one, the coat today has transcended fashion; worn by cosmopolitan bankers and aristocrats alike, it has become an international statement of style as well as a symbol of country life.

Loden Frey's Wallach shop, close to its flagship store, specialises in traditional dress – or *Tracht* – and wonderfully old-fashioned accessories, as well as beautiful hand-painted clothing, tablecloths and bedspreads.

Loden Frey
Maffeistrasse 7-9, D-80333 Munich, Germany
Tel: +49-89-21 03 90   Fax: +49-89-21 03 92 50

LISSON GALLERY

This is arguably London's most influential and exciting showcase for young artists with a higher number of Turner Prize laureates than any other dealer. Established in 1967 by Nicholas Logsdail, the gallery deals mainly in European and American contemporary art with a strong emphasis on new British artists of the 1990s and minimalist work.

Lisson Gallery
52-54 Bell Street & 67 Lisson Street
London NW1 5DA, UK
Tel: +44-20-77 24 27 39   Fax: +44-20-77 24 71 24

LISMORE ESTATE

Set on the River Blackwater, this estate – the Duke of Devonshire's Irish country home – is centred on a magnificent 12th-century castle. However, for sportsmen, the real attraction is the celebrated Careysville salmon fishery nearby, which is also part of the estate. With almost two miles of double bank fishing and average catches of over 550 salmon per season, it offers some of Europe's most glorious fishing. Private parties of up to 12 people can be accommodated in the castle and, for slightly smaller groups, there is a comfortable Georgian house next to the fishery.

Lismore Castle
Fermoy, Co. Cork, Ireland
Tel: +353-58-54 288   Fax: +353-58-54 896

LION D'OR, LE

If you have been to a smart party in Geneva where the cooking and service were exceptional, the chances are that your hostess will have called in Thomas Byrne and Gilles Dupont's catering service. Renowned perfectionists, they insist that everything is of the same standard as you get in their Michelin-starred restaurant. The 'local' for Cologny's élite residents, it is generally regarded as the best in town. Byrne and Dupont focus their gastronomic offerings around seasonal products and Mediterranean flavours.

L'Auberge du Lion D'Or
Place Pierre Gautier 5, CH-1223 Cologny
Geneva, Switzerland
Tel: +41-22-736 4432   Fax: +41-22-786 7462

LOMBARD ODIER

Founded in 1798, Lombard Odier is one of Switzerland's oldest and largest private banks. The Lombard family was involved from the start, while the Odiers joined up in the course of the 19th century. The Alexis Lombard-James Odier team was, from 1850 onwards, a particularly forceful combination, attracting the attention of - among others - Jules Verne (who mentioned the bank as one of the backers of the inter-planetary project described in his novel, From the Earth to the Moon), and it was the idea of these partners that the bank should branch out into financing international ventures. It has been building up expertise in international financial markets ever since.

Having survived some dramatic historic events, the bank is understandably proud that its excellent and distinctive methods have been handed down through the generations regardless of politics. Today the bank prides itself on its combination of tradition and innovation, its experienced, loyal staff and its emphasis on absolute discretion. The eight partners of Lombard Odier stand behind the bank's liabilities to the full extent of their own assets. Its clients - mostly long-standing and drawn from all over the world - can rely on a high standard of bespoke services and there are personal advisers for every customer.

Lombard Odier & Cie
11 rue de la Corraterie, CH-1204 Geneva,
Switzerland
Tel: +41-22-709 2111   Fax: +41-22-709 2897

LOCK & CO.

Having creating the definitive hats for gentlemen since 1676, this is the oldest hatter in the world. The one-guinea silk tricorn was the original bestseller, while the equivalent today is the £110 trilby. The originator of the bowler (first created for the Earl of Leicester's gamekeepers) the company heads into the 21st century with its own web-site and a new ladies' department under the auspices of milliner Sylvia Fletcher.

James Lock & Co.
6 St. James's Street, London SW1A 1EF, UK
Tel: +44-20-79 30 88 74 Fax: +44-20-79 76 19 08

LOEWE

Fired by the rich cultural heritage of Spain, as personified by Velazquez and Balenciaga, Narciso Rodriguez has made an assured start at the house of Loewe. His newest offerings include beautifully cut leather suits and delicious suede dresses, offset by garnet-beaded shell tops and elegant trench coats. Luxurious skins, notably ostrich, python and alligator also feature.

Loewe
54 avenue Montaigne, 75008 Paris, France
Tel: +33-1-44 20 84 24   Fax: +33-1-44 20 84 98

LODEN PLANKL

Founded in 1830, this is Vienna's oldest specialist shop selling top-quality, traditional Austrian clothes. Richard Plankl, a hunter, took over the firm in 1880, and it has been in the same family ever since – a fact reflected in the consistent quality and charmingly old-world service. Today, in addition to the traditional 'Himalaya-loden' for capes and classical hunting coats, the firm has developed 'silk-loden' and 'cashmere-loden', which are wonderfully light and extra-smooth. The store also stocks knitwear, dirndls and Tyrolean accessories.

Loden Plankl
Michaelerplatz 6, A-1010 Vienna, Austria
Tel: +43-1-533 8032   Fax: +43-1-535 4920

G. LORENZI

Straight out of another era, the Lorenzi family's shop - an endearingly quaint anachronism amid its glitzy via Montenapoleone neighbours - has been charming visitors since it opened in 1929, when the grandfather of its present director - a blade grinder from Trentino – arrived in Milan. Its products, likewise – a huge range of scissors, knives, shaving equipment and smokers' accessories, made of wood, horn, leather, copper and brass - need no modern gimmickry to ensure their desirability.

G. Lorenzi
via Montenapoleone 9, 20121 Milan, Italy
Tel: +39-02-76 02 28 48   Fax: +39-02-76 00 33 90

LOCH LOMOND GOLF CLUB

This superb golf club could hardly be in a more beautiful location. Designed by Tom Weiskopf and Jay Morrish and built with no expense spared, the course is the venue for several prestigious tournaments: the Solheim Cup – regarded as the Ryder Cup of the women's game – in October 2000 and the Standard Life Loch Lomond Golf Tournament in the week before the Open Championship 2000. After a round of golf – or, indeed, an afternoon's fishing, members of this private club can relax in its impressively restored Georgian clubhouse.

Loch Lomond Golf Club
Rossdhu House, Luss, by Alexandria
Scotland G83 8NT, UK
Tel: +44-1436-65 55 55 Fax: +44-1436-65 55 00

LORETTA CAPONI

If Lewis Carroll had described the source of Alice in Wonderland's wardrobe, it might well have looked like the splendid frescoed room where Loretta Caponi and her daughter, Lucia, display their ravishing children's clothes. In an adjoining workshop you can glimpse the embroiderers at work, creating the sublime bed-linens, towels, table cloths and ravishing silk lingerie which fill the rest of the store. The staff here receive every client with exquisitely old-fashioned courtesy.

Loretta Caponi
Piazza Antinori 4r, 50123 Florence, Italy
Tel: +39-055-21 36 68   Fax: +39-055-29 31 18

LORO PIANA

The subtle colours and fine quality of Loro Piana's cashmere and *vicuña* scarves and throws – and, more recently, its signature collection of knitwear and fine

tailoring – have made them style icons among the *cognoscenti*.

Already renowned as one of the world's leading manufacturers of cashmere and fine fabrics, the Loro Piana family has been trading in and processing fabrics since in 1812. Today, underlining its philosophy of timeless elegance – so perfectly in tune with today's definition of 'luxury in simplicity' – Loro Piana has begun establishing stores under its own name. Its three-floor flagship, which opened in Milan in autumn 1998, has already been joined by stores in Rome, Florence and Venice (the New York store had opened eight years earlier), with further expansion planned for 2000.

Lanificio Loro Piana
Corso Rolandi 10, 13017 Quarona, Italy
Tel: +39-0163-2011   Fax: +39-0163-43 00 99

LOPEZ DE ARAGON, FELIX

This family business has been the leading dealer in Spanish antiques for over 30 years. López was first inspired by his father's collection of medieval art and is now working with his own sons, Gonzalo and Diego. He has sold works to Spain's great art centres, including the Prado and the National Archaeological Museum.

Félix López de Aragón
Jorge Juan 9, E-28001 Madrid, Spain
Tel & Fax: +34-91-576 0012

LOUIS ROEDERER

First made for the Tsars of Russia, Roederer's famed Cristal is one of the greatest of all champagnes. For the millennium a special bottling of Cristal has been made. 2,000 Methuselahs (equivalent to eight bottles each) have been produced from the 1990 vintage, in a blend with more chardonnay than the standard bottlings. Surely the finest cork you could pop when the big night comes. Failing that, try the Cristal Rosé 1989.

Louis Roederer
21 boulevard Lundy, 51100 Reims, France
Tel: +33-3-26 40 42 11   Fax: +33-3-26 61 40 35

LOUIS VUITTON

Nothing is ever marked down to sale price in Louis Vuitton's 200-odd stores world-wide. As Artistic Director, Marc Jacobs has successfully spear-headed the company's expansion into ready-to-wear and shoes, although these sectors are believed to represent a very small percentage of overall sales. Classic accessories are still the company's backbone and newer best-sellers include the trophy 'Pegasus' carry-on bag and the 'Monogram' range of dog accessories.

Louis Vuitton
101 avenue Champs Elysées, 75008 Paris, France
Tel: +33-1-45 62 47 00   Fax: +33-1-45 62 90 43

LOUIS BENECH

Having begun his career as a gardener in England, Louis Benech has become one of France's foremost landscape designers, credited with redefining the formal French garden. Whether set against the backdrop of a rustic manoir or a grand château,

Benech's gardens are traditional yet deeply romantic. His painterly approach to the handling of plant colour and texture creates wonderful floral and foliage contrasts within a structured landscape. Among Benech's public commissions, his mid-1990s restoration of Paris' Jardin des Tuileries is considered to be a benchmark of excellence.

Louis Benech
175 avenue Victor Hugo, 75116 Paris, France
Tel: +33-1-44 05 00 21   Fax: +33-1-44 05 95 65

LOUIS XV, LE

A meal in the awesome, gilded room or on the terrace of Le Louis XV is pure theatre. Each guest uses no less than 50 pieces of the service-silverware, glasses and plates – and, between the main course and dessert, the entire table, from candles to napkin rings, is redecorated. Ably assisted by Franck Cerruti, Alain Ducasse produces a subtly Mediterranean menu that fully justifies his demi-god status.

Le Louis XV
Hôtel de Paris, MC 98000 Monaco
Tel: +377-92 16 30 01   Fax: +377-92 16 69 21

LOUISENLUND

This excellent girls' boarding-school in northern Germany combines tradition with progressive ideas. Established in 1949, it owes its creation to Duke Friedrich of Schleswig-Holstein, who was inspired by the ideas of Professor Kurt Hahn, founder of Salem College and Gordonstoun. Headmaster Henning Kraack encourages education of the whole person – independent thinking, social skills and sports – as well as academic excellence. Bilingual instruction is offered from the fifth grade onwards and the school attracts a cosmopolitan mix of students.

Stiftung Louisenlund
D-24354 Güby, Germany
Tel: +49-4354-9990   Fax: +49-4354-99 97 83

LUCIANO BARBERA

"I really consider the fabric to be the root of my clothing," says Luciano Barbera. This is especially fitting, since he is the son of Carlo Barbera, whose eponymous fabric mill, one of Italy's finest, produces all of the fabrics for the collection. The menswear line, launched in 1971, is designed in the Milanese manner with an English twist – understated and luxurious, with narrow, softly padded shoulders and a gently tapered waistline. Barbera's women's line, introduced in 1989, is informed by the same classical elegance

Luciano Barbera Showroom
via Montenapoleone 19, 20121 Milan, Italy
Tel: +39-02-76 00 55 14   Fax: +39-02-76 03 21 17

LUCIEN PELLAT-FINET

The advent of his own boutiques in Paris and, most recently, London and New York assures cashmere king Lucien Pellat-Finet of a high profile - denied him in the days when his office was also his apartment. His deluxe men's and women's collections reflect Pellat-Finet's distinctive sense of colour and cut, while his new children's line is delighting society mothers.

Lucien Pellat-Finet
1 rue de Montalembert, 75007 Paris, France
Tel: +33-1-42 22 22 77   Fax: +33-1-44 22 86 86

LUCKNAM PARK

A mile-long avenue of beech trees leads up to this beautiful Palladian-style mansion. Built as a family home in 1720 and set in 500 acres of parkland, it opened as a hotel in 1989. Since then it has been showered with praise – notably for its award-winning spa and for Paul Collins' cooking. Far from resting on its laurels, though, it was refurbished throughout during 1999. The recent appointment of Claire Randall as General Manager has added a warm femininity to the already excellent service.

Lucknam Park
Colerne, Wiltshire SN14 8AZ, UK
Tel: +44-1225-74 27 77   Fax: +44-1225-74 35 36

LOUISE KENNEDY

"Women today have complex enough lives without having to worry about how they dress," asserts Louise Kennedy, "I hope my clothes make things easier for them". Her admirers would certainly agree; Kennedy has dressed numerous women in public life, notably Irish Presidents Mary McAleese and Mary Robinson, as well as Tony Blair's wife Cherie. She has designed uniforms for Aer Lingus and the Ulster Bank and has pride of place in Ireland's premier department store, Brown Thomas.

Her stylish suits and fluid evening wear are beautifully showcased at her headquarters – a lovely 18th-century house in Merrion Square – which have been transformed into a lifestyle retail salon. Here, Kennedy's distinctive ready-to-wear and accessories collections are displayed alongside Philip Treacy's hats, Lulu Guinness' bags and decorative items by David Linley. The designer's 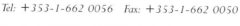 winter 1999 collection – entitled 'Pure Indulgence' – emphasises knitwear over tailoring, features full-length shearling coats and introduces an exquisite new line of hand-beaded evening dresses.

A further exciting development for Kennedy is her collaboration with Tipperary Crystal to produce a collection of modern tableware bearing her unique signature. Three distinct and individualistic designs have been produced – 'Earth Star', 'Sea Aster' and 'Spindle Tree'; each comprises elegant variations on stemware, jugs, bowls, vases and candlesticks.

Louise Kennedy
56 Merrion Square, Dublin 2, Ireland
Tel: +353-1-662 0056   Fax: +353-1-662 0050

LUIGI BORRELLI

"The perfect gentleman is the one who is neither doubtful nor hasty in taking decisions". This, one of Luigi Borrelli's favourite maxims, can be seen to characterise the discriminating international clients who choose his fluid, beautifully-cut and entirely hand-stitched bespoke shirts. Following the rich tradition of Neapolitan shirtmaking, Borrelli attributes his expertise to his mother, Anna; his son, Fabio, now at the helm of the company, continues the line.

Luigi Borrelli
Largo S. Orsola a Chiaia 3bis, 80040 Naples, Italy
Tel: +39-081-41 00 70   Fax: +39-081-93 95 77
Email: anto@luigiborrelli.com

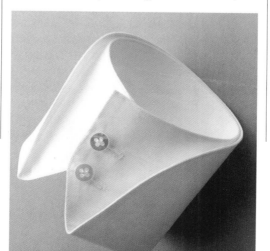

PHOTOGRAPH SNOWDON

Maria Lalaounis is wearing a necklace and earclips in 22 carat hand-hammered gold.
The necklace is inspired by jewellery found in the ruins of Troy from the 3rd Millennium b.c
and the earclips are inspired by pre-Columbian art.

ilias LALAoUNIS

5 SLOANE STREET, LONDON, SW1X 9LA.
TEL: (0171) 235 9253   FAX (0171) 235 9257

ATHENS • PARIS • NEW YORK • GENEVA • ZURICH • TOKYO • HONG KONG • CORFU • MYCONOS • RHODES

LUIGI BOCCHI

Located in one of Rome's smartest areas, this flower shop is filled with all manner of exquisite creations. Luigi Bocchi, who took over the management of the shop from his father in 1967, has a remarkable talent for presentation. His shop is built to his own ultra-modern design, with imaginative, daring lighting and a central, indoor fountain. Bocchi's architectural sense extends to his floral work, where his love of exotic flowers is married to a strong commitment to quality and careful planning. Bocchi's courteous and attentive treatment of his clients place him in much

demand for weddings and elegant social events.
Luigi Bocchi
Corso Vittorio Emanuele 136, 00186 Rome, Italy
Tel: +39-06-68 89 09 31 Fax: +39-06-68 89 25 69

LUIS ALEGRIA

The eclectic collection of *objets d'art* and antiques in the Porto gallery of this respected dealer ranges from medieval English religious carvings to 19th-century Dutch pistol sets. There are also perfect examples of 18th-century Portuguese ceramics, with a more exotic element represented by the fine selection of Chinese porcelain. Refined and soft-spoken, Alegria has an international presence, most notably with his regular appearances at the annual Grosvenor House Art & Antiques Fair.
Luís Alegria
Avenue Dr. Antunes Guimaraes 142
4100 Porto, Portugal
Tel: +351-2-610 2124 Fax: +351-2-610 5446

LUIS ELVIRA

Combining experience and erudition, this art dealer has built up a first-class international reputation. His gallery, on the slopes near Oropesa Castle, offers

fine works from the Medieval, Romanesque and Gothic periods. As well as exhibiting at important art fairs, Luis Elvira has edited a number of monographs on art. He also plays an active role in his local cultural life, participating in a project to turn Oropesa into a museum. In autumn 1999, Luis Elvira opened a new gallery to show his magnificent collection of *rejas* (forged iron window grates).
Luis Elvira
Ramón y Cajal 1, E-12594 Oropesa del Mar
Castellón, Spain
Tel: +34-964-31 07 51 Fax: +34-964-31 20 91

LUISING MANOR

Thanks to its rich variety of sport —moufflon and wild boar hunting, fallow and red deer stalking, partridge, pheasant and duck shooting) and its wonderful setting, two hours' drive from Vienna, this sporting estate is virtually unique in Europe. Owned by Count Menzdorf-Pouilly, it offers first class hospitality (with mini-banquets laid on every night by the exceptional staff) in the family's elegant shooting lodge. Remarkably, for all this you don't need unduly deep pockets.
Luising Manor
A-7522 Luising, Austria
Tel: +43-33-24 73 66 Fax: +43-33-24 61 87

LURSSEN

With credits ranging from the 72.5m Jon Bannenberg-designed *Coral Island* to the classic 31-metre sailing yacht, *Aschanti IV*, which Lürssen completely rebuilt — and in late 1999 the world's largest-ever private motor yacht at 130 metres — this shipyard's reputation for technological expertise and fine craftsmanship goes from strength to strength. More than just a constructor, though, this fourth-generation family-owned company (run today by Friedrich and Peter Lürssen) also offers design and engineering services, logistical support and first-class crew training.
Lürssen Yachts
Friedrich-Klippert-Strasse 1, D-28759 Bremen, Germany
Tel: +49-421-660 4166 Fax: +49-421-660 4170

LYNTON AVIATION

One of the most dynamic players in the international corporate aviation industry, Lynton Aviation (formerly Lynton Group, Inc) is a fully-integrated business, offering aircraft sales, charter and management, engineering services and FBO (Fixed Base Operator) services. Its charter and management division offers an impressive selection of aircraft for charter, from bases at Luton and London City airports in the UK and the Morristown Municipal Airport near New York.
Lynton Aviation
Denholm Airport, Hangar Road
Uxbridge, Middlesex UB9 5DF, UK
Tel: +44-1895-83 50 00 Fax: +44-1895-83 25 64

LULU GUINNESS

Known for her trademark flower-basket handbags sported by the likes of the Queen of Greece, the Duchess of York and Viscountess Linley, talented girl-about-town Lulu Guinness is on the up and up. Her second shop has newly opened in Chelsea: as well as stocking an expanding collection of bags, it will have club facilities for customers, a bespoke service and a bridal collection.
Lulu Guinness
66 Ledbury Road, London W11 2AJ, UK
Tel: +44-20-72 21 96 86 Fax: +44-20-72 43 21 67

THE MACALLAN

This renowned single malt whisky producer adheres religiously to traditional methods - some of which have a unique twist. Maturing the whisky in sherry casks from Spain is key and in this respect, The Macallan stands alone among single malts. The company's "Six Pillars of Spiritual Wisdom" also dictate the use of the rare and expensive Golden Promise barley; a unique combination of four yeasts in the fermentation process; small, hand-beaten copper stills rather than larger, more economic versions; the purity of cut taken during distillation; and finally, the deter-

mination that The Macallan should have a pure, natural colour. Available from a 10- to a 30-year-old bottling, this malt achieves a wondrous marriage of dried fruits, spices, toffee and a hint of sherry sweetness.

The Macallan
Highland Distillers plc
West Kinfauns, Perth PH2 7XZ, Scotland, UK
Tel: +44-1738-44 00 00   Fax: +44-1738-63 34 55

GALERIE MAEGHT

This Paris gallery, opened in 1957, remains an important showcase for contemporary art. Its founder, Adrien Maeght, has exhibited most of the 20th century's great names, from Chagall to Giacometti and Miró to Braque and currently hosts around 12 exhibitions a year covering everything from sculpture to photography. Famous works in the permanent collection include Miró's *Nord-Sud*, Braque's *Les Oiseaux Noirs* and Giacometti's *Le Portrait de Marguerite Maeght*

Galerie Maeght
42 rue du Bac, 75008 Paris, France
Tel: +33-1-45 48 45 15   Fax: +33-1-42 22 22 83

MAESTRO DI CASA, IL

For this party organiser, good food (and theirs is superb) is only part of a successful event. Impact means a lot – the company uses some of the most stunning locations in and around Milan and, within them, creates marvellously theatrical effects – and so does detail. Director Melania Sala prides herself on being even more obsessive about the 'small things' than her most finicky clients. With a list that ranges from Calvin Klein and Patek Philippe to several of Milan's grandest families, she's obviously getting it right.

Il Maestro di Casa
via Udine 85, 20010 Canegrate, Milan, Italy
Tel: +39-0331-41 13 40   Fax: +39-0331-41 13 41

MAGGIO MUSICALE FIORENTINO

This music festival is not just about opera but also adventurous ballet productions, imaginative set design and a proud tradition of stagecraft. This explains the quality of the artists who have performed here – Callas made her debut and Karajan, Solti and Bernstein have all conducted at the festival; Nureyev and Baryshnikov have graced the stage and audiences have enjoyed the talents of such artist-directors as Visconti and Zeffirelli. *Pelléas et Mélisande* and *Giselle* were among the works performed in the 1999 programme.

Maggio Musicale Fiorentino
Teatro Comunale, Corso Italia 16, 50123 Florence, Italy
Tel: +39-055-21 11 58   Fax: +39-055-277 9410

MAGGS BROS

To visit this antiquarian bookseller is to take a trip into the past – not least because John Maggs, the charming fourth-generation head of the family firm, would prefer to sit down over a pot of tea and inspire you, rather than merely sell you a book. The five floors of this Georgian house are stuffed with an amazing assortment of antiquarian books (including a specialist T.E Lawrence section), precious bindings, rare autographs and manuscripts.

Maggs Bros
50 Berkeley Square, London W1X 6EL, UK
Tel: +44-20-74 93 71 60   Fax: +44-20-74 99 20 07

MAISON BLANCHE & GRAND BAIN, HOTEL

The Alpentherme spa is the focal point of this hotel, which – together with its ovely surroundings – may explain why a team of top Eurocrats recently chose to hold important meetings here. Facilities include indoor and outdoor thermal pools, a grotto pool heated to 40°C and a sports pool. There is a formidable team of therapists on hand, from masseurs and dieticians to a rheumatologist and an acupuncturist.

Hôtel Maison Blanche & Grand Bain
Loèche-les-Bains, CH-3954 Leukerbad, Switzerland
Tel: +41-27-470 5161   Fax: +41-27-470 3474

MAISONS DE BRICOURT, LES

Seafood is the star here – naturally enough, as Olivier Roellinger grew up within sight of Cancale's oyster beds – but forget those accompanying clichés of haute cuisine, olive oil and caviar. Roellinger scents his dishes – ever so delicately – with exotic spices which allow the full flavour of the fish to shine; it's all in the name – *Saint Pierre retour des Indes*, for example. His wife, Jane, presides over this lovely restaurant. Set in the 18th-century *malouinière* that was Roellinger's childhood home, it is luminous and peaceful, overlooking a lovely garden where ducks disport themselves in the pond.

Les Maisons de Bricourt
1 rue Duguesclin, 35260 Cancale, France
Tel & Fax: +33-2-99 89 64 76

MALLETT AT BOURDON HOUSE

Founded in 1865, Mallett continues to prosper and innovate. Its Bond Street showroom displays English furniture and paintings from the 18th and 19th centuries while Bourdon House specialises in European art and was re-modelled in 1999 to include a new 'Great Room'. Mallett also shows contemporary art, such as the glass sculpture of Danny Lane.

Mallett
141 New Bond Street, London W1Y OBS, UK
Tel: +44-20-74 99 74 11   Fax: +44-20-74 95 31 79

MALO

That this cashmere company has become such a cult brand is due to two clever strategies. First it got the styling and quality dead right: multi-ply thicknesses for winter, body-hugging little tops for summer and a gorgeous array of colours. Then it opened boutiques in Europe's most sophisticated resorts – Cortina d'Ampezzo, Capri, Portofino, Porto Cervo, St. Moritz and Sylt – guaranteeing that girls with time on their hands would come in their droves. Obvious, really, isn't it.

Malo

Corso Monforte 30, 20122 Milan, Italy

Tel: +39-02-76 00 83 83   Fax: +39-02-76 01 32 42

MANGANI

This producer of fine hand-made porcelain (mostly inspired by 18th-century designs) has a long family tradition: the Manganis had a sculpture workshop in Florence in the early 19th century. Their products appealed to a small market of local connoisseurs until a director from Tiffany's spotted one of Mangani's exquisite coffee cups, found its maker and ordered over 1000 pieces. Now the company employs more than 50 artisans and has added contemporary designs to its signature range.

Mangani

via Pietro Arentino 20, 50040 Settinello, Florence, Italy

Tel: +39-055-882 5132   Fax: +39-055-887 3258

MANOIR "INTER SCALDES", LE

Kees and Maartje Boudeling have run this Relais & Châteaux retreat since 1968. Set in a beautiful, thatched manor house, the conservatory-style restaurant is filled with light (in summer tables spill out onto the terrace) and overlooks a ravishingly pretty English-style garden. Maartje Boudeling's outstandingly good cooking, for which she has been rewarded with two Michelin stars, is based on the local seafood – notably lobster, oysters and turbot. Sleepy diners have a choice of 12 cosy bedrooms.

Le Manoir "Inter Scaldes"

Zandweg 2, NL-4416 NA Kruiningen Yerseke

The Netherlands

Tel: +31-113-38 17 53   Fax: +31-113-38 17 63

LE MANOIR AUX QUAT'SAISONS

Perfection of the order of Raymond Blanc's Pigeon baked in a salt crust and the beautifully-presented starter of John Dory, red mullet and scallops with marinated vegetables serves as a reminder of the fickleness of the Michelin star system. (Why only two?) The conservatory dining room is airy and relaxed; like the rest of this gorgeous 15th-century Cotswold manor, it has just been skilfully

transformed by designer Emily Todhunter from its old cushions-and-chintz character into a stylish and contemporary country house idiom. Blanc runs excellent cookery courses for those inspired by his magic.

Le Manoir aux Quat'Saisons

Church Road, Great Milton, Oxfordshire OX44 7PD, UK

Tel: +44-1844-27 88 81   Fax: +44-1844-27 88 47

MANOLO BLAHNIK

As Manolo Blahnik celebrates the success of his new Manhattan town-house boutique, increasing numbers of his delicious shoes are being snapped up on both sides of the Atlantic. Iman, Donatella Versace and Aerin Lauder worship the ground he walks on, and fashion designers are also clamouring for Blahnik's services, among them Marc Jacobs and Antonio Berardi, for whom Blahnik created shoes decorated with 18 carat gold.

Manolo Blahnik

49-51 Old Church Street, London SW3 5BS, UK

Tel: +44-20-73 52 38 63   Fax: +44-20-73 51 73 14

MARBELLA CLUB, THE

Established shortly after World War II by Prinz Alfonso Hohenlohe, the Marbella Club was a home from home for the likes of James Stewart and Maria Callas. By the time entrepreneur David Shamoon bought it in 1994, however, both Marbella and the Club had gone rather to seed. Now, after a £6.5 million expansion and redesign by Jean-Pierre Martel, it is an oasis of gardens, colonnaded squares and fountains and its suites, cottages and spacious rooms are attracting a new-generation élite – confirming Marbella's rehabilitation as a chic destination.

The Marbella Club

Marbella, Malaga, Spain

Tel: 34-952-82 22 11   Fax: +34-952-82 98 84

MARESCALCHI, GALLERIA

This gallery, founded in 1973, remains a very important venue for 19th-century and contemporary European art. Its permanent collection reads like a 'Who's Who' of modern masters, with works by Chagall, Kandinsky, Klee, Magritte and Picasso and 20th-century Italian artists Botero, De Chirico and Morandi. Exhibitions in recent years have paid homage to Miró, Guttuso and Casorati.

Galleria Marescalchi

via Mascarella 116/B, 40126 Bologna, Italy

Tel: +39-051-24 03 68   Fax: +39-051-25 13 41

MARGAUX, CHATEAU

For over 20 years now the Mentzelopoulos family has striven to restore Margaux's reputation after an earlier period of decline. There can be no doubt that they have succeeded and the wines being produced now, under the direction of Paul Pontallier, will eventually rival those of such fabled vintages as 1953.

Château Margaux

33460 Margaux, France

Tel: +33-5-57 88 83 83   Fax: +33-5-57 88 31 32

MARIA LUISA

This enclave of three boutiques (women's, men's and accessories) stocks some of the most sought-after names in fashion. With a great instinct for the *zeitgeist* its owner – self-confessed clothes addict Maria Luisa Poumaillou – has, over the last 12 years, introduced numerous emerging talents who have gone on to become major fashion stars. Hot names of which she is currently the sole stockist in Paris include Marc Jacobs, Sarah Dearlove (men's and women's collections from both), Olivier Theyskens, Manolo Blahnik and Lulu Guinness.

Maria Luisa

2 rue Cambon, 75001 Paris, France

Tel: +33-1-47 03 96 15   Fax: +33-1-47 03 94 17

MARIABRUNA BEAUTY WORKSHOP

Widely regarded as the beauty therapist in Italy, Mariabruna Zorzi studied graphic design and psychology before discovering her true vocation. She set up her first studio 20 years ago in Brescia and later moved to a 16th-century former convent, where the treatment rooms are arranged around a cloistered courtyard. Her relaxing and utterly revitalising spa therapies include a sublime steam treatment with aromatic oils and her private-label cosmetics and perfumes have a devoted following among the cognoscenti.

Mariabruna Beauty Workshop

Piazza Vescovato 1/C, 25125 Brescia, Italy

Tel: +39-030-45 194   Fax: +39-030-42 092

MARINA B

Constantine Bulgari's daughter, Marina, developed her training as an engineer into a skill for jewellery design, creating a range of ingeniously versatile pieces and even developing a unique stone cut which bears her name. Although she has now virtually retired from designing, her team continues to innovate, producing the interchangeable semi-precious stones, reversible pieces and stackable designs which had become her

distinctive trademark. These key elements are combined in Marina B's new signature 'Multi Ring'.
Marina B
40 rue de Rhône, CH-1204 Geneva, Switzerland
Tel: +41-22-817 0212   Fax: +41-22-817 0201

MARIO BUCCELLATI

The styles may have changed but the breath-taking artisanship - beloved by poet Gabriele D'Annunzio - which has distinguished Mario Buccellati's jewellery since 1919 remains unchanged. The house's revision of traditional gold and silver-working techniques has led to an extraordinary variety of pieces, the finest of which resemble fabrics such as lace and damask.
Mario Buccellati
via 4, 20121 Milan, Italy
Tel: +39-02-76 00 21 53   Fax: +39-02-78 09 03

MARLBOROUGH FINE ART

A Mark Rothko exhibition shortly after this gallery opened in 1946 put Marlborough's name (and that of its founder, Frank Lloyd) firmly on the map and the gallery has continued to hold ground-breaking exhibitions. Artists it has promoted include Auerbach, Bacon, Chadwick and Freud. Its 1999 exhibition of Stephen Conroy — which achieved 100% sales — and Sarah Raphael continued this tradition, while a major retrospective of Pasmore's work waas also held in 1999.
Marlborough Fine Art
6 Albemarle Street, London W1X 4BY, UK
Tel: +44-20-76 29 51 61   Fax: +44-20-76 29 63 38

MARK'S CLUB

Housed in a discreet Mayfair townhouse, without even the tiniest brass plaque to announce its presence, this is Mark Birley's luxurious and subtly sophisticated alternative to the old-fashioned ambience of the traditional St. James's gentlemen's clubs.

While its quintessential Englishness is reflected in the cooking — the world's finest manifestation of English 'nursery food' — and even the waitresses in their traditional nanny-style uniforms, the level of perfection is decidedly un-English. It is, rather, a precise reflection of Birley's own taste and renowned attention to detail; Landseers from his private collection line the red silk-covered walls and Bugatti bronzes stand on highly polished antique sideboards. While the mellow colours, the richly upholstered sofas and the open fires glowing in the grates do, indeed, convey a sense of the English country house, this is not a 'look' so much as an ambience which has developed organically over the almost 30 years since the club opened its doors.

This island of cosy serenity is a home-from-home for discreet movers and shakers rather than the glossy international set — one over which Bruno, more diplomat than maître d'hôtel, presides with exquisite courtesy.
Mark's Club
46 Charles Street, London W1X 7PB, UK
Tel: +44-20-74 99 29 36

MARLIES MOLLER

In addition to owning Hamburg's smartest salon — where the social élite and visiting celebrities come to receive her expert attention — award-winning hairdresser and make-up artist, Marlies Möller, works for film, television and magazines. The setting of her huge studio — in a former palace — adds to the glamour and Moller's speciality "dry cuts" are equally in demand from both men and women.
Marlies Möller
Tesdorpfstrasser 20, D-20148 Hamburg, Germany
Tel: +49-40-444 0040   Fax: +49-40-45 36 42

MARNI

Madonna and a host of models pay court to Consuela Castiglione, the designer behind Marni. Folkloric chic defines Castiglione's current collection — exceptional detailing, flawless seams, gorgeous colours and the best bohemian fabrics money can buy. The key looks to watch are wrapped, decorated dresses along with hopsack embroidered coats.
Marni
via Sismondi 70
20133 Milan, Italy
Tel: +39-02-74 81 91   Fax: +39-02-70 10 19 77

MARLFIELD HOUSE

Huge log fires in the winter and flowers in the summer form the *leitmotif* of this intimate and ravishingly pretty Relais & Châteaux retreat. Formerly a residence of the Earls of Courtown, it is set on a 36-acre estate with woodlands, a water garden, a wildfowl reserve and outstanding formal gardens. Its owner, Mary Bowe's exquisite taste is reflected in every corner – particularly in the bedrooms, each named after its decorative theme: the Print Room (which opens onto a private patio) has walls decorated in print panels; the Morland is adorned with coloured engravings by the artist; the Sheraton with original antique furniture from the celebrated Regency firm.

The service, led by Mrs. Bowe's charming daughter, Margaret, is impeccable and the Modern Irish cooking – based on vegetables and herbs from the hotel's own gardens – of an equally high standard; Mrs Bowe is renowned for nurturing young talent in the kitchen, with many of her protegés becoming acclaimed chef-proprietors in their own right. Marlfield's peace and tranquillity clearly appeal to celebrities in search of R&R; recent guests include Tom Hanks, Stephen Spielberg and Robert Redford. Two miles from the sea, the hotel is surrounded by enough golf courses to play on a different course every day for two weeks and it also offers fishing, riding and lovely countryside walks.

Marlfield House
Gorey, Co. Wexford, Ireland
Tel: +353-55-21 124   Fax: +353-55-21 572
Email: marlf@iol.ie
Website: www.marlfieldhouse.com

E. MARINELLA

"It is the tiniest of details that make up the elegance of the whole man," declared Don Eugenio Marinella, who founded this company in 1914 with a burning desire to change the way stylish men dressed. His grandson, Maurizio, maintains this philosophy, creating what are, indisputably, the world's finest ties. What is it about this basic wardrobe item that makes such paragons of elegance as Gianni Agnelli, Luca di Montezemolo and Prince Charles go weak at the knees? Marinella's made-to-measure ties (60 percent of its production) are beautifully hand-crafted; each made to the precise length, width and weight desired by the client. Maurizio Marinella designs all of his own fabrics, working closely with English fabric mills, which print myriad colour variations of each pattern – in sufficient quantity to make only four ties from each.
E. Marinella
Riviera di Chiaia 287
80121 Naples, Italy
Tel: +39-081-764 4214   Fax: +39-081-764 3265

MARTIN BERASATEGUI

Berasategui is a hero to aspiring young Spanish chefs. Beginning his career in a tapas bar, he quickly developed his own 'modern Basque' style. He takes risks but succeeds brilliantly – as with his sublime *Millefeuille au caramel d'anguille fumée au foie gras, à l'oignon et à la pomme verte*. Ten years later, Berasategui has two Michelin stars (and is hotly tipped to win a third); his flagship restaurant, in an elegant country house, was made a member of Relais & Châteaux in 1999 and his mini-gastronomic empire includes the restaurant at the Guggenheim Museum.
Martin Berasategui
Loidi 4
E-20160 Lasarte, Spain
Tel: +34-943-66 471   Fax: +34-943-36 61 07

MCKENNA & CO.

In 1983 Catherine MacMillan and Michael McKenna set up this company with the objective of selling exquisite, one-of-a-kind items of vintage jewellery. Despite coming from entirely different professional backgrounds, the couple shared a love of the fine arts, believing that each jewel is a work of art in miniature. As luck would have it they also shared an 'eye' – the ability to alight on something special and single it out for its beauty and investment value. After completing a gemmology course, they spent three years travelling the world seeking out rare and exceptional *bijoux*. Thousands of lovely jewels have since passed through their hands and they have subsequently broadened their reach to include more recent jewellery and contemporary collections.

After outgrowing their first shop, the partners found their present, picturesque location – an oak-panelled, Regency town-house in Knightsbridge. Clients – who range from royalty to media figures – praise the McKennas' discretion, along with their special instinct for matching the right piece with the right client – whether a simple charm bracelet or a high-Victorian, gem-encrusted dragonfly brooch, a simple, modern adornment for a few hundred pounds or a show-stopper for six figures.

McKenna & Co.
28 Beauchamp Place, London SW3 1NJ, UK
Tel: +44-20-75 84 19 66   Fax: +44-20-72 25 28 93
Website: www.mckennajewels.com

MARTIN PIPE

This champion trainer of steeplechasers and 1996 Grand National winner seldom goes through a week without a winner, flying to meetings all over Britain in his helicopter. The Cheltenham Festival is one of his favourite meetings, although his two wins there in 1999 fell well short of his usual record. Among Pipe's current prodigies are *Auetarler*, owned by

Liverpool Football Club, Paul Green's *Hors La Loi*, described by one leading pundit as "a serious goer", and *Lady Cricket*.
Martin Pipe
Pond House, Nicholashayne, Wellington
Somerset TA21 9QY, UK
Tel: +44-1884-84 07 15
Fax: +44-1884-84 13 43

MAS DE TORRENT

Here, the Figueras family has created a sophisticated Relais & Châteaux retreat. The original, 18th-century Catalan farmhouse has been beautifully restored and another wing of suites added, each with its own private garden (there are plans to add private pools to some). The restaurant – decorated with works in homage to Picasso by Spain's leading contemporary artists – opens onto a shaded verandah overlooking the gardens. The food, wine and service are beyond reproach but the real joy is its laid-back elegance.
Mas de Torrent
Afueras de Torrent, E-17123 Girona, Catalonia, Spain
Tel: +34-972-30 32 92   Fax: +34-972-30 32 93

MAURITSHUIS

For an overview of the Golden Age of Dutch painting, there are few better places than this gem of a gallery. Built in 1640 by Van Campen and Post, the two leading architects of their day, this was originally the house of Johan Maurits, Governor-General of Dutch Brazil. It now houses an important collection of Flemish paintings, including striking pieces by Vermeer, Hals, Rembrandt, Rubens and Van Dyck, and also has the honour of holding the Royal Cabinet of Paintings.
Mauritshuis
Koret Vijverberg 8, 2513 AB The Hague, The Netherlands
Tel: +31-70-302 3456   Fax: +31-70-365 3819

MAX HETZLER, GALERIE

Max Hetzler, one of Germany's leading contemporary art dealers, prides himself on the diversity of his gallery, where he represents everything from painting and drawing to photography, sculpture and video art. 1999 saw exhibitions of work by American painter Ellen Gallagher, French furniture designer Jean Prouvé and East German artist Georg Herold.
Galerie Max Hetzler
Zimmerstrasse 89, D-10117 Berlin, Germany
Tel: +49-30-229 2437   Fax: +49-30-229 2417

MENDEL, J.

This fifth-generation furrier was established in St. Petersburg in 1870 by Mendel Breitman, himself the son of a fur trader, and later moved to Moscow, Warsaw, Vienna, Berlin before settling in Paris in 1914. Renowned for the creativity and fine craftsmanship of its *Haute Fourrure* collections (which have won it the Grand Prix de la Création de la Ville de Paris) Mendel also has a genius for transforming boring old classics into fresh and chic new staples.
J. Mendel
396 rue Saint-Honoré, 75001 Paris, France
Tel: +33-1-42 61 76 77   Fax: +33-1-42 60 36 94

MEURICE, LE

A home from home over the years for archdukes and kings, literary lions and great artists, this legendary hotel closed its doors in March 1999 for an ambitious nine-month restoration. The 'new' Meurice is the same – grand, gilded and stuffed with antiques – only better. The décor is still 18th-century but is softer, less overwhelming and a

fabulous Royal Suite with a wraparound terrace has been added on the top floor. The heart of the hotel is the Winter Garden, with its stunning, restored Art Nouveau glass ceiling.

Le Meurice
228 rue de Rivoli, 75001 Paris, France
Tel: +33-1-44 58 10 10   Fax: +33-1-44 58 10 17

MICHAEL STOUTE, SIR

Best known as the trainer for the Aga Khan, Lord Weinstock and members of the Maktoum family, Barbados-born Stoute has been one of the giants of the business for over two decades. His spectacular track record – including two Derby wins, one with the great *Shergar* – was instrumental in persuading Gary Stevens to ride in England in 1999. *Blueprint*, which he trains for The Queen was a hot favourite for the 1999 Melbourne Cup.

Sir Michael Stoute
Freemason Lodge, Bury Road
Newmarket, Suffolk CB8 7BT, UK
Tel: +44-1638-66 38 01   Fax: +44-1638-66 72 76

MERRION, THE

Since opening in the autumn of 1997, Dublin's most beautiful hotel has been showered with accolades, among them 'Best Hotel Room in Dublin' from Fortune magazine, admission to the Leading Hotels of the World consortium after only six months and, in 1999, a Five Star Diamond Award.

Created from four beautifully restored Georgian townhouses and a contemporary wing, enclosing two private 18th-century style gardens, The Merrion is announced only by a tiny brass name-plate. This perfectly sums up the hotel's attitude. It is not the sort of place which thinks that five stars mean gilt, grandeur and obsequious service.

Rather, The Merrion seems designed for relaxation. The Front Hall has no imposing reception desk; it is a beautiful space given over to the perfectly proportioned simplicity of the architecture. You are soothed by the scent of fresh flowers and of smoke from the turf fires which burn in the Drawing Room grates. In the bedrooms – decorated in (authentically Georgian) muted colours – the myriad high-tech accoutrements are discreetly positioned so as hardly to impose on the sense of being in a serene private house. The Tethra Spa (named after the legendary land of the young), with its ozone-filtered pool, is a magical retreat from urban stress.

But there is plenty for sophisticates, too. Patrick Guilbaud's two-Michelin star restaurant is here and The Merrion's lively Cellar Bar has become a Dublin institution.

The Merrion
Upper Merrion Street, Dublin 2, Ireland
Tel: +353-1-603 0600   Fax: +353-1-603 0700

MICHAEL ZINGRAF

Twenty years' experience of handling top-of-the-range properties on the Côte d'Azur have brought German-born Michaël Zingraf a clientele which ranges from British financiers to Michael Schumacher. Quality rather than quantity is his forte. Add to this a solid reputation for integrity and good, old-fashioned Teutonic efficiency and it becomes clear why, even when others have complained of a dip in the market, Zingraf has emerged triumphant.

Michaël Zingraf
34 La Croisette, 06400 Cannes, France
Tel: +33-4-93 39 77 77   Fax: +33-4-93 39 79 45

MICHEELS, DR. PATRICK

Emphasising non-invasive aesthetic treatments for both men and women, Dr. Micheels' expertise ranges from hair transplants and the natural remodelling of lips to laser treatment of facial veins and the treatment of wrinkles. For the latter he uses several methods, including collagen, hyaluronic acid and 'Botox'. Renowned for his discretion and reassuring manner, Dr. Micheels works both in his own office and in a private clinic in the smart residential area of Conches.
Dr. Patrick Micheels
58 rue de la Terrassière, CH-1207 Geneva, Switzerland
Tel: +41-22-735 9116   Fax: +41-22-735 1734

MIDLETON VERY RARE

With its numbered bottles, signed by master distiller Barry Crockett, this is the most exclusive of all Irish whiskeys. An ultra-smooth, premium blend, created by

the Jameson distillery, it caresses the palate rather than exploding onto it in the manner of its more vigorous cousins. It is worth lingering over to discover its full range of subtle flavours – silky at first, followed by a touch of sweetness and finishing with a hint of spice. Distilled three times to ensure its distinctive mellowness, it is carefully aged in hand-picked oak casks. Although a new Vintage is released each year, fewer than 100 casks are selected and then bottled to become what the Irish call *"uisce beatha"* – the water of life.
Midleton Very Rare
Irish Distillers Ltd
Bow Street Distillery, Smithfield, Dublin 7, Ireland
Tel: +353-1-872 5566   Fax: +353-1-872 3109

MICHEL BRAS

Born and bred in the wild Aubrac area, Michel Bras – who received his third Michelin star in 1999 – has a passion for nature, which is reflected in the powerful rusticity of his dishes: *Gargouillou* of vegetables with country herbs and germinated seeds; Kid goat slow-roasted with herbs; a savoury, truffle-infused sorbet. The wine list is excellent and – refreshingly – the sommelier, Sergio, doesn't push you towards the most expensive bottles. The severe architecture of the metal, granite and glass building – perched on a high bluff – reflects the austerity of the landscape.
Michel Bras
Route de l'Aubrac, 12210 Laguiole, France
Tel: +33-5-65 51 18 20   Fax: +33-5-65 48 47 02

MILLE FEUILLES, LES

This delightful shop, established 12 years ago by self-taught florists Philippe Landri and Pierre Brinon is an oasis of calm. The house style is pure *'jardin de curé'*, with masses bunches of old-fashioned flowers – delicately coloured and deliciously scented roses, peonies, sweet peas, lily-of-the-valley and lilac – offset by an eclectic selection of vases, mirrors, chandeliers and candlesticks. Special events decorated by the florists range from the couture shows to the Cannes Film Festival and smart weddings, including, recently, one in Japan.
Les Mille Feuilles
2 rue Rambuteau, 75003 Paris, France
Tel: +33-1-42 78 32 93   Fax: +33-1-44 54 89 15

MILLESIMES

"We try to have the best," is the simple way in which the manager of this superb wine merchant explains its philosophy. This translates into a list of over 1000 wines, including all the *grand cru* Bordeaux, a remarkable selection of rare Burgundies (notably some exceptional Romanée-Conti and Comte de Vogüe vintages) and even the 1859 Château d'Yquem. That its clients include the Louis XV restaurant says it all.
Millésimes
Verger d'Entreprises de la Capelette
13520 Maussane, France
Tel: +33-4-90 54 49 45   Fax: +33-4-90 54 49 44

MILLFIELD SENIOR SCHOOL

Willing to Accept pupils from any academic or social background, Millfield represents an impressive 54 nationalities. Founded by R.J.O. Meyer in 1935, it occupies 120 acres of parkland which contain superb - if widely scattered – modern facilities for educational and recreational life. An internationally recognised Language Development Unit supports those with language difficulties and the plush new tennis facilities are a magnet for would-be sports stars.
Millfield Senior School
Buckleigh Road, Somerset BA16 OYD, UK
Tel: +44-1458-44 22 91   Fax: +44-1458-44 72 76

MODERNA MUSEET

A major international centre in the 1960s, this contemporary art museum has been reborn in the last two years, since its collection (which ranges from Picasso to Warhol) was moved to a new building designed by Spanish architect Rafael Moneo. Its new British director, David Elliott, has an exciting vision for the future: his main exhibition in 1999 reviewed art, film, photography and music in post-Communist Europe.
Moderna Museet
Skeppsholmen Island, 11149 Stockholm, Sweden
Tel: +46-8-51 95 52 00   Fax: +46-8-51 95 52 16

MOLLAND

Part of the joy of this sporting estate is that the partridge and pheasant pose a challenge even to the best shots, flying both high and fast. The 2,500-acre estate, centred on the lovely village of Molland in the English West Country, is perfect country for game

birds, with deep, grassy valleys and mature woodlands. Parties are generally small – eight guns – and guests stay in one of several charming country inns nearby.
Molland
near Tiverton, Devon, UK
c/o Holland & Holland, 31-33 Bruton Street
London W1X 8JS, UK
Tel: +44-20-74 99 44 11   Fax: +44-20-74 99 45 44

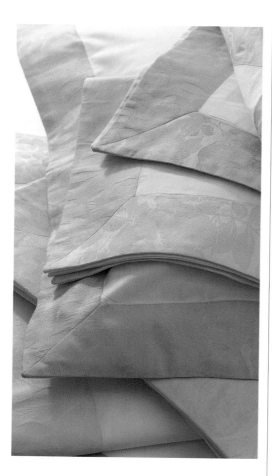

MONOGRAMMED LINEN SHOP

Expanded to twice its original size, Anne Singer's enchanting shop stocks a glorious collection of hand-smocked and embroidered children's clothes, bed and bathroom linens and accessories. As well as classical white, there is a range of almost 100 colours and, for truly shameless sybarites, there are cashmere blankets and heavy silk sheets. Commissions undertaken by its bespoke service range from the simple monogramming of stock items to the creation of whole sets of special linens.

Monogrammed Linen Shop
168-170 Walton Street, London SW3 2JL, UK
Tel: +44-20-75 89 40 33   Fax: +44-20-78 23 77 45

MONT CERVIN, HOTEL

To wake up here with a grandstand view of the Matterhorn from your bedroom window is sheer heaven. Alexander Seiler took over the village inn in 1852 and the Mont Cervin (still owned by the Seiler family) has become Zermatt's smartest hotel. Set right in the centre of this traffic-free village, it was completely refurbished last year, the bar — the hub of Zermatt's social life — was extended and, in time for the winter 1999 season, an additional conservatory-style bar added.

Hotel Mont Cervin
CH-3920 Zermatt, Switzerland
Tel: +41-27-966 8888   Fax: +41-27-967 2878

MONTALEMBERT, HOTEL

This luxurious retreat on the Left Bank matches bigger hotels in every way except that it feels much more exclusive and secluded. Built in 1926 and named after the politician and man of letters Charles Montalembert, the hotel was bought by Grace Leo-Andrieu in 1989 and redesigned by Christian Liaigre. The result is subtle and simple interiors and its relaxed elegance is perfectly complemented by a refreshingly unpretentious staff.

Hôtel Montalembert
3 rue de Montalembert, 75007 Paris, France
Tel: +33-1-45 49 68 68   Fax: +33-1-45 49 69 49

MONTE CARLO BEACH CLUB

The younger Grimaldis come to La Vigie, perched out on the rocks, for family lunches and meanwhile, by the pool, nannies and bodyguards keep watch over the children — whose fathers are playing backgammon over a good cigar in the main restaurant and whose bejewelled mothers are fully occupied with their suntans and gossip (only the Americans wear bikini tops). The waiting list for the front-row cabanas is years long and, when they do change hands, it is for thousands.

Monte Carlo Beach Club
avenue Princess Grace, MC 98000 Monaco
Tel: +33-4-93 28 66 66   Fax: +33-4-93 78 14 18

MONTBLANC

Montblanc's Meisterstück fountain pen enjoys iconic status and its limited editions (two different models of which have been introduced each year since 1992) are prized by collectors. However, the most luxe pieces of all are the 'Ramses II' and 'Tsar Nikolai I' models from the Solitaire collection, which combine gold with *lapis lazuli* and *malachite*. Montblanc's distinctive wing nib — whose production requires 150 separate operations — was created in 1955. The company, which became known as Montblanc in 1934, was established in 1906 when a stationery merchant and a banker from Hamburg joined forces with a Berlin engineer.

Montblanc
100 Hellgrundweg, D-22525 Hamburg, Germany
Tel: +49-40-84 00 10 Fax: +49-40-84 00 13 50

MOSER

In a city where crystal shops abound, this is the best — a grand establishment richly decorated with engraved Doric columns, elaborate chandeliers and highly varnished wood — reflecting Moser's status as one of Europe's finest crystal manufacturers. Traditionally known for its gilded baroque style, Moser has more recently introduced elegant and more simple pieces. Unique for containing no lead, Moser's crystal is renowned for its bright lustre; its complicated chemical make-up is the reason behind its clarity.

Moser
Na Prikope 12, Prague 1, Czech Republic
Tel: +42-02-24 21 12 93 Fax: +42-02-24 22 86 86

MOULIE

The doyen of Parisian florists, Monsieur Moulié is adored by his clients as much for his courtly charm as for the exquisite classical bouquets that he sends all over the city and the wonderful *mises-en-scène* that he creates for smart society parties and weddings. White and scented flowers and camellias are his favourites. M. Moulié has assembled an eclectic collection of garden ornaments — from the 18th-century onwards — in the adjoining boutique.

Moulié
8 Place du Palais Bourbon, 75007 Paris, France
Tel: +33-1-45 51 78 43   Fax: +33-1-45 50 45 54

MOUNT JULIET

This golf course - with its testing and superbly maintained fairways - is where Nick Faldo and Bernhard Langer have both won Irish Opens. It forms part of a sizeable estate - the origins of which go back to the 12th century - which spreads across the rolling, wooded hills of south-eastern Ireland. Its centrepiece, the former mansion home of the Earl of Carrick, was AA Hotel of the Year in 1999.

Mount Juliet
Thomastown, Co. Kilkenny, Ireland
Tel: +353-56-24 455 Fax: +353-56-24 522

MOUSSAIEFF

Some of the necklaces that appear in the window of this unprepossessing shop in London's Hilton hotel may be spectacular but they pale into insignificance next to the private commissions that these ultra-discreet jewellers undertake. That Sam and Alisa Moussaieff are reckoned to be among the few people whose buying power influences the world market for important stones says it all. Daughter of the house, Dorrit Moussaieff has been an aficionado of the newly-fashionable black diamonds for some time and employs them in her own designs.

Moussaieff
The Hilton Hotel, Park Lane, London W1Y 4BE, UK
Tel: +44-20-74 99 12 26 Fax: +44-20-74 99 05 97

MOUTON ROTHSCHILD, CHATEAU

Barrels of inky dark Mouton complete their first year's ageing in this château's 100-metre long chai, the beginning of a process that may last 20 or 30 years before this brooding giant of a wine is ready to reveal itself. Be prepared for the characteristic waft of blackcurrants and the rich, substantial flavour.

Château Mouton-Rothschild
33250 Pauillac, France
Tel: +33-5-56 73 20 20   Fax: +33-5-56 73 20 44

MUSEE CARNAVALET

This fascinating museum in the heart of the Marais traces the history of Paris from earliest times to the 20th century through art, maps, topographical models, memorabilia and majestic, reconstructed versions of 17th- and 18th-century interiors. The building itself – a 16th-century *hôtel particulier* inhabited from 1677 to 1696 by Madame de Sévigné and its 17th-century neighbour – has a particularly impressive grand staircase and mural paintings by Brunetti.

Musée Carnavalet
23 rue de Sevigné, 75003 Paris, France
Tel: +33-1-42 72 21 13   Fax: +33-1-42 72 01 61

MUSEE COGNACQ-JAY

This museum, founded in 1929, was relocated in 1990 to a restored 16th-century *hôtel particulier* in the Marais. Philanthropist and businessman Ernest Cognacq and his wife, Louise Jay, chose to channel their shared love for fine and decorative arts into a museum. The result is this collection of furniture, paintings and wonderful porcelain. Works are mostly 18th-century but there are some good 17th-century pictures (Rembrandt, Ruisdael). The museum's intimacy adds an irresistible charm.

Musée Cognacq-Jay
8 rue Elzévir, 75003 Paris, France
Tel: +33-1-42 72 21 13

MUSEE DE LA CHASSE ET DE LA NATURE

This impressive collection of weapons, animal trophies and hunting-themed pictures and tapestries is housed within its own piece of history – a stunning mansion built by François Mansart in 1654. The hunt, more than nature, is the Leitmotif of the museum and exhibits include everything from Stone Age arrow-heads to Persian helmets and ancient elephant guns. The paintings include works by Cranach, Dürer, Rembrandt and Monet.

Musée de la Chasse et de la Nature
60 rue des Archives, 75003 Paris, France
Tel: +33-1-42 72 86 43   Fax: +33-1-42 77 45 70

MUSEE DES ARTS FORAINS

Jean-Paul Favand's museum elevates the fair-ground to high art, with carousels and galleries by such 19th-century artists as Toulouse-Lautrec. The Salon de Musique can be hired for memorable evening parties while the new Salon Vénétien recreates the intrigue of an 18th-century Venetian palace during carnival time.

Musée des Arts Forains
53 avenue des Terroirs de France
75012 Paris, France
Tel: +33-1-43 40 16 22   Fax: +33-1-43 40 16 89

MUSEE NATIONAL PICASSO

This is the Picasso collection par excellence, housed in the magnificent 17th-century Hôtel Salé. Every phase of the artist's career is shown – hung in chronological order – from the Blue Period through Cubism to Picasso's witty bathing scenes and late works. Many of the paintings on display were his own personal favourites. Significant space is also given to Picasso's private collection of work by his contemporaries – Cézanne, Braque and Matisse, *inter alia*.

Musée National Picasso
5 rue de Thorigny, 75003 Paris, France
Tel: +33-1-42 71 25 21   Fax: +33-1-42 71 12 99

MUSEO THYSSEN-BORNEMISZA

The previous Baron Thyssen-Bornemisza had amassed a vast collection of Old Masters and other great European paintings by the time of his death in 1947. The Spanish state acquired the collection from the present Baron in 1993, housing it in the Villahermosa Palace, near the Prado. Art-lovers can see everything from early Italian painting to German Expressionism.

Museo Thyssen-Bornemisza
8 Paseo del Prado, E-28014 Madrid, Spain
Tel: +34-91-420 3944   Fax: +34-91-420 2780

MUSEE JACQUEMART-ANDRE

There can be few better showcases for French 18th-century and Italian artists than this compact museum – originally the home of banker Edouard André and his artist wife, Nelie Jacquemart. The most intimate and atmospheric area is the Italian Renaissance room; particularly striking here are Paolo Ucello's *Saint George Restraining the Dragon* and the *Virgin and Child* by Botticelli. Attributed officially to the painter only after cleaning in 1995, the latter is testimony to the couple's gift for choosing the most outstanding works of art on the market during their time.

Musée Jacquemart-André
158 Boulevard Haussman, 75008 Paris, France
Tel: +33-1-42 89 04 91

NATIONAL GALLERY OF IRELAND

One of Ireland's finest cultural attractions, this museum houses an outstanding collection of Irish historic paintings as well as an impressive array of works by European masters from Caravaggio and El Greco to Rembrandt and Gainsborough. A new Yeats museum was opened in 1999 while a gallery extension is currently in progress.

National Gallery of Ireland
Merrion Square (West), Dublin 2, Ireland
Tel: +353-1-661 5133   Fax: +353-1-661 5372

NATIONAL GALLERY OF SCOTLAND, THE

This gallery, housed in a magnificent neo-classical building, contains a major international collection which includes important works by Vermeer, El Greco, Raphael, Titian, Rembrandt and Turner. There is also a local flavour with some memorable works by such Scottish artists such as Ramsay and Raeburn. Exhibitions in 1999 varied from The Draughtsman's Art, a look at five centuries of European draughtsmanship, to The Tiger and The Thistle, specially held to commemorate the bi-centenary of the Scottish military campaign in South India.

The National Gallery of Scotland
The Mound, Edinburgh EH2 2EL, UK
Tel: +44-131-624 6200   Fax: +44-131-343 3250

NATIONAL, HOTEL

Four years and $80 million were lavished on restoring Alexander Ivanov's architectural gem to the glory it enjoyed as Russia's finest hotel at the beginning of this century. The suites, filled with antiques — number 101 has an extraordinary German Baroque mirror and fabulous marquetry bedroom furniture and number 107 was Lenin's favourite — overlook the Kremlin and St. Basil's cathedral and the Bolshoi theatre is just a short walk away. Marina Akhmeteley, the charming concierge, is a genius at getting tickets for the ballet and anything else worth doing in Moscow.

Hotel National
15/1 Mokhovaya Street, 103009 Moscow, Russia
Tel: +7-095-258 7000   Fax: +7-095-258 7100

NAUTOR'S SWAN

With Luciano Scarmuccia (ex-Perini Navi) at the helm for the past three years, this yacht-builder goes from strength to strength. Renowned for its classically-styled and superbly crafted yachts (there are 12 models, from 40 feet upwards) it launched the first of its semi-custom Germán Frers-designed 112-foot series in spring 1999. Swan owners have all the luck; their regattas — especially the biennial Rolex World Cup in Porto Cervo — are furiously competitive and fiendishly social.

Nautor's Swan
Oy Nautor Ab, P.O. Box 10
Fin-68601 Pietarsaari, Finland
Tel: +358-6-760 1111   Fax: +358-6-766 7364

NAVA, LA

The Medem family's aim is to re-create the great old days of sportsmanship — and their superb partridge shoot, two hours from Madrid, succeeds brilliantly. The birds are completely wild, reared naturally, and beats — across spectacularly beautiful countryside — follow the traditional pattern. Hospitality is equally important, they believe. Parties of up to 12 guns are accommodated in great comfort, with food and wine to match and every expense, from arrival at the airport to the moment you leave, is included.

La Nava
Calle Lagasca 126 Bajo
E-28006 Madrid, Spain
Tel: +34-91-564 5730   Fax: +34-91-563 4988

NEICHEL

As much a Barcelona social landmark as it is a monument to outstandingly good Mediterranean cooking, Jean-Louis and Evelyn Neichel's sleek, modern restaurant occupies a tranquil corner of the exclusive Pedralbes area, its glass wall facing out into greenery. Neichel's cooking is richly aromatic and bursts with the flavours of southern Europe. The sweet trolley is irresistible and sommelier Javier Petrirena presides over an excellent cellar — with an awesome selection of old armagnacs.

Neichel
16 bis Beltran i Rózpide
E-08034 Barcelona, Spain
Tel: +34-93-203 8408   Fax: +34-93-205 6339

NELAHOZEVES CASTLE

This 16th-century castle represents the peak of Renaissance architecture in Bohemia. Returned to the Roudnice-Lobkowicz family in 1993, the castle houses one of the richest and most important private collections in Europe, comprising thousands of works of art by artists from Bruegel, Cranach and Rubens to Velasquez and Canaletto. There are also significant *objets d'art*, books, musical instruments and manuscripts and the castle is a prestigious venue for music festivals, concerts, receptions and other private and business functions. It also includes a Museum shop, an enticing restaurant and further strings to the family bow are the Roudnice wine production, established in 1603, the brewing of Lobkowicz beer since 1466, and an exclusive travel services company.

Nelahozeves Castle
Lobkowicz Travel Services, 27751 Nelahozeves
Czech Republic
Tel: +420-205-78 53 31   Fax: +420-205-78 53 33
Email: wel@login.cz

NELLA LONGARI, GALLERIA

This gallery in the heart of Milan has played an important role in the Italian art world since its inception some 70 years ago. Always a centre for Italian Renaissance art, it also houses medieval miniatures, impressive bronzes, marble sculptures in different colours, historic tapestries and Florentine furniture. The gallery has recently been published in a set of beautiful catalogues, distributed to the major European and American museums.

Galleria Nella Longari
via Bigli 15, 20121 Milan, Italy
Tel: +39-02-79 42 87   Fax: +39-02-78 03 22

NEOTU, GALERIE

Regarded as a leading light in contemporary French furniture design, Pierre Staudenmeyer and Gérard Dalmon's gallery showcases the work of young, *avant-garde* talents. Many have launched their career as a result of Neotu exhibitions. The gallery, which opened in 1984, hosts two new collections a year; works are by Neotu's own designers as well as artists from around the world, who are regularly invited to contribute.

Galerie Neotu
25 rue du Renard
75004 Paris, France
Tel: +33-1-42 78 96 97   Fax: +33-1-42 78 26 27

NEUHAUS KUNSTHANDEL

August art dealer, Albrecht Neuhaus, has been in the business for more than 30 years. His areas of speciality are broad, ranging from medieval sculpture and *objets d'art* to baroque pieces, German gold- and silverwork and some important European furniture. The Neuhaus reputation is one of discretion, excellent advice and long experience in the art of salesmanship.

Albrecht Neuhaus Kunsthandel
Heinestrasse 9, D-9070 Würzburg, Germany
Tel: +49-931-56 849   Fax: +49-931-54 286

NEW & LINGWOOD

One of Jermyn Street's most distinguished shirtmakers, New & Lingwood has also acquired Bowring & Arundel, the last bespoke shirtmaker on Savile Row. In addition to its bespoke and off-the-peg shirts – renowned for their impeccable cut and construction – the company sells its own-label collection of fine, bench-made shoes. 'Catch them young' could be the motto here, for New & Lingwood's Eton High Street branch is practically the in-house tailor for the famous college.

New & Lingwood
53 Jermyn Street, London SW1Y 6LX, UK
Tel: +44-20-74 93 96 21   Fax: +44-20-74 99 31 03

NICKY CLARKE

Made a household name by the celebrity press, award-winning hairdresser Nicky Clarke has focused his styling abilities on his own three-storey salon,

giving it a major overhaul in 1999. The maestro and his team not only tend the hair of celebrities but they also work closely on catwalk presentations with designers such as Calvin Klein. The Nicky Clarke Beauty Suite has pampered Hollywood's finest, from Gwyneth Paltrow to Brad Pitt.

Nicky Clarke
130 Mount Street, London W1Y 5HA, UK
Tel: +44-20-74 91 47 00   Fax: +44-20-74 91 95 64

NICOLA RESTAURI

Maria Rosa Nicola inherited her passion for handling art from her father, an antique dealer and restorer in Turin and Genoa. This was also how she met her husband, Guido Nicola, who founded the business over 50 years ago. They have since undertaken countless public and private projects, often using progressive methods, and their daughter Anna Rosa and son Aldo are now key members of the company. The Nicolas' team of 50 craftsmen restores everything from paintings and frescoes to sculpture and Egyptian artefacts.

Nicola Restauri
via Santa Giulia 65, 10124 Turin, Italy
Tel & Fax: +39-011-812 2780

NIGEL BURGESS

Specialising only in yachts of over 36 metres, this yacht brokerage firm provides a highly focused service, whether that should involve charter, sales, new construction or yacht management. It has, for example, handled the sale of *Kingdom* (ex-*Nabila* and *Trump Princess*) twice and has managed the yacht for three successive owners. Approximately 80 motor and sailing yachts are offered for charter and recent new construction projects included a 52-meter yacht launched at the end of 1999 by Amels shipyard, for which it is the European agent.

Nigel Burgess
16-17 Pall Mall, London SW1Y 5LU, UK
Tel: +44-20-77 66 43 00   Fax: +44-20-77 66 43 29

NINA CAMPBELL

Her sure sense of colour and the relaxed ease of the rooms that she creates ensure Nina Campbell's status as the doyenne of English decorators. Her second shop – recently opened – houses her design studio, as well as selling antiques and her fabrics, wallpapers and new range of carpets. The original shop stocks witty or unusual accessories and gifts. While writing her third book, Campbell's current projects include an office in Moscow and a residence in Beirut.

Nina Campbell
7 Milner Street, London SW3 2QA, UK
Tel: +44-20-72 25 10 11   Fax: +44-20-72 25 06 44

NIEPOORT

This small, Dutch-owned, port house may not enjoy the same high public profile as some of its competitors but Niepoort is as sure a source of top quality vintage port as you could want. The 1955 is still superb, a silky-smooth marriage between succulent fruity wine and vigorous spirit. The 1994 shows every sign of following in its footsteps.

Niepoort (Vinhos) S.E.

rue Infete D. Henrique 39-2-Ñ, 4000 Porto, Portugal

Tel: +351-2-200 1028   Fax: +351-2-332 0209

NOBILIS FONTAN

Nobilis, the Latin for 'noble', was chosen by Adolphe Halard as the name of the company he started in 1928, close to Paris' Ecole des Beaux Arts. In this artistic milieu, Halard created his first wallpapers. Later, Suzanne Fontan introduced a co-ordinated fabric and paper collection. Today, under the direction of Adolphe's son, Denis Halard, Nobilis' creative, eclectic range also encompasses trimmings, rugs and furniture.

Nobilis Fontan

38-40 rue Bonaparte, 75006 Paris, France

Tel: +33-1-43 29 12 71   Fax: +33-1-43 29 77 57

NOEL

For lovers of beautifully embroidered household linens and traditional baby wear, Adeline Dieudonné's serene boutique is heaven. Founded in 1883, its collection of designs – now 13,000 – is constantly enriched and expanded (for the millennium, for instance, Dieudonné created a limited-edition collection embroidered with the constellations) and much work is done to private commission. Noël also offers special services which are increasingly hard to find; articles lost from past collections can be replaced and delicate linens taken in for maintenance and repairs.

Noël

1 avenue Pierre Ier de Serbie, Place d'Iéna

75116 Paris, France

Tel: +33-1-40 70 14 63   Fax: +33-1-40 70 05 25

NORLAND NANNIES

Since 1892 Norland has been synonymous with the world's best nannies and nursery nurses – distinguishable (in more traditionally-minded households, at least) by their brown-and-beige uniforms and by their quiet competence. Its selection criteria are rigorous and the two-year training (both theoretical and practical) covers all aspects of child care – from nutrition and psychology to social and legal matters – as well as equipping nannies with all-important parent-handling skills.

Norland Nannies

Denford Park, Hungerford, Berkshire RG17 OPQ, UK

Tel: +44-1488-68 22 52   Fax: +44-1488-68 52 12

NYMPHENBURG PORZELLAN-MANUFAKTUR

The porcelain works at Nymphenburg were founded in 1747 in a fairy-tale setting which compliments the magical quality of its dinner services and figurines; their designs are drawn from an archive of 30,000 exclusive designs, including menagerie models and renderings of Bustelli's *Commedia dell'Arte* players. Especially renowned for the high artistic quality of

its hand-painting, the Manufactory draws on the skills of around 80 craftsmen. Each piece is made entirely by hand; relief details are modelled free-hand and painstakingly applied, one by one, before painting. Gilding is done using 24-carat gold, applied in layers three times as thick as the more commonly-used gold leaf and the hand-burnishing takes longer even than the entire painting process.

Porzellan-Manufaktur Nymphenburg

Nördliches Schlossrondell 8, D-80638 Munich, Germany

Tel: +49-89-179 1970   Fax: +49-89-17 91 97 50

Email: info@nymphenburg-porzellan.com

Website: www.nymphenburg-porzellan.com

O'SULLIVAN ANTIQUES

The largest antiques business in Ireland, O'Sullivan Antiques now has an outpost on East 10th Street in New York, where American devotees can stock up on covetable Irish furniture from the 18th and 19th centuries. Owner Chantal O'Sullivan regularly

lends exquisite pieces to Hollywood film sets, while Liam Neeson and Mia Farrow have both browsed among her Victorian armchairs, Georgian tables, chandeliers and brass candle-sticks – further underlining the cordial transatlantic relationship. Celebrated decorator David Mlinaric admires her blend of the regal and eccentric and has introduced a wealth of well-connected clients, including Pia Getty.

O'Sullivan Antiques

43-44 Francis Street, Dublin 8, Ireland

Tel: +353-1-454 1143   Fax: +353-1-454 1156

OAK ROOM, THE

However much his gastronomic empire may expand, Marco Pierre White's flagship restaurant continues to serve the sort of food that can only be inspired by genius — or something as near to it as makes no difference. The grandiose room — wood panelled and hung with art — is the perfect setting and the value of the wine cellar approaches that of an Eaton Square house. The Oak Room is frightfully grown-up, so expect nothing less than a performance.

The Oak Room – Marco Pierre White
Le Meridien, 21 Piccadilly, London W1V 0BH, UK
Tel: +44-20-74 37 02 02 Fax: +44-20-74 37 35 74

OCEANCO

Richard Hein has never been one to think small. He has, since merging his naval architecture and yacht design practice with Oceanco six years ago, been the driving force behind Oceanco's development into

the world's largest constructor of custom-built private motor yachts. With two Dutch shipyards, one in South Africa and an international sales office in Fort Lauderdale, Florida, Oceanco currently has eight yachts of over 50 metres under construction. By early 2000 the company will have launched three yachts of 80 metres-plus within six months. The 80-metre *Constellation* (originally *Stargate I*) hit the water in late summer 1999, followed by the 95-metre *Trick One* at the end of the year and the 80-metre Stargate II a couple of months later. It's not all huge yachts, though. The roll-call also includes the 42-metre *Aspiration*, winner of the 1999 Showboats International Award for Technical Excellence, the 57-metre *Sunrise* and — still under construction — the 49-metre *Avalon*, a collaboration with Andrew Winch.

Oceanco
Gildo Pastor Centre, 7 rue du Gabian
MC 98000 Monaco
Tel: +377-93 10 02 81 Fax: +377-92 05 65 99

ODILE LECOIN

To say that your beautician gave you "a new skin" — as Paloma Picasso has said of Odile Lecoin — is praise indeed. Lecoin's deep-cleansing treatment, unique in Paris, uses aluminium crystals, which lift away dead cells and embedded pollution, leaving the skin wonderfully luminous. Lecoin's equally celebrated body massages use one of four specially-formulated lotions, all plant-based, as are her anti-wrinkle and cellulite treatments.

Odile Lecoin
75 avenue Paul Doumer, 75016 Paris, France
Tel: +33-1-45 04 91 85 Fax: +33-1-45 04 98 26

ODIOT

This gold and silversmith holds a rare distinction: its craftsmen still make exquisite cutlery by hand, according to the methods they have used since the firm was established in 1690. The styles are traditional, too. 'Nemours', is a Second Empire baroque model and 'Potocki', with its mouldings of thread fastened with acanthus is a Directoire design. Odiot's most intricate design, 'Compiègne', commemorates a Louis XVI hunting trip in 1776.

Odiot
7 Place de la Madeleine, 75008 Paris, France
Tel: +33-1-42 65 00 95 Fax: +33-1-42 66 49 12

OHANA, DR. SYDNEY

Author of *La Beauté en Harmonie*, Dr. Ohana runs Paris' most elegant clinic for cosmetic surgery — a striking *hôtel particulier* decorated with fine art. But the surroundings are not the point. Ohana specialises in the skilful remodelling of faces and breasts, with remarkably natural results. His clients also value his sensitive approach; Ohana's earlier experience as a surgeon working with cancer patients impressed upon him the importance of a patient's emotional well-being to the success of an operation.

Dr. Sydney Ohana
6 Square Petrarque, 75116 Paris, France
Tel: +33-1-53 70 05 05 Fax: +33-1-44 05 97 61

OLIVIER CREED

Grace Kelly swept up the aisle to marry Prince Rainier in a cloud of her very own Creed Fleurissimo. For the woman who has everything, what could be more spoiling than commissioning an exclusive scent? Olivier Creed will do just that; six generation's of his family have produced fragrances since 1760 and the scion of this illustrious line is justifiably proud that his is the world's only remaining family-run company producing artisan-quality perfumes. There are more than 200

existing perfumes to choose from, including vintage scents which can be recreated to order - yours exclusively for a year.

Olivier Creed
38 avenue Pierre 1er de Serbie
75008 Paris, France
Tel: +33-1-47 20 58 02 Fax: +33-1-47 20 71 32

OMAS

Established by Armando Simoni in 1925 and now run by his daughter, Raffaella Malaguti and her family, Omas has, since its earliest days, made some of the world's most sought-after pens. Its finest range from museum-quality works of art, such as the 'Jerusalem 3000', with *repoussé* scenes of the Holy City, to quirky collectibles, such as the 1930s 'Doctor's Pen' which contained a thermometer and two reservoirs for different coloured inks and the recent limited-edition model honouring Lech Walesa's Nobel Peace Prize.

Omas
via del Fondatore 10
40138 Bologna, Italy
Tel: +39-051-53 24 46 Fax: +39-051-601 0074

ONE ALDWYCH

A year after its opening, Gordon Campbell Gray's hotel has proved to be a hit with low-key celebrities and stylish bankers. Why? Having travelled the world for a year — staying in the best hotels — before embarking on its construction, Campbell Gray distilled what he saw as the essence of real luxury into his 'baby'. In practice that means quiet chic, wonderful service and an absence of what he calls "extras that guests don't really use". Special touches include 300 works of art (some antiquities, some contemporary), exceptional flowers by Stephen Woodhams (changed daily), a swimming pool with underwater music and a private cinema.

One Aldwych
London WC2B 4BZ, UK
Tel: +44-20-73 00 10 00 Fax: +44-20-73 00 10 01

OPERA MUSEO STIBBERT

This museum houses the richly diverse 19th-century art and artefacts of Frederick Stibbert's bequest. Lying in its own extensive park, it has a large space where changing exhibitions from the museum's own collection are shown. After a successful run of costume exhibits, 1999-2000 will feature masterpieces of Japanese art and armour.

Opera Museo Stibbert
via F. Stibbert 26
50134 Florence, Italy
Tel: +39-055-47 55 20 Fax: +39-055-48 69 49

SAL. OPPENHEIM JR. & CIE.

Founded in 1789 by Salomon Oppenheim, this prestigious private bank enjoys a strong relationship of mutual trust with its clients. The Oppenheim and Pferdmenges families still play a central role in the running of the bank – along with other partners, including former Bundesbank President Karl-Otto Pöhl – and are proud of this independence. In recent years, the bank has successfully withstood a number of international economic pressures and, in 1999, made a smooth switch to Euro compliance.

In addition to its traditional expertise in handling stocks, bonds and funds, the bank's Private Banking division now offers customers private equity investment. Sal. Oppenheim jr. & Cie. has seen an impressive rise in its underwriting of business securities and has worked on some very notable projects, such as the DaimlerChrysler merger.

Recently, the bank has seen even greater demand for its institutional asset management, which has contributed to the profitability of the group. The bank's principal interests in Zürich, Luxembourg and the Oppenheim-Esch Group have also helped. The commercial activities of the latter include the Cologne Arena, opened in a flamboyant ceremony in October 1998.

Sal. Oppenheim jr. & Cie. never strays far from its basic objectives, however: to increase customer satisfaction and achieve an acceptable return on equity, to expand asset management and investment banking activities, to strengthen its risk profile and to offer the best possible training to its talented staff.

Sal. Oppenheim jr. & Cie.
Unter Sachsenhausen 4, D-50667 Cologne, Germany
Tel: +49-221-14 501   Fax: +49-221-145 1512
Website: www.oppenheim.de

ORIENT EXPRESS TRAINS

Having bought two run-down sleeper coaches from the old Orient Express in 1977, James Sherwood set about recreating the glamour which defined the Golden Age of train travel. As Charlotte Rampling, Gunther Sachs and Peter Ustinov have already discovered, it's all terribly romantic – dining like a prince and being waited on hand and foot by your Personal Steward as you make your stately two-day progress across the Continent. The entire train is also available for private charter to almost any European destination.

Orient Express Trains
Sea Containers House, 20 Upper Ground
London SE1 9PF, UK
Tel: +44-20-78 05 50 60   Fax: +44-20-78 05 59 08

THE ORIENTAL AT THE DORCHESTER

Kenneth Poon's Cantonese cooking is of the highest order (Michelin thinks so, too, having made it Europe's first Chinese restaurant to receive a star – and so do Sharon Stone and Harrison Ford). Poon's *tours de force* include Braised superior shark fin with crab meat and Chilled shredded chicken with

jellyfish. The setting is exotic-opulent – the cleaner lines of the main, mezzanine dining-room complementing the richness of its three private rooms below.

The Oriental Restaurant
The Dorchester, Park Lane, London W1A 2HJ, UK
Tel: +44-20-76 29 88 88

~

ORLIK CASTLE

Reclaimed by the Schwarzenberg family since the fall of communism (having been established by royalty in the 13th century), this 9,700-hectare estate offers an extraordinary variety of game – stag and roebuck, wild boar, hare and pheasant. The 19th-century lodge, to which Ceaucescu, Brezhnev and Honneker gravitated in search of their sport now hosts American plutocrats and European aristocrats; cosy rather than stylish, it contains a fascinating museum of a selection of hunting trophies and weaponry.

Orlik Castle, Czech Republic
c/- Czech Forestry Administration
Tel: +420-362-84 11 16

7 PORTES

The best and most authentic Catalan food is served at this legendary restaurant (whose name translates as 'seven doors') from one in the afternoon until

one in the morning. For over a century, its hallowed dining room has been a haven for gourmets and glamorous celebrities alike; there are small plaques above the tables naming illustrious regulars of the past, including Dalí, Che Guevara, Orson Welles and Maria Callas. The menu lists over ten varieties of *paella*, all of which are sensational.

7 Portes
Po Isabel II 14, E-08003 Barcelona, Spain
Tel: +34-93-319 3033   Fax: +34-93-319 4662

PAÇO DA GLORIA

In Portugal's lovely Minho valley, Paço da Gloria — available for private rental — is perfect for those in search of profound serenity and singular beauty. The magnificent, 18th-century stone palace, surrounded by vineyards (the estate produces its own vinho verde), is owned by a Portuguese antiquarian and collector, who has filled it with works of art (some of which may be bought). The Long Gallery, for instance, is lined with Baroque busts and precious tapestries and other rooms are filled with *Boulle chiffoniers*, exquisite porcelain and chinoiserie cabinets, as well as contemporary paintings.

Paço da Gloria
near Ponte de Lima, Northern Portugal
c/ Earth, 2 Durrand Gardens
London SW4 OPP, UK
Tel: +44-20-77 93 99 93   Fax: +44-20-77 93 99 94

PALACE HOTEL, MADRID

In Madrid the Palace and the Ritz have always been arch-rivals but, since its 1997 restoration, the Palace has emerged the clear winner. As classical and as grand as they come, it was originally conceived by King Alfonso XIII and inspired by the French Baroque style. There can be no finer antidote to the noise of the streets than to sit quietly under its magnificent stained-glass cupola, marble gleaming reassuringly all around, and sip a glass of champagne.

Palace Hotel
Plaza de las Cortes 7, E-28014 Madrid, Spain
Tel: +34-91-360 80 00   Fax: +34-91-360 81 00

PALACE HOTEL GSTAAD

A home from home for all the Greek shipping magnates who own holiday houses here — and for the Euro-élite who choose not to — The Palace has been described as "Switzerland's largest family boarding-house". Indeed, the Scherz family makes a virtue of its low-key approach and the simple rusticity of its interior decoration. But we are talking millionaire-simple here. The spa is run by La Prairie and, for six weeks each summer, no less a legend than Roy Emerson runs tennis clinics.

Palace Hotel Gstaad
CH-3780 Gstaad, Switzerland
Tel: +41-33-748 5000   Fax: +41-33-748 5001

PALACIO DE CAMPO REAL

Set in the centre of old Jerez, this stunning 13th-century palace — declared a national monument in 1990 — has been in the hands of the same family since the early 1600s. Available for private rental, its vast rooms surround a Moorish courtyard and fountain and overlook two lovely gardens. Beautifully restored, many of the rooms have Renaissance architectural details — and the archive room contains museum-quality documents, dating back to 1264.

Palacio de Campo Real, Jerez, Spain
c/- Blandings, The Barn, Musgrave Farm
Horningsea Road, Fen Ditton
Cambridge CB5 8SZ, UK
Tel: +44-1223-29 34 44   Fax: +44-1223-29 28 88

PALAIS SCHWARZENBERG, HOTEL IM

Still owned by the Prince of Schwarzenberg, whose forebears built it as their summer palace in 1716, this heavenly retreat — located in a private, 7.5 hectare park — was opened as a hotel in 1962. Last year the celebrated architect Paolo Piva oversaw the restoration of a new wing of six suites, where fine antiques are offset by original contemporary art works. Rooms 18 and 19 are of special historical interest (they were the private quarters of the Princess of Schwarzenberg until destroyed in World War II) and room 27 has a romantic open fireplace.

Hotel im Palais Schwarzenberg
Schwarzenbergplatz 9, A-1030 Vienna, Austria
Tel: +43-1-798 4515   Fax: +43-1-798 4714

PALAZZO SASSO

At night, instead of a chocolate on your pillow, you find a tiny tub of sun cream, made by the monks in the monastery up the road. In the morning, particularly in Room 1, 201, 204 or 301 (the ones with the private terraces), you wake up to views of the Mediterranean that will stun you into silence. In Rossellini's restaurant 30-year old Antonio Genovese is tipped as a hot new culinary star. And the building – Moorish, originally 12th-century, exquisitely restored – is a knockout.

Palazzo Sasso
via San Giovanni del Toro 28, 84010 Ravello, Italy
Tel: +39-089-81 81 81   Fax: +39-089-85 89 00

PAOLO OLBI

Passionate about reviving the Renaissance hand-crafts of his native Venice, Paolo Olbi has his own workshop, where skilled artisans create beautiful hand-made notebooks and albums covered in calf-skin, into which glass and silver are inlaid. It was Olbi who first revived carta marmorata, the marbled paper originated by the Turks and Chinese, which was wildly popular during Venice's Golden Age; however, so disillusioned was he by its crass commercialisation that he now refuses to deal in it.

Paolo Obli
Calle della Mandola 3653, 30100 San Marco
Venice, Italy
Tel: +39-041-528 5025   Fax: +39-041-522 4057

PAOLO PEJRONE

Despite credits including gardens for Marella Agnelli, Sir Jimmy Goldsmith and the Aga Khan (at the latter's former hotels) this designer is far too discreet to discuss his projects in any detail, preferring his work to speak for itself. A garden, in his view, is like an item of clothing which reflects the mentality of its owner and he regards their creation as a philosophical rather than a physical exercise. Signor Pejrone considers it vital to get to know the clients and their view of life well before accepting a commission, and claims to have turned down lucrative offers because "the feeling was not right".

Paolo Pejrone
via san Leonardo 1, 12036 Ravello, Italy
Tel: +39-01-75 25 19 58   Fax: +39-01-75 25 72 65

PAOLO TEVERINI

There is a delightfully old-world charm about Paolo Teverini's intimate little restaurant and the hotel which houses it; set on a river bank, it has been in his family since the 17th century. The decor is country-cosy and a tinkling piano adds to the atmosphere. Teverini is a genius with vegetables – for example Terrina Primavera (a delicious terrine of spring vegetables) and Ravioli filled with vegetables and dresses with a fish-infused sauce.

Paolo Teverini
Hotel Tosco Romagnolo, via del Popolo 1, 47021 Forli, Italy
Tel: +39-0543-91 12 60   Fax: +39-0543-91 10 14

PARIS BAR

This enclave of Berlin will be forever France – right down to the waiters' distinctly Parisian 'charm'. But that – along with its unspoken seating code – is all part of the appeal. Next to the huge front window sit the film and TV folk; on the red leather banquettes are the artists, sugar-daddies and young aristos and discreetly hidden away at the back are the superstars (Jack Nicholson, David Bowie, Alfred Brendel, Claudia Schiffer). The food is excellent – brasserie classics, such as steack frites, escargots and oysters.

Paris Bar
152 Kantstrasse, D-10623 Berlin, Germany
Tel: +49-30-313 8052   Fax: +49-30-313 2816

PARNESS

The superb quality of her own-label pet toiletries, as well as her exquisite, made-to-order dog-kennels and pet beds – exact replicas of those used in the 18th-century French royal court – have made Sheila

Parness a cult heroine among the owners of the world's most pampered pets. Parness is soon to open a sumptuous pets' pleasure-dome in the heart of Mayfair. Here, indulgent owners will find luxurious food items (including 'cat-viar' - sturgeon eggs for felines) and a wide range of accessories, from dog collars (bridle leather for country dogs, diamond-encrusted for their city cousins) to hand-painted china, crystal and silver bowls and stylish pet-carrying bags. The pet pampering extends to a state-of-the-art grooming parlour, staffed by highly experienced stylists.

Parness
London, UK
Enquiries:
Tel: +44-20-78 38 94 66   Fax: +44-20-78 38 94 67

PARTRIDGE FINE ART

Still in family hands after 100 years in business, Partridge is a pre-eminent dealer in 18th-century French furniture, silver and works of art. Its picture department, while long established, has recently emerged as a key player at auctions, snapping up an 1830s racing picture by John Ferneley for over $600,000 in spring 1999.

Partridge Fine Art
144-146 New Bond Street
London W1Y OLY, UK
Tel: +44-20-76 29 08 34   Fax: +44-20-76 29 22 92

PARTY PLANNERS

The original *maîtresse* of ceremonies and consummate party organiser Lady Elizabeth Anson has the added distinction of being the Earl of Lichfield's sister. Her Ladyship was one of the first to put her considerable social skills to commercial advantage by starting Party Planners. This successful operation continues to source everything an aspiring hostess might command – from staff and caterers to music, flowers and venues – and stage-managed Princess Alexia of Greece's recent wedding celebrations.

Party Planners
56 Ladbroke Grove, London W11 2PB, UK
Tel: +44-20-72 29 96 66   Fax: +44-20-77 27 60 01

PASCAL BARY

Longchamp is special to every French trainer but none more so than Pascal Bary, who won the Group I Prix d'Ispahan there with *Croco Rouge* in 1999. Following wins in both the French and the Irish Derby in 1998 with *Dreamwell*, it confirmed – if confirmation were needed – that he's the among the best in the business. His dynamism and perfectionist nature are appreciated by the Niarchos family, Prince Abdullah and Wafic Said, whose horses are among his 120-strong stable.

Pascal Bary
5 Chemin des Aigles, 60500 Chantilly, France
Tel: +33-3-44 57 14 03   Fax: +33-3-44 67 20 15

PASTICCERIA MARCHESI

The best coffee in town is served in fine porcelain cups by *suave baristi* who could all be David Niven clones and is accompanied by irresistibly light pastries (notably the barely-sweet apple tart). Giorgio Armani joins the pre-Christmas crush here to get his favourite Panettone, filled with Chantilly cream. A Milan institution since 1824, it still looks the part, with tasselled window shades keeping the sun off the sweets.

Pasticceria Marchesi
via Santa Maria alla Porta 11a, 20123 Milan, Italy
Tel: +39-02-87 67 30

PATEK PHILIPPE

No watch appreciates in value quite as much as a vintage Patek Philippe – in 1996 a world record $1.7 million was fetched at auction by a 1939 'Calatrava'. These are the ground-breaking mechanical watches that make a connoisseur's heart beat faster, especially as little more than a dozen are made of the most complicated models (hardly surprising, as each takes a year to make). At the 1999 Basel show a new model – 'Ref. 5054' – with moon, date and power-reserve indicators was launched and the same spring saw the company's Moscow launch of its new 'Sculpture' collection, exclusive to the Russian market.

Patek Philippe SA
Chemin du Pont du Centenaire
CH-1228 Plan Les Ouates, Geneva, Switzerland
Tel: +41-22-884 2020 Fax: +41-22-884 2040

PATRICK BARBE

President of the French bloodstock agents' association (A.F.C). Patrick Barbe, does most of his business in Japan these days – notably with the Yoshida family, for whom he bought 'Arc' winner *Helissio* and champions such as *Hector Protector* and *Groom Dancer*. Barbe is always a very active agent at the Deauville Agence Francaise Sales, his long list of successful purchases includes *Deep Roots* (champion French two-year-old) and *Fabulous la Fouine* (champion Japanese filly).

Patrick Barbe
via Montenapoleone 19, 20121 Milan, Italy
Tel: +39-02-76 00 55 14 Fax: +30-02-76 02 31 17

PAUL SMITH

British Menswear Designer of the Year for the last two years running, Paul Smith is planning to celebrate spring 2000 with the launch of a new fragrance. His menswear endears itself to clients with its discreet luxury, enlivened by off-beat fabrics and colours, while the parallel wit and whimsy of his four-year old women's line numbers Kate Capshaw and Helena Christensen among admirers. In mid-1999 Smith opened a bespoke tailoring service at his flagship shop.

Paul Smith
Westbourne House, 122 Kensington Park Road
London W11 2EP, UK
Tel: +44-20-77 27 35 53 Fax: +44-20-77 27 38 47

PATRICK GUILBAUD, RESTAURANT

Opened 20 years ago (at a previous address) by Brittany-born chef, Patrick Guilbaud, Ireland's most fashionable restaurant fully justifies its two-star Michelin ranking – the only such commendation in Ireland – while packing in the *haute monde* of Dublin. Head Chef Guillaume Lebrun interprets Guilbaud's signature Modern French cooking with immense panache, his use of the finest local produce giving it a subtle yet distinctively Irish twist. In the sleek dining room, enlivened by regular visits from the charismatic Guilbaud himself, Stephane Robin leads a highly professional team. Add to this a superb wine list and a wonderful location in the heart of Georgian Dublin and you have a world-class restaurant. The *prix fixe* lunch at £22 is exceptional value.

Restaurant Patrick Guilbaud
Merrion Hotel, Upper Merrion St., Dublin 2, Ireland
Tel: +353-1-676 4192 Fax: +353-1-661 0052

PECK

From its expanded premises, Peck purveys a smörgasbord of cold cuts, the best of local and international cheeses, and a wealth of delicacies from truffles to caviar. A glass lift descends to the new basement wine cellar where fourteen thousand bottles of wine are displayed. On the first floor you will find tea and coffee shops, an ice-cream parlour and bar.

Peck
via Spadari 9, 20123 Milan, Italy
Tel: +39-02-86 10 40 Fax: +39-02-869 3017

PELLICANO, IL

Built on a series of terraces dipping to the extraordinarily limpid sea on an isolated corner of Monte Argentario, Il Pellicano is an utterly private and deeply pampering place. It was conceived as a hideaway in the 1960s by two lovers, British aviator Michael Graham and Hollywood denizen Patsy

Daszel and the sense of romance continues. The rooms – in cottages scattered amongst the pine woods – are wonderfully secluded; G1 is perfect for lovers and G3 has a private pool. New chef, Stefano di Salvo, works wonders with seafood.

Il Pellicano
Loc. Lo Sbarcatello, 58018 Porto Ercole, Italy
Tel: +39-0564-85 81 11 Fax: +39-0564-83 34 18

PENDULERIE, LA

For 22 years Christophe Guérin and Stéphane Gagnon have specialised in clocks dating from the 17th- to the 19th century. Guérin travels widely, unearthing exciting finds, which are painstakingly restored. The clocks – more than 200 at any time – are complemented by a wonderful cache of 18th- and early 19th-century decorative *objets*, particularly bronze chandeliers, torches and candlesticks. The shop is utterly enchanting at noon, when the clocks all chime in unison.

La Pendulerie
134 rue du Faubourg Saint Honoré, 75008 Paris, France
Tel: +33-1-45 61 44 55 Fax: +33-1-45 61 44 54

PENHALIGON'S

Established in 1870 by the barber to the Royal court, this perfume company has stayed true to its roots; fragrances like 'Bluebell', 'Blenheim Bouquet' and 'Violetta' have a delightfully old-fashioned

resonance (some are reinterpreted classics; others use Mr. Penhaligon's original *formulae*) and the packaging – including collectors' edition solid silver year bottles – reeks of establishment grandeur. Among Penhaligon's countless fans, Franco Zeffirelli adores 'Hammam' and Taki Theodoracopulos loves its most recent creation, Quercus.

Penhaligon's
16 Burlington Arcade, Piccadilly, London W1V 9AB, UK
Tel: +44-20-76 29 14 16

PETIT MATELOT, LE

Founded in 1790, this is France's most exclusive outdoor clothing boutique. As the name suggests, it has always been linked to the development of sailing as a sport – the company created the classical pea-jacket and Jacques Cousteau's distinctive sailing hat. Today, while retaining traditional fabrics, owner Jean-François Lion has added goretex and similar high-performance fabrics to his range. He has also introduced a collection of casual sportswear for both men and women; made of classical cottons, tweed and loden, it has a relaxed, BCBG elegance.

Le Petit Matelot
27 avenue de la Grande Armée, 75016 Paris, France
Tel: +33-1-45 00 15 51 Fax: +33-1-40 67 12 95

PETROSSIAN

Rich in history, Petrossian pioneered the introduction of caviar to the West in the 1920s. Founded by Mouchegh and Melkoum Petrossian, this specialist shop has become the largest and best-known importer to France and America from Russia's Caspian Sea. In keeping with its gourmet image, Petrossian now offers other delicacies, ranging from the finest smoked fish and salmon eggs to its own-label, caviar-enhancing vodka.

Petrossian
18 boulevard de la Tour Maubourg, 75007 Paris, France
Tel: +33-1-44 11 32 22 Fax: +33-1-44 89 67 66

CHATEAU PETRUS

The relentless pursuit of excellence at this château meant that no wine was made in 1991, a poor vintage, while in 1987 a helicopter was employed to hover just above the vines in an effort to dry them after heavy rainfall at harvest time. The resulting wine has its own folklore attached: incredibly rare, astronomically priced, intense and profoundly flavoured.

Château Petrus
Jean-Pierre Mouiex, 54 quai du Prieurat
33500 Libourne, France
Tel: +33-5-57 51 93 66 Fax: +33-5-57 51 79 79

PIAGET

Piaget won the Watch of the Year award at the end of 1998 for the 'Altiplano' - a superlative men's hand-wound mechanical watch in 18-carat white gold with an ultra-thin, square face. This is just another milestone in the company's distinguished history – a story that began in a Jura village in 1874, when the business was originally devoted to making watch movements alone. In 1940 a decision was made to sign their own watches and, nine years later, Gérald and Valentin Piaget (respectively the father and uncle of current President, Yves Piaget) formed today's Piaget SA.

Throughout the 1950s and 1960s the company played a pioneering role in the development of ultra-thin mechanisms – notably, in 1956, launching the celebrated ultra-thin 9P mechanical movement, still used in the classic collections. This was followed in 1959 by the 12P, the world's thinnest self-winding mechanical movement at 2.3mm, and the calibre 7P, the thinnest quartz movement made to date.

Piaget subsequently added jewellery to its portfolio of products, launching its first line in 1990. Designed to complement its watches and characterised by a relaxed, contemporary edge, the jewellery lines are a great success – notably the 'Possession' collection, with its inimitable concept of a 'ring within a ring'.

Piaget International SA
61 route de Chêne, CH-1208 Geneva, Switzerland
Tel: +41-22-707 3232 Fax: +41-22-707 3888
European shops in Geneva, Paris, Monaco, Barcelona and London (at Harrods)

PEVERO GOLF CLUB

Thanks to the Aga Khan's funding, Sardinia's wild terrain was no obstacle to the execution of Robert Trent Jones' design for this spectacularly-sited golf course; any rocks in the way were simply blasted into oblivion. The result is 18 challenging holes which give no quarter to a player who is over-ambitious or imprecise; the rough here, a mix of fragrant juniper and myrtle, may be very beautiful but it's famously unforgiving. As befits the celebrity-studded Costa Smeralda, the clubhouse is immensely stylish, with a swimming pool, a restaurant and a bar overlooking the 9th and 18th greens.

Pevero Golf Club
07020 Porto Cervo
Sardinia, Italy
Tel: +39-0789-96 072 Fax: +39-0789-96 572

PENUELA, LA

To rent Fermín Bohórquez's magnificent Andalusian Cortijo is to live like an aristocratic Spanish landowner in the 18th century – albeit with every modern comfort. Bulls are tested in the private bull-ring, flamenco dancers will come to perform in the flamenco gallery, coachmen will take you for picnics on the 2,500-acre estate in one of the antique coaches and, for riding, there are Pure Spanish horses, which are bred on the estate.

La Peñuela
near Jerez, Spain
c/o Blandings, The Barn, Musgrave House
Horningsea Road, Fen Ditton, Cambridge CB5 8SZ, UK
Tel: +44-1223-29 34 44 Fax: +44-1223-29 28 88

PERBELLINI

Don't be put off by the industrialised area near Verona in which this restaurant is set; Perbellini is a delight. Paolo Perbellini presides over a pair of refined and tasteful rooms – one pink, the other blue – with Murano chandeliers and masses of flowers. Meanwhile, Giancarlo Perbellini, named "best young chef" in 1987 lives up to his earlier promise. Wonderful seafood starters, presented on a crystal tray, include Sea bass with chives, Red mullet with apples and St. Pierre with ginger.

Perbellini
via Muselle 10, 37050 Isola Rizza, Italy
Tel: +39-045-713 5352 Fax: +39-045-710 3727

PERINI NAVI

Apart from designer Ron Holland, nobody has had a greater influence on the market for large, custom-built sailing yachts over the last 15 years than Fabio Perini. His notion that a large and luxuriously fitted yacht could be handled by one person – revolutionary in 1984 – is now the norm and his company has since built 23 yachts over 45 metres. Recent launches include the 49-metre *Phryne* in February 1999 and (resisting the temptation simply to keep getting bigger) the 33-metre *Heritage* at the end of 1999. The 53-metre *Atmosphere* will follow in early 2000.

Perini Navi
via M. Coppino 114, 55049 Viareggio, Itlay
Tel: +39-0584-4241   Fax: +39-0584-42 42 00

PERLE DE PRAGUE, LA

This is undoubtedly Prague's smartest restaurant - and its owners go so far as to fly in international chefs for a month at a time to create the unforgettable *haute cuisine* on which La Perle de Prague's reputation is based. Such dishes include Nuggets of foie gras and free-range chicken in candied ginger and lemon. The buzz to your tastebuds is enhanced by the visual experience of the restaurant's bold violet and green decor and its spectacular view over the city.

La Perle de Prague
Rasin Building, Rasinovo Nabrezi 80
Prague 2, Czech Republic
Tel: +420-2-21 98 41 60   Fax: +420-2-22 19 84 179

PERRIN ANTIQUAIRES

The Perrin family has been handling important works of art for four generations. Jacques Perrin and his sons, Patrick and Philippe, buy pieces together but display them separately in their own galleries. Their particular interests are 18th-century French paintings, furniture and *objets d'art*, described as being in "perfect millionaire taste" and always of superb quality. The Perrins' expertise is often called upon by museums and heritage organisations and they are an important presence at international art events. Jacques Perrin's showroom was redecorated by François-Joseph Graf in 1999.

Perrin Antiquaires
98 rue du Faubourg Saint-Honoré, 75008 Paris, France
Tel: +33-1-42 65 01 38   Fax: +33-1-49 24 04 08

PETER INSULL YACHT MARKETING

Since establishing his yacht brokerage firm in the South of France in 1980, British-born Peter Insull has built up an excellent reputation, based on his expert knowledge of the market and his constant search for ways of developing the services offered to clients. Insull pioneered the concept of a specialist crew employment agency, for instance, and remains the leader in this field.

One of the first to recognise the evolution in the market during the late Eighties, when a division emerged between yachts of under 100 feet and those above this size, the firm has, for over a decade, specialised in the larger yachts. It offers a fully-integrated service, comprising brokerage, new construction, chartering and management.

A mark of any good business, Insull's firm has retained many clients as they have progressed through the ownership of several yachts – most notably Sir Donald Gosling, whose third (and current) yacht is the 75-metre *Leander*. The most expensive yacht on the charter market today, its charter management is also handled by Insull. Recent successes include the top-secret sale of a 58-metre newly-built yacht and the signing of a two-month charter of *Savarona*, the classic 140-metre yacht formerly owned by Ataturk. In 1994 Insull was also appointed the marketing representative of British shipyard Devonport Yachts, whose credits include the reconstruction of *Talitha G*.

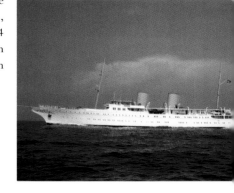

Peter Insull Yacht Marketing
Résidences du Port Vauban, Place de l'Acqueduc
Avenue du 11 Novembre, 06600 Antibes, France
Tel: +33-4-93 34 44 55   Fax: +33-4-93 34 92 74
Email: yacht-marketing@insull.com
Website: www.insull.com

PHILIP KINGSLEY

It is much more than his urbane charm that has endeared trichologist Philip Kingsley to Candice Bergen, Barbra Streisand and Jerry Hall. He is simply the best in the business of trichology. But it may not have been so, as Kingsley originally wanted to pursue a career as a doctor. Consultations begin with a dietary and lifestyle analysis and the treatments and take-home products are all personalised accordingly. Kingsley's worst nightmare? "I used to dream that I would wake up completely bald." Given his expertise, there's little chance of that.

Philip Kingsley
54 Green Street, London W1Y 3RH, UK
Tel: +44-20-76 29 40 04 Fax: +44-20-74 91 98 43

PHILIP TREACY

Grace Jones led a cavalcade of models, including Honor Fraser and Naomi Campbell, down the catwalk for Philip Treacy's first New York fashion show. Fresh from designing hats for the film *Plunkett & Maclean*, the milliner's dazzled the audience with crowns of fluorescent feathers, Mohican head-dresses, diamante visors and Mad-Hatter styles.

Philip Treacy
69 Elizabeth Street, London SW1W 9PJ, UK
Tel: +44-20-72 59 96 05 Fax: +44-20-78 24 85 59

PHILIPPE ROCHAT - RESTAURANT DE L'HOTEL DE VILLE

Philippe Rochat has made this restaurant, set in a pretty maison bourgeoise near Lausanne, very much his own since he took over from his former mentor, Fredy Girardet a few years ago. A new generation is enjoying his culinary wizardry, characterised by the same sure hand and lightness of touch as his predecessor. Rochat's expertise shines in such dishes as *Canard nantais cuit rosé au vin de Brouilly*, followed by a sublime *Conversation tiède de fraises des bois, glace à la vanille*.

Restaurant de l'Hôtel de Ville - Philippe Rochat
1 rue d'Yverdon
CH-1023 Crissier, Switzerland
Tel: +41-21-634 0505 Fax: +41-21-634 2464

PHILLIPS, S.J.

Specialising in British and Continental silver, *objets de vertu* and antique jewellery – from the early 16th century to late Victorian – this family business, founded in 1869, is currently run by Martin Norton, grandson of S.J. Phillips, and his nephew. Signed jewels include 19th-century pieces by such craftsmen as Castellani of Rome and Devos, who was the Belgian royal jeweller. Phillips' collection of 18th-century gold snuff boxes is particularly outstanding

S.J. Phillips Ltd.
139 New Bond Street, London W1A 3DL, UK
Tel: +44-20-76 29 62 61 Fax: +44-20-74 95 61 80

PIC, RESTAURANT

"What matters is what is on the plate," the great Jacques Pic used to insist. His daughter, Anne Pic-Sinapian – who took over here from her brother, Alain, in October 1998 – agrees wholeheartedly. But she also understands the importance of setting. She has blown the cobwebs off the place (and has transformed the adjoining building into the 15-room Auberge du Pin) creating a serene and exquisitely tasteful Provençal retreat. On the plate, some of her late father's great classics are complemented by her own lighter and fresher dishes.

Restaurant Pic
285 avenue Victor-Hugo
26000 Valence, France
Tel: +33-4-75 44 15 32 Fax: +33-4-75 40 96 03

PICHON-LALANDE, CHATEAU

Since taking over the reins of Pichon-Lalande (formerly known as Pichon-Longueville Comtesse de Lalande) in 1978 May Eliane de Lencquesaing has elevated the status of this château to a level just below that of first growth. Approachable when quite young due to its high merlot content, this wine is capable of giving pleasure for decades. Packed with elegant fruit, it is never a blockbuster but, rather, a soft yet serious statement of all that is good about fine claret.

Château Pichon-Lalande
33250 Pauillac, France
Tel: +33-5-56 59 19 40 Fax: +33-5-56 59 29 78

PIERO CASTELLINI BALDISSERA

One of Italy's most sought-after interior designers, architect Piero Castellini (a grandson of Portalupi, one of Italy's leading early 20th-century architects) is renowned for the sensitivity with which he restores old villas and castles. His decorative schemes are distinguished by warm Mediterranean colours, with subtle hints of the Far East – the result of his frequent travels there. As well as his recent work for Pirelli on the 15th-century palazzo, Bicocca degli Arcimboldi, Castellini's private clients include some of Italy's most prominent industrialists, aristocrats and film actors.

Piero Castellini Baldissera
via Marozzo della Rocca 5, 20123 Milan, Italy
Tel: +39-02-48 00 53 84 Fax: +39-02-469 2068

PIERINO PENATI, RISTORANTE

The cooking here is based in tradition but sparked with imagination. Star dishes – which include Roasted king prawns with ginger and vegetables and an awesomely good Pasta with watercress, rabbit and black truffles – are each credited on the menu with the name of the individual chef who cooked them.

Established by Pietro Paolo Penati in 1940, this elegant restaurant – set in a large country house north of Milan, with a lovely garden for summer dining – is now run by his son, Pier Giuseppe, and other family members. Everything is in the best of taste, with beautiful flowers, crystal and table linen, yet the atmosphere is remarkably relaxed. The restaurant runs a first-class catering service, too, creating a magical atmosphere with flowers, music and fireworks to complement its superb signature cooking.

Ristorante Pierino Penati
via XXIV Maggio 36
23897 Viganò, Lecco, Italy
Tel: +39-039-95 60 20 Fax: +39-039-921 1400

PIERRE CELEYRON

Arguably Europe's most talented party organiser, Pierre Celeyron has, in the past year, organised weddings in Germany and Austria and a ball in Rome, as well as the most glamorous private events in France. The June 1999 *soirée* at the Orangerie of Versailles on behalf of the American Friends of Versailles – generally regarded as the party of the year – was also his work. Celeyron's great gift is his unique combination of the ability to create wonderful settings – always in exquisite taste and always one-offs – with the most minute attention to detail.

Pierre Celeyron
44 avenue Gabriel
75008 Paris, France
Tel: +33-1-42 89 58 45 Fax: +33-1-42 89 58 48

PIERRE FREY

Increasingly known for its contemporary designs, this fabric house draws much of its inspiration from 18th- and 19th-century French patterns. Indeed, it was his love for this period – and especially for the

work of the celebrated fabric and carpet house, Braquenié – that prompted Patrick Frey (son of Pierre, who founded the firm in 1935) to buy that company and re-launch its collections. The Pierre Frey boutiques stock fabrics both by the metre and made up into cushions, bed-covers and lampshades.
Pierre Frey
47 rue des Petit Champs, 75001 Paris, France
Tel: +33-1-42 97 44 00   Fax: +33-1-42 97 46 00

PIERRE GAGNAIRE

Tables at this wunderkind-chef's restaurant are among the hardest to come by in Paris. And no wonder. He is a great risk-taker and the names of his dishes are Proustian in their complexity – *Salpicon de tourteau, gnocchis d'agria à la pimprenelle, girolles et amandes fraîches* – but his combinations (almost always) succeed brilliantly. In his hands, too, a simple *pot-au-feu* is equally sublime. The wine list – unusually short and constantly changing – is as adventurous as the cooking.
Pierre Gagnaire
6 rue Balzac, 75008 Paris, France
Tel: +33-1-44 35 18 25   Fax: +33-1-44 35 18 37

PIET OUDOLF

Oudolf's training as an architect prior to becoming a garden designer is evident in his use of space, structure and dramatic focal points, yet he is a true plantsman at heart. (With his wife, Anja, he runs one of Europe's best plant nurseries.) Having pioneered the trend to use grasses and meadow plants in borders, Oudolf combines plants to look as stunning in winter as in summer, anchored by evergreen topiary and hedges. Possibly Europe's most sought-after *paysagiste*, Oudolf is booked up years ahead.
Piet Oudolf
Broekstraat 17, 6999 De Hummelo, The Netherlands
Tel: +31-314-38 11 20   Fax: +31-314-38 11 99

PIERRE MARCOLINI

The sublime products of this highly creative *chocolatier-pâtissier* (awarded World Champion of Pâtisserie in 1995) are, quite simply, as good as chocolate gets. Marcolini combines the finest cocoa from Madagascar, Venezuela and Equador with exotic flavourings, including Earl Grey or Jasmine tea and thyme with orange, as well as such classics as

PIERRE MARCOLINI
CHOCOLATIER BRUXELLES

CHAMPION DU MONDE
DE PÂTISSERIE LYON 1995

violet and ginger. This year Marcolini's three Brussels boutiques are joined by a fourth, together with boutiques in Paris and Anvers and an outlet at Fortnum & Mason in London.
Pierre Marcolini
Avenue Louise 75M
1050 Brussels, Belgium (inside Hotel Conrad)
Tel: +32-2-216 8215 (for general information)

PIGUET & CIE

Founded by the Piguet family, this bank has, for nearly 150 years, been an integral part of the Swiss banking scene, establishing an almost unequalled reputation for excellent services, a highly professional team of staff and what it proudly calls the "maintenance of a human dimension" whenever dealing with clients. The bank is now part of the Banque Cantonale Vaudoise, which owns a 75% majority share in Piguet.
Banque Piguet & Cie S.A.
Place de l'Université 5, CH-1204 Geneva, Switzerland
Tel: +41-22-322 88 00   Fax: +41-22-322 88 22

PINEIDER

Since Francesco Pineider founded this firm in 1774 it has made the finest, hand-finished papers, engraving onto them decorations and crests for the likes of Napoleon and Byron, Piero Antinori and Riccardo Muti. The papers were – and still are – complemented by leather book-bindings and desk accessories. Now developing into a global brand (under new owners since 1997) its collections include small leathergoods, watches and pens. In 1999 Pineider released a limited-edition calligraphy pen, the 'Medici'.
Pineider
via del Roseto 54, Vallina, Florence, Italy
Tel: +39-02-659 8647   Fax: +39-02-655 5883

PININ BRAMBILLA

A pupil of Pellicolli, legendary art restorer Pinin Brambilla succeeded him in overseeing the restoration of Leonardo's *Last Supper* in the church of Santa Maria delle Grazie in Milan. Enormously respected internationally, Brambilla has written numerous pamphlets and several learned books on the problems of art preservation. Credits during her 40-year career include the renovation of Giotto's *Crucifixion* in Padua and paintings by Caravaggio, Tiepolo and Titian.
Dottoressa Pinin Brambilla
via Savona 43, 20144 Milan, Italy
Tel & Fax: +39-02-423 4350

PITRIZZA, HOTEL

Luigi Vietti's design and the hotel's location make the sense of seclusion here absolute. The Pitrizzia's rooms are spread between six bungalows, scattered through the grounds and the entire complex is set on its own point of land, with Sardinia's crystalline sea on three sides. Built into the landscape – even the swimming pool is punctuated by huge granite rocks – every part of it faces the sea and the décor (painted furniture and glazed floor tiles) is appropriately understated 'beach house'.
Hotel Pitrizza
07020 Porto Cervo, Sardinia, Italy
Tel: +39-0789-93 01 11   Fax: +39-0789-93 06 11

PIPPA POP-INS

When Pippa Deakin pioneered her concept of a hotel exclusively for children under 12, it was a sensation. Eight years on it has proved a brilliant

success; children love the fairy-tale setting with its 'midnight' feasts and cuddles-with-everything, provided by an excellent staff of trained nannies. For all the apparent whimsy, Deakin's approach to child-care is deadly serious. Her day nursery gives children from two to five the most wonderful start in life and there is also an imaginative programme of school-holiday excursions and workshops.

Pippa Pop-Ins
430 Fulham Road
London SW6 1DU, UK
Tel: +44-20-73 85 24 58   Fax: +44-20-73 85 57 06

PLAZA ATHENEE

Completely renovated in 1999 under the auspices of the Brunei Royal Family (its owners since 1997) the redoubtable Plaza Athénée has regained the splendour for which it is justifiably famous. This beautiful hotel is quintessentially French – guests can soak up the lush glamour of the place, confident that they will be treated like kings, thanks to the inspired management of Hervé Houdré, a hotelier of rare wit and wisdom. Favourite people-watching haunts include the cosy basement Scottish Bar, the leafy courtyard and the magnificent Gobelins gallery.

Hotel Plaza Athénée
25 avenue Montaigne, 75008 Paris, France
Tel: +33-1-53 67 66 65   Fax: +33-1-53 67 66 66

PLOUMIS-SOTIROPOULOS

Located in an elegant neo-classical building just off Athens' Constitution Square, this firm is the leading source of prime properties in Greece, whether a grand house in Athens or a dream villa on the islands, from Corfu to the Cyclades. Established in 1924, it is still family owned – under the direction of John Ploumis – and has been affiliated with Sotheby's for a decade. Its multi-lingual staff is noted for its expertise and discretion.

Ploumis-Sotiropoulos
Panepistimiou 6, GR-10671 Athens, Greece
Tel: +30-1-364 3112   Fax: +30-1-363 8005

POGGIO DEI MEDICI GOLF & COUNTRY CLUB

Tuscany. The very word evokes visions of ravishing countryside, great food and wine and beautiful architecture. This club has them all – and very good golf to boot. With five tees to each hole, the course challenges the best players while not intimidating those who play considerably 'more' golf to complete a round. The clubhouse – the lovely 16th-century Villa di Cignano – is a highly sociable gathering place for the Florentine élite and the seasonal residents of the surrounding villas.

Poggio dei Medici Golf & Country Club
via S. Gavino 27, 50038 Scarperia, Florence, Italy
Tel: +39-055-843 0436   Fax: +39-055-843 0439

POLO CLUB DU DOMAINE DE CHANTILLY

The creation of Patrick Guerrand-Hermès, this four-year old club is set on a 150-hectare estate in the heart of France's racing country. Not surprisingly, then, it counts the sons and wives of several leading owners and jockeys, as well as some junior Rothschilds among the members of its polo school. *Le tout Paris* gathers around the old English-style clubhouse for the season's key events: the Open de Paris in spring, the Trophée de Coquedier d'Or in July and the Coupe Hermès in September.

Polo Club du Domaine de Chantilly
La Ferme d'Apremont, 60300 Apremont, France
Tel: +33-3-44 64 04 30   Fax: +33-3-44 64 04 32

POLO DE DEAUVILLE

Although polo is played throughout the summer, this club truly sparkles in August when, between the end of the English season and the beginning of the American and Southern Hemisphere ones, many top players pass through. In fact, Deauville is in serious 'horse mode' in August, with racing and the bloodstock sales taking place at the same time. In a relaxed, holiday atmosphere, this is very much polo for polo's sake.

Polo de Deauville
45 avenue Hocquart de Turlot, 14800 Deauville, France
Tel: +33-2-31 98 95 34

POMMERY

If champagne were to have seasons, Pommery would be summer; its Brut Royal is "lively, floral, with lots of freshness on the finish", according to one respected wine writer. This style has been identified with the house since Madame Louise Pommery produced the first Brut champagne in 1874. Prince Alain de

Polignac, Madame Pommery's great-great-grandson, who created the blend, describes it as "a champagne without shadows"; in other words, nothing can be hidden in such a light style. Pommery's real show-stoppers, however, are its 'Louise' and 'Louise Rosé'; made only in exceptional years, each is blended from three grands crus and matured for seven years.

Pommery
5 Place du Général Gouraud, 51053 Reims, France
Tel: +33-3-26 61 62 63   Fax: +33-3-26 61 62 99

PORTHAULT

Established in 1920 Porthault caused a sensation five years later when it introduced the first coloured and printed household linen. Since then it has continued to innovate, with lace and *appliqué* borders and braid-trimmed towels, for example, and by marrying state-of-the-art production with traditional handcrafts – but the house is renowned, above all for its quality and restrained good taste. Its design studio, directed by Madeleine Porthault, also undertakes dozens of special commissions for both hotels and private clients.

Porthault
18 avenue Montaigne, 75008 Paris, France
Tel: +33-1-47 20 75 25   Fax: +33-1-40 70 09 26

PORTMARNOCK GOLF CLUB

The Irish Muirfield in terms of both prestige and challenge, Portmarnock – founded in 1894 – is set on a windswept peninsula which was once part of the whisky-making Jameson family estate. The gabled clubhouse – populated by cream-of-Dublin members – overlooks a demanding, serpentine course. The only PGA European Tour Course in Ireland, it possesses some legendary holes; the 14th was Henry Cotton's "best ever", the 15th is the best par-3 in the world, according to Arnold Palmer and – unusually – even Portmarnock's 9-hole course is worthy of praise in its own right.

Portmarnock Golf Club
Co. Dublin, Ireland
Tel: +353-1-846 2968 Fax: +353-1-846 2601

POSTA VECCHIA, LA

John Paul Getty's former home, this 17th-century villa on the edge of the sea, is still adorned with stunning works of art from his collection, Gobelin tapestries, Venetian lamps and – beneath the music room – its own archaeological dig. For all that, its spirit is far from intimidating; the young director, Henry Sció, wanders around in shirt sleeves, encouraging his guests to relax and help themselves to drinks at the bar. And, when you want to escape, he will arrange the rental of a Ferrari for you.

La Posta Vecchia
Loc. Palo Laziale, 00055 Ladispoli, Italy
Tel: +39-06-994 9501 Fax: +39-06-994 9507

PRADA

While Miuccia Prada's modern art foundation gathers momentum in Milan and her company buys up shares in other major brands, the trend-setter still continues to be a fashion innovator. Turning her attention to the outdoors, she has launched the highly successful red-strip sportswear line and sponsored the Italian yacht in America's Cup 2000.

Prada
Galleria Vittorio Emmanuele 60-65, 20121 Milan, Italy
Tel: +39-02-87 69 79 Fax: +39-02-72 00 21 85

PRATESI

The world's luckiest babies sleep on Pratesi's cot sheets and are wrapped in its ultra-soft cotton *piqué* robes. Famous for its *appliquéed* and embroidered household linens, the firm was established by Remigio Pratesi four generations ago in the Tuscan hills, to furnish his aristocratic patrons. Complementing its classical sheets and towels, Federico Pratesi and his mother, Dede, have introduced a 'Yachting' line and developed 'Pravoile', a specially woven, ultra-light cotton muslin for its bed sets.

Pratesi
via Montenapoleone 27E, 20121 Milan, Italy
Tel: +39-02-76 01 27 55 Fax: +39-02-78 35 74

PRATT'S

This private dining club was once the rooming house where the 7th Duke of Beaufort's steward, William Nathaniel Pratt, stayed when in London and where the Duke occasionally dropped in for a little kitchen supper. Given that its present owner, the Duke of Devonshire, is among England's most well-read men, the conversation around its basement dining tables is lively and wide-ranging, Though ladies are resolutely barred, an annual cocktail party does allows them into Pratt's – perhaps to discover exactly why all the staff have come to b e known as 'George'.

Pratt's
14 Park Place, London SW1A 1LP, UK
Tel: +44-20-74 93 03 97

PYMS GALLERY

Since establishing Pyms Gallery in 1975, Alan and Mary Hobart have become widely recognised as specialists in the field of late 19th- and early 20th century French, British and Irish art, acting on behalf of both private collectors and museums from around the globe.

Their reputation in Irish art is particularly strong. In 1990 the gallery published A Free Spirit – Irish Art From 1860-1960 to coincide with its exhibition at the Royal Hibernian Academy in Dublin, which featured Jack B. Yeats, Lavery and O'Connor – all of whose works feature regularly at the gallery. 'The Irish Revival' (1982) and 'An Ireland Imagined' (1993) are among the titles of past exhibitions, which have charted the rise in value and prestige of Irish painting.

In more recent years the gallery has extended its catalogue, acquiring for private collectors works by such old masters as Poussin, Ribera and Canaletto. They have also handled French Impressionists, including Monet, Manet and Pissarro and recently acquired a 1947 portrait by Picasso of Françoise Gilot, mother of his daughter Paloma.

Offering advice on forming collections, insurance, restoration, valuing and selling paintings, the Hobarts also hold three exhibitions each year in their 19th-century premises on Mount Street – noted for their convivial atmosphere – and show newly acquired works at the Grosvenor House Art and Antiques Fair.

Pyms Gallery
9 Mount Street, London W1Y 5AD, UK
Tel: +44-20-76 29 20 20 Fax: +44-20-76 29 20 60

PRE CATALAN, LE

A Sunday lunch-time table on the terrace here is one of the loveliest places to be in Paris – the sunlight filtering through the trees, the sound of horses' hooves, the quiet conversation from neighbouring tables (smartly dressed bourgeois families – perfectly *coiffed* women, perfectly mannered children) and Frédéric Anton's superb cooking. Dishes such as his Pigeon breast with *foie gras* and an almond jelly won him a second Michelin star in 1999. It is only fitting, then, that the wines are almost exclusively grands crus, with prices to match.

Le Pré Catalan
Route de Suresnes, Bois de Boulogne, 75016 Paris, France
Tel: +33-1-45 24 55 58

PRES ET LES SOURCES D'EUGENIE, LES

The Empress Eugénie, a regular visitor here in the 19th century, would feel at home in the exquisitely tasteful surroundings that Christine Guérard has created from three old colonial houses – where the finesse of the interiors is matched only by the beauty of the gardens. The restless creative genius of Michel Guérard, celebrated for his *cuisine minceur*, is reflected in a menu which suggests a return to his roots, with such sublime and powerfully flavoured dishes as his *Tourte rustique du caneton et caille au foie gras*.

Les Près et les Sources d'Eugénie
40302 Eugénie-Les-Bains, France
Tel: +33-5-58 05 06 07   Fax: +33-5-58 51 10 10

PROFESSIONAL SECURITY

The devastatingly simple motto of brothers Gianni and Roberto Fagnoni – "What you cannot see you cannot steal" – is behind their invention of the first pro-active burglary response, the Smoke-Cloak. Trained as electrical engineers, they have worked throughout the world, applying their technical know-how to the design and setting up of this and similar security systems, to protect private houses, art collections, banks and individuals.

Professional Security
Via Ghibellina 69, Florence 50122, Italy
Tel: +39-055-24 15 06   Fax: +39-055-24 15 62

PROSE SA

Established in 1974, this is the oldest security company in Spain; however its first-class reputation is due to more than just experience. Offering systems installation and maintenance, personal protection and consultancy services, it adapts solutions to each client, according to their needs and priorities. Furthermore, it is rigorous in the training of its personnel, invests heavily in support technology and underlines the quality of its service with international ISO 9002 certification.

Prose SA
Calle Lezama 4, E-28034 Madrid, Spain
Tel: +34-91-631 0900

PRIVATAIR

Underlining its claim to offer the highest standards of safety, security and service (not to mention confidentiality) PrivatAir became Europe's first certified ISO 9002 private charter airline in May 1999. The fleet expanded in the autumn to include

two all-new high-performance Boeing Business Jets for 18 and 28 passengers respectively. The first of their type available for charter, they enable the company to offer non-stop service on such routes as Geneva to Los Angeles.

PrivatAir
33 Chemin de l'Avanchet, P.O. Box 53
CH-1216 Cointrin-Geneva, Switzerland
Tel: +41-22-929 6730   Fax: +41-22-929 6731

PRUM, J.J.

The image of German wines has suffered horribly in recent years but, thankfully, producers such as Prum have stuck to their principles and continue to turn out wines which are models of their kind. Low in alcohol, Prum wines rely on a delicious acidity to give them life and longevity. In a world seemingly addicted to ponderously flavoured Chardonnay, these Rieslings provide an uplifting and utterly refreshing alternative.

J. J. Prum
Uferallee 19, D-54470 Wehlen an der Mosel, Germany
Tel: +49-65-31 30 91   Fax: +49-65-31 60 71

PUIFORCAT

In the 1920s and '30s Jean Puiforcat established his company's signature, modernistic style – taking it away from the formal style for which the silversmith had been renowned in his father's day – while retaining the house's fine tradition of craftsmanship. Today, under the ownership of Hermès, this philosophy continues. A number of Jean Puiforcat's distinctive, sculptural pieces have been re-edited and new collections added – including, in 1998, the stainless steel 'Wave' flatware and, in 1999, the 'Central Park' tea and coffee service.

Puiforcat
48 avenue Gabriel, 75008 Paris, France
Tel: +33-1-45 63 10 10   Fax: +33-1-42 56 27 15

PULBROOK & GOULD

Founded over 40 years ago by Lady Susan Pulbrook and Miss Rosamund Gould, this grand florists' exuberant, country-inspired style has influenced a generation of florists throughout the world. The founders' philosophy – that cow parsley is as important as lilies – still holds true, although the company has moved forward, with a range of luxurious beauty products and a school, set up by Lady Pulbrook, where skills and secrets are shared.

Pulbrook & Gould
Liscartan House, 127 Sloane Street, London SW1X 9AS, UK
Tel: +44-20-77 30 00 30   Fax: +44-20-77 30 07 22

PUPI SOLARI

The more conservatively elegant of Milan's ladies revere Pupi Solari's classical tailoring and finely-detailed children's clothes. Vivacious Pupi sources her precision-cut suits and ravishing hats from artisan tailors and milliners in both Milan and Naples – and it shows in the quality; much of her collection is hand made and the fabrics are wonderful. Pupi's son, Andrea Host, has equally elegant men's clothes at his nearby boutique, Host.

Pupi Solari
Piazza Tommaseo 2, 20145 Milan, Italy
Tel: +39-02-46 33 25 Fax: +39-02-481 9210

PUSHKIN MUSEUM, THE

If seeing first-rate works by Monet, Cézanne, Chagall, Renoir and Degas in relatively uncrowded surroundings is your idea of heaven, this museum is the perfect place to do so. The superb collection was amassed before the Revolution by Sergei Shchukin and Ivan Morosov – merchants enriched by business who, in turn, enriched the city with art. The museum's vast collections of Flemish, Gothic and Byzantine art are less well known but equally fascinating.

The Pushkin Museum of Fine Art
12 Volkhonka Ulitsa, 101000 Moscow, Russia
Tel: +7-095-203 9578

QUARTIER 206

Anne Maria Jagfeld has brought the style of a Harvey Nichols or a Bergdorf Goodman to Berlin in the form of the superb Quartier 206. Housed in a marble shopping arcade designed by I.M. Pei, this 27,000 square-foot luxury department store is a Mecca of sharply-edited and artfully displayed must-haves from Michael Kors to Acqua di Parma, lingerie and porcelain to books, flowers and cigars and even twice-yearly measuring sessions for John Lobb's bespoke shoes.

Quartier 206
Friedrichstrasse 71, D-10117 Berlin, Germany
Tel: +49-30-20 94 68 00 Fax: +49-30-20 94 68 10

QUINZI E GABRIELI

The tables are Lilliputian (which adds to the buzz), the décor charmingly simple (aquamarine walls and huge vases of gladioli) and the wine list, curiously, doesn't list vintages (there are some good ones) but the point of this marvellous restaurant is seafood. Forget culinary *tours de force*; in its simplicity and purity this is as good as it ever gets, anywhere. The Alzata of mixed seafood. The Crudo of scampi, sea bass and squid. The grilled lobster. And, best of all, the Spaghetti with *langoustines*. Prepared on a little stove beside your table, the pasta is cooked in sea-

THE QUEEN OF SCOTS PRIVATE TRAIN

At the end of the 19th century, the railways provided the last word in luxury for wealthy travellers; families would own or charter whole trains to transport them to their Scottish estates. Rick Edmondson and his family own one of the last of these great private trains, which they have restored to its original glory.

The Observation Car has, as its livery, the original and beautifully evocative "plum and spilt milk", which was chosen as the colour scheme for the Royal limousine. The Family Saloon contains a library and the Dining Car, the world's oldest – commissioned for 19th-century cotton barons, is a marvel of polished wood and deep red velvet.

Now the Edmondson family's private train, The Queen of Scots is also available for charter and will take you anywhere you wish in Britain. Recent clients include a group of French plutocrats who travelled from London to St Andrews for a golfing holiday – but the train will go even to the tiniest station and, depending on the tracks being used, can be hauled by a classic steam locomotive.

The service on board is first-rate and no detail is too small for the company's attention, whether sourcing a rare vintage to be served with dinner or – a recent case – providing the same day's newspapers from Beijing for a Chinese client.

The Queen of Scots Private Train
The Scottish Highland Railway Co. Ltd., Bedford House
62 London Road, Maidstone, Kent ME16 8QL, UK
Tel: +44-1622-68 88 99 Fax: +44-1622-68 88 55

water, the *langoustines* tossed in a miraculously fresh tomato sauce. Enzo Gabrieli, looking down from that great kitchen in the sky, would certainly approve. You will think that you have died and gone to heaven.

Quinzi e Gabrieli
via delle Coppelle 5-6, 00186 Rome, Italy
Tel: +39-06-687 9389 Fax: +39-06-687 4940

RACO DE CAN FABES, EL

Santi Santamaria might have been an artist or a writer – indeed, he has just published a fascinating book, *L'Etica del Gusto* (The Ethics of Taste). His formidable energy, though, is channelled into creating extraordinary dishes from the humblest ingredients; described simply as "Veal" or "Neck of" or "Pig's trotters" it is truly 'peasant food' fit for kings. In what has become an industrial suburb, Santamaria and his wife, Angels Serra, have transformed his family's former country home into one of Europe's most outstanding restaurants. Every detail – from the china and flowers to the staff uniforms – is their own creation and is in the most marvellous taste.
El Raco de Can Fabes
Sant Joan 6, Sant Celoni, E-08080 Barcelona, Spain
Tel & Fax: +34-93-867 2851

RADI DI MONTAGNA

Comprising a castle, two houses and de-consecrated Romanesque church in a beautiful 34-acre park, this exquisite medieval hamlet can be rented as a whole or its houses rented individually. Set on a hill and surrounded by woods, vineyards and olive groves, it was rescued from ruin by an American couple in the 1970s. Keen collectors of early Italian art, they have filled it with beautiful furniture and objects and every imaginable modern luxury so as to create a magical retreat.
Radi di Montagna near Siena, Italy
c/- Villas and Apartments Abroad, 402 Madison Ave New York, NY 10017
Tel: +1-212-759 1025   Fax: +1-212-755 8316

RAFAEL, HOTEL

There can be few finer places in Munich on a summer's evening than the roof-top pool of the Raphael, as the sun sets behind the city's spires. Unless it is a cosy winter's evening in Suite 608, set in the round tower. Small and intimate, this is Munich's most stylish retreat, where glitz has been forsaken in favour of restrained luxury and, in place of obsequious staff, there is a young team who perfectly understand the maxim "God is in the detail."
Hotel Rafael
Neuturmstrasse 1, D-80331 Munich, Germany
Tel: +49-89-29 09 80   Fax: +49-89-22 25 39

RAIMONDO BIANCHI

Much in demand among Milan's fashion circle, Raimondo Bianchi makes daringly original and wonderfully stylish bouquets and floral arrangements. His style is guided by the season and the mood and his shop is a feast for the senses. Bianchi's creations delight through their mix of the chic and the surprising – wild flowers with nettles and roses surrounded by a halo of branches.
Raimondo Bianchi
via Montebello 7, 20121 Milan, Italy
Tel: +39-02-655 5108

RAMONET, DOMAINE

Even connoisseurs of white burgundy are astounded at the massive concentration of fruit that the Ramonet brothers manage to pack into their wines. Such is the staggering opulence of their Montrachet that, at one tasting, a taster implored his colleague not to spit out her sample for it almost broke his heart to see Montrachet treated thus. Go to any lengths to secure a bottle.
Ramonet
11 rue de Grand Puit, 21190 Chassagne, France
Tel: +33-3-80 21 30 88   Fax: +33-3-80213565

RAMPOLDI

Now the unofficial *arbiter* of Monte Carlo's social pecking order, owner Luciano was Régine's star waiter in Paris in the early seventies. Here, this master of placement decides whether multi-millionaire racing drivers should have precedence over Milanese bankers and rock stars and who should sit at the coveted tables in the back room. The menu is a brasserie-simple mix of French and Italian dishes – the latter, according to Karl Lagerfeld, including some works of genius.
Rampoldi
3 avenue des Spélugues, Monte Carlo, Monaco
Tel: +377-93 30 70 65   Fax: +377-93 50 43 84

RAVASI

An open secret among Italy's best decorators – among them Piero Castellini – Gabriella Ravasi and Guido Lamperti have a remarkable talent for restoring upholstered furniture that seems, even to a well-tutored eye, beyond redemption. Whether for private clients or decorators, they are as happy with a brocade-covered sofa as with a tiny needlepoint foot-stool. Their work is not, however, confined to antiques; they recently did a superb job on some rare 1930s pieces.
Ravasi
via Como 34, 23807 Merate, Italy
Tel: +39-039-59 93 97

RAVENEAU, DOMAINE

For those who are enchanted by the steely austerity of great chablis, the wines of François and Jean-Marie Raveneau form a benchmark. The grand crus possess amazing complexity and a good vintage can age for 10 or more years before reaching its apogee. Then it will deliver a taste experience that is clean and pure, with subtle mineral hints and a distinct flintiness. A wine for purists.
Domaine Raveneau
9 rue Chichée, 89800 Chablis, France
Tel: +33-3-86 42 17 46   Fax: +33-3-86 42 45 55

RELILAX

There has been a thermal spa on this site for 1000 years and the treatments offered today by the Braggion family and their formidable team of therapists combine this long tradition with state-of-the-art innovation and expert medical advice. Established in 1982, the spa has developed a programme of over 50 treatments – many based on its own products – which will tackle anything from stress to cellulite. A return rate of over 75% of guests underlines their excellence.
Relilax Club-Hotel Terme Miramonti
Piazza Roma 19, 35036 Montegrotto Terme
Padua, Italy
Tel: +39-049-891 1755   Fax: +39-049-891 1678

REM KOOLHASS

Fearsomely intelligent and described by Architectural Digest as "perhaps the world's most astonishing architect", Rem Koulhass creates the most extraordinary houses. His ideas often appear to confound gravity – like placing a swimming pool on the roof with little evident means of support. Uncompromisingly modern yet poetic, intricate rather than cosy (he prefers aluminium floors to carpet) his houses are full of surprises – capturing views from an unexpected angle or juxtaposing the cheapest with the most noble materials.
Rem Koolhass
Office for Metropolitan Architecture, Heer Bokelweg 149
3032 AD Rotterdam, The Netherlands
Tel: +31-10-243 8200   Fax: +31-10-243 8202

REMY MARTIN

Packaged in a dark green, frosted bottle, adorned with the company's famous centaur logo, Rémy Martin's VSOP cognac has become a byword for quality. So, too, has its top-of-the-range Louis XIII, a superb cognac which is presented in a Baccarat crystal decanter. Its flavour is rich and fruity and extraordinarily vibrant for a spirit that will be at least 50 years old before it is released.

Rémy Martin
rue Société Vinicole, BP 37
15112 Cognac Cedex, France
Tel: +33-5-45 35 76 00   Fax: +33-5-45 35 02 85

RENA LANGE

Sophisticate Rena Lange's business is very much a family affair. The wife of Peter Gunthert, CEO of M. Lange & Co, she has now been joined by her son Daniel. Born in Berlin, Lange worked in Paris and Munich as a designer before setting up alone. Her signature unlined tweed jacket, beautifully finished inside and out, is typical of her cool, calm and collected style. Lange's latest departure is the 'Red' collection, a working wardrobe for career women which features such classics as pinstripe and seersucker suits with a natty twist.

Rena Lange
Rosenheimer Strasse 139
D-81671 Munich, Germany
Tel: +49-89-41 86 61 12   Fax: +49-89-49 18 48

RENE CAOVILLA

When Rene Caovilla asserts that his shoes are "the last objects that a woman should take off", it is clear that he regards them as serious instruments of seduction. Characterised by clean, refined lines and hand-decorated with pearls, lace and beads, they are also minor works of art, which have gained the admiration of Sharon Stone, Elizabeth Taylor, Caroline of Monaco and Valentino – for whose couture shows Caovilla has made the shoes for over 20 years.

René Caovilla
via Paradisi 1, 30032 Fiesso D'Artico, Venezia, Italy
Tel: +39-049-980 1300   Fax: +39-049-980 1315

RESERVE DE BEAULIEU, LA

To arrive at La Réserve's private jetty by boat before dining in its Michelin-starred restaurant is to evoke memories of the Côte d'Azur in its 1930s' heyday. Since being bought by the Delion family in 1994, this pink stucco Italianate villa has been restored to its former glory and the Delions have been rewarded by the return of an exceedingly elegant clientele. The view of Cap Ferrat from the best suites can only be described as utterly seductive

La Réserve de Beaulieu
5 Boulevard du General-Leclerc
06310 Beaulieu-sur-Mer, France
Tel: +33-4-93 01 00 01   Fax: +33-4-93 01 28 99

REPOSSI

Strongly identified with Monaco, where he opened his first shop in 1977 (his Place Vendôme boutique opened in 1985) Alberto Repossi is a third-

generation jeweller. Often reflecting his fascination with India and his love of antique stones, Repossi's jewels are designed for high-impact glamour. As jeweller-by-appointment to Prince Rainier, Repossi created a special collection of jewels to commemorate the 700th anniversary of the Grimaldi dynasty.

Repossi
6 Place Vendome, 75001 Paris, France
Tel: +33-1-42 96 42 34   Fax: 33-1-40 15 07 89

RESIDENCE DE LA PINEDE, LA

If you are not seeing St. Tropez from the seclusion and luxury of a very large yacht, this hotel is certainly the next best thing. Hidden away from the frenetic activity of the town, it has lovely shaded gardens and a private beach of talc-fine sand facing towards Le Port – a view shared by all of its rooms and suites. Since falling in love with the place in 1985, Jean-Claude and Nicole Delion have turned it into a sybarites' paradise.

La Résidence de la La Pinéde
Plage de la Bouillabaisse, 83990 Saint Tropez, France
Tel: +33-4-94 55 91 00   Fax: +33-4-94 97 73 64

RESIDENCIA, LA

The brainchild of Richard Branson, this lovely retreat in the village of Deià – where Michael Douglas is a neighbour – was created from two old manor houses. Furnished in traditional Mallorcan style, they offer great luxury without the glitz. Perched on the cliffs, with wonderful views of the sea and mountains, La Residencia has countless secluded terraces, two swimming pools and a private beach nearby. Its upgraded hydrotherapy centre and gymnasium opened in October 1999.

La Residencia
Deià, E-07179 Mallorca, Spain
Tel: +34-971-63 90 11   Fax: +34-971-63 93 70

RESIDENZ HEINZ WINKLER

In 1981 the youngest-ever holder of three Michelin stars (at Munich's Tantris restaurant), Tyrolean-born chef Heinz Winkler returned to his roots in 1989, buying this 14th century residence and transforming it into a sumptuous Relais & Château establishment. Accolades have been heaped upon Winkler's deliciously light interpretations of French classics such as Goose liver parfait with grapes in a

Traminer jelly and Ballotine of lobster in saffron. His exceptional 25,000-bottle cellar includes rarities dating back to 1874.

Residenz Heinz Winkler
1 Kirchplatz, D-83229 Aschau im Chiemgau, Germany
Tel: +49-8052-17 990   Fax: +49-8052-17 99 66
Website: www.Residenz-Heinz-Winkler.de

RHODE SCHOOL OF CUISINE

This excellent cookery school offers week-long spring and autumn courses in two luxurious villas, one in Tuscany, the other on the Côte d'Azur. Groups are small and former students praise the sublime blend of some of the finest scenery and food in the world – and the masterly and imaginative teaching of chefs Frédéric Rivière and Valter Roman. Their book, *From Our Table to Yours*, was published in October 1999 and, in spring 2001, the school opens a third venue, in Marrakech.

Rhode School of Cuisine
c/- Skybridge Design Ltd, 11A Porchester Terrace
London W2 3TH, UK
Tel: +44-20-72 62 71 62 Fax: +44-20-72 62 71 63
Email: rhode@btinternet.com
Website: www.togastronomy.com

RESTAURANT DIETER MULLER

Thomas Althof, owner of the lovely Schlosshotel Lerbach and a stickler for quality, certainly got it right when he invited Dieter Müller to establish his eponymous restaurant here in 1992. A modern glass-walled wing was built overlooking the gardens and Müller has turned it into a major destination restaurant. Widely travelled and cosmopolitan in outlook, the classically-trained Müller imbues his cooking with a remarkable lightness and a deft use of Asian herbs. The wine cellar is stupendous.

Restaurant Dieter Müller
Schlosshotel Lerbach, Lerbacher Weg
D-51465 Bergisch Gladbach, Germany
Tel: +49-2202-2040 Fax: +49-2202-20 49 40

RICARDO DO ESPIRITO SANTO SILVA FOUNDATION

In 1953 the banker and art collector Ricardo do Espírito Santo Silva set up a Foundation and created the Portuguese Decorative Arts Museum-School, which houses part of his personal collection – almost 2,000 pieces of Portuguese furniture, tiles, textiles, rugs and silverware from the 15th- to the early 19th-century – as well as 18 workshops.

Here, highly skilled craftsmen perform wood-work and metal-work, gilding, decorative painting and book binding and undertake the restoration of glassware, porcelain and faïence and the making of

Arraiolos rugs. They reproduce items in the Foundation's collection, as well as creating replicas of originals belonging to other museums and private collectors. The Foundation also runs two schools – the College of Decorative Arts, and the Arts and Crafts Institute.

Ricardo do Espírito Santo Silva Foundation
Largo das Portas do Sol 2, 1100 Lisbon, Portugal
Tel: +351-1-886 2183 Fax: +351-1-887 4930
Website: www.fress.pt

RICHARD GINORI 1735

Celebrated for the timeless classicism of its Chinese-inspired cockerel design (created before 1750) and its 'Impero' collection, this was one of Europe's earliest porcelain makers. Established in 1735 by Marchese Carlo Ginori, it became known as Richard-Ginori in 1896, when it merged with the Ceramica Richard Society. Limited-edition collections include its 'Liberty' lamps and vases, its re-editions of 1930s Gio Ponti museum pieces and its annual 'Medici' collectors' plates. The company recently opened a museum in Florence's Palazzo Rucellai.

Richard Ginori 1735
via Giulio Cesare 21, 50019 Florence, Italy
Tel: +39-055-42 04 91 Fax: +39-055-420 4954

RICHARD GREEN

Having joined his father's gallery aged 15, Richard Green set up on his own before he was 20 and attributes his success to a good eye, a passion for paintings and sheer hard work. Green's flagship gallery (once the home of Admiral Nelson's mistress, Emma Hamilton) opened a couple of years ago and is a six-floor mansion with a top-lit 19th-century picture gallery. 1999 exhibitions included a remarkable collection of 17th century 'Cabinet Pictures' by Dutch and Flemish Masters including Jacob van Ruisdael and Gerrit Dou.

Richard Green
147 New Bond Street, London W1Y 9PE, UK
Tel: +44-20-74 93 39 39 Fax: +44-20-76 29 26 09

RICHEMOND, LE

Miró and Chagall are just two of the artists who have doodled in Le Richemond's Livre d'Or since the hotel opened in 1875. Decorated in theatrically grand style, with heavy drapes and rich panelling, it nevertheless has the atmosphere of a private club – one which recently-appointed General Manager, Victor Armleder will, no doubt, maintain. The best rooms in the house have lovely views of the lake – particularly the Colette Suite, named for the writer, who adored the place.

Le Richemond
Jardin Brunswick, CH-1201 Geneva, Switzerland
Tel: +41-22-715 7000 Fax: +41-22-715 7001

RIEDEL

For lovers of the finest wines there are no better glasses than the 'Sommelier' line produced by Georg Riedel in Austria. One fan even went so far as to describe them as "lingerie for wine"! The range is wide, with a particular glass painstakingly designed for each style of wine. Form and function combine beautifully, to enhance the wine while at the same time adorning the dinner table.

Riedel Crystal
Weissachstrasse 28, A-6330 Kufstein, Austria
Tel: +43-5373-64 896 Fax: +43-5372-63 225

RITZ, LONDON

Thanks to Director Giles Shepard's passion for detail and the Barclay family's deep pockets, this Sleeping Beauty has reawakened. Nothing has really changed (the Empire-style *décor*, the stunningly beautiful Restaurant) yet everything has changed. The doormen once again turn away the scruffily-dressed who would take afternoon tea in the Palm Court. And the tea is, once again, served in the

Ritz's famous forget-me-not patterned porcelain. Again, too, it is the venue for some of London's smartest parties (Camilla Parker Bowles and Prince Charles are practically regulars now). And a small fortune has been spent 'upstairs' – particularly restoring the suites overlooking Green Park into some of the most splendid in London.

The Ritz
150 Piccadilly, London W1V 9DG, UK
Tel: +44-20-74 93 81 81   Fax: +44-20-74 93 26 87

RITZ, PARIS

A 20th-century legend, The Ritz's glamour was defined in the past by Ingrid Bergman and Ernest Hemingway and today by Sharon Stone and Kim Basinger. Elton John's favourite Diptyque candles are lit in his suite before he arrives and, for other regular guests, the Head Housekeeper takes photographs of the night tables to ensure that favourite objects are arranged 'just so'. How sad, then, that the tourists in the Bar Vendôme haven't the courtesy to observe the "jackets-must-be-worn" dress code – or that the staff apparently haven't the authority to enforce it.

The Ritz Paris
15 Place Vendome, 75001 Paris, France
Tel: +33-1-43 16 30 30   Fax: +33-1-43 16 36 68

RIVA

Since its takeover a few years ago by the Stellican group, this great marque (which traces its origins back to Pietro Riva's boat-repair business on the Italian lakes in the mid-19th century) has taken huge strides toward reclaiming its former pre-eminence. The range now comprises five models, the latest of which – introduced in October 1999 to great acclaim – is the sleek, 25.6-metre *Riva 84 Open*. Next to come will be a 21-metre *Open* and a 30-foot sports boat to replace the legendary *Aquarama*.

Cantieri Riva
24067 Sarnico, Italy
Tel: +39-035-91 12 02   Fax: +39-035-91 10 59

RIVER CAFE, THE

Their introduction (through their best-selling cookery books) of Tuscan cooking to London's dinner-party circuit and their adoption as patron saints of Tony Blair's New Labour élite may have made owners Ruth Rogers and Rose Gray into media stars but nothing has changed at their restaurant. The cooking is wonderfully simple, bold and singing with flavour; the staff are young and breezy; the short and constantly evolving wine list contains delicious surprises and an outdoor table overlooking the Thames is one of the best places to be on a summer day.

The River Café
Thames Wharf, Rainville Road, London W6 9HA, UK
Tel: +44-20-73 81 88 24

ROB VAN HELDEN

The stunning flowers which decorate Elton John's parties are the work of this modest but immensely talented young man. Entirely self-taught (his first job was delivering flowers by bicycle in his native Holland), van Helden favours flowers such as tuberoses, peonies, lily of the valley and blue hyacinths. His arrangements – which often incorporate fruit and candles – are distinguished by strong structures and unusual containers, though never at the expense of the natural beauty of the flowers.

Rob Van Helden Floral Design
Unit 8, Tun Yard, Peardon Street
London SW8 3HT, UK
Tel: +44-20-77 20 67 74   Fax: +44-20-77 20 95 68

ROBBE & BERKING

Now more than 125 years old, this distinguished company was the first silversmith to introduce Northern European design to the wider world in the 1950s. Underlining the value which the company places on design, 17 European museums include its 1980s 'Alta' pattern, designed by Wilfried Moll, in

their collections and several of its other patterns – characterised by sculptural lines and superb workmanship – are recognised as modern classics.

Robbe & Berking
Zur Bleiche 47, D-24941 Flensburg, Germany
Tel: +49-461-90 30 60   Fax: +49-461-903 0622

ROBERGE

Although the Robergé marque first appeared in 1972, owner Robert Mouawad's family have been jewellers since the mid-19th century, originally in Beirut. Robergé's establishment of its own manufactory in 1995 gives it total control over the entire watch-making process. Its collection – all named after the constellations – ranges from chronographs and grand complications to *haute joaillerie* watches. The firm has also launched a collection of pens, the most

dazzling of which is set with almost 3,000 diamonds.
Robergé
68 rue de Rhone, CH-1204 Geneva, Switzerland
Tel: +41-22-310 7093   Fax: +41-22-311 1874

ROBERT NATAF

The *doyen* of French bloodstock agents, Nataf has bought more than 50 Group I winners during his career – notably *Triptych*, which he bought as a yearling for $2.15 million on behalf of Alan Clore. At the other end of the scale, he has a great instinct for a bargain, purchasing a 'claimer' for FF220,000 in 1990 that went on to win the French Derby. Nataf has done business with practically every big name French breeder and owner and is the French representative of both John Magnier and Michael Tabor.

Robert Nataf
Horse France, 49 avenue Pierre Grenier
92100 Boulogne, France
Tel: +33-1-46 94 84 00   Fax: +33-1-46 94 00 14

ROBERT SCHMIT, GALERIE

This gallery, founded in 1929 by Jean Schmit, always has impressive pieces by 19th- and 20th-century masters. Its most significant exhibition of 1999, 'Delacroix à Chagall', with works by such artists as Renoir, Van Gogh, Modigliani and Picasso, showed the calibre of the place. Its excellent reputation is also reflected in its sale of key *œuvres* to the Musée d'Orsay, the Metropolitan Museum of Art and the National Gallery in Washington.

Galerie Robert Schmit
396 rue Saint-Honoré
75001 Paris, France
Tel: +33-1-42 60 36 36   Fax: +33-1-49 27 97 16

ROBERTO, RESTAURANT

Sean Connery, the Duke of Aosta and other members of the jet-setting establishment make this their first stop on arriving in Geneva, settling into the cosy wood-panelled room as if they had come home. For over three decades Roberto Carugati has been delighting them with his urbane charm and chef Antonio Martignetti's fresh pasta, *ossobuco and bollito misto*. Roberto's passion for wine – Italian, naturally – means a cellar-full of great names alongside some little-known treasures.

Restaurant Roberto
110 rue Pierre-Fatio
CH-1204 Geneva, Switzerland
Tel: +41-22-311 8033   Fax: +41-22-311 8466

ROBERTO PEREGALLI

The former collaborator of Renzo Mongiardino, Roberto Peregalli established his own interior design practice in 1986. Now working in partnership with the architect, Laura Sartori Rimini, Peregalli is celebrated as the master of the 'old palazzo' look although, in his hands, this is no mere reconstruction of antiquity; his interiors are bold fantasies, imbued with a stunning theatricality, while furniture – often kept to a minimum – is relaxed and comfortable, mixing flea-market finds with fine, 18th-century pieces.

Roberto Peregalli
via Passione 11, 20122 Milan, Italy
Tel: +39-02-76 01 41 40   Fax: +39-02-76 00 16 40

ROLAND BARTHELEMY

The extraordinary smell that wafts into the street confirms that this is a cheese merchant *par excellence* (he supplies the Elysée Palace, no less). As well as the classics – Camembert, Roquefort, Maroilles et al – which he ripens to perfection in his cellars, Barthélemy makes his own, deliciously creamy

Fontainbleau on the premises. Mountain cheeses are a Barthélemy speciality (perhaps a throwback to his ski-instructor days) as are *recherché* goats' and ewes' milk cheeses from the farthest corners of France.

Roland Barthélémy
51 rue de Grenelle
75007 Paris, France
Tel: +33-1-45 48 56 75   Fax: +33-1-45 49 25 16

ROLEX

This giant of the watch-making industry began as a watch distribution company in London in 1905, the brainchild of *émigré* Bavarian, Hans Wilsdorf, who coined the brand name three years later. His big break came in 1926 with the invention of the first truly waterproof and air-tight watch, the Oyster, now the world's most instantly recognisable luxury sports watch. Each Oyster movement, assembled by hand, contains almost 220 components, including the Perpetual rotor, which it patented in 1931.

Rolex SA
3-6 rue François Dussaud
CH-1211 Geneve 24, Switzerland
Tel: +41-22-308 2745   Fax: +41-22-308 2583

ROMANEE-CONTI, DOMAINE DE LA

Of all the stars in the Burgundian firmament none shines more brightly than this magnificent *domaine*. Its wines appear to go just that bit further than their rivals, packing in a seemingly endless stream of flavour that is a marvellous balance of power and finesse. A top vintage from the Leroy and Villaine families' estate can easily command in excess of £1,000 per bottle.

Domaine de la Romanée-Conti
1 rue Demiére Le Fou
21700 Vosne Romanée, France
Fax only: +33-3-80 61 05 72

ROMEO SOZZI

Romeo Sozzi comes from a family of furniture-makers but began his career representing other designers (notably producing and selling Christian Liaigre's furniture and Philippe Starck), before launching his own company 'Promemoria' in 1987. Drawing on a training in fine art, his beautiful furniture designs are classical and precise, yet feature a wealth of details like dark woods, artisan silver and leather.

Romeo Sozzi
via Montanapoleone 8
20121 Milan, Italy
Tel: +39-02-76 00 07 85

RON HOLLAND

Ron Holland has had a seminal influence on the market for large sailing yachts in the last two decades. His premise – obvious now but radical in the early eighties – was simple: why should an owner have to make the choice between a fast yacht or a luxurious one? Combining high performance with a comfortable, large-volume interior, *Whirlwind XII*, launched in 1985, proved to be a turning point. Since then, Holland has been responsible for designing more sailing yachts of over 100 feet than

any of his competitors. Current projects include a 150-foot motor yacht, being built at Delta Marine, and a 210-foot ketch, the largest private sailing yacht at present under construction.

Ron Holland Design
P.O. Box 23, Kinsale, Co. Cork, Ireland
Tel: +353-21-77 48 66   Fax: +353-21-77 48 08
Email: rhd@iol.ie

RONALD PHILLIPS

This family-run antiques business, set up in 1952 by Ronald Phillips, is now owned and managed by his son, Simon. Its Mayfair showroom (where invitations to discreet lunches in the magnificent Chinese dining room are highly coveted) houses an impressive selection of English furniture, clocks,

glassware, *objets d'art* and probably the finest selection of antique mirrors in the UK. The company regularly assists clients to find specific pieces and exhibits at such prestigious events as the Grosvenor House Fair.

Ronald Phillips Ltd.
26 Bruton Street, London W1X 8LH, UK
Tel: +44-20-74 93 23 41   Fax: +44-20-74 95 08 43

ROSALP, HOTEL

Deliciously cosy, the Rosalp's 18 rooms get booked up months in advance for the ski season. This is partly due to its prime position in the centre of Verbier but also has a lot to do with the cooking. Chef-owner Alain Pierroz is good. Very good indeed. Named Chef of the Year a couple of years ago, he is also a larger-than-life personality and a wonderful host. Full of wit and wisdom, he is affectionately known among his fellow Relais & Châteaux members as 'The Ayatollah'.

Hotel Rosalp
Route de Medran, CH-1936 Verbier, Switzerland
Tel: +41-27-771 6323   Fax: +41-27-771 1059

ROSE & VAN GELUWE

That the style of a Rose & Van Geluwe suit is traditional and discreetly elegant – with a recognisable hint of Savile Row and the quality to match – can be explained by the firm's origins. Robert M. Rose and Gustave Van Geluwe met while working as tailors in London in 1916 and, twelve years later, set up shop together in Van Geluwe's native Brussels. Today the business is run by Bernard Van Geluwe, great-nephew of the founder, whose clients include the cream of Belgian nobility and top Eurocrats.

Rose & Van Geluwe
2 avenue de Tervuren, B-1040 Brussels, Belgium
Tel: +32-2-735 7800   Fax: +32-2-734 5995

ROSEMARY VEREY

Her 1997 book *The Making of a Garden* was a best-seller; Prince Charles is an admirer, and devotees in Europe and America flock to her lectures – Rosemary Verey is a garden design phenomenon. Her garden at home, now run by her son Charles and open to the public, features all of her favourite motifs: *vistas*, *allés*, knot gardens and potagers. She is currently creating a Vegetable Garden for the New York Botanical Gardens.

Rosemary Verey
Barnsley House, near Cirencester
Gloucestershire GL7 5EE, UK
Tel & Fax: +44-1285-74 02 81

ROSEY, LE

Le Rosey describes itself as a "school for life" – particularly apt in view of its unparalleled old boy/girl network. Much admired, it reflects Switzerland's international and humanist traditions and has consistently attracted an elite, multi-lingual cross-section of pupils since 1880. Seventy-two full-time staff educate 330 pupils in Swiss, French, American and British grade programmes.

Institut Le Rosey
Château du Rosey, CH-1180 Rolle, Switzerland
Tel: +41-21-822 5500   Fax: +41-21-822 5555

ROSSINI OPERA FESTIVAL

Held in Pesaro, the composer's birthplace, this festival is a showcase for Rossini's best-loved, as well as his lesser-known works. Performances take place in the Teatro Rossini and the Palace of Sport, which allows staging on a larger scale. The 1999 programme included the operas *Tancredi* and *Il Viaggio a Reims*. A number of the productions are new and all performed by world-class musicians.

Rossini Opera Festival
via Rossini 37, 61100 Pesaro, Italy
Tel: +39-0721-30 161   Fax: +39-0721-30 979

ROTHSCHILD & CIE

The Rothschild family's reputation for the skilful management and investment of capital goes back 200 years, yet the Banque Rothschild (represented in London as N.M. Rothschild Services Ltd.) has moved with the times, dealing successfully with corporate investment portfolios as well as private accounts. The firm is legendary for its discretion, as well as its financial acumen.

Banque Rothschild & Cie
17 avenue Matignon, 75008 Paris, France
Tel: +33-1-40 74 40 74   Fax: +33-1-40 74 98 01

THE ROXBURGHE ESTATE

While rods are usually available here for spring fishing, you will have to join the waiting list if you want to fish in the autumn. The River Tweed is legendary for its salmon fishing and two of its finest beats – the Upper and Lower Floors – are on the Duke of Roxburghe's estate. They provide double-bank fishing for four rods each, in a mix of slack and flowing water. The luxurious Roxburghe Hotel is also on the estate.

The Roxburghe Estate
Estate Office, Kelso, Roxburghshire TD5 7SF
Scotland, UK
Tel: +44-1573-22 33 33   Fax: +44-1573-22 60 56

ROXTON BAILEY ROBINSON

Everyone who works for this specialist sporting travel consultancy sleeps, eats and breathes shooting and fishing and their tremendous knowledge and infectious enthusiasm engender almost fanatical loyalty among their clients. Trips range from salmon fishing in Iceland to saltwater fishing in Cuba and from partridge shooting in Patagonia to classic African safaris. Roxton's also arranges access to some of the UK's finest sporting estates, with accommodation in superb private homes, as well as hotels.

Roxton Bailey Robinson
25 High Street, Hungerford
Berkshire RG17 0NF, UK
Tel: +44-1488-68 32 22   Fax: +44-1488-68 29 77

ROYAL COPENHAGEN

This porcelain factory was established 1775 and several of its earliest patterns are still crafted and painted by hand today – most notably the delicate 'Flora Danica'. Created in 1790 as a gift for Catherine the Great but still incomplete at the time of her death, it was taken into use by the Danish Royal Court. Its 'Blue Fluted' pattern, created in 1775, is made in three versions, including 'Full Lace', which has hand-pierced borders. For its 225th anniversary in 2000 Royal Copenhagen is creating a limited-edition, one-off series of collectors' items.

Royal Copenhagen
Amagertorv 6, 1160 Copenhagen K, Denmark
Tel: +45-38-13 71 81   Fax: +45-38-14 99 40

ROYAL COUNTY DOWN

Consistently rated among the world's top 10, the Championship Course here is as spectacular to look at as it is challenging to play. Set on the dunes between the Mountains of Mourne and the Irish Sea, it owes its design as much to nature as to Old Tom Morris and Donald Steel. Its first three holes are among the best openers in the game and the bunkering – especially on the 3rd – is formidable. This being Northern Ireland, an added delight is the club's complete lack of stuffiness or pretension.

Royal County Down
Newmarket, Co. Down
Northern Ireland BT33 0NA, UK
Tel: +44-13967-23 314   Fax: +44-13967-26 281

ROYAL COUNTY OF BERKSHIRE POLO CLUB

Bryan Morrison spent a small fortune creating this club in 1985 and he has succeeded well, for it is a serious rival to Smith's Lawn. But the two could hardly be more different in style – a reflection, no doubt, on Morrison's music industry background. However, for all its laid-back glamour (Stephanie Powers bases her team here and Mike and Angie Rutherford are *habitués*) the polo is taken seriously. The prestigious Prince of Wales Trophy is played here each May and polo continues through the winter in the indoor arena.

The Royal County of Berkshire Polo Club
North Street, Winkfield, Berkshire SL4 4TH, UK
Tel: +44-1344-89 00 60   Fax: +44-1344-89 03 85

ROYAL HUISMAN

From the classical beauty of the 44-metre schooner, *Borkumriff III* to the cutting-edge technology incorporated into *Hyperion - Netscape* founder, Jim Clark's 47.5-metre aluminium sloop launched in late 1998, the Huisman family's shipyard is renowned for its superb craftsmanship. The classical 34.5-metre Ted Hood sloop, *Pamina*, will be launched in spring 2000 and *Unfurled*, a 34-metre high-performance German Frers design, is due for completion in early summer 2000. Orders are also in hand for a 50-metre schooner and a 40-metre Bruce King design.

Royal Huisman Shipyard BV
Flevoweg 1, 8325 PA Vollenhove, The Netherlands
Tel: +31-527-24 31 31   Fax: +31-527-24 38 00

ROYAL TROON GOLF CLUB

Tradition is all at this dignified club. Ladies may not play the Old Course, there is a strict dress code in the Smoking and Dining Rooms and a mobile phone is deemed a mortal sin. The front nine holes run out to the end of the course (its tricky 8th – 'The Postage Stamp' – is the shortest on the Championship rota) and the back nine return against the prevailing wind. Visitors may play between May and October on Mondays, Tuesdays and Thursdays only.

Royal Troon Golf Club
Troon, Ayrshire, Scotland KA10 6EP, UK
Tel: +44-1292-31 15 55   Fax: +44-1292-31 82 04

ROYAL DORNOCH

There are records of golf being played at Dornoch in 1616, although it was 1877 before the club was officially established. It is so far north that, in mid-summer, you can begin a round at 8pm with every confidence of completing it. Most fairways are lined

by gorse bushes, which severely punish any transgressors and pin-point accuracy to the well-guarded greens is essential. Tom Watson's favourite hole here is the 5th, played from a high tee to a plateaued green.

Royal Dornoch
Golf Road, Dornoch, Sutherland, Scotland IV25 3LW, UK
Tel: +44-1862-81 02 19   Fax: +44-1862-81 07 92
Website: www.royaldornoch.com

ROYAL YACHT SQUADRON

The sound of sailors piping the Duke of Edinburgh ashore sets the scene at the world's most august yacht club. The Squadron sticks to tradition in every way (ladies – except Princess Anne – must still use the tradesmen's entrance) and remains as particular about its membership today as it was when it blackballed Sir Thomas Lipton "because he was in trade". However, given that sailing is a great leveller, the atmosphere inside is relaxed and friendly.

The Royal Yacht Squadron
The Parade, Cowes, Isle of Wight PO32 6QT, UK
Tel: +44-1983-29 21 91

RUBELLI

The fact that this celebrated fabric house has supplied the Royal Households of Spain, Saudi Arabia, Denmark and Great Britain gives an insight not only into the richness of its style but the superb quality of its fabrics. Established in 1858 by Lorenzo Rubelli, it remains immensely proud of its artisanal traditions (the Venice weaving factory is one of the few where 16th century *soprarizzi* or hand-embossed velvets are still produced), Rubelli is unusual in embracing computer technology to enable it to translate its design ideas into the finished product.

Rubelli
San Marco 3877, 30124 Venice, Italy
Tel: +39-041-521 6411   Fax: +39-041-522 5557

RUSSELL SIMPSON

Property consultant Alan Russell probably knows more about every £2million-plus house in Kensington, Chelsea and Belgravia than anyone else in London: who lives there, when it might come onto the market and – just as importantly – who is longing to buy or rent it. His determination to match the right clients to the right property (on occasion, he even advises them not to buy) coupled with an unshakeable commitment to confidentiality has – largely by word-of-mouth recommendation – won Russell a matchless client list. His low profile is such that, eschewing the usual shop-front premises, he operates out of a discreet Chelsea townhouse.

Russell Simpson
5 Anderson Street, London SW3 3LU, UK
Tel: +44-20-75 84 78 76   Fax: +44-20-75 81 38 59

RUSSIAN MUSEUM

Housed in a palace which was built in 1819 for the younger brother of Alexander I, this museum is worth seeing for its interiors alone. However, although its fame is eclipsed by The Hermitage, it contains the most impressive collection – arranged chronologically – of Russian art. Its 300,000 exhibits, some dating back to the 14th century, include countless classical icons, as well as illustrating the development of secular art, right up to the 1930s.

The Russian Museum
Inzhenernaya ul, 4, St. Petersburg, Russia
Tel: +7-812-219 1615

50 ST. JAMES

A monumental, Grade II-listed building – designed by Benjamin and Philip Watt, who also worked on the Duke of Wellington's Apsley House – houses London's newest casino. Opened in autumn 1998, it has rapidly won over an élite corps of international high rollers. Its magnificent interiors, which have been restored to their original late Regency baroque style, include a grand first-floor gaming room (which looks directly across the street into the ultra-traditional gentlemen's club, White's) and two *Salles Privées*, one with a private dining room.

50 St. James
London, UK
At the time of writing, UK law prohibits the publication of contact details for British casinos. The law is currently under review.

SALIMBENI

Founded in 1891, Salimbeni hand-crafts exquisitely detailed picture frames, pill-boxes, jewellery boxes, cuff links and other pieces in sterling silver and gold offset by the finest enamels and a variety of precious substances ranging from ivory and jade to wood and crystals. The family firm, headed today by Franco and Giorgio Salimbeni, reproduces and interprets many historical styles – Art Deco, Art Nouveau, Fabergé, Empire and Baroque among them – and willingly undertakes private commissions on request.

Salimbeni
via dell'Olivuzzo 70/A, 50143 Florence, Italy
Tel: +39-055-71 12 96   Fax: +39-055-71 07 30

SALON

One of the most highly prized of all champagnes, Salon is unique in almost every respect: it is made entirely from chardonnay, all the grapes come from Le Mesnil-sur-Oger and only grapes from vines with a minimum age of 40 years are used. Add to that the distinction of its being the only wine in the world which isn't made every year (only good vintages are considered) and you begin to understand what makes it special. The result is an intensely dry champagne that gets better and better as the decades roll by.

Salon
B.P.3, 51190 Le Mesnil-sur-Oger, France
Tel: +33-3-26 57 51 65   Fax: +33-3-26 57 79 29

SALZBURG FESTIVAL

Both musically and socially this festival has, since its foundation in 1922, stood out as one of the greatest in the world. Its setting, in one of Europe's most beautiful cities, is the perfect backdrop for the exciting music and world-class performances on offer. 1999's programme included the première of Berio's new opera and new productions of Busoni's *Doktor Faust* and Mozart's *Don Giovanni*, while its stars included Willard White and Simon Rattle.

Salzburg Festival
Postfach 140, Hofstallgasse 1
A-50610 Salzburg, Austria
Tel: +43-662-804 5791   Fax: +43-662-804 5700

SAM FOGG

Art historian Sam Fogg trained at the Courtauld Institute before setting up in business in 1979 and continues to make his name as a source of some of the world's finest manuscripts. In addition to his stalwarts - which range from Medieval Illuminated manuscripts of the Western Middle Ages to Himalayan Buddhist manuscripts from the 7th and 8th centuries - Fogg has introduced a growing number of Indian and Persian paintings and manuscripts.

Sam Fogg
35 St. George Street, London W1R 9FA, UK
Tel: +44-20-74 95 23 33   Fax: +44-20-74 09 33 26

SATER

Established in Rome in 1963, Sater's chauffeur service operates throughout Italy and prides itself on upholding four key tenets: experience, tradition, precision and exclusivity. The company uses a fleet of top-quality Mercedes and Lancias and counts embassies and banks among its clients, as well as private individuals. It is not surprising, then, that visitors on grand tours of Italy and organisers of everything from small gatherings to political events (such as the G7 summit in Naples) and State visits (including the Japanese Emperor's most recent tour of Rome and Tuscany) turn to this service, relying completely on its rigorous quality, trustworthiness and punctuality.

Sater
via Licia 64, 00183 Rome, Italy
Tel: +39-06-77 20 46 42   Fax: +39-06-70 45 03 88

SAN LORENZO

Although San Lorenzo has never hosted a major championship, that has everything to do with its owners' desire to maintain its exclusivity and nothing to do with its superb quality. Designed by Joe Lee and Rocky Roquemore and set against the wetlands of the Ria Formosa estuary, it is beautiful and challenging and many top players regard it as second only to Valderrama in continental Europe. Fellow players will be the elegant northern Europeans who own holiday homes on the surrounding estates.

San Lorenzo
Quinta do Lago, P-8135 Almancil, Portugal
Tel: +351-89-39 65 22   Fax: +351-89-39 69 08

SANT'ANDREA IMMOBILI DI PRESTIGIO

The directors of this property consultancy quite rightly believe that buying a prestigious property involves more than simply questions of logistics and necessity. Taste, culture and history all have an influence. Backed by the experience and financial muscle of the giant Gabetti real estate group, Sant'Andrea specialises in buildings of architectural merit – whether contemporary or historic – in the best locations in Italy. Utterly discreet, it has no 'shop front' and operates by appointment only.

Sant'Andrea Immobili di Prestigio
Corso Venezia 5, 20121 Milan, Italy
Tel: +39-02-77 55 47   Fax: +39-02-78 19 96

SCHULE SCHLOSS SALEM

Three separate castles house the junior, middle and upper schools of this prestigious establishment, under the headmastership of Dr. Bernhard Bueb. The co-educational boarding school has 560 students who are encouraged to "develop a sense of fair play and team spirit", as much in academic life as on the playing field. Their holistic education is famously well-grounded and multi-cultural.

Salem College
Schule Schloss Salem
D-88682 Salem, Germany
Tel: +49-755-38 13 17   Fax: +49-755-38 13 90

SANTA MARIA POLO CLUB

It is a tribute to club founder Enrique Zobel's determination and high standards that in August, after the English polo season ends, the international stars all decamp to Sotogrande for the Gold Cup. It was not always so; 32 years ago the serious players regarded it as little more than 'beach polo'. These days, however, while the style remains resolutely casual, the spectators are a mix of celebrities and social high-flyers.

Santa Maria Polo Club

Ramiro El Monje, Sotogrande, E-11310 Cadiz, Spain
Tel: +34-956-79 64 64   Fax: +34-956-79 41 57

THE SAVOY

A breath of fresh air has swept through this great London landmark, evident immediately you step into the front hall – masterfully restored by Nina Campbell and David Linley. Its location gives The Savoy much of its unique flavour. Close links with the theatre have taken it from Gilbert & Sullivan to Gwyneth Paltrow and *Notting Hill*, while its proximity to Westminster has made The Savoy Grill

a de facto annexe of Parliament (maître d' Angelo Maresca arguably wields as much influence as the Speaker of the House). Monet painted his views of London's bridges from a 5th floor suite and, today, you can gaze at Big Ben while standing in the shower of one of the newly created 7th floor rooms.

The Savoy
Strand, London WC2R 0EU, UK
Tel: +44-20-78 36 43 43   Fax: +44-20-72 40 60 40
Email: info@the-savoy.co.uk

SAVONLINNA OPERA FESTIVAL

There can be few more stunning settings for opera than Olavinlinna, this 15th-century water-fortress built on an islet in Finland's largest lake. The new production of *Faust* in 1999 celebrated the life and work of Aino Ackté,

who first put on musical productions here in 1912 and for whom this was a key work. Opera lovers also savoured performances of *La Forza del Destino* and *Cavalleria Rusticana*. In July 2000 the festival will stage, *The Age of Dreams*, newly-commissioned from a triumvirate of Finnish composers, Rechberger, Kortekangas and Aho.

Savonlinna Opera Festival
Olavinkatu 27, FIN-57130 Savonlinna, Finland
Tel: +358-15-47 67 50   Fax: +358-15-476 7540
Email: info@operafestival.fi
Website: http://www.operafestival.fi

SCHLOSS WASSERBURG

What gives this Baroque-style castle its unique charm? Perhaps it's the sense of history – it has been owned by Count Seilern's family for eight centuries. Or is it the dreamy setting, in the middle of a lake with willows dipping into the water – where you skate when it freezes over in winter. Or perhaps the grand proportions of its rooms – furnished largely with English antiques. Above all, the Seilerns have a great gift for making guests who rent their home feel as if it were their own.

Schloss Wasserburg
St. Polten, Austria
c/- Villas and Apartments Abroad Ltd.
420 Madison Avenue, New York, NY 10017, USA
Tel: +1-212-759 1025   Fax: +1-212-755 8316

SCHLOSSHOTEL KRONBERG

Built in 1889 by the Empress Friedrich, this grand, Tudor-style palace was sensitively restored by the Hesse family and transformed into an unashamedly luxurious hotel. Filled with antiques – many from the Empress' own collection – and paintings (some by her own hand), it retains all the glamour of that era. As well as having wonderful formal gardens and an Italianate rose garden, the hotel just happens to own Frankfurt's most prestigious and elegant golf club – the playground of the city's banking and business czars. Adjoining the hotel, its 18 holes are set on gentle terrain among beautiful, mature trees.

Schlosshotel Kronberg
Hainstrasse 25, D-61476 Kronberg/Taunus, Germany
Tel: +49-61-73 70 10   Fax: +49-61-73 70 12 67

SCHLOSSHOTEL LERBACH

In transforming the former home of Siemens heiress, Anna Zander into this lovely hotel less than 10 years ago, Thomas Althoff created a magical retreat that feels like a centuries-old country house. The service, too, is what you would expect of an excellent private home. Picnic supper in some secluded spot in the 70-acre grounds? No problem – out go the crystal, candelabra and white linen. Miss your Harley Davidson? No problem – one is waiting for you on arrival and they have planned a perfect touring route and called ahead to four other Relais & Châteaux to arrange overnight stays.

Schlosshotel Lerbach
Lerbacher Weg, D-51465 Bergisch Gladbach, Germany
Tel: +49-2202-20 40   Fax: +49-2202-20 49 40

SCHLOSSHOTEL RITZ-CARLTON

The management of this splendid hotel was taken over by Ritz-Carlton in January 1999. Built as a private home in 1912, the Baroque-style villa was restored in 1994 under the creative direction of Karl Lagerfeld. (When he is not in town you can stay in the suite which he took as payment for his work). It is deliciously plush and – set in leafy grounds in the chic Grünewald area – wonderfully quiet. The all white Roman-style pool – centrepiece of a first class spa – is a treat.

Schlosshotel Ritz-Carlton
Brahmsstrasse 10, D-14193 Berlin, Germany
Tel: +49-30-89 58 40   Fax: +49-30-89 58 48 00

SCHUBERTIADE FESTIVAL

This late June festival provides a perfect blend of fine music and harmonious surroundings. Although Schubert's prolific output is the basis for the festival, homage is paid to others, too, with the 1999 programme featuring works for orchestra, chamber groups, individual instruments and voice by Beethoven, Brahms, Dvorak and Strauss, amongst others. Visitors enjoy world-class performances; Alfred Brendel,was among the leading lights to appear in 1999.

Schubertiade Festival GmbH
Villa Rosenthal, Schweizerstrasse 1
A-6845 Hohenems, Austria
Tel: +43-5576-72 091   Fax: +43-5576-75 450

SCHOLTESHOF

Everything about Roger Souveyren's little corner of paradise is magical. A passionate antique collector, he spent four years restoring this lovely 18th-century farmhouse. An equally passionate gardener, he has transformed its 28 acres into a dream-world of orchards, ponds, vegetable patches (where he grows the produce for his kitchen) and formal gardens. Above all, a passionate and immensely talented chef, he creates the most exquisitely fresh and perfectly balanced dishes. His staff is charming – happy in the knowledge that they are part of something so special.
Scholteshof
Kermstraat 130, B-3512 Stevoort Hasselt, Belgium
Tel: +32-11-25 02 02   Fax: +32-11-25 43 28

SCHWARZWALDSTUBE

In Harald Wohlfart the Finkbeiner family – owners of the delightful Hotel Traube Tonbach – have a chef of rare genius who has made their Schwarzwaldstube into a gourmet Mecca. (Note that he doesn't cook in the hotel's other restaurants.) Wohlfahrt's cooking is classically French and unspeakably good – Wild duck *consommé* with little dumplings of foie gras and truffles; Pheasant with a juniper sauce and purée of parsley root – Stéphane Gass presides over an excellent cellar and the view of the Black Forest countryside is enchanting.
Schwarzwaldstube
Hotel Traube Tonbach, Tonbachstrasse 237
D-72270 Baiersbronn, Germany
Tel: +49-7442-4920   Fax: +49-7442-49 26 92

SEABOURN CRUISE LINE

Following the 1998 merger of Seabourn – which set the benchmark for small, luxury cruise liners a decade ago – with Cunard, the Seabourn fleet has expanded to six ships: the original *Seabourn Pride*, *Spirit and Legend*, *Seabourn Goddess I & II* and *Seabourn Sun*. The latter – the flagship of the fleet – underwent a major refit at the end of 1999.

The new company brings together three styles under one flag: the sophistication of *Seabourn Pride*, *Spirit and Legend*, the casual elegance of the *Goddesses'* and the country club ambience of *Seabourn Sun*.

The line's ethos, however, remains unchanged: to offer ultra-luxury cruises to destinations which range from the classically glamorous – Monte Carlo, Portofino and St. Barthélelmy, for instance – to the exotic and rarely visited, such as the Amazon and the Yangtze River, and to special events, such as the Sydney Olympics in September 2000.

The ships share a distinctively sophisticated ambience; guests, the majority of whom return year after year, are cosmopolitan, highly-educated (and, sometimes, famous) and the service is impeccable. The officers and crew – mainly northern European – are refreshingly un-stuffy, though faultlessly professional.

Seabourn's cruises incorporate special-interest presentations by world-class lecturers (ranging from former US Attorney General, Edwin Meese to award-winning anthropologist and film-maker, Dr. Lawrence Blair) and exceptional land programmes of up to five days' duration.
Seabourn Cruise Line (a division of Cunard Seabourn Limited)
Mountbatten House, Grosvenor Square
Southampton SO15 2BF, UK
Tel: +44-23-80 71 65 00   Fax: +44-23-80 71 58 43

SEBAGH, DR J.L.

In an ideal world, avows Dr Sebagh, women should look upon a face-lift as a last resort. "If a woman comes to me in her early thirties, she should be able to avoid surgery for 20 years," he asserts. To this end the dynamic young doctor-aesthetician advocates lipostructure, or fat injections, which plump the face; 'Botox' to erase and prevent lines and 'Dermalive', a new, non-allergic anti-sag technique from France. So

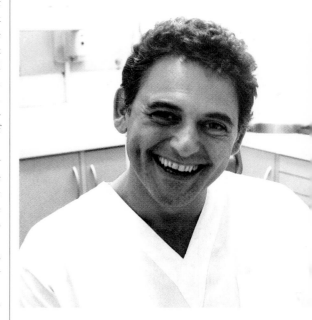

successful has his practice been that Sebagh is taking on two new doctors as well as a surgeon and has plans for a teaching institute – good news for the fashionable admirers who besiege his surgery.
Dr. J.L. Sebagh
The French Cosmetic Medical Company Ltd.
25 Wimpole Street London W1M 7AD, UK
Tel: +44-20-76 37 05 48   Fax: +44-20-76 37 51 50
64 rue de Longchamp, 75016 Paris, France
Tel: +33-1-47 04 65 75 Fax: +33-1-45 33 45 18

SEGOURA, GALERIE

In his gallery, an elegant *hôtel particulier* decorated by François-Joseph Graf, Maurice Segoura displays a fabulous selection of 18th-century French works of art. Connoisseurs will find Louis XIV bronzes, fine Enlightenment-era clocks, old lacquerwork, excellent furniture (particularly Boulle) and paintings by Watteau, Fragonard, Boucher and Vernet. There are also exquisite *Famille Verte* porcelains from China and Japan. Monsieur Segoura, whom Hubert de Givenchy describes as "a very civil gentleman", works closely with his sons, Pierre and Marc.

Galerie Segoura
14 Place François 1er, 75008 Paris, France
Tel: +33-1-42 89 20 20   Fax: +33-1-42 89 64 13

SELLERIE LOPEZ

Andalucia has a long equestrian tradition and this shop has supplied its landed grandees with their riding kit for many years. Everything is made in-house – mostly by hand – including the traditional saddles called *vaqueras*, which are teamed with the orange and yellow striped fabric, *Lola Sarga*. There is a wide range of other saddles, as well as harnesses and riding boots – and a collection of stylish hand-made leather shoes for men.

Sellerie Lopez
Calle Cuna 34, E-41001 Seville, Spain
Tel & Fax: +34-95-421 6923

SEVEN ONE SEVEN

Set in a 17th-century building overlooking the Prinsengracht canal, with just eight suites and a small brass plaque to announce its name – but not its function – this magical haven was created by ex-fashion designer Kees van der Valk in 1996. Four years later, in a case of the guest loving the hotel so much that he bought the company, it has changed hands (the new owner prefers to remain anonymous) but the magic continues. The décor is marvellously eclectic – African masks, classical busts, Murano glass – and, as in a private house, you are welcome to help yourselves from the drinks cabinet (it's included in the price).

Seven One Seven
Prinsengracht 717, 1017 JW Amsterdam
The Netherlands
Tel: +31-20-427 0717   Fax: +31-20-423 0717

SHEEN FALLS LODGE

Winning a Five Star Diamond Award in 1999 confirmed Sheen Falls' excellence but the real joy of this place is its sense of total escape. It is tempting simply to choose one of the 1200 books from the library, curl up in front of the fire and watch the falls cascading past the windows. But, with 300 acres of woodland and 15 miles of private salmon and trout fishing on its own stretch of the Sheen River, it is a paradise for riding and fishing – and they will even smoke your salmon for you.

Sheen Falls Lodge
Kenmare, Co. Kerry, Ireland
Tel: +353-64-41 600   Fax: +353-64-41 386

SERGIO VALENTE

More an exercise in TLC than a mere trip to the hairdressers, the experience of visiting Sergio Valente's salon is an unforgettable luxury. A stickler for detail – as much for the calibre of the hairdressing as its surrounding environment – the charismatic Valente personally supervises all of the

hair and beauty treatments undertaken by his highly experienced team. Located on the first floor of a beautiful 15th-century *palazzo* – decorated to within an inch of its life – the salon also boasts a coffee shop and a library. Such is Valente's status that – in addition to his celebrity clients – he has met many luminaries, most notably the Pope.

Sergio Valente
via Condotti 11, 00187 Rome, Italy
Tel: +39-06-679 4515   Fax: +39-06-69 94 06 96

SILVA NETTO, ARTHUR

This discreet and expert cosmetic surgery practitioner specialises in eyes, noses and breasts implants "with no scars". Brazilian-born Dr. Silva Netto is also a prolific writer, with over 20 publications to his name, including the recent *Sanctuary of Plastic Surgery*, a guide to international cosmetic surgery techniques.

Arthur Silva Netto
Galleria del Corso 4, 20122 Milan, Italy
Tel: +39-02-76 02 33 80   Fax: +39-02-78 27 65 11

SILVERSEA

Established in 1994 by the Rome-based Lefebvre family, Silversea won the 1998 *Condé Nast Traveler Readers' Award* for Best Cruise Line and its Best Overall award, ahead of the world's finest resorts and hotels. Its success is due, no doubt, to the style of its two ships (suites only, 75 percent with private verandahs) and its emphasis on special-interest cruises to some of the world's most exotic destinations. Additional ships are to be launched in September 2000 and May 2001.

Silversea Cruises
77-79 Great Eastern Street, London EC2A 3HU, UK
Tel: +44-20-77 39 40 29   Fax: +44-20-76 13 29 99

SIMON C. DICKINSON

Acting on behalf of clients, this company provides a discreet alternative to buying and selling works of art at public auction. Simon Dickinson, formerly head of Old Masters paintings at Christie's in London, founded the firm in 1993 and was soon joined by two other ex-Christie's experts, Ian Kennedy and James Roundell, as well as English painting specialist and dealer David Ker. Their collective expertise in European painting has proved irresistible to many private clients and institutions.

Simon C. Dickinson Ltd.
58 Jermyn Street, London SW1Y 6LX, UK
Tel: +44-20-74 93 03 40   Fax: +44-20-74 93 07 96

SIR ANTHONY VAN DIJCK

In 1978, aged 28, Marc Paesbrugghe became one of Europe's youngest Michelin-starred chefs; four years later he gained a second star. Then, in 1991, he did something extraordinary. He gave them back. And tripled his clientele. The food is as good as ever; Michelin-style dishes (Galantine of lobster) sit next to simpler offerings (Cod with *stoemp* – the traditional Belgian mix of potatoes with whatever green vegetable is in season). Contemporary art now hangs alongside Old Masters and the clientele is as smart as at any star-spangled establishment.

Sir Anthony van Dijck
Oude Koornmarkt 16, B-2000 Antwerp, Belgium
Tel: +32-3-231 6170   Fax: +32-3-225 1169

SIMON HORN

Over almost 20 years, Simon Horn has effected a renaissance of the classical bed. Much of the splendid furniture created by his team of craftsmen

is inspired by antique pieces, especially French styles, such as Empire and Louis XV. His range of 'metamorphic' nursery furniture is designed to grow up with the children for whom it's made, while his 'pull-out' *lits de repos* are a boon in this age of limited interior space. Items can be made to order in a variety of woods, from walnut to rosewood, and are distinguished by fine craftsmanship and attention to detail.

Simon Horn Classical Beds
117-121 Wandsworth Bridge Road
London SW6 2TP, UK
Tel: +44-20-77 31 12 79 Fax: +44-20-77 36 35 22

SIR JOHN SOANE'S MUSEUM

The home of the great architect, Sir John Soane (1753-1837), who designed and built it himself, was established as a museum in 1833. It holds annual exhibitions which, in 1999, included *Visions of Ruin*, an exploration of 19th-century follies, and *Frank Gehry at the Soane*, a display of work by the leading modern American architect.

Sir John Soane's Museum
13 Lincoln's Inn Fields, London WC2A 3BP, UK
Tel: +44-20-74 05 21 07 Fax: +44-20-78 31 39 57

S.I.R.

The introduction of security via a global positioning system, allowing precise intervention and the blocking of escape routes, has revolutionised the capabilities of this excellent security company. Established in 1978, S.I.R. prides itself on its confidentiality and its willingness to work with other networks when the situation demands. Experienced specialists are recruited from a wide cross-section of the security industry to provide a comprehensive service. Uniformed or plain-clothed units will cover top-level events and a house key-holding service is also provided.

S.I.R.- Service d'Intervention Rapide
Chemin de la Crétaux, Case Postale 29
CH-1196 Gland, Switzerland
Tel: +41-22-364 4644 Fax: +41-22-364 4873

SIRENUSE, LE

Condé Nast Traveler rated it second in Europe only to the Hôtel du Cap but its relaxed style could not be more different. You descend from a deceptively modest entrance to a jumble of terraces (spilling over with bougainvillea and potted lemon trees) peaceful sitting rooms and labyrinthine corridors which tell you that Le Sireneuse is utterly unlike any other hotel. This was originally the summer retreat of Director Antonio Sersale's family and his staff wins huge points for treating you as a house-guest, not a hotel guest. The pool has a ravishing view of Positano and the bar and restaurant (where dinner is candle-light only) were redecorated recently by Fausta Gaetani.

Le Sirenuse
via Cristoforo Colombo 30
84017 Positano, Italy
Tel: +39-089-87 50 66 Fax: +39-089-81 17 98

SMYTHSON OF BOND STREET

Calling Smythson a stationer is rather like calling champagne a fizzy wine. Established in 1887, it has made bespoke stationery for dozens of crowned heads (British and otherwise) together with myriad accessories: notebooks, desk sets and small leather goods. With a new, young management team since early 1999, it is gently re-orienting itself and modernising its lines ('Wardrobe Notes' and 'Packing Notes' in lipstick-pink covers have been added to the notebooks series, for instance) while remaining true to its traditional clientele.

Frank Smythson Ltd.
40 New Bond Street
London W1Y 0DE, UK
Tel: +44-20-76 29 85 58 Fax: +44-20-74 95 61 11

SOCIETE PRIVEE DE GERANCE

If ever one of those coveted apartments in Geneva's Vieille Ville were to come onto the open market, the chances are that SPG would be handling it. Founded in 1960 and ably directed today by Thierry Barbier-Müller, this is the leading full-service real estate company in French-speaking Switzerland. Its skills range from appraisals and brokerage to investment advice for Swiss or foreign investors and the firm has an excellent rental portfolio of top-drawer Geneva properties.

Société Privée de Gérance
36 Route du Chêne, CH-1208 Geneva, Switzerland
Tel: +41-22-849 65 50 Fax: +41-22-849 61 04

SOLEDAD LORENZO

Soledad Lorenzo has played a major part in the development of contemporary Spanish art, yet she became a dealer by chance 25 years ago, when she took part in a gallery project as a way of dealing with her husband's death. Now one of Spain's most respected gallery owners, Lorenzo is recognised both for her expertise and for the rapport that she has with the artists. Those she has brought to international prominenence include Tàpies and Palazuelo.

Soledad Lorenzo
Orefila 5, E-28010 Madrid, Spain
Tel: +34-91-308 2887 Fax: +34-91-308 6830

SOTHEBY'S INTERNATIONAL REALTY

Sotheby's yardstick for whether a property fits its portfolio is that it is of exceptional character or quality and that it is less likely to appeal to the local market than to an international buyer. Established in Europe for 12 years Sotheby's has its own office in Paris in addition to its new London headquarters – an elegant Georgian house into which it moved in spring 1999 – and has formed a network of alliances with the most prestigious property consultants in several other European cities.

Sotheby's International Realty
123 Sloane Street, London SW1X 9BW, UK
Tel: +44-20-75 98 16 00 Fax: +44-20-75 98 16 99

SOURCES DES ALPES, LES

Named Best Health Farm in Switzerland in 1998, this Relais & Châteaux retreat is set in a serene alpine valley, where the crisp air and peaceful outlook do much to assist the winding-down process. There are thermal pools and the huge variety of treatments are tailored into individual programmes, from de-toxing to weight-loss. The contemporary style and soothing colours of the rooms add to the sense of peace.

Hotel Les Sources des Alpes
CH-3954 Loèche-les-Bains, Leukerbad, Switzerland
Tel: +41-27-470 5151 Fax: +41-27-470 3533

SOTHEBY'S

Founded in 1744 by Samuel Baker, Sotheby's held the status of the world's largest seller of books by auction for its first 200 years. In the last half-century, it has also become a major international auctioneer of fine art, as well as jewellery, classic cars, coins, wine and celebrity memorabilia. Supplementing its 110 offices in 46 countries, Sotheby's newest salerooms opened in Zürich in March 1999 and in Amsterdam the following autumn.

Its place as one the world's pre-eminent auction houses was underlined by such 1999 successes as the sales of the contents of decorator Alberto Pinto's Paris apartment, collector Giuseppe Rossi's 1400-lot collection of furniture and decorative arts – which raised £21 million – and the sale in New York of Seurat's *L'Ile de la Grande Jatte* for $35.2 million and Cézanne's *Rideau, Cruchon et Compotier* for $60.5 million (a record for the artist). Sotheby's also handled the sale of the spectacular Château Groussay, formerly owned by the renowned collector, Charles de Bestegui.

The company continues to develop new services for its clients and, in autumn 1999, pioneered a new Internet auction business, sothebys.com and has formed a partnership with amazon.com to establish another on-line auction site.

Sotheby's
34-35 New Bond Street, London W1A 2AA, UK
Tel: +44-20-72 93 50 00   Fax: +44-20-72 93 59 89

SPA'DEUS

Days here begin with a long walk in the unspoilt Tuscan hills (an idea inspired by devoted client Donna Karan) and continue with blissful hydrotherapy, shiatsu or *ayurvedic* treatments and end with aromatic oil massages to induce a deep and revitalising sleep. In between, you eat extraordinarily well, for Hungarian-born Christina Newburgh, the spa's founder, believes that the best way to lose weight is not through suffering but by de-stressing, de-toxifying and re-balancing your life.

Spa'Deus
Via Le Piane 3
53042 Chianciano Terme Italy
Tel: +39-0578-63 232   Fax: +39-0578-64 329

SPERONE

The sheer beauty of this Robert Trent Jones-designed golf course (centre-piece of Guy and Jacques Dewez's real estate development) has well-travelled players comparing it with Pebble Beach or Cypress Point. The first big sea view is at the 11th and for sheer spectacle it's hard to beat, although the 16th is the most impressive and challenging – a 500-yard par five which follows a sweep of cliffs from tee to green. Sperone can be so quiet on weekdays that you can stop for a swim after the 13th without losing your place.

Golf de Sperone
Domaine de Sperone, 20169 Bonifacio, Corsica, France
Tel: +33-4-95 73 17 13   Fax: +33-4-95 73 17 85

SPIELBANK BADEN-BADEN

Established in 1855 by Jacques Benazet and described by Marlene Dietrich as "the most beautiful of all casinos", the casino at Baden-Baden still evokes a sense of the golden summers before World War I when frail *contessas*, whiskery Archdukes and wide-eyed American *ingénues* came to the resort to take the waters. Today, in addition to offering blackjack, American roulette and *punto banco*, the casino plays host to three prestigious international baccarat competitions every year.

Spielbank Baden-Baden
Augustaplatz 2, D-76530 Baden Baden, Germany
Tel: +49-7221-21 060   Fax: +49-7221-21 06 54

ST.-NOM-LA-BRETECHE

Established in 1959, this club is the favourite of grand Parisian golfers and, during the prestigious Lancôme Trophy every September, of fashionable Parisians with no interest in golf but a burning desire to see and be seen. Fred Hawtree's Blue Course contains plenty of water hazards, while the slightly more hilly Red Course has some fast, sloping greens. Lunch in the clubhouse – a pretty, restored farmhouse – is as good as you'll get in many Parisian restaurants.

St.-Nom-La-Bretêche Golf Club
78860 Saint-Nom-La-Bretêche, France
Tel: +33-1-30 80 04 40   Fax: +33-1-34 62 60 44

ST. ANDREWS

If golf is a religion this is its Mecca. Every golfer worth his putter dreams of following the steps of the game's great legends across the Swilken Bridge and any golfer with a handicap may play the Old Course – although demand is so great in summer that there is a daily ballot for tee times. The club is remarkably hospitable for one so exalted. The Open returns here in 2000.

St. Andrews Links Club House
West Sands Road, St. Andrews, Fife, Scotland KY16 9XL, UK
Tel: +44-1334-46 66 66   Fax: +44-1334-46 66 64

SQUARE, THE

Nigel Platts-Martin and Philip Howard have proved that two Michelin stars needn't mean stuffiness in either attitude or décor. This large, light room, its deep terracotta walls hung with four large abstract landscapes is as modern and relaxed as the (impeccably professional) staff and the room resounds with the lively conversation of Mayfair's movers and shakers rather than the hushed tones of awe-struck foodies. Howard's cooking continues to delight with such star dishes as Cappuccino of *langoustine* with shellfish *cannelloni*.

The Square
6-10 Bruton Street, London W1X 7AG, UK
Tel: +44-20-74 95 71 00   Fax: +44-20-74 95 71 50

ST. MARY'S ASCOT

This Catholic girls' boarding school, established in the 1800s enrolls a predominantly British intake with a fair list of Europeans. It's first lay headmistress, appointed at the end of 1998, Mary Breen, is the first appointed woman in it's 115-year history. Mrs Breen is deeply committed to academic achievement coupled to a spiritual dimension, which gives girls the "right perspective on their relationships with the rest of the world". The school has a new purpose-built language faculty, which should help its already excellent record in this area of development. An expanded music school and good sports facilities means St. Mary's excels in these leading fields. Past pupils include Lady Antonia Fraser and Princess Caroline of Monaco.

St. Mary's Ascot
Ascot, Berkshire SL5 9JF, UK
Tel: +44-1344-62 37 21   Fax: +44-1344-87 32 81

STEFANOBI

Although Stefanobi was established in 1991, its hand-sewn shoes – only 85 pairs of which are made each day – are classics of the Italian cobbler's art.

Owned by LVMH since 1994, the firm was the brainchild of Stefano Branchini (who is no longer involved in the company). Styling is 'classical with a twist'. The sturdy but elegant 'Norwegian' lace-up model superbly illustrates Stefanobi's ethos; its construction method is the most complete, the firm believes, because three separate seams join the last to the sole.

Stefanobi
Manifattura Ferrarese, via Cimarosa 7
44100 Ferrara, Italy
Tel: +39-0532-90 30 20   Fax: +39-0532-90 18 13

STEIRERECK, RESTAURANT

The Reitbauers' restaurant has become known as a gastronomic landmark, thanks to their talented but exceedingly modest chef, Helmut Österreicher. In both style and presentation, his is a *haute* interpretation of the classical dishes from the Austrian regions. As well as the expected classical French vintages, the wine list provides an excellent opportunity to discover just how good some of Austria's wine-makers are and, as befits the baronial surroundings, there is an excellent selection of cigars.

Restaurant Steirereck
Rasumofskygasse 2, A-1030 Vienna, Austria
Tel: +43-1-713 3168   Fax: +43-1-71 31 56 82

STRESA, LE

Pasta is the staple here, including *Spaghetti carbonara à la Jean-Paul Belmondo* (with tomatoes, olives, garlic and spices) and Ravioli with white truffles – and it's delicious. But above all, Tony and Claudio Faiola run the smartest celebrity restaurant in Paris. Valentino and Alain Delon rub shoulders with John Travolta and the Rothschilds but the welcome is warm for all comers. The front room – especially the first table by the door – is the place to sit for those who want to see and be seen.

Le Stresa
7 rue de Chambiges, 75008 Paris, France
Tel: +33-1-47 23 51 62

SUNNINGDALE

Thanks to its location, amongst the heather and rhododendrons near Ascot, its two excellent courses and its superb catering, Sunningdale is a kind of gentlemen's club in the country and a favourite haunt for tour professionals and celebrities alike. The debate rages as to whether the Old or the New (1922) course is the better but holes from both regularly appear in serious golfers' favourite lists. Outstanding holes on the Old Course are the 5th to the 7th and the 10th to 12th – including the blind 11th.

Sunningdale
Ridgemount Road, Sunningdale
Berkshire SL5 9RR, UK
Tel: +44-1344-62 16 81   Fax: +44-1344-62 41 54

STUBBEN

This family business, founded in Germany and now in its fourth generation, is renowned throughout Europe for its equestrian accessories. Its celebrated saddles, which come in six varieties (dressage, jumping, all-purpose, pony, Iceland and endurance), are famous for their durability, range of sizes and crafted individuality – each one is mostly hand-stitched. In addition, Stübben offers everything from bridlework to stirrups. The current generation believes that their great-grandfather, Johannes Stübben, would be proud to see how few of the traditional production methods, which he introduced, have changed.

Stübben
Langmattring 32, CH-6370 Stans, Switzerland
Tel: +41-41-610 6061 Fax: +41-41-610 7684 Website: www.stuebben.de

SUNSEEKER INTERNATIONAL

Producing craft from 34 to 84 feet, Sunseeker is now the world's largest privately owned and managed power boat manufacturer. A notable example of its perfect balance of good looks and technical quality is the *Hawk 34*; owners include Nigel Mansell and Roger Moore and it will feature in the 19th Bond movie, currently being filmed. Following the announcement of plans to build the new *105 Superyacht*, Sunseeker launched four new models in September 1999, including a new version of its *Manhattan 84*.

Sunseeker International
27-31 West Quay Road, Poole, Dorset BH15 1HX, UK
Tel: +44-1202-38 11 11 Fax: +44-1202-38 22 22

SUVRETTA HOUSE

Set slightly apart from the frenetic centre of St. Moritz, with uninterrupted views of the mountains and lakes, Suvretta House is much loved by the more discreet members of the international élite – and by serious skiers, who appreciate its private ski lift leading directly to Corviglia. Opened in 1912 by the Bon family, it is now run with considerable grace and charm by the Jacob family. Far more low-key than Badrutt's Palace, though no less luxurious, its décor owes much to the English country house style.

Suvretta House
CH-7500 St. Moritz, Switzerland
Tel: +41-81-832 1132 Fax: +41-81-833 8524

SWEERTS DE LANDAS

Within the impressive setting of the stately Dunsborough House, Baron Dolf Sweerts de Landas and his wife, Caroline, display the finest garden statuary, urns and furniture, ranging from 18th-century pieces by the Flemish sculptor Jan Pieter Baurscheit to early 20th-century English pottery by Compton. Their newly-restored greenhouses provide the perfect showcase for their exquisite collection, viewings of which can be arranged by appointment. They also exhibit annually at the Maastricht and Grosvenor House fairs.

Sweerts de Landas
Dunsborough Park, Ripley, Surrey GU23 6AL, UK
Tel: +44-1483-22 53 66 Fax: +44-1483-22 45 25

SWINLEY FOREST

One of the treasures of English golf – and possibly Europe's most private club – Swinley Forest is hidden away in the heathland of Ascot. One of the world's best short inland courses, it is a delightful anachronism, insofar as there is no PGA pro and not even a par – they prefer to list the old 'bogey' scores. Although access is possible through one of the few corporate days, it is worth getting to know a member – probably a CEO, a posh lawyer or a Prince (Andrew) – in order to get a game followed by a great lunch.

Swinley Forest Golf Club
Coronation Road, South Ascot
Berkshire SL5 9LE, UK
Tel: +44-1344-87 49 79

SWAINE ADENEY BRIGG

Swaine Adeney Brigg received its first Royal Warrant from King George III – for riding whips – shortly after it opened in 1750. While still making equestrian-related leather goods, its ranges have long since expanded into travel goods and other accessories. Notable particularly for its use of bridle leather, the company's style is classical and its craftsmanship superb. The firm also makes the Brigg umbrella, justly celebrated as the world's finest and, in 1996, joined forces with hat-maker Herbert Johnson. Together they opened a slick, new flagship store in St James's in 1998.

Swaine Adeney Brigg
54 St. James's Street, London SW1A 1JT, UK
Tel: +44-20-74 09 72 77 Fax: +44-20-76 29 31 14

SYMPOSIUM

The flamboyant owner, Lucio Pompili, has returned to the kitchens while his wife and a French sommelier share front-of-house duties. The welcome is just as warm and their celebrity guests are still treated like normal customers – which is how they like it. Pompili's star dishes include a delicious *Escalope of foie gras alla sapa* (grape must be cooked until it thickens and becomes very sweet) and, this being the Adriatic side of Italy, *Buzara* of seafood cooked in a light onion broth with sweet garlic and parsley – an old Croatian fishermen's recipe. Eat in the garden in summer.

Symposium
via Cartoceto 36, 61030 Serrungarina, Italy
Tel: +39-0721-89 83 20 Fax: +39-0721-89 84 93

TABLE DU MARCHE, LA

An open secret on the Côte d'Azur, Christophe Leroy's St. Tropez restaurant and *boulangerie-patîssserie* is the source of the best catering in the area. Leroy specialises in Provençal cuisine and, as may be expected of a former Alain Ducasse protégé, it is excellent – robustly flavoured and singing with the freshness of its ingredients. However, Leroy is equally adept at Oriental cuisine. Yacht parties are a speciality and Leroy has catered to many during the Cannes film festival.

La Table du Marché
38 rue Clemenceau, 83390 St. Tropez, France
Tel: +33-4-94 97 85 20

TAG AVIATION

Formed as a result of the 1999 merger between Geneva-based Aeroleasing and Aviation Methods Inc., one of America's leading business jet management companies, TAG Aviation now offers a fully-integrated, world-wide service for business jet users. Its charter fleet, comprising 20 of the finest business aircraft – from transoceanic to medium-range jets – benefits from Aeroleasing's 33 years of experience in the market. In addition, TAG now offers aircraft management services in Europe, maintenance for third-party planes and aircraft sales.

TAG Aviation
P.O.Box 36, CH-1215 Geneva Airport, Switzerland
Tel: +41-22-717 0000   Fax: +41-22-717 0007

TAGE ANDERSEN

Tage Andersen's florist shop – set in an 18th-century house – is a magical world, where rich displays of flowers and greenery are set between antique cages, in which birds of every description sing. Andersen seeks out the rare and unusual as well as the enchantingly pretty; according to the season, there may be blue grape hyacinths, massed in their hundreds, or tiny violets in pots, or the rare and spicy-scented woodruff woven into wreaths. For Andersen – a contemplative man who dresses in plus-fours and muted colours – flowers are an emotional statement and every bouquet is unique.

Tage Andersen
12 Ny Adelgade, Copenhagen K, Denmark
Tel: +45-33-93 09 13   Fax: +45-33-93 21 13

TAILLEVENT AND LES CAVES TAILLEVENT

The perfect embodiment of French classicism, this *grand restaurant* has a new private dining room, exquisitely decorated with 18th-century Chinese paintings. Jean-Claude Vrinat has inherited the gift of hospitality-as-art-form from his father; nothing here is showy or gratuitous. The same goes for Philippe Legendre's cooking; his *andouilette de pieds de porc aux truffes* redefines the word 'sublime'. The astonishingly rich wine list thoughtfully includes several wines for under £20. The same degree of thought has gone into the selection available from Taillevent's nearby wine shop, where the staff take particular delight in encouraging clients to discover lesser-known names, as well as the great vintages.

Taillevent
15 rue Lamennais, 75008 Paris, France
Tel: +33-1-44 95 15 01   Fax: +33-1-42 25 95 18
Les Caves Taillevent
199 rue du Faubourg St. Honoré, 75008 Paris, France
Tel: +33-1-45 61 14 09   Fax: +33-1-45 61 19 68

TANTE CLAIRE, LA

Despite his resolutely low profile, Pierre Koffman is one of Britain's most revered chefs; it is he who introduced London to the flavours of his native Gascony when he opened La Tante Claire (originally in Chelsea) in the late 1970s and it is he who became Britain's first holder of three Michelin stars. It was therefore a shock to many that he lost one of those stars after moving to his new address in November 1998. The room is light and attractive in its lilac, green and dark blue colour scheme (with striking arrangements of flowers which match perfectly). Determinedly anti-fashion in culinary matters and equally determined to regain the lost star, Koffman continues to turn out his superb signature dishes: Pig's trotters with morel mushrooms (copied by at least half a dozen other leading chefs); Salmon in goose fat and Galette of foie gras with shallots and Sauternes.

La Tante Claire
The Berkeley Hotel, Wilton Place
London SW1X 7RL, UK
Tel: +44-20-78 23 20 03   Fax: +44-20-78 23 20 01

TANNER KROLLE

Tanner Krolle is now two years into its reincarnation as a fashion-forward leather accessories brand. Having remained a best-kept secret for 140 years among the royalty and international jet set who travelled the world with its classical bridle-leather luggage, Tanner Krolle has,

with a new designer in place, taken on a stylish, contemporary edge. However, every handbag, jewellery case and briefcase is still made using the fine craftsmanship and attention to detail which the firm has honed to perfection since 1856. The luggage, too, has been updated with the use of rich colours to supplement the classic neutrals. Having opened its first-ever store – on London's Old Bond Street – in 1997, Tanner Krolle now has 15 outlets worldwide.

Tanner Krolle
38 Old Bond Street, London W1X 3AE, UK
Tel: +44-20-74 91 22 43   Fax: +44-20-74 91 87 02

TALISKER

The only distillery on the Isle of Skye, Talisker was founded in 1831. Said to be one of the original ingredients in Drambuie, it thankfully stands on its own these days. Light and almost lemony sharp at first, the flavour explodes across the palate. Its peppery, peaty ruggedness inspires rave reviews and a loyalty among its followers that is the envy of its rivals.

Talisker
United Distillers UK, Templefields House, River Way
Harlow, Essex CM18 2EA, UK
Tel: +44-1279-62 68 01   Fax: +44-1279-63 33 00

TANTRIS

The jewel-coloured, Eastern-inspired room and the summertime terrace of this restaurant are the favoured haunts of Munich's élite (appropriately its name means 'enjoyment' in Indian). With two Michelin stars to their name and a best-selling book each, chef Hans Haas and sommelier Paul Bosch are the powerhouses behind the place. Haas is a master of subtle flavouring – from his red mullet with a *gazpacho* jelly to the delicious finale of cherry and cinnamon tart.

Tantris
Johann-Fichte-Strasse 7, D-80805 Munich, Germany
Tel: +49-89-36 20 61   Fax: +49-89-361 8649

TAPIS ROUGE INTERNATIONAL

With programmes such as an Orient Express ride along the Silk Route, this travel agent will appeal to anyone wishing to plunge into an exotic culture while enjoying money-no-object comfort. France's renowned historian, Jean de Carrs, organises more intensely intellectual tours – assembled in the 'Athenaeum' brochure – to cultural centres world-wide. Tapis Rouge also works closely with Silversea cruise line and was instrumental in organising its successful autumn 1999 gastronomic cruise in the Mediterranean, in conjunction with Relais & Châteaux.

Tapis Rouge International
39 rue Marbeuf, 75008 Paris, France
Tel: +33-1-42 56 55 00   Fax: +33-1-45 63 01 51

TASSINARI & CHATEL

Founded in 1680 by gold and silver weaver Louis Pernon, this fabric house has been owned by a series of venerable families and, since 1998, by the prestigious Lelièvre group. Its sumptuous velvets, silks and damasks attracted clients such as Catherine the Great and Napoleon I during the 18th and 19th centuries and today its fabrics – reproduced from originals in its vast archives – can be seen in the White House and Versailles. Its showroom is open only to professionals.

Tassinari & Chatel
13 rue du Mail, 75002 Paris, France
Tel: +33-1-43 16 88 00   Fax: +33-1-42 61 49 99

TAYLOR'S

The bluest of blue-chip ports, Taylor's splendid vintages are full bodied and rounded and worthy of the highest acclaim. The declaration of a vintage is a time-honoured ritual here; a tasting is held on St. George's Day and only then, if the wine is judged good enough, will it be given vintage status. Ahead of it may lie decades of quiet maturation before it is ready to enchant a future generation of wine lovers.

Taylor's
rue de Choupelo 250, 4450 Villa Nova Gaia, Portugal
Tel: +35-123-71 9999   Fax: +35-123-70 7321

TATTERSALLS

Tattersalls, the world's first bloodstock house, was founded in 1766; now it accounts for nearly 90% of the British thoroughbred auction market. Some 10,000 horses are offered in 17 sales each year at Newmarket and in Ireland, which are attended by buyers from over 50 countries. In 1999 records tumbled at Tattersalls' April 'Breeze Up' sale; at 99,000 guineas, *Phone Trick* set a European record for a training 2-year old.

Tattersalls Ltd.
Terrace House, Newmarket, Suffolk CB8 9BT, UK
Tel: +44-1638-66 59 31   Fax: +44-1638-66 08 50

TEFAF MAASTRICHT

With over 170 leading dealers from 13 different countries participating, Maastricht is the world's greatest non-contemporary art fair. The fair is in seven sections; the largest, Antiques and Works of Art, is followed by Paintings, Drawings and Prints. Twentieth Century Art is third in size, followed by Textiles, Classical Arts and Antiquities, Illuminated Manuscripts, Maps and Rare Books and Haute Joaillerie. Each object is carefully vetted and some dealers work all year towards the fair, bringing their best wares.

TEFAF Maastricht
The European Fine Arts Foundation, oude Dieze 17
5211 KT Den Bosch, The Netherlands
Tel: +31-73-614 5165   Fax: +31-73-614 7360
Annually, over 8 days in March

TERENCE DISDALE DESIGN

The launch of the Disdale-designed *Sussurro* in spring 1999 – his 41st yacht – set a new standard in yacht interior design. It was, he says, "probably the only boat on which I have had a completely free hand" and the result perfectly encapsulates today's glitz-free definition of luxury, using simple, natural materials to brilliant effect. Much more than just a stylist, however, Disdale insists that good looks are irrelevant unless a design is based on excellent space planning and a thorough understanding of how a yacht operates, areas in which he is noted for his expertise. Disdale currently has at least six projects under construction.

Terence Disdale Design
3 Portland Terrace, Richmond-on-Thames
Surrey TW9 1QQ, UK
Tel: +44-20-89 40 14 52   Fax: +44-20-89 40 59 64

THADDAEUS ROPAC, GALERIE

Thaddaeus Ropac spent his formative years rubbing shoulders with Andy Warhol and Sandro Chia. His gallery – a favourite stop-off for denizens of the Salzburg Festival – opened in 1983 and focuses on cutting-edge contemporary art, with a special interest in American abstract painting and pop art. A second gallery, founded in Paris in 1990, shows lively annual exhibitions. Ropac's fabulous rococo villa – once Count Esterházy's summer residence – is hung with masterpieces by, amongst others, Hockney and Flanagan.

Galerie Thaddaeus Ropac
Mirabellplatz 2, A-5020 Salzburg, Austria
Tel: +43-662-88 13 93   Fax: +43-662-881 3939

THEO FENNELL

Theo Fennell's fascination for jewellery stems from his art school training as a miniaturist. His refreshingly unpretentious approach to selling jewellery and the clean, contemporary styling of his collections have proved a huge hit since he established his business in 1982. He has also triumphed with his private commissions – notably

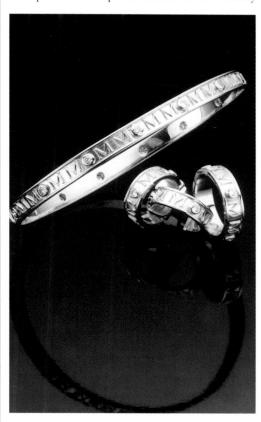

perfectly-scaled silver models of their cars, guitars and yachts for several rock stars. In 1999 Fennell introduced his second watch collection, 'The Pelham', and a new range of 'Key' pendants.

Theo Fennell
169 Fulham Road, London SW3 6SP, UK
Tel: +44-20-75 91 50 00   Fax: +44-20-75 91 50 01

THALGO LA BAULE – HOTEL ROYAL THALASSO

With glass walls facing towards the Atlantic, the futuristic design of this spa building provides an unusual foil to the Belle Epoque style of the adjoining Hotel Royal Thalasso. The spa provides a vast array of sea-water based treatments in a variety of tailor-made programmes – including special courses for men. Catherine Deneuve's favourite is the 'Diamond', a six-day course of therapies ranging from seaweed wraps and hot mud baths to aquatonic classes.

Thalgo La Baule – Hôtel Royal Thalasso
6 avenue Pierre Loti, 44504 La Baule, France
Tel: +33-2-40 11 48 48   Fax: +33-2-40 11 48 45

THERME DEL PARCO SPA

Set in peaceful gardens in the midst of a smart Sardinian holiday resort, this oasis of calm is renowned for its exceptional thalassotherapy treatments, including the remarkable Sea-Oil pool. Unique to this spa, it uses water extraordinarily rich in magnesium salts and marine oligo-elements and so high in salt that you float without effort. The atmosphere is relaxed and friendly but, given its glossy Euro clientele, bring your jewellery for the evenings. Bring your children too; while you de-stress, they are brilliantly entertained in the resort's children's club.

Terme Del Parco Spa
The Forte Village, 09010 Santa Margherita di Pula
Cagliari, Sardinia, Italy
Tel: +39-070 9218 033   Fax: +39-070 921 246

THERMES MARINS, LES

A cliff-side palace of marble, glass and blonde wood, this is certainly the most luxurious spa on the Mediterranean. (The fact that you stay in the Hermitage or the Hôtel de Paris is an added bonus.) It's anti-cellulite programme is reputed to be one of the best in the business but its *massage sous affusion* – warm sea water rains down on you during a four-handed massage with essential oils – is possibly the best thing this side of heaven.

Les Therme Marins
Société des Bains de Mer, MC 98000 Monaco
Tel: +377-92 16 49 46   Fax: +377-92 16 49 49

TSITOURAS COLLECTION, THE

Distinguished Greek artist Yannis Tsarouchis was commissioned to design Dimitris Tsitouras' laurel wreath logo and the same attention to aesthetic detail is common throughout his distinctive line of luxury products. Drawing on inspirations from ancient Greece to 17th-century Venice, it ranges from bath and table linens, scarves and ties to glassware, china, picture frames and scented candles, which are crafted from natural materials, including gold, silver, wood, leather and the finest cotton and silk. The company's concern for the environment is reflected in the donation of proceeds from its 'Arcturus' teddy-bear to the Greek brown bear preservation fund. The ultimate show-case for this collection is the eponymous hotel on the island of Santorini, where items are artfully displayed amongst the fine antiques and works of art which decorate its rooms. Commanding a spectacular view of the Santorini caldera from its cliff-top location, the hotel comprises five traditional Cycladic houses. The 'House of Portraits', at the core of the 18th-century mansion, is filled with beautiful drawings and engravings depicting, amongst others, Lord Byron and the other Houses - 'Porcelain', 'The Winds', 'Nureyev' and 'The Sea' - are each named according to their decorative themes. However, for all of its sophisticated refinement, this hotel encourages a barefoot ease and provides a deliciously private sanctuary from the bustle outside.

The Tsitouras Collection
(Showroom) 80 Solonos Street, 10680 Athens, Greece
Tel: +30-1-362 2326   Fax: +30-1-363 6738
Email: tsitoura@otenet.gr   Website: www.tsitouras.gr
(Hotel) Firostefani, 84700 Thera, Greece
Tel: +30-286-23 747   Fax: +30-286-23 918

THIRLSTANE CASTLE

According to the late Sir Joseph Nickerson, author of *The Shooting Man's Creed*, this magnificent shoot delivers "the most difficult birds" – the sort of birds, indeed, which provide a perfect challenge for the *Forbes* 500 types who regularly visit. The shoot extends over 15,000 acres surrounding Captain The Hon. Gerald Maitland-Carew's Thirlstane Castle and the accommodation is equally impressive. Guests are received at some of the finest castles and country mansions in the Scottish Borders, including Manderston, the home of Lord Palmerston.

Thirlstane Castle
Berwickshire, Scotland, c/o Eskdale Shooting, 3 Market Place, Lauder, Berwickshire TD2 6SR Scotland, UK
Tel: +44-1578-72 27 03   Fax: +44-1578-72 27 73

THOMAS GIBSON FINE ART

As a gallery owner from 1969 to 1996 Thomas Gibson brokered some of the most important Old Master, 19th- and 20th-century paintings to come onto the international market. Now styling himself as an art advisor, Gibson works with museums and a small number of major collectors, dividing his time between London and a private showroom in New

York, where works by such artists as Degas, Cézanne, Picasso, Matisse, Giacometti and Freud can be viewed by appointment.

Thomas Gibson Fine Art Ltd.
44 Old Bond Street, London W1X 4HQ, UK
Tel: +44-20-74 99 85 72   Fax: +44-20-74 95 19 24

THOMAS GOODE

This quintessentially English establishment with its elegant, historic interior, has been the purveyor of exquisite objects and gifts to royalty and connoisseurs since 1827. As well as stocking

collections from the world's greatest names in porcelain, crystal, silver and linen, Goode's produces its own fine china, ranging from the traditional to the *avant-garde* - the latter designed by its Creative Director, Peter Ting - and frequently works to private commission. Among recent clients of its Bridal Registry service were Prince Edward and Sophie Rhys-Jones.

Thomas Goode Ltd.
19 South Audley Street, London W1Y 6BN, UK
Tel: +44-20-74 99 28 23   Fax: +44-20-76 29 42 30
Website: www.thomasgoode.co.uk

THOMAS HENEAGE ART BOOKS

From modest beginnings in the early 1970s this would-be art collector has become recognised as the definitive source of reference books for other collectors. A regular exhibitor at the Grosvenor House Fair (where he is often called upon to provide a quick reference to items on other stands) Heneage sources rare, antiquarian volumes for collectors all over the world, as well as holding an extraordinarily comprehensive stock of current titles. (His thrice-yearly newsletter, *The Art Book Survey*, reviews new and forthcoming art reference books.) Strategically positioned next to Christie's, his shop is a regular port of call for collectors, who drop in for advice before the sales.

Thomas Heneage Art Books
42 Duke Street, St. James's, London SW1Y 6JD, UK
Tel: +44-20-79 30 92 23   Fax: +44-20-78 39 92 23

TJS INTERNATIONAL

Don't ask Thierry Meunier whose hair he cuts; he is too discreet to name names but the location of his barbershop – in the hotel Le Bristol and just down the street from the Elysée Palace – suggests that his veiled allusion to politicians, movie stars and top bankers is right on the mark. For 16 years now the charming, bow-tied Meunier has been cutting hair, offering trichological advice and giving the best shaves in town.

TJS International
Le Bristol, 112 rue du Faubourg St-Honoré
75008 Paris, France
Tel: +33-1-42 66 47 07

TOM PONZI INVESTIGATIONS

Having completed a masters degree in criminology at Cambridge, Miriam Ponzi collaborated with her father – a famous detective – for over 20 years. She now runs the agency and, in addition to the backbone business (personal and industrial infidelities, blackmail and missing persons investigations), Ponzi has greatly expanded her financial investigation and personal protection divisions. She recently began a collaboration with world data banks to retrieve stolen artwork and other precious items.

Tom Ponzi Investigations
via Veneto 116, 00187 Rome, Italy
Tel: +39-06-487 0007   Fax: +39-06-488 0590

TOMASZ STARZEWSKI

Tomasz Starzewski's profile continues to grow – thanks in part to the patronage of Sophie Rhys-Jones and Camilla Parker-Bowles – and capitalising on this, the designer has now bought his company back from Asprey in conjunction with his Managing Director David Phillips. His winter 1999 collection was shown in New York for the first time, along with his new menswear line, and featured lady-like signature suits and duchesse satin *panniered* ball-gowns.

Tomasz Starzewski
177-178 Sloane Street, London SW1X 4AS, UK
Tel: +44-20-72 35 45 26 Fax: +44-20-72 35 53 50

TONI CORDERO

Regarded as something of an iconoclast throughout his 40-year career, this architect today dismisses minimalism as "egocentric". His is a complex rather than a simple architectural language, often full of surprises – including the juxtaposition of unexpected materials, for instance. While tight-lipped about their names, Cordero has designed remarkable houses for several high-profile clients. The Turin football stadium is among his most notable public projects.

Toni Cordero
Strada Communale Mongreno 71, 10132 Turin, Italy
Tel: +39-011-898 7295   Fax: +39-011-898 0601

TRAVELLERS CLUB, LE

The headquarters of this very traditional club is an architectural gem – a grand *hôtel particulier* built in 1870 for the Russian-born Marquis de Paiva. It features several fine salons and an exceptional onyx spiral staircase. The original bathroom, complete with immaculately preserved silver-plated bronze tub, now serves as a private dining room. Its 800 members – mostly, though by no means all, French but certainly all very 'establishment' – also enjoy an excellent restaurant and wine cellar.

Le Travellers Club
25 Champs Elysées, 75008 Paris, France
Tel: +33-1-43 59 75 00   Fax: +33-1-45 62 95 16

TRIANON PALACE – PHYTOMER SPA

The luxuries in this three-floor complex (extended again last year) are both big and small – acres of marble and a huge, pillared pool; pre-warmed robes and towels. The vast array of therapies, available individually or grouped into programmes tailored for anti-stress, jet lag and so on range from Hydrojet treatments to *shiatsu* and seaweed wraps. Gérard Vié's celebrated cooking at the hotel's restaurant, Les Trois Marches, is the finest way imaginable to re-tox before the following day's treatments.

Phytomer Spa –Trianon Palace Spa
Hotel le Trianon Palace, 1 Boulevard de la Reine
78000 Versailles, France
Tel: +33 1 30843800   Fax: +33 1 39490077

TROIS POMMES

Since opening her first boutique in 1973, Trudie Götz has created a fashion empire. Her fashion eye is as acute as her business sense and she has introduced countless top designer labels to Switzerland. In addition to her Trois Pommes boutiques (four in Zürich, three in Basel and one in St. Moritz) which stock brilliantly edited collections from a variety of labels, Götz is behind the own-name boutiques of such stars as Ralph Lauren, Jil Sander, Giorgio Armani and the jeweller, Barry Kieselstein-Cord.

Trois Pommes
Weggengasse 1, CH-8001 Zürich, Switzerland
Tel: +41-1-211 0622   Fax: +41-1-212 2163

TORRES

Founded in 1870, Miguel Torres' firm can justly claim to have become the standard bearer for Spanish winemaking in recent years. With associated vineyards in California, Chile and, most recently China, this is now a worldwide concern. But it is still from the original base in Penedes that the finest wines emanate,

most especially the Gran Coronas Mas La Plana, a wine that can hold its own even against the best clarets.

Miguel Torres
Comercio 22, Vilafranca del Penedes
E-08720 Barcelona, Spain
Tel: +34-93-817 7400   Fax: +34-93-817 7467

TURNBULL & ASSER

One of the world's leading shirtmakers, this distinguished firm was founded in 1885 by Mr Reginald Turnbull and Mr Ernest Asser and is noted for the quality of its cutting and the calibre of fabrics used. Master shirt-cutters Paul Cuss and Steven Quin currently heads its bespoke division. By Royal Appointment to the present Prince of Wales, it has been patronised by a host of other famous names, ranging from Winston Churchill and Pablo Picasso to Sean Connery and David Bowie - as well as the cream of European aristocracy.

The company first found recognition back in the 1880s with the introduction of a yellow silk hunting shirt and matching stock tie, which became the established attire of the hunting set. Flamboyant pyjama suits and dressing-gowns in silks, moirés and old English prints characterised the 1920s and later, T&A (as it is affectionately known), introduced checked and striped shirting, as well as the kipper tie which was infamous to the 1960s pop generation.

The Turnbull & Asser look remains as distinctive as ever today and, as well as bespoke and ready-made shirts in hundreds of variations, it stocks nightwear, underwear, suits, jackets and knitwear.

Turnbull and Asser Ltd.
71/72 Jermyn Street, London SW1Y 6PF, UK
Tel: +44-20-78 08 30 00   Fax: +44-20-78 08 30 01

TROISGROS

It would be easy for a dynasty such as this to slip into complacency, so exalted is it in the annals of French gastronomy, yet the wonder is that Pierre and Michel Troisgros continue to add subtle twists to their cooking. (The *céléri rémoulade* which accompanies the frogs' legs, for instance, is lightly scented with *cumin*.) The other wonder is that the standard remains so consistently high. The cellar is bursting with wonderful Burgundies — at sensible prices.

Troisgros
Place Jean Troisgros, 42300 Roanne, France
Tel: +33-4-77 71 66 97   Fax: +33-4-77 70 39 77

TURF CLUB, THE

With a tradition dating back to the 1860s, this august club was in danger of dying on its feet until the dynamic Marquess of Hartington took the helm in 1977 and encouraged an influx of younger members. The grandeur of Carlton House Terrace is an entirely appropriate setting for its patrician members who, for many years, have enjoyed a reciprocal relationship with the equally exclusive Paris Jockey Club.

The Turf Club
5 Carlton House Terrace, London SW1Y 5AQ, UK
Tel: +44-20-79 30 85 55

TURNBERRY

Three times host to The Open, Turnberry's Ailsa course (named for the Marquess of Ailsa, who built a private course here in 1902) is one of the most celebrated in the game. What makes Turnberry such a special place for golfers, though, is all the extras that have little to do with the game: a first-class resort, a state-of-the-art spa (it is entirely appropriate that therapies include an hour-long Golfers' Foot Treatment) and miles of deserted shore for walking.

Turnberry Hotel & Golf Club
Ayrshire KA26 9LT, Scotland, UK
Tel: +44-1655-33 10 00   Fax: +44-1655-33 17 06

TRUSSARDI

The heritage of this company dates back to 1910, when Dante Trussardi established a glove-making business in Bergamo. However, Trussardi's transformation into a leading luxury brand over the last 30 years is due to the vision of the founder's grandson, the late Nicola Trussardi.

In the early 1970s he translated the fine workmanship and high-quality materials used in glove-making into a collection of luggage and small leathergoods, establishing his own tannery and developing new techniques for the processing and finishing of leather. The success of this collection led naturally to a line of leather clothing and, in due course, to a complete ready-to-wear line for men and women.

Trussardi's love of the Arts has been expressed through costume designs for ballet and opera (notably Jose Carreras' Macbeth at Verona in 1986) and through the choice of fashion show venues – including the Pavilion of Contemporary Art and La Scala. At the Marino Alla Scala, the company's headquarters since 1996, Trussardi hosts regular exhibitions of contemporary art.

A philanthropist of some note, Nicola Trussardi sponsored the third of Pavarotti's 'War Child' concerts in 1996. It is fitting, therefore, that, following his tragic death in a car accident in April 1999, Nicola Trussardi's family has created a charitable fund, 'Trussardi per il Kosovo', in his name.

Trussardi
Piazza Della Scala 5, 20122 Milan, Italy
Tel: +39-02-80 68 82 99   Fax: +39-02-80 68 82 79

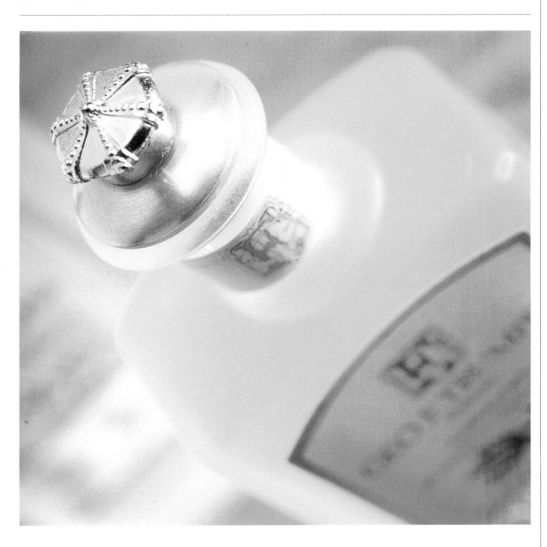

TRUMPER, GEO. F.

Established in 1875 in Mayfair, this is London's most prestigious barber, with branches on Curzon and Jermyn Streets. As well as providing impeccable hair cutting – delivered with perfect old-school courtesy – Trumper provides all of a gentleman's essential grooming services, from perfect shaves to manicures and head massages. There is even a special shaving 'school' to teach customers the best techniques to practise at home. The company also sells its own fine colognes, shaving creams, hair dressings, skin foods and soaps and a new fragrance, GFT, was launched in 1999. With its unflinching commitment to excellence, Trumper continues to be a favourite with key members of London society, as well as attracting a new and younger clientele.

Geo. F. Trumper
9 Curzon Street, London W1Y 7FL, UK
Tel: +44-20-74 99 18 50

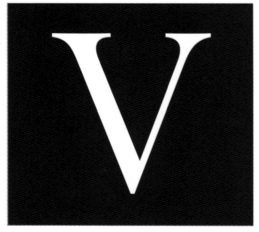

U ZLATEHO TYGRA

Local connections can be a good thing when travelling, which may be why Bill Clinton had Vaclav Havel accompany him to 'The Golden Tiger' – for you may be treated with disdain if not accompanied by a regular. Homely cooking and great Pilsner are what attract a lively mixture of ageing Czech counts, young British royals, artists, writers (Milan Kundera) film folk (Milos Forman), and the cream of Prague's new capitalist class here.

U Zlateho Tygra
Husova 17, Prague 1, Czech Republic
Tel: +420-2-24 22 90 20

UBERSEE CLUB

Created in 1922 as a meeting place for the leaders of politics and industry, this private club is housed in a patrician residence which was built in 1831 for the merchant Gottlieb Jenish. Guest speakers have included John Maynard Keynes, François Mitterand and every post-war German Chancellor. Of its present 1800 members, 100 are women, who have been allowed to join this previously male domain since 1951. Its excellent restaurant is run by the equally august Hotel Atlantic Kempinski.

Übersee Club
Jungfernsteig 19, D-20354 Hamburg, Germany
Tel: +49-40-355 2900   Fax: +49-40-34 53 14

UNGARO

A decade ago, it was Emanuel Ungaro's short and sassy subtly bohemian dresses in brightly coloured silk; today it is his *Haute Couture* collection, which is getting the rave reviews. And it's attracting a clutch of new, younger clients (some 20% of them under 30) such as Comtesse Mina d'Ornano and the Duchess of Montoro, daughter of the Duchess of Alba. Ungaro formed a partnership with Ferragamo in 1996, introducing his accessories collection two years later.

Emanuel Ungaro
2 avenue Montaigne, 75008 Paris, France
Tel: +33-1-53 57 00 00 Fax: +33-1-47 23 82 31

VACHERON CONSTANTIN

Although Vacheron Constantin does not create its own movements, its chronometers and 'complications' are so finely crafted and made in such limited numbers that they become collectors' items overnight. Founded in 1755, Vacheron is immensely proud of its heritage. Its 245 model, in white gold on a crocodile strap, with a see-though sapphire case back – introduced at the Geneva show in 1999 – is a perfect blend of retro and contemporary styling.

Vacheron Constantin
1 rue des Moulins, CH-1204 Geneva, Switzerland
Tel: +41-22-310 3227   Fax: +41-22-310 3228

VALDERRAMA

What began as Sotogrande's second course has become Europe's answer to Augusta, due to the vision of two men: its designer Robert Trent Jones Sr. and its owner, Jaime Ortiz Patiño (grandson of the legendary Bolivian 'Tin King', Simon Patiño), who bought it in the early 1980s. He is a very hands-on owner, delighting in his early morning sorties to oversee the green-keeping work. Everything about Valderrama is exceptional; it is the only course to have hosted the Ryder Cup (in 1997) outside its traditional homelands of Britain and the USA; it's the only course to have a Michelin-starred restaurant and it has a museum filled with priceless golf antiques and memorabilia.

Valderrama
E-11310 Sotogrande, Cadiz, Spain
Tel: +34-956-79 57 75   Fax: +34-956-79 60 28

VALENTINO

British actress Emily Watson is a fan and Meryl Streep sported one of his creations at the last Oscars. Valentino Garavani has been dressing the stars for decades and, in the process, has become one himself. Despite selling his company for a huge profit last year, he is still fully involved in the design process, never losing sight of the femininity and mature sexiness which are his trademarks. His winter 1999 collection featured racy lace hot-pants, red silk jeans and wispy satin skirts.

Valentino
Piazza Mignanelli 22, 00187 Rome, Italy
Tel: +39-06-67 391   Fax: +39-06-679 0275

VANDERVEN & VANDERVEN

Founded in 1968, this Dutch family firm specialises in Asiatic art, particularly Chinese and Japanese export porcelain, although its collection ranges from antique bronzes and terracotta objects dating back to 3000 BC right up to Dutch colonial furniture.

Vanderven deals, by appointment only, from lovely Edwardian-style premises in the medieval town of 's-Hertogenbosch.

Vanderven & Vanderven Oriental Art
Peperstraat 6, 5211 KM 's-Hertogenbosch
The Netherlands
Tel: +31-73-614 6251   Fax: +31-73-613 0662

VAN CLEEF & ARPELS

Van Cleef & Arpels has been in the vanguard of jewellery design since the merger of the two families, by marriage, in 1906. Since then the house has become synonymous with glamour, its

distinctive style emerging with the appointment of designer, René Slim Lacaze, in 1922. Flower motifs became the main theme after 1925 and, in 1933 the house pioneered the mosaic-like *Serti Mystérieux*, or invisible setting. Its jewels have adorned world-class beauties from Vanderbilts and Kennedys to Sharon Stone.

Van Cleef & Arpels
22 Place Vendôme, 75001 Paris, France
Tel: +33-1-53 45 45 45   Fax: +33-1-53 45 45 00

VARENNE, LA

A leading authority on French food and cooking (author of 11 books on the subject), British-born Anne Willan established this cookery school 25 years ago. Based at the Château de Feÿ in Burgundy, the five-day courses are held in June and July. As well as learning cookery techniques, classes of up to 10 pupils visit local markets, restaurants and wineries. Anne Willan also hosts courses at the Cipriani in Venice, Turnberry in Scotland and in America.

La Varenne

Château de Feÿ, 89300 Villecien, France
Tel: +33-3-86 63 18 34 Fax: +33-3-86 63 01 33

VARZUGA RIVER

One of the world's most prolific salmon rivers, the Varzuga yields huge quantities of prime quality fish (an average of 81 fish per rod over a week in late May on the Lower Varzuga). The river offers a tremendous variety of water conditions – from its fast-flowing upper reaches to the wide and shallow lower river. The camps are overseen by a British manager but guides are all local. While May and June are the traditional season, excellent September fishing has recently begun.

Varzuga River, Russia
c/o Roxton Bailey Robinson, 25 High Street
Hungerford, Berkshire RG17 0NF, UK
Tel: +44-1488-68 32 22 Fax: +44-1488-68 29 77

VAU

Sleek, modern, mellow-toned and hung with fine contemporary art, this restaurant (designed by star architect Meinhard von Gerkan) is packed at lunch time with Berlin's fashion and business élite and in the evening with opera and theatre folk. Kolja Kleeberg's cooking is the best of modern German cuisine – particularly game in season – and Petra Fontaine is a great hostess. In the bar, the former coal cellar, once a month, actors or writers give readings – a recollection of its origins as the home of literary hostess Rahel Varnhagen.

Vau

Jägerstrasse 54-55, D-10117 Berlin, Germany
Tel: +49-30-202 9730 Fax: +49-30-20 29 73 11

VEGA SICILIA

Vega Sicilia's relative anonymity is perhaps due to its remote location, high in Spain's Duero Valley. Here the climate is harsh and the resultant wine is potent and full bodied, reaching up to 16 percent alcohol. So quickly does its loyal band of followers snap up this treasured wine that it is seldom to be seen for sale. Should you acquire a bottle, be prepared for such a panoply of flavour as your palate has never experienced before.

Vega Sicilia

Ctra. N-122, Km. 322, E-47359 Valbuena de
Duero, Valladolid, Spain
Tel: +34-983-68 01 47 Fax: +34-983-68 02 63

VERDE VISCONTI DI MODRONE

Since establishing her business 30 years ago, interior decorator Verde Visconti di Modrone has worked all over the world. She looks upon her residential projects (anything from flats to palaces) as stage sets, into which she incorporates the quirky personal traits of her clients and has a particularly good eye for texture and for architectural elements which define and delineate space. Visconti has also turned her talents to film sets and the decoration of grand balls and events.

Verde Visconti di Modrone

via Gregoriana 5, 00187 Rome, Italy
Tel: +39-06-6992 04 20 Fax: +39-06-678 8925

VENINI

With the collaboration of some of the 20th century's most creative spirits, Paolo Venini – a former lawyer, who founded this company in 1921 – revolutionised artistic glass-making. Combining Murano's great glass-blowing tradition with daring new techniques, the likes of Carlo Scarpa and Tapio Wirkkala created pieces which are now held in some of the world's finest museums. Versace, in 1997, is one of the most recent designers to have collaborated with the company.

Venini

Fondamenta Vetrai 50, 30141 Murano, Venice, Italy
Tel: +39-041-73 99 55 Fax: +39-041-73 93 69

VEREL DE BELVAL

The swathes of jewel-coloured silk fabrics on display in this tiny shop are difficult to resist – myriad prints and complex weaves, rich taffetas and lampass, jacquards and brocade. The four families of craftsmen behind the business are driven by a passion to maintain the *savoir-faire* which made Lyon a centre of the world's silk-weaving business in the 18th century, reviving historic patterns and techniques and creating new designs inspired by their heritage.

Verel de Belval

4 rue de Furstenberg, 75006 Paris, France
Tel: +33-1-43 26 17 89

VERGER DE LA MADELEINE, AU

While some may be content to celebrate the millennium with a wine that is up to a century old, others may want something even more venerable - and with something to say for itself too. Perhaps a Madeira from 1789, the year of the French Revolution? You will find it at this magnificent shop, along with a great array of old Armagnacs and many vintages of Bonnezeaux, the ageless sweet white wine from the Loire Valley.

Au Verger de la Madeleine

4 boulevard Malesherbes, 75008 Paris, France
Tel: +33-1-42 65 51 99 Fax: +33-1-49 24 05 22

VEUVE CLICQUOT

Popularly known as 'The Widow', Veuve Clicquot is famed for its restrained power and its absolute consistency from year to year, making it the first choice of many connoisseurs. The 1990 Rich Réserve, with its predominantly silver label, and slightly higher dosage, is the perfect champagne to go with food. Try it, as suggested by Veuve Clicquot themselves, with *foie gras chaud aux pommes* and let yourself be enchanted by the combination.

Veuve Clicquot Ponsardin

12 rue du Temple, 51100 Reims, France
Tel: +33-3-26 89 54 40 Fax: +33-3-26 40 60 17

VICTORIA COIFFURE

Recently refurbished to provide an even more relaxing backdrop to a first-rate hair-cut by the amiable and talented Antony or a beauty routine courtesy of Leonor Greyl and Carita, Victoria Coiffure is Geneva's pre-eminent hairdresser. It now offers the option of a little electronic wizardry, too – with the aid of former fashion stylist Fabiana Ripari, new hairstyles or make-up looks can be tested for their suitability to a client's face via computer imaging.

Victoria Coiffure

4 rue Saint Victor, CH-1206 Geneva, Switzerland
Tel: +41-22-346 2512 Fax: +41-22-789 1342

VIER JAHRESZEITEN, HOTEL

Overlooking the Inner Alster lake, this grand hotel is remarkable for its warmth and intimacy. The staff remember even the smallest foibles of their regular guests, while the atmosphere is a mix of English country house and Hanseatic elegance, with a series of cosy lounges. Doc Cheng's restaurant, which opened in the building last year, has proved a roaring success with the city's movers and shakers and extensive refurbishment in 1999 included the opening of a new fitness centre.

Hotel Vier Jahreszeiten Hamburg
Neuer Jungfernsteig 9
D-20354 Hamburg, Germany
Tel: +49-40-34 940 Fax: +49-40-349 4602

VILLA CIPRIANI, HOTEL

This beautiful Palladian-era villa in the hill village of Asolo has had some eminent owners. Acquired by Robert Browning in 1889, it eventually passed to the Guinness family in the 1950s before being taken over in 1962 by Giuseppe Cipriani, founder of Harry's Bar in Venice. Its guests are equally eminent; over the years the Duke of Edinburgh, Aristotle Onassis, Orson Welles and the Queen Mother have all passed through. Rooms have a rustic grandeur – exposed beams and terracotta-tiled floors – and timeless views across the perfect garden to the Veneto plains beyond. Dining in the

restaurant is an event in itself. Chef Secondo Ceccato seasonal menus are based on the Veneto tradition; his signature dishes include the delectable *Risotto all'asolana* with seasonal greens.

Hotel Villa Cipriani
via Canova 298, 31011 Asolo-Treviso, Italy
Tel: +39-0423-95 21 66   Fax: +39-0423-95 20 95

VILLA EPHRUSSI DE ROTHSCHILD

It took Baroness Béatrice de Rothschild and her team of architects seven years to build the sumptuous Villa Ephrussi, set amid its exotically-themed gardens on Cap Ferrat. Today the salons and private apartments of the eccentric Baroness' home is a museum filled with 5,000 treasures - including a breathtaking porcelain collection.

Villa Ephrussi de Rothschild
06230 Saint-Jean-Cap-Ferrat, France
Tel: +33-4-93 01 45 90   Fax: +33-4-93 01 31 10

VILLA D'ESTE

Not merely a grand hotel, the Villa d'Este is a dreamlike refuge from the hurry and harshness of the late 20th century. Why? Its setting, amid ravishing gardens on the shore of the utterly seductive Lake Como; the magical light – silvery in the morning, turning to molten gold in the evening; architecture on a grand scale, though decorated in unpretentious good taste with the addition of some fine antiques; the swimming pool which floats directly on the lake. All of these things play a part but much of the magic comes from Claudio Ceccherelli and his staff – their total lack of stuffiness, the sense they give that you are part of the family. So much does the Villa d'Este care about its guests that it reopened specially for the millennium, inviting its regulars back for a week-long party. The cost? Regular room rate, not a lira more. That's class. A superb hydrotherapy-based spa opened here in summer 1999, its stunning design providing a perfect foil for state-of-the-art treatments.

Villa d'Este
22012 Cernobbio, Lago di Como, Italy
Tel: +39-031-3481 Fax: +39-031-34 88 44

VILLA LA LOGGIA

The simple façade of this 17th-century hillside villa gives little clue to the beauty within – vast rooms with rare antiques, set against a backdrop of magnificent frescoes, and exquisitely comfortable contemporary furniture – all chosen with faultless taste. The villa's sweeping views, across the Trevisan-Venetian plain, are equally dreamy. The Brandolini family built the villa in 1610 on the site of an earlier fortress and now make it

available for limited private rental. Focal point of its lovely, terraced gardens is the swimming pool, with a beautiful arcaded *loggia*, smothered in climbing roses.

Villa la Loggia
c/o The Best In Italy, via Ugo Foscolo 72, 50124 Florence, Italy
Tel: +39-055-22 30 64   Fax: +39-055-229 8912
Email: thebestinitaly@thebestinitaly.com

VILLA LA RIVELLA

To stay at this spectacular villa at the foot of the Euganean hills is to live in a work of art. Designed by Andrea Palladio, it was built by his pupil, Vincenzo Scamozzi, in 1588. The villa's strikingly harmonious, symmetrical exterior is complemented by the grandeur of the frescoes and furnishings inside. Its magnificent, terraced gardens are dotted with statuary and ponds and filled with 30,000 rose bushes – with an excellent outdoor pool hidden amongst the fruit trees.

Villa La Rivella
c/o The Best in Italy, via Ugo Foscolo 72
50124 Florence, Italy
Tel: +39-055-22 30 64 Fax: +39-055-229 8912
Email: thebestinitaly@thebestinitaly.com

VILLA GALLICI

Set in light-dappled Florentine gardens, Villa Gallici is a treasure-filled manoir decorated in sunshine colours and furnished with Provençal antiques and elegant bric-à-brac. Picturesque yet utterly *mondaine*, it is the brainchild of two interior designers who gave up their careers in 1996 in favour of creating one of France's most desirable hotels. The bedrooms open onto private, lavender-scented gardens and the heart of the house is its lovely courtyard restaurant.

Villa Gallici
avenue de la Violette, 13100 Aix-en-Provence, France
Tel: +33-4-42 23 29 23   Fax: +33-4-42 96 30 45

VILLA PARADISO

Despite the undeniably luxurious allure of this elegant lakeside villa, Villa Paradiso takes its role as a centre of preventative medicine very seriously. Its regimes are aimed at those with specific health and fitness goals – supplemented by a wide range of beauty treatments – and an accomplished team of medics and therapists assess you accordingly. The clinic's *Vacanza Salute Bellezza* is highly recommended and consists of a week of invigorating treatments which range from the detoxifying to the slimming.

Villa Paradiso
via Zanardelli 254, 25080 Fasano del Garda, Italy
Tel: +39-0365-21 883   Fax: +39-0365-20 269

VINCENT CALABRESE

Establishing his workshop 23 years ago, self-taught watch-maker Vincent Calabrese pioneered the re-emergence of the independent watch-makers with whom the craft originated over two centuries ago. An inventor of exceptional imagination, he first created a movement which appears suspended in space within the watch case. Launched as his 'Personelles' line, it won a gold medal at the 1977 Geneva International Inventors Show and became, like all of his watches, a prized collector's item. His '52' model combines eight complications in a thickness of only one millimetre and his 'Italia' contains the first-ever platinum movement.

Vincent Calabrese
19a Boulevard de Grancy
CH-1006 Lausanne, Switzerland
Tel: +41-21-617 0834   Fax: +41-21-617 0835

VISSANI

It's a sign of the times that having high-profile friends in politics and entertainment has led to criticism of Gianfranco Vissani in certain sections of the Italian media. It is an equally turn-of-the-century phenomenon that his restaurant (rustic in style and filled with antiques) is separated into two rooms, one where you can smoke and use your mobile phone, the other where peace reigns. Gianfranco Vissani is that he is probably the most exciting chef working in Italy today. The inventiveness and technical brilliance of his dishes is as near perfection as makes no difference – for example Asparagus soup with red prawns, Lasagne with broad beans, peas and *baccalà* and Saddle of roe deer with hazelnut sauce. Vissani has recently added a few gem-like bedrooms to his restaurant.

Vissani
Loc. Civitella del Lago
Strada per Todi 448
05020 Baschi, Italy
Tel: +39-0744-93 34 82   Fax: +39-0774-95 03 96

VILLA SAN MICHELE

Set on the hillside of Fiesole, this is a serene retreat from the crowds of Florence. Originally a 15th-century Franciscan monastery, with a façade by Michelangelo and a fine collection of antiques, it has a timeless magic. The grand Loggia is a wonderful place for evening drinks, with its breathtaking view of Florence shared by the swimming pool and terraced gardens. The most secluded suites are in the Limonaia.

Hotel Villa San Michele
via di Doccia 4, 50014 Fiesole
Florence, Italy
Tel: +39-055-59 451   Fax: +39-055-59 87 34

VOYAGES EXCELLENCE, LES

This travel company designs dream holidays in extraordinary parts of the world, catering as much for those in search of hyperactivity as sybaritic excess. Aware of how difficult it is today to have an experience which is truly out of the ordinary, Bernard Fromageau, who founded the company 20 years ago, insists that all trips should be made-to-measure and that the hotels used – many of which appear in few other companies' itineraries – should offer real atmosphere rather than just standardised luxury. Furthermore, as a guarantee of quality, he refuses to work through intermediaries, appointing his own, hand-picked representatives in each of the 110 countries in the company's portfolio. Fromageau has recently launched a new VIP division, which takes guests to luxurious estancias in Argentina and to private islands, on heli-skiing trips to northern Canada and 4X4 expeditions across northern Namibia, the Libyan desert or the Andes. Perhaps the most amazing trip is a 44-day trans-African odyssey by private plane, landing in and flying over places such as Ethiopia which are normally closed to outsiders.

It's not simply the destinations which are exceptional, though. Fromageau's guests receive the most wonderful service, including such thoughtful touches as their favourite coloured flowers in their hotel suites and even ready-stamped postcards awaiting their arrival.

Les Voyages Excellence
13 rue de Tournon, 75006 Paris, France
Tel: +33-1-46 34 54 54   Fax: +33-1-44 07 21 33
Email: bfexcell@cybercable.fr

VILLA REALE

Guests who rent this stunning Tuscan villa are surrounded by history. Magnificently decorated and filled with antiques, it has been home to distinguished families and royalty ever since it was created. Napoleon's sister, Elisa, who ruled Tuscany from here, transformed the estate by combining the Villa Orsetti with the former grounds and palace of the Bishops of Lucca and it was later owned by the King of Italy. The villa is surrounded by exquisite gardens with grottoes, fountains and sculptures and its own tennis court and swimming pool.

Villa Reale
c/o The Best in Italy, via Ugo Foscolo 72
50124 Florence, Italy
Tel: +39-055-22 30 64   Fax: +39-055-229 8912
Email: thebestinitaly@thebestinitaly.com

VILLEROY & BOCH

During eight generations of family ownership, Villeroy & Boch has devoted itself to ceramic design, supplementing its core product ranges with other tableware items. These include bone china, top-quality lead crystal, table linens and cutlery. This

forward-looking company took a global approach to marketing as early as the mid-19th century and has always employed the services of the leading designers of each period including, currently, Paloma Picasso.

Villeroy & Boch
S.à.r.l. 330 rue de Rollingergrund, L-1018, Luxembourg
Tel: +352-46 82 11   Fax: +352-46 25 80

VLADI PRIVATE ISLANDS

Farhad Vladi set up his company in the late 1970s after he discovered that there was a nascent market for private islands (he had bought his own in the Seychelles not long before). The business now operates from Hamburg and Nova Scotia and its portfolio includes islands for sale or rental in areas from the Scottish Hebrides to the Indian Ocean. Those for sale are all suitable for development and not too far from the nearest mainland.

Vladi Private Islands
Ballindamm 7, D-20095 Hamburg, Germany
Tel: +49-40-33 89 89   Fax: +49-40-33 00 81

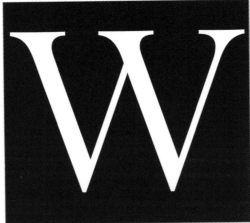

WADDESDON MANOR

Built in French château-style in the 19th century to house the art collection of Baron Ferdinand de Rothschild, Waddesdon Manor contains a remarkable array of French 18th-century furniture, Sèvres porcelain and Old Masters paintings. Although bequeathed to the National Trust, the family maintains an active interest in running the house (and retains private apartments there). 1999 saw a special carpet bedding display by artist John Hubbard, part of a new initiative by Lord Rothschild to invite a major international artists to produce a contemporary design for this part of the garden's celebrated gardens every year.

Waddesdon Manor
Waddesdon, near Aylesbury
Buckinghamshire HP18 0JH, UK
Tel: +44-1296-65 12 82   Fax: +44-1296-65 12 93

WADDINGTON GALLERIES

Leslie Waddington, whose name is synonymous with that of Cork Street — the heart of London's contemporary art market — has never set himself up as the champion of any particular practice. Working within a broad twentieth-century, Modernist remit, he prefers to hunt out the best works within a given genre and, in his galleries, museum-quality 20th-century works rub shoulders with a selection of older and younger contemporary artists. Waddington artists include Peter Blake, Patrick Caulfield, Antoni Tàpies, Barry Flanagan, Michael Craig-Martin, Ian Davenport and Fiona Rae.

Waddington Galleries
11 Cork Street
London W1X 2LT, UK
Tel: +44-20-74 37 86 11   Fax: +44-20-77 34 41 46

WAGNER FESTIVAL BAYREUTH

Run by Wagner's grandson, Wolfgang, and held in the theatre that the composer himself built, this annual music festival is (despite bitter family in-fighting and an alleged lack of artistic innovation) one of the finest of any genre in the world. Productions of *Parsifal*, *Tristan and Isolde* and *The Flying Dutchman* all graced the 1999 season. As well as serious opera-lovers, the festival is a meeting-point for cultured international socialites. Not surprisingly, tickets are extremely hard to come by.

Wagner Festival Bayreuth
Festspielhügel 1-2, D-95445 Bayreuth, Germany
Tel: +49-921-78 780   Fax: +49-921-787 8130

WALD & SCHLOSSHOTEL FRIEDRICHSRUHE

A delight for all the senses, this hotel – originally a 17th-century summer palace and hunting lodge – is set in a magnificent park and surrounded by miles of unspoilt countryside. Its owners, the Prince and Princess zu Hohenlohe-Oehringen, insist that you should be treated as if you were guests in their own home and Lothar Eiermann succeeds brilliantly in his dual role as chef and General Manager. The estate's own Verrenberg wine complements a collection of rare Burgundies.

Wald & Schlosshotel Friedrichsruhe
D-74639 Friedrichsruhe-Zweiflingen, Germany
Tel: +49-7941-60 870   Fax: +49-7941-61 468

WALLACE COLLECTION, THE

This gallery, housed in the former home of the Fourth Marquess of Hertford's heir, Lady Wallace, has just completed a major restoration programme. Its sumptuously decorated rooms display outstanding arms

and armour, one of the world's finest collections of Sèvres porcelain, Boulle furniture and paintings by a dozen leading Old Masters, including Frans Hals' *Laughing Cavalier* and Nicolas Poussin's *A Dance to the Music of Time*, capturing perfectly the tastes and interests of single wealthy family in the second half of the 19th century.

The Wallace Collection
Hertford House, Manchester Square
London W1M 6BN, UK
Tel: +44-20-79 35 06 87   Fax: +44-20-72 24 21 55

WALLY YACHTS

The brainchild of sailor and entrepreneur Luca Bassani, this company creates large cruising yachts that are as simple to handle as a dinghy and as fast as a Maxi racer — yet with no sacrifice of luxury, safety and comfort. Among more recent innovations are the 1998 *Tiketitan*, with its

revolutionary 'terrace on the sea' aft deck and architects Lazzarini & Pickering's loft-style interior for the 107-foot *Wally B*, launched also in 1998. Ranging in size from 67 feet upwards and characterised by clean lines, flush decks and advanced sail-handling systems, every yacht is custom-designed and built; Wally Yachts works as an independent contractor allowing it total flexibility in finding the most effective design and building solutions.

Wally Yachts
Seaside Plaza, 8 avenue des Ligures, MC 98000, Monaco
Tel: +377-93 10 00 93   Fax: +377-93 10 00 94
Email: sales@wallyyachts.com

WARTSKI

This royally-appointed firm has an international reputation for works by Carl Fabergé dating back to the 19th century. Wartski later acquired such masterpieces as the *Rosebud*, *Peacock* and *Winter Imperial Eggs* and swiftly developed the Fabergé market in Europe. It has played host to some significant exhibitions which, in 1999, focused on Falize, the French jewellery dynasty.

Wartski
14 Grafton Street, London W1X 4DE, UK
Tel: +44-20-74 93 11 41   Fax: +44-20-74 09 74 48

WATERFORD CRYSTAL

Waterford crystal was first manufactured by businessmen George and William Penrose in 1783 in the Irish town which gives the brand its name; since then it has developed into the world's largest manufacturer of premium quality crystal.

It now produces three unique brands, Waterford Crystal, Marquis by Waterford Crystal and a new range, introduced in 1997, designed by fashion guru John Rocha at Waterford Crystal. The latter is moderately priced and distinctly stylish, dovetailing with Marquis, also moderately-priced and transitional in concept, while the original adheres to Waterford's classical roots. In addition, Waterford produces unique works of art for prestigious clients, particularly in the Middle East and the US; these specially-commissioned pieces have won admiration for their intricate patterns and remarkable beauty. Waterford's artisans — all of whom undergo a five-year apprenticeship, followed by a further five years' experience before being granted the status of master craftsmen — still employ 18th-century techniques and implements which have scarcely changed since that time, combining them with state-of-the-art technology when appropriate, to produce pieces of outstanding beauty.

Far from resting on its laurels, Waterford recently expanded into gift ware by introducing complementary ranges, such as linens, writing instruments, china and jewellery.

Waterford Crystal
Kilbarry, Waterford, Ireland
Tel: +353-51-373 311   Fax: +353-51-378 539

WATERSIDE INN, THE

Set on one of the most bucolic stretches of the River Thames, Michel Roux's Waterside Inn is reputedly The Queen's favourite restaurant — and no wonder. Since opening it in 1972, Roux (once a chef for the Rothschilds in France) has won every accolade in the book for his classical cooking and a devoted clientele of international plutocrats. There are seven pretty bedrooms for overnight guests and a private dining room in the next-door River Cottage.

The Waterside Inn
Ferry Road, Bray, Berkshire SL6 2AT, UK
Tel: +44-1628-62 06 91 Fax: +44-1628-67 87 10

WESTRA PIREN

The excellence of this restaurant — set in a futuristic, glass-walled building overlooking the old Gothenburg docks — is due to young brother-and-sister team, Mikael and Annelie Öster. She is out front; he is in the kitchen. Östler's Michelin-starred cooking is based on seafood — the freshest imaginable, given Westra Piren's location. Dishes such as *Marbre de bouillabaise froide aux merveilles de la mer du Nord* indicate his mastery of classical French technique.

Westra Piren
Dockepiren, S-41764 Göteborg, Sweden
Tel: +46-31-51 95 55   Fax: +46-31-23 99 40

WENTWORTH

Think Wentworth and you will, no doubt, think golf - thanks to its high profile as the venue of the Volvo PGA and the World Matchplay Championships. Yet this club was conceived over 75 years ago as a high-quality residential estate centred on a mixture of golf and other sporting facilities.

The opening of a spectacular tennis and health centre in January 1999 underscored a renewed commitment to this original vision; an indoor pool, gymnasiums and a superb spa now complement the 11 outdoor courts. And then there is the golf. Harry Colt's East course was inaugurated in 1924 and his West (described by Ballesteros as "the ultimate examination") three years later. They were supplemented in 1990 by the Edinburgh course.

While the quality and range of its facilities may, indeed, mirror the finest American country clubs, Wentworth's relaxed elegance and unpretentious ambience are unmistakably English – as its unique sense of magic. Perhaps it is the setting: 800 acres of beautiful countryside, smothered with rhododendrons and towering beeches, birches and oaks. Or is it the sense of history? Its famous, castellated clubhouse – beautifully refurbished in 1993 – was once a stately home and the club has inaugurated or hosted most of the world's major golf events, including, in 1926, the forerunner to the Ryder Cup. Sports entrepreneur Mark McCormack speaks for many when he says, "I fell in love with Wentworth almost at first sight."

Wentworth
Wentworth Drive, Virginia Water, Surrey GU25 4LS, UK
Tel: +44-1344-84 22 01   Fax: +44-1344-84 28 04

WHITE NIGHTS FESTIVAL

This annual music festival in St. Petersburg is so called because it takes place in midsummer, when the sun doesn't set. With Valery Gergiev, the Maryiinsky Theatre's dynamic Artistic Director at the helm, the repertoire is always varied and the cream of Russian singers and musicians come to perform. The 1999 programme featured the original St. Petersburg version of *La Forza del Destino* and a concert performance of Rimsky-Korsakov's *The Snow Maiden*.

White Nights Festival
Maryiinsky Theatre, 190000 St. Petersburg, Russia
Tel: +7-812-114 3039   Fax: +7-812-314 1744

WHITE'S CLUB

White's is one of the last bastions of polite society to stand firm against even the most lucrative advances of the corporate age and its tent at Royal Ascot is (apart, of course from the Royal Box) the last remaining enclave of civility. The club's elegant bay-windowed headquarters in St. James's is a gentlemanly Eden where very little has changed (and that includes the patrician membership) since its inception in 1674.

White's Club
37 St. James's Street, London SW1 AJG, UK
Tel: +44-20-74 93 66 71

WEDHOLM'S FISK

A landmark on Stockholm's culinary scene, this restaurant is a must for lovers of fish. Its simple yet *avant-garde* décor focuses attention on a display of paintings by contemporary Swedish artists and the service is suitably upbeat. Bengt Wedholm calls his cooking "plain and no-nonsense" but his creativity has been rewarded by a Michelin star; highlights

include Sweet pickled herring with red onion, dill and melted butter and a mouthwatering Grilled turbot with Dijon hollandaise.

Wedholm's Fisk
Nybrokajen 17, 111 48 Stockholm, Sweden
Tel: +46-8-611 7874   Fax: +46-8-678 6011

WILKINSON

Chandelier maker and glass restorer by appointment to The Queen, this family-run business was founded in 1920 by the pioneering Wilkinson brothers. (Their far-sighted polishing and glass-cutting methods were later adopted around the world.) The company specialises in the faithful re-creation of virtually any style of chandelier, as well as producing table candelabra and mirrors and its Mayfair shop is a fitting showcase for Wilkinson's gloriously ornate confections.

Wilkinson
1 Grafton Street, London W1X 3LB, UK
Tel: +44-20-74 95 24 77   Fax: +44-20-74 91 17 37

WILLIAM H. C. MONTGOMERY

William Montgomery progressed naturally from selling antiques to selling property when, in 1987, clients who owned a castle asked him to handle its sale on their behalf. Already Sotheby's Representative in Ireland, Montgomery played a pivotal role in the establishment of Sotheby's

International in Europe. Properties which he handles range from fine Georgian country houses to castles (Tulira, in Co. Galway, was sold to a member of the Disney family) and sporting estates – including, in 1999, Humewood Castle.

William H. C. Montgomery

Grey Abbey, Newtownards, Co. Down, Northern Ireland, UK

Tel: +44-12477-88 668   Fax: +44-12477-88 652

WILTONS

A *de facto* annexe of the august gentlemen's clubs of St James's (not least because, unlike those clubs, it admits ladies), Wiltons restaurant has been delighting the Establishment since the 1740s. Famed as much for its oysters (and its oysterman, Patrick Flaherty) as for its stupendous cellar, it offers fine 'country estate' cooking – from salmon and trout to venison and pheasant, depending on the season. *Habitués* range from aristocrats and government ministers to art dealers and at least one celebrated artist, Lucian Freud.

Wiltons

55 Jermyn Street, London SW1Y 6LX, UK

Tel: +44-20-76 29 99 55   Fax: +44-20-74 95 62 33

WINGS OF DESIRE

Recognisable by its drivers – who sport the smartest livery in London – and its car registration plates (PAW), Wings of Desire has rapidly become the chauffeur company favoured by Hollywood's finest since it was established in the mid-1990s. Its fleet of

navy blue Bentleys is supplemented by a fleet of BMW motorbikes and the more prosaic Renault Espaces, as well as a Sikorsky S76 Agusta helicopter. Self-drive cars, such as Porsches and Ferraris, are also available.

Wings of Desire

2-5 Old Bond Street, London W1X 3TB, UK

Freephone: Tel: +08000-283 932   Fax: +08000-283 934

WESTERN & ORIENTAL

In an age when even the luxury end of the travel market is over-crowded with people vying for the same patch of what they consider to be paradise, Western & Oriental stands out for the incomparable journeys that it organises for its clients. "We are obsessed by the idea of tailor-made trips," says its founder, Bruce Palling, whose background – as a foreign correspondent for *The Times* and travel editor of *Tatler* magazine – has given him not only a unique knowledge of the exotic and luxurious destinations which he recommends – notably in India, South East Asia and the Mediterranean – but a vast network of contacts who constantly relay back insider information.

The question of what constitutes real luxury is another of Palling's preoccupations. "We *want* clients who are demanding and discerning," he says, "not just those in search of gold taps and upgrades." Thus there is an emphasis on hideaways which are filled with atmosphere – privately-owned villas, forts and palaces and

intimate hotels, such as the Amanresorts, rather than grand places with little atmosphere. W&O's reward is a client list which includes some of the most prominent names in society and the music industry, as well as clients based as far afield as California and Australia.

Expanding upon its definition of luxury, Western & Oriental will, in the spring of 2000, launch *theluxury.net*, bringing together a wide variey of luxury goods and services.

Western & Oriental

King House, 11 Westbourne Grove, London W2 4UA, UK

Tel: +44-20-73 13 66 00   Fax: +44-20-73 13 66 01

WOODHAMS

The pared-down urban style of Stephen Woodhams' bouquets and floral arrangements have made him a huge hit among London's taste-makers – his client list ranges from Lady Weinberg to Pink Floyd and Robert Sangster. Still disarmingly modest for all his success, Woodhams also designs some of the capital's most spectacular parties – for example, creating a magnificent Snow Queen fantasyland in

an empty office building for the opening of jeweller de Grisogono's London shop. A trained horticulturist, he is rapidly expanding his landscape design business and his latest book, *Flower Palettes*, was published in spring 1999.

Woodhams

One Aldwych, London WC2 4BZ, UK

Tel: +44-20-73 00 07 77   Fax: +44-20-73 00 07 78

WOLTERINCK

Marcel Wolterinck, who opened his shop in Laren near Amsterdam in 1986, is a leading floral stylist and interior designer, both at home and abroad. His beautiful shop is a showcase for his talents, with generous floral arrangements offset by ceramics, furniture and antique *objets d'art*. In the last five years,

Wolterinck has successfully worked on several prestigious commissions in Washington, from arranging exhibitions in the Dutch Ambassador's house to creating all of the floral decorations for the first major American exhibition of Vermeer's paintings. In 1998, he was the first non-French designer to be chosen by L'Art du Jardin to work on the Hippodrôme's 50th anniversary celebrations in Paris.
Wolterinck Bloemen BV
Naarderstraat 13, 1251 AW Laren, The Netherlands
Tel: +31-35-538 3909   Fax: +31-35-531 6872

WYCOMBE ABBEY SCHOOL

Pauline Davies took over as headmistress here at the end of 1998 and the exceptional academic record of this all-girls school shows no signs of flagging. Top results are regularly achieved in History, English and Art, as well as Music and Photography. Pupils have the benefit of a new music hall and recital centre, a splendid lakeside arts building and an unusually rich variety of societies to join.
Wycombe Abbey School
High Wycombe
Buckinghamshire HP11 1PE, UK
Tel: +44-1494-52 03 81   Fax: +44-1494-47 38 36

YACHTING PARTNERS INTERNATIONAL

With over 25 years' experience in yacht chartering, founding Directors Alex Braden and Mike Everton-Jones and their team have an intimate knowledge of the worlds finest cruising waters - from the Mediterranean and Caribbean to more exotic destinations, such as the Indian Ocean and Alaska. Furthermore, in order to ensure that their clients' style and needs are perfectly matched to the right yacht, they go to considerable lengths to get to know not only the yachts which they represent but many of their senior crew. The firm's expertise in such mundane matters as tax regulations, insurance and safety ensures problem-free charters, allowing their clients to focus only on the pleasurable aspects, such as the choice of yacht and destination.

Yachting Partners' portfolio ranges from a classical, 23-metre cutter-rigged sailing yacht (available in the Eastern Mediterranean in summer and the Seychelles in winter) to the futuristic, 36-metre motor yacht, *Antipodean*, based in South East Asia. In addition to its chartering activities, Yachting Partners continues to expand its brokerage and management divisions. Having realised the successful sale of the owner's original, 46-metre *Liberty*, for instance, it now handles charter arrangements for his new yacht of the same name, an exceptional, 52-metre ketch built, like the original, by Perini Navi.
Yachting Partners International Ltd.
28-29 Richmond Place
Brighton BN2 2NA, UK
Tel: +44-1273-57 17 22
Fax: +44-1273-57 17 20
Email: ypi@ypi.co.uk
French office: Residence du Port Vauban
avenue du 11 Novembre
06600 Antibes, France
Tel: +33-4-93 34 01 00
Fax: +33-4-93 34 20 40
Email: ypifr@ypi.co.uk

YQUEM, CHATEAU D'

Château d'Yquem is, by a long shot, the most famous sweet wine in the world. Even its near rivals have to concede that it always possesses that extra dimension – an almost buttery overlay of richness, which amplifies and supports the sublime sweetness without ever making the wine clumsy. A long struggle for ownership has now been resolved, with LVMH taking 64 percent of the shares. Alexandre de Lur-Saluces stays on as President and Manager, a welcome sign of continuity for lovers of this luscious nectar.
Château d'Yquem
33210 Sauternes, France
Tel: +33-5-57 98 07 07   Fax: +33-5-57 98 07 08

YACHT CLUB COSTA SMERALDA

Established by the Aga Khan in 1967, this is the most glamorous of Europe's yacht clubs. Centred on a sleek clubhouse in Porto Cervo (whose pool is frequented by equally sleek members), it has a membership of around 400 international yachting luminaries, berths for 650 yachts and a second clubhouse at Porto Rotondo. The real joy is that it really works as a club, both socially and in sporting terms. Combining urbane charm with serious professionalism, Club Commodore, Gianfranco Alberini presides over such blue-chip regattas as the Swan World Cup and the Maxi Yacht World Championship.

Yacht Club Costa Smeralda
07020 Porto Cervo, Sardina, Italy
Tel: +39-0789-90 22 00   Fax: +39-0789-91 213

YACHT CLUB DE MONACO

Thanks to the combined efforts of its patron, Prince Albert (a passionate sailor, he takes a more active role than might be expected) and its director, Bernard d'Alessandri, the Yacht Club de Monaco has been transformed over the last 10 years from a somewhat snobbish social club into an active sporting club – with its fair share of glossy parties thrown in for good measure and a growing (and increasingly young and international) membership. Events range from Offshore powerboat racing to the Monaco Classic week and the Showboats International Rendezvous.

Yacht Club De Monaco
16 Quai Antoine 1er, MC 98000, Monaco
Tel: +377-93-10 6300   Fax: +377-93-50 80 88

YVES SAINT LAURENT

There's enough news at YSL these days to fill a book. While Saint Laurent himself continued to head up Haute Couture – producing a wonderful Winter '99 collection, Alber Ebaz (poached from Guy Laroche after only three collections) made a big hit with his début Autumn 1999 ready-to-wear collection for the house, subtly reinterpreting the master's familiar silhouettes and trademark colouring. Saint Laurent also introduced his first tableware collection – influenced by Morocco, Matisse and Picasso – in spring 1999. However, the media was full of another story. Following François Pinault's white knight takeover of YSL, the fashion world worked itself into a frenzy of speculation that Saint Laurent's long-time mentor and business partner, Pierre Bergé, could be eased aside so that Domenico de Sole and Tom Ford can manage the company. Will we be seeing 'Gucci II'? And where would that leave Ebaz and Yves?

Yves Saint Laurent
5 avenue Marceau, 75008 Paris, France
Tel: +33-1-44 31 64 00   Fax: +33-1-47 20 62 13

ZAFFERANO

Winning a Michelin star in 1999 saw a transformation towards a stylish refurbishment. Although nothing appears to have changed upfront within this leading establishment, behind the scenes Zafferano has dramatically refined its already successful menu. It certainly confirms its status among this very grown-up 'neighbourhood' Italian restaurant – to the relief of such fans as Joan Collins, George Michael and Eric Clapton. Giorgio Locatelli's superb and unique cooking – Italian regional-with-a-twist – simply keeps on getting better and better, and familiar faces (familiarity or patience being the pre-requisites of securing one of Zafferano's tables) are greeted with the usual charm, warmth and inviting hospitality. The slightly awkward jumble of its two rooms and close-together tables (19 in total) add to the excitement and buzz of dining.

Zafferano
15 Lowndes Street
London SW1X 9EY, UK
Tel: +44-20-72 35 58 00

ZOFFANY

Zoffany's archives contain countless 18th- and 19th-century documents, as well as fragments of wall-coverings and fabrics recovered from English and Continental stately homes dating back to the early 16th century. Reproducing the colourings, materials and hand-printed effects of the originals, the house produces a vast collection of classical, elegant and subtly-coloured wall-coverings. These are all complemented by furnishing fabrics, floor coverings and trimmings and can be reinterpreted for bespoke orders.

Zoffany
63 South Audley Street
London W1Y 5BF, UK
Tel: +44-20-74 95 25 05   Fax: +44-20-74 93 72 57

ZUBER

This firm, founded in the 1700s, still uses traditional printing methods. Drawing on an archive of over 100,000 antique patterns dating from 1797, Zuber produces extraordinary wallpapers. If you have marvelled at a wonderful *trompe l'oeil* landscape scene on the wall of a château in the Loire valley, the chances are that it was produced by this company with such a vast history. In addition to its signature panoramas, patterns include subtly tinted rose borders and marbled and damask papers. Zuber also produces a range of fabrics in complementary patterns.

Zuber
5 boulevard des Filles-du-Calvaire, 75003 Paris, France
Tel: +33-1-42 77 95 91   Fax: +33-1-42 77 17 98

ZUR TRAUBE

Having pioneered the light, modern style of classical French cooking, Chef Dieter Kauffmann is practically a national treasure. Mastering his culinary skills in his native Germany over 20 years ago, his wife, Elvira, also enjoys quasi-legendary status as one of the country's best sommeliers (she presides over a 30,000-bottle cellar and is a passionate ambassador for German wines). Dieter and Elvira are renowned as Germany's most welcoming hosts. Set in an imposing 19th-century townhouse, their restaurant continues to uphold its status as a gastronomic landmark.

Hotel Restaurant Zur Traube
Bahnstrasse 47
D-41515 Grevenbroich, Germany
Tel: +49-2181-68 767   Fax: +49-2181-61 122

BVLGARI

CONTEMPORARY ITALIAN JEWELLERS

The Trika watch

In 18 kt white gold and with pavé diamonds.

100 RISING STARS

*This selection comprises 100 names which, the Editors believe,
will soon make it to the very top in their particular field. Some of
them have been around for quite some time and have already
achieved a considerable degree of success; others are just starting out.
But all, we believe, bear the indefinable mark of true greatness.*

112 HARLEY STREET

A uniquely elegant refuge for patients recovering from surgery and in sore need of rest and relaxation, the Kelly Hoppen-designed interiors of 112 Harley Street are more reminiscent of a hotel than the certified nursing home that it is. Guests enjoy round-the-clock nursing, gourmet food and all mod

cons – including an infra-red remote control system which controls the automatic beds, the temperature and a huge plasma, internet-connected television /video screen.

112 Harley Street
London W1N 1AF, UK
Tel: +44-20-72 98 89 00   Fax: +44-20-72 98 89 19

ACQUA DI PARMA

Once a favourite of David Niven and Audrey Hepburn, the Acqua di Parma range of toiletries has been saved from obscurity by new owners, Ferrari chief, Luca di Montezemolo and J.P. Tod's supremo, Diego della Valle. The product's 1930s recipe remains unchanged and the distinctive flacon and packaging are still hand-made. In this shop you will also find bath oils and scented candles, as well as a capsule collection of cashmere clothing.

Acqua di Parma
via Gesú 3, 20121Milan, Italy
Tel: +39-02-76 02 33 07
Fax: +39-02-76 02 33 22

ALBERETA, L'

The taste and style of the Moretti family, who are prominent Italian industrialists, is evident in this lovely country hotel, a member of Relais & Châteaux since 1999. Converted by Carmen Moretti de Rosa from a 19th-century manor house, it is set on a hilltop, surrounded by the family's Bellavista vineyards. As irresistible in the snow as in the heat of summer, this corner of northern Italy, Franciacorta, has remained hidden from mass tourism; as a result its prettiness is untarnished, its quietness complete.

You enter this serene domain as you would a private house – ringing the bell on the imposing wrought-iron gates. And the sense that you have come to stay with friends continues – albeit friends with the most amazing staff, who combine perfect, old-school manners with real warmth and charm. The 'cook' is pretty sensational, too, for he is no less than super-chef Gualtiero Marchesi, who moved his restaurant from Milan to l'Albereta six years ago.

The bedrooms all have balconies or direct access to the gardens but the best of them are No.1, with its four-poster bed draped in pistachio-coloured silk and its truly vast bathroom, from whose oversized tub you can gaze out over the vineyards and – Pavarotti's favourite – the duplex suite, No.9, with its two balconies overlooking Lake Iseo.

L'Albereta
via Vittorio Emanuele 11, 25030 Erbusco, Italy
Tel: +39-030-776 0550   Fax: +39-030-776 0573
Email: albereta@terramoretti.it
Website: www.terramoretti.it

ANNEN ETAGE

Annen Etage was a long-standing gastronomic landmark in Oslo, where the city's cultural élite headed before or after an evening at the theatre. After a much-mourned two-year absence the restaurant is open for business again, with Norway's largest private wine cellar and Chef Pal Christian Suarez in the kitchen. His delicate dishes, such as Sea salt-flavoured rack of lamb and Nordic Lobster Tartare, indicate that this restaurant is regaining its former glory.

Annen Etage
Strortingsgaten 24-26
Oslo, Norway
Tel: +47-22-42 33 15

ANGOLO D'ABRUZZO

These days *terroir*, roots, or what have you are much-abused gastronomic buzz-words but this restaurant is the real thing. In a rustic dining room in the middle of nowhere – halfway between Rome and L'Aquila – self-taught chefs Lanfranco Centofanti and his wife, Maria Lugange, serve up food that tastes the way it did in the good old days. *Prosciutto crudo* is hand-sliced at your table; it is followed by divine pasta – *Tagliolini with lamb ragù* or *Papardelle alla pecora* – and main courses such as *agliu cutturu* lamb, which requires hours of preparation.

Angolo d'Abruzzo
Piazza Aldo Moro 8-9, 64061 Carsoli, Italy
Tel & Fax: +39-0863-99 74 29

D'AMICO

Gianni Versace's long-term companion Antonio D'Amico has started designing under his own name. His well received debut collections for men and women benefited from Elton John's presence in the audience. Definitely one to watch, D'Amico has the benefit of a Versace atelier training and plans to open four stores over the next five years.

Antonio d'Amico
Piazzale le Baiamonti 4, 20159 Milan, Italy
Tel: +39-02-63 28 41   Fax: +39-02-63 61 06 66

ASTOR, L'

The legacy of Joel Robouchon is everywhere in evidence here; Antoine Hernandez, his former sommelier is restaurant director and Eric Lecerf is the man behind the stoves. They have done the master proud, earning a second Michelin star in 1999. The constantly changing menu includes such delights as *Ris de veau aux morilles* and Robuchon's celebrated *Crème de chou-fleur au caviar et gelée de crustaces*. Frédéric Méchiche was responsible for the arresting 1940s-style interior decoration.

L'Astor
11 rue d'Astor, 75008 Paris, France
Tel: +33-1-53 05 05 31   Fax: +33-1-53-05 05 30

AUBERGE DU LAC

A combination of its idyllic setting on the Brocket Hall estate and Pascal Breant's inspired cooking places this newcomer firmly on the 'must visit' roster. Based on the classical tradition, with a subtle use of Oriental ingredients the cooking is light and executed with considerable finesse. The wine list is a well-chosen mixture Old World and New and there is a great selection of really worthwhile wines by the glass. The front-of-house team is young, highly competent and notably charming.

Auberge du Lac
Brocket Hall, Welwyn, Hertfordshire AL8 7XG, UK
Tel: +44-1707-36 88 88   Fax: +44-1707-36 88 98

AUX ARMES DE CHAMPAGNE

In an area of France which reveres classical cooking, the precociously talented Gilles Blandin is a breath of fresh air. A former disciple of Ducasse, he brings a lightness of touch and perfect mastery of technique to such dishes as *Pied de veau glacé au four, avec son jus vinaigré*. The welcome is warm, there is a cosy bar and the restaurant has a charming view of the village church.

Aux Armes de Champagne
avenue du Luxembourg 31, 51460 L'Epine
Châlons en Champagne, France
Tel: +33-3-26 69 30 30   Fax: +33-3-26 66 92 31

BAGATELLE

Chef-owner Eyvind Hellstrøm's talent with seafood is equalled only by his expertise with game — as his constantly changing menus reflect, with such dishes as Sole steamed in seaweed and Roasted rabbit with basil. He is also a great wine enthusiast and runs a series of spring and autumn tastings for his clients. The place is packed with Oslo's movers and shakers and, despite its sophistication, the atmosphere is informal and clubby.

Bagatelle
Bygdøy Allé 3
0257 Oslo, Norway
Tel: +47-22-44 63 97   Fax: +47-22-43 64 20

BELINDA ROBERTSON

Kate Moss, Sharon Stone, Nancy Reagan and Joan Collins are all fans of cashmere's hottest young name, Belinda Robertson. Her talent has also been recognised by Michael Kors and Karl Lagerfeld, for whom she has produced cashmere collections.

However, Robertson was virtually unknown in London before early 1999, when she opened her first shop there. From her base in Edinburgh, she had spent 12 years establishing a solid business and, until now, 90 per cent of her production was sold abroad, particularly in Japan and the USA.

Robertson's clothes are clean-lined and understated but unmistakably of the moment. Featuring covetable cardigans, cowl-necked sweaters, streamlined dresses and slouchy trousers, her collections are remarkably easy to understand. In the shop — created in collaboration with designer Anthony Symonds — the predominantly neutral colour palette of the clothes is enlivened by bright accent colours which change every week and any item can be made to private order in any of 120 colours.

Self-trained, Robertson insists that she is a business-woman as much as a designer. Realising that building her brand requires "more than just sweaters", she has added a capsule collection of 'home' items, including cushions and throws. In the future accessories, baby clothes and menswear are also on the agenda.

Belinda Robertson
4 West Halkin Street
London SW1X 8JA, UK
Tel: +44-20-72 35 05 19 Fax: +44-20-72 35 05 23

BALENCIAGA

Since his first show for this august house, in October 1997, Nicholas Ghesquière has been receiving rave reviews for his refined take on modern elegance. Although his architectural styles are reminiscent of the great Cristobal Balenciaga, Ghesquière has not simply reinterpreted archives; rather he is following his own path, while expressing the spirit of the house's heritage. Self-taught and still only in his twenties, Ghesquière's complete disinterest in fashion industry hype makes him something of an anomaly in that world.

Balenciaga
10 avenue Georges V, 75008 Paris, France
Tel: +33-1-47 20 21 11   Fax: +33-1-53 96 03 34

BELLA FREUD

Sigmund Freud's great-granddaughter, the fashion designer Bella Freud, was recently immortalised in the film *Hideous Kinky*, based on her sister Esther's novel about their peripatetic childhood. The designer's life is hardly less colourful now that she is creating clothes for the likes of Sophie Dahl and Elizabeth Hurley. Her autumn-winter 1999 collection was portrayed in *Strap-Hanging*, a short film directed by John Malkovich.

Bella Freud

48 Rawsthorne Street, London EC1V 7ND, UK

Tel: +44-20-77 13 64 66   Fax: +44-20-77 13 64 77

BOETTNER'S

One of Munich's oldest restaurants, Boettner's has been reincarnated. Everything was moved from the site it has occupied in Theatinerstrasse since 1901 – even the wood-panelled interior and the guest book with its Andy Warhol and Lovis Corinth sketches – and has been faithfully reproduced in the Orlandohaus in the old Platzl quarter of the city. The menu, too, reflects Boettner's origins – as an oyster house – with some excellent fish dishes alongside classical Bavarian specialities. The old, patrician clients are back, joined by a stylish new generation.

Boettner's

Pfisterstrasse 9, D-80331 Munich, Germany

Tel: +49-89-22 12 10   Fax: +49-89-29 16 20 24

BOVET

Founded in 1822 and renowned for its extraordinary enamelled gold watches, Bovet is, after a 50-year hiatus, making a remarkable comeback. The quality of today's timepieces compares well with such historic examples as the pair commissioned by the Emperor of China and a prize-winner at the 1855 Paris Universal Exhibition.

Reflecting this, Bovet won both the Watch of the Year 'Prix du Public' in 1997, and Best Watch-case in 1998, for its 'Fleurier' ladies' pocket watch on a gold bracelet.

Bovet Fleurier S.A.

8 rue de la Cloche, CH-1211 Geneva 21, Switzerland

Tel: +41-22-731 4638   Fax: +41-22-731 4686

BULOW RESIDENZ, HOTEL

Since Germany's reunification, Dresden – nicknamed "the second Florence" and one of Germany's most beautiful cities – has been completely restored and is emerging once again as a key destination. One of its lovely Baroque manor houses is the setting for this charming Relais & Châteaux hotel. Its inner courtyard is a delightful spot for summer lunches and its Carousel Bar – the former wine cellar – is a favourite local haunt.

Bülow Residenz

Rähnitzgasse 19, D-01907 Dresden, Germany

Tel: +49-351-800 30   Fax: +49-351-800 31 00

BLAKES AMSTERDAM

Anouska Hempel who effectively invented the designer hotel genre when she opened Blakes in London 15 years ago, opened this sister hotel in the Dutch capital in spring 1999. Inspired by the beauty of the 18th-century building – originally an alms house – set around a leafy courtyard garden, Hempel has spent 18 months transforming it into one of Europe's most exciting new hotels.

Each of its 26 rooms are decorated differently, in Hempel's celebrated, theatrical style. She describes it as an evolution of the ideas which she developed in her two previous hotels, blending the lushness of Blakes with the oriental simplicity of The Hempel. With a subtle nod to Amsterdam's historic Indonesian connections, it is decorated in a predominantly blue, black and white palette, its spaces divided by sliding screens; the sense of mystery and discovery is enhanced by wonderful lighting. The clean-lined monochrome of the public rooms gives way to a richer colour palette in the bedrooms; details include piles of lacquered Japanese trunks and sisal runners set into the mahogany floors. The cooking in Blakes' restaurant – already one of Amsterdam's hottest locations - reflects the East-West mix which informs that of the two London hotels but it, too, is an evolution of Hempel's ideas, as she introduces a Szechuan twist to certain dishes.

Blakes Amsterdam

Keizersgracht 384, 1016 GB Amsterdam, The Netherlands

Tel: +31-20-530 2010   Fax: +31-20-530 2030

BURBERRY

With a fresh CEO in the person of Rose Marie Bravo, and a new designer, Roberto Menichetti on board, establishment favourite Burberry is taking on a new energy. Bravo has streamlined the logo, spruced up the 1912 London flagship and authorised a re-interpretation of the famous check. Add to this some cutting-edge fashion and a new home collection, and you have a directional label which shows every sign of becoming a serious player in the luxury market.

Burberry

18-22 Haymarket, London SW1Y 4DQ, UK

Tel: +44-20-79 30 33 43   Fax: +44-20-78 39 25 40

BYE BYE BLUES

Antonio and Patrizia Barracco's restaurant is set amongst villas and gardens – with a shady terrace for summer dining – near the sea on the outskirts of Palermo. Patrizia's dishes – predominantly seafood – are simple but bursting with the freshness of their ingredients: fragrant raw prawns; strips of fried tuna that are quite out of this world. The puddings (at least 10 at any time) are also sensational, particularly the Ricotta *semifreddo* with watermelon sauce. As the restaurant's name suggests, it's a perfect antidote to the blues.

Bye Bye Blues
via del Garofalo 23, Valdesi, 90151 Mondello, Sicily, Italy
Tel & Fax: +39-091-684 1415

CA SON NET

This traditional Mallorcan *finca* was the summer home of golf course developer David Stein – until he realised that his house guests spent more time there than he did. Now he has transformed it into the most stylish hotel to have opened in Europe in the past couple of years. The interiors, done by a local decorator, are rustic-luxe at its best; there are Hockneys and Warhols on the walls and every detail is perfectly thought out. The setting is magical – vast acres in an unspoiled valley, with the feel of Mallorca as it was 40 years ago.

Ca Son Net
E-07194 Pulgpunyent, Mallorca, Spain
Tel: +34-971-14 70 00   Fax: +34-971-14 70 01

CARNOUSTIE

A phoenix rising and host to the British Open Golf Championship in 1999 after a 24-year gap, Carnoustie Golf Links appears to have been restored to its former glory. Every hole has been altered or re-structured, under the direction of forward-thinking greens superintendent, John Philip, and a luxurious new hotel, overlooking the first tee, completes the transformation.

Carnoustie Golf Links
3 Links Parade, Carnoustie DD7 7JE, Scotland, UK
Tel: +44-1241-85 24 80   Fax: +44-1241-85 64 59

CASA NOVA

Although Baron Wessel von Loringhoven established his interior design practice in 1972, it is now – more than ever – that his pared-down yet deeply comfortable style accords perfectly with the prevailing aesthetic mood. Casa Nova's interiors are modern classics – recognisable by their clean lines and the use of a limited amount of very good furniture, together with tribal, contemporary and naïve artworks. Von Lohringhoven's palette is usually anchored by greys – every shade from lichen grey to taupe to silvery tones.

Casa Nova
Konigsallee 30, D-40212 Dusseldorf, Germany
Tel: +49-211-32 69 52   Fax: +49-211-32 84 46

CELIN, DR. JOHN F.

Having built his clientele largely by word of mouth, Dr. Celin's skill as a cosmetic surgeon has remained something of a best-kept secret in London until the last few years. Venetian born, Celin is a former Clinical Teaching Fellow at Harvard Medical School and still practises regularly in the United States. Charming, relaxed and unpretentious, with a calm and reassuring bedside manner, Celin believes deeply in cosmetic surgery as a tool for gently and subtly improving existing looks rather than for a radical transformation.

Dr. John F. Celin
34 Hans Road, London SW3 1RW, UK
Tel: +44-20-72 25 01 79   Fax: +44-20-72 25 20 16

CHATEAU DE GERMIGNEY

The Marquis de Germigney's 18th-century country manor was first transformed into a hotel in 1830. Now, under the ownership of interior designer Roland Schön and his wife, Verena, it has been transformed once again. Restored and redecorated in a wonderfully tasteful mixture of Napoleon III and contemporary style, it is surrounded by seven acres of fairy-tale parkland, with woods, waterfalls and a lake with a private island. In 1999 it became a member of Relais & Châteaux and chef Pierre Basso Moro won his first Michelin star.

Château de Germigney
rue Edgar Faure, 39600 Port-Lesney, France
Tel: +33-3-84 73 85 85   Fax: +33-3-84 73 88 88

CELTIC MANOR RESORT, THE

Driven by fierce pride in his Welsh roots and the vision of creating the most spectacular golf, leisure and convention resort in Europe, Terry Matthews bought this 1400-acre estate – set in the beautiful Usk River Valley – in 1981. Its 19th-century manor house (his birthplace – at the time a maternity hospital) was transformed into a luxurious 73-bedroom hotel and Robert Trent Jones Sr. was called in to design two 18-hole golf courses. First came Roman Road, named for the Via Julia which bisected the estate, then Coldra Woods, an excellent short course. Ian Woosnam was engaged as Touring Pro and state-of-the-art Golf Academy created – along with the largest and best-equipped clubhouse in Europe.

Enough? No, for in 1999 the full scale of Matthews' vision was revealed – and, by European standards, it's awesome. In the spring a third course opened. Called Wentwood Hills and designed by Trent Jones Sr. & Jr., it was immediately hailed as "a jewel" by the PGA European Tour. A few months later a new, 400-bedroom hotel – featuring a spectacular glass-domed atrium – was opened, along with a vast new Health Club and Spa, a host of other sports facilities and a major convention centre. That's not all, though, for Matthews has another burning ambition: "No matter how much it costs or how long it takes.... I'm going to bring the Ryder Cup to Wales."

The Celtic Manor Resort
Coldra Woods, Newport, Gwent NP18 1HQ, Wales, UK
Tel: +44-1633-41 30 00   Fax: +44-1633 41 29 10
Email: postbox@celtic-manor.com   Website: www.celtic-manor.com

CHRISTIAN DIOR HAUTE JOAILLERIE

Dior's new venture into *Haute Joaillerie* comes under the aegis of taste-maker Victoire de Castellane, who previously spent 14 years working as Chanel's accessories designer under Karl Lagerfeld and her uncle, Gilles Dufour. Eschewing the formality of classical Place Vendôme style, de Castellane has created jewels as playful and as colourful as a candy jar and – the real show stopper – a lily-of-the-valley necklace encrusted with diamonds, pearls and 3,000 emeralds.

Christian Dior Haute Joaillerie
28 avenue Montaigne, Paris 75008, France
Tel: +33-1-47 23 52 39   Fax: +33-1-47 20 00 60

CHRISTOPHE DECARPENTRIE

"It's about magic really," says Christophe Decarpentrie of the interiors that he designs. This former theatre designer believes in creating dreams and his extensive travels in India, Greece and Nepal have endowed him with a sense of eclecticism and exoticism. He mixes styles and periods with great skill – for instance, making a huge wrought-iron wall clock the focal point of an otherwise classical room or placing an Indian rug in a neo-Gothic setting.

Christophe Decarpentrie
Avenue des Saisons 18, B-1050 Brussels, Belgium
Tel: +32-2-640 3376   Fax: +32-2-657 1275

CHRISTOPHER FARR

Trained as an artist, Christopher Farr's exposure to pre-Colombian art during a trip to Peru in 1975 awakened his passion for ancient art. This influence

allied to his love of 20th century modern art has resulted in a striking collection of rugs and flatweaves in subtle and intensely rich colours. Made from the best hand-spun Anatolian wool, the rugs are all hand-knotted – and thus extremely enduring. Farr has also pioneered the use of contemporary designers from various fields, such as Kate Blee, Georgina von Etzdorf, Allegra Hicks, Gary Hume, Romeo Gigli and Gillian Ayres. Farr's work is also sold in New York (through Pucci International), San Francisco and Sydney.

Christopher Farr
212 Westbourne Grove, London W11 2RH, UK
Tel: +44-20-77 92 57 61   Fax: +44-20-77 92 57 63
Email: info@cfarr.co.uk   Website: www.cfarr.co.uk

CORTIJO LAS FLORES

What began as a hobby for British-born Linda Cockerell in the early 1990s has become a hugely successful floral business – which is now expanding into interior decorating. It was Cockerell who did all the flowers for the 1997 Ryder Cup at Valderrama and she has also decorated countless private parties and does the Christmas decorations for several leading hotels. Her richly artistic floral style sits perfectly with the smart rusticity of her interior schemes.

Cortijo Las Flores
22 Calle Las Flores, E-11311 San Enrique de Guadiaro,
Sotogrande, Spain
Tel & Fax: +34-956-61 51 43

DENIS MARTIN, RESTAURANT

Denis Martin took over the running of the 16th-century Taverne du Château in Vevey in 1996, gave it his own name two years later and has since transformed the dining rooms into a sleek, contemporary space (there is also a terrace overlooking the lake for warm days). Martin has just won his first Michelin star for his sophisticated cooking, in which he mixes Oriental spices and Mediterranean flavours to brilliant effect.

Restaurant Denis Martin
La Taverne du Château, Rue du Château 2
CH-1800 Vevey, Switzerland
Tel: +41-21-921 1210   Fax: +41-21-921 4552

DOMINIQUE KIEFFER

Dominique Kieffer's signature feather-edged linen and cashmere throws have become a must-have accessory in the most chic of today's contemporary interiors. Kieffer's early career, as a journalist and stylist for interiors magazines, led to a commission in 1980 by Boussac, to design a collection of furnishing fabrics and, seven years later, to the

establishment of her own company. In 1999, with her fabrics now in demand world wide, Kieffer has opened her own-name boutique.

Dominique Kieffer
8 rue Hérold, 75001 Paris, France
Tel: +33-1-42 21 32 44   Fax: +33-1-42 21 31 90

ELSPETH GIBSON

Winner of the New Generation category at the 1999 British Fashion Awards, Zandra Rhodes-trained Elspeth Gibson is the mistress of crossover day- and evening-wear and is particularly noted for her distinctive, wearable pieces, such as cashmere twinsets atop beaded chiffon skirts. Her predictions for the next twelve months include softer dressing and below-the-knee skirts in leather, animal skins, velvets or felts, worked in a palette of vanilla, green and navy.

Elspeth Gibson
7 Pont Street
London SW1X 9EJ, UK
Tel & Fax: +44-20-72 35 06 01

ENZO-VRONY

Entrepreneur Heinz Julen had the extremely canny idea of bringing together two rival restaurateurs – his sister, Vrony Julen Cotting and Enzo Andretta – when he established this restaurant. As a result, Zermatt now has cooking (Risotto with Gorgonzola, marsala and pears and Breast of duck with Chinese mandarin oranges, raisins and port) which is as spectacularly good as its skiing. The decor of the 18th-century chalet reflects Julen's background as an artist. Be warned, though, it is closed during the summer.

Enzo Vrony
CH-3920 Zermatt, Switzerland
Tel: +41-27-967 8484

FREDERIC MECHICHE

Méchiche's recent Thirties-style redecoration of the two Michelin-starred restaurant at the Hotel Astor demonstrates the interior architect's assured hand in creating period rooms. Yet he is equally impressive when working in a contemporary idiom. His own home, a soaring, loft-like space which he reinvented from three cramped flats, is unashamedly modern, with works by Warhol and Basquiat taking centre stage. If you need someone who can conjure volume from thin air and subtly blend cutting-edge modernism with period pieces, Méchiche could be your man.

Frédéric Méchiche
4 rue Thorigny
75003 Paris, France
Tel: +33-1-42 78 78 28   Fax: +33-1-42 78 23 30

GUY LASSAUSAIE

Since Guy Lassausaie took over his family's long-established restaurant 15 years ago, it has gone from strength to strength. A master of classical technique, he brings real creative flair to his dishes. There is a clear hint of rusticity in his signature dish, *Pigeon cuit au foin en cocotte lutée, ragoût de fenouil, chataîgnes et lentins de chêne* but Lassausaie considers that fish allows him the greatest creative possibilities. The dining room has recently been enlarged and a terrace added. The young *sommelière*, Marie-Annick, is a delight.

Guy Lassausaie
rue du Belcize, 69380 Chasselay, France
Tel: +33-4-78 47 62 59   Fax: +33-4-78 47 06 19

HEIBERG CUMMINGS DESIGN

Before establishing their decorating firm in Oslo in 1990, Norwegian Bernt Heiberg studied interior design in California and American William Cummings gave up a business career to study photography, before becoming an antique dealer – backgrounds which explain perfectly their decorating style. Cool, contemporary and post-modern, it is clearly influenced by the Scandinavian tradition. They will, for instance, happily set elegant 18th-century style *bergères* against a backdrop of tongue-and-groove panelling and polished floorboards. To date they have worked in London, the South of France and the USA, as well as Norway.

Heiberg Cummings Design
Gimleveien 22, 1266 Oslo, Norway
Tel: +47-22-12 98 70   Fax: +47-22-55 68 14

HISTORICAL PORTRAITS

During his 15-year career as an art dealer, Philip Mould has discovered several lost masterpieces – including, in 1991, the missing half of the earliest known portrait of Gainsborough. However, despite being Britain's leading specialist dealer in historical portraits and Works of Art Advisor to the Palace of Westminster, he has studiously maintained a low profile, working out of a discreet first floor office. However, with the opening of his gallery in spring 1999, all that is changing and his star is sure to rise even further.

Historical Portraits Ltd.
31 Dover Street, London W1X 3RA, UK
Tel: +44-20-74 99 68 18   Fax: +44-20-74 95 07 93

IBU POILANE

After helping her husband, Lionel Poilane, to build up his celebrated bakery business, this former interior designer's strong creative instincts have re-emerged, this time focused on jewels. The textured,

sculptural quality of her gold and silver necklaces, such as the 'Mangled Heart' series, and white gold rings inset with coral or turquoise, make them *objets d'art* as much as accessories.

Ibu Gallery Edition
8 rue du Cherche Midi, 75006 Paris, France
Tel: +33-1-44 39 26 62   Fax: +33-1-42 22 16 51

IMPERIAL GAROUPE, HOTEL

This little gem of a hotel, which opened in spring 1998, has two distinct advantages. One: its owner, Gilbert Irondelle learned hotel-keeping at the knee of his father, Jean-Pierre – Director of the Hôtel du Cap just down the road. Two: Its concierge is (for the first reason) better than anyone at getting you a table on the Eden Roc terrace. There are other pluses, too. The hotel is ravishingly pretty; the beach is three minutes' walk away and Room 35 has a lovely private terrace.

Hotel Imperial Garoupe
770 chemin de la Garoupe, 16600 Cap d'Antibes, France
Tel: +33-4-92 93 31 61   Fax: +33-4-92 93 31 62

INDIA MAHDAVI HUDSON

Cosmopolitan by both nature and nurture, designer India Mahdavi Hudson has recently opened her first Paris shop. After working for seven years with Christian Liaigre, Mahdavi started her own architectural, interior, furniture and product design company and has rapidly become known for her elegant, linear but comfortable designs. London-based retailing supremo, Joseph, is a key client and she recently created a deluxe capsule furniture collection for him.

India Mahdavi Hudson
3 rue Las Cases, 75007 Paris, France
Tel: +33-1-45 51 63 89   Fax: +33-1-45 51 38 16

INTERIORS

After travelling the world as a diplomat's wife, Françoise de Pfyffer settled in Geneva and, with her partner, Andrea Waidele, opened Interiors (followed in 1998 by Interiors bis, in London) as a showcase for their very personal style. "There is no such thing as a national style in design," says De Pfyffer, who mixes one-off antiques with their own-design pieces and furniture and *objets* from a hand-picked group of Europe's most talented contemporary designers.

Interiors
15 rue Verdaine, CH-1204 Geneva, Switzerland
Tel: +41-22-310 4135   Fax: +41-22-311 4203

ISABELLE DE BORCHGRAVE

Artist, decorator and designer Isabelle de Borchgrave has opened this eponymous boutique in Brussels' exclusive Sablons district. In the ambience of an exquisite bazaar, she stocks a range of *art de vivre* items, much of it – like her 'Oiseau Bleu' faïence dinnerware, scattered with depictions of fruit – hand-painted in predominantly pastel colours. In addition she stocks hand-decorated furniture, throws, rugs and pillows, and pictures of garden scenes and farmyards.

Isabelle de Borchgrave
27 rue de Rollebeek, B-1000 Brussels, Belgium
Tel: +32-2-514 3639   Fax: +32-2-514 1639

JEAN-PIERRE HEIM

This multi-talented, multi-lingual architect-designer is the person to whom French luxury goods firms (Van Cleef & Arpels, Revillon, Baccarat) turn when defining their image in America. Heim's private commissions include houses in Monaco, Switzerland and Greece, where he has also done a large yacht. Despite having begun his career as a muralist, Heim insists that he is not a decorator, summing up his style as "symmetrical, subtle and neo-classical".

Jean-Pierre Heim & Associates Inc.
39 rue Scheffer, 75116 Paris, France
Tel: +33-1-47 55 67 85   Fax: +33-1-47 55 81 70

JEROME ABEL SEGUIN

The luxury of Seguin's streamlined, monumentally proportioned wooden furniture and *objets* lies in their simplicity and raw beauty; every piece is a one-off, hand-carved from a single piece of hardwood. "I don't really think in terms of furniture," he has said. "The wood inspires the shapes." After training as a sculptor, Seguin's visual talent led to design work with such luxury goods companies as Hermès and Louis Vuitton, before he discovered the Indonesian island of Sumbawa and the team of craftsmen with whom he now works.

Jérôme Abel Seguin
36 rue Etienne Marcel, 75002 Paris, France
Tel: +33-1-42 21 37 70

KATTEGAT GASTRONOMI

The genial Nilsson brothers, Robert and Rikard – both multiple award-winning chefs – opened this restaurant in the charming old fishing port of Torekov in 1996. In 1999 it was made a member of Relais & Châteaux – a sure sign of rising stardom. The Nilssons produce superb 'Modern Swedish' cuisine, with an emphasis on fish and game (the Venison with plum sauce is superb) and have one of the biggest selections of Californian wine in Europe.

Kattegat Gastronomi
Storgatan 46, S-26093 Torekov, Sweden
Tel: +46-431-36 30 02   Fax: +46-431-36 03 03

LAPA, HOTEL DA

Set in the heart of Lisbon's Embassy district overlooking the city and the Atlantic, the Lapa Palace was built in 1870 as the home of the Count of Valenças. Set in luxuriant gardens with fountains, streams and a swimming pool and furnished with Portuguese antiques, the hotel still retains much of its original glamour. After major renovations in 1992 it became part of the Orient Express group in 1998, which suggests that further improvements are on the way.

Hotel da Lapa
Rua do Pau de Bandeira 4, 1200 Lisbon, Portugal
Tel: +351-1-395 0005   Fax: +351-1-395 0666

LAZZARINI PICKERING

Rome-born Claudio Lazzarini and Australian Carl Pickering, who established their architectural practice in 1983, are one of Italy's hottest names – thanks, not least, to their sleek, loft-like 1999 design for the interior of the yacht *Wally B*. The fact that this was their first yacht was a distinct advantage, the partners say; their experience in re-designing historical buildings (in Tuscany, Capri and Sicily) had taught them to "respect the container" and their inexperience in yachts enabled them to overturn all the old assumptions of the genre.

Lazzarini Pickering Architects
via Cola di Rienzo 28, Rome 00192, Italy
Tel: +39-06-321 0305   Fax: +39-06-321 6755

LA MAISON DU CHOCOLAT

The aroma in this shop is of singularly fresh, sharp, dark chocolate, far removed from the cloying sweetness of other varieties – like the difference between eau de vie and Drambuie. The citrus fruit flavours, which have a sheer tang, are particularly good. The packaging – in tones of dark brown and caramel to match the shop's interior – is pure Parisian chic. The *chocolatier* has four other branches in the French capital.

La Maison du Chocolat
225 rue du Faubourg St.-Honore, 75008 Paris, France
Tel: +33-1-42 27 39 44

MARIE DAAGE

"I was studying for a degree in management but spent all my time at the Louvre instead," laughs Marie Daâge, explaining the beginnings of her career as a hand-painter of fine porcelain. Working with small family firms in Limoges, which produce the 'blanks' on which she and her team of skilled artisans paint floral and fruit designs, Directoire-inspired motifs or bold stripes, she brings freshness and an exuberant sense of colour to her mix-and-match collections of tableware.

Showroom Marie Daâge
14 rue Portalis, 75008 Paris, France
By Appointment:
Tel: +33-1-44 90 01 36   Fax: +33-1-43 87 59 36

MAS DE PEINT, LE

Lucille and Jacques Bon run their tiny hotel like a private wing of their house – and treat their guests accordingly. Lucille, an architect, worked with a local interior designer, converting a 17th-century barn into one of the most deliciously tasteful settings in France, filled with locally-sourced antiques. Set on a working farm (where Jacques Bon runs a traditional *manade*, breeding bulls and horses) it is surrounded by the wild beauty of the Camargue. Chef Raik Sert, who joined the Bons in mid-1999, cooks wonderful Mediterranean-rustic food.

Hotel Le Mas de Peint
Le Sambuc
13200 Arles, France
Tel: +33-4-90 97 20 62   Fax: +33-4-90 97 22 20

MATTHEW WILLIAMSON

Matthew Williamson may have graduated from St. Martin's only in 1994 but he is already being romanced by Paris fashion houses, according to rumour. Best buddy to Jade Jagger and, with the likes of Kate Moss and Jodie Kidd queuing up to be in his shows, Williamson is hot! A-list youth is snapping up the current 'Glomad' collection of hessian, knits and brocade, decorated with feathers and chinoiserie.

Matthew Williamson
Tel: +44-20-72 53 42 00 (for stockists only)

MOULIN DE LOURMARIN, LE

In 1999, at the precocious age of 28, Edouard Loubet – already the youngest chef ever to be awarded a Michelin star – won his second star. His restaurant is set in a restored 18th-century oil mill (with 20 bedrooms) in an unspoiled village in the Lubéron. Infused with the herbs of the surrounding countryside, dishes such as *Pigeon des Alpilles aux aromates des champs, au petit lait de Roquette du Ventoux* demonstrate Loubet's spontaneous and imaginative style – a legacy, no doubt, of his training with Marc Veyrat.

Le Moulin de Lourmarin
rue du Temple, 84160 Lourmarin, France
Tel: +33-4-90 68 06 69   Fax: +33-4-90 68 31 76

MUNKENBECK & MARSHALL

Since Alfred Munkenbeck & Steve Marshall established their architectural practice in 1985 they have become increasingly recognised as masters of modernity. Using a mixture of materials to create warmth and texture, their spaces are an understated backdrop for objects and furnishings, rather than the main focus. The firm's residential work includes a house for Charles Saatchi, and 'The Woodlands', one of the most expensive houses to be built in England for decades. Current projects include a resort hotel in Zanzibar, due to open in 2001.

Munkenbeck & Marshall
3-11 Pine Street, London EC1R 0JH, UK
Tel: +44-20-78 33 14 07   Fax: +44-20-78 37 54 16

MUSEE D'ART ET D'HISTOIRE DU JUDAISME

This outstanding museum, which opened in the 17th-century Hôtel de Saint Aignan in December 1998, provides a unique overview of the Jewish diaspora. Drawing on public collections, loans from institutions and private donations assembled over 13 years, its galleries contain an extraordinary range of treasures celebrating Jewish history, festivals and ritual. Arranged both geographically and chronologically, exhibits range from 16th-century Italian Hanukkah oil lamps to Sephardic costumes from Uzbekhistan.

Musée d'Art et d'Histoire du Judaïsme
71 rue Temple, Paris 75003, France
Tel: +33-1-53-01 86 53   Fax: +33-1-53 01 86 63

MUSEO NAZIONALE ROMANO

This museum, which contains one of the world's most outstanding archaeological collections, is housed in three different facilities, which have been the subject of a 15-year restoration programme. The 15th-century Palazzo Altemps reopened in late

1997, the 19th-century Palazzo Massimo in summer 1998 and, finally, the Baths of Diocletian – the largest in the ancient world – will reopen at the end of 1999. In addition to antiquities, reliefs and frescoes, the museum houses Italy's premier collections of mosaics and antique statues.

Museo Nazionale Romano
viale E. De Nicola 79, 00155 Rome, Italy
Tel: +39-06-488 0530   Fax: +39-06-481 4125

~

MUSEU DE SERRALVES

Newly opened in 1999, this is Portugal's first major museum dedicated entirely to contemporary art. Its stylish concrete-and-glass building is the work of local architect and Pritzker Prize winner Alvaro Siza. Permanent exhibitions showcase work from the mid-1960s onwards by such Portuguese artists as René Bértholo and Alvaro Lapa, as well as international figures like Richard Serra; its opening show, 'Circa 1968', focused on art from that year of international political drama.

Museu de Serralves
rua de Serralves 977, 4150 Porto, Portugal
Tel: +351-2-618 0057   Fax: +351-2-617 3862

~

NAÇIONAL, LE

Paris may have been slower than New York and London to realise the appeal of cigar bars but Le Naçional, which opened in October 1999, has set matters right, proving an instant hit with sophisticated Parisians. Set in the basement of the hotel Balzac and right next door to Pierre Gagnaire's restaurant, the space – originally designed by Philippe Starck – has been re-worked by Adam Tihany (of Le Cirque fame). As well as an unparalleled selection of Havana's finest there is a vast list of champagnes.

Le Naçional
Hôtel Le Balzac, 6 rue Balzac, 75008 Paris, France
Tel: +33-1-44 35 18 00   Fax: +33-1-42 25 24 82

~

NINA GILL

Nina Gill created embroidery for the top fashion houses – Dior, Lacroix and Armani among them – for 15 years before launching her own accessory lines five years ago. These consist of a couture collection of velvet, silk and beaded evening bags, silk stoles and cashmere shawls, as well as a second line, 'Starlette', of witty, pretty bags. The response has been so encouraging that last year she opened her own boutique in Paris.

Nina Gill
17 rue Saint-Florentin, 75008 Paris, France
Tel: +33-1-42 86 04 29   Fax: +33-1-49 24 93 80

MASON ROSE

Established six years ago by Tanya Rose and Sarah Mason – both of whom had many years' experience in the luxury hotel industry, ten of which were with the Savoy Group – this consultancy represents a hand-picked selection of the world's finest, privately owned 5-star properties. They range from the exotic, such as Parrot Cay and Necker Island, to the traditionally grand – Hôtel Le Bristol and The Carlyle – and country retreats, such as Chewton Glen and the Kildare Club.

The firm not only handles enquiries and reservations but arranges VIP privileges which enable travellers to circumvent many of the systems which are a seemingly unavoidable part of travel today, such as strict check-in and check-out times. Other services, on request, include airport pick-ups and restaurant recommendations.

The company is punctilious about keeping abreast of developments at each property – staff members visit all of them regularly – and is praised by clients for the honesty of its advice. Indeed, they have even recommended properties which they do not represent on occasions when their own have not matched the client's criteria.

Its discreet and highly efficient service has won Mason Rose a client list which ranges from film director David Puttnam and members of the Royal Family to the directors of top city companies, such as Goldman Sachs and Deutsche Bank.

Mason Rose
8A Bradbrook House, Studio Place, Knightsbridge
London SW1X 8EL, UK
Tel: +44-20-72 35 32 45   Fax: +44-20-72 35 32 46
Email: hotel@masonrose.bdx.co.uk

OLIVIA PUTMAN

Winner of the 1998 Parfums Caron Award for the *L'art du jardin* flower-show at Longchamp, Olivia Putman discovered a passion for plants when she was 17. After an eight-year career in contemporary art, she turned to her real love, gardening. Armed with a degree and two years' experience working for Louis Benech, she set up her own business in 1994 and has now designed gardens as far afield as Japan.

Olivia Putman
41 rue Boulard, 75014 Paris, France
Tel & Fax: +33-1-45 39 82 76

PALAZZO ARZAGA

Filled with frescoes and huge fireplaces, this 15th-century monastery has been transformed into a sumptuous hotel, which opened in spring 1999. It sits among vineyards and lemon groves on a 450-hectare estate near Lake Garda and has two golf courses – an 18-hole course designed by Jack Nicklaus II and a Gary Player 9-hole course. Those of gentler persuasion head for the Saturnia Spa, join a cookery course or attend concerts in the chapel.

Palazzo Arzaga
25080 Carzago di Calvagese della Riviera, Brescia, Italy
Tel: +39-030-68 06 00   Fax: +39-030-680 6168

OFFICINE PANERAI

Re-launched after its 1997 acquisition by the Vendôme Group, Officine Panerai rapidly became a must-have brand; Silvester Stallone ordered 200 for his friends and Schwarzenegger wore one in *Eraser*. However, their appeal is based on more than just a rugged image and retro styling. Founded in Florence in the mid-19th century, the company manufactured precision military equipment. Its first wristwatch – the 'Radiomir', which became the official watch of the Italian Navy in 1938 – has been reissued today, along with its more sophisticated successor, the 'Luminor' series.

Officine Panerai
via L. di Breme 45, 20156 Milan, Italy
Tel: +39-02-38 00 02 08   Fax: +39-02-38 00 05 19

OLD HEAD GOLF LINKS

The location is awesome and the golf is not half bad either; *Links* magazine wrote that no other course offers such 'heart-pounding excitement'. The spit of land on which it sits, the Old Head of Kinsale (an Irish national monument), was bought in 1989 by property developers John and Patrick O'Connor and, almost £10 million later, veteran designer Ron Kirby's course opened for play in June 1997. Its design may be rather simple but its water hazards are quite something; no fewer than nine holes play alongside the cliffs, with the Atlantic pounding in 300 feet below.

Old Head Golf Links
Kinsale, Co. Cork, Ireland
Tel: +353-21-77 84 44   Fax: +353-21-77 80 22
Email: info@oldheadgolf.ie

PECA

From starters such as Langoustine and artichoke casserole with polenta or Snails with artichoke *stracciata* to puddings such as Pear mousse with crushed almonds, Nicola Portinari's wonderfully creative cooking takes Venetian tradition into new and unexplored territory. Gigi Portinari heads an excellent team in the relaxed and elegant first-floor dining room (wooden floors, straw-backed sofas, beautiful place-settings) and in summer, tables are set on a vine-covered terrace with a lovely view of the Veneto hills.

Peca
via Principe Giovannelli 2, 36045 Lonigo-Vicenza, Italy
Tel & Fax: +39-0444-83 02 14

PARMIGIANI

Master horologist Michel Parmigiani's eponymous company was founded in 1975 and has been 51% owned by the Sandoz family trust since 1996. Its three divisions undertake, respectively, the restoration of antique watches and clocks, the manufacture of one-off timepieces and the creation

of its own exclusive collection sold under the Parmigiani Fleurier marque. All of the latter are acknowledged masterpieces, with one included in the world's most definitive horology exhibition, The Story of Time, at Greenwich, throughout 2000.

Parmigiani
33 rue de l'Hôpital , CH-2114 Fleurier, Switzerland
Tel: +41-32-862 6630   Fax: +41-32-862 6631

PRAIA D'EL REY

If stunning landscapes and a dramatic view of the Atlantic surf put you off your game, this golf course is probably not for you. The centrepiece of a new real estate development, it opened in 1997 and, unlike the Algarve, remains blissfully uncrowded. A serpentine course, it winds over sand dunes and has fast greens and a fine finishing stretch. Beware the rough, though. Dotted with seaside wild flowers, is as fierce as it is pretty.

Praia d'El Rey
Vale De Janelas, Aparpapto 2, 2510 Obieos, Portugal
Tel: +351-62-90 50 00   Fax: +351-62-90 50 09

PRINCE JARDINIER, LE

The gardening tools and clothes sold under this name are probably the finest available, combining utility with great style and quality. They are the product of a real 'Prince gardener', Louis Albert de Broglie. Promised to a brilliant banking career, de Broglie instead channelled his passion for history, art and nature into the Château de Bourdaisiene, which he bought with his brother, Philippe Maurice, and has turned into an incredible garden – open to the public – and a laboratory for his ideas. A 'Le Prince Jardinier' boutique will open in Paris in late 1999.

Le Prince Jardinier
Le Château de Bourdaisiene
37270 Mont-Louis-sur-Loire, France
Tel: +33-2-47 50 89 34   Fax: +33-2-47 45 03 32

RICHARD WARD

The young pretender to London's hairdressing throne, Richard Ward counts socialites and beauties – Normandie Keith, Elizabeth Hurley, Ines Sastre and Juliette Binoche – as well as Richard E. Grant, John Cleese and Gary Oldman among his clients. A 55-strong team offers over 80 hair and beauty treatments, ranging from expert cutting and colouring (book a month ahead for head colourist, George) to Reiki massage and 'City Dweller' facials. Stylist Joy Miller was nominated for the 1999 'Afro Hairdresser of the Year' award.

Richard Ward
162b Sloane Street, London SW1X 9BS, UK
Tel: +44-20-72 45 61 51   Fax: +44-20-75 84 79 49

RIGA OPERA FESTIVAL

Inaugurated in 1998, the Latvian National Opera Company's summer festival was immediately praised by critics for the high standards of it performances – notably by *The Times*, which described it as heralding "a return to a Baltic state of operatic grace". Staged in Riga's neo-classical opera house, its 1999 season included acclaimed interpretations of Don Giovanni and Eugène Onegin. The latter will feature again on the millennium programme, along with Die Zauberflöte and La Bohème.

Riga Opera Festival
Latvian National Opera, Aspazijas bulvaris 3
LV-1050 Riga, Latvia
Tel: +371-722-5803   Fax: +371-722-8240

ROSA ALPINA

Paolo and Daniela Pizzinini and their family run this magical hotel – set against the coral-pink rocks of the Italian Dolomites – like a family home and therein lies much of its unique charm. The decor, while anchored to its surroundings, is in restrained good taste rather than stereotypically kitsch mountain style; good paintings and antiques from the Ladin valley are set against a backdrop of linen, wood and marble. In

the spa Daniela's sister, Ulrike Steiner, pampers guests with her natural essences and oils, made with materials gathered from the mountains.

In the St. Hubertus restaurant, Norbert Niederkofler, who served time in some of the world's finest hotels before returning to his roots, creates unique and delicious dishes such as Fillet of beef cooked in mountain hay and Venison dumplings in a nettle crust with pumpkin purée. Skiing is, of course, the main attraction in winter but in summer there can be nothing finer than taking a picnic lunch up to the hotel's own mountain hut, high on Piz Sorega.

Rosa Alpina
Via del Centro 61, 39030 San Cassiano in Badia
Bolzano, Italy
Tel: +39-0471-84 95 00   Fax: +39-0471-84 93 77
E-mail: info@rosalpina.it

ROYAL TOKAJI

The drab hand of communist rule in Hungary wrought terrible damage upon her wine industry. Thankfully, since 1989, Royal Tokaji – co-founded by British wine writer, Hugh Johnson – has been steadily reversing that decline. The wines echo the legendary nectar that was once the talk of the courts of Europe; they are thrilling, vibrant expressions of what can be achieved through attention to detail and sheer determination.

Royal Tokaji Wine Company
Rackoczi Ut 35, 3909 Mád, Hungary
Tel: +36-47-34 80 11

ROSENTHAL

What makes this porcelain manufacturer (founded in 1879 and already well known for the great breadth of its ranges) a rising star is its recent, high-profile collaborations with Bulgari and Versace, which suggest a conscious move up-market. Rosenthal's Bulgari venture resulted in the creation of silverware, crystal and bar ware, as well as porcelain, for the jeweller's 'Home Designs' collection, introduced in 1999. The company's earlier 'Studio' line includes contributions from Dalì and Lichtenstein.

Rosenthal
Wittelsbacherstrasse 43, D-95100 Selb, Germany
Tel: +49-9287-72 344   Fax: +49-9287-72 271

SABINA FAY BRAXTON

Fabric designer Sabina Fay Braxton's big break came when Christian Lacroix discovered her in 1989. Braxton's peripatetic childhood impressed upon her the value of tradition and gave her a passion for the Far East – both of which inform her work. Reviving the 16th-century art of *gaufrage*, she added her own special technique, crushing gold leaf and metallic powders onto the fabrics. Suffused with colour and shimmering with light, they suggest the wonders of Byzantium or ancient Indian temples. Now concentrating on interiors fabrics, Braxton works to private commission.

Sabina Fay Braxton
5 rue Daguerre, 75014 Paris, France
Tel: +33-1-46 57 11 62   Fax: +33-1-46 57 02 52

SHEEKEY, J.

Re-created, re-jigged and re-furbished by the Le Caprice team, the venerable J. Sheekey restaurant nonetheless manages to look very much as it would have done when Joseph Sheekey opened it in 1896 under the patronage of Lord Salisbury. The nostalgic, oak-panelled decor was supervised by David Collins and features a fine collection of paintings from 1910-1940. Celebrity patrons enjoy the predominantly fish and shellfish menu.

J. Sheekey
28-32 St. Martin's Court, London WC2N 4AL, UK
Tel: +44-20-72 40 25 65   Fax: +44-20-72 40 81 14

SHOZAN

Attracting a mix of the fashionocracy and sophisticated Japanese, Jihei Isawa's restaurant is third millennium East-meets-West in the best possible sense. The restrained aesthetic of its Christian Liagre-designed interior (purple banquettes, dark wood walls, giant ceramic pots – and a terrace for summer dining) is a perfect foil for the cooking, which combines Japanese delicacies with French technique, as in *Carré d'agneau en croûte de thé vert à l'infusion d'algues*. The excellent sake is produced in Japan by the restaurant's owners.

Shozan
11 rue de la Tremoille, 75008 Paris, France
Tel: +33-1-47 23 37 32   Fax: +33-1-47 23 67 30

SARA NAVARRO

A legacy, no doubt, of her background as the granddaughter of Juan Navarro, the founder of Kurhapies – one of the world's leading makers of orthopaedically-designed shoes – Sara Navarro insists on the importance of comfort as well as style. The result? Even her most feminine, strappy high heels – made in a variety of pastel, pearlised and metallic leathers – are beautifully balanced. Since establishing her company at the age of 22, Navarro

has also collaborated on collections with Martine Sitbon and John Galliano.

Sara Navarro
Madrid, Spain
Tel: +34-91-547 3454 (for stockists)

SIECLE

Although their limited edition, gilded cutlery, dinner services and table linens have a distinctly

contemporary feel, Ecole du Louvre graduates Marisa Osorio-Farinha and Philippe Chupin are inspired by techniques devised by European goldsmiths and craftsmen of past centuries. One example of the traditional *savoir-faire* that they have revived is *Arte Povera*, otherwise known as *découpage*, an 18th-century technique of applying cut-out engravings onto tableware. The designers have also created table linen using such almost-forgotten techniques as needle painting and Elizabethan 'Black Work' embroidery.

The quality and originality of their tableware have brought the couple an impressive roll-call of clients, including Jack Nicholson, Barbra Streisand, Sharon Stone and Isabelle Adjani, and their book, *Leçons de la Table*, is published in late 2000.

Siècle
24 rue du Bac, 75007 Paris, France
Tel: +33-1-47 03 48 03   Fax: +33-1-47 03 48 01

SOURCES DE CAUDALIE, LES

Capitalising on the success of Mathilde Cathiard-Thomas' grape extract-based Caudalie beauty products (Isabelle Adjani is a devotee) the Cathiard family has opened the world's first Vinothérapie spa at its vineyard, Château Smith Haut Lafite. Treatments include the Merlot Wrap, which contains crushed grape seeds and wine yeast extract (for improving circulation) and the Bain Barrique, an anti-cellulite red-wine soak. The spa's fine restaurant is run by Didier and Marie-Louise Banyols.

Les Sources de Caudalie
Chemin de Smith Haut Lafitte, 33650 Martillac, France
Tel: +33-5-57-83 11 26   Fax: +33-5-57 83 11 20

ST. CLERAN'S

Nobody has yet been able to define its magical serenity but everyone who visits this beautiful Georgian manor is spellbound. Film director John Huston called St. Cleran's "a world apart" when it was his home during the 1950s and 60s and now Merv Griffin has been seduced. After painstakingly restoring the house and filling it with art treasures, he opened it as a country house hotel (with just 12 bedrooms) in 1998. It's a perfect base for exploring

the west of Ireland and excellent fishing, fox hunting and golf (at Ballybunion) are right on the doorstep – but the chances are that you will be content simply to wrap yourself in its magic and stay put.

St. Cleran's
Craughwell, Co. Galway, Ireland
Tel: +353-91-84 65 55   Fax: +353-91-84 66 00

ST. DAVID'S HOTEL & SPA

Set on Cardiff Bay, surrounded by water on three sides, this is the cornerstone of Sir Rocco Forte's new 'RF' group of hotels. Already a member of Leading Hotels of the World, St. David's opened in early 1999 to rave reviews – not least for its spectacular modernist architecture. Combining the benefits of salt-water hydrotherapy with the philosophy of the E'spa product range, its spa offers a vast range of de-stressing and revitalising treatments.

St. David's Hotel & Spa
Havannah Street, Cardiff Bay, Cardiff CF10 5SD, Wales, UK
Tel: +44-1222-45 40 45   Fax: +44-1222-448 70 56

STEFAN HAFNER

Although creative master-jeweller, Stefan Hafner has been designing superbly-crafted, gem-set pieces for over 30 years, his name has only recently emerged onto the international scene. Of Italian-Swiss descent, his design training included precision watchmaking,

which has given him an eye for the technically complex, as well as the fashionable, in fine jewellery. A favourite among jet-set customers is the 'Diamonds in Motion' range. For the new millennium Hafner is looking to organic shapes, Eastern influences and special, free-floating settings for inspiration.

Stefan Hafner
via Vallescura 12/2, 40136 Bologna, Italy
Tel: +39-051-51 58 05 90   Fax: +39-051-58 21 61

STEPHEN WEBSTER

Newcomer Stephen Webster is taking the jewellery scene by storm. His innovative designs include the well-received crystal-faceted jewels, "Crystal Haze" and, most recently, his black Tahitian pearl "Thorn Noir" and hand-faceted "Pearl Boa" collections. Connoisseurs avidly collect his interpretations of rare stones and ancient artefacts.

Stephen Webster
1A Duke Street, London W1M 5RD, UK
Tel: +44-20-74 86 65 75   Fax: +44-20-74 86 64 39

STOKE PARK

A marvellous 18th-century confection of white stucco and pillars, Stoke Park was bought last year by a British businessman who has transformed it into a splendid hotel. It sits amid parkland designed by Humphrey Repton and 'Capability' Brown which, in 1908, became the Stoke Poges Golf Club. Club members still us it as their HQ and in return hotel guests can use the course. A new tennis and spa complex is scheduled to open in late summer 2000.

Stoke Park
Park Road, Stoke Poges, Buckinghamshire SL2 4PG, UK
Tel: +44-1753-71 71 71   Fax: +44-1753-71 71 81

TEAROSE

The scent of candles, colognes and massed flowers will leave you breathless when you enter Alessandra Rovati Vitali's florist shop – and the charm of Rovati and her assistants will leave you with a smile on your face.

Originally based in Monza, Tearose opened in Milan in May 1998 and its fresh and naturalistic arrangements (in ravishing colour combinations) have been a hit with fashionable Milanese. Tearose also stocks an eclectic collection of antiques and accessories.

Tearose
via Santo Spirito 18, 20121 Milan, Italy
Tel: +39-02-76 01 54 67

THERME VALS

Since architect Peter Zumthor's strikingly futuristic stone and glass building opened two years ago, this spa (there has been one here for 60 years) has hit the big time. Some state-of-the-art equipment has been added, too, to assist with the exercise programmes – including an electrode machine which evaluates the movements of individual muscles and the Vigor Unweighting harness, which stabilises fragile necks. Treatments in the thermal pools range from the pampering Flower Bath (using wild flowers from the alpine meadows) to the invigorating Fire Bath.

Therme Vals
CH-7132 Vals, Switzerland
Tel: +41-81-926 8080   Fax: +41-81-926 8000

TIM HEYWOOD

After working with Jon Bannenberg for many years, Tim Heywood opened his own yacht design practice in 1996. He recently completed a major refit of a 42-metre Dutch-built motor yacht and current projects include an interior refit of an 86-metre yacht, the exterior of a 95-metre yacht – under construction in Germany and due for launching in 2001 – and the interior of a Boeing 737. The most important lesson that he has learned in his career, Heywood says, is "the value of listening – really listening – to clients".

Tim Heywood Design
1e Oliver's Wharf, 64 Wapping High Street
London E1 9PJ, UK
Tel: +44-20-74 81 89 58   Fax: +44-20-74 81 41 33

TERROIRS

Though only five years old, Terroirs has rapidly established itself as a wine merchant of rare style and charm. Husband-and-wife-team, Seán and Françoise Gilley, have created an exquisite emporium, stocked with marvellous wines as well as select foodstuffs such as caviar, foie gras and hand made chocolates.

Glassware is another speciality. In all, it's one of the most seductive shopping experiences you are ever likely to encounter.

Terroirs

103 Morehampton Road, Donnybrook, Dublin 4, Ireland
Tel: +353-1-667 1311   Fax: +353-1-667 1312
Email: info@terroirs.ie

TIMOTHY EVEREST

When Tom Cruise was dressed in Timothy Everest suits for *Mission: Impossible*, he was so taken with them that he not only kept the suits but persuaded Stanley Kubrick to use Everest for *Eyes Wide Shut*. Nicole Kidman became a client, too – and, when Gordon Brown became Chancellor in 1998, he went to Everest for his new image. Based in an 18th-century East London house, Everest – once a protégé of Tommy Nutter – has taken the tradition of Savile Row and subtly moved it forward.

Timothy Everest

32 Spitalfields, London E1 6BT, UK
Tel: +44-20-73 77 57 70   Fax: +44-20-73 77 59 90

TIMOTHY HATTON

Architect Tim Hatton appears to lead a charmed life. Having been awarded not one but two scholarships, he graduated from both Cambridge University and Harvard's Graduate School of Design with honours. Since setting up his practice in 1985 Hatton's clients have included Lord Rothschild and Mick Jagger. His adaptable and sympathetic style, coupled with his innate good taste, has meant that most clients – whether private or commercial – remain firm friends long after the builders' dust has settled.

Timothy Hatton

6 St. Luke's Road, London W11 1DP, UK
Tel: +44-20-77 27 34 84   Fax: +44-20-77 92 11 85

TMT

Having started their careers with celebrated designer Luigi Sturchio, Luciano Di Pilla and Milena Rotta Loria established their own business ten years ago, specialising in the architecture and interior decoration of yachts, private houses and offices. They create spaces which skilfully combine aesthetics and practicality and mix styles and periods with great flair. Working closely with a team of talented Italian craftsmen, TMT also produces furniture – whether one-off pieces or as part of their recently launched XOM collection. Current projects include a large private yacht and *The World of Residensea* – the latter in conjunction with Nina Campbell and Juan Pablo Molyneux.

TMT Design by Di Pilla

Via Bagutti 14, Palazzo Greco
CH-6900 Lugano, Switzerland
Tel: +41-91-972 1316   Fax: +41-91-972 1317

THORNTON'S

With the intimate atmosphere of a private dining room and decorated with wonderful, exotic flowers, this restaurant has become the toast of Ireland since it opened in 1995, thanks to the talents of its chef-owner, Kevin Thornton.

Thornton's training included stints at The Four Seasons in Toronto and at Paul Bocuse in Lyons; however, it is his own almost religious passion for his ingredients and his craft which have made him Ireland's premier chef. Thoroughly deserving of the Michelin star that he received in 1996, Thornton reveres his ingredients, choosing his techniques to elicit the optimum results from them; his lobsters are slowly drowned, rather than boiled, for instance, to avoid toughness.

It is this passion which makes Thornton a traditionalist at heart; in his hands the Irish favourite of bacon and cabbage becomes as near to sublime as makes no difference, while his Suckling Pig and Trotter dish is – in the opinion of composer and sometime restaurant reviewer, Andrew Lloyd Webber – superior to the versions produced by Marco Pierre White or Pierre Koffmann.

The 'front of house' is the domain of the restaurant manager, Oliver Meisonnave (formerly of Alain Chapel), who has been with Thornton's since its inception, together with Thornton's wife, Muriel, he oversees the serenely impeccable service by a mainly French staff.

Thornton's

1 Portobello Road, Dublin 6, Ireland
Tel: +353-1-454 9067   Fax: +353-1-453 2947

ULTIMATE TRAVEL COMPANY, THE

This travel consultancy may be little more than a year old but its founder, Martin Thompson – former director of Abercrombie & Kent's London office – and his nine staff have 170 years in the business between them. In addition to tailor-made trips, Ultimate organises some exceptional escorted tours for small groups (described by one happy client as "travelling house parties"). You might, for instance, go riding in Bolivia with polo champion Patrick Beresford or visit the castles of Bohemia with Helen de Borchgrave

The Ultimate Travel Company

20 Pimlico Road, London SW1W 8LJ, UK
Tel: +44-20-72 59 02 59   Fax: +44-20-72 59 02 56

VERROCCHIO, IL

Set in Villa La Massa, a Renaissance palazzo near Florence which was renovated and reopened in spring 1999 by the owners of Villa d'Este, Il Verrocchio is a delight. Decorated in sunshine yellow, it has a huge, shady terrace on the edge of the River Arno, where you can have lunch in summer. Andrea Quagliarella's menu of regional specialities includes a delicious Purée of white beans with crayfish and the service is every bit as good as you get at its grand 'big sister' on Lake Como.

Il Verrocchio

via Della Massa 24, 50012 Candeli, Florence, Italy
Tel: +39-055-62 611   Fax: +39-055-63 31 02

VILLA BELROSE

Designed in the Italianate style and set on a hill overlooking the sea, this immensely stylish hotel has changed the social order in Saint-Tropez since it opened in 1997. Its owner, Thomas Althoff, proprietor of the splendid Schlosshotel Lerbach near Cologne, knows exactly what his sophisticated clientele wants – and Relais & Châteaux exercised typically perfect judgement by inviting it into its consortium in 1999.

Villa Belrose sits at the end of a long driveway, lined on both sides with bougainvillea. It is a deeply civilised place – somewhere that, after a bare-feet-and-bathing-suits day, you *dress*, jewels and all, for dinner. (And what a dinner; Thierry Thiercelin's Mediterranean-accented cooking is tremendously accomplished.) Indeed, it is a place from which you may feel no need to venture forth. The pool, built on the lowest of three terraces, is sublime. From the bedrooms – all large, airy and beautifully appointed – as from every point on the property, you revel in the magnificent views across Saint-Tropez....and say a silent word of thanks that you are not down there, jostling for space.What really sets Villa

Belrose apart, though, is the service. Brazilian-born Jean-Pierre Hall is an outstanding director, inspiring from his team the same intuitive and utterly unobtrusive service that one usually finds only in the finest private homes.
Villa Belrose
Boulevard des Crêtes, 83580 Gassin, France
Tel: +33-4-94 55 97 97   Fax: +33-4-94 55 97 98

VIAGGI DELL'ELEFANTE

Inveterate traveller Vittorio Ducrot turned his all-consuming passion into a business 25 years ago and today, with his son – the author and archaeologist, Enrico Ducrot – working alongside him, Ducrot still tests in person every destination and every service his company uses before offering them to clients. The trips which he offers – whether individual or in small, escorted groups – to destinations including China, India, Peru and Iran, are characterised by a perfectly judged mix of nature, archaeology, culture and adventure.
Viaggi dell'Elefante
61a via dei Condotti, 00817 Rome, Italy
Tel: +39-06-678 4541   Fax: +39-06-679 6164

VIP NATIONAL CLUB MOSCOW

This private club and casino is an oasis of class in the maelstrom of Moscow life. It was opened in late 1998 by Timur Karchava, a genial and sophisticated Georgian, who knows all his guests – including Moscow's mayor, Yuri Luzhkov and the country's leading film director, Nikita Mikhalkov – personally and whose fascination with London's gentlemen's clubs is reflected both in the décor and in his choice of an English management team. The restaurant overlooks The Kremlin and, in addition to the 12-table Gaming Room, there is a Salle Privée where high rollers can keep a low profile.
VIP National Club Moscow
15/1 Mokhovaya Street, 103009 Moscow, Russia
Tel: +7-095-797 6000   Fax: 7-095-797 6006

VAN DER STRAETEN

After graduating from the Ecole des Beaux Arts in 1985, Hervé Van der Straeten designed jewellery in hammered metal and semi-precious stones for such luminaries as Saint Laurent, Givenchy and Lacroix. His gallery, opened in 1999 and showcases his jewellery, furniture and decorative accessories, inspired by nature and mythology. It also brings together the work of other individualists, hand-picked by Van der Straeten, such as Thomas Boog and Olivier Gagnère.
Galerie Van der Straeten
11 Rue Ferdinand Duval, 75004 Paris, France
Tel: +33-1-42 78 99 99   Fax: +33-1-42 78 99 90

WALSERHOF, HOTEL

Until Beat and Gabi Bolliger opened their hotel and restaurant a decade ago, the best food in Klosters was served in the homes of its royal and discreetly chic winter residents (as were the smartest places to stay). Not so any more; Beat's dishes are modern classics and the hotel is a new member of Relais & Châteaux. The Bolligers are marvellous hosts; for them 'sophistication' is no substitute for cosy rusticity and treating their guests like long lost friends.
Hotel Walserhof
Landstrasse 141, CH-7250 Klosters, Switzerland
Tel: +41-81-410 2929   Fax: +41-81-410 2939

WILLIAM YEOWARD

Having trained with Designer's Guild and Nicky Haslam, William Yeoward set up his furniture company in 1989, making his own designs, based on 18th- and 19th-century painted gothic pieces. A creamware collection followed four years later and, in 1995, he launched his successful glassware, also based on 18th- and 19th-century designs. The glassware is displayed in its own pretty Chelsea shop, while furnishings are showcased across the river at Yeoward South.
William Yeoward
336 Kings Road, London SW3 5UR, UK
Tel: +44-20-73 51 54 54   Fax: +44-20-73 51 94 69

WISLEY GOLF CLUB

This private members' club, which opened in 1991, nestles in pretty countryside less than an hour from central London. The excellence of both the course and the members' facilities (the clubhouse was inspired by the work of Edwardian architect Sir Edwin Lutyens) has attracted a membership which now embraces 27 nationalities. The first in the UK to be designed by Robert Trent Jones Jr., the course presents a challenge to golfers of all levels.
Wisley Golf Club
Woking, Surrey GU23 6QU, UK
Tel: +44-1483-21 12 13   Fax: +44-1483-21 16 62

THE INSIDERS GUIDE TO AMERICA

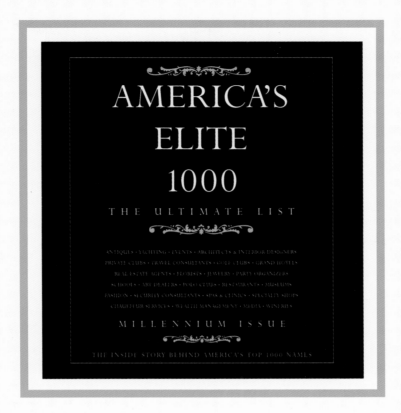

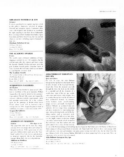

Acclaimed internationally — a spectacular directory of the best of the best in America listing a broad range of luxury goods and services. This stunning publication will appeal to sophisticated travellers to America — a must for any library or coffee table.

To order the most beautiful book in the world:

Tel: +44-20-78 23 74 45   Fax: +44-20-72 25 29 42

Cadogan Publications

50 Hans Crescent, Knightsbridge, London SW1X ONA, UK

email: cadogan@dircon.co.uk

Lombard Odier

Our first 200 years
as private bankers

11, rue de la Corraterie
1204 Geneva - Switzerland

GSPP 1999

trust
in the art of asset management

Lombard Odier

Geneva - Zurich - London - Amsterdam - Frankfurt - Gibraltar - New York - Montreal - Bermuda - Tokyo - Hong Kong

100 BEST-KEPT SECRETS

The 100 names on the following pages are all magical places and specialist shops and services, some of them quirky and most of them hardly known outside the inner circle of Europe's cognoscenti. All of them, however, offer outstanding quality and an indefinable 'something special'.

AI MONASTERI

Situated in Rome's historic centre, Ai Monasteri sells a heavenly range of creams, lotions, tonics and elixirs, all of which are hand-made by monks and nuns. Four generations of the Nardi family have purveyed the rarefied, natural formulas, which include a lavender-scented hand-cream, the curative Tintura Imperiale, and the (reputedly) aphrodisiac Count Igor's Waters.

Ai Monasteri

Corso Rinascimento 72, 00186 Rome, Italy

Tel & Fax: +39-06-68 80 27 83

ANSELMI

The son of a wine merchant, Roberto Anselmi began buying up vineyards in 1948 – to the benefit of connoisseurs everywhere. To most of us, for whom Soave means rather thin and acidic white wine, the first sip of his 'Capitel Croce' will come as a revelation.....and by the third you will be in raptures; it is rich, mellow and beautifully structured. His 'I Capitelli' – like 'Capitel Croce', 100% garganega, but barrel-fermented for 16 months – is conclusive proof that Château d'Yquem is not the only sweet wine worth drinking.

Anselmi

via San Carlo 46, 37032 Monteforte D'Alpone, Italy

Tel: +39-045-761 1488   Fax: +39-045-761 1490

ANTIQUA

The owner of this Aladdin's cave of a book shop, Ulf Egelius, is a serious bibliophile with a particular passion for architecture, city planning and the decorative arts. The tiny shop is stuffed to the rafters with both antiquarian and contemporary volumes on the subject, books overflow onto the floor and more are listed in a catalogue which Egelius updates. Must-haves for those interested in design include such tomes as Architektur, a three-volume work by Joseph Olbrich.

Antiqua

Karlavägen 12, 11431 Stockholm, Sweden

Tel & Fax: +46-8-10 09 96

AU TROU GASCON

This pint-sized bistrot is packed with Parisians who have neither forgotten how good it is nor are put off by its unfashionable location. It's where star chef Alain Dutournier started and his wife, Nicole, still runs it beautifully. The cooking (now done by Jacques Faussat) is the honest-to-goodness regional fare that Dutournier grew up with and is the best of its kind in Paris: Cassoulet, Chalosse ham, Foie gras and potato terrine. The wines and armagnacs are outstanding for a place of this style.

Au Trou Gascon

40 rue Taine, 75012 Paris, France

Tel: +33-1-43 44 34 26   Fax: +33-1-43 07 80 55

BELLAVISTA

The Moretti family, who have lived in the wine region of Franciacorta since the 15th century, have a passion for excellence – reflected today in their development of Bellavista into the producer of Italy's finest sparkling wines. Bellavista's Cuvée Brut is rich in ripe fruits, with small and long-lasting bubbles, while its premium cuvées, made from a

single year's harvest, give full rein to oenologist Mattia Vezzola's skills. Its elegant and intense vintage Gran Cuvée Pas Operé, bottle-aged for six years, comes from vines that are over 20 years old; the Gran Cuvée Brut Rosé is graceful yet intense and its 100% chardonnay Gran Cuvée Satèn, is deliciously feminine in character.

Bellavista

via Bellavista 5, 25030 Erbusco, Italy

Tel: +39-030-776 0276   Fax: +39-030-776 0386

Website: www.terramoretti.it

BLAIRQUHAN

This privately-owned Scottish castle on the banks of the River Girvan is as grand and baronial as they come – and is available for limited private rental. A three-mile driveway lined by lime trees leads up to it. There is a beautiful galleried Hall, the grand dining room seats 24 at its Regency table and there

is a billiards room, a library, two drawing rooms and 15 bedrooms. Turnberry Golf Course is a mere 14 miles away.

Blairquhan

Ayrshire, Scotland, UK

c/o George Goldsmith, Catchpell House, Carpet Lane

Edinburgh EH6 6SP, UK

Tel: +44-131-468 8535   Fax: +44-131-467 0099

LE BONAPARTE

This postage-stamp sized restaurant, which opened in 1998, is a perfect emblem for post-communist Estonia. One the one hand, there is French savoir faire (the restaurant's owner imported Gaston Grenier straight from France and his signature Honey-glazed duck breast with red berries is sensational) and on the other, there is the sense of history. This was the home of a 14th-century Baltic baron and, later, the home of the city's mayor. In such surroundings the absence of prices on the ladies' menu is an entirely appropriate anachronism.

Le Bonaparte

Pikk 46, Tallinn, Estonia

Tel: +372-646 4444   Fax: +372-646 4263

BURINI

This fine shirtmaker, now part of the Brioni group, was founded in 1950 in Bergamo. Its 80 craftsmen produce an amazing 80,000 shirts a year and the firm is justifiably proud of the styling, construction

and assembly of each precious garment which, it believes, combines the "originality of the artisan with the perfection of industry". Burini uses over 1,000 different fabrics, ranging from silk and poplin to Egyptian and Sea Island cotton.

Burini
Tel (for stockists only): +39-06-462 0161

C & M

This exclusive travel consultancy seeks out the best hotels and villas in the world's most glamorous places, as well as the most exclusive hideaways around the globe. Destinations range from the traditionally chic – London, New York, the Côte d'Azur – to the exotic and mysterious. Founder and Managing Director Stephanie Elingshausen and her team regard VIP treatment as entirely normal and

are praised by clients for their knowledge and professionalism, as much as for their unerring ability to match their tailor-made itineraries precisely to the travellers' tastes.

C & M Reise GmbH
Kaisershofstrasse 6
D-60313 Frankfurt-am-Main, Germany
Tel: +49-69-920 0600   *Fax:* +49-69-28 70 00
Website: www.c-und-m.de

CASA LUCIO

A native of Ávila, Lucio Blázquez Blázquez has been in and out of restaurants since he was 12. He opened Casa Lucio in 1974 and his unpretentious, home-style dishes have won him an intensely loyal following. Local and international celebrities, from Carolina Herrera – who loves the speciality tiny lamb chops – to the Prime Minister of Spain are among its acolytes. Blázquez' staff are equally loyal and his three children, all qualified lawyers, have chosen to go into the family business.

Casa Lucio
Cava Baja 35, E-28005 Madrid, Spain
Tel: +34-91-365 3252   *Fax:* +34-91-365 8217

CHARLES PLANTE FINE ARTS

Former Washington DC art dealer Charles Plante spent so much time in London that he moved there last year. He specialises in 18th- and 19th-century European neo-classical water-colour drawings, dealing privately and at London's Olympia Fine Arts Fairs. His clients – connoisseurs rather than those needing the reassurance of big-name artists to define their taste – are a mixture of private collectors and decorators. One leading Italian decorator was so charmed by Plante's display – pictures are densely hung, grouped in room sets and always set in period frames – that she bought an entire wall of his stand (over 50 pictures) at Olympia.

Charles Plante Fine Arts
50 Gloucester Street, London SW1V 4EH, UK
Tel: +44-20-78 34 33 05
Fax: +44-20-78 28 34 99
By appointment only

CHARLTON HOUSE

17th-century Charlton House was acquired, in 1996, by Roger and Monty Saul of the Mulberry Design Company who converted it into a cosy country retreat. Set in the rolling hills of Somerset, it is beautifully decorated with fabrics, furnishings and curios from the company's home furnishings range. Adam Fellowes' cooking has already earned its Mulberry Restaurant a Michelin star.

Charlton House
Charlton Road, Shepton Mallet, Somerset BA4 4PR
(near Bath), UK
Tel: +44-1749-34 20 08   *Fax:* +44-1749-34 63 62

A. CODOGNATO

Attilio Codognato was founded in 1866, the same year that its birthplace Venice was incorporated into the Italian kingdom. Cameos, ancient intaglios, jewelled moors (Moretto brooches), neo-Renaissance objets, diamond-studded serpents and a host of other gem-set curios characterise the unique stock. The company numbers among its clients English, Italian and Russian royalty, as well as members of the European aristocracy; the beau monde has a similar appreciation of the works of this ancient Venetian firm.

A. Codognato
San Marco 1295, 30124 Venice, Italy
Tel: +39-041-522 5042   *Fax:* 39-041-524 2882

CHATEAU CORDEILLAN BAGES

Set in its own vineyard, this Relais & Châteaux property – a restored, 17th-century chartreuse – is a key address for amateur oenophiles and wine professionals alike. Is is not, however, just its location, in the heart of the Médoc, nor Thierry Marx's excellent cooking that makes it special. It is the headquarters of the Ecole du Bordeaux, where courses ranging from weekends to week-long seminars are offered. Pupils not only learn the secrets of the regions great wines, they taste many of its rare vintages and meet the experts who create them.

Château Cordeillan Bages
Route des Châteaux, 33250 Pauillac, France
Tel: +33-5-56 59 24 24   Fax: +33-5-56 59 01 89

CORDINGS

Established in 1839, this traditional men's outfitters has garnered a cult following in the late 1990s, especially among stylish Italians in search of the real English country look. Fashionable Brits, such as Sir Terence Conran, Damien Hirst and Marco

Pierre White are also customers. It was Cordings who invented the now classical covert coat, a version of which is exhibited at the V&A museum.

Cordings
19 Piccadilly, London W1V OPE, UK
Tel:+44-20-77 34 08 30 Fax: +44-20-74 94 23 49

CRACOW FESTIVAL

Poland's second city, which escaped the Second World War largely unscathed, is a medieval jewel and the perfect setting for this excellent, up-and-coming music festival. Performances are held in the fin-de-siècle Slowacki Theatre and the rich spread in 1999 included such operatic magic as Nabucco, Faust, La Traviata, Carmen and Tosca.

Cracow Festival
Bracka 12, Cracow, Poland
Tel: +48-12-422 7807   Fax: +48-12-422 0879

CRISPIN DE MOWBRAY

The only English bloodstock agent to be based in France, Crispin de Mowbray got hooked on racing at the age of 10, when he attended a meeting with his brother, who worked for Pacemaker magazine. An agent since 1992, the 39-year old de Mowbray has been cutting deals for savvy owners – including Martyn Arbib and Chris Wright – from California and Japan to Germany. His successes include St Leger winner, Snurge and several Group 1 winners.

Crispin de Mowbary
49 rue Monsieur le Prince, 75006 Paris, France
Tel: +33-1-46 33 63 08   Fax: +33-1-43 25 33 73

LE CYGNE VERT

The exquisite busts and figurines in Olivier Dufay's handkerchief-sized gallery are by the greatest French sculptors of the 1920s and '30s, most notably Despiau, Wlerick, Gimond, Drivier and Malfray. Producing work which was a reaction against the declamatory style of the 19th-century masters, yet eschewing abstract art, these artists were brushed aside by the French art establishment – as they still are today. The deeply reflective, almost mysterious, mood of these works will seduce true connoisseurs.

Le Cygne Vert
41 rue de Verneuil, 75007 Paris, France
Tel: +33-1-40 20 08 41

DA GIGGETTO

Forget pretensions to Michelin stars, this simple and lively trattoria has, for three generations, served some of the best traditional cooking in the Eternal City – and is packed with stylish Romans who know that glamour is usually no substitute for simple goodness. Appropriately, as the restaurant is located in the old Jewish ghetto, its signature dish is the delicate and delicious Carciofi alla giudia (fried baby artichokes).

Da Giggetto
Via del Portico d'Ottavia, 21/A, 00186 Rome, Italy
Tel: +39-06-686 1105   Fax: +39-06-683 2106

DIDIER LUDOT

For more than 20 years, this guru of vintage couture has run his shop near the Palais Royal. Ludot specialises in French Haute Couture from 1920 to 1980 and stocks such items as original Hermès and Chanel handbags and high heels from Perugia and Roger Vivier. Clients fly in from all over the world to inspect the treasures on offer, including fashion celebrities Naomi Campbell and Stephanie Seymour and Hollywood princess Demi Moore.

Dider Ludot
20 & 24 Galerie Montpensier, Jardin du Palais Royal
75001 Paris, France
Tel & Fax: +33-1-42 96 06 56

EL CASTELL, HOTEL

Jaume Tapies (Chairman of the Spanish members of Relais & Châteaux) and his German-born wife, Katja, run this delightful hotel in the Spanish Pyrenees. Designed in mountain lodge style and set immediately below the 1000-year old fortress, El Castell de Ciutat, it was opened by Tapies' father 25

years ago. Over the years the family has restored the castle itself, creating a wonderful venue for parties, and the remaining wing will soon be transformed into additional hotel rooms. The views of the countryside and mountains are as delicious as the cooking, which features superb game and mushrooms in season.

Hotel El Castell
Route N-260 km 229, Apto.53
E-25700 Seu d'Urgell, Spain
Tel: +34-973-35 07 04   Fax: +34-973-35 15 74

EARTH

Set up 10 years ago by Glen Donovan as an antidote to the large, faceless travel agencies which dominate the market, this exclusive consultancy finds little-known hotels and holiday homes for a highly select clientele. Earth's ethos is to look for unusual places with a distinct character – and there is a strong emphasis on personal service. Donovan and his team strive to understand the lifestyles of their clients before recommending a property.

For Donovan the real definition of luxury is style, rather than glitz, and, as the company readily concedes,

taste is a highly individual matter. Thus Earth has perfected the art of dreaming up unconventional ideas. Houses might be in the middle of Florence, half-way up a Jamaican mountain or – constructed entirely of ice – within the Arctic Circle. The company is also proud to offer such gems as the late Diana Vreeland's extraordinary Marrakesh house and several elusive properties in the south of France.

Eschewing publicity on its own account, Earth has a special understanding for clients who require absolute privacy. Many of them – famous names in film, music and art – who have been recommended to Earth by word of mouth have become dedicated repeat clients.

Earth
2 Durand Gardens, London SW9 OPP, UK
Tel: +44-20-77 93 99 93   Fax: +44-20-77 93 99 94

ENCINAR DE LA PARRA, EL

This sporting estate is centred on a 17th-century monastery, which has been restored and converted into an exquisite hunting lodge by Beatriz Abello Gallo – whose brother owns the celebrated Campillo du San Juan estate. It is set in magnificent countryside, where red deer, moufflon, fallow deer

and wild boar roam among forests of evergreen oaks. That each shooting party restricted to two guns and two observers guarantees both wonderful hunting and superb hospitality.
El Encinar de la Parra
Pl Maria Guerrero 6, Madrid, Spain
Tel: +34-91-563 9983   Fax: +34-91-562 7301

EVE LOM

Beauty insiders rave about Czech facialist and treatment guru Eve Lom. Once married to Herbert Lom of Pink Panther fame, she is known as "the healing hands of Marylebone". Her legendary facials – a combination of lymphatic drainage and reiki massage – are diagnostic as well as healing. Lom's products, such as her celebrated cleansing cream are treasured by discerning acolytes.
Eve Lom
2 Spanish Place, London W1M 5AN, UK
Tel: +44-20-79 35 99 88   Fax: +44-20-72 24 05 15

FAGUAIS

Since 1912, three generations of the Faguais family have run this very special grocery store. Specialising in coffee, they carefully choose plantations around the world whose coffee best represents the characteristics of the particular region. The shop is also packed with home-made French jams and condiments. Equally enticing are the ceramic jars in which much of the shop's merchandise is sold; beautifully hand-painted by Italian artisans, they are made exclusively for Faguais.
Maison Faguais
30 rue de la Trémoille, 75008 Paris, France
Tel: +33-1-47 20 80 91. Fax: +33-1-47 20 14 85

FATTORIA CERRETO LIBRI

Olive oil producers since the end of the 18th century, the Baldini Libri family is rightly proud of its superb, organically-produced products. Picked by hand, the olives are pressed using a traditional stone frantoio and the oil is matured in terracotta jars before being decanted into bottles for sale. Charming hosts, Massimiliano Baldini Libri and his family welcome visitors to their fattoria, located in a beautiful hilltop villa surrounded by ancient cypresses.
Fattoria Cerreto Libri
via Aretina 90, 50065 Pontassieve - Florence, Italy
Tel & Fax: +39-055-831 4528

FLORENCE LOPEZ

Working out of a ravishing Saint-Germain attic studio decorated in the manner of a cabinet d'amateur, Florence Lopez is a decorator and antique dealer who also produces her own range of limited edition objets. Having trained for 8 years with Jacques Garcia of Hotel Costes fame, Lopez set up alone in 1993 and has since found favour with Paris' artistic set, notably Charlotte Rampling and Gerard Depardieu.
Florence Lopez
18 rue du Dragon, 75006 Paris, France
Tel & Fax: +33-1-40 49 08 12

FRANCESCO RUBINATO

Presented in apothecary-style glass bottles with hand-written labels and wax lids, the inks that Francesco Rubinato produces will inspire you to forget your fax and e-mail and start writing letters. Each of the 21 shades is perfumed to match its colour, such as rose, pine or lavender. At his Treviso factory, Rubinato also makes historically perfect reproductions of other writing accoutrements, including seals, sealing wax and glass pens – the nibs of which are of brass, hand-chiselled by jeweller Bruno Ceoldo.

Francesco Rubinato
via Reginato 69, 31100 Treviso, Italy
Tel: +39-04-22 43 62 50 Fax: +39-04-22 43 62 36

FRAY

Mrs Randi, who founded this company in 1962, is so protective of her hand-sewn dress shirts, boxer shorts, robes and pyjamas that, as soon as a garment is finished, she lays it on a tray and covers it with a linen cloth so that not a speck of dust will get on it. Her craftsmen produce fewer than 1,000 garments a week; the ready-to-wear is snapped up by prestigious retailers and the bespoke items are made for a mainly Italian clientele.

Fray
via G. Fanin 1, 40033 Casalecchio di Reno, Italy
Tel (for stockists): +39-051-571 036
Fax: +39-051-59 21 11

FUKIER

Magda Gessler's five year-old restaurant could be a set for the Peter Greenaway film, The Cook, The Thief, His Wife and Her Lover with its candle-light, lush décor and extravagant displays of food and flowers. The cooking is the best traditional Polish food you will find anywhere – Duck with apples and herbs and Venison with cranberries – the cellar first-rate (though the pricing of some bottles is rather steep) and there is a pretty patio garden for warm days.

Fukier
Old Town Square 27, 00272 Warsaw, Poland
Tel: +48-22-831 1013 Fax: +48-22-831 5808

GALERIE MICHEL DESCOURS

Michael Descours and Charles Dauphin attribute much of the success of their 25-year old antiques business to their ability as buyers; many of their pieces come via their connections with patrician French families – especially in Burgundy, where there are still many untouched châteaux. However, they have the added benefit of a great eye; every item is chosen as much for its aesthetic appeal as for its intrinsic value and their stock ranges from Louis XV and Régence to Art Deco and the 1940s.

Galerie Michel Descours
44 avenue Auguste Comte
69002 Lyon, France
Tel: +33-4-78 37 34 54 Fax: +33-4-72 41 90 67

GARSINGTON

Leonard Ingrams' refusal to bow to years of protests by neighbours, who evidently preferred the sound of lawnmowers to that of beautiful music, has finally been rewarded by official sanction for his midsummer opera festival. Held in the grounds of his home, which formerly belonged to flamboyant society hostess Lady Ottoline Morell, the festival's three-opera season always includes a rare work; in 1999 it was the little-known Loves of the Danae by Richard Strauss.

Garsington Opera
Garsington
Oxford OX44 9DH, UK
Tel: +44-1865-36 16 36 Fax: +44-1865-36 15 45

GALLERIA NAZIONALE DELL'UMBRIA

This collection of regional art, housed in one of the oldest buildings in Perugia, covers works from the 13th to the 19th century. They range from frescoes to sculpture and goldwork to fabrics, all created by artists who lived locally. A perfectly-preserved Piero della Francesca triptych is one of the gallery's highlights.

Galleria Nazionale dell'Umbria
Palazzo dei Priori, Corso Vannucci, 06100 Perugia, Italy
Tel: +39-075-574 1257 Fax: +39-075-572 0316

GLOBE-TROTTER

Founded in Saxony in the late-1800s, and relocated to Britain in 1901, Globe-Trotter is that rare bird, an unreconstituted luxury brand which defies technology and trends. Its traditional, largely hand-made suitcases are sturdy, plain and practical. Used by such demanding travellers as The Queen (on her honeymoon), Princess Diana and John McEnroe, as well as explorers and foreign correspondents, they might flout fashion but they are built to last several lifetimes.

Globe-Trotter
Tel: +44-1992-76 45 45 (for stockists only)

HEMISPHERE

Established in 1992 by Raymond Paynter, Hemisphere specialises in fine French furniture and decorative arts from 1930-1960. Elegant proportions, strong clean lines and modernity characterise the work of featured designers such as Jean Besnard, Marc du Plantier, Line Vautrin and Jean Royère. Insiders such as David Mlinaric, Peter Marino and David Collins are all clients, although the gallery, while popular with Americans, is less well known to Europeans.

Hemisphere
173 Fulham Road, London SW3 6JH, UK
Tel: +44-20-75 81 98 00 Fax: +44-20-75 81 98 80

GOETHES WOHNHAUS

Goethe made Weimar his home for almost 60 years, dividing his time between a country mansion nearby and this town house, which escaped the destruction of World War II and has been lovingly restored and reopened in 1998. Although there are larger collections of Goethe memorabilia in various German museums, this house, with its original study, library, parlour and art collection, reflects Goethe's fascination with colour theory and the prodigious number of books, drawings and prints the amassed.

Goethes Wohnhaus
Frauenplan 1, P.O.Box 2012, 99401 Weimar, Germany
Tel: +49-3643-54 53 00 Fax: +49-3643-54 53 03

D.R. HARRIS

Clubmen in search of hangover pick-me-ups and super-models requiring 'crystal eyes', head to this, London's oldest apothecary. The delightful shop is a cornucopia of old-world toiletries and remedies. Opened in 1790, the business is still family-owned and Kate Moss, Joanna Lumley and Melanie Griffith are all fans.

D.R. Harris
29 St James's Street, London SW1A 1HB, UK
Tel: +44-20-79 30 39 15 Fax: +44-20-79 25 26 91

HELENE AGUER

Hélène Aguer's talent for mixing antiques with modern pieces has been inherited by her daughter, Maite, to whom she handed over this delightful shop in 1996, after running it for three decades. Early 20th-century dinner services and 19th-century Chinese armoires are arranged with contemporary items such as Provençal bed covers by Elsa C, lamps from Julie Prisca and furniture from Mis en Demeure. It's done with such panache that you will want to buy everything.

Hélène Aguer
16 boulevard Thiers, 64500 Saint-Jean-de-Luz, France
Tel: +33-05-59-51 07 73 Fax: +33-59-26 97 71

HIGHCLERE CASTLE

The Earl of Carnavon, best known as the owner of Highclere Stud and The Queen's racing manager, has begun to make his spectacular home available for private parties. The castle was designed by Sir Charles Barry in the 1830s, at the same time as he was building the Houses of Parliament. Set on a 3,000-acre estate with its own cricket ground, it is filled with marvellous art and artefacts, including the legacy of the present Earl's grandfather, who discovered the tomb of Tutankhamun in 1922.

Highclere Castle, Berkshire, UK
c/- Mason Rose, 8A Bradbrooke House
Studio Place, London SW1X 8E, UK
Tel: +44-20-72 35 32 45 Fax: +44-20-72 35 32 46

HOTEL D'EUROPE

Built by the great architect Gabriel (responsible for the Crillon Hotel in Paris) this hotel retains the ambience of the aristocratic town house it once was – exquisitely decorated with antiques that have been part of the establishment for generations. It has a far from dusty image, however. Every inch of the hotel is beautifully maintained and the courtyard, with its great plane tree, is perhaps the most civilised place in Avignon to take Sunday lunch.

Hôtel d'Europe
12 Place Crillon, 84000 Avignon, France
Tel: +33-4-90 14 76 76. Fax: +33-4-90 85 43 66

HOTEL DE VIGNY

This Parisian gem has all the luxuries of its grandiose cousins with none of their pretensions. Decorated by Nina Campbell, it has the feel of an English town-house in Paris – complete with a log fire in the lobby – and the young staff treat you as they would a house guest. Little wonder then, that word-of-mouth recommendation brings the likes of Mel Gibson to stay here – most likely in Suite 504, a duplex at the top of the building, with a glass cupola and a terrace.

Hotel De Vigny
9-11 Rue Balzac, 75008, Paris, France
Tel: +33-40-75 04 39 Fax: +33-42-99 80 40

HOUSE OF BRUAR

This is a vast emporium for everything Scottish (cashmere, food, books) but, above all, it is an excellent source of country sports clothing. The staff, many of whom shoot or fish themselves, give not only expert advice about the clothing best suited to the conditions but also useful tips on dress etiquette for those who have been invited on a shooting party. A mail order service and a new department for that other great Scottish sport – golf – opened in 1999.

House of Bruar
by Blair Atholl, Perthshire PH18 5TW, Scotland, UK
Tel: +44-1796-48 32 36 Fax: +44-1796-48 32 18

JAN KIELMAN

This bespoke shoe- and boot-maker is run today by the third and fourth generation descendants of its founder (all have borne the Christian name of Jan). Established in 1883, its heyday was in the 1920s and '30s, when the movers and shakers from across Europe (including the young Charles de Gaulle) were clients. Many Poles supplied themselves from the burning shop as they fled the Warsaw Uprising – and wrote after the War to thank the family. Having struggled to keep going under communism, the firm is now enjoying a new lease of life. Both men's and women's shoes are made entirely by hand from the finest leathers and Kielman's made-to-measure riding boots are particularly sought-after. Depending on seasonal demand, delivery may take from four to 12 weeks.

Jan Kielman
ul. Chmielna 6, 00-020 Warsaw, Poland
Tel & Fax: +48-22-828 4630

JEAN D'ALOS

Jean D'Alos, one of France's most expert affineurs, has a remarkable instinct for knowing to the moment when a cheese will have matured to perfection. To him cheese-ripening is an art form, influenced even by such considerations as where the animals grazed and when they were last milked. Particularly memorable among the countless varieties maturing in the three-level caves beneath his shop are his Ossau, from the Pyrénées, and the long-ripened Comté, from the Jura, sold by its vintage year.

Jean D'Alos
4 rue Montesquieu, 33000 Bordeaux, France
Tel: +33-5-56 44 29 66 Fax: +33-5-56 51 67 82

JEAN-PIERRE RENARD

Founded in 1940 by Joseph Renard, this tiny leather goods company remained unchanged until January 1999, when the founder's son, Jean-Pierre, retired. Now Gisèle Millot heads the atelier of just four staff, who continue to produce entirely hand-made bags, belts and suitcases in sober or sumptuous colours. Camouflaged by rhododendron bushes at the end of a courtyard, this workshop offers a charming and very personal service.

Jean-Pierre Renard
3 Place du Palais-Bourbon, 75007 Paris, France
Tel & Fax: +33-1-45 51 77 87

JEANNETTE MINER

Sandwiched between the big shots on avenue Montaigne, Jeannette Miner's tiny boutique is hidden in a courtyard behind a wrought iron gate. For chic Parisiennes, who want something a little less obvious (and less expensive) than designer labels but who move in circles where it is almost de rigeur, Miner is a godsend. She creates fuss-free, confidence-inspiring looks which ooze panache and femininity and, mindful of her clients' demanding lives, will open any time by appointment, given enough notice.

Jeannette Miner
49 Avenue Montaigne, Paris 75008, France
Tel & Fax: +33-1-47 20 47 30

JOELLE CIOCCO

The launch of Chanel's 'Precision' line of beauty products, based on individual diagnosis of skin types, may seem revolutionary but a number of women, including Cher and Madonna, may not find it especially innovative. They are the clients of beautician-cum-dermatologist Joëlle Ciocco who has, for years, been producing made-to-measure formulas for patients after extensive skin testing. Better still, her treatments and massages leave you feeling utterly serene.

Joëlle Ciocco
8 Place Madeleine, 75008 Paris, France
Tel: +33-1-42 60 58 80   Fax: +33-1-34 90 00 88

JOHN MAKEPEACE

As a young man in search of a cause, John Makepeace briefly considered theology before discovering his talent for furniture-making which, he says, "was something to which I could commit myself". With a team of eight virtuoso craftsmen,

Makepeace designs to private commission, creating one-off pieces, which he describes as "a personal statement of patronage" by each client and a legacy for their descendants. The result, whether a functional piece or a more decorative one, every item is both highly original and exquisitely crafted.

John Makepeace
Parnham House, Beaminster, Dorset DT8 3NA, UK
Tel: +44-1308-86 22 04   Fax: +44-1308-86 38 06

JOHN MINSHAW

The fact that this designer's work rarely appears in glossy magazines is no reflection on his considerable talent; it is simply that his clients are the sort of

people who do not allow publicity. Minshaw is adept at finding architectural solutions which transform good houses into great ones – rebuilding the façade of a classical villa in Geneva, for instance, or adding a new wing to an Arts and Crafts-style house in London. His decorative schemes – often inspired by a single item, such as a classical urn or a 1930s chair – are characterised by superb bespoke cabinet-making and a restrained colour palette.

John Minshaw
119 George Street, London W1H 5TB, UK
Tel: +44-20-72 58 06 27   Fax: +44-20-72 58 06 28

JOURNE

Although considered a genius by many of his peers, Journe is little-known outside the Swiss watchmaking community, where he has worked behind the scenes for many of the most prestigious brands. Recently, however, he launched his own signature watch collection. One timepiece, designed

with a gold face in a platinum case, features an equalising system to help the balance wheel maintain constant amplitude as the spring unwinds, thus achieving a more accurate watch. The second model has a dual movement for optimal cancellation of the effects of the movement of the wrist.

Francois-Paul Journe - Chez T.I.M Horlogerie S.A
5 rue des Maraîchers, CH-1205 Geneva, Switzerland
Tel: +41-22-320 49 90

KATE DE ROTHSCHILD

Since she began dealing in 1974, Kate de Rothschild has sold works of art to several of the world's greatest museums, including the British Museum and the Art Institute of Chicago. The fact that she eschews her own gallery in favour of dealing privately is, to the serious collectors among her clientele, a bonus. De Rothschild sells works from all major European schools, except English, from Old Masters to 19th-century decorative drawings.

Kate de Rothschild
186 Brompton Road, London SW3 1XJ, UK
Tel: +44-20-75 89 94 40   Fax: +44-20-75 84 52 53

KATHARINA BEER

Katharina Beer makes dramatic, one-of-a-kind Cinderella dresses crafted in strong, vivid colours often offset by beading. The young couturier favours Swarowski crystals and fabrics imported from Paris and Milan for her creations, which are worn by both career women and such supermodels as Vendela. She has recently introduced a ready-to-wear line.

Katharina Beer
Artillerigatan 29, 11445 Stockholm, Sweden
Tel: +46-8-66 19 41 40   Fax: +46-8-665 3081

KINNAIRD

Formerly a private shooting lodge, this grand Edwardian mansion has been converted by Constance Ward into a deeply cosseting nine-bedroom hotel. Every room is decorated in perfect taste, with antiques, beautiful fabrics, open fireplaces and sublime views over the Tay valley. It is a perfect base for salmon fishing, deer stalking or simply walking on a 9,000 acre estate and eight secluded cottages on the estate are also available for rental.

Kinnaird Estate
By Dunkeld, Perthshire PH8 0LB, Scotland, UK
Tel: +44-1796-48 24 40   Fax: +44-1796-48 22 89

KRAGGA HERRGARD

Owned by Leif Bonér and run with tremendous charm by his wife, Louise Hindmarsh Bonér and her sister, Sophie, this idyllic hotel is set on the edge of

Lake Mälarens. The herrgård (manor house), which dates back to the 1800s, has been decorated in exquisite taste and life follows a magical country-house rhythm: picnics and tennis in the grounds, afternoon tea in the library, evening drinks at the water's edge and a fine dinner, prepared by chef Lasse Strutz, from the freshest produce.

Krägga Herrgård
S-74693 Bålsta, Sweden
Tel: +46-171-53 280   Fax: +46-171-53 265

LORENZO VILLORESI

Based in a 15th-century palazzo overlooking Florence's River Arno, Lorenzo Villoresi cuts a romantic figure in his laboratory. He is a bespoke perfumer, calling upon an armoury of a thousand essences, woods and spices with which to conjure a customised fragrance for each of his clients – Cherie Blair and the late Jacqueline Kennedy among them. Entirely self-taught, he is fascinated by the process of identifying each client's individuality and creating a scent to enhance it.

Lorenzo Villoresi
via de' Bardi 14, 50125 Florence, Italy
Tel: +39-055-234 1187   Fax: +39-55-234 5893

MARBLEHEAD COMPANY, THE

Two of the world's most spectacular yachts – both designed by Jon Bannenberg – are managed by and available for charter through this ultra-discreet

company, run by Bannenberg's son, Dickie: the 235-foot *Talitha G*, which Bannenberg recreated within a classical 1929 hull, and the ultra-modern *Thunder*, a 50-metre, 40-knot gas turbine-powered flyer. In organising the charters – in the Mediterranean, Caribbean and Baltic – Marblehead's atttention to detail is remarkable. It has, for instance, arranged a special broadcasting feed to one of the yachts for a cricket Test match in Barbados and has sourced silver sixpences to match the charterers' dates of birth for their Christmas pudding on board.

The Marblehead Company Ltd.
6 Burnsall Street, London SW3 3ST, UK
Tel: +44-20-73 52 84 37   Fax: +44-20-73 51 53 73
Email: yachts@marblehead.co.uk

MARITIME MUSEUM

This monument to the Golden Age of Dutch exploration offers a fascinating glimpse into a lost world. The brainchild of a few individuals who believed in preserving something of their country's maritime past, the collection is housed in a 17th-century naval base and features such gems as a life-size replica of the East Indiaman, Amsterdam, as well as valuable globes, maps and paintings. Temporary exhibitions are presented twice a year and one can occasionally ride on the historic steamship, Christiaan Brunings.

Maritime Museum
Kattenburgerplein 1
1018 Amsterdam, The Netherlands
Tel: +31-20-523 2311   Fax: +31-20-523 2213

MAS DE LA BRUNE

Only a tiny roadside sign announces that you have reached this inn but, once inside the gates – kept closed for privacy – you will discover something as good as (no, better than) owning your own Provençal mas. Built in 1572, it has every luxury inside – a Renaissance fireplace, Provençal antiques – and stunning grounds outside, including a recently planted 'alchemists garden'. Even when its 10 rooms are full the chances are that you will have the Roman-style swimming pool to yourself.

Mas de la Brune
13810 Eygalières en Provence, France
Tel: +33-4-90 95 90 77   Fax: +33-4-90 95 99 21

MCL GARDEN DESIGN

French-born Marie-Christine de Laubarède came to her profession by chance. Having inherited an Oxfordshire house with three acres of garden nine years ago, she gradually realised that she had "quite a plant collection". Enrolling in the English

Gardening School at Chelsea Physic Garden, she studied horticulture, plantsmanship and design and her first commissions soon followed. Working in a 'modern classical' style, she has, so far, completed projects in Morocco, Japan and the UK.

MCL Garden Design
30 Prairie Street
London SW8 3PP, UK
Tel: +44-20-76 22 84 14

MOZART WEEK

What the Salzburg summer Festival is to the international social set, this more discreet celebration of Mozart's work and influence (held every January) is to the true connoisseur. The millennium programme opened with a new production of The Magic Flute, followed by orchestral, chamber and choral concerts performed by such outstanding conductors Sir André Previn, Nikolaus Harnoncourt and Trevor Pinnock and famed Mozart interpreters, pianist Mitsuko Uchida and soprano, Barbara Bonney.

Mozart Week
c/o Internationale Stiftung Mozarteum
Schwarzstrasse 26, A-5020 Salzburg, Austria
Tel: +43-662-889 4032   Fax: +43-662-88 24 19

MUSEE DE L'ANNONCIADE

This chapel-turned-museum is testimony to the blossoming of art in Saint-Tropez at the beginning of this century. It came into being in 1955 through the passion of one man, Georges Grammont, who converted the building and donated 56 paintings from his private collection. Art-lovers can now view works of world renown, from Seurat's Le Chenal de Gravelines to La Gitane by Matisse.

Musée de l'Annonciade
Place Grammont
83990 Saint-Tropez, France
Tel: +33-4-94 97 04 01   Fax: +33-4-94 97 87 24

NORD PINUS, HOTEL

This little hotel in the centre of Arles (one wall is formed by part of a Roman ruin) is where the matadors stayed while performing in the nearby arena. Now owned by Anne Ygou – wife of fashion photographer Peter Lindbergh – it has a different, albeit laid-back glamour. You may well bump into Christian Lacroix – Arles' celebrated son and a friend of the Lindberghs – who redecorated it or Ines de la Fressange having Sunday brunch on the terrace with her family.

Hôtel Nord Pinus
14 Place du Forum, 13200 Arles, France
Tel: +33-4-90 93 44 44   Fax: +33-4-90 93 34 00

MUSEO MONTEMARTINI

Built in 1912, this cultural centre has a special place in Rome's artistic life. Originally the city's first power station with the original machinery restored, it now houses part of an extensive archaeological collection from the Capitoline Museums and plays host to a vibrant blend of theatre, television shows, exhibitions and conferences.

Museo Montemartini
Centrale Montemartini, via Ostiense 106
00154 Rome, Italy
Tel: +39-06-699 1191   Fax: +39-06-69 92 05 63

MUSICA NEL CHIOSTRO BATIGNANO

This very special opera festival takes place at the monastery of Santa Croce and appears small-scale, although this belies the range and quality of productions. Past programmes have covered Baroque revivals, 18th-century masterpieces and specially-commissioned new works. Batignano was the brainchild of Englishman Adam Pollock in 1974 and, through creativity and sheer nerve, he has sustained the idea, regularly attracting top-level musicians.

Musica nel Chiostro Batignano
Santa Croce, 58041 Batignano, Grosseto, Italy
Tel: +39-0564-33 80 96   Fax: +39-0564-33 80 85

NICK ASHLEY

Frustrated at the lack of stylish biker clothes, motorcycle fanatic Ashley, who honed his eye as design director at family-owned Laura Ashley, decided to make his own. Now Tom Cruise and assorted action men flock to his eponymous shop to stock up on his high-performance, high-style kit, including Gore-Tex biker jackets, fleece crombies and 'powerstretch' suits.

Nick Ashley
57 Ledbury Road, London W11 2AA, UK
Tel: +44-20-72 21 12 21   Fax: +44-20-77 27 42 21

PALAIS DES THES, LE

This Parisian tea emporium gives new meaning to the ancient drink, with its comprehensive selection of everything tea-related. The 300 varieties – sourced from the Far East, India, Africa and South America – range from the classics to flavoured and scented blends and there are all the tools needed for proper tea appreciation: pots in pewter, glass and porcelain, samovars, tea cases, and books on tea, as well as tea-based jams, confectionery and beauty products.

Le Palais des Thés
25 rue Losserand, 75014 Paris, France
Tel: +33-1-43 21 97 97

PALAZZO TERRANOVA

Sarah and Johnny Townsend took ten years to transform this stately, early 18th-century villa from a ruin into an exquisite country retreat. Opened in spring 1999, it feels like a much-loved family home

rather than a hotel and guests rave about the warmth of Sarah's hospitality as much as they do about the palazzo's ravishing views of the surrounding hills. With just eight bedrooms it is also perfect for a private house-party.

Palazzo Terranova Umbria
Loc. Ronti Morra, 06010 Perugia, Italy
Tel & Fax: +39-075-857 0083/0014
Email: sarahft@krenet.it

PAM

This third-generation family firm, established in 1926 by Odoardo Mecatti, prides itself on its national loyalty – every piece of its sumptuous household linen is created from Italian materials by Italian craftsmen, according to time-honoured Italian methods. Its traditional hand-embroidered linens are supplemented by bed, bath and table sets – fluffy towels edged in raw linen and jacquard cloths with honeycomb-weave borders, for instance – which are perfectly in tune with contemporary taste.

PAM di Piccarda Mecatti s.a.s
via Bartolomeo Scala 2R-10N
50126 Florence, Italy
Tel: +39-055-681 3375   Fax: +39-055-681 3320

PARIONE

The hand-combing method by which Parione's marbled paper is produced yields only 50 sheets a day; however, the firm's owner, Stefano Viliani refuses to compromise on the traditional skills employed by his craftsmen. Parione's Amatruda

paper – a style which originated on the Amalfi coast – is woven one page at a time, meaning that no two sheets are identical, and four master book-binders make albums and books to special order. Parione's admirers include the Marchese Pucci who, in 1999, invited Viliani to move his workshops to the Palazzo Pucci.

Parione
via del Parione 10/r, 50123 Florence, Italy
Tel & Fax: +39-055-21 56 84

THE PELHAM

1999 saw the tenth anniversary of Tim and Kit Kemp's sophisticated English town-house hotel, The Pelham, as well as the completion of 13 elegant bedrooms (designed, like the rest of the hotel, by Kit) in the newly-acquired building next door. The hotel is tranquil and traditionalist but with a stylish

twist to its grand decor with an admiring coterie of urbane guests to match. Good old-fashioned service reflects perfectly the Kemps' vision of creating an antidote to the impersonality of traditional grand hotels.

The Pelham Hotel
15 Cromwell Place, London SW7 2LA, UK
Tel: +44-20-75 89 82 88   Fax: +44-20-75 84 84 44
Email: pelham@firmdale.com
Website: www.firmdale.com

PETERSON

In addition to selling its own-label Dominican cigars, this Dublin company is keeping alive the esoteric art of pipe-making. Taking the root briar of a 150-year old Erica Arboria, for instance, each pipe is hand-shaped, sanded, drilled, lacquered and polished before being fitted with its vulcanite mouth-piece (also shaped by hand) and, finally, its silver rim cap. Limited-edition pipes include a commemorative model for the millennium.

Peterson of Dublin Ltd
Peterson House, Sallynoggin, Co. Dublin, Ireland
Tel: +353-1-285 1011   Fax: +353-1-285 6593

PETTINAROLI

Assisted by a team of green-aproned clerks, Francesco Pettinaroli, great-grandson of the founder, runs this wonderfully old-fashioned business where Milan's élite come to choose the thick cards with which to celebrate the milestones in their lives. The craftsmen downstairs still do real lithography (literally, 'stone writing') writing backwards on granite blocks with diamond-tipped pens. Upstairs the papers and cards are supplemented by hand-tooled leather desk sets and beautiful boxes in cherry and briar wood.

Pettinaroli

Piazza San Fedele 2, Milan, Italy

Tel: +39-02-86 46 46 42

PHILIPPE DUFOUR

Philippe Dufour has created watches for some of Switzerland's most celebrated firms, yet it was not until he began making watches under his own name in 1992 (crafting every component and assembling the movements himself) that he became known to more than a handful of people outside the industry. Dufour's *tour de force* is his gold medal-winning clock watch (grande et petite sonnerie) with minute repeater – so complicated, that only one has ever been made.

Philippe Dufour

Chemin Aubert 1, CH-1347 Le Sentier, Switzerland

Tel & Fax: +41-21-845 4195

PRESTAT

Established in 1902 and still family-owned and run, Prestat is one of London's oldest chocolate houses. Chocolate-maker to The Queen, Prestat is praised for its fine, hand-made chocolates and cocoa-dusted truffles, which are still sold according to the old imperial measures. Its Napoleon III truffles are made to a secret 150-year old recipe and its Easter eggs were the outright winner of a 1999 survey organised by *The Times*.

Prestat

14 Princes Arcade, London SW1Y 6DS, UK

Tel & Fax: +44-171-629 4838

QUINTARELLI

Now in his mid-seventies Guiseppe Quintarelli is one of the world's finest winemakers. His vineyard is tiny and his winery is, quite literally, the large garage at the back of his house. But, if you want to drink the best Valpolicella, this is it; for more power and vigour, try his Recioto or Amarone and, if you want something really special, get your hands on a bottle of his rarely available Cabernet Franc, Alzero.

Azienda Agricola Quintarelli

via Cere 1, 37024 Negrar, Verona, Italy

Tel & Fax: +39-045-750 0016

RAGLAN CONSULTANTS

Chartered Surveyor Charles Mackintosh works on behalf of would-be purchasers, providing a unique hand-holding service throughout the complex process of finding and buying a property on the Côte d'Azur and acting as project manager when renovations are required. Many clients come by word-of-mouth recommendation – and Mackintosh's reputation is such that several of the leading agents in the area contact him when high quality properties come onto the market.

Raglan Consultants

Mas du Roc, 90 Chemin de la Dragonniere

06130 Grasse, France

Tel: +33-4-93 09 21 11   Fax: +33-4-93 09 85 13

RAYMOND MASSARO

By 1968, when Raymond Massaro took over the company founded by his father, it had become the leading shoemaker for the major couture houses. He created Chanel's signature two-tone models and his workshop of 10 artisans still produces the shoes for that house's *haute couture* collections. Massaro's private clients include women with a preference for sleek, classical models and men of refined taste, such as Pope John Paul II.

Raymond Massaro

2 rue de la Paix, 75002 Paris, France

Tel: +33-1-42 61 00 29   Fax: +33-1-42 61 19 55

RELAIS IL FALCONIERE

Set in an idyllic part of southern Tuscany, this charming hotel was the 19th-century home of the poet, Antonio Guadagnoli. Originally built in the 16th-century, it has been beautifully restored by the Baracchi family, who have filled it with antiques, while remaining true to its rustic spirit. The cooking is simple and authentic Tuscan country food and the terrace, where tables are set in summer, has a dreamy view of the surrounding hills.

Relais Il Falconiere

Localita San Martino 370, 52044 Cortona, Italy

Tel: +39-0575-61 26 16   Fax: +39-0575-61 29 27

ROYAL ASCOT RACING CLUB

As Royal Ascot becomes increasingly crowded, this recently established club is an oasis of style and civility for serious race-goers. Managed by Claire Kay-Shuttleworth, a former Personal Assistant to Mark Birley, its superb Club Room is almost adjacent to the Royal Box, and leads to a private grandstand area. More importantly, its 300 members reap the rewards of the Club syndicate whose six horses are selected by John Warren, managed by the Hon. Harry Herbert and trained by Michael Stoute, among others.

The Royal Ascot Racing Club

Ascot Racecourse, Ascot, Berkshire SL5 7JN, UK

Tel: +44-1344-87 85 43   Fax: +44-1344-62 82 99

RENAUD PELLEGRINO

This accessories designer with a passion for 20th-century art has created a boutique which is as enticing as a candy store. His three collections per year include such original ideas as open bags with

hologram patterns (fish which turn into butterflies, for instance) and tiny straw ones with handles of rock crystal and untreated stones. That renowned Parisian fashion plate, Catherine Deneuve, is a devoted client.

Renaud Pellegrino

14 rue du Faubourg Saint-Honoré, 75008 Paris, France

Tel: +33-1-42 65 35 52   Fax: +33-1-47 42 57 07

SABBADINI

The Sabbadini family has been in jewellery for several generations and, in 1986, introduced its 'invisible setting' collection in rubies, sapphires and yellow sapphires – including its signature bee brooches and flexible diamond rings. However, since Sabbadini sold its beautifully crafted pieces through other jewellers, its name was little-known until 1998, when it opened a boutique on Milan's Via Montenapoleone. The shop's décor was conceived by the late Renzo Mongiardino and executed by Roberto Peregalli.

Sabbadini

via Montenapoleone 6, 20121 Milan, Italy

Tel: +39-02-76 00 82 28   Fax: +39-02-76 00 19 94

LA SARACINA

A magical and very private hilltop hideaway set amidst the vineyards of southern Tuscany, this 100-year old farmhouse was transformed by an American couple into an exquisitely tasteful inn. When they retired recently, they sold it to the charming Simonetta Vessichelli and her husband, whose love for the place is inspiring. Its three suites all have open fireplaces, huge bathrooms and dreamy views of the countryside. There is a buffet breakfast but no restaurant – a bonus, as there are several good ones nearby.

La Saracina
SS. 146 – KM 29, 53026 Pienza, Siena, Italy
Tel: +39-0578-74 80 22   Fax: +39-0578-74 80 18

SCHNIEDER

Rudolf Schnieder is fiercely proud of the riding boots which his firm produces – and with good reason. Such is their quality that they are worn by the Household cavalry, the Olympic equestrian teams of several countries and the world's best polo players. His craftsmen employ traditional skills which have been handed down since his factory was established in 1857, making both off-the-shelf and bespoke models – each of which is specially designed for a particular equestrian discipline.

Schnieder
16 Clifford Street, London W1X 1RG, UK
Tel: +44-20-74 37 67 75   Fax: +44-20-72 87 25 36

SCOTT BARNES

Six years ago, former New York antiques dealer Scott Barnes settled in Rome and quickly realised two things: its antiques market was largely untapped by Americans and, with the cultural and language difference it was likely to stay that way – unless he stepped in. Today he sources furniture and decorative objects on behalf of clients (including several serious private collectors), advising on pricing and provenance and negotiating on their behalf – as well as organising "the fun part of their trips", such as restaurants, hotels and cultural events. Such is his success that Barnes recently took on a partner, Salvatore Loriga.

Scott Barnes
via delle Terme di Tito 94, 00184 Rome, Italy
Tel & Fax: +39-06-482 0694
By appointment only

SENNELIER

Gustave Sennelier founded this treasure-trove of artists' materials – a stone's throw from the École des Beaux-Arts – in 1887, later opening a Montparnasse branch, in 1936. The shop is still in the hands of the family, who have preserved the atmosphere that charmed Cézanne, Gauguin, Modigliani, Kandinsky, Picasso and Cocteau. Amongst the easels, brushes and wonderful selection of artists' papers, there are rare pigments derived from lapis lazuli and malachite, four types of gold leaf and hundreds of shades of oils, pastels and watercolours.

Sennelier
3 quai Voltaire, 75007 Paris, France
Tel: +33-1-42 60 72 15   Fax: +33-1-42 61 00 69

LES SENTEURS

Heaven-scent fragrance boutique, Les Senteurs, was established in 1984 by Betty and Michael Hawksley to provide an outlet for perfumes from Europe's smaller and less well-known houses including the then recherché names Creed, Diptyque and Annick Goutal. Recently re-located in Belgravia, this olfactory paradise offers customers mail-order, a beauty treatment room and its very own three-day perfume course.

Les Senteurs - Specialist Perfumery
71 Elizabeth Street, London SW1W 9PJ, UK
Tel: +44-20-77 30 23 22   Fax: +44-20-72 59 91 45

SHELLEY ASHMAN INTERNATIONAL

Ask Sean Shelley what he does for a living and he says, "I fix things." What that means in practice is that, thanks to his amazing contacts book, he can get three private jets to JFK airport at 8pm on a Saturday at 30 minutes' notice or can organise a 40-metre yacht in St Tropez within half a day. He's just as good at the mundane things, too, like scheduled flights – if his clients need them.

Shelley Ashman International
New Barn Farm, Bucklebury Village
Reading, Berkshire RG7 6EF, UK
Tel: +44-1189-71 47 14   Fax: +44-1189-71 48 00

SIMONE DE LOOZE

Everything that is inside the villa, from where antiques dealer Simone de Looze operates, is for sale. "I've even sold during dinner parties," she confesses. The daughter of an antiques dealer, she chooses objects – which may range from a 17th-century wooden chest or 19th-century stone eagle to a Balinese drum or a Mexican bowl – for their decorative impact and not necessarily their value. The only thing that she shuns is English Victoriana – "the Ralph Lauren look", as she calls it.

Simone de Looze
v.d Oudermeulenlaan 11a
2243 CR Wassenaar, The Netherlands
Tel: +31-70-514 1051

STEINBERG & TOLKIEN

This labyrinthine little shop is where fashion's big league shops for ideas, for its racks are crammed with impeccable vintage couture: Chanel, Lanvin, Schiaparelli – and once a great 1950s Givenchy evening dress that had belonged to Jackie Kennedy. Narciso Rodriquez, Jean-Paul Gaultier, Donna Karan and Tom Ford have all been seen in person but others are not quite so up-front. John Galliano, for instance, sends his assistant, Vanessa Bellanger along to truffle out ideas.

Steinberg & Tolkien
193 Kings Road, London SW3 5ED, UK
Tel: +44-20-73 76 36 60   Fax: +44-20-73-76-36 30

TERRA INCOGNITA

Formed early in 1999, UK-based Terra Incognita represents a dozen luxurious and well-established, owner-operated camps, lodges and mobile safaris in Africa. Off the 'commercial safari' circuit, these places – such as Campi ya Kanzi, in the Chyulu Hills, Loisaba and Galdessa – have built their reputation among connoisseurs of the 'real' Africa by word of mouth. The company is currently expanding its portfolio to include owner-operated wilderness properties around the world.

Terra Incognita
Tel: +44-1488-68 32 22 (All enquiries)
Fax: +44-1488-68 29 77
Email: Stephie@terrra-incognita.com

TRETYAKOV GALLERY

In 1892 prominent Moscow merchant and collector, Pavel Tretyakov, donated his gallery to the city, forming the basis of what has grown to a collection of over 100,000 works. It includes a collection – unique in the world – of icons from the 11th to the 17th century, as well as secular painting from the early 18th century onwards. More recent works include pre-Revolutionary avant-garde paintings and a remarkable collection of iconoclastic Soviet poster art and sculpture.

Tretyakov Gallery
10 Lavrushinsky Pereulok, 109017 Moscow, Russia
Tel: +7-095-231 1362   Fax: +7-095-233 1051

VALVONA & CROLLA

Benedetto Valvona started importing Italian food into Edinburgh in the 1860s to supply the growing number of Italian immigrants there. In the early 1920s, Alfonso Crolla joined the family business and the venerable Scottish deli, Valvona & Crolla was born. Wine and food is sourced from small growers and producers and fresh vegetables arrive from Milan twice weekly.

Valvona & Crolla
19 Elm Row, Edinburgh EH7 4AA, Scotland, UK
Tel: +44-131-556 6066   Fax: +44-131-556 1668

GALERIE DE VERNEUIL

Anyone with a superb, yet incomplete, set of 17th- or 18th-century French silver cutlery should certainly make the acquaintance of Bernard Sève, who is so well-informed on silverware hallmarks that he can identify 17th-century tableware right down to the week the pieces were manufactured. He is also adept at uncovering fine late 18th-century commodes and armchairs, particularly those signed by the great cabinet-maker, Jacob.

Galerie de Verneuil
45 rue de Verneuil, 75007 Paris, France
Tel & Fax: +33-1-40 15 01 15

VIAJES TEAM 3

Package holidays are anathema to Ignacio Crespo and Eduardo Gianello, who founded this travel consultancy in 1997. Working from a private house they receive clients by appointment and, over coffee or champagne, will simply ask where they would like to go and, just as importantly, why. Then the 'back room' experts and their huge network of contacts come into play. The result? A one-off trip which may not necessarily be the client's initial idea but which precisely matches his or her taste, budget and time available.

Viajes Team 3
Marqués de Riscal 5, Bajolzda
28010 Madrid, Spain
Tel: +34-91-308 2344   Fax: +34-91-310 3882

VICTORIA BRIDGEMAN

Following a degree from the Courtauld Institute and four years with antique dealer John Hobbs, Victoria Bridgeman set up on her own as a scout and researcher on behalf of both decorators and private clients. Saving them vast amounts of travelling time, she will track down anything from an Art Déco chair to an 18th-century chest, anywhere in Europe. The likes of Juan Pablo Molyneux and Bunny Williams praise her combination of good taste, tenacity and total discretion.

Victoria Bridgeman
21 Chepstow Road, London W2 5BP, UK
Tel: +44-20-72 21 68 64   Fax: +44-20-77 27 58 85

VILLA FIORDALISO

An exquisite lake-side Renaissance-style hotel built at the end of the last century, Villa Fiordaliso was once leased by the poet Gabriele d'Annunzio and, later, Mussolini's mistress, Claretta Petacci. Now a hotel, it is an extremely special place to stay, with just seven rooms, wonderful views across the gardens and private beach, as well as a Michelin-starred restaurant.

Ristorante Villa Fiordaliso Hotel
via Zanardelli 150, 25083 Gardone Riviera, Italy
Tel: +39-0365-20 158   Fax: +39-0365-29 00 11

VILLA PISANI

Hailed as one of the earliest masterpieces of Andrea Palladio, Villa Pisani was built between 1541 and 1544. Standing in 10,000 square metres of parkland between Verona and Vicenza and owned today by the Countess Ferri de Lazara, it is a superb venue for parties. The nine-metre high ceilings of the atrium are decorated with frescoes painted by Bernardino India, a student of Raphael, the Great Kitchen, with its 18th-century fireplace and vast dining table, is delightful on winter evenings while the Loggia is perfect for summer drinks. The villa also has an adjoining cottage for rent.

Villa Pisani
via Risaie 1, 36045 Bagnolo di Lonigo, Italy
Tel: +39-0444-83 11 04   Fax: +39-0444-83 55 17

VINTAGE HOUSE HOTEL

In the heart of the Douro valley, this 18th-century quinta, owned by Taylor's port, has been transformed into a 45-room hotel, filled with Portuguese antiques and azulejos tiles. Its best rooms – 103, 104 and 105 – have ravishing views of the river and the Pinhão bridge. The bar is a joy: set in the estate's original lodge, it has book-shelves and fireplaces, leather sofas and stone pillars. But most importantly it has a matchless selection of over 100 ports.

Vintage House Hotel
Lugar da Ponte, 5085 Pinhão, Portugal
Tel: +351-54-73 02 30   Fax: +351-54-73 02 38

B&L WAHLSTROM

This shop, in Stockholm's elegant Östermalm quarter, is a favourite of American decorating guru David Easton. Its owners, Barbro and Lennart Wahlström, have a keen eye for 18th- and 19th-century century furniture and objets, drawn mainly from Nordic sources. Typical of their finds are such pieces as a Swedish gilt and bronze chandelier decorated with sculpted owls and swans, a set of 1820 'Swedish Biedermeier' chairs or a *faux* marble-topped console table supported by carved wooden Egyptian caryatids.

B&L Wahlström
Nybrogata 42, 11440 Stockholm, Sweden
Tel: +46-8-662 3337   Fax: +46-8-661 1061

VILLA

Brothers Filippo and Marco Villa are the fourth generation of their family to have overseen this jewellery business, which was established by Benvenuto Villa in 1876. Imaginative and eccentric, Benvenuto was known for his incorporation of new precious alloys in his creations, notably 'black gold'. Between the wars, the firm began creating jewellery

for the Italian Royal Family and has, since then, been patronised by discerning Milanese grandees. Villa continues to be renowned for its innovative techniques - from the original gold maille parures that were woven like a fabric wire twill, to today's 'micromosaic' multi-toned precious pieces and innovative range of cufflinks.

Villa
via Manzoni 23, 20121 Milan, Italy
Tel: +39-02-80 42 79   Fax: +39-02-87 69 00

EUROPEAN DECORATING STYLE

By Caroline Clifton-Mogg

Defining the key moods and influences in European decorating, we identify Europe's leading designers and how their decorative style is evolving as we enter the new millennium.

Contemporary interior design and decoration is — as it always was — an amalgam of past and present influences, tempered by that endlessly fascinating, imponderable quantity known as taste. Taste — so elusive, so difficult to track down, so satisfying to find — is a constantly shifting quantity, influenced by events, comment and the visual face of the world around us. To have taste is a claim made by few, but apportioned by many, to those rare people who seem to be able to justify and make sense of an arrangement of rooms where all is original and unique, yet harmonious and pleasing.

Today, although the subject of interior decoration has never been more fashionable, it is certainly not a question of fashion — although one might be forgiven for thinking otherwise when glancing

Previous page: In the entrance hall of a Milanese apartment, Roberto Peregalli's trademark theatricality is expressed through his use of trompe l'oeil painting and greco-roman antiquities. Above: Architect John Pawson's credo of pure minimalism, seen here in his own home, has had a huge influence on decorative style in the 1990s.

through magazines where the virtues of shocking pink bed linen or the merits of brushed steel light switches are variously and endlessly extolled. What is true, however, is that we are all, whether we admit it or not, interested in how houses — our own and others' — look and most of us like to pass comment, silent or vocal, on others' decorative arrangements. And why not? How people live and what they live with tells us as much about their characters and social aspirations as any pseudo-psychological tome would — and is far more interesting to boot.

So, as we slip towards the new, as yet uncharted century, it seems a good moment to ponder on how one would currently describe the particular style — or styles — of decoration that we currently espouse and which, if any, will be influential tomorrow.

In historical terms there was not, before the 17th century, much decorative style of any kind, with the notable exception of Renaissance Italy. Such

essentials as warmth, privacy and practicality were, for most people at that time, far more important. It is a matter of argument as to when the art or profession of interior decoration began to evolve. Some say it was first commented on at the end of the 19th- and beginning of the 20th centuries by such indomitable ladies as Edith Wharton, Mrs H. R. Haweis, and Elsie de Wolfe. Others point to the confident instructions issued by such architect-designers as Robert Adam in England in the 1760s and Fontaine and Percier in France in the early 1800s, all three of whom effectively dictated every element of the schemes in which they were involved, from the design of the carpet to the moulding on the ceiling. But, for all their influence on the styles of the time, they were nothing like as influential as the designers and decorators of our current style-obsessed era, whose taste affects not only those who commission them to design their homes but also all of us who buy a metre of wallpaper, a litre of paint or even a new cushion cover.

To understand what is happening at the end of the century, we must look at its beginning. In many ways we are only just starting to appreciate the legacy of the great early 20th-century designers like Eileen Gray and Robert Mallet-Stevens and later architect-designers such as Luis Barragan and Frank Lloyd Wright. In their different ways they each considered internal space, furnishings, decorative details and colour, took each element as intrinsic to the architecture and developed forms and a language which still have a resonance today. Both they and interior decorators were engaged in doing the same thing — seeking to create a harmonious interior space. Decorators like Elsie de Wolfe saw rooms not as recreations of any past 'period' style but as new rooms — rooms which were both 'fresh' and 'simple' (oft-used adjectives then). This simplicity was the new modernity and it really is this studied simplicity with a contemporary take which is as much admired today as it was then.

But simplicity alone does not completely describe contemporary *fin-de-siècle* decoration. The best-designed schemes are an evolution of what has gone before, coupled with a new understanding and application of modern technology and materials. This understanding takes several forms and, indeed, results in distinct and distinctive styles of decoration based, on the one hand, on the reductivist and functional tendencies of Modernism and, on the other, a more exuberant and 'decorative' spirit, reflecting what Stephen Calloway of the Victoria & Albert Museum has described as "man's inherent desire to ornament his possessions and surroundings".

The former has found its purest expression in minimalism, which, at its most uncompromising, is perhaps best exemplified by the work of John Pawson, who, though an architect, has been

Above: With his exuberant use of colour and skillful mixing of furniture, paintings and objets from the 17th- to the 19th centuries, Jacques Garcia has created a richly comfortable environment in this Parisian apartment. Left: Alberto Pinto's sketch for the drawing room of an English castle, which he is restoring for a Saudi Arabian client, reflects his opulent signature style.

Above: Renowned for his love of classicism and his cerebral approach to decorating, David Mlinaric achieves an informal grandeur in the private suites which he has restored for Lord Rothschild at Waddesdon Manor. Left: Christian Liaigre's use of dark woods mixed with soft colour and texture, all edited into a sleek new definition of modernism, is epitomised by his own holiday house on France's Atlantic coast.

extremely influential in the refining of design, stripping away, as he does, every unnecessary element from a scheme.

The austerity of this style has evolved into a soft-edged minimalism, an altogether gentler and easier-to-live-with version, as seen in the work of such designers as Christian Liaigre. His is a new modernism which, in his work at New York's Mercer hotel and the new Joseph shop in London, combines natural materials and a soft palette. So influential is this new aesthetic that even such renowned lovers of the grand, the classical and the flamboyant as Valentino and Karl Lagerfeld have turned to Liaigre for their latest decorative schemes.

At the other extreme is the grand, almost baroque lushness of Alberto Pinto, Jacques Garcia and the late Renzo Mongiardino and Henri Samuel, whose work reflects a love of detail, rich texture and exuberant colouring – an element of the rich that will never entirely disappear. Their work, however, in common with that of Liaigre and all of the style-makers in between, demonstrates one of the most important characteristics of current decorative style: an eclectic approach to style and period.

There was a time when a carefully decorated room would be furnished with pieces that all related – drawn from the same period or culture. But that has changed. The combining of different styles and periods is one of the most important directions of late 20th-century decoration and is espoused by many decorators, both modernist and classical.

A deep understanding of both the architecture and art of earlier periods informs the work of many of them. François-Joseph Graf, for instance, mixes styles with great skill. The son of a Paris antique dealer, he studied at both the Ecole des Beaux Arts and the Ecole du Louvre, followed by a period at the Ecole des Monuments Historiques and is as much at home discussing Louis XVI furniture as he is the works of Charles Rennie Macintosh or Frank Lloyd Wright.

Others take a more instinctive approach. Hotelier-cum-decorator Anouska Hempel has created the interiors for all of her hotels with considerable imagination and flair. To create the lush environment of Blakes, she has drawn on influences as diverse as Imperial Russia and the old Colonies, while the cool minimalism of The Hempel owes a clear debt to the architecture and culture of Japan.

On the modernist front Christian Liaigre, in particular, is known for his masterful mixing of the styles and objects of East with West. He is not the only one. There is a new understanding of the power of ethnic art and its place in contemporary Modernism and it is one of the most powerful influences at the end of this century.

The Fondation Beyeler in Riehen near Basel, designed by Renzo Piano to house the collection of Ernst Beyeler, and where Matisse and African art are displayed together, exemplifies this trend. Interior decorators who mix pieces from every country and culture include the heroic Frédéric Méchiche, who also is a master at combining different periods of strongly different approach - such as the 18th century and the 1950s. In Britain Jonathan Reed's interiors could be nothing but contemporary. But

they mix styles and times, all edited into a sleek whole. And David Champion uses an East/West language when he manipulates interior spaces, a particular language, however, which is injected with a wit and eccentricity that is the essence of contemporary Englishness.

But there is another sort of Englishness in decoration, a most important – and influential – style, which is difficult to classify but which can perhaps best be described as the redefining of what was once known as the 'country house look', reinterpreted in

Roberto Peregalli's confident mixing of periods is seen in the hallway of this Milanese palazzo. Against walls painted to resemble Roman bas-reliefs, he has placed an 18th-century commode and a 17th-century chair; the sculpture is 14th-century.

a way that is relevant for today. This look has not had an altogether good press over the years. Originally supposed to represent the way that old English houses looked when they had been lived in continuously for many years – a combination of slightly shabby comfort, soft faded tones and personal possessions – this deeply misunderstood style degenerated during the 1980s, in the hands of

Above: Decorators such as Jane Churchill have reinterpreted the much-misunderstood 'English look' in a way which is sophisticated, comfortable and relevant to both city and country living, as seen in the hallway of this London house. Opposite page: For British partnership, Collett Zarzycki, who designed this London house, the crispness and correctness of classicism provide a canvas on which they can play with detail and colour, creating a contemporary ease within a formal framework.

inexperienced and unsympathetic decorators, into a pastiche of country life; ghastly stage sets of overcrowded rooms were crammed with small cloth-covered tables, overstuffed chairs, over-swagged curtains, chintz everywhere and enough bric-a-brac to furnish a junk shop.

But today the new mood in decorating and the new interest in simplicity have revived the look in a way that is sophisticated, comfortable and, especially, relevant to both city and country living. The layers have been peeled back to expose the fine bones of traditional decorating, where the colours are appropriate, the furniture comfortable

and the mix is of old and new, though always with a classical reference.

Exemplified in Britain by such taste-makers as Christopher Hodsoll, Christopher Gibbs and Robert Kime, it has been perfected by such exponents as Wendy Nicholls and Vivien Greenock at Colefax & Fowler and Emily Todhunter. Nina Campbell, too, creates houses that look as if they have been lived in for years but she does so with a relaxed humour and a decidedly contemporary sense of colour – bronze, aubergine, terracotta and olive green, rather than pretty pastels.

Distinctive versions of this style are also found in the work of such pan-European designers as John Stefanidis (whose brash modernism of the 1960s has long been superseded by a restrained and refined eclecticism), as well as in the 'old palazzo' look of Roberto Peregalli and Piero Castellini Baldiserra. In France, too, the chameleon Jacques Garcia has decorated a Normandy chateau in a very rich, eclectic version of the style – more country castle than country house. Spain, likewise, has decorators working in similar style, enlivened with contemporary references – particularly Jaime Parladé, whose work has an edge and a definition and whose use of colour and textiles is legendary.

The glue which holds these diverse styles together is classicism. However, late 20th-century classicism is not mere pastiche but an appreciation of its order and symmetry, which enables designers to create a decidedly contemporary sense of ease within a formal framework. For British partnership, Collett Zarzycki, it "provides the ground rules," according to partner Tim Flynn. "Its crispness and correctness provide a canvas on which we can play more with details and colours."

David Mlinaric, whose cerebral approach, married to the informal grandeur of his work have made him one of Europe's most sought-after and respected interior designers, likewise sets great store by the control and discipline provided by a classical framework.

"Once you have made a classic house, you can break it – add things which make it a bit 'off'," he has said. "The decoration can answer the architecture rather than the other way around."

This respect for architecture is an underlying theme, for both traditionalists and modernists, and the architect-decorator is an important phenomenon as we approach the millennium.

Chester Jones, who trained as an architect before moving into decoration, notes that, as his career has progressed, he is "returning to the beginning of the circle" in his approach to his work.

Belgian duo Claire Bataille and Paul Ibens, who regard themselves more as architects than decorators, stress the importance of purity, natural light and good space distribution; their work reflects the

An understanding of the power of ethnic art is one of the most important influences on late 20th-century decorating. Clockwise from above: Anouska Hempel deftly mixes East and West at the The Hempel hotel in London; Guinevere Antiques' arrangement of a Chinese Tang Dynasty terracotta horse on a Chinese 19th-century vellum trunk for a contemporary London house; French architect-decorator Gilles Saint Gilles draws on Mediterranean and North African influences for many of his schemes.

The mixing of different periods and styles is a defining theme of current style. Clockwise from above: John Minshaw's drawing of classical pillars, made while travelling in Egypt, provides a counterpoint to furniture from the 1930s and the 1990s in this London drawing room; a pair of 18th-century stone urns provided Minshaw's inspiration for this recently-built pool house; Collett Zarzycki mixes items from the 18th- to 20th centuries in this Georgian London house.

sober functionalism of Bauhaus, coupled with the beautiful perspectives of the 18th century.

Many of today's decorators design their own furniture and accessories, carrying their themes right through from the architectural bones of a scheme to its smallest detail. Christian Liaigre's pieces are sculptural in feeling, using woods like the nearly black (and very contemporary-feeling) wenge. This use of dark woods mixed with soft colour and texture is epitomised in the comfortable lines of his own holiday house on the Atlantic coast.

In Italy, Romeo Sozzi combines forward thinking with classical restraint; he believes in quality and craftsmanship – often using hand-stitched leather – and his meticulous attention to detail is well-known. Milan-based Angelica Frescobaldi designs and makes not only furniture but also lights and any other essential elements needed for her decorating schemes. She describes her style as "Italian-International" – part classical, part contemporary and never overdressed.

Even in the hands of more traditionally-minded designers, it is not reproduction but a reinterpretation of antique styles with a contemporary edge. Christopher Hodsoll has designed a traditional, curved back wooden chair which he has then upholstered in lipstick pink leather. This perhaps defines the look – the traditional with the unexpected, the comfortable with the intelligent, the luxurious with the eclectic.

Pondering on the concerns and aims of so many different talents across Europe, it fast becomes evident that, at the end of the 20th century, where the best decorators are concerned, there is no longer any such thing as a 'national' decorating style. Nor is there an unbridgeable abyss dividing the modern and the classical and perhaps this is what millennium decorating is all about – the ability to keep the best of the past and confidently add to that the best of the present and the promise of the future." E

HAUTE HORLOGERIE

Tourbillon sous trois Ponts d'or, Président

GP
GIRARD-PERREGAUX
MANUFACTURE DEPUIS 1791

For further information:

GIRARD-PERREGAUX
1, place Girardet • CH-2301 La Chaux-de-Fonds
Tel: (+41)32 911 33 33 • Fax: (+41)32 913 04 80

E-mail: com@girard-perregaux.ch
http://www.girard-perregaux.ch

ASSOCIATION
INTERPROFESSIONNELLE
DE LA HAUTE HORLOGERIE

EUROPE'S MOST STYLISH GOLF CLUBS

By Michael McDonnell

While some of Europe's leading golf clubs are famed for their challenging fairways, others are equally renowned for their social cachet. We visit Europe's most stylish clubs.

Previous page: The 3rd hole at St-Nom-la-Bretêche, near Paris. Above: The 11th hole and clubhouse at Valderrama. Dubbed "the Augusta of Europe", it is the creation of Bolivian multi-millionaire Jaime Ortiz-Patino (pictured).

From earliest times there has been an exhilarating social aspect to the game of golf that has carried as much importance as any playing prowess. Indeed, more than two centuries ago, the game's Scottish forefathers would gather after their round in some nearby inn to enjoy good fellowship and camaraderie until the wee small hours.

The Leith golfers in 1768 could always be found in Luckie Clephan's tavern. Their St Andrews counterparts across the Firth of Forth met up in Bailie Glass's inn while, in southern England, the Blackheath golfers gathered in the Chocolate House and, later, the Green Man Hotel. Therein lie the origins of what is now known as the golf club.

Yet, just as the royal and ancient game has taken on many different forms of play around the world so, too, has the golf club itself risen beyond those dim and distant origins. It now takes many imaginative forms, from the splendour of a Palladian-style mansion north of London to the rustic charm of an old French farmhouse or the architectural magnificence of a residence on the outskirts of Madrid.

Moreover, the very best golf clubs in Europe observe a standard and a style that extends beyond the greens and fairways and embraces every aspect of good living. At the Kildare Club south of Dublin, for example, there is the finest collection of mainly Irish art treasures in private hands, acquired by club owner Dr Michael Smurfit for the pleasure of his guests, while the Valderrama Club in southern Spain has assembled a priceless and growing array of golf antiques and memorabilia. At a handful of similarly outstanding clubs good taste and quality combine to provide a unique atmosphere in which elements other than just golf play an important role in the fulfilment of their leisure time for those fortunate enough to enjoy them.

This emphasis on quality invariably attracts a discerning and obviously affluent membership which, for the most part, strikes a welcome balance between maintaining its own privacy and permitting the outside world a glimpse of golf – and life – at its very best.

Some clubs, nevertheless, still remain reluctant to open their doors. The Real Club de la Puerta de Hierro, set on the hilltops just a few minutes drive from Madrid, is one. An exclusive playground which attracts the cream of Spain's aristocratic and wealthy families, it satisfies most of their needs – both spiritual and physical.

Just inside the gates of the long drive to the clubhouse stands the children's nursery, where parents deposit their offspring into safe and experienced hands on the way in and collect them on the way out at the end of the day. There is a chapel by the first tee where enthusiasts can attend to their spiritual needs, perhaps gaining a little supernatural help before they play, and there was

This page: The brainchild of industrialist, Dr Michael Smurfit and the club of choice for Dublin's new élite, Ireland's Kildare Club will host the Ryder Cup in 2005. Played across the River Liffey, its 7th hole is overlooked by the original Barton mansion, now a sumptuous Relais & Châteaux hotel.

Top: Set in 1500 acres near Kilkenny, Mount Juliet was once the home of the Earl of Carrick. Above: Entrepreneur Peter de Savary named his Carnegie Club after the 19th-century tycoon, Andrew Carnegie, whose Scottish home it once was.

once even a school in which young caddies acquired a formal education in between their stints of bag-carrying. The road from the main gate also passes the polo ground and equestrian centre, while the swimming pool and tennis courts are located at convenient distances so as not to disturb the more elderly members taking lunch on the verandah.

In contrast, the Valderrama club at Sotogrande has eschewed the country club role and boasts no recreational facility other than the awesome golf course that has been dubbed "the Augusta of Europe". The creation of Bolivian multi-millionaire Jaime Ortiz-Patino, who bought the club with a few friends for their private use then transformed it into one of the major venues of world golf, Valderrama has already hosted the Ryder Cup and is scheduled to hold a World Championship.

For all its fame, Valderrama maintains the assured informality of a comfortable private club, where the standards of cuisine are among the highest in Europe and the legendary Bloody Marys have a potency that should carry a health warning. There is no accommodation on the premises but most members have their own villas on the surrounding estate and, in any case, the next-door

resort of San Roque has an excellent hotel where both Ryder Cup teams stayed for the 1997 match.

The Meriden Penna resort in southern Portugal's Algarve region stands as an enduring tribute to the creative genius of the late Sir Henry Cotton, three times British Open champion, who transformed what was a rice field into one of the best-known golf courses in the world. Moreover, the elegant hotel that stands alongside serves to confirm that this brilliant concept – the first in the Algarve – set the standards by which other complexes along the coast had to judge themselves.

Further north, near Sintra, the Penha Longa course, a regular venue on the European PGA Tour, is the place to play if, for once in your life, you fancy the idea of getting around a circuit ahead of Damon Hill or Michael Schumacher. For this is where they play during the Portuguese Grand Prix week; from the highest points on the course they can actually see the race track.

Yet the curious aspect of such supreme standards in golf is that they are not necessarily linked to antiquity or longevity, as two relative newcomers to the Irish scene demonstrate.

The Kildare Club (affectionately known as the

K Club) is the brainchild of Irish industrialist Dr Michael Smurfit who, in 1988, assembled Arnold Palmer and a team of experts to transform the Straffan estate, on the banks of the River Liffey, into one of Europe's premier hotel and golf resorts. His efforts have been duly rewarded by the decision to take the Ryder Cup to the club in 2005, the first time in history that the contest will be played on Irish soil.

The K Club exudes quality, particularly in the old house, based on the design of the great Château of Louveciennes near Paris, which has now been enlarged into a luxurious hotel. Once a great centre for Irish society, Straffan House was where the North Kildare Hunt met for lavish breakfasts before their day's sport. Later it became the home of film producer Kevin McClory, whose guests during his tenure included Peter Sellers, Sean Connery and Shirley MacLaine. Nearby, a slick, modern clubhouse is the gathering place of choice for the cream of Dublin's new society, enriched by the booming Irish economy.

Mount Juliet, on the outskirts of Kilkenny, is a 1,500 acre estate set in woodlands, with extensive pastures and formal gardens. Standing on the banks

Top: With all of the facilities of the finest American country clubs, the Wentworth Club, set in 800 wooded acres near London, retains an unmistakably British ambience. Above: At Penha Longa during the Portuguese Grand Prix week you are likely to cross paths with Michael Schumacher.

Above: Hardelot, in northern France, is a magical place, set amid a pine forest near the sea.

of the River Nore, it was once the home of the Earl of Carrick and, following in the great tradition of Irish country homes, boasts all manner of leisure activities, including coarse fishing, rough shooting and an equestrian centre. Mount Juliet achieved golfing prominence when Jack Nicklaus decided to build his first course in Ireland there in 1991.

In the same year, property developers Guy and Jacques Dewez inaugurated the Robert Trent Jones-designed course which forms the centrepiece of their spectacularly-sited Sperone estate in the south of Corsica. Here, rich Parisians have their holiday homes – designed in timber-clad Big-Sur-meets-the-Med style and perched among the *maquis* – and club membership costs £10,000 plus £1,500 a year subscription. For them it is a rewarding investment because the rugged beauty of Sperone, with its seaward holes perched on rocky crags overlooking the Mediterranean, stands genuine comparison with the classic Californian charm of Pebble Beach. For all its exclusivity, though, Sperone is welcoming to visitors; play during the week and you can even stop

for a swim at the beautiful beach between the 13th and 14th holes without losing your place.

Perhaps the best example of a club serving both the wider public and its own members is to be found at Wentworth, a private, gated estate in the rich stockbroker belt south west of London, where new properties start at well over £1 million. The club has become a haven for the great and the good and attracts a broad spectrum of members, from entertainers to professional golfers, including Nick Faldo and Sandy Lyle.

From its inception in 1924 Wentworth has been a fashionable club, which has figured as prominently on the gossip pages as in the sport sections. But it was transformed into one of the world's outstanding venues thanks to the perceptiveness of property magnate Elliott Bernerd and the hands-on direction of his Chief Executive, Willy Bauer, who had previously established a solid reputation at London's Savoy Hotel.

St Andrews apart, Wentworth is probably the most sought-after venue in Britain and keeps its three courses – the West, the East and the Edinburgh – in constant daily use. It is also the headquarters of the PGA European Tour and

provides a wide range of other sports facilities, including a fully equipped fitness centre, as well as high-quality grass tennis courts where Martina Navratilova and other world-class tennis players have practised during Wimbledon.

Just a few miles down the road stands the Sunningdale Club, strictly devoted to golf – although a little backgammon in the clubhouse and quite a lot of high-stakes gambling on the course have also been known to occur. Past captains include the Prince of Wales, who later briefly became King Edward VIII, as well as his younger brother, who was King George IV.

It has always been an extremely sociable club where golf is treated as serious fun and where matches are kept evenly balanced by the club's special handicapping system. Its high-profile stalwarts number England cricket legend Ted Dexter, as well as several television commentators, former Ryder Cup golfer Michael King and Prince Andrew, who lives virtually next door – all of them still too young to join the famous 'Bay Window Brigade' of senior members who used to sit in the main lounge every day, watching the world go by and putting it to rights.

Across the Channel, the French are immensely adept at combining the demands of both visitors and members to equal satisfaction and nowhere is the art better demonstrated than at St-Nom-la-Bretêche, near Versailles, where the grandees of Paris gather to play. The course itself is the permanent venue for the Lancôme Trophy, which is now so much a part of the social calendar that even Parisians with no interest in golf turn up just to be seen.

The main building, once a farmhouse, has been sensitively transformed to provide two high-quality restaurants, as well as a spike bar where golfers in a hurry can consume a baguette and whatever shade of *vin* preferred. The cuisine of St-Nom stands supreme; its *crême caramel* has not been matched anywhere in the world, while its speciality of lamb on the bone makes the mouth water even at the memory. But beware the ducks — the live ones that inhabit the pond behind the 9th and 18th greens; their cackling strikes a particularly derisory note after a short putt has been missed.

Hardelot, a short drive from Boulogne, is a magical place, set amid a pine forest close to the sea. This tranquil setting offers all of the

Above: Resolutely private, the Real Club de la Puerta de Hierro, near Madrid, attracts the cream of Spain's wealthy and aristocratic families.

Above: In the 1920s a visit to Gleneagles for the grouse shooting or golf was part of the social calendar; today Gleneagles is a full-scale, five-star resort, with three golf courses and a shooting school run by ex-Formula One World Champion, Jackie Stewart, among its facilities.

essential leisure facilities – riding, tennis and so on – which make life as enjoyable for visitors as it does for its members. Here, the French bring their own refreshing Gallic casualness to a game that, at times, can be rather tight-lipped.

There are two courses, although many habitués prefer the original 'Pins' through the trees, where each hole is instantly committed to personal memory, particularly the 16th where the late British newspaper magnate and golf devotee, Lord Rothermere, was once observed heading a procession that included a buggy for his clubs, another for his iced champagne and a special handler for his dogs.

Of course it helps, when travelling, to be able to play golf as close as possible to cultural attractions, as well as the other amenities of comfortable living. One joyous coincidence of any golfing visit to Italy is

that arguably its finest course stands barely 15 kilometres from the Eternal City. Olgiata sits among the hills that surround Rome in an affluent and extremely private residential development, where the elite can play without fear of intrusion. Underlining its stature and reputation, it has hosted the World Amateur Team Championships as well as the World Cup of Golf but, even so, Olgiata remains a pocket of discreet privilege.

On Sardinia, the Golf Club Pevero, near Porto Cervo, offers a contrast in style. It goes without saying that when the Aga Khan puts his hand to a project the result will be stunning and so it is here on the Costa Smerelda – an exotic resort in a magical setting, where ocean-going yachts tie up alongside luxurious hotels and the globe-trotting glitterati can relax without being disturbed.

The fact that volcanic rock had to be dynamited

to carve a path for the fairways was a minor obstacle in the creation of the spectacular Robert Trent Jones course. As may be expected in such an elegant playground, the clubhouse is an exercise in luxury, where your non-golfing companions would be happy to while away the hours. Three terraces — one with a bar, another with the restaurant and the third with a swimming pool — overlook the 9th and 18th greens.

In Germany, the Frankfurt Golf Club underlines one enduring aspect of golf, in that Henry Cotton won the German Open on its tree-lined fairways in 1938; a year later, after winning again on another course, he had to beat a hasty retreat when the threat of World War II loomed. He even left without his prize money, which was sent on to him in 1946 by the German Golf Federation. After the hostilities Frankfurt was restored to the European Tour rota for a number of years and still remains a favourite haunt for international visitors because of its history and proximity to the city.

There can, however, be few more fairytale settings anywhere in the world than the Kronberg Club, some 16 kilometres north west of Frankfurt, the regular — and very exclusive — haunt of the legion of international bankers who live and work in the city.

The woodland course threads a hilly route around an enchanting castle — Schloss Friedrichshof, owned by the Hesse family — which serves not only as the clubhouse but also as a fashionable and shamelessly opulent hotel and restaurant. The course was opened in 1954 and, so far, the shrewd members have refrained from encouraging big golf tournaments, thereby avoiding the consequent circus atmosphere and disruption.

Inevitably this cursory glance at the golf clubs of Europe must end back in Scotland, where it began, though in sharp contrast to those spit-and-sawdust beginnings. The game and its establishments have moved on — and nowhere more so than at Gleneagles, a five-star resort with its own railway station, set in 850 acres close to the foothills of the Highlands.

In the 1920s a visit to Gleneagles for the grouse shooting or the golf was part of the social calendar, along with yachting at Cowes, polo at Deauville and the London Season of parties. It still holds a Jazz Age opulence while meeting modern-day needs. In keeping with its 'everything, but only the best' philosophy, Gleneagles' shooting school is run by ex-Formula One World Champion and crack shot, Jackie Stewart, while Captain Mark Phillips, former husband of Princess Anne, is the guiding light behind its equestrian centre. The kitchens here are famed for their dishes based on freshly-caught game from the estates, Border lamb, Tay salmon and Black Angus beef.

For the golfer there are three courses, including

the latest creation of the ubiquitous Jack Nicklaus. Moreover, the teaching staff has a high reputation; it was here that Sean Connery underwent a week of intensive golf tuition for his James Bond role in the film *Goldfinger*. He has been a golf addict and a regular visitor ever since.

And so to St Andrews, the Home of Golf. It is a Mecca — the shrine which every golfer aspires to visit

at least once in a lifetime. There are six courses in the town, all of them public, so that even the august Royal and Ancient Golf Club, which governs the game throughout most of the world, is allocated only certain tee times for its members. Nevertheless, St Andrews is not given over completely to golf, as the ranks of red-gowned university students around the town underline.

Of course, Bailie's 18th-century tavern is no longer there but many other establishments have sprung up to take its place, ranging from the Old Course Hotel beside the 17th hole to tiny establishments tucked into almost every street and square and, in contrast, the grand, 17th-century mansion, Strathtyrum (adjacent to the course of the same name) which is available for rental to private parties.

When legendary American golfer Bobby Jones was given the freedom of St Andrews he declared, "I could take out of my life everything but my experience at St Andrews and I'd still have a full, rich life." In so doing he defined the charm of the "auld grey toon" and revealed also its fascination for all who tirelessly follow the little white ball. **E**

Above: In the clubhouse at St-Nom-la-Bretêche — originally a farmhouse — the social élite of Paris enjoys cuisine the equal of many of the capital's fine restaurants. The Lancôme Trophy, played here, has become such a social fixture that even Parisians with no interest in golf come to be seen.

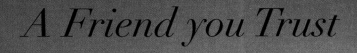

EUROPE'S BEST ADDRESSES

By Marina Dudley

A guide to Europe's most desirable addresses —
the grandest apartments, the smartest squares,
the most chic avenues — and who lives there.

Europe's great cities present a conundrum: how to live within about five minutes of their heart and still enjoy space and peace, to have a garden, keep a dog, park your car, revel in a view of something more inspiring than your neighbour's windows. Where do you look if you have several million to spend on a home in Europe?

Some cities answer these needs better than others. Take Geneva. At home in Cologny, the likes of Edmund Safra, John Latsis, Nana Mouskouri and The Aga Khan are, indeed, only five minutes from the banks and the smart shops of the rue du Rhône. (But then, as Martin Denning of Geneva's Société Privée de Gérance points out, nowhere in Geneva is much more than five minutes away; it's a relatively small city and traffic is never a problem.)

All of the other needs seem to be answered, too: peace, privacy, gardens and a view. Especially a view. Cologny climbs the slopes of Geneva's Left Bank, so houses on the principal streets, such as the Chemins de Bonnevaux, Coudrée, Nant d'Argent and Ruth not only face the setting sun but offer ravishing views

across the lake to the Jura mountains. An added joy is that the sensible Swiss have passed laws obliging developers to leave the view open to the property behind any new building.

In Paris neither the traffic noise nor their northerly aspect is enough to reduce the desirability of the quai Voltaire and quai d'Orsay, with their views over the Seine. On the latter, Count and Countess Hubert d'Ornano have a magnificent, 15-room duplex in the same building as über-decorator Alberto Pinto and, a few doors along, Valentino's partner, Giancarlo Giammetti bought a place last year. Ask a clutch of Paris real estate agents which is the most beautiful building in Paris and the consensus is likely to be Number 73 quai d'Orsay, built about 30 years ago in 18th-century style.

The quieter alternative is to overlook one of the parks: Parc Monceau, which straddles the 8th and 17th *arrondissements*, or the Jardins de Luxembourg in the sixth. São Schlumberger's grand quarters overlook the wide open spaces of the Champs de Mars while, on the ultra-smart rue Barbet-de-Jouy, Hachette Publishing and Matra supremo, Jean-Luc Lagardère and his wife Betty, have an *hôtel particulier* next door to that of Emanuel and Laura Ungaro; both overlook Les Invalides.

In London, the plethora of green space means that park views don't necessarily command such a premium. Far more sought-after are properties on one of the private garden squares, most notably Eaton, Chester and Cadogan Squares. While the river would provide a wonderfully open outlook, there is little property worth having along its banks. The exception is Cheyne Walk in Chelsea - a row of exquisite red-brick 17th- and 18th-century houses, home to the likes of Lord Weidenfeld and decorator John Stefanidis.

Views command a big premium in the crowded Principality of Monaco. This, combined with parking, porterage and high security explains the continuing desirability of the Rocabella (despite its rather ugly 1970s exterior), as well as the attraction of the pretty, Belle Epoque-styled Hôtel de Rome, built seven years ago, at the opposite end of town. The elegant Hermosa Palace, nearing completion next door to the Hôtel de Rome, will be another jewel.

However, the pick of the Principality's buildings, in terms of view and proximity to the centre, must be Porto Bello. Built five or six years ago right on the port, it has direct access to the Casino Square from its upper levels; agents KnightFrank sold a three-bedroom apartment here for 365 million French Francs in 1999. In contrast, 3 Place du Palais, on 'The Rock' is ultra-discreet, its façade (and its internal lift which takes residents' cars to its underground garage) giving the tourists outside the Palace no clue to the elegance within.

Previous page: Apartments overlooking the Parc Monceau in Paris' 8th arrondissement are highly sought-after. Below: The elegant façade of an apartment building just off the avenue Montaigne in the 'Golden Triangle' of Paris' Right Bank.

Views of London: Clockwise from above: The beautiful 18th-century houses of Cheyne Walk; Earl Cadogan's crest adorns the gate to the residents' communal garden in Cadogan Square; the 19th-century stucco-fronted terraces of Eaton Square.

In Europe's more northerly cities light is dramatically important. Thus, in London, the northern side of Eaton Square, for instance, where the principal rooms face south is the more desirable. The same goes for avenue Foch in Paris, although, according to Donelle Higbee, Director of Sotheby's Real Estate in the French capital, the unevenly-numbered south side of the street was – and remains – preferred by serious collectors of art and antiques. "The strong sunlight pouring in through the south-facing windows on the other side will simply destroy their valuables," she points out.

On the other hand, the best garden to have is a west-facing one. Thus, in London, the western side of Phillimore Gardens, in Kensington, has private back gardens with the bonus of a view onto the open space of Holland Park. However, in Regent's Park, where the houses generally have no private gardens, Chester and Cumberland Terraces on the eastern side (facing the afternoon light and the view across the park) are more desirable than those on the opposite side. In Geneva, it is the houses on the 'downhill' side of those streets in Cologny whose back gardens face the lake.

Hamburg and Munich, the only truly smart cities in Germany, are blessed with abundant gardens and greenery. The most sought-after gardens in Hamburg run right down to the River Alster, making mini-paradises of such quiet streets as Leinpfad (with the water on both sides.) Blumenstrasse and Agnesstrasse, all of which have lovely old villas. Schöne Aussicht, as its name suggests, has the added benefit of a magnificent view. In Munich, the best houses – big, turn-of-the-century villas on very large plots of land – are on Ebersbergerstrasse and Delpstrasse in the Altbogenhausen area while, in Herzogpark, Pienzenauerstrasse and Flemingstrasse overlook the Englischer Garten and the River Isar. As Marianne Detlefsen of Engel & Völkers points out, the great joy of such properties is their almost rural sense of peace and seclusion less than ten minutes from the best shopping streets of their respective cities.

Milan, on the other hand, is not generally a city for gardens at all – not unless you are the happy owner of a top floor apartment with a roof terrace or one of the 18th-century *palazzi* on via Mozart or via Vivaio. In the Magenta area, west of the Duomo – where some properties date back to the Middle Ages – the *palazzi* which are still in use as private houses are generally owned by the old, aristocratic families – such as the Radices, on via Cappucio. However, as Giorgio Viganò, doyen of Milan's estate agents, points out, "These really prime properties hardly ever come onto the market. A top floor apartment is such a rarity that price is no object – a 50% premium is normal. And if the *palazzi* change hands, it is between members of the

Opposite and top: In the principality of Monaco, open views command a high premium.
Above: A classical Hamburg villa, set in expansive grounds near the Alster.

In Geneva, Cologny is home to the élite, where the large villas have uninterrupted views of the lake and the Jura mountains beyond.

old families who have owned them for centuries."

The Versaces' solution was to buy an entire building on via Gesù, using the lower floors for their business and the upper floors as living quarters. Top people's tailor, Gianni Campagna is doing the same with the *palazzo* he bought in early 1999 on via Palestro, a few minutes' walk away.

The big question, of course, is: house or apartment? In Milan there is little choice. The best properties are all within five or ten minutes' walk of via Montenapoleone and this means apartments within the beautifully proportioned 18th- and 19th-century buildings, ideally on the quieter lateral streets, such as via Gesù and via Santo Spirito. From here you simply go downstairs to the shops — and what shops they are; the world's greatest fashion and style merchants are right on your doorstep, not to mention the florists, food shops and other necessities of life. You walk to the best restaurants and you stroll to the top of the street to take your children to and from school.

In the centre of Geneva — the Old Town — it's a similar story. Built from the 16th century onwards, the properties on the rue des Granges and Grande Rue remain largely in the hands of such old Geneva families as the de Saussures. If you could ever get your hands on one, an apartment on the unevenly-numbered side of rue des Granges, with a terrace overlooking Place Neuve, would be the ultimate prize. The same is true of apartments on Rome's via Giulia and the surrounding streets.

Generally, though, most people's ideal would be a house, rather than an apartment, right in the centre of a city. For this Paris is a good bet, as it is so compact, although, as Sotheby's Higbee points out, the sale of an *hôtel particulier* in the heart of the city is notable, above all for its rarity: "It's usually only through divorce or death that we would see the most exceptional properties — somewhere like avenue Marigny or Ile St-Louis, for example — on the market." Bearing out this view, it took the Lagardères, for instance, six years to find their current home.

London, a city composed of many villages which simply grew together rather than being the product of town planners, is full of by-ways and backwaters which contain some very unusual 'hidden' houses — low-built, wide and elegant. Chelsea's Old Church Street has two such gems — Sloane House and The Old Rectory — and nearby Chelsea Square has another two, both with big, west-facing gardens. In South Kensington, Mick Flick's home, Park House, is completely hidden by the surrounding stucco-fronted terraces and Mark Birley shares a quiet little lane nearby with just one neighbour. Hyde Park Gate is an enclave of similar houses, as is Lowndes Place in Belgravia. Although the houses in London's character-filled mews are generally small — they

were, after all, originally built as stables — Belgravia's Wilton Row is a notable exception, with a couple of really substantial houses. The very top end of the London market is driven by such special, individual houses as these, rather than by particular streets.

That said, it is universally accepted that Eaton Square is the most prestigious of all London's addresses. Why, then, would composer Andrew Lloyd Webber sell his house there (one of only six intact houses remaining in the square) in favour of an apartment in nearby Chester Square (still very smart — Baroness Thatcher is a resident — but without quite the cachet of its neighbour)?

Part of the answer lies in that peculiarity of central London's architectural style: the predominance of tall, narrow terraced houses — mostly built in the early 19th century on the estates of the great aristocratic landlords, Grosvenor, Cadogan and, north of Oxford Street, Howard de Walden among them. Not everybody enjoys the effect, as a leading London agent put it, of "living in a lighthouse", particularly in an age of fewer household staff and less formally structured family lives. What Lord Lloyd Webber may have sacrificed in prestige, he has gained in convenience: a vast penthouse with several roof terraces, converted across the top three floors of three adjoining buildings.

Any developer worth the name understands this and the canniest among them acquire several houses at a time, converting them laterally into spacious apartments. The recent redevelopment of Chesham Place has turned a smart, though unexceptional Belgravia terrace into one of London's finest buildings — a fact reflected in the prices; at over £1,000 per square foot, a would-be neighbour of Sir Evelyn de Rothschild will pay as much as £4.5 million for a two-bedroom flat.

The prime areas of London and Paris are both characterised by a 'great divide'. In Paris, while the quality of the best Right and Left Bank properties is the same, the people who inhabit them tend to have different outlooks — more arty/intellectual on the Left, more overtly jet-set (together with old money) on the Right. As one Left Bank socialite jokingly remarks, "We would choose a cashmere coat lined with fur; they would wear their fur on the outside."

London's two distinct markets are loosely termed North and South of the Park — Hyde Park, that is. 'South' runs across Belgravia and Chelsea to Kensington and Holland Park, while 'North' means the beautiful, Nash-designed terraces of Regent's Park — the freehold of which is owned by the Crown Estate — and St John's Wood, with its large, detached houses.

While Europe's best addresses have, for the most part, always enjoyed that status, there has been a shift in fortunes — or at least fashions — in some cases. In Paris, for instance, the Right Bank has lost

some of its most glamorous denizens to St Germain (an area that they would not have considered 20 years ago) and a 16th *arrondissement* postal code is no longer the guarantee of pre-eminence that it once was. That said, the Muette area, bordering the Jardins de Ranelagh, remains as gold-plated as ever. The Thysssens' Paris home is here and Bernard Arnault lives on rue d'Andigné. Also on the Right Bank, the 'golden triangle' – that area of the 8th arrondissement bounded by avenues Montaigne and George V and running up to avenue Gabriel and avenue Marigny, next to the Elysée Palace, is still 22-carat.

It's a similar story outside Europe's principal cities. As the French Riviera, from Monaco to Cannes, became increasingly crowded, St Tropez grew in stature. However, the entire coast is now so over-built that the smart money is leaving altogether, much of it going inland. The only truly civilised areas nowadays are Cap Ferrat, Cap d'Antibes and Cap Martin, where the best houses are hidden from the public gaze in a *domaine privé*, with large gardens running down to the water. Here, Daisy Fellowes' former estate, Les Zoraïdes, where, in the Thirties, she treated her guests to fashion shows on the

Although filled with character, London's mews houses are generally small. This property, in the highly sought-after Wilton Row, is a notable exception.

265

Marbella has begun a major renaissance in the late 1990s. While houses on the sea-front are scarce and in great demand, some of the finest properties, are to be found in the hills behind the town, such as these properties at El Almendro, on the road to Ronda.

72-step staircase leading from the house to the swimming pool, sold last year for £15 million.

Both sides of Cap Ferrat remain seriously smart and, while mid-market houses (that is to say, houses in the FF2-3 million bracket) are openly available, the best houses change hands by word of mouth. The western side of avenue Général de Gaulle provides a grandstand view of Villefranche Bay, as well as catching the evening sun, while the

handful of houses on the little St-Hospice Point on the eastern side have a pretty and intimate outlook onto St-Jean and Beaulieu – and it's a mere stroll down to the port.

Southern Spain has suffered a similar fate to the Côte d'Azur. Marbella, which the stylish, seriously rich and (often) famous made their playground in the 1970s had fallen right out of favour by the late Eighties. However, its fortunes are undergoing a real renaissance. But, while the finest sea-front properties are back in demand, the real excitement is in the hills above the coast. Hidden in the Benahavis hills 450 metres above sea level, with breathtaking views of the coast, La Zagaleta is the hottest of the new developments.

Formerly Adnan Khasshogi's estate, it has been transformed into a self-contained community with first-rate sporting facilities and state-of-the-art security. It has been sub-divided into 400 separate building plots but, with many buyers snapping up more than one plot at a time, the

eventual number of houses will be less than 300.

It is not just within these established areas that shifts have taken place; whole new cities are emerging. While it is true that, at least until recently, the only truly chic cities in Germany were Hamburg and Munich, Berlin's reinstatement as its country's capital will attract a new power class and with it, presumably, a social and financial élite. Where will they live? According to agents Engel & Völkers, the traditional areas immediately to the south west of Kurfürstendamm are still the best. In Grünewald, the quiet streets near the forest and lakes, such as Griegstrasses, Regerstrasse and Königstrasse are highly favoured while, in Dahelm, Miquelstrasse and Im Dol have lovely villas.

Ireland's booming economy has focused attention on Dublin and two areas of the capital in particular. In Killiney, overlooking Dublin Bay, the best streets – Vico Road, Killiney Hill Road and Sorrento Terrace – are home to the likes of Bono, of rock band U2, and racing driver Eddie Irvine.

But the real prize in Dublin is a house in one of its beautifully-proportioned Georgian Squares. Fashion designer Louise Kennedy, for instance, lives in Merrion Square and Tony and Chryss O'Reilly have a splendid house on the western side of Fitzwilliam Square. These houses have all of the attributes: peace, space, private gardens, an open outlook over the square, gorgeous architecture and they are a mere five-minute walk from the heart of this increasingly vibrant city.

However, the same rule applies in these emerging cities as it does to all of Europe's finest addresses. The very best properties are extremely difficult to come by; they are snapped up within days of coming onto the market or, indeed, never come to the market at all, changing hands privately instead.

As Martin Denning of SPG in Geneva puts it, "You have to get out of bed very early if you want the best." Either that or be a close, personal friend of the vendor. E

Cap Ferrat will never be anything but smart. Bathed in the afternoon sun, properties on its western side, including the charming Le Petit Rocher (top) command sweeping views of Villefranche Bay.

Kiton

Ciro Paone S.p.A.

10022 New York N.Y. • 689, Fifth Avenue
Tel. +1 (212) 2651995 Fax +1 (212) 7029117

20121 Milano • Via della Spiga, 46
Tel. +39.02.76013049 Fax +39.02.76013051

40474 Düsseldorf • Kaiserswerther Str. 144
Tel. +49 (211) 4543328 Fax +49 (211) 4543422

80022 Arzano (NA) • Viale delle Industrie
Tel. +39.081.5733175 Fax +39.081.7318611

YOUNG STARS FOR THE MILLENNIUM

Research by Virginia Mucchi and Ruth Hillenbrand

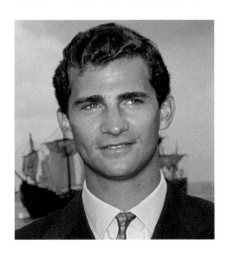

A selection of Europe's finest young talent, whose commitment and flair have already made them stars of society, stage, sport and industry — names the world will be watching in the new millennium.

AHMED▲

Ajaz Ahmed eats, drinks, sleeps and talks websites; that is how he has become one of Britain's youngest and wealthiest entrepreneurs. At 27, he runs Britain's biggest Internet and New Media Company, AKQA. Not surprisingly, Microsoft's Bill Gates is one of his heroes.

He inherited his brother's PC when he was 11 but soon got bored with the standard computer games on offer and decided to write his own, complete with sound and animation. While most teenagers were collecting football stickers and posters of pop stars, Ahmed was going through the annual reports of advertising agencies and software companies. He watched television more for the commercials than for the programmes.

Success came at an early age. When he was 14, he wrote down an idea for a television commercial for Swatch watches and sent it to the company. It was such a hit that Swatch asked Ahmed to direct the ad himself and it became one of the most successful TV spots of the decade.

In 1994 he launched his Internet consultancy, AKQA. Within a year, the company had made its mark by signing such important clients as Coca Cola, BMW, Microsoft, Sony and Rover. AKQA

websites were quickly recognised for their innovative technology and the company was soon receiving prestigious awards: the *Sunday Times* International Web Site of the Year in 1996, the *New Media Age* Best Digital Advertising Campaign (for BMW) and the *Advertising Age* International Media Innovator of the Year in 1998.

It would seem that Ahmed's interests revolve entirely around work, except, that is, for his car – a snazzy, technically advanced BMW. Still living in his parents' house outside London, it takes him two hours to get to the office and back.

"The good thing about driving is that you can think about the things that happened in the day and find ways to fix what went wrong," he says. But very little seems to go wrong for Ahmed.

ÅKERLUND

What does it take to be the best in the world of music video-making and advertising? Jonas Åkerlund, one of Sweden's hottest properties, should know. For him, the winning formula seems to involve controversy, honesty and being able to turn down demands – even from Steven Spielberg and the Rolling Stones. Despite having worked with some of the music industry's biggest players, Åkerlund remains unaffected by his success.

His route to the top was suitably unorthodox for a creative non-conformist. Born in Stockholm in 1965, Åkerlund's first love was music. Rejecting an academic path, he joined a rock band, Bathory, as its drummer. Then came military service – where Åkerlund first experimented with film-making when he helped to put together information programmes – and a stint in London, where Åkerlund worked as a builder and later ran a solarium. From there, he became a production assistant at a Swedish film company, Mekano, in 1986. He had picked the name at random from the telephone directory.

"Jonas came in looking like a hard rocker," recalls Lars Pettersson, who was working at Mekano at the time and is now Åkerlund's partner in their production company, Pettersson Åkerlund. "About 200 young hopefuls pass through the film and production companies in Sweden each year. Only a few stay."

Despite being hugely sought-after as a maker of music videos and commercials, Åkerlund generally prefers time spent at home with his partner and young son to celebrity nights out – and he still dresses a bit like a rocker.

He seems entirely secure about what matters most to him: "A few years ago, I looked at my finished products," he explains. "I realised that everything I did well had come from my heart, my experience and my dreams, and from my son. I've tried to make the most of that."

ALAJMO▼

If, while playing in the backyard with his brother (pictured below) and sister, the seven-year-old Massimiliano Alajmo ever noticed his mother cooking in the kitchen, no game could keep him from joining her and baking biscuits, his speciality at the time.

Since then he has gone on to take his mother's place as chef at the family's restaurant, Le Calandre, near Padua. Alajmo belongs to the sixth generation of a family of restaurateurs who have delighted the region with exquisite food since 1860. But Alajmo is special. In 1997, at the age of 23, a couple of years after he had succeeded his mother at Le Calandre, the restaurant was upgraded to a second Michelin star and experts believe that he has all the qualities needed to become a three-star chef very soon.

As a teenager, he tried to gain as much culinary experience as possible by working with his mother in the restaurant. During his summer holidays, he did *stages* in some of the best restaurants in France, including the Auberge de l'Eridan, with Marc Veyrat, and Les Prés d'Eugénie, with Michel Guérard. One of the best-known Italian food critics soon hailed him as the "Mozart of the cooking stove".

Experience, talent and – in his words – "the genes" have served to make him one of the finest young chefs in Europe and his commitment will definitely take him far.

ANDSNES ▲

There is a certain contrast between the boyish looks of Leif Ove Andsnes and the power and talent as a pianist that have so rapidly made him a star. And this contrast perhaps best explains the fascination for the phenomenon called Leif Ove Andsnes.

His parents, both music teachers, brought music into Andsnes' life soon after he was born in Norway in 1970; but, as he stresses, "they never told me that I should become a pianist. I decided on my own". It didn't take his parents long, though, to recognise their son's gift.

Andsnes entered the Bergen Music Conservatory in 1986. These were the years of discovery when, from an initial obsession, as he called it, for Russian player Sviatoslav Richter, he found his own, very personal style – lighter, charming but still potent. This style has been his hallmark ever since.

An international career soon followed, with concerts in the US, Canada, Germany and Japan, and he was named 1998 Gilmore Artist by the Irving S. Gilmore International Keyboard Festival. Following the release of one of his latest recordings – Brahms Concerto No.1 – one critic wrote that "even the most ardent Brahms-hater would find it difficult to resist Andsnes's sense of space and majesty or, indeed, the beguiling quality of the sound itself".

Andsnes' little free time is spent between Bergen and Copenhagen; while he admits that continuous travelling has made it difficult for him to form a relationship, fortunately for all of us he seems unlikely to change the beautiful one he has with the piano.

ANELKA ▶

When the English football club, Arsenal, bought the little-known, though prodigiously talented player, Nicolas Anelka, from Paris St. Germain for an undisclosed fee in February 1997, eyebrows were raised in France, where there is an unwritten rule that young players should show loyalty to the clubs that nurtured them.

Arsenal waited patiently for Anelka to fulfil his potential and was soon rewarded when he scored one of the winning goals in its 1998 FA Cup Final victory. French supporters expressed surprise when Anelka was omitted from the 1998 World Cup-winning team, since many team-mates believe that the media-shy Anelka is the cream of their striking talent. They were vindicated when Anelka, playing for the national team, scored one goal of a hat trick in a friendly match against England in February 1999. The French captain, Didier Deschamps, says, "He's our very own Ronaldo," suggesting that the 21-year-old Anelka is destined to become one of the world's finest footballers.

Anelka plays alongside Emmanuel Petit and is managed by Arsène Wenger. Despite the fact that Arsenal is a very Gallic team, the reserved Anelka – who hails from a poor suburb of Paris – apparently feels a little lonely. Although Arsenal signed Anelka until 2003, it is unlikely to hold on to him as, at time of writing, he has been the subject of fervent interest from clubs in Italy, France and Spain, including Lazio in Milan and Real Madrid. This scramble to sign the young star comes as little surprise to seasoned football observers who recognise that Anelka is one of Europe's hottest properties.

ARZUAGA

With her own label sold in 600 shops in 36 countries worldwide, Amaya Arzuaga, at 30, has made it in the fashion industry. Arzuaga's passion for designing clothes comes from her mother, who controls one of Spain's most successful knitwear manufacturing labels, while her love for audacious, luxurious textures and colours probably comes from her father's well-known wine, Tinto Arzuaga. And she could be said to get her head for business from them both.

After her design studies, Arzuaga entered the family fashion business but her dream was to have her own label. Her wish came true in 1994 when she launched her very first collection, mostly knitwear, and her success has been growing ever since. In Spain she was named Designer of the Year 1996, and in 1997 she showed her work in London, alongside Vivienne Westwood and Alexander McQueen.

Her clothes are sexy, young and made in fabrics which can sometimes hardly be recognised for what they are. "I work with everything, from plastic to 100 per cent cashmere," she says. "I want to make clothes that surprise." And she certainly does, especially in Spain where, as she recently declared, "We don't have the mixture of races. Wear a sari in London and nobody even notices; wear a sari in Madrid and everyone would stop and stare. Although we are a creative and cultured people, for some reason it is not reflected in our clothes." She can proudly consider her clothes the exception.

BERNADOTTE◀

Crown Princess Victoria was born on 14th July 1977 in Stockholm, the first child of King Carl XVI and Queen Silvia.

In 1979 the Swedish constitution was changed to the effect that the monarch's eldest child, whether male or female, could inherit the throne – which meant that Victoria's status as heir to the throne was confirmed when she was just two years old.

Victoria was raised with her younger brother Carl Philip, and sister Madeleine, at Drottningholm Palace outside Stockholm. And when it came to her education, there was some controversy – it was decided that she would go to an ordinary state school rather than a private one. If anything, this boosted her growing popularity with all generations in Sweden and the rest of Europe.

After gaining A-levels in Science and Social Studies, Victoria began travelling. At 18 she enrolled for a year at the Centre International d'Études Françaises in Angers to improve her French.

Then in 1998 she decided to go to the US to begin studying for her degree at Yale University. Originally it had been thought that she would attend Sweden's renowned Uppsala University, but part of the reason for choosing the States lay in her desire to avoid the media attention that had followed her so intensely in Europe since she became the official heir to the throne.

In addition to her formal academic studies, Victoria has pursued a long-term programme especially designed to acquaint her with the workings of the Swedish government. Experts believe that she will be the perfect queen because of her attitude, charm and commitment; certainly she has already conquered her countrymen's hearts.

BERNINGER

When Matthias Berninger was elected to Parliament in 1994, he was the youngest-ever German to sit in the Bundeshaus. "The reason I entered politics is linked to a certain fear I have of the future," he says.

Evidently, compared to that fear, Parliament was less frightening. In fact, politics has always been a part of his life; Matthias' father, uncle and grandfather were all members of the Social Democratic Party. However, notwithstanding family pressures, he joined the Green Party, making the protection of the environment his top priority. At university, where he read Chemistry and Economics, Matthias sold bicycles to earn some money and involved himself part-time with the Green Party, organising environmental campaigns and getting cross with his sister when she wanted to buy a car.

In Parliament, to which he was re-elected in 1998, he is making his mark as spokesperson for General and Higher Education. He supports the idea of student loans for everyone, a system which has become known as 'Baff', as opposed to the existing system, 'Bafog', where loans are calculated according to the income of student's parents.

In the evenings, when he's not at home with his wife and their young son, he sometimes meets other young MPs in the basement of Sassella, an Italian restaurant in the heart of Bonn where it is not unusual for cross-party discussions to go on until the early hours of the morning.

BOUCHEZ ▼

If Leslie Caron has a successor, it is probably the beautiful and captivating Elodie Bouchez — for whom the past two years have been golden. Now 26, Bouchez has been showered with awards at home and abroad, making her one of France's most sought-after young film actresses.

Bouchez established herself in some key films of recent French cinema: the coming-of-age drama, *Les roseaux sauvages* ('Waterlilies In The Wild'), for which she won the 1994 Most Promising Actress César; *Clubbed to Death* (1996), the controversial, nihilist study of French youth culture; and her biggest triumph so far, *La vie rêvée des anges* ('The Dream Life of Angels') released in 1998.

This last film, showing the friendship between two urban outsiders in northern France, has won Bouchez four coveted prizes: joint Best Actress award at the Cannes Film Festival and the European Film Awards (with her co-star Natacha Régnier), and the Best Actress title at the Lumière and César awards.

Bouchez especially cherishes her Cannes award: "It was just incredible to hear my name being spoken by Martin Scorsese [president of the Cannes jury]. Winning the award was like being swept up by a tidal wave. I felt extremely proud," she declares.

Bouchez has been acting in films since she was 17, when she made her debut in the late Serge Gainsbourg's feature, *Stan The Flasher*. After a few years spent completing her education and learning to dance, she returned to films and has been prolific ever since. Critics are watching Bouchez's next moves with interest. It's not known if she will stay in European cinema but one point is clear — she most enjoys working with young film-makers.

"I love the idea of growing up with actors and directors of my own generation and making films together," she asserts.

BOYD ▲

Dermot Boyd is full of ideas — on space, light, art and its possible threat from technology. One of Ireland's most prominent architects, he has a confident style, very much his own, influenced in part by the time he spent working abroad. Architecture, which he describes as "the mother of all arts", is best when simple and unadorned, he believes.

Boyd's accession to the dizzy heights of awards, high-profile teaching and the presidency of the Architectural Association in Ireland in 1997 has come via long study, work in Spain and the UK and the influence of his parents.

"My father was an architect and my mother an architectural conservationist," he says. "I enjoyed art at school, but also wanted to be involved in business. I thought architecture would give me the freedom to be creative — but with tangible results."

The 33-year-old Boyd has worked for Dublin architects McCullough Mulvin since 1994, on prestigious projects including renovation of part of the historic Abbey Theatre, and has undertaken private commissions since 1993 — a real chance to express his ideas.

Boyd's freelance work, sometimes commissioned outside Ireland, often involves interior design. "I call it interior 'architecture'," he says. "You can bring architecture into anything, whether it's an apartment or a restaurant."

Again he tries to cut out the decoration that might interfere with a living space. He is also a perfectionist, determined to work on a project until it is exactly as he wants it.

Born in Belfast in 1967 and raised in Dublin, Boyd studied in Ireland but cites his time spent under the tutelage of Alberto Campo Beeza, a professor of architecture in Madrid, as pivotal. "He's my mentor," Boyd explains.

Work is central to Boyd's life. He has taught at University College, Dublin, and the University of Strathclyde, Glasgow; currently, he is a tutor at his alma mater, the Dublin Institute of Technology. He has just completed the building of his own house and, in his free time, he enjoys walking and visiting art galleries. "Art uplifts me, particularly contemporary work," he says.

BRAINE ◄

British sculptress Kate Braine first became interested in making things with her hands at six. Little could she have known that, in later life, she would be sculpting the portrait heads of some of the world's most flamboyant men.

After a London childhood, Braine began a modelling career which took her as far afield as Japan before she took the decision to study sculpture at evening classes. In 1984 she went to Carrara in Italy, a place famous for its marble and an inspiration to Michelangelo. The experience proved to be an epiphany. "It was in Carrara that I decided to sculpt as a career," she says.

Braine followed up her trip with four years at City & Guilds School of Art in London studying sculpture. Here she found her niche: body casting and portrait heads. A series of important commissions has followed with Braine sculpting in marble and bronze. She has made busts of David Tang, Colin Wilson, Shakespeare (commissioned by Sam Wanamaker) and Francis Bacon, and fashioned a sculpture in collaboration with David Bowie in 1996.

Now 36, she has exhibited her work on numerous occasions. She prefers to make portrait heads of men: "Bronze is not flattering," she explains. "I work an inch and a half larger than life — and beauty is a matter of a millimetre. Women like to be flattered but men don't mind."

Braine sees art all around her: one of her biggest pleasures is exotic shells. She is also fascinated by stuffed animals which she views as "sculptures".

With a three-year-old son and some demanding projects to work on, Braine is kept busy. "I want to get to the stage where people with interesting faces approach me for sittings rather than the other way around," she says.

BRITTI

One of the most original and interesting talents on Italy's music scene, Alex Britti has suddenly become a hot property in the media. It has surprised many but most of all Britti himself: "I have always wanted to be successful," he says, "but going into platinum sales in three months has made me dizzy."

Britti was voted Best Newcomer of the Year for 1998 at the Premio Italiano della Musica (the Italian Music Awards) and came first in the New Proposals Category at the 1999 San|remo Festival, Italy's main music festival.

Born in 1968 in Rome, Britti started playing the guitar at the age of eight and joined a blues trio group when he was 17. His perfect technique was soon noticed by two of the world's leading blues musicians, Buddy Miles and Billy Preston, who were performing in Italy and asked him to join their band for the remainder of their tour. Britti left on his own European tour with a member of the band, Rosa King, in 1990. Since then blues has become a recurrent characteristic of his music.

With musical maturity came the idea of writing songs instead of just performing blues music. Finally, in 1998 and after a couple of extremely successful singles, his first CD, *It.pop*, which he wrote, produced and performed himself, displayed his abilities and ideas to a much wider audience. The people who know him say that, despite his success, Britti is the same "smart, determined and funny man" and that his love for music will take him further still.

BYNG▲

In 1997, Jamie Byng came up with a revolutionary idea: to re-publish the King James Bible as individual pocket-sized books. Viewing the books as works of literature, Byng commissioned introductions from such authors as Will Self and Louis de Bernières, in order to explain the significance and personal relevance of each text. His *Pocket Canons* came out in 1998 and have been selling successfully ever since.

At just 30, the precociously talented and ambitious Byng is nothing short of a radical publishing phenomenon.

A key figure in Scotland's recent cultural renaissance, Byng left Edinburgh University in 1993, joining Canongate Books — the respected Scottish publishing house — as an unpaid publicity officer. When Canongate went into receivership in October 1994, Byng stepped in buying the company for a knockdown price and became joint managing director.

Continuing Canongate's traditional publication of Scottish classics, he also created his own imprint, Payback Press. Its purpose was to bring back into print unknown or forgotten works by black American authors, many of whom were neglected in the United States. Byng's passion for Afro-American literature began with his college thesis on hip-hop music and the black oral tradition. One of the new imprint's first successes was Iceberg Slim's *Pimp*, which attracted publicity in *Esquire*, *GQ* and the music press, giving Canongate a considerable youth culture following. Canongate now has the power to sign prominent black writers, such as Gil Scott Heron and S. H. Fernando.

As well as possessing a maverick literary vision, Byng, now sole managing director at Canongate, has shown a true instinct for marketing. Although his numerous connections include his stepfather, Sir Christopher Bland, Chairman of the BBC, who gave him business advice initially, it is Byng himself who has made Canongate worthy of international attention with his ability to pinpoint niche markets. The publishing house has grown rapidly since he took over — it recorded a 1997 turnover of £1.8m — and it looks as if Byng's ambition will propel him into a constant realisation of new visions.

CAMENZIND & GRÄFENSTEINER▼

"We always thought it would be exciting to combine the building cultures of Switzerland and the UK," says Stefan Camenzind, 37, of Swiss/UK architects Camenzind & Gräfensteiner. "We want to take the precision of Swiss architecture and combine it with the forward-looking attitude of the UK."

It has been a cutting-edge combination: Camenzind and his partner Michael Gräfensteiner, 36, won the 1999 UK Young Architect of the Year Award. Their prize-winning building was the sports centre at Buchholz near Zürich, praised by judges for its "maturity", "elegance", "rationality" and "energy-effectiveness". It was a mark of their ability that their Zürich-based practice, only opened in 1995, was immediately entrusted with such a big commission.

Camenzind and Gräfensteiner are both from Zürich. They decided to become architects after their 'building technician' apprenticeships, a standard preliminary period under the Swiss system, which involves draughtsmanship and supervising building sites. They met on the architectural diploma course at Technikum Winterthur three years later, in 1984. After college, Gräfensteiner joined Lausanne firm Atelier Cube Architectes, moving to Angélil/Graham Architecture in Los Angeles in 1992. Camenzind stayed in Europe, spending six years in London at Nicholas Grimshaw & Partners and one year at Renzo Piano Building Workshop in Paris. His work for Nicholas Grimshaw included the Berlin Stock Exchange and the new international terminal at Waterloo Station in London. He has maintained this UK connection: there is a Camenzind & Gräfensteiner office in Brighton.

The pair are ambitious for the future. They hope to continue what they call an "international exchange" — opening more European offices and working with the best designers and technicians from every country.

Camenzind divides his time between Switzerland and the UK and spends his few free moments mountaineering. Gräfensteiner is married and enjoys sailing. As always there is an architectural explanation for what they do: "We are very interested in the difference between built-up and natural environments," says Camenzind, "and need the balance in our lives."

CASTA ▲

Discovered in 1994 on a Corsican beach when she was only 15, French model Laetitia Casta shot to international fame almost instantly and the demands put on her have meant she has had to grow up fast.

Vivienne Westwood is reported to have said about her, "I don't believe in God but, when I see Laetitia, I consider changing my mind". And French photographer Dominique Issermann has called her "the most beautiful girl in the world".

Accurate as this praise may be, it fails to do her complete justice, for the remarkable distinctiveness of her appeal and persona is difficult to put into words. Frequently compared to Brigitte Bardot, Casta stands out in a fashion industry that continues to search for ever-thinner models —she is voluptuous and proud of it. When asked about her favourite foods, Casta says she makes a point of eating the same as everyone else in her family, with whom she still lives, including puddings and home-made cookies. Likewise, she refuses to become a slave to stringent exercise regimes, preferring instead to remain in shape by riding horses and taking long walks.

Casta's has, so far, landed contracts and assignments with the likes of Chanel, Dior and Ralph Lauren but, crucially, her activities are not confined to the fashion industry. She played a part in France's most expensive film ever, *Astérix and Obélix*, and conquered millions of Italian hearts as the most charming presenter the San Remo Song Festival has ever had.

Experts believe that the enormous success of this gracious 21-year-old model owes much to her calm and laid-back character, but more to her refreshing attitude to beauty. "Beauty never stays with anyone," she asserts simply. "It passes."

CATHIARD-THOMAS▲

Wine has always been the dominant theme in the life of French entrepreneur Mathilde Cathiard-Thomas. Her parents own the Château Smith-Haut-Lafitte winery in Bordeaux and one of her early jobs was direct wine sales and showing tour parties around the Château. But it is her love of the beauty industry, combined with this instinctively comfortable attitude to wine, that has produced her groundbreaking Caudalie vinotherapy treatments.

Cathiard-Thomas, now 28, graduated from business school in Nice in 1994. She had already gained important cosmetic industry experience in 1991, at L'Oréal in Madrid, where her brief was to market Cacharel products. After a succession of posts at high-profile companies, including the beauty divisions of Van Cleef and Cartier, Cathiard-Thomas seized on the chance to combine her two interests.

In 1994 she paid a visit to her parents during the grape harvest, accompanied by her future husband Bertrand Thomas (pictured left with Mathilde), and met a team of researchers from the Bordeaux Faculty of Pharmacy. The meeting led to the momentous discovery that the grape seeds left over from wine-making are rich in polyphenols – far more active in combating premature ageing than are the vitamins C and E commonly used in cosmetic creams.

Caudalie was set up in 1995 and over the next three years 13 products were introduced; it rapidly became a cult brand with a client list that includes Caroline, Princess of Hannover, Isabelle Adjani and Claudia Cardinale. In June 1999 Cathiard-Thomas opened the luxurious Sources Caudalie spa, incorporating the Institut de Vinothérapie, in the grounds of Château Smith-Haut-Lafitte; it offers treatments based on Caudalie's products. A keen sportswoman, Cathiard-Thomas' own health regime includes walking races, hiking, snow boarding, wind surfing and roller-blading.

CHARPENTIER

Robert Charpentier's professional achievements are partly explained by his childhood. From a banking family, Charpentier grew up in Finland as part of the Swedish-speaking minority.

"I was already interested in stocks and shares at 11, when my grandfather taught me about them, and I started up a small company at school," he recalls.

Now, at 34, he is Senior Vice-President at Swedbank Markets in Stockholm. Charpentier has succeeded at everything he has tried: during military service he rose to the highest possible rank in the time available. In 1989 he was top of a class of 220 on his Masters degree course in international finance at business school in Helsinki. From there, he went straight to Goldman Sachs in London, where he worked in debt capital markets for the Nordic region for eight years. He left in search of a new challenge – and so that he could see more of his family.

Already promoted as one of Europe's major young financial leaders in surveys by *WorldLink* and *Euromoney* magazines, Charpentier was further honoured when he was appointed to the Board of Directors of Finnish commercial bank AKTIA in March 1999. To have achieved all this, he ought to be ruthlessly ambitious, yet he is broad-minded and quietly confident: "I don't believe nice guys finish last," he says, "although you have to be tough. I've seen a lot in my life and I try to maintain high moral standards."

Charpentier has clear plans for the future: "…to be a CEO or President one day." In the meantime, he balances work with his wife and children, fishing and following Formula One racing.

A citizen of the world, Charpentier speaks five languages and his ancestry goes back to a 17th-century French mercenary soldier who was ennobled by the King of Sweden.

But on his national identity, he remains firmly loyal: "I'm very proud to be Finnish."

CHURCH▶

"I was watching *This Morning* on TV and they said they were looking for talented kids. No-one else was in the room, so I phoned up," says Charlotte Church, when asked how her music career got started. "The producers said I had to sing on the phone, so I did *Pie Jesu* and that was it – I was invited to appear on the show and Mum and Dad were the last to find out!"

That show – in 1997 – would be the first in a series of successful television appearances. Sony Chief Executive Paul Burger spotted her during one show and, impressed with both her voice and personality signed her almost immediately. Her first album, *Voice Of An Angel*, released in December 1998, has been a staggering success, selling more than half a million copies and reaching the Top 40 in the United Kingdom and the United States. Charlotte was just 12 at the time – the youngest artist ever to achieve this.

Born in Llandaff, Wales, in 1986, Church has been singing for as long as she can remember. By the age of 8 she already knew several operas by heart. Church's young age is reflected in her love of confectionery and pop music. However she has no dreams of becoming a pop star. "I don't have the voice for pop music," she asserts. "My real dream is to sing my favourite opera, *Madame Butterfly*, at La Scala – and get a standing ovation, of course."

CORRS▲

Irish-based band, The Corrs, defies categorisation with its blend of pop, rock and folk accompanied by traditional Celtic instruments. It has taken a while to persuade the world to listen to their sound but their determination has paid off.

The group's first real break came in 1990 when Irish musician, John Hughes, heard them and offered to be their manager. Then, in 1994, the group was performing in a small Dublin club when Jean Kennedy Smith, then US Ambassador to Ireland, spotted them; an invitation followed to represent Ireland at a World Cup celebration in Boston. The Corrs tried to launch their US career from there but it was only on the day they were due to fly home that they met Jason Flom of Atlantic Records, who was about to start his own recording label, Lava. He signed the band immediately, leading to The Corrs' debut album, *Forgiven Not Forgotten*. This was followed in 1997 by *Talk On Corners*. Both albums went into platinum several times.

The Corrs are a family partnership: Andrea Corr, 26, lends the main vocals, while her sisters, Sharon, 30, and Caroline, 27, provide violin and drums and her brother Jim, 32, plays guitar and keyboards. He is joined by Conor Brady on guitar and Keith Duffy on bass. Brought up in Dundalk near the Northern Irish border, The Corrs were given musical encouragement from an early age; their parents played in a local band. "We grew up with a lot of music in our house," Andrea explains. "It was always our intention to become a band."

The past few years have been a whirlwind of touring, recording and media interviews and Andrea has had film parts in *The Commitments* (1990) and *Evita* (1996). But the band members remain down-to-earth. "People will always think of us as a stereotypical, old-fashioned Irish family, which is enough to keep anybody's feet on the ground," says Andrea.

DE BORBON ▶

Prince Felipe's birth in Madrid on January 30 in 1968 was greeted with enormous joy. He is the first son of King Juan Carlos and Queen Sofia, so this was a true dynastic event, for it secured a male successor.

Felipe's education began at the co-educational Santa Maria de los Rosales School in Madrid, where he proved to be hard-working and an avid scientist. Despite his family's attempts to make sure he fitted in to 'normal' life, his royal duties were never far away and in 1977 he was given the title of Prince of Asturias.

Following his secondary school studies, he went on to do a year's preparation for university at Lakefield College in Ontario, Canada. Felipe has fond memories of the time and believes it helped to build his character. "In Canada I had to learn to stand on my own two feet a bit more, in surroundings where there was no reason why anybody should know about me," he has said.

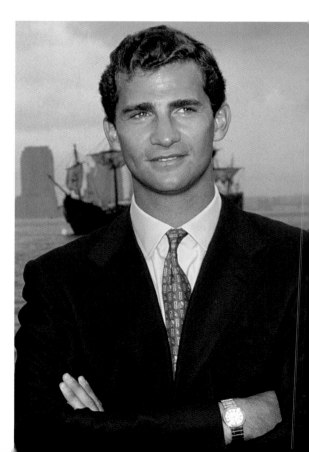

From 1985-1988, Felipe received a thorough military training at Spain's national academies for the three services. Again, keen not to be treated differently from his peers, he followed the cadet tradition of having his hair shaved into a T-shape on graduation as a pilot from the Air Force Academy. Felipe graduated from Madrid's Autonomous University with a law degree in 1993, following up with another North American stint when he went to Georgetown University for a Masters in International Relations.

To think that Felipe's life thus far has just been about preparing himself for the day when he accedes to the throne would be a mistake. Rather than merely contemplating the future, he enjoys the moment. A keen sailor, he was a member of the Spanish national sailing team during the 1992 Barcelona Olympic Games and he is also frequently seen enjoying the Madrid night-life.

DE TAILLAC

Exoticism is part of Marie-Hélène de Taillac's make-up. The 35-year-old jewellery designer is French but was born in Libya, grew up in Lebanon, and her aristocratic family is believed to be descended from Porthos of The Three Musketeers fame.

"My first memory of a beautiful *bijou* was the crown jewels of the Shah of Iran," she recalls. "I was about six and my parents had brought back some postcards of his incredible pieces." Unsurprisingly, her jewellery now draws on cosmopolitan influences, particularly from India.

After completing her education in Paris, de Taillac moved to London to improve her English in readiness for a course at the Gemological Institute of America in New York. A chance meeting with costume jeweller Nicky Butler of Butler & Wilson led to her joining that company instead and staying in London for ten years, during which time she also worked for John Galliano,

couturier Victor Edelstein and milliner Philip Treacy. Then, in 1995, de Taillac decided to go East again, travelling in Japan, Thailand, Indonesia and India where her life took a new direction.

While buying stones in Jaipur in June 1996, she visited the Gem Palace, where the Kasliwal brothers have been court jewellers to the maharajas for centuries. "Munnu Kasliwal gave me a ring of smoky quartz, so beautiful and simple," she reveals. "It felt magical, balancing the heat around me amazingly; it was like carrying an oasis at my fingertips." Inspired by the skill of the Jaipur craftsmen, de Taillac designed her first collection there. She now divides her time between Jaipur and Paris.

De Taillac's pieces have been praised for their femininity and understated chic. "I admire the sort of woman who would put on one of my pieces and then take the Metro," she says, "safe in the knowledge that only the *cognoscenti* would recognise its value."

DOMMERMUTH

At the ripe old age of 25, with the money he saved as a computer salesman, a yellow desk, a grey chair and a PC – all three rented – Ralph Dommermuth has built one of Europe's most successful new media and software companies, 1&1, which derives its name from his idea of the perfect relation between supplier and user.

In the early stages – the company was founded in 1988 – this modern-day Cinderella figure decided to take responsibility for practically everything. However, the enormous success of the business brought changes; today, 37-year-old Dommermuth is just one of the managers of a company that achieved a profit of DM135m in 1997 and had approximately 950 employees.

The organisational changes have given him more free time but, as with many others who have had similar success, Dommermuth lives for his work. "No parties, no luxury, no travel, no real extravagances – I prefer a quiet life," he insists. "Anyway, 1&1 is fun every day!"

There must be some particular attraction, however, between new media fanatics and fast cars, since driving them is, for Dommermuth – like several of his fellow young IT tycoons – pretty much his only distraction from work. He is reported to have sold his Ferrari but a Porsche, a Mercedes Cabriolet and a Range Rover can still be seen in his garage.

EIJGENSTEIN ▶

"Stop fighting your business enemies, start loving your clients" is one of the slogans that summarises the innovative management philosophy advocated by Yolanda Eijgenstein. "Instead of sending a reminder to a client who does not pay on time," she says, "you should send flowers to the one who does."

Since she started her own direct marketing research company, Wie Mailt Wat?, at the age of 24, her career has gone from strength to strength. At the end of 1995 Eijgenstein was appointed CEO of

ARA/ABBD, one of the leading advertising agencies in the Netherlands. In 1998 she decided to leave to set up a new company called Why?, which focuses on internal communication and motivation training.

Unlike most management consultants, she emphasises the value of open communication, emotion and intuition – to be productive, she insists, employees need to be happy. Hence the title of her best-selling 1998 book, *The Happy Worker*. Keen to provoke, she once said that all people in leadership

positions should first go into psychoanalysis

Since the early Nineties, she has picked up national and international prizes at an impressive rate. She was voted Dutch Commercial Communication Woman of the Year in 1991 and was later awarded a prize for the most innovative and creative direct marketing campaign in the world. At just 31 she was voted Dutch Businesswoman of the Year. Judging by her success, emotional management seems to be a winning strategy.

ELKANN

The Agnelli family and Italy's premier industrial empire, FIAT, have always been inextricably linked. This was amply demonstrated when, in January 1998 at the incredible age of 21, John Philip Elkann – or Iachi, as his family calls him – the son of Gianni Agnelli's daughter, Margherita, and Franco-American writer, Alain Elkann, was co-opted onto the board of FIAT.

Crucially it was Gianni Agnelli himself, currently Honorary President, who made public the decision to bring his grandson on board. "John's arrival is the most significant way in which the Agnelli family can express its continuing affinities with FIAT and I, myself, was only 22 when I took my place on the board back in 1943," he said in response to those who raised an eyebrow about Elkann's age. "John is very young but he has already shown himself to be capable and sound." With such a public blessing and in an environment where family lineage matters greatly, Elkann's career looks extraordinarily promising.

Born in the US, but quintessentially Italian, Elkann has followed the traditional family path in many crucial respects. As with every Agnelli, he has had an international education and internships in many FIAT operating companies across Europe. An impressive linguist, fluent in English, French and Portuguese, he has also dabbled in another family tradition, this one paternal – journalism. While he was studying engineering and management at Turin's prestigious Polytechnic, he was also an editor of the university magazine, *La Scheggia* ('The Splinter').

Although it is still early days, Elkann has the right qualifications, on paper at least, to play a leading role in running one of Europe's largest industrial empires – and his pedigree is certainly no hindrance.

FIENNES◄

Few actors can suggest characters from 400 years ago more persuasively than Joseph Fiennes, who, at 30, has emerged as one of Britain's most exciting talents on stage and screen.

Younger brother of Hollywood star, Ralph Fiennes, and the son of creative, although not theatrical, parents (his father was a photographer, his mother a painter and writer), Fiennes' childhood in England and Ireland was nomadic - the perfect preparation for a career in acting.

"When you're thrown into a new school every few years, you learn tricks for adapting," he says, "I was forever re-inventing myself."

Fiennes trained at the Guildhall School of Music and Drama in London. After several years of working in small theatres across London, he progressed to the Royal Shakespeare Company in 1996, building up an impressive classical reputation with parts in *As You Like It* and *Troilus and Cressida*.

His television break came in 1995 when he starred as Willy in the adaptation of Mary Wesley's novel, *The Vacillations of Poppy Carew*.

Fiennes' cinematic début was in Bertolucci's *Stealing Beauty*, with American actress, Liv Tyler, in 1995. But it was in 1998 that he really exploded onto the screen, establishing himself as a dynamic and versatile talent in *Elizabeth* and *Shakespeare in Love*. His performance as Elizabeth I's lover, Robert Dudley, was an essentially serious role, while the title part of Shakespeare in the latter film displayed his comic talents.

But he is keen not to become typecast, explaining good-naturedly, "I'd like to get out of tights." The modern-day satire on relationships, *Martha – Meet Frank, Daniel and Laurence*, also released in 1998, and a new dark comedy thriller entitled *Rancid Aluminium*, and *Forever Mine*, a love story, should ensure that he remains an excitingly unpredictable talent.

FISICHELLA ▶

Anna Maria Fisichella, mother of the Formula 1 Benetton racing driver and his biggest fan, has a duty which she takes very seriously. Every week she polishes her son's trophies, which number around 150 and are scattered all over the family home, just outside Rome. She has every reason to be proud. Her son Giancarlo's results in the last F1 World Championship have made him Benetton's biggest hope for the future.

Like many before him, Fisichella's introduction to motor racing came through go-karting; he first took to the track at the age of 11, and his potential was immediately obvious.

His breakthrough came in 1992 when, at the age of 19, he drove for the first time in the Italian Formula 3 Championship, becoming one of the few drivers to win a race in his first season in the category. His performance in F3 was so remarkable that Giancarlo Minardi, owner of the Minardi F1 team, offered him a testing contract in 1995 and Fisichella finally made his F1 debut in 1996. Since switching to the Benetton team in 1998, he has taken second place a number of times, confirming his reputation as a tenacious and challenging opponent.

Born in Rome in 1974, Fisichella now lives in Monaco with his partner and their young daughter. Although he has settled abroad, his love for his home town remains strong and success has not changed his character in the slightest.

Only his Porsche Carrera and his expensive taste in clothes reveal that there is another side to the reserved, modest and extremely motivated young man that he has always been.

FISCHER ◀

Financial *wunderkind* Leonhard Fischer's career has been meteoric. At 37, he is already a member of the Board of Managing Directors at Dresdner Bank, Germany's second-largest bank, and a respected voice on economic matters in the German financial press.

Fischer's love affair with finance started when he studied Economics in Germany and the United States. He joined J. P. Morgan as a trainee in Frankfurt and New York and, in 1991, was made head of trading and then head of Global Markets the following year. Fischer's promotion to Managing Director of J. P. Morgan in Germany in 1994 reflected the huge confidence he inspired in the people around him. This comes, at least in part, from his genuine passion for economic affairs – both national and international.

But Fischer needed a new challenge and left the relative security of J. P. Morgan to join Dresdner Bank in 1995, quickly rising through the ranks. He is excited about his future, though confident enough not to feel under pressure: "I am happy learning and reflecting on issues," he maintains, "but it's important not to slide, mentally or physically, which is why I struggle to improve my tennis and skiing!" The German – and international – financial media will continue to watch Fischer's progress with interest.

GAINSBOURG ▶

Hailing from French entertainment's aristocracy – her father was the singer-songwriter, Serge Gainsbourg, and her mother, the English actress, Jane Birkin – Charlotte Gainsbourg had a difficult act to follow, at least when it came to scandalising her audience.

It would have come as little surprise if she had turned her back on show-business. Nevertheless, becoming an actress was a logical step; entertaining is in her blood. It is a credit to the young actress' talent and originality that the 29-year-old actress has achieved success in her own right.

Gainsbourg started making films at the tender age of 13 in 1984. She also collaborated with her father in a record of one of his songs. Since then she has appeared in some 18 films, often with big names.

An early feature, *La petite voleuse* (1989), was based on the late François Truffaut's last script; in 1990 she starred in the Italian production *Il sole anche di notte* with Nastassja Kinski and in 1995 she was Jane Eyre to William Hurt's Mr. Rochester in a new film version of Charlotte Brontë's classic.

Gainsbourg usually steers clear of the kind of wild parties that made her parents famous. She and her partner, the French actor Yvan Attal, recently bought a house in Provence, where they have settled with their three-year-old son, Ben. Gainsbourg refused to make any films in the year after his birth.

Unlike her father, Gainsbourg considers privacy sacred and in 1998 she successfully sued the magazine *France Dimanche* for its publication of candid photographs taken during her pregnancy. "I'm very different from them," she says of her parents, "but I'm still proud of my upbringing."

Clearly she considers her family an inspiration. After her father died in 1991, she bought his apartment in Paris with the aim of turning it into a museum. That hasn't happened yet, but she still uses it as a second base.

Gainsbourg wears her heritage well; while refusing to depend on her parents' reputation, she acknowledges her upbringing as a creative spur.

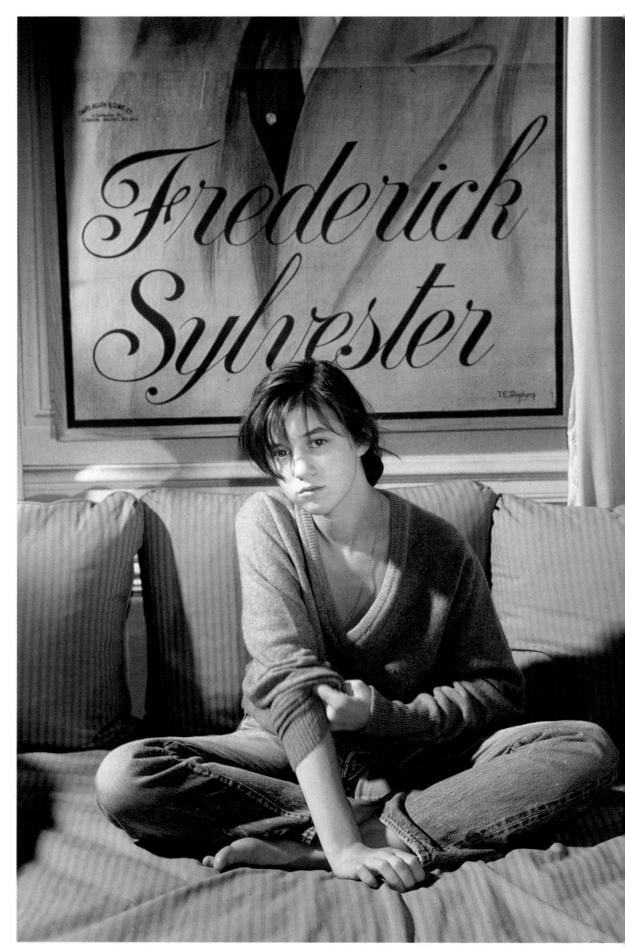

GARCIA▼

Golf may be 600 years old but, as in the case of Sergio Garcia, a Spanish John McEnroe-lookalike, its players are getting younger. In 1998, before his 20th birthday, he had won the British Amateur Title, and experts believe that he will turn professional sooner than anyone expects – himself included.

People in Spain call him 'El Niño' because he was just one-and-a-half metres tall when he was noticed for the first time.

"He is a cocky kid who thinks he can beat the world. And he may be right," remarked Tom Lehman. Comparisons are increasingly being drawn with Severiano Ballesteros; undoubtedly, Sergio Garcia has the same self-confidence and determination and an equally enormous talent. Garcia points out that Ballesteros, whom he considers a second father, became professional at the age of 19 and he seems to be hoping to follow in his hero's footsteps.

His adult behaviour on the golf course is balanced by his passions off the course – not long out of his teens, Garcia unashamedly admits that fast food and television are his weaknesses.

When asked what he likes most about playing on the professional circuit, he gets excited about the free buffets, the lavish attention and the strong competition. But question him about his opponents or his strategies on the course and his winner's eyes really light up.

GARLAND▲

Alex Garland initially wanted to follow in his cartoonist father's footsteps and he started his career as a comic illustrator of school books. But it's probably just as well that he decided he wasn't talented enough for drawing, turning to writing instead. *The Beach*, his first novel, published in 1996, has become an international literary hit. Fellow novelist Nick Hornby claimed it has "all the makings of a cult classic". Danny Boyle, director of *Trainspotting*, has filmed a big-budget adaptation of the book, starring Leonardo DiCaprio.

With two novels already under his belt Garland has, at 30, been described as "the new Graham Greene" and his heroes, J. G. Ballard and Kazuo Ishiguro, have both sung his praises. His second novel, *The Tesseract*, is (like *The Beach*) set in South-East Asia, an area Garland toured extensively when he graduated from Manchester University.

Garland lives an upside-down sort of life. "During the day – I tend to work at night – I do chores, watch a lot of films and videos, meet people and play computer games. I probably would have written more books by now, if I didn't spend all my time playing computer games." He believes his work habits interfere with the rest of his life, especially when it comes to relationships. But that said, he's definitely attached – he's involved with the up-and-coming actress, Paloma Baeza.

He loves Formula One, occasionally writing magazine/newspaper articles about it and is currently at work on his third novel, which will be set in Europe. This has given rise to great speculation about his analysis of his own continent and from where he will derive his next inspiration.

GHESQUIÈRE

Designers recently taken on by the major Paris fashion houses come from very similar backgrounds: American, British or Belgian, they all studied at either Central St. Martins or Parsons. This makes 28-year-old Nicolas Ghesquière an anomaly – he is French and he didn't even go to fashion school.

It also may explain why there wasn't the normal huge crowd when he made his debut at Balenciaga in October 1997. "No one knew me or what to expect," Ghesquière says. But word spread and, the next day, people began turning up at his showroom. Since then he has become the one to watch. The number of Balenciaga stores has doubled since he took over and his collections are always very well received.

Ghesquière was 13 and on vacation with his parents when he first discovered his artistic potential. "I was at that age where you realise there are more interesting things to do than go on holiday with your parents," he admits. "I was bored to death and my escape was drawing." His aunt noticed the obvious – every drawing was a fashion sketch.

After high school, desperate to work for Jean-Paul Gaultier, Ghesquière sent sketches and called him every day until he finally got an interview and, shortly afterwards, a job, thus beginning his fashion career. "He is an incredibly strong person, with a lot of determination and willpower," says Dutch photographer Inez van Lamsweerde, with whom he has been working on the Balenciaga advertising campaign.

When asked if his current relatively low profile makes him at all envious of the level of media attention that other couture houses attract, Ghesquière simply says, "I have another place in the scheme of things. My place is in the long term".

GILLAIN▼

Belgian-born Marie Gillain, the new 'face' of Lancôme, is also an accomplished star of stage and screen, who relishes difficult roles, especially in theatre. Her first film was the 1991 comedy, *Mon Père, Ce Héros* ('My Father, The Hero'), where she played Gérard Depardieu's rebellious teenage daughter. This was followed by the lead role in *Marie*, for which she won the Best Actress award at the 1994 Paris Film Festival.

Since then she has worked with some of the finest European directors, including Bertrand Tavernier, Ettore Scola and the Taviani brothers. Yet, although *Mon Père, Ce Héros* was shown internationally, 25-year-old Gillain has yet to make the move into global cinema.

(It is perhaps something of a compromise that her current project, *Le Dernier Harem* – 'The Last Harem' – is being filmed by a Turkish director, Feran Ozpetek, in Istanbul).

Gillain's impressive portfolio of parts keeps her close to her European roots. Her most rewarding role so far was Anne Frank, whom she portrayed on stage, earning a Molière nomination (France's equivalent of a Tony award).

Critics praise Gillain's natural instinct for acting. "Whatever part I play, I let my emotions guide me," she says. She is doing what she loves most. "I enjoy the sense of trust that binds you together when you're working on a film. But I don't like watching myself on screen. I'm never completely satisfied with my performance and I'm always trying to improve."

This seems modest, coming from an actress whose films have won her several César nominations already. Widely regarded as more than just the latest beautiful French starlet, Gillain should continue to inspire her audiences for years to come.

GOMEZ▲

Aida Gomez knew that it wouldn't be easy to be Director of the Spanish National Ballet at the same time as being its principal ballerina. She likens the difficulties of her profession to a war zone but has managed to juggle her responsibilities very well so far.

Gomez was made for dancing. She began Spanish dance when she was seven, switched to classical ballet four years later and graduated at the age of 12 from the Conservatorio de Madrid. She was only 14 when she first started dancing for the Spanish National Ballet and has never left, becoming – in January 1998 – the youngest Director the Ballet has ever had.

Under her supervision there have been major changes. First, she called in the painters because the grey walls seemed too oppressive, and had the whole theatre decorated with what she called a "vitaminic salmon pink". Second, and more importantly, she wanted to revive a National Ballet which used to be considered one of Spain's most prestigious institutions but which has recently remained too firmly anchored to its past. Achieving this is a big challenge; Gomez has had to face numerous bureaucratic setbacks and questions over her artistic choices but this has not thrown her: "I don't mind criticism," she says. "I've learnt a lot from my mistakes."

Her career as a ballerina has obviously been affected by her duties as Director but she has already fulfilled much of her potential as a dancer. In 1998, when she was already in charge of the National Ballet, she was awarded the Max Performing Arts Prize for Ballerina of the Year.

Gomez enjoys her new directing role and she also frequently choreographs productions. "I couldn't stop dancing, though," she admits. "If I didn't dance, I would go crazy!"

GRIMA▼

Once she discovered that she had a talent for creating jewellery, 20-year-old Francesca Grima had two of the best teachers she could have hoped for – her parents. Daughter of Andrew Grima, the celebrated jeweller, and his wife Jojo, also a designer, Grima joined the family company in April 1998 and since then has immersed herself in every aspect of the business.

"My parents have been very supportive and inspirational throughout the learning process," she says. "They've allowed me plenty of scope for my ideas. To date I've concentrated on things like chunky pendants and unusual rings – the kind of pieces young people my age might like to wear."

With an Anglo-Italian father and a South African mother, Grima had a cosmopolitan upbringing. An equally multicultural education took her to the prestigious Swiss boarding schools, Le Rosey and Aiglon College, where she studied English. She made friends with a broad range of people there, and became fluent in several languages in the process.

Jewellery is in her blood and she has already competed in the De Beers Diamonds International Awards for the year 2000, getting as far as the European finals with her innovative design for a jewelled cuff.

Currently involved in company communications as well as jewellery design, Grima looks set to remain involved in the family business indefinitely, gaining greater responsibility, sharpening her skills and contributing ideas as she hones her talents. Appropriately, she is the latest jewel in the family crown.

HARDING ▶

While most conductors' true potential emerges only when they are in their 30s or 40s, Daniel Harding has proved a rare exception. At 25, he has already led the Berlin Philharmonic, London Symphony, Rotterdam Philharmonic, City of Birmingham Symphony, Los Angeles Philharmonic and Oslo Philharmonic Orchestras.

Harding began assisting Sir Simon Rattle at the City of Birmingham Symphony Orchestra (CBSO) at the age of 18, soon becoming his conducting protégé. He made his professional debut with the CBSO the following year, winning the Royal Philharmonic Society 'Best Debut' Award. In the 1995-1996 season, Harding was assistant to Claudio Abbado at the Berlin Philharmonic, culminating in his debut with the orchestra at the 1996 Berlin Festival. At the end of 1995, he was invited to take over from Carlo Maria Giulini at the Orchestre de Paris but had to decline the offer because of his busy schedule.

Harding is believed to be the youngest person ever to conduct the London Symphony Orchestra at the Barbican Hall (in 1996) where, according to one critic, "he swept the orchestra through an electrifying performance".

Newly appointed as Music Director of the Deutsche Kammerphilharmonie in Bremen, Harding returns to Birmingham to conduct the CBSO in the 2000/2001 season. He is considered to be significantly more than a brilliant and exciting conductor; his performances reveal an exceptional musical mind and a deep musical maturity – extraordinary at such a young age.

HAJI-IOANNOU

With a fabulously wealthy tycoon father, a private education, a shipping business handed to him after graduation, homes in some of Europe's most glamorous locations and a 110-foot yacht, Greek entrepreneur Stelios Haji-Ioannou could hardly be said to be lacking in anything. Yet the 33-year-old was desperate to prove himself when he set up the no-frills, UK-based airline, easyJet, in 1995.

EasyJet's success has come rapidly, thanks to both Haji-Ioannou's drive to achieve and to his engagingly innovative formula – flights are inexpensive and booked directly with the airline, while food must be paid for on board. In-flight style is informal – pilots are the only staff to wear ties – and Haji-Ioannou himself flies on easyJet, mingling with the passengers at least five times a week. The package has proved massively popular, making easyJet the airline of choice not only for budget travellers, but for a host of British celebrities flying to destinations such as Nice, Barcelona and Athens. The company made a £2.3m profit in 1998.

After studying at the London School of Economics, he was preoccupied by a problem which provides the answer to why he strives so hard: "The biggest stigma for the son of a rich father is that he is not anything himself," he explains. Although grateful for the start-up capital provided by his father, Loucas, for Stelios Haji-Ioannou, easyJet was a chance "to prove myself in a business my father knows nothing about".

His meeting with Virgin Atlantic founder Richard Branson also proved crucial: "A Greek company was flying a franchised route for Virgin from Athens to London and I was asked to buy a stake. I decided not to, but I caught the airline bug from Branson."

Haji-Ioannou often works 17-hour days and has branched into new areas: he recently launched a chain of Internet cafés in London and plans to set up the first Internet-based car rental business.

HIRST ▼

Damien Hirst's works of art have provoked powerful reactions: admiration and loathing – in equal measure – from art world *cognoscenti* and the general public alike. But this divide in opinion ensures that, whenever Hirst exhibits his work, he's talked about. Controversy is a vital part of his magic.

Born in Bristol in 1965, he studied Fine Art at Goldsmith's College, London, and while there, established himself as a minor celebrity among his peers when he organised *Freeze*, an exhibition of his own and fellow students' work, in an East London warehouse in 1988. Although some critics suggested that curating his own work while still a student had made Hirst "too big for his boots", he managed to pull off the exhibition perfectly, while drawing attention to his own work at the same time.

Hirst has become most famous for a set of ironically-entitled, modern-day *memento mori*, where dead animals are embalmed in formaldehyde. His 1994 piece, *Away from the Flock*, simply shows a sheep preserved in a box. *The Physical Impossibility of Death in the Mind of Someone Living* goes even further, presenting a 14-foot tiger shark. Hirst has emerged triumphant through his unique blend of black humour, an unflinching preoccupation with traditional themes in art – mortality, especially, but also love and beauty – and an innovative approach.

Awarded the prestigious UK Turner Prize in 1995, Hirst has also been acclaimed in the United States and Europe. Judging from the speed with which the prices of his work go up, one can assume that Hirst will continue to satisfy the demand for his shocking surprises.

HASHEMI ▲

Her early background belies the direction that entrepreneur Sahar Hashemi's career has taken lately. Co-founder of Coffee Republic, the highly successful chain of US-style espresso bars, she was initially set for a lifetime in law.

Born in 1967 in the UK, Hashemi studied at Bristol University and was a solicitor with a corporate law firm, specialising in the entertainment industry, but she soon became dissatisfied with her work. "No-one would involve you in the fun side of the business – that is, the decision-making," she explains. She hoped a sideways move to an entertainment company as its in-house lawyer would provide the solution, but the sudden death of her father in 1994 made Hashemi change her plans entirely.

With five years' experience as a lawyer at the time, she thought she deserved a break and decided to travel first to Argentina and then to New York. "In New York, I always started my mornings in espresso bars with a skinny cappuccino and a fat-free muffin," she recalls. "When I returned to England and started going for interviews with entertainment companies, I couldn't believe there was nowhere in London with any kind of buzz where I could read the papers and have a delicious, foamy cappuccino and a muffin."

When Hashemi mentioned this gap in the market to her brother, an idea slowly came to life: why not step in themselves? They first discussed the project in 1994 and, in 1995, opened their first store. The company is now a multi-million pound outfit with 34 stores in the UK. Coffee Republic bars could be seen to represent 33-year-old Hashemi's character – wholesome, modest and with an impressive capacity for exciting future developments.

HORSTING & SNOEREN ▼

Viktor Horsting and Rolf Snoeren went to the same college, Arnhem Academy of the Arts in The Netherlands. They both studied fashion, they both wanted to become famous and they were both penniless – but they made it. Their label, Viktor & Rolf, is now the talk of the fashion world.

Every morning Horsting and Snoeren meet in their riverside studio – permanently in disarray – in Amsterdam and work together on their new collection. They started to build up their reputation with a number of exhibitions in Europe, well received by the art world, and even before their big break, they provoked attention by launching a 'virtual' fragrance in a bottle that wouldn't open. In 1996, as a protest at the lack of support for their fashion, they declared themselves "on strike" for a season and, a year later, unable to finance their couture collection, they tried it out entirely on dolls.

"We were wondering if we should get ready for the biggest party ever or for the end of the world, predicted by Nostradamus." Talking about the dawn of the new millennium, they declared, "We decided to combine end-of-the-world and party-esque elements in our collection." And that is how their 'atomic bomb' silhouette – a model wearing a dress emblazoned with a replica of a bomb – came about and, with it, success. Their presence at the Paris couture shows in 1999 ensured maximum shock effect.

While commercial satisfaction has arrived at last, Horsting and Snoeren insist on their artistic abilities and the retrospective of their work, promised by the Groningen Museum in The Netherlands in 2001, is the proof that the years leading up to stardom have their value.

KARNÉUS ▲

How does a female singer capture the essence of a young boy infatuated with an older woman? The usual answer is: with some difficulty. But for Swedish mezzo-soprano Katarina Karnéus, the part of Sesto in Mozart's *La Clemenza di Tito* was a triumph. She took on the role for Welsh National Opera in 1997 and captivated UK critics, who were dazzled by her acting and her voice, describing her performance as "electrifying" and "impeccable". Wales has been a lucky place for Karnéus, who was made Cardiff Singer of the World in 1995.

Born in 1965, she is unquestionably one of the most exciting young talents to hit European opera in recent years. Educated in London at Trinity College of Music and the National Opera Studio, her work has been with the UK's leading opera houses, orchestras and choral societies, although she is seen on the international stage more and more frequently.

Karnéus has sung some of opera's most classic, popular and meaty roles: Rosina in Rossini's *Barber of Seville*, Cherubino in Mozart's *Marriage Of Figaro* and Carmen, the latter at the Opéra-Comique in Paris. She received praise for her performance in all three roles, especially from the French press for her portrayal of Carmen; they even commented on the fluency of her French.

Karnéus launched her recording career with EMI in February 1999. Meanwhile, her current and future activities are suitably ambitious: a debut at the Metropolitan Opera in New York, roles in Germany and the Netherlands and a reprisal of her performance as Carmen at the Opéra-Comique and in Tokyo.

KJUS ▲

As Norway's new star of skiing – a sport at which his countrymen have shone over the last decade – Lasse Kjus has established impeccable credentials. Overall World Champion in 1996 and 1998, Kjus made history at the 1998 Winter Olympics as the first person to capture two medals on the same day. It didn't matter to him that they were silver. In a sport where all-rounders are rare, Kjus stands out – he started as a downhill skier but has managed to take on other events *and* come first. He has also blossomed somewhat later than most skiers.

His achievements are all the more exceptional in that he has faced adversity. In 1991, while training in Chile, Kjus crashed and dislocated his left shoulder, ripping the nerve and losing muscle sensation. He still races with an upper arm that is effectively paralysed. "The muscle isn't really there," says Kjus, "I can't use it. I went through a long rehabilitation – I just had to work on it every day." Kjus belittles the problem but friends and competitors express great respect for his stoicism.

The 29-year-old Kjus had a relatively normal childhood. His father was Director of an electrical company and his mother ran a clothes shop. They were supportive when he started skiing lessons just outside Oslo – and especially when he began to compete. "To race, the whole family had to go away at weekends to events which were up to five hours away by car," he recalls. "I have to thank my family for my success." Despite the rigours of competition, Kjus still found time to socialise as a teenager.

Kjus is also noted for his long friendship with his fellow Norwegian, the former world champion Kjetil Andre Aamodt. Direct contemporaries, they began training together at the age of six and remain close friends with a healthy rivalry. Kjus has quietly accepted celebrity status in Norway, where he remains close to his family and girlfriend and enjoys boating near his holiday cabin on a small island off the coast.

KNUTZEN

Tom Knutzen believes that European industry has an exciting future: "We're moving towards globalisation and greater efficiency," he asserts. "Methods are changing dramatically and there is more competition." His attitude is characteristically positive but this is a subject close to his heart. Knutzen, now 38, is Executive Director of one of Denmark's biggest industrial companies, NKT Holding.

Keen to work in business from an early age, Knutzen spent five years at Copenhagen Business School, where he studied Economics at undergraduate level and financial and strategic planning as a postgraduate. He was a high-flying student, joining Denmark's prestigious Faellesbanken part-time in 1985. He left in 1988 to work for the Niro Group, an international engineering company based in Denmark; two of his eight years with the company were spent in the United States. "My move to the US was probably the high point of my career so far," he says. "American business life is fascinating – they have such different methods – and it equipped me with the skills to work in an international company."

On his return to Denmark in 1993, Knutzen was made Niro Group Vice-President and, subsequently, Executive Director, moving to his current post at NKT in 1996. He has already become something of a pillar of the Danish business community; happily married, with two small sons, he sits on several business and educational boards in Denmark.

Meanwhile, his quixotic, cheerful management style gives some clue as to why he has been so successful: "I believe in openness and in setting a good example," he says. "You must have humour on both the good days and the bad."

KOPECKÝ

When the Berlin Wall came down in 1989 and political changes swept Eastern Europe, Petr Kopecký, an Economics student at Prague University, was so impressed by events that he decided to make politics the subject of his PhD. He has since become one of the leading experts on the Czech political system, contributing to the difficult process of democratisation.

After graduation in 1991 Kopecký left his country, first for the UK where he did a Masters in European Government and then for the Netherlands, where he has just finished his PhD. at Leiden.

Kopecký's publications record is quite impressive for such a young academic. His 1995 article, 'Developing party organisation in East-Central Europe', published in the international journal *Party Politics* is what has pushed his career forward. While still a PhD. student, he was appointed Lecturer in Politics at Sheffield University in the UK, teaching and researching Eastern European politics.

The politics of the Czech and Slovak Republics remain Kopecký's focus and a number of Czech MPs have found his advice and research extremely useful during their relatively new, free election campaigns. Kopecký is a frequent visitor to the Czech Republic, where he keeps a house and the Czech media believe he will soon be very influential in local politics. For the moment he is happy living in the UK with his Dutch girlfriend and managing to find time for his hobby: collecting fine wines and studying oenology.

KOURNIKOVA ▶

The tennis world sees its fair share of prodigies but, among them, Anna Kournikova stands out; she is beautiful, Russian and became professional at only 15.

Like most of today's tennis stars, Kournikova has been playing since she was a toddler. She grew up practising with fellow Russian player Marat Safin, whom she often beat. "I was happy that he would always play with me, even though I was a girl," she recalls. "He just wanted to play tennis and so did I."

Her determination has paid off; she was spotted by IMG's talent scouts in 1989 while playing in the Kremlin Cup in Moscow and whisked away to the United States, where she enrolled at Nick Bollettieri's famous tennis academy in Florida. It was just a matter of time before her professional debut at an ITF Women's Circuit satellite event in Michigan, which she won. Her first Grand Slam championship was the US Open in 1996 and since then, she's played in all the major international tennis tournaments, with increasing success.

Ranked among the world's top 20 female players, the 19-year-old Kournikova has yet to attain Grand Slam glory. She is clearly ambitious but insists that she takes one match at a time. She has also adapted with youthful flexibility to the American way of life, embracing the opportunities to play better tennis there, while maintaining her links with Russia. "I often talk to my grandparents," she says.

With her unflappability, considerable critical and popular following and natural glamour, she looks set to be a great future champion.

LEONARD ▼

The Foreign Policy Centre (FPC) on London's Haymarket is a small but influential establishment. A think-tank set up in March 1998 by UK Foreign Secretary Robin Cook, its aim is to provide fresh, independent ideas on modernising Britain's foreign relations. Mark Leonard, its Managing Director, was just 24 when he was offered the job.

Leonard is in a good position to form ideas on European politics. He was brought up in Brussels, where his British father (a former Labour MP) was a political analyst and his German mother was a university professor. After school, he worked as a political researcher for British Labour MP Calum Macdonald, later studying social and political science at Cambridge University. His conviction about the importance of ideas has propelled Leonard from one coveted job to another at an age when most people are still finding their way. He joined Demos, an older UK think-tank, in 1996 after a brief spell at UK news magazine *The Economist*.

It was at Demos that Leonard's name really became known, thanks to a series of controversial pamphlets. His most influential was *Britain: Renewing Our Identity* (1997) which spoke of the country's need to modernise or 're-brand' itself. Leonard threw down the gauntlet, challenging such British values as fair play, great institutions and the sanctity of the English language. *Modernising The Monarchy* (1998) called for an overhaul of royal traditions. Unsurprisingly, Leonard's moniker is 'the moderniser's moderniser'.

With his gift for memorable phrases and his unofficial role as Tony Blair's connection to young people's ideas, Leonard looks set for a golden future. He is already a member of Blair's élite Panel 2000, a committee of advisers from outside party politics which advises the British government on how it should present the country abroad.

LÉVY ▶

French fashion designer José Lévy is not content with traditional couture; a glance at his career shows that he is happiest when facing new challenges.

Lévy was born in Paris in 1963. His decision to study fashion came shortly after he left school and he graduated from ESMOD, one of the best fashion schools in Paris, in 1983. His first menswear collection, under the label *José Lévy à Paris*, appeared in 1990 and won First Prize at the Salon de l'Habillement Masculin, the highly competitive French trade gathering. "Men's fashion is a very conservative market," he says. "I wanted to bring something new to it while making sure the clothes stay masculine."

Bright colours instead of the ever-popular black have been part of his strategy and clothes must be wearable. Designing for women is also exciting for Lévy, who believes that their clothes should not "have to show everything" in order to be feminine.

After his first collection, Lévy established his clothing line across Europe and Asia, worked as a consultant for Nina Ricci, and was Artistic Director at Cacharel Homme. In 1998 he brought out his first women's collection and in 1999 became Creative Design Consultant at classic British country sports clothier, Holland & Holland.

Some might ask what this very Parisian designer could have in common with a bastion of Britishness. "I've always loved England," he explains, "so I was excited to work on the Holland & Holland fashion line. Anyway, the two styles are complementary."

Work consumes most of Lévy's time but he enjoys cinema, travel and art. The latter interest

developed as a child, when his parents took him to countless museums. When abroad, one of his favourite pursuits is visiting a local supermarket. "I love to see what people buy for their everyday use," he enthuses.

LINLEY ▶

For British furniture designer David Linley, fine craftsmanship is a passion: "Furniture is a legacy, a tangible object that can be handed down from one generation to the next," he says. His heroes include the 18th-century master Thomas Chippendale, whom he describes as "a supreme craftsman, as well as a delegator and businessman" – qualities that Linley appears to share.

Linley's design philosophy is to mesh traditional and creative elements. "Design should not be outrageous," he explains. "We aim to produce contemporary classics with subtle details – hints of colour, contrasting textures and fine marquetry." The result is a range of beautifully individual pieces and a private client list that ranges from Elton John to aristocrats and international business people.

Born in 1961, Linley is the son of Princess Margaret, sister of the Queen, and photographer Lord Snowdon; despite his royal status, his was a happy, pressure-free upbringing. "My father had a workshop and we used to execute wonderful projects together," he recalls. "Complex boats, detailed boxes, toys that actually worked. I knew early on that I wanted to do something creative." More early inspiration came from Linley's teacher at Bedales school, David Butcher: "His ethos was to concentrate on making things to the best of your ability," says Linley, "rather than designing something that would fetch a lot of money and then fall apart."

At 18, Linley went to Parnham House, John Makepeace's school for wood craftsmanship, graduating in 1982. The next three years were spent honing his skills at his workshop just outside London, before he opened his first retail shop in 1985. Following its move to bigger premises in 1993, Linley introduced a 'ready-made' range in 1998, which went on sale in the US the following year.

He is married to Serena, a sculptor and the daughter of Viscount Petersham, an affluent Anglo-Irish peer. At time of writing, Serena was expecting the couple's first child. The Linleys spend their free time at their home, a converted school-house which they decorated from scratch, in Battersea, south London.

LÓPEZ ESCOBAR

At many of the summer festivals in Spain, France and Latin America, you may see a beautiful boy with a charming smile being paraded triumphantly by a crowd of older and apparently stronger people.

The boy is called Julián López Escobar but everyone knows him as 'El Juli'. He has probably just won another *corrida*, killing a bull which weighed around 500 kilos. Previous victories have already made him a nationally-acclaimed hero in his native Spain.

For his ninth birthday in 1990, El Juli's parents gave him a present that would change the direction of his life: he was allowed to enrol in Madrid's prestigious Escuela de Tauromaquia. His natural talents were immediately clear to everyone around him and he was just ten years old when he killed his first bull. Throughout his time at the school, El Juli's bullfighting performance was impressive and in 1997 he graduated with distinction.

By the age of just 13, El Juli had already participated in at least 130 bullfighting events, achieving a great deal of success and publicity. The commentators who followed his first tour of Latin America in 1997 were incredulous and it seemed that, even in the world's largest bullring – Plaza México – he was fearless.

"This is a phenomenon that happens once every 50 years," one reporter said when he saw El Juli's triumph in the bullring at Nîmes in 1998, where he carried – as tradition demanded – the bull's ears in his hand. "El Juli's is obviously still an evolving talent," says the President of the Peruvian Association of Bullfighting Magazines. "But his geniality, inspiration and capacity to communicate with the public need no further training."

El Juli is still just 18. The title of his biography suggests the honest answer to how he has managed such a stunning achievement: *El Juli – A Story of Will*.

MAIER ▲

Although he loved skiing as a child, 28-year-old Hermann Maier's early life gave few clues that he would become a world champion. Born in Flachau, in the mountains near Salzburg and close to Sportwelt Amadé, one of Austria's most popular ski resorts, Maier dabbled in junior racing as a child but gave up because of knee problems. He was also too short and light for skiing as a child. "As a kid I was very small, only 50kg," he remembers.

At 16, Maier began a bricklayer's apprenticeship during the summers so that he could work as a ski instructor at his father's ski school during winter. Professional skiing seemed a long way off. Then, after seven years, Maier broke into competitive skiing with a splash. In the 1995-96 season, he was chosen for the Austrian World Cup Team, winning the European Championships. He was World Cup Champion for 1997-98 but his finest hour – so far – was yet to come. In the 1998 Winter Olympics Maier took home gold medals for the Super-G and Giant Slalom. Bricklaying was, he says, "good training" for the strength and stamina needed to compete at international level.

Famed for his friendliness and courtesy, Maier is seen as a model for the super-successful Austrian team; he is an all-rounder, capable of winning in downhills, giant slaloms, super-Gs and combined events. His high-octane performance ups the stakes for fellow Austrians, who aspire to reach his level. In the new millennium, it will be interesting to see how long he continues to compete before he adopts the role (surely perfect for him) of ambassador for the sport.

LUCAS PIRES

Finding new and more inspiring ways to communicate seems to be Jacinto Lucas Pires' biggest ambition. At the tender age of 26, he is one of Portugal's most versatile and best-loved young talents; he is a poet, a theatre writer and a film director.

The son of a prominent Portuguese politician, Lucas Pires was born in Porto in 1974. His first choice of career was law, which he studied at university in Lisbon. But it was at university that he embarked on writing – a very different road from the one that his father would probably have liked.

After a workshop at New York's Film Academy, where he directed his first short film, *Black and White and Grey*, he put together a successful exhibition of his photographs back in Portugal and wrote his first book of short stories, entitled *Para Averiguar do Seu Grau de Pureza* ('In Search of His Level of Purity', published

in 1996). The book won critical and public acclaim and Lucas Pires produced another success the following year with *Universos e Frigoríficos* ('Universes And Refrigerators'), a play about contemporary values, which turned him into a literary star in Portugal.

Lucas Pires' smile is disarmingly shy and his illusions and ideals are typical of a young man in his twenties. These qualities are in peculiar contrast to the acute and clinical eye with which he observes people's feelings and behaviour in his texts. "For me, writing is like a game that permits you to reveal what is otherwise hidden," he says.

Certainly with the publication of his third book, *Azul-Turquesa* ('Turquoise-Azure'), no-one can have any doubts about the blossoming of Lucas Pires' talent.

MAJOLI ▶

Born in 1971 in Italy, Alex Majoli is one of celebrated photo agency Magnum's youngest members. His pictures are an extraordinary reflection of different world realities and range from a project on psychiatric institutions around the world to a report on the life of *favelas* children in Brazil. Trying to portray and understand social problems has been his main objective throughout his relatively brief career and Magnum membership in 1996 was confirmation of the value of his work.

"My family was relatively poor, so I didn't have the money to attend one of those big photography schools," Majoli says. "My luck was being brought up in Ravenna which, in spite of its small size, is Italy's photography capital."

In 1985, while still at school and working as an assistant chef to earn some money, Majoli was "adopted", as he puts it, by Ettore Malanca, a great Italian photographer, who had a studio in Ravenna. "I used to spend all my free time at Ravenna's studios and that is where I learned everything I know today," he says. "In that summer of 1985, I understood that cooking could not be my future."

After a few years of newspaper and magazine projects in conjuction with Magnum – especially a captivating essay on the Kosovar-Albanians during the refugee crisis in 1999 – Majoli became keener on developing his own projects. In order to fund them, he shot a number of CD covers for his friends in the music business.

Among the many ideas that have passed through his creative mind, Majoli is currently working, also with Magnum, on an ambitious, long-term project, started in 1997, called *Neither Land Nor Sea* on port cities – Bombay, Rotterdam, Genoa and many more – whose life evolves around their harbour. "My plan is to make a documentary out of it," he explains, "with a soundtrack and interviews, showing my pictures at the same time."

MARCEGAGLIA ◀

In the Italian business community it is very difficult to succeed as a woman, which makes Emma Marcegaglia's achievements all the more remarkable. Together with her brother Antonio, she is Director of the Marcegaglia Group, a metal manufacturing company based in Mantua and set up in 1959 by her father. She is also a popular figure.

Her public standing derives from the fact that, since 1996, she has been Head of the Young Employers' Organisation, a branch of the Italian Employers' Confederation. As the voice of the Organisation, her qualities as leader and visionary have shone through.

Marcegaglia is Mantua-born and bred. Now 35, she followed the classical route for a successful Italian entrepreneur, graduating with distinction from Bocconi, the famous Business University in Milan, in 1989 and going on to receive a Masters in Business Administration from New York University.

After joining the family business, she started her involvement with the Employers' Confederation back in Mantua and was soon advising on the national structure of the Organisation. Her commitment and fortitude captured the attention of her European colleagues who selected her as Head of the European Entrepreneurs in 1997.

Marcegaglia is living proof of how much can be done with determination. Her strong pro-Europeanism has pushed her to promote greater European integration. This is borne out by her Presidency of the research organisation, Yes For Europe. Marcegaglia's work schedule is punishing and leaves her little time for other activities; however, she remains an avid reader and compulsive observer of current affairs.

MATIC

It is extremely difficult to be an independent journalist in Serbia. And Veran Matic can tell you everything about it. His radio station, B92, founded in 1989 in Belgrade, was banned from broadcasting several times but, thanks to international pressure, has managed to continue its work throughout the last nine years. The risk of being shut down is a constant element in Matic's job but he is a fighter; he started working as a journalist in 1984 and, since then, has always battled for freedom of expression and against any kind of censorship.

At B92 radio, 17 of the staff of 35 are journalists, paid one third of the average salary for a senior reporter at Belgrade Television; the radio has a very weak signal and its transmitter is 40 years old. But Matic's ingenuity has enabled him to find ways of compensating for these drawbacks. His greatest success has been in making creative use of the Internet. Matic has set up his country's first Internet provider and has established mirror web sites in the Netherlands and the United States to facilitate distribution and diminish government control.

At the radio station, they are very proud of their firebrand reputation: "We are the only station that is reporting what is actually happening on the streets of Belgrade," says the current director. "When they ban us, it is the greatest advertisement we can hope for."

For Veran Matic, however, being chairman of the Association of Independent Electronic Media in the former Yugoslavia (ANEM) is probably his greatest achievement, since promoting democracy – the purpose of this organisation – has always been Matic's top priority.

MATTILA▼

With her compelling stage presence, beauty, dramatic ability and extraordinary voice, Finnish soprano Karita Mattila is widely regarded as a rare-voiced nightingale of opera.

Mattila began her singing life at the Sibelius Academy in Helsinki but first came to international attention in 1983 when she won the Cardiff Singer of the World competition. After that, it wasn't long before she was singing at some of the world's most important opera houses.

Her repertoire is wide – everything from Mozart to Wagner and Verdi to Bernstein – but she remains patriotic, frequently performing music from the Finnish classical pantheon: Sibelius and the contemporary composer Kaipainen, in particular. She also remains fervently loyal to her long-time collaborator, the accompanist Imo Ranta.

Now 39, Mattila is often regarded as a younger, European answer to Kiri Te Kanawa: remarkably talented, she is also widely regarded as possessing the beauty of a natural diva and she combines a lyric soprano tone with a growing musical resonance. Her 1999 New York season, during which she appeared at the Metropolitan Opera and the Carnegie Hall, brought her widespread critical acclaim.

Commentators believe that she is currently reaching her prime and her career looks set to flourish well into the next century.

MARIK▲

"I've always wanted to be my own boss," explains French entrepreneur François Marik – and at 40, his wish has come true. Before setting up the cosmetics house, Ayers, in 1996, he had an eclectic international career.

Marik began his odyssey in 1986 when, after university in Lyon, he opted out of French military service and into industrial experience in Australia with the international air freight company, Clasquin. This was not, perhaps, the obvious place for a man with a doctorate in Pharmacy but Marik had developed a taste for marketing while studying for his MBA. After four years in Australia, Marik moved to Spain in 1990 to set up Clasquin España. Two years later he was back in France as International Vice-President.

In 1995, seeking fresh challenges, he set up a new company, MFM, which specialised in art products, with his father in the Czech Republic (Marik's grandparents were Czech). Marik remains the majority shareholder in MFM but moved back to Paris and his pharmaceutical roots after a year in Prague, setting up Ayers. "It was hard to get back into the cosmetic industry after so many years," he says. Ayers has its own beauty product line and sends its specialists to clients' homes. Marik's formula has worked in our appearance- and health-conscious times.

Something of a Renaissance man, Marik was a junior show jumper in France and a footballer for the Australian non-professional league; he has also been a triathlete, golfer, rugby player and parachutist. Married with two children, his idea of relaxation is to go on expedition challenges, often to Africa, and to make television programmes with his best friend, a film director. "This is a real passion of mine," he says. "I may even end up going into film-making full time."

McCOY▲

For most jockeys a leg injury early in their career, followed by a weight gain, would spell disaster. For the teenaged Tony McCoy, however, it was a blessing in disguise, as it forced him to divert his ambitions from flat racing to jumping, with spectacular results.

Born in 1974, the son of a horse breeder in County Antrim, Northern Ireland, McCoy was sitting on a horse almost before he could walk. A the age of 12, he started working in a neighbour's racing stables and at 15 joined top trainer Jim Bolger. Then the leg injury intervened. However by the end of the 1994-95 season, he was crowned champion conditional jockey, becoming outright champion jockey just a year later, ahead of such established stars as Richard Duwoody. He retained that title for three successive seasons.

Few who watched the 1997 Cheltenham Festival will ever forget how the 22-year old jockey stole the show, entering the record books by winning two races – one on a particularly difficult horse, Mr. Mulligan – and this was after breaking two shoulder bones a month earlier. After the Festival, former Irish flat champion jockey Christy Roche was reported as saying, "Tony McCoy should be handicapped, he's that much better than all his rivals."

By late 1997 the Grand National seemed to be the only trophy missing from McCoy's haul; however he was denied his chance that year, being stood down on medical grounds after a fall. "Being barred from riding in the Grand National was one of the biggest disappointments of my life," he declared – especially when, as it turned out, the doctor in question had make a mistake. But he bounced back with typical brilliance, winning the Scottish Grand National a fortnight later.

Although the Grand National remains tantalisingly out of his grasp, McCoy was again top jockey at the 1998 Cheltenham Festival and also did very well in 1999. During the 1998 National Hunt season he reached 100 wins faster than any other jockey – an all-time record.

McDEAN

"Reality is all around us," says British fashion photographer Craig McDean. "I want to create fantasy." This single-mindedness and originality have made 37-year-old McDean one of the world's most sought-after photographers, his reputation underlined by his work with Calvin Klein, Prada, Givenchy and Levi's.

Now based in New York, McDean has come a long way from his Northern English boyhood, when he aspired to be a moto-cross ace. Failing to excel, he switched to photographing his motorbiking friends instead. Accepted on to the prestigious photography course at Blackpool College, he soon became disenchanted. "I seemed to fall out with every lecturer," he says.

His ambition dampened, McDean threw his energies into ju-jitsu, reaching black belt standard. Moving to London, he struggled for recognition until his break came in 1989, when he was accepted as the assistant to respected photographer Nick Knight.

Knight was dazzled by his young protégé, passing numerous commissions on to him. "I took Craig in because of the way he looked – more like David Bowie than David Bowie," he recalls. "But he was one of the best assistants I ever had. It was like having Superman on the team." McDean's new portfolio launched him into the ranks of international photographers. He shot all nine of the current Calvin Klein advertising campaigns, creating their now unmistakable image, and has also worked for *Harper's Bazaar*, Italian *Vogue* and *W*.

McDean is in demand because his work pushes back boundaries with subjects that are often new to him. One unpublished project was on Sumo wrestlers and for a shoot for *W*, McDean used cowboys as his theme and worked with an unknown model and a local girl, with extraordinary results. McDean was a finalist in the 1998 Alfred Eisentaedt Awards with fantastical pictures of the model Karen Elson, one of them inspired by a children's book about pixies.

Colleagues speak of McDean's uncompromising approach, discipline and vision. He is also loyal, staying with the same team of stylists on all projects. It will be exciting to see what image the man with so many ideas creates next.

McDONNELL ◄

"I have always loved magazines," says Jane McDonnell, Managing Director and Editorial Director of Image Publications, the Irish magazine group, and for ten years Editor of its flagship title *Image*.

Born in Dublin in 1962, McDonnell's roots are firmly planted in Ireland. Accepted by Trinity College, Dublin, to study English, McDonnell switched to Natural Science instead. She graduated in 1984 and got a job in London working with *Vogue*. "Studying science was not the normal route into publishing," she explains, "but, when I left university, there were very few jobs in Dublin and lots of people were emigrating. The chance to work in London and with famed *Vogue* Editors, Beatrix Miller and Anna Wintour, was a dream come true."

In 1987, she left *Vogue* to work as a writer on the highly acclaimed British edition of *W* and in 1989 was headhunted to become Editor of *Image* magazine. McDonnell went on to create *Image Interiors* in 1992 and in 1998, masterminded the launch of *Himself*, Ireland's first men's magazine. McDonnell was appointed Group Managing Director in 1999.

Deeply committed to excellent editorial standards in both writing and photography, she has attracted high-profile writers and photographers and *Image* magazine has gained international recognition as well as enormous influence in the local market. "I intend Image Publications to maintain its position as Ireland's premier quality publishing house," she says, "and to develop its stable of magazines."

Outside her rigorous work schedule McDonnell's interests include interior design, literature and spending time with her husband and two small children.

MELANDRI

Every time Italian politician Giovanna Melandri appears on television, her party probably gains a couple of thousand votes. There are at least two reasons for this. Firstly, she is both attractive and charming. Secondly – and probably more importantly – she feels passionately about three causes: peace, human rights and the environment, all issues which strike a chord with the general public.

Her personal attributes, her global perspective on political issues and her status as a role model for working mothers have all served to make her one of the most recognised young politicians in Italy. She has held the position of Minister for Culture and Sports under two successive centre-left Prime Ministers, Romano Prodi and Massimo D'Alema.

Born in 1962, Melandri studied economics at university; her thesis looked at Ronald Reagan's fiscal reforms. Over the next few years, Melandri worked in the private sector and, during this period, began to develop her interest in environmental issues as a member of 'Legambiente', one of Italy's most committed pressure groups on the environment. In 1991 she entered the national board of the erstwhile left-wing party Partito Democratico della Sinistra (PDS) and was elected to Parliament for the first time in 1994 at the age of 32. Since then, her career has progressed quickly, with her installation as one of the youngest female ministers in Italy's political history.

In Italy's volatile political atmosphere – one that has, in recent decades, focused obsessively on the short term and on party political posturing at the expense of meaningful action – Melandri's gentle ways, seriousness about issues and attention to ethics have shown how much success a different kind of Italian politician can have.

MENDES ►

How on earth did British director Sam Mendes manage to persuade Nicole Kidman to take on a role in an obscure play, *The Blue Room*, at a small London theatre for a mere £250 a week? If you look at his life so far, the answer is easy to find. Mendes has achieved more at 35 than many might hope to achieve in a lifetime. Everything he touches turns to gold.

His cosmopolitan background may have something to do with it; his mother is Italian, of Polish-Jewish extraction, while his Portuguese father was brought up in Trinidad. His grandfather was Alfred Mendes, the novelist and legendary *bon viveur*.

After graduating from Cambridge University, Mendes' lucky break came in 1989 when, while working as a lowly assistant at Chichester Festival Theatre, he was asked to take over an important production at the last minute after the main director walked out. The play, *London Assurance*, was an unexpected success and soon transferred to the London stage. Within a few years, Mendes had directed high-profile London and Stratford productions of Shakespeare, Chekhov and Sartre and triumphed commercially with the musical, *Cabaret*, on Broadway.

But Mendes' greatest challenge came in 1992 when he took over the ailing Donmar Warehouse theatre in London's Covent Garden. Through a combination of attracting new plays, staging old classics and bringing in Hollywood talent, Mendes has created a glittering international centre for theatre.

His Broadway work attracted the attention of Steven Spielberg and, in September 1998, he went to Hollywood to direct the film *American Beauty* with Kevin Spacey and Annette Bening.

Many qualities are talked of in connection with Sam Mendes – intelligence, creativity, talent,

energy, vision, charm – but the one most often associated with this exciting young star is chutzpah, and it is this drive which will propel him to keep achieving the impossible well into the new millennium.

entrepreneurial flair was not dampened by the accident, neither were her creativity or humanity. Noticing how many prosthetic arms and limbs were thrown away, she came up with a plan to ship unwanted prostheses to Croatia.

After the publication of *Out on a Limb,* her best-selling autobiography, in 1997, Mills' modelling career, which had been lacklustre since her accident, received a new boost when the Italian cosmetics firm, Pascal, signed her for a three-year contract. Pascal had wanted "more than a face" and Mills was, clearly, just that.

Mills' life has been extraordinary so far. She has demonstrated not just an impressive determination to remain independent but something more too. "Overcoming adversity and, ultimately, denying it the right of passage, has become a constant and perpetual motive throughout my life," she says.

MORÉ

Even as a small child, Luis Moré displayed the gift which has made him one of Europe's most important living sculptors.

The artist, born in Barcelona in October 1971, was only 15 when he made his first important sculpture, from a one-ton block of marble, entitled *Christ Dead on the Rocks*. Moré subsequently embarked on a passionate search for the realism found in classical sculpture and, determined to work in marble, set off for Carrara in Italy, to follow a course at the Accademia delle Belle Arti.

Since Moré organised his first one-man show at the age of 20, sponsored by UNESCO, the Spanish Consulate and the City of Florence, his career seems to have mirrored those of his Renaissance predecessors. In 1992 he was awarded the commission of a lifetime — an ambitious, 3.5-metre marble statue of Lorenzo de' Medici, the father of the Italian Renaissance, for a public *piazza* in Florence.

In the same year he was granted an audience with Pope John Paul II, who made the sign of the cross on Moré's forehead, saying, "My son, blessed be your art". A commission from the Catholic Church followed in 1994, for a bust of one of its dignitaries in Rome. Since then he has worked between there and Mexico City, in the process of developing an interesting sideline — designing his own limited-edition jewellery in silver and enamel.

Moré, who, by the age of 20, had done more marble sculptures than Michelangelo at the same age, has been compared to the Italian master. But he modestly replies, "I only share his technical skill in my use of materials."

For most critics, however, he is more than just a technician. Art expert Juan Carlos Pérez has said of Luis Moré, "He knows what chisel he would shape eternity with."

MILLS ▲

British model Heather Mills has a lot more to her than just glamour. Her life has been shaped and reshaped by truly dramatic events and her real interests lie far outside the glossy world of fashion.

Mills' early years were marked by unhappiness. Born in 1968, she ran away from home at the age of 13, sleeping under Waterloo Bridge in London while working in a bakery.

She became a model in the late 1980s when her husband secretly sent her picture to a newspaper beauty competition but her life took a momentous turn in 1991 when war broke out in Slovenia while she was on holiday there. Instead of returning to the safety and comfort of Britain, Mills set up a refugee crisis centre and, for the next two years, shuttled between Britain and the former Yugoslavia, continuing her modelling career to earn money for the centre. She also founded the Heather Mills Trust, to help young and disabled victims of war.

During one of her return visits to Britain, disaster struck when Mills was involved in a serious road accident, which resulted in the partial amputation of her left leg. Once more Mills rose to the challenge; using this tragic experience as a business opportunity, she summoned the press to her hospital room and sold them her story. If her

MYERSCOUGH ◀

Ishbel Myerscough spent her twenties building up her reputation as a portraitist and scooping up most of the major awards along the way. One of her greatest honours was being asked to paint the actress Helen Mirren, who praised the artist's skill and beauty, for the National Portrait Gallery in London in 1997.

Myerscough's style is traditional, but original; she likes to paint her subjects in minute detail. The result is a slightly stylised realism. "What fascinates me is the fact that everyone is completely individual," she says. "It's the odd, small things that make the difference." Her subjects welcome Myerscough's honesty and praise her ability to bring out facial qualities which are not immediately apparent.

Myerscough, born in London in 1968, started her career at Glasgow School of Art, winning prizes and mentions in a string of competitions, from the Van Gogh Self-Portrait Award to the Natwest 90s Prize for Art. From Glasgow, she moved on to London's prestigious Slade School of Art, where she studied fine art and received a distinction. Portraits were emerging as her natural milieu and her biggest break came in 1995 when she won first prize in the English National Portrait Gallery's BP Portrait Award. This was the springboard to celebrity portraiture and, after the Mirren painting, Myerscough's place as one of the finest portrait painters of her generation was assured.

Portraits are not the whole of Myerscough's craft; food is another object of fascination and critics have praised her grittily realistic depictions. However her interest in people remains undimmed. "I never get bored with looking at people," she explains. "You're always amazed by something you hadn't noticed before."

NIKOLOV

Bulgarian scientist Stavri Nikolov is fascinated by images or, more precisely, imaging: the process of analysing 2-D and 3-D images in order to achieve a better understanding of the world around us. Image processing has taken Nikolov across Europe and given him access to some key research projects in several diverse fields.

Presently carrying out research at Bristol University in the UK, the 33-year-old Nikolov's chosen path was influenced by his parents, both academics. His father is a Chemistry professor at Sofia University, his mother an interpreter and former lecturer in English.

After his first degree – in computer science – at Sofia University, Nikolov went to the Vienna University of Technology and completed his Ph.D. in Microscopy Image Processing in 1996. "In Vienna I worked on images of the surface of diamonds," he explains, "which are essential for physicists and chemists trying to analyse the chemical content of gems."

This work was followed by two years in Portugal at the University of Algarve, working on a very different area – sonar data processing or the designing of maps of the sea floor. "The practical application of this is that we can monitor transatlantic cables and any other objects embedded in the sea bed," he says.

Nikolov's most significant project is arguably his current work on medical imaging. Through a fusion of different types of image, he and his team are working towards earlier cancer detection. He is challenged by the responsibility involved: "My question is how we can use these images meaningfully," he says.

Leaving Bulgaria in 1992 was a necessity because the country lacked the facilities essential for his work. Portugal and the UK have provided opportunities but Nikolov is now looking to the United States as well. "I would like to start a company for software development, computer graphics and image processing," he says. "As a combination, they are increasingly used to solve problems, especially in America." If Nikolov's award-winning research record is anything to go by, his business career will be a big success.

O'REILLY ◀

Managing Director of Independent Newspapers (Ireland), 33-year-old Gavin O'Reilly is an important figure in modern Ireland. Since his appointment at the end of 1998 he has had the task of expanding Independent Newspapers in such areas as circulation, advertising and technology.

Involved in the Independent Group since 1993, when he developed the Independent Directories – a version of the *Yellow Pages* – O'Reilly moved to the Newspapers division in 1996, first as Director of Production Operations and then as Deputy Managing Director.

Educated at Georgetown University Business School in Washington DC, O'Reilly comes from a privileged background; his father, who owns the Independent Group, is Tony O'Reilly of Heinz Foods fame. The younger O'Reilly has inherited his father's drive, charisma and capacity for hard work and seems calmly to have accepted the inevitable pressure to emulate his father's success.

Although he could sit back and enjoy his wealth, O'Reilly makes little time for relaxation; his motivation is to turn Independent Newspapers into a significant international media group.

Married to actress Alison Doody, he lives in a beautiful home in Dalkey, near Dublin. He is already making his mark as a philanthropist, sitting on the boards of six charities. He directs the Irish Heart Foundation, Angel's Quest (a foreign adoption charity) and the Ireland Fund of Great Britain (for children with serious illnesses). A member of one of Ireland's most important families, O'Reilly has, it seems, assumed the mantle of business heir apparent with authority and confidence.

OBRIST ▼

"Galleries should be adaptable places where things are produced, rather than static, neutral white spaces," according to Swiss art curator Hans-Ulrich Obrist. This philosophy has worked for a man who has won international recognition in his field at a notably young age.

Born in Zürich in 1968, Obrist was already visiting art studios at 16. His passion persisted and by 1990, he was curating his own exhibitions. His first, 'The Kitchen', marked his experimental tastes; one half of the show was Hans-Peter Feldmann's work which was exhibited in Obrist's refrigerator, the other half displayed pieces by Paul-Armand Gette, this time in Obrist's bathroom. His second exhibition, 'Hotel Carlton', took place in his hotel room and his third, 'Santis 2500', was a show of postcards at the top of a 2,500 metre-mountain. In a world of conservative curators, Obrist was a revelation.

His concession to the conventional art world was to take on the role of Resident Curator at the Musée d'Art Moderne de la Ville de Paris in 1993 – but on his own terms. He is often on the move, arranging exhibitions in Vienna, Rome, Berlin and London; he is also a prolific editor, responsible for 20 publications, and, within his Paris base, exhibitions are avant–garde. 'Migrateurs', an ongoing project at Obrist's museum in Paris, is intended to be a series of exhibitions by young artists whose work will shown in unexpected parts of the gallery – for example, in the passageways and under exit signs.

Obrist is described by friends and colleagues as compulsively interested in everything and full of energy but he is modest about his talents. "Things have become very rigid in the art world," he says. "The big challenge is to keep things elastic. A curator should be a trigger, not an attraction in himself – art should be all about the artist."

O'TOOLE

Every information market has its answer to Bill Gates and for Ireland, one of Europe's fastest-growing economies, Annrai O'Toole could just be that. Executive Vice-President and Chief Technical Officer of the formidably successful software provider Iona Technologies, O'Toole has gone from university research assistant to millionaire and voice of Irish IT in the space of just eight years.

In 1991 O'Toole switched from his job at the Department of Computer Science in Trinity College, Dublin, to the more precarious role of entrepreneur when he set up Iona with Chris Horn (now Chief Executive) and Sean Baker. O'Toole attributes the company's success to the simplicity of its products and its ability to read the market: "Our experience showed us that real people didn't want tons of technology shoved down their throats," he explains, "so we produced something very open and easy to extend." This has won them such high-profile clients as Boeing, Chase Manhattan Bank and Motorola. Iona went public in 1997, floating on the Irish Stock Exchange and NASDAQ and raising around $140m.

Despite the lure of working abroad, O'Toole remains committed to Ireland. "Seventy per cent of our sales are to the United States and we must attend to that market, but the pool of engineering talent in Ireland is exceptional. We considered moving to America but chose to stay here."

The 36-year-old prodigy has not only stayed close to his national roots, but he has also remained modest in the face of success. With a personal fortune estimated to be around £46m, he has just one extravagance – his silver Porsche.

OWEN▶

The quality that most surprises people about British teenage football sensation Michael Owen is his calmness. His talent — many say his genius — on the football pitch and his achievements at the 1998 World Cup have given him every excuse to be arrogant but he remains refreshingly modest and sensible.

Owen was 18 and had already been playing for English club Liverpool for a year when he was chosen for the England World Cup squad. He proved his precocious ability in two of England's four matches, where the goals he scored were viewed as perfect in their balance and technique. England's then coach, Glenn Hoddle, was criticised for not using his new star in more games but he believed that Owen was still too young for the burden of international matches.

Yet, being the youngest player to represent England this century, Owen has kept his cool and, despite tempting offers from foreign clubs, he remains loyally committed to Liverpool.

His composure and maturity were evident at the end of 1998 when he was made BBC Sports Personality Of The Year and gave a confident speech in front of millions of television viewers.

Owen, born in 1979, is one of the UK's youngest millionaires, thanks to a series of lucrative sponsorships. So what is the secret of his inner peace and charming demeanour? It's probably a blend of strong family ties, a father who played professional football before him, respect for people with more experience than he has, enough free time to play golf and snooker — and a determination to indulge in none of the prima donna antics often seen in the super-class of world footballers.

PALUMBO◀

One might not expect the founder and owner of the night club-cum-music business, Ministry of Sound, to come from such a traditional background; after Eton and Oxford, James Palumbo, son of Lord Palumbo, the property magnate, went into the City to work as a merchant banker.

Restless and unhappy with his work, he decided to invest in the music industry. By the following year, he had transformed a derelict warehouse in a dubious neighbourhood of London into one of the world's most successful nightclubs. Despite its troubled start in 1991, the Ministry of Sound has grown into an international empire, including a music-publishing business, a global radio show and a clothing company. Sales in 1997 topped $40 million, of which $6 million came from the club. While most nightclubs fall out of fashion after a year or two, the Ministry of Sound has become a British institution. The right staff, a perfect team of marketers and the decision to

change the look of the club every six weeks to give it freshness and an air of innovation could be the secret of its success.

The 37-year-old Palumbo doesn't visit the club very often; he prefers to go to the opera or stay at home and read to his son. Most of his days are spent going through marketing reports. Once asked what he thought about the dance music he sells, he said: "I understand it, but I don't find it intellectually interesting. Now Beethoven, there was a real innovator!" However, Palumbo has said that he aims for the Ministry of Sound brand to be the defining name for dance music, as Motown was for rhythm and blues in the 1960s.

And what about Palumbo's future? There are rumours that he may branch into politics, but, as one commentator remarked, "a man who has been used to wielding unaccountable power and influence, and all this at the age of 36, is unlikely to be happy in Parliament."

PASTORI

In most countries, traditional music is slowly dying out but the flamenco tradition in Spain is still very much alive – and it is young singers such as Niña Pastori who are making it more popular by the day.

Born in 1978 near Cádiz, Pastori started to sing at a very young age. After winning a number of singing contests, she was eventually discovered and introduced to the wider public by the singer Camaron at the tender age of eight. Her voice and warmth won over the audience and she released her first album, in 1996, at the age of 18. The album was so successful that Pastori was nominated for the Spanish equivalent of the Grammies as Best Flamenco Artist.

Her second album, *Eres Luz* ('You are Light') which came out in 1998, launched her as a star in her native country.

People close to her say that what is so special about Pastori is her contagious enthusiasm, which she manages to express so strongly when she is singing. She is not just a performer, though, and uses her high public profile to promote charitable organisations, such as Amnesty International and UNICEF. She does this for perhaps the same reason as her commitment to what is called 'pure flamenco' – a sincere need. "My flamenco is pure because it comes from my heart," she says.

PÉREC▲

After ten minutes of watching the 19-year-old French track athlete Marie-José Pérec in action, her future coach knew he had a star on his hands. Following this fateful meeting in 1987, Pérec went on to win Olympic gold in the 400 metres in both the 1992 and 1996 Games. The feat of winning gold medals back-to-back in this event is unprecedented in the history of the Games. She also captured Olympic gold in 1996 in the 200 metres.

Now one of France's most popular sports personalities, thanks to her mixture of self-possession, strength of character and humour, Pérec is famous for her no-nonsense handling of both the French sports establishment and the press. But her spirited behaviour has periodically landed her in difficulties; her association with the veteran coach, Jacques Piasenta, was terminated after the 1992 Olympics because of personality clashes. Perhaps it is simply that the woman known as 'The Gazelle' refuses to be tamed, although her subsequent collaboration with the celebrated Californian coach, John Smith, has been a happy one. She has trained in Los Angeles since 1994. "With John, everything is calm and quiet. I have more confidence in myself," she says.

Brought up by her grandmother, Pérec was so tall and athletic when she was growing up that her teachers were confounded and her contemporaries didn't want to play against her for fear of losing. After an idyllic, tropical childhood in Guadeloupe, Pérec moved to France at 14 for a rigorous academic and sporting education.

It has paid off. Now the question on everyone's lips is whether Pérec will score a hat trick and win Olympic gold in the 400 metres at Sydney 2000. Whether she does or not, the 32-year-old Pérec, with her combination of artistry and efficiency on the track, will remain an historic champion and an inspiration to younger athletes.

PIC-SINAPIAN ◄

"I like to do things fast," says Anne Pic-Sinapian, speaking of her plans for her family's celebrated restaurant, Pic, at Valence in France's Rhône valley, where she took over the kitchens in October 1998. "Maybe it's because I learned to cook very late."

Her formal training may, indeed, have started relatively late – in 1992, when she was 20 years old – but Pic-Sinapian had been absorbing a knowledge of fine cuisine since birth. The fourth generation of one of France's most renowned cooking dynasties, she grew up in the kitchens of her father, Jacques Pic.

Seeing how hard her parents worked, the young Anne Pic took a different course. "I wanted to make my own way in the world, rather than automatically following the family path," she says. Besides, her brother, Alain, was there to succeed their father.

Management studies in Paris, New York and Tokyo led to a job in the export department of Moët & Chandon, followed by a position at Cartier, with responsibility for YSL accessories. She had just begun the latter job when her father died suddenly.

Pic-Sinapian (who, by now, had married David Sinapian, a fellow Valençois whom she met for the first time in Paris) returned immediately to the family fold, working the front-of-house while her brother cooked, and instigating plans to, as she puts it, "blow the cobwebs off the place". This included the purchase and conversion (employing the aid of an architect and her own exquisite taste) of an adjoining building into the 15-bedroom Auberge du Pin.

Disagreeing with this expansion, as well as her wish to modernise the menu, Alain Pic sold his share of the business to his sister, who put her brief training to work behind the stoves. Determined to recapture the third Michelin star, lost on her father's death, Anne Pic-Sinapian has retained several of her father's classic dishes, while introducing her own, fresher and lighter style. Already she has passed her first major test, retaining two stars, but there is little doubt that her eye for quality, her drive and her obvious natural talent will take her much further.

PINKAVA

Czech-born Jan Pinkava has always loved animation and his talent emerged early on; at just 16, he won the BBC Young Film Makers' Competition with a highly original feature, *The Rainbow*. The UK magazine *Movie Maker* hailed him as a "born animator". Almost 20 years later, in 1998, Pinkava won the Oscar for Best Animated Short Film. His feature, *Geri's Game*, showing an old man's chess game with his alter ego, broke new ground in computer animation.

Born in 1963, Pinkava moved to England with his family in 1969, after the Russian invasion of Czechoslovakia. In his early teens, he watched a television programme showing 'do-it-yourself animation' and begged his parents for a Super-8 camera. This was a turning-point and Pinkava worked endlessly on home animations in his spare time, while still managing to excel at school.

Nevertheless, animation seemed too time-consuming. "I realised that animation is difficult and demands tenacity and patience," he says and he went,

instead, to university, coming away with a degree in Computer Science and a PhD in Theoretical Robotics from Aberystwyth University. "But I kept a close eye on the exciting world of computer graphics," he explains.

After graduation, Pinkava got a job at Digital Pictures, one of the best computer animation companies in London, where he worked on television commercials. In 1993, he moved to the Californian animation studio Pixar, responsible for Academy Award-winning features *Tin Toy* and *Toy Story*. His first advertisement there won him a Gold Clio Award in 1994.

Pinkava, who is married with a young son, believes animation should be about telling stories and expressing ideas in an intelligent way. Pinkava's directorial debut, *Geri's Game*, a four-and-a-half-minute feature, took two years to make. If he continues as he has started, there will be no limit to what he can achieve.

PONTES

"I want to show that there's a way of preserving our traditions at the same time as developing them," says Portuguese singer Dulce Pontes, "a way of remaining loyal to one's culture whilst also giving it a new face." This means that, in addition to singing conventional rock ballads, 30-year-old Pontes has revived the *fado* (traditional Portuguese folk music) for a new generation, as the celebrated Amália Rodrigues did before her in the 1940s.

Pontes began to sing when she was seven and could not get the compulsion out of her system. By 16, she was lead vocalist in her older brother Luis' band but her break came in 1991 when she won the Portuguese Song Festival. Her first album, *Lusitania*, released in 1992, was an international best-seller. *Lágrimas*, a follow-up album, came soon after and Pontes went on to tour extensively.

Dulce Pontes strives to be her own woman. "Although people often say I am Amália Rodrigues' successor, I am not the same. I have borrowed some of her ideas but I improvise as well." When it comes to comparisons – made by some commentators – with pop diva Céline Dion, Pontes is "flattered" but insists that their styles are "like different colours".

Still based in Lisbon, Pontes remains patriotic. Although she admits that singing in English can "open doors", she sticks mostly to songs in Portuguese. "I love my language and I'm proud of it," she says. "It's not that I think Portuguese is the best language but I do find its sounds beautiful. Anyway, music is the universal language." Pontes' wide use of metaphors only adds to her image as poet, artist and one of Portugal's greatest assets.

PUTMAN

"Landscape designers are not subject to the same trend cycles as fashion designers," says French landscape gardener Olivia Putman, "because people who commission a design for their garden are keener to reproduce 'the garden of their childhood', without a real sense of time or trendiness."

Her passion for plants and gardens began early in life. "When I was 17, I had friends who had great plans for their gardens," she recalls. "We had 'gardening weekends' and my interest grew steadily after that."

Born in 1964 and the daughter of the renowned architect Andrée Putman and the art dealer Jacques, she initially planned to follow in her father's footsteps and graduated in History of Art from the Sorbonne, Paris. However, she now admits to wishing that she had attended the landscape gardening school in Versailles instead. Her first job – as an organiser of contemporary art exhibitions in outdoor locations – lasted two years, during which time she also created exciting new gardens for several friends.

The switch from exhibition organiser to full-time garden designer came in 1996, when she became assistant to Luis Benech, the *paysagiste* responsible for the restoration of the Jardin des Tuileries. In 1997 Putman became a qualified landscape architect, after receiving a diploma, for which she had studied by correspondence. It was a short step from there to becoming independent in 1998.

Her creativity and originality express themselves especially in her work on Parisian garden terraces where plants and colours are chosen to complement the urban landscape; Putman's singular approach is seen in her preference for plants with contrasting leaves rather than flowers.

Putman's star is certainly on the rise; she has already completed her first foreign project – a garden in Japan – was the winner of the 1999 Parfums Caron competition for the exhibition, L'Art du Jardin, and she is working on several major projects in France.

POLGAR ▼

If there is one game which has always been dominated by men, it is chess. Zsuzsa Polgar has become, as she puts it, the "queen of a kings' game", and a very young queen indeed. Wandering around the house when she was four years old, she found a chess board in a cupboard at home and it didn't take long for her father, a chess enthusiast, to realise that she had real talent. She won ten out of the ten games in the Budapest chess championship for children under 11, later becoming, at the age of 12, world champion for girls under 16. Since then, Polgar has amassed a series of victories in the world's most prestigious tournaments.

"I had to face a lot of discrimination as a woman. No other female player before me had ever challenged and beaten male chess champions, such as Anatoly Karpov and Nigel Short," she recalls.

Because of Polgar's participation, championship organisers had to change their tournament names from just 'men's' to 'mixed'. More and more women started playing chess – including Polgar's two sisters, both now champions as well – and Zsuzsa Polgar rightly considers herself a pioneer of the women's chess game. Now living in the US with her American husband, she recently opened a chess centre, where she teaches, and remains the undisputed women's chess champion of the world.

SCHNEIDER ▲

To write literature, some believe, you have to experience your own dramas first. But, for Robert Schneider, life has been notably peaceful. Perhaps his inspiration comes, instead, from the beauty of the Austrian Alps, where he was raised and to which he returned after university in Vienna.

Schneider had been writing plays for eight years, funding himself through scholarships, before his first novel, *Schlafes Bruder* ('Brother of Sleep'), brought him massive, overnight success. Published in 1992, it was scarcely advertised, yet the first print run sold out within a few weeks. The book had soon been translated into 24 languages and Schneider showered with national and international awards, notably the Prix Médicis in France and the Premio Grinzane Cavour, Italy's most important prize for foreign-language literature. The book has since become a staple text on German university syllabuses.

Schneider's childhood is, perhaps, at odds with his intellectual creativity. Born in 1961 and adopted by a farming couple, he says, "There were no books or music in the house. My family were normal people with no cultural interests. They didn't really understand why I wanted to be a writer but they let me get on with it." Nevertheless, he was expected to muck in with work on the farm. "I had to make hay, which I hated," he recalls. "But now I've come to enjoy working with my hands. I make all my own furniture."

On the creative process, Schneider is straightforward. "I can't start writing until I know what's going to happen," he explains. "I must have the title, the ending and the important events clear in my mind, otherwise there's no point in sitting down to write. Writing is just a technical process."

This clarity may explain the passionate emphasis of Schneider's writing – one of his most distinctive features.

Since *Schlafes Bruder*, he has written the award-winning play, *Dreck* ('Filth'). For the time being, at least, he eschews the glamour of literary parties, happy to live near his parents' farm. His imagination is clearly more than enough to keep him occupied: "I'm finding myself in the age-old author's position," he says. "I live through my manuscripts!"

SCHOLL

Ever since German singer Andreas Scholl burst onto the musical scene, he has been showered with praise. One review concluded that Scholl was "probably the finest counter-tenor of our time," while another lauded his voice for its "crystalline, translucent purity."

Scholl has become one of the leading lights in the current revival of early music, having worked with most of the major conductors of the genre. The soft-spoken Scholl, however, claims not to be ambitious. "I sing because I love it," he explains. "It is a way to praise God and to earn a good living."

Born in 1967 near Wiesbaden in Germany, Scholl began singing at the tender age of seven when he enrolled in the Kiedricher Chorbuben, a children's choral training institution with origins that go back to the 12th century. His formal training came at the Schola Cantorum in Basel where his mentors included Richard Levitt and, most importantly, René Jacob.

Since 1993 Scholl has followed a demanding concert schedule as well as frequent recording projects. For both he has received numerous prizes and accolades. His recording of Caldara's oratorio, *Maddalena ai piedi di Cristo*, was voted Best Disc of the Year by the BBC Music Magazine and also won a 1997 *Gramophone* Award for Best Baroque Vocal Recording. In 1998 Scholl made his operatic debut at Glyndebourne in Handel's *Rodelinda*, an experience which confirmed the versatility of his voice.

When asked, Scholl plays down the effort required to perform so successfully. Appropriately enough, he describes his singing philosophy as "the art of not showing that this is an art".

SEWELL ▼

The British actor Rufus Sewell may not like it but beauty is one of his defining characteristics. Reviewers routinely praise his Byronic looks: dark curly hair, big green eyes, high cheekbones and pale skin. And, more than just a pretty face, Sewell is honest, down-to-earth and a major talent on stage and screen.

Born in London in 1967, he is the son of an Australian animator and a Welsh delivery driver. His childhood was uninhibited and happy and marked by a love of acting. However school drama made him restless. "I thought of playing the hunchback of Notre Dame or some political activist," recalls Sewell. "I wanted to be actor and anarchist rolled into one." He won a place at London's Central School of Speech and Drama in 1986.

Sewell has always believed in waiting for the roles he wants and now has an enviable body of work behind him. His professional stage debut in *Making It Better* (1992) won the London Critics' Circle Best Newcomer Award and his performance in New York as Owen in *Translations* received the Broadway Theatre World Award in 1995. In 1999 he relished the chance to play Macbeth, again on the London stage.

His film roles include the volatile artist in *Carrington* (1995), the lustful son in *Cold Comfort Farm* (1996) and the embittered would-be actor in *Martha – Meet Frank, Daniel and Laurence* (1998), all British projects. Foreign films include the American sci-fi fantasy *Dark City* (1998) and the Australian period drama *Destiny of Her Own* (1999). He was delighted to film in his late father's home country. "He described it as a place of sun and good steak," says Sewell.

Sewell, who married fashion buyer Yasmin Abdullah in 1999, has also starred in television dramas, particularly historical series, although he is keen to move away from the romantic, period leads for which he made his name.

SIEGHART

British publisher William Sieghart is a rare combination: entrepreneur, intellectual and philanthropist. Educated at Eton and Oxford University where he studied Politics, Philosophy and Economics, Sieghart's career began at Rank Xerox (UK) where he rose to become Manager of Corporate Communications picking up valuable experience in public affairs and sponsorship.

After four years, he made a bid for independence, setting up Forward Publishing with an old friend, Neil Mendoza, in 1986. Since then, the company has published high-quality magazines around the world and won over 75 editorial and design awards.

Not content with just running his publishing business, 40-year-old Sieghart established the Forward Poetry Prizes for the UK, Ireland and the British Commonwealth in 1992 and then, in 1994, the National Poetry Day for Britain and Ireland. "Poetry has always been a great companion in my life," he explains. "It voices emotions which you can't always express. Many people love poetry but have been quiet about it."

Married with a young daughter, Sieghart is praised by friends and colleagues for his charisma, energy and intellect. Outside work he enjoys travel, golf, architecture and spending time with his family. Sieghart is also a notable philanthropist; he is Chairman of Streetsmart Action for the Homeless, Governor of the British Institute of Human Rights, Director of the Young Children's Television Charity and Director of the Writers & Scholars Educational Trust.

He traces his humanitarian work to his upbringing: his father was a human rights lawyer, while his mother was involved in public service and both were committed to charitable causes. "I believe you must put in what you take out," he says simply.

SIELICKI

1998 was remarkable for Polish information technology whizz-kid Tomasz Sielicki, President of ComputerLand SA in Poland. He has won three major accolades: Leader of Polish Business (from the Business Centre Club), a place in the *Wall Street Journal*'s Top 10 Executives in Central Europe and one of the World Business Forum/*WorldLink* magazine prizes for a Global Leader for Tomorrow. All this at just 39.

ComputerLand was a minor presence in Eastern Europe when Sielicki, a computer science graduate, joined the company shortly after its establishment in 1991. He became President the following year and the company, a leading integrator of information systems, has flourished ever since. Sielicki's dynamic strategy has been to increase his staff, float on the Warsaw Stock Exchange, acquire competitors – not only from his home market, but also from the UK and the US – and to move into wider areas of information technology.

Amid all this activity, Sielicki still has time for a range of local business and philanthropic interests. Vice-President of the Polish Business Round Table, he's also engaged in national politics, working towards the reshaping of his country through involvement with the Committee for De-Bureaucratisation of the Polish Economy, and he loyally supports local charities, such as the Litewska Children's Hospital Foundation.

Not surprisingly, Sielicki has become something of an industry guru in Eastern Europe. His latest challenge is to take ComputerLand into Hungary, Slovakia and the Czech Republic – and he also has Western Europe within his sights.

SLUTSKAYA ▲

Irina Slutskaya's entry into the international figure-skating world was dramatic. In her first-ever appearance, she won the 1996 European Championships, an achievement she repeated the following year – and she was the first Russian woman to win the ladies' title in the 40-year history of the Championships.

Slutskaya, born in Moscow in 1979, comes from a non-sporting background. Neither of her parents skates although it was her mother, an engineer, who placed Slutskaya on the ice at four. "My mother told me I should get more fresh air!" she remembers. "When I first started skating I cried but, after a while, I began to enjoy it."

Soon afterwards, she began ballet classes, which remain an important part of her training schedule. Experts have pointed out that it is through this early exposure to ballet that Slutskaya can perform a double Biellmann spin with a foot change, a move which demands particular skill.

Slutskaya's recent record includes fourth place in the 1997 World Championships and fifth in the 1998 Winter Olympics. Her greatest ambition is to take the gold at both contests; again she would be making history as the first Russian woman to win either and she continually strives to improve, resolute that she prefers to skate alone. "All the best skating is singles skating," she says. "I love jumps but they are difficult – I have to think about them and put in a lot of work."

At home she is a sporting heroine and, loyal to her parents, sends them money from her earnings. Eschewing the media spotlight, Slutskaya enjoys music and reading when she has free time.

SOLDINI

Although he doesn't think of himself as a hero, racing yachtsman Giovanni Soldini has certainly become one, having risked his life to save fellow-competitor Isabelle Autissier when her yacht was wrecked by a storm in the Southern Atlantic Ocean during the third leg of the Around Alone race (formerly known as BOC Challenge). Autissier has no doubts about Soldini's qualities. "Giovanni is a gentleman of the sea and also on shore," she says. "If I can stand here and laugh now, it's because he saved my life." Soldini's own attitude is simply that anyone would have done the same.

Before he hit the world's headlines, though, Soldini was already an undisputed champion in the tough world of single-handed sailing, having set a new record in the 1998 Atlantic Alone race on board FILA. Soldini's progression from being just another sportsman to celebrity status was rapid. Born and raised in Milan – a land-locked city that he never liked – Soldini made his first ocean crossing in 1984, at the age of 17, beginning with transfers and offshore competitions. Since then, he has made at least 18 ocean crossings – both single-handed and two-man races – winning 11 times.

Short and strongly built, with a mass of untamed brown hair, he has a charismatic presence, although success has not remotely changed his attitude or his passion for his sport. The secret behind his records is his perfect combination of a good training, positive thinking and the right amount of sleep (a point he emphasises with conviction). Sleep is a crucial factor in single-handed races, but Soldini's philosophy is touchingly simple: "You sleep when the boat tells you you can sleep."

Soldini's only luxury on board is, as may be expected of a good Italian boy, pasta. "The only problem was cooking it properly," he laughs, "but I have learned to use a pressure cooker and now I can make perfect pasta at sea."

SÖRENSTAM ▲

For someone who claims not to have been immediately captivated by golf, Annika Sörenstam has come a long way. Indeed her exceptional golfing career easily justifies this 30-year-old Swede's reputation as one of the world's leading women golfers.

She grew up near a golf course and, at 12, her parents introduced Sörenstam and her sister, Charlotta (now a successful golfer in her own right),

to the game. Despite her initial misgivings, Sörenstam soon discovered that not only did she have a real talent for golf, it was a sport that she enjoyed playing. As an amateur, she was a member of the Swedish National Team from 1987-1992 and the World Amateur Champion in 1992. During her studies at the University of Arizona, she made what turned out to be an important discovery: that she could make a living playing golf. Her decision to turn professional was soon rewarded with the Rolex Rookie of the Year Award in 1994, on the strength of three top-10 finishes and the next year brought her an impressive victory at the US Women's Open.

Even more convincingly, she repeated her success at the same tournament in 1996. Her tour statistics since then have been no less impressive: in 1998, she was the Rolex Player of the Year for the third time in four years. What is more, Sörenstam also won the 1998 Vare Trophy Award for the third time in four years, setting an all-time Ladies' Professional Golf Association record for the lowest scoring average with 69.99. Sörenstam's reputation is therefore built as much on individual victories as on the exceptional consistency of her performance.

Despite her constant travelling on the competition circuit, Stockholm remains Sörenstam's official home and she is careful to nurture her outside interests, which include other sports – principally skiing (on both water and snow). Surprisingly, perhaps, for someone who spends most of her time outdoors, she describes herself as domesticated too, enjoying life at home where she likes cooking meals for her husband and friends.

STEWART ▲

Dazzling, fantastical dresses with their inspiration drawn from film and fairy tale are the flavour of the young Northern Ireland-born designer John Stewart's work.

Now 26 and still in the midst of his degree course in fashion at Central St. Martin's College of Art & Design, Stewart has already scored some notable successes in this notoriously competitive industry.

Stewart came second in the 1995 and 1996 Northern Ireland heats of the Smirnoff International Fashion Awards. His promise was especially clear in the second year, with his bold, Hitchcock-inspired pieces. He provided a new take on the 1950s/60s classic chic of such heroines as Tippi Hedren with, for example, the sinister mystery of his 'Birds' dress.

In 1998, Stewart was asked to enter the prestigious charity-based Dolls Against Addiction competition, along with established fashion glitterati John Galliano, Joseph and Stella McCartney. His entry – a striking, white, silk-and-velvet dress embellished with tiny crystals – went on to win him first prize and small wonder with its exciting blend of sexy, feminine appeal and exotic intricacy.

Stewart is hard-working and ambitious, as well as talented. His current goal is to work for Yves St. Laurent: "I'd love to work there – it would be a dream." To have achieved so much while still a student suggests that Stewart's star will continue to shoot upwards – after all, designing clothes has been a lifelong passion: "Ever since I was very small, fashion has been something within me," he says.

SVĚRÁK

"When I was 12, Poppa bought a small Super-8 camera, which he let me use," recalls Czech film-maker Jan Svěrák, 35. "That was the decisive point in my life. It made me realise that what I really wanted to do was direct films."

Svěrák has gone on to make award-winning features: Oscar-nominated *Obecna Skola* ('The Elementary School', 1992) and *Kolya*, which won the Oscar for Best Foreign Language Film in 1997 – the Czech Republic's first Academy Award. His international successes follow a string of other home triumphs.

Svěrák's father is the writer, actor and television presenter Zdenek Svěrák, whose fame in the Czech Republic is second only to that of Vaclav Havel. When Svěrák was accepted to study documentary film-making at Prague's exclusive Film Academy some eyebrows were raised. "Having a famous father opens doors but they open at a price," explains Svěrák. "I knew that because Poppa was so well-known, I needed to establish my own reputation." Undoubtedly he has achieved that, although father and son have collaborated on both of his internationally-acclaimed features.

Svěrák is seen as a bridge between the new generation of Czech directors and the 1960s New Wave, made famous by Milos Forman. His films steer clear of political messages, although their Czech backdrop inevitably reflects political change. The characters in Svěrák's 1994 film *Jizda* ('The Ride') notice, for example, that newspapers no longer refer to people as 'comrades'.

Svěrák, who spends his free time with his wife and two children, has not rested on his laurels. He is looking to his next challenge: to make a successful English-language film. "You can make the most wonderful film of your life," he says. "But if it's not in English, the audience will be too small."

THEYSKENS ▶

"Olivier could make a modern, stunning dress from a tea towel," enthuses Dutch fashion editor Matthias Vriens of this 23-year-old Belgian-born designer who has suddenly hit the big time.

Olivier Theyskens' speciality is opulent, 18th-century-inspired gowns with such wild touches as jet-beaded neck corsets, hair used for embroidery and crows as decoration. It's precisely this kind of detail that, most famously, has attracted the attention of singer Madonna.

In 1998, Theyskens had not sold a single dress when his publicist forwarded some pieces to Inez van Lamsweerde, who was photographing Madonna. The singer's stylist, Arianne Phillips, was so taken with Theyskens' work that she decided to visit him personally in Paris. Phillips returned to the States with a selection of dresses for Madonna to wear on her forthcomng European tour, resulting in massive exposure for the young designer.

His route to such dreamed-of exposure was a spell at La Cambre Fashion School in Brussels, which he left after six months ("I hated the spirit of an art-fashion school," he says). He started to work, instead, from a spacious 18th-century house in Brussels, where he still designs and makes all his clothes.

Every garment presented at his first collection in March 1998 was produced by him personally – "I prefer to do as much of the work as possible myself," he says. Perhaps it is this practicality and hard work which supports his creative imagination and ensures such beautifully ornate clothes keep a very personal signature.

With his clothes now going on sale at boutiques in Europe and America, Theyskens has big plans to dress more of the world's beautiful and prominent women. Meanwhile, even fashion competitors are generous in their praise for his talent.

THIMISTER

Dutch-born designer Josephus Thimister is as famous in Paris for his showroom with its eccentric choice of decoration – stuffed tigers and elephants – as for his superb designs. One of fashion's hottest properties, he is articulate, confident and original. Clothes must be "relevant" and wearable but Thimister's sources of inspiration are more whimsical, from as far away as India and as far back as World War II military uniforms and 19th-century Basque fishing communities. His intelligence is manifest in the forethought put into his shows.

The 38-year-old Thimister was educated at the Royal Academy of Fine Arts in Antwerp. His first important post was designer for Parisian fashion house Balenciaga, where he worked from 1992 to 1997. His relationship with the company was impeccable. In 1997 he set up his own design label, and the following year, was taken on as the new designer for the Italian Genny range.

Thimister loves to innovate. He has invented new fabrics – fusing plastic and chiffon – and revived old ones, like the white silk worn by British soldiers in colonial India. His haute couture follows a minimalist, perfectionist approach: dresses are sometimes cut and re-cut four or five times before they are ready.

"For me, couture is about cutting, not feathers," says Thimister. "Bias-cut dresses are actually more difficult to make than very decorated ones because every stitch shows." His beautiful, yet practical, women's clothes have made him the toast of the fashion *cognoscenti*, with such high-profile customers as Inès de la Fressange and Carole Bouquet. Thimister will most certainly continue to experiment and surprise the fashion world for some time to come. But his emphasis remains simple. "A dress is just a piece of fabric with a hole for the head and two holes for the arms," he says. "What transforms it is the woman who wears it."

VAN ALMSICK ◀

Swimmer Franziska van Almsick is viewed as one of the first true sports stars of the new Germany. Her popularity is not confined to young or old, east or west. She is beautiful and down-to-earth – a darling of the German advertising industry and media.

Born in East Berlin in 1978, she toyed with the idea of being a vet or an interior designer but had established her credentials as a swimmer while still at junior school. She remains close to her roots, still living in Berlin and describing her family as a "constant support". It was her performance at the 1992 Barcelona Olympic Games that shot van Almsick to fame. Taking a silver and two bronze medals, she invited comparisons with the 17-year-old Boris Becker's Wimbledon victory in 1985. Her highest point was probably the 1994 World Championships in Rome where she set a new world record for her best event, the 200 metres freestyle.

Although commentators are unequivocal about van Almsick's enormous talent, it has not been an easy ride for the superstar since her spectacular debut. The 1996 Olympic Games, where van Almsick failed to take home a gold medal, were a disappointment but the Games were also testament to her ambition. Her 'failure' actually meant two silver medals and a bronze – quite a stash. But injury, illness, self-doubt and no Olympic gold – in the face of so much expectation – took their toll and van Almsick threatened to leave the sport; a motorcycle accident in 1997 also caused her to re-assess and take a break. But, after two months, van Almsick was desperate to get back into a pool.

Her goal now is to win gold in the 2000 Sydney Olympic Games. She has applied her considerable determination to achieving this aim and scooped up gold and silver medals in the 1998 World Championships in Perth. Commentators believe she is swimming better than ever and could reach another peak of achievement in Sydney.

VAN ORANJE

The youngest of Queen Beatrix's three sons, Prince Constantijn van Oranje has lived his life as a typical Dutch royal, trying to meet the public expectations that come with his family's historical role, while maintaining a degree of privacy and normality that has eluded most of Europe's other royal families. He feels committed to the 'public cause', as both his academic pursuits and his career choice have demonstrated so far.

Born in 1969, he spent his early youth at the family residence Drakensteyn Castle. Constantijn remembers that period as one of the best in his life, since all the family seemed to live in an 'ordinary' style. When his mother was crowned Queen of the Netherlands in 1980, he moved to the Hague.

At the University of Leiden, Constantijn proved himself an active and prominent member of the Netherlands' oldest and largest student union, Minerva. Here, as well as satisfying his pan-European interests, developed during extensive travels through -out the continent, he demonstrated an artistic side, with his drawings and illustrations – a talent which probably comes from his mother, who is known for her impressive sculptures.

A true polyglot, Constantijn finally launched his European career in 1995, moving to Brussels to work for the Dutch commissioner at the European Commission. Although not entirely immune to glamour, he also clearly feels at ease in the political world of Brussels. He has demonstrated the talent and the tact necessary to become a true statesman and although his brother's eventual accession to the Dutch throne is not in any doubt, some say that Constantijn would be as well-suited as his older brother to performing the careful balancing act that the role of a European king in the 21st century involves.

VAN LAMSWEERDE ▲

Avant-garde photographer Inez van Lamsweerde doesn't believe in just reflecting what she sees. A simple shot of a model becomes, in her hands, a startling urban collage, the woman's face sandwiched between classic images of Times Square in New York. This is just one example of Van Lamsweerde's award-winning work, which she describes as "surreal and hyper-real" and which have attained shock value through their juxtaposition of conventional images with computer-generated effects. Her ground-breaking experiments have put the Netherlands on the international map for art and fashion.

Van Lamsweerde, born in 1963, began her career in her native Amsterdam, spending four years at Rietveld Academy of Arts. Her big break was a photo assignment for Vital Statistics in 1991, which won her the PANL and European Kodak Awards as well as widespread attention. In 1992 she took up a one-year artist's residency at the Institute of Contemporary Arts in New York.

Since then she has mounted numerous solo and group exhibitions at top contemporary art venues in Europe and the United States. Van Lamsweerde's work can be divided between fashion, advertising and art-for-art's-sake. With her long-time business partner, Vinoodh Matadin, she has created the images for international advertising campaigns ranging from Kodak to Yohji Yamamoto. Her exhibitions are often inspired by the idea of women: their natural beauty, how it can be experimented with and how it is portrayed by the media.

Van Lamsweerde remains an enthusiastic exponent of her special form of photo-montage, especially the opportunities it gives to find the ideal backdrop. "It's fantastic being able to pretend to travel anywhere in the world without being there," she says. "We get the most intense sunsets. Colours shift when you blend them over one another, so things happen that you could not have planned. A lot of great things can be done digitally, but I don't think it will ever threaten conventional photography." Her words play down her achievements – some of the most exciting to hit photography for decades.

VINTERBERG

Danish film director Thomas Vinterberg has long been considered a prodigious talent at home but it was only in 1998 that he really hit the world stage with his second feature, *The Celebration*.

Vinterberg came to prominence as part of an avant-garde cinematic movement in Denmark, Dogme 95, spearheaded by Lars von Trier. Their credo, which amounts to a set of rules agreed on by four directors, precludes artificial light, music and sound effects. The director must hold the camera by hand and should not be included in the film credits.

"I am a confused, chaotic sort of person," says Vinterberg, "so I appreciate this kind of regularity. The collective feeling arising from making the leap together has been extremely stimulating."

Vinterberg tasted success relatively early. He was born in 1969 and graduated from the National Film School of Denmark in 1993. As a student, his promise shone through; his film, *Last Round*, won the jury prize and producer's prize at the International Student Film Festival in Munich in 1993. Two early, short films also scooped up international awards. Vinterberg's first feature film was *The Greatest Heroes* (1996), directed according to more usual conventions. He used the cast of his first film for *The Celebration*, which received the Special Jury Prize at Cannes and the New York Film Critics Circle award for Best Foreign Film.

He remains committed to Danish cinema but also draws inspiration from abroad. "I am fond of *The Godfather*," he says, "and it would be interesting to see Coppola or Scorsese do a Dogme film."

VENGEROV▲

Young female musicians do not have the monopoly on beauty, charisma and sex appeal. Maxim Vengerov has them all, as well as exceptional talent.

Born in Novosibirsk, Western Siberia, in August 1974, Vengerov recalls the time his mother went to hear David Oistrakh playing the Tchaikovsky violin concerto: "I was in my mother's belly and very noisy, apparently, kicking around, so clearly I was moved by the performance!"

His grandfather wanted him to become a weight-lifter but Vengerov, instead, began violin lessons at the age of five with a local teacher, Galina Turtschaninova. "Galina gave me a passionate love for the violin," he recalls. "Playing it soon became as much of an instinct as walking, speaking or eating. For me, the violin has never been just a tool – it was always an extension of my soul."

Vengerov first came to international attention in 1989 when, at the age of 14, he gave a recital at the Concertgebouw in Amsterdam, which has now become his home. Five years later he was named *Gramophone*'s Young Artist of the Year and the magazine fêted him again in 1995, naming his recording of the Shostakovich and Prokofiev violin concertos its Record of the Year.

Now aged 26, Vengerov has worked with some of the world's greatest conductors and played alongside some of the best international orchestras. But his happiest memory was getting to know the great Rostropovich: "There are many great interpreters today, but here was one who actually knew the composers. He talked about Prokofiev, Shostakovich or Britten as if he was talking about his own father."

As Vengerov reaches out for ever greater challenges, among them a concerto being composed especially for him by Schedrin, critics speak of the parallels between the young violinist and Rostropovich praising their "effortless brilliance and ability to hold audiences in the palm of their hand".

VENTOLA▶

Currently playing for Inter Milan, where his contract ends in 2003, Nicola Ventola belongs to a team that already has some of the best footballers in the world. Probably because of this wealth of talent, Ventola's skills were properly recognised only when his team-mates, Roberto Biaggio and Ronaldo, were both injured during the 1998-99 season. Not only did he succeed in his duty to make their absence as invisible as possible to the public, he instantly became the player that everyone was watching.

Ventola, the son of a lawyer, was brought up in the southern Italian town of Bari. His fascination with football began as a small child and was quite normal in a part of the world where sportsmen are idolised.

He started playing for the premier Bari team in 1994, based close to his home. After three very successful years, Inter Milan took a £10 million gamble on Ventola and brought him to Milan.

Even when Ronaldo recovered from his injury, Ventola remained in the limelight with excellent performances throughout 1999. Despite his youth, he has already given careful thought to what he wants to do in the future; he will finish his law studies, at which he excelled in his first year and which he started before he became committed to Inter Milan. He may then go on to work with his brother, Domenico, who is a successful sports manager. But, for now, his place is definitely on the pitch.

WILKINSON ▶

English rugby can hardly believe its latest star, Jonny Wilkinson. Brought on for the first time to play against Australia in 1998, Wilkinson, who was just 18, was the youngest person to have played for England since 1927.

Observers questioned the wisdom of using such an inexperienced player but Wilkinson silenced his critics with his fifth international appearance, in March 1999, in England's Five Nations victory over France.

The match was a glittering showcase for his talents – he scored all the match points England needed to secure the important victory.

Wilkinson, who has been playing for Newcastle Rugby Football Club (the 'Falcons') since 1997, has remained calm in the face of praise and pressure.

"What has happened to me has been so sudden," he says. "One minute I was in the England Schools team, the next I was being asked to join the full England squad. It was an enormous surprise but I have to stay level-headed."

His father and agent, Phil, is seen as a steadying influence, as is his coach, veteran England player Rob Andrew.

Born in 1979 into a rugby-mad family, as a schoolboy Wilkinson chose rugby over cricket and tennis, in which he also excelled. He was also academically successful but, for the time being, has turned down offers of a university place.

Meanwhile, endorsement offers are flooding in, not least because Wilkinson has the youth, good looks and clean playing skills that both the English game and the media have been looking for. The French newspaper, *Journal du Dimanche*, dubbed him "angel face" after his Five Nations triumph.

But Wilkinson's real joy lies in playing rugby, not publicity. "I don't listen to what the press says," this reluctant hero insists. "It is very flattering sometimes but it's something I don't need." **E**

The oceans' best address.

Oceanco has taken the lead. A daring expression of excellence to grace the world's oceans.

A fresh approach combining the ultimate in engineering technology and the traditional Dutch skills of the hand and the eye.

The passion, enthusiasm and attitude of all the people at Oceanco elevate our yachts above the rest.

International networks give creative designers and project managers the computer power and tools to produce a far better product.

Whatever the reason, Oceanco is constantly exploring better ways to give the customer what they want.

The Oceans' best address.

INDEX I

LISTING BY ALPHABET

ALPHABETICAL INDEX

PLEASE NOTE:

Entries which begin with a definite article (*The, Le, La, Il, El, Der, Die* etc.) appear under the first letter of the name proper, as do entries which begin with initials.

Hotels and restaurants normally appear under the first letter of the name proper, except in a few cases where the name cannot stand alone. (For example, Hôtel du Cap is listed under 'H', whereas the Hotel Imperial and the Hotel Cala di Volpe are listed under 'I' and 'C' respectively).

Wine châteaux and domaines are listed under the name proper; however, entries such as hotels or properties whose name begins with Château or Domaine are listed under 'C' or 'D' respectively.

INDEX I

INDEX I

INDEX I

INDEX II

LISTING BY COUNTRY

INDEX BY COUNTRY

PLEASE NOTE:
Entries which begin with a definite article (*The, Le, La, Il, El, Der, Die etc.*) appear under the first letter of the name proper, as do entries which begin with initials.

Hotels and restaurants normally appear under the first letter of the name proper, except in a few cases where the name cannot stand alone. (For example, Hôtel du Cap is listed under 'H', whereas the Hotel Imperial and the Hotel Cala di Volpe are listed under 'I' and 'C' respectively).

Wine châteaux and domaines are listed under the name proper; however, entries such as hotels or properties whose name begins with Château or Domaine are listed under 'C' or 'D' respectively.

PREVIOUS PAGE: *Flower table-setting courtesy of Thomas Goode*

INDEX II

INDEX II

INDEX II

This earth has a

continent that has a

nation that has a

city that has a

street that has a

store that has

precisely what you want.

Did we mention we deliver?

WWW.BESTSELECTIONS.COM

BestSelections.com

INDEX III

LISTING BY PRODUCT CATEGORY

INDEX BY PRODUCT CATEGORY

PLEASE NOTE:

Entries which begin with a definite article (*The, Le, La, Il, El, Der, Die etc.*) appear under the first letter of the name proper, as do entries which begin with initials.

Hotels and restaurants normally appear under the first letter of the name proper, except in a few cases where the name cannot stand alone. (For example, Hôtel du Cap is listed under 'H', whereas the Hotel Imperial and the Hotel Cala di Volpe are listed under 'I' and 'C' respectively).

Wine châteaux and domaines are listed under the name proper; however, entries such as hotels or properties whose name begins with Château or Domaine are listed under 'C' or 'D' respectively.

(RS) and (BKS) denotes entries which appear in the Rising Stars and Best Kept Secrets listings respectively.

AIR CHARTER
Air Harrods **59** *UK*
Flexjet Europe **110** *UK*
Lauda Executive Service **143** *Austria*
Lynton Aviation **151** *UK*
PrivatAir **175** *Switzerland*
TAG Aviation **192** *Switzerland*

ANTIQUES
Adrian Sassoon **58** *UK*
Alberto Di Castro, Antichità **61** *Italy*
Antichi Maestri Pittori **65** *Italy*
Apolloni, Galleria Antichita **66** *Italy*
Aveline, Galerie **69** *France*
Axel Vervoordt **69** *Belgium*
Bernard & Benjamin Steinitz **74**
    France
Carlo Orsi, Galleria **82** *Italy*
Christopher Gibbs **89** *UK*
Christopher Hodsoll **89** *UK*
Davide Halevim **97** *Italy*
Didier Aaron & Cie **99** *France*
Eskenazi **106** *UK*
Fallani **107** *Italy*
Florence Lopez **229** (BKS) *France*
François Léage **111** *France*
Galerie Michel Descours **230**
    (BKS) *France*
Giovanni Pratesi **116** *Italy*
Guinevere Antiques **122** *UK*
Jacques Kugel Antiquaires **135** *France*
John Eskenazi **137** *UK*
John Hobbs **138** *UK*
Kraemer & Cie **141** *France*
Lopez de Aragon, Felix **148** *Spain*
Luis Elvira **151** *Spain*
Mallett **152** *UK*
Nella Longari, Galleria **162** *Italy*
Neuhaus Kunsthandel, Albrecht **162**
    Germany
O'Sullivan Antiques **163** *Ireland*
Partridge Fine Art **167** *UK*
Perrin Antiquaires **170** *France*
Phillips, S.J. **171** *UK*
Ronald Phillips & Sons **182** *UK*
Sam Fogg **184** *UK*
Scott Barnes **236** (BKS) *Italy*
Segoura, Galerie **187** *France*
Simone de Looze **236** (BKS)
    Netherlands

Sweerts de Landas **191** *UK*
Vanderven & Vanderven
    Oriental Art **198** *Netherlands*
Victoria Bridgeman **237** (BKS) *UK*
Wahlström, B & L **237** (BKS) *Sweden*

ARCHITECTS & DECORATORS
Alain Demachy **60** *France*
Alberto Pinto **61** *France*
André de Cacqueray **63** *UK*
Angelica Frescobaldi **64** *Italy*
Bruno Lafourcade **79** *France*
Casa Nova **213** (RS) *Germany*
Chester Jones **87** *UK*
Christian Liaigre **88** *France*
Christophe Decarpentrie (RS)
    214 *Belgium*
Claire Bataille & Paul Ibens Design N.V. **90**
    Belgium
Colefax and Fowler - Wendy Nicholls
    91 *UK*
Collett-Zarzycki **92** *UK*
David Collins Architecture & Design
    97 *UK*
David Mlinaric **97** *UK*
Frédéric Méchiche **214** (RS) *France*
Gabhan O'Keeffe **113** *UK*
Gilles Saint-Gilles **116** *France*
Graf, Ariodante **121** *France*
Heiberg Cummings Design
    215 (RS) *Norway*
Holger Stewen **129** *Germany*
Jacques Garcia **135** *France*
Jacques Grange **135** *France*
Jaime Parladé **135** *Spain*
Jane Churchill Interiors **135** *UK*
Javier Barba **136** *Spain*
Jean-Pierre Heim & Associates **215**
    (RS) *France*
Jean Pierre Martel **136** *Spain*
Jérôme Abel Seguin **215** (RS) *France*
John Pawson **138** *UK*
John Minshaw **232** (BKS) *UK*
John Stefanidis & Assoc. **138** *UK*
Lazzarini Pickering **216** (RS) *Italy*
Nina Campbell **162** *UK*
Munkenbeck & Marshall (RS)
    216 *UK*
Piero Castellini Baldissera **171** *Italy*
Rem Koolhass **177** *Netherlands*

Roberto Peregalli **181** *Italy*
Toni Cordero **195** *Italy*
Tim Hatton **220** (RS) *UK*
Verde Visconti di Modrone **199** *Italy*

ART FAIRS
Art Basel **67** *Switzerland*
Art Cologne **67** *Germany*
Biennale Internationale des Antiquaires
    75 *France*
Biennale Internazionale dell' Antiquariato
    75 *Italy*
Grosvenor House Art & Antiques Fair
    122 *UK*
TEFAF Maastricht **193** *Netherlands*

ARTS DE LA TABLE
Antonietta Mazzotti Emaldi
    66 *Italy*
Baccarat **70** *France*
Barovier & Toso **73** *Italy*
Bernardaud **74** *France*
Christofle **89** *France*
Cristalleries Saint Louis **95** *France*
De Lamerie **99** *UK*
Frette **111** *Italy*
Georg Jensen **114** *Denmark*
Herend **128** *Hungary*
KPM **141** *Germany*
Lalique **142** *France*
Mangani **153** *Italy*
Moser **159** *Czech Republic*
Nymphenburg Porzellan- Manufaktur
    163 *Germany*
Porthault, D. **173** *France*
Pratesi **174** *Italy*
Puiforcat **175** *France*
Richard Ginori 1735 **179** *Italy*
Riedel Crystal **179** *Austria*
Robbe & Berking **180** *Germany*
Rosenthal **219** (RS) *Germany*
Royal Copenhagen **182** *Denmark*
Venini **199** *Italy*
Villeroy & Boch **202** *Germany*
Waterford Crystal **203** *Ireland*

AUCTION HOUSES
Antiquorum **65** *Switzerland*
Christie's **89** *UK*
Etude Tajan **106** *France*
Sotheby's **189** *UK*

CASINOS
50 St James **184** *UK*
Ambassadeurs, Les **62** *UK*
Aspinalls **67** *UK*
Casino de Divonne **83** *France*
Casino de Monte-Carlo **83**
    Monaco
Crockfords **95** *UK*
Spielbank Baden-Baden **189** *Germany*

CASTLES & VILLAS
Blairquhan **226** (BKS) *UK*
Blandings **76** *UK*
Chalet Brames **85** *France*
Château de Puyricard **86** *France*

Château de Tourreau **87** *France*
Glin Castle **117** *Ireland*
Hatton Castle **127** *UK*
Highclere Castle **231** (BKS) *UK*
Paço da Gloria **166** *Portugal*
Palacio de Campo Real **166** *Spain*
Penuela, La **170** *Spain*
Radi Di Montagna **177** *Italy*
Schloss Wasserburg **185** *Austria*
Villa La Loggia **200** *Italy*
Villa la Rivella **200** *Italy*
Villa Pisani **237** (BKS) *Italy*
Villa Reale **201** *Italy*

CHAUFFEUR SERVICES
Geneva Limousine **114** *Switzerland*
Inpersau **133** *France*
Sater **184** *Italy*
Wings of Desire **205** *UK*

COSMETIC SURGEONS
Basra, Dr. Dev **71** *UK*
Besins, Dr. Thierry **74** *France*
Bezzola, Dr. Alain **75** *Switzerland*
Bowen, Dr. John **76** *UK*
Campiglio, Dr. Gianluca **82** *Italy*
Celin, Dr. John **213** (RS) *UK*
Cornette De St Cyr, Dr. Bernard
    93 *France*
Davies, Dr. Dai **97** *UK*
Lavezzari, Dr. Emilio **145** *Italy*
Micheels, Dr. Patrick **158**
    Switzerland
Ohana, Dr. Sydney **164** *France*
Sebagh, Dr. J.L. **186** *UK*
Silva Netto, Dr. Arthur **187** *Italy*

EMPLOYMENT AGENCIES -
DOMESTIC STAFF
AgenC, The **58** *UK*
Lady Apsley School for Butlers & Butler
    Agency, The **142** *UK*

FASHION & ACCESSORIES
A. Ugolini & Figli **58** *Italy*
Alberta Ferretti **61** *Italy*
Alfred Dunhill **61** *UK*
Alice Cadolle Lingerie **61** *France*
Anderson & Sheppard **62** *UK*
Anouska Hempel Couture
    65 *UK*
Antonio D'Amico **211** (RS) *Italy*
Arnys **66** *France*
Artioli **67** *Italy*
Balenciaga **211** (RS) *France*
Balmain **70** *France*
Belinda Robertson **211** (RS) *UK*
Bella Freud **212** (RS) *UK*
Berluti **74** *France*
Birger Christensen **75**
    Denmark
Bogner **76** *Germany*
Bonpoint **76** *France*
Brioni Roman Style **76** *Italy*
Burberry **212** (RS) *UK*
Burini **226** (BKS) *Italy*
Campagna **82** *Italy*

INDEX III

INDEX III

INDEX III

INDEX III

EUROPE'S ELITE 1000
THE ULTIMATE LIST
THE MILLENNIUM ISSUE

CHAIRMAN
EDITOR-IN-CHIEF
Kevin Kelly

SENIOR EDITOR
Sandra Lane
Managing Editor: Lynda Weatherhead
Picture Editor: Nicole Bettelley

Editor, France: Nicola Mitchell
Contributing Editor: Caroline Kellett

CONTRIBUTING WRITERS & RESEARCHERS
Raymond Blake, Barbara Gurawska, Mark Kelly, Ruth Hillenbrand,
Nessrin Gräfin zu Königsegg, Louise Lamb, Virginia Mucchi,
Michael McDonnell, James O'Connell, Trevor White

FEATURE WRITERS
CAROLINE CLIFTON-MOGG is one of Britain's most respected writers on the subject of decoration.
Her latest book, Inspired by Antiques was published in September 1999.
MARINA DUDLEY has lived in France, Italy and Germany, as well as London, and writes about property and travel.
RUTH HILLENBRAND writes for several international publications, primarily about art and antiques.
MICHAEL McDONNELL was golf correspondent of The Daily Mail for 35 years. His best-selling books
include Complete Book of Golf and A Round to Remember.
VIRGINIA MUCCHI is a writer for both magazines and television, specialising in international current affairs.

ADVERTISING
Associate Publisher: Patricia McEntee
Senior Sales Executive: Christine Blanc
Senior Sales Executive: Gianfranco Caputo

DESIGN & ART
Design: Gowers Elmes Publishing Limited, London, UK
Contributing Designers: Helen Harris, Jane Phillips
Contributing Art Editor: Phyl Clarke

PHOTOGRAPHIC CREDITS
Paul Massey: *page 65 (Annouska Hempel Couture)*
Michel Guillard: *pages 9-19 (Château Margaux)*
Terry Murphy: *page 203 (Waterford Crystal)*
Bill Munke: *page 30 (Interior shot of Tigre D'or from Terence Disdale)*
All Sport: *page 311 (Johnny Wilkinson), page 283 (Sergio Garcia),*
page 306 (Annika Sorenstan), page 305 (Irina Slutskaya),
page 310 (Nicholas Ventola), page 281 (Giancarlo Fisichela)
Katz Pictures: *page 276 (Laeticia Casta)*
Rex Features: *page 272 (Victoria Bernadotte), page 273 (Elodie Bouchez),*
page 278 (The Corrs), page 282 (Charlotte Gainsbourg), page 284 (Marie Gillian),
page 286 (Damien Hirst), page 288 (Lasse Kjus),
page 291 (David and Serena Linely), page 296 (Sam Mendes),
page 301 (Marie-Jose Perec), page 299 (Gavin O'Reilly and wife)
La Fototech Agency: *pages 259, 260 (All Paris shots)*
Phil Sheldon: *page 250 (Valderrama), pages 249 & 257 (St Nom La Breteche),*
page 255 (Peuto de Heirro), page 254 (Hardelot Les Pins), page 253 (Penha Longa),
Fritz von Schulenburg: *page 64 (Annabels),*
page 154 (Mark's Club), page 126 (Harry's Bar), page 72 (The Bath and Raquets Club)
Massimo Listri: *pages 239 & 243 (Roberto Peregalli shots)*

CHARTER · ANTIQUE DEALERS · ARCHITECTS & DECO
UCTION HOUSES · CASINOS · CASTLES & VILLAS · CHAU
OMESTIC EMPLOYMENT AGENCIES · FASHION & ACCESS
AUTY · HOTELS · JEWELLERY & WATCHES · MUSEUMS
CTURE DEALERS · POLO CLUBS · PRIVATE BANKS · PRO
ENTS · RESTAURANTS & BARS · SCHOOLS · SECURITY C
TATES · SPORTS CLUBS & GYMS · TRAVEL CONSULTANT
OKERS, DESIGNERS & BUILDERS · YACHT CLUBS · AIR C
NTIQUE FAIRS · ARTS DE LA TABLE · ARTS DE VIVRE · AU
RVICES · COOKERY SCHOOLS · COSMETIC SURGEONS ·
ORISTS · GARDEN DESIGNERS · GOLF CLUBS · HAIR & B
STIVALS · NANNIES · PARTY ORGANISERS & CATERERS ·
ONSULTANTS · RACING, TRAINERS AND BLOODSTOCK A
PAS & CLINICS · SPECIALIST SHOPS · SPORTING ESTATE
ERCHANTS · WINES, CHAMPAGNES & SPIRITS · YACHT B
NTIQUE DEALERS · ARCHITECTS & DECORATORS · ART
USES · CASINOS · CASTLES & VILLAS · CHAUFFEUR SE
MPLOYMENT AGENCIES · FASHION & ACCESSORIES · FL
OTELS · JEWELLERY & WATCHES · MUSEUMS · MUSIC F
EALERS · POLO CLUBS · PRIVATE BANKS · PROPERTY CO
STAURANTS & BARS · SCHOOLS · SECURITY CONSULTA
ORTS CLUBS & GYMS · TRAVEL CONSULTANTS · WINE M
ESIGNERS & BUILDERS · YACHT CLUBS · AIR CHARTER ·
IRS · ARTS DE LA TABLE · ARTS DE VIVRE · AUCTION HO
OKERY SCHOOLS · COSMETIC SURGEONS · DOMESTIC
ARDEN DESIGNERS · GOLF CLUBS · HAIR & BEAUTY ·
ANNIES · PARTY ORGANISERS & CATERERS · PICTURE D
CING, TRAINERS AND BLOODSTOCK AGENTS · RESTAU
INICS · SPECIALIST SHOPS · SPORTING ESTATES · SPOR
NES, CHAMPAGNES & SPIRITS · YACHT BROKERS, DESI